OKANAGAN UNIV/COLLEGE LIBRARY

P9-DUJ-445

CHANGING
CHARACTER

OKANAGAN UNIVERSITY COLLEGE
LIBRARY
BRITISH COLUMBIA

CHANGING
CHARACTER

*Short-Term Anxiety-Regulating
Psychotherapy for Restructuring
Defenses, Affects, and Attachment*

LEIGH McCULLOUGH VAILLANT

BasicBooks
A Division of HarperCollins*Publishers*

Figure 2.1 on p. 63 is reprinted with permission from the *Diagnostic and Statistical Manual of Mental Disorders* (4th ed., p. 32). Copyright © 1994 American Psychiatric Association.

Excerpt on p. 78 is from Adrienne Rich, *Diving into the Wreck: Poems 1971–1972.* Copyright © 1973 W. W. Norton. Reprinted with permission.

Copyright © 1997 by BasicBooks, A Division of HarperCollins Publishers, Inc.

All rights reserved. Printed in the United States of America. No part of this book may be reproduced in any manner whatsoever without written permission except in the case of brief quotations embodied in critical articles and reviews. For information, address BasicBooks, 10 East 53rd Street, New York, NY 10022–5299.

Library of Congress Cataloging-in-Publication Data

Vaillant, Leigh McCullough.
    Changing character : short-term anxiety-regulating psychotherapy for restructuring defenses, affects, and attachment / Leigh McCullough Vaillant.
        p. cm.
    Includes bibliographical references and index.
    1. Personality disorders—Treatment.   2. Brief psychotherapy.   3. Psychodynamic psychotherapy.   4. Defense mechanisms (Psychology).   I. Title.
    [DNLM: 1. Personality Disorders—therapy.   2. Psychotherapy, Brief—methods. WM 190 V131c   1996]
RC554.V35   1996
616.89'14—dc21
DNLM/DLC
                                                                            96-39634
                                                                            CIP
    for Library of Congress

97 98 99 00 ❖/HC 9 8 7 6 5 4 3 2 1

To George
whose love made this happen

Contents

Acknowledgments
and Historical Evolution
of This Treatment Model

This integrative model of psychotherapy has had a lengthy period of gestation and has grown and evolved in a series of "holding environments" over the past twenty years. In looking back I am struck by the amount of support I have received and feel extremely fortunate. This book truly is a melting pot of ideas. At the start I would like to acknowledge the invaluable contribution of the patients who have permitted their therapy to be videotaped and/or transcribed, without whose generosity the scientific study of psychotherapy would not be possible.

Such a book as this could not be accomplished by a single individual alone; I therefore would like to take the opportunity to thank many teachers and colleagues without whom this book could not have been written. The first teacher I wish to thank is Bill Redpath, author of *Trauma Energetics* (1995), who deserves credit for forever shaping the way I view the world, and in 1972, propelling me back into psychology. His course, called the "Psychology of Space" at the Boston Architectural Center where I was a student, was so inspiring that I audited it the following year and discovered that I had to go back to study psychology, my first love.

Returning to psychology, I was blessed by superb teaching. First, at Wheaton College in Norton, Massachusetts, Paul Sprosty, Jerry Zuriff, David Wolfe, and others gave me a solid foundation in the field. Another form of excellent teaching came from the minister of the Unitarian church in Providence, Rhode Island, Tom Ahlburn, who has for two decades inspired me and helped develop my understanding of the place of spirituality in psychology. However, in 1975, because I had young children and was limited geographically, I was having trouble finding a graduate school. One Sunday, during coffee hour at the Unitarian church, I happened to describe my dilemma to a stranger who told me that at Boston College, Joseph Cautela offered a clinical program to one or two people per year. (The stranger was David Barlow.)

I was fortunate to be accepted into Cautela's program, and his brilliant instruction in behavioral observation and the impact of conditioning on learning forever altered the way I view human behavior. Many psychodynamically oriented friends and colleagues warned me not to study behavior therapy, but I cared about "what works," and at that time behavior therapy offered the clearest means of behavioral change. For this reason I feel thankful that I began by learning behavioral principles. Although psychodynamic theory is fascinating and compelling, had I studied it first I would not have appreciated the power of learning principles to effect behavior change. Furthermore, if I had not studied with Cautela (nor happened to speak that day to David Barlow), this book would not exist. Perhaps not coincidentally, Barlow's research is noted throughout the book.

Although my behavioral training was outstanding, I noticed that there were still patients I could not reach: those with personality disorders. The frustration with such patients led me on a quest to find superb supervision. I made extensive inquiries, went to workshops by leaders in the field, and read everything I could find. In 1979, a friend of mine, Julie Parsons, called from England and said, "I know you're looking for top-notch supervision, and I have the best supervisor in the world—David Malan at the Tavistock Clinic. Come visit me." After one week of sitting in one of Malan's courses and watching his videotapes, I knew I wanted to learn his method of therapy. Because I lived in the United States, Malan suggested that I contact Habib Davanloo in Montreal. I first attended a Davanloo workshop in 1980 and saw his dramatic methods with severely resistant patients. I applied and received training from him from 1983 to 1985 with the first Core Training Group in Manhattan. As a cognitive behaviorist I was at a disadvantage and had to struggle to learn his psychodynamic approach. However, I feel deeply indebted to Davanloo for his teaching how to persist with defensive patients. Although I no longer use his challenging style, I have sought throughout this book to retain his spirit of "relentless healing." Though our methods differ, I feel our goals ultimately are the same, that is, the seeking of deep and lasting character change.

More than any other individual, David Malan's thought has shaped this book, and he, too, seeks long-lasting change in long-standing problems. With each passing year I become more impressed by the conceptual clarity of the Two Triangles in guiding both clinical work and research in dynamic psychotherapy that form the conceptual foundation of this book. I feel honored that David Malan has read and made substantive comments to the manuscript and am deeply appreciative of his wisdom and mentorship.

From 1980 to 1983, I was hired by George Vaillant as a behavioral consultant to the Study for Adult Development at Harvard Medical School. My task was to operationally define and code ego defenses based on specific behaviors exhibited by the subjects in the study. This exercise laid the groundwork for my continuing operationalization of dynamic constructs. (Incidentally, upon hearing about my job some of my colleagues exclaimed, "Why did Vaillant hire you? You're a behaviorist!" They did not realize that George Vaillant, although a psychoanalyst, had spent two years working in a Skinnerian laboratory and knew the value of integrating theoretical orientations.)

At the same time I was concerned that research be conducted on short-term treatment. I had seen too many charismatic clinicians profess to have all the answers, and I did not want to learn a therapy model without researching it. David Malan had inspired me with a lengthy history of research on brief psychotherapy, and I wanted to continue in his tradition. In 1983, I was most fortunate when Manuel Trujillo and Arnold Winston invited me to join their research group at Beth Israel Medical Center in Manhattan. I became research director of the project from 1985 to 1990. Arnold Winston deserves much credit for his vision of research in short-term psychotherapy and for his ability to keep such a research program going to the present day. Without the support of Manuel Trujillo and Arnold Winston, I would not have had a laboratory in which to study the techniques set forth in this book. I am deeply grateful to them.

My colleagues and friends during those years were invaluable resources. For seven years, Debra Kaplan, director of psychology training, and I taught the short-term psychotherapy workshop to the psychology interns at Beth Israel, where we continually learned from each other. Other colleagues, Michael Laikin and Isabel Sklar, also were resources, always there to struggle with a puzzling question, review a tape, and give feedback. Barry Farber at Columbia University Teachers College supervised many dissertations on this model. Unfortunately, I am not able to list all the students who contributed over the years, but some deserving of special mention include Franklin Porter, Monica Salerno, Jeffrey Foote, Marcelo Rubin, Christine Joseph, Clarissa Bullitt, Sara Bacheldor, Nick Samstag, Bennett Hanig, and Nahama Broner. Other colleagues in Philadelphia who were most helpful in talking through concepts are Anita Simon, Claudia Byrum, Yvonne Agrarian, and Dick Peters. Four colleagues read early drafts of this book and gave many helpful comments: Christine Cooke, Clarissa Bullitt, Nan Shiowitz, and Andrea Solomon.

Two groups in particular served as important crucibles for the development of this short-term model. The first group is Michael Alpert, Isabel Sklar, Diana Fosha, and their colleagues, who developed their own form of short-term therapy, accelerated empathic therapy (AET). My friend Diana Fosha deserves special mention for her theoretical clarity, helping me to better understand the difference between anxiety-provoking and anxiety-regulating approaches. When I was confused about a patient's behavior, Isabel Sklar often encouraged me to "see it as defensive." Michael Alpert deserves special credit for working to resist the "splits" that seem inevitable in groups of theory builders. He encouraged an acceptance of disagreement that provided budding theorists a place to grow and evolve, and we are all richer for it.

The other crucible that has become inestimably dear to me is the research group at the University of Trondheim, Norway. I want to express my deepest gratitude to each of these colleagues, who spent eight years learning, helping to develop, and then submitting this treatment model to rigorous testing. This collaboration began in 1987, when the director, Martin Svartberg, attended my presentation at the Society for Psychotherapy Research and invited me to supervise his short-term dynamic therapy group. He is not only an excellent methodologist and statistician but also a skilled clinician—a combination of gifts that make him an outstanding researcher of psychotherapy. He challenged me from the start to operationalize constructs that were not clear, and read and critiqued each chapter, making significant contributions throughout. The research therapists Trond Haug, Ottar Hummelsund, Per Johan Ingstad, Bente Jansen, Tore Johnsen, Ronnaug Leland, and Monika van Beelen have a profound understanding of psychotherapeutics and were invaluable resources. Together with Martin Svartberg they pushed me conceptually to place the intrapsychic self *within* (not beside) the interpersonal holding environment, giving birth to self–other restructuring and the mandala signifying the self–other integration that appears on the book jacket. Special thanks goes to my close friend Ronnaug Leland, a psychiatrist and psychoanalyst-in-training, who provided me with the hospitality of her beautiful home on the Trondheim fjord over these eight years, gave excellent feedback on the manuscript, and guided me on concepts of transference and relational theory.

I also have been fortunate, since coming to Harvard Medical School, to have had support and encouragement from Fred Frankel and Nick Covino in the Department of Psychiatry at Boston's Beth Israel Hospital. With their help, I have been able to establish a research program to continue in the intensive study of short-term dynamic psychotherapy in a single-case experimental design format. Collegial support has been abundant from Dina Hirshfeld, David Rosenberg, Stephanie Meyer, Xing Ja Cui, Stewart Andrews, Nat Kuhn, and others.

As the treatment model took shape, I have been asked to present workshops on it. During the past eight years, I have spoken to almost 10,000 therapists in Europe and America and have received heartwarming encouragement and support. Audiences have repeatedly challenged me in ways that have greatly improved and enriched the model. I can remember so many excellent questions and suggestions from people whose names I did not know that forever improved what I did. Therefore, I send my deepest thanks to the audiences who have served as the whetstone for the polishing and refinement of this treatment approach.

In closing, I want to give special appreciation to Judy Freedman, my dear friend and psychoanalyst in New York City, who for the last ten years has been tossing ideas back and forth with me about long-term versus short-term treatment. Her inquisitive and exciting mind has been a constant resource. She helped me to better understand analytic theory and often read psychoanalytic literature to me over the telephone to help clarify my confusion on certain points. She read early and late drafts of the manuscript and gave many helpful comments, as well as encouragement, every step of the way.

The final acknowledgment is most special, to my husband, George Vaillant, who not only read and edited each sentence at least three times, but who took over the bulk of the domestic chores and cooked for us both as the deadline for publication bore down upon me. Without his help, this book would have been years longer being born, and would have been decidedly less pleasant to read. I have felt truly blessed by his support.

Leigh McCullough Vaillant
June 1996

Foreword

David Malan

A key factor in the technique of all dynamic short-term psychotherapy is the ability to break free from the passivity of classical psychoanalysis and transfer control into the hands of the therapist. In our investigations at the Tavistock Clinic we developed the principle of *planning* therapy from the beginning in terms of a *focus,* that is, a basic theme for interpretations, and actively trying to maintain this focus throughout each therapeutic session. As we later realized, however, the ability to maintain a focus depended on selecting patients who were well-motivated and responsive to interpretation. In the absence of these essential qualities, our purely interpretive technique was powerless.

It was Habib Davanloo who took *activity* on the part of the therapist to the limit, abandoning interpretation in the initial stages and exercising control by the relentless *confrontation* of defenses until a breakthrough was achieved. By this means he managed to bring into the sphere of short-term therapy many highly resistant patients suffering from severe personality disorders, who often lacked the motivation to give up their lifelong maladaptive patterns.

In 1982, a team at the Beth Israel Medical Center in New York of which Leigh McCullough Vaillant was research director began to investigate the effectiveness of short-term psychotherapy in a controlled study using as patients entirely those suffering from personality disorders. Among their results was the observation that confrontation of defenses, even when prolonged, did not in itself correlate with improvement.

This entirely ran counter to predictions based on the extreme effectiveness of Davanloo's work as seen on videotape; but the apparent contradiction can be simply resolved by the supposition that, in the hands of anyone but those most comfortable with a confrontational technique, confrontation in itself is ineffective and indeed may actually do harm. Put another way, if you are going to use persistent confrontation then you *must resolve the situation in that session* by breaking through into the hidden feeling that will give the patient relief. If you fail, you leave the patient merely antagonized or traumatized (4 out of the 64 in the aforementioned study described this phenomenon exactly, and 2 dropped out and refused further treatment of any kind).

One may ask, Did this lead to an impasse? The answer is no, since a second observation was that confronting interventions did correlate with improvement provided they contained in addition an element of empathy and support. Moreover, the factor that was most effective in eliciting feeling and ultimately in producing therapeutic effects was not so much *confrontation* of defenses but *clarification*. Finally, it appeared that using a more gentle approach did not lead to any decrease in effectiveness.

There are two main reasons why these observations are of immense importance. The first is that the *statistical* study of *clinically relevant* variables led to meaningful results and produced a major change in clinical practice— an event almost unprecedented in the field of dynamic psychotherapy.

The second is even more important. These statistical observations exactly confirmed three crucial clinical impressions: first, that a highly confrontational technique is extremely difficult to learn and does not suit the personalities of the majority of therapists; second, that the therapists' deeply felt inclination to back off and not to press the patient too hard was vindicated; and third, that there does exist an effective technique with which most therapists are comfortable. This technique uses the Two Triangles, as first made explicit in our work at the Tavistock Clinic, but it is nearer to that of Davanloo in the degree to which it concentrates on the defenses. On the other hand, the style of intervention is different from Davanloo's. Anyone who reads the many verbatim transcripts in this book cannot fail to be impressed with the warmth and sympathy that run through the author's interventions.

Here is a single, highly abbreviated, example (see pp. 131–132). The patient was a man suffering from a lifelong inhibition of feeling, of which he was hardly aware. In this vignette, the reader can see both the influence of Davanloo and the marked softening that represent the author's own particular style:

THERAPIST: There must be some really uncomfortable feelings here, because each time we get on a sad topic you quickly shut down. . . . Well, it takes strength to contain emotion that much, but now it's doing you no service. Isn't it sad that you come here needing to pour out the grief you've been carrying, but you don't feel free to do so?

This example is taken from the first stage of the author's system of therapy, namely, *defense recognition*. She goes on to enumerate the other three main stages, *defense relinquishing* and *affect experiencing*, both in the therapeutic session, and *affect expression* in the patient's life outside. This simple but profound schema offers an overall structure for therapy that enables the therapist to keep control not only of each individual session but also of therapy itself, against which therapists can measure the progress they are making. It represents an example of the author's exceptional clarity of thought, and makes the teaching of her technique relatively easy.

The combination of deep empathy, psychodynamic insight, and scientific rigor shown here is indeed rare. Leigh McCullough Vaillant comes to dynamic psychotherapy from behavior therapy, and she integrates in her work the techniques and theories not only of behavior therapy but also, for example, of the gestalt and cognitive schools as well. These techniques are almost certainly used covertly by many dynamic therapists: for instance, the technique of concentrating on emotions to *desensitize* the patient to the accompanying anxiety, guided fantasy to bring out feeling, and challenging the patient's mistaken beliefs. The author uses them deliberately and openly, however, at the same time basing them entirely on an understanding of the psychodynamics and, thus, on the patient's psychodynamic needs.

The clinical examples that abound in this book for the most part include follow-up after a substantial period, and the therapeutic results are extremely impressive. Clinical examples with lengthy follow-up are crucial in any book of this kind (it would be useless to write a manual for a technique whose efficacy is unknown), and I would like to make a special plea to the author, here in print and therefore more binding, that what is needed is publication of a *continuous series* of case histories with long follow-up, in which the *living details* of changes in the patient's life, specific to each individual, are recorded. This is precisely what Ferrucio Osimo and I attempted in *Psychodynamics, Training, and Outcome in Brief Psychotherapy* (1992). As an example of such changes described in the present volume, the patient mentioned earlier eventually formed a deep and lasting relationship with a woman—something he had never been able to achieve before—and was able to cry in her arms about the losses of his childhood and the ways in which these losses had caused him to waste the whole of his life hitherto. Obviously, the ability to feel sadness was one of the "target problems" of his therapy that can be rated on a scale, but the details of this incident make clear to the world, as no score on any scale can convey, the true quality of the therapeutic result. I do not believe such a result could be achieved by any form of therapy other than one based on the fundamental principles of psychodynamics, that is, defense, anxiety, and hidden feeling. Moreover, if the publication that I propose were based on a *continuous* series it would make clear the overall, quantitative effectiveness of the form of therapy used, which represents essential information needed for its acceptance by other professionals.

Although Leigh Vaillant's technique differs markedly from that of Davanloo, the principle that it retains and that makes it so effective is the persistent concentration on the defenses. In this connection I have often thought of two parallels: in 1953, Edmund Hillary and Tenzing Norgay climbed Mount Everest, and in 1954 Roger Bannister ran a 4-minute mile. Both of these feats, once demonstrated, became not only repeatable but actually routine (recently, there were as many as 30 people at the summit of Mount Everest at the same time!). Likewise, perhaps Davanloo's most important contribution is not so much his technique of confrontation but simply his demonstrating that by concentrating on the defenses, short-term psychotherapy with apparently intractable personality disorders became possible, thereby encouraging other therapists to find their own way to similar results. All the evidence suggests this is what the present author has achieved, and because her technique is that much more acceptable to the majority of therapists, perhaps it will lead to the psychotherapeutic equivalent of 30 people standing on the summit of Everest in years to come.

CHAPTER 1

Introduction and Overview
of the Treatment Model

Passio, ergo sum;
"I feel, therefore I am."

Part 1: Basic Principles

THE CENTRALITY OF EMOTION TO MENTAL HEALTH

The mechanism of emotional change is the most central issue in the mental health field. "It is primarily emotional change that lies at the heart of human suffering associated with mental disorders and constitutes much of our work in psychotherapy and pharmacotherapy" (Robinson, 1995, p. 327). It is emotional change that is necessary for healing the long-standing painfulness of character pathology. Yet emotional change is the least studied and most misunderstood area in the field.

This book is, at heart, about emotion: how to get to it, how to flow with it and follow its lead, but equally important, how to use cognition to guide, control, and direct it. This is a treatment manual with the goal of helping patients to live joyfully and spontaneously—but mindfully—with themselves and others through the adaptive responsivity to experience. The thrust of this book is in demonstrating how to assist our patients (and ourselves) in, first, identifying and removing characterological obstacles to emotional experience and, second, delving deep into that experience, putting reins on it, and harnessing the tremendous adaptive power that emotions provide. The ultimate goal is to have emotions without letting emotions have us.

Although one's skills in the art of living, one's character style, are never perfect, the more one can laugh when happy, cry when sad, use anger to set firm limits, make love passionately, and give and receive tenderness fully and openly, the further one is from suffering. And the fuller one is with the

1

joy of existence, the more generous one can be toward others. Toward these ends, this chapter begins with an overview of the entire book by defining the active, involved change mechanisms of short-term therapy and the basic foundations of the treatment model, in which the healing connection between the therapist and patient is the director, and healthy emotional responsivity and the obstacles to it are the central players.

Unfortunately, most therapists who do effective work practice in one manner and talk about it quite differently. There is a huge gulf between what people do and what people say they do. There is an even greater gap between what they do and what they write. Given this reality, what is needed is some way to bring together all of the theories that therapists use in their practice and to intertwine them in such a manner that they make sense and contribute to a focused, efficient, relatively brief psychotherapy. A treatment manual worth its salt should describe as accurately as possible what is done in clinical practice. That is the task of this book.

DEFINING SHORT-TERM PSYCHOTHERAPY

The meaning of the expression *short-term psychotherapy* is much misunderstood. My colleagues and I have struggled for years to find a better term. Rather than continue to struggle for the words, I describe here what we do in clinical practice. A workshop participant once told me that *short-term therapy* should mean "not one session more than what is necessary for change." Whew! After watching many videotapes of myself and my colleagues struggling longer than we wished to find the pathways to healing, that seemed a tall order. A more reasonable standard, "not more than a *few* sessions more than what is necessary for change," is closer to what we can realistically strive for, and we do not always achieve it.

Although *short-term* and *brief* are the most popular labels, the process of psychotherapy to be described in this book is not always short in an absolute sense; it is to be accomplished in the shortest time possible given the nature of the problem and the character structure of the patient. Many other adjectives have emerged in an attempt to improve on the terminology. *Time-limited* was the term used by James Mann (1973) to refer to therapy with a strict limit of 12 sessions, which brought many issues to the forefront rapidly. However, therapists often have found it difficult to limit the number of sessions arbitrarily to a fixed number. *Time-efficient* is closer to what is strived for, yet the term is somewhat unsavory, bringing to mind a perfunctory nurse who says, "Spit-spot, time's up. You'd better be finished!"—not the impression I wish to convey, nor the ambience I wish to create. *Time-effective* is an improvement, but I prefer a label that describes the treatment process rather than the hoped-for outcome. Finally, there is the term *time-conscious*, which is an even more accurate description of the process. Such an approach is well described in Jeffrey Binder, William Henry, and Hans Strupp's (1987) article on the "time-limited attitude"; rather than setting rigid limits, the therapist retains a constant mindfulness of *limiting treatment to the shortest time possible*. In other words, the therapist aims for "what will yield the best results to the greatest number of people in the *shortest period of time*" (Lazarus & Messer, 1991, p. 153).

In this book, I retain the expression *short-term* to refer to a form of psychotherapy in which the therapist is (a) focused on specific objectives, (b) highly active and involved, and (c) working through therapeutic objectives in the shortest possible time; however, the treatment duration varies depending on the needs of the patient.

As James Sabin (1994) put it, "in any given clinical situation, the best treatment is the least intensive, least extensive, least intrusive and least costly one that can *successfully* address the patient's current need for care" (p. 31). Nick Cummings and Mike Sayama (1995) sum up these principles as follows: "Our contract with the patient should be: I shall never abandon you as long as you need me, and I shall never ask you to do anything until you're ready. In return for this, you'll be joining me in a partnership to make me obsolete as soon as possible" (p. 1).

How Long Does It Take for Behavior to Change?

According to James Prochaska's naturalistic studies, *behavior takes time to change* (e.g., Prochaska, Rossi, & Wilcox, 1991). For addictions, his diverse samples of people who had changed such behavior reported taking 7 years, with two to three relapses, before stable change was achieved (Prochaska, DiClemente, & Norcross, 1992). For other behaviors (e.g., simple phobias, unresolved grief), the time needed for change is less clear and varies greatly. However, a year or two can often be needed for the individual to recognize the problem, take action, and maintain the gains. Prochaska and his colleagues have begun to raise our consciousness about the naturalistic course and stages of behavior change. Given that natural course, how much therapy do we need for each stage? One might ask how much time is needed for each of the following phases of treatment:

1. To encourage motivation for change and build the necessary alliance or trust between the patient and therapist.
2. To help individuals recognize various problems (narcissistic disorders are not as easily recognized by the patient as are phobias).
3. To make the shifts in behaviors, desensitize conflicts, and acquire new habits (the action phase).
4. To stabilize changes.

The point of short-term treatment is not to complete all aspects of the character change but to get it started and sufficiently stabilized so that patients can continue the growth process with relationships in their lives. Therapists need to put the tools of treatment into the hands of patients as soon as possible. An important question is, therefore, how many sessions are required to get that process started? Just because a long-standing behavior pattern may require a year or two of attention for change to occur, constant psychotherapy during this entire time often is not necessary. Some cases may require one or more sessions per week over extended periods (e.g., a patient who lacks motivation or basic trust; a patient who has difficulty with the therapeutic alliance; a patient with an identity disturbance). For other problems, less impaired individuals may be able to do the bulk of the work of change in fewer, intermittent sessions.

Providing "batches" of sessions (e.g., 10–20) with some weeks or months in between can be a valuable method of giving patients the opportunity to digest, metabolize, and implement the newly acquired skills on their own. Learning is dependent on the state in which it occurs; if all change is experienced in a context of weekly therapeutic encounters, patients may not integrate into that change process the experience of relying on their own resources.[1] This is an extremely important factor in the maintenance of change. Therapists strive to discover the balance between specific patient needs and the "floors," or *minimum numbers of sessions for effective treatment*. When psychotherapy is viewed as inherently a change-facilitating process, the therapist's function can be more *catalytic* than *analytic* (Bennett, 1989).

As researchers in short-term treatment continue to study single cases, patterns begin to emerge. Many symptomatic changes can be achieved in a relatively short time (1–10 sessions) by more than one form of short-term treatment (e.g., cognitive, dynamic, interpersonal). There are also data that indicate that the work of 10–20 sessions can improve interpersonal relationships (e.g., Malan, 1979; Malan & Osimo, 1992). Thus far, these results represent the limits of what can be accomplished in most managed-care settings, and many health maintenance organizations (HMOs) are labeling this treatment "crisis intervention," not therapy.

Character change in chronic personality disorder is the major challenge in psychotherapy. When characterological issues are not dealt with, relapse is more likely. It is whispered among colleagues of short-term persuasion—from both cognitive and dynamic schools—that after the dramatic symptom reduction of a few sessions, most therapists end up recommending longer treatment for the "deeper" issues that have emerged. *Because this is a common occurrence in the field, it should be faced and dealt with.*

My colleagues and I have been inspired by Malan and Osimo's reports that character changes[2] frequently have been noted after 30 sessions or fewer (1992, pp. 93, 223–228). Similarly, at the Short-Term Psychotherapy Research Program at Harvard Medical School, it is increasingly evident that therapy for these deeper characterological issues does not have to drag on endlessly but can lead to resolution or at least improvement in a finite number of sessions for many patients.[3] Our accumulating body of cases, therefore, also

[1]Such recommendations must always be considered in light of patient characteristics, which are discussed in detail in chapter 11. The more dependent an individual is, the more I encourage intermittent breaks, to help develop autonomy. In the counterdependent individual, I encourage close connection until healthy dependency (i.e., attachment) is comfortable. Ultimately, the goal with any individual is an adaptive balance between autonomy and relatedness.

[2]Malan and Osimo (1992) operationally define *character change* as change in "repetitive and inappropriate (or maladaptive) patterns of behavior" (p. 93). I use this definition throughout this book.

[3]My colleagues and I provide treatment in batches of 20 sessions for moderately

supports Malan's finding: that it is possible to effect significant changes in character or basic sense of self, in moderately impaired patients with personality disorders, in weeks or months of treatment. More severe impairment generally necessitates lengthier treatment, but not always. (Patient motivation and personal strengths make a difference.)

For every case, we strive for *demonstrable steps toward healing every month*. Furthermore, short-term methods should not be limited to a small percentage of healthy patients. Ideally, time-conscious interventions should be used in all treatments. Much more research is needed regarding what can be accomplished for whom, in what amount of time, because time-conscious intervention is the optimal objective of short-term dynamic psychotherapy. The challenge before us is to discover which interventions are most time-effective for patients with different degrees of impairment. Case examples of short-term treatments with patients at various levels of impairment are presented at the end of the chapter.

Do Short-Term Approaches Rush the Patient?

One of the most frequent criticisms of short-term therapy by conscientious therapists is that limiting time in treatment robs the patient of experiences that are desperately needed. *Overly extending* time in treatment may also rob the patient of experiences that are desperately needed, however. How do we strike a balance? On one hand, concerns such as Strupp's (1989) that modern therapy threatens to "hurry" the patient are substantive and should make us stop and think. In the healing of a wound, there is a natural course and time period. Some patients need more time than others to build a bond with the therapist. Processes such as grief, separation–individuation, and development of trust seem eminently "unrushable." Certainly it is not healing to rush a patient through treatment in an unnatural way. Such a process is not likely to sustain change in the long run and, indeed, would suggest a false or superficial change, if any.

Just as physicians can maximize the natural healing process by decreasing the deterrents to physical healing, so can the short-term psychotherapist help to *remove the deterrents* to psychological and emotional healing. Our patients avoid healing through maladaptive defensive maneuvers. What we want to rush patients through is *the defensive avoidance of doing what they desperately need to do*, which is allowing closeness, building compassion for themselves and others, learning to feel once more, finding their voice. These are all capacities that patients fervently avoid acquiring or even facing; however, *defenses must never be dealt with in a manner that causes the patient to be overwhelmed or left without support*. That is not healing; it is abuse. For that reason, this book is dedicated to altering defensive patterns in the least

---

impaired patients with personality disorders. Unless there is a serious crisis, we end after the first set of 20, for the majority of cases. When there are serious, unresolved issues, we either continue without a break or, if possible, break for 6 months to allow change to metabolize and then offer a second set of 20 sessions. Our goal is to begin to document the minimum number of sessions necessary to resolve long-standing character patterns.

painful and most constructive manner. Short-term therapists need to be conscious of the time that is wasted and the suffering that continues when destructive behaviors are maintained. *Much defensive behavior can be given up more readily than we realize, and there are many safe ways to do so.* There is one caveat, however: that the patient be ready for change.

Patient Readiness for Change

James Prochaska and his colleagues have noted a paradigm shift in the understanding of behavior change. It formerly was thought that behavior changed from "bad" to "good" (e.g., smoking to nonsmoking, alcoholic to sober). As noted earlier, Prochaska's research (e.g., Prochaska, Rossi, & Wilcox, 1991) demonstrated not only that behavior takes time to change, but also that behavior changes in stages and that patients vary widely in their degree of readiness for change (Prochaska, Norcross, & DiClemente, 1994). Their research has identified six stages in change. The *precontemplative stage* ("what's the problem?" or "it's not my problem") is often seen in husbands dragged into marital counseling by their wives, teenagers brought by their parents, and criminal offenders sentenced to treatment by the courts. The next stage is the *contemplative stage* ("I guess I have a problem, but I'm not sure, and I don't know if I want to change anything and rock the boat"). The *preparation stage* is third, in which plans for action and resolution to change are made. The fourth *"action" stage* involves actively working on changing the problem, and the fifth or *maintenance stage* involves maintaining of the therapeutic gains. The sixth and final stage is *termination*, where change is well-established without fear of relapse (Prochaska, Norcross, & DiClemente, 1994, pp. 38–50).

This extensive research on readiness for psychotherapy demonstrates, therefore, that many patients are not prepared for the action-oriented approach of short-term psychotherapy. If a therapist mistakenly jumps into an "action-oriented" mode of behavior change, patients who are in the pretreatment stages will be lost. Such patients are less motivated; for example, if their identity is built on being long suffering or compliant, change will be resisted until they have a viable alternative to replace that behavior.

When patients are functioning within these two pretreatment stages, the therapeutic focus in this model would be, for the first stage, "Let's see if we can find a reason that you might benefit from treatment" and, for the second, "Let's see what could be gained by resolving this problem. What difficulties might we prepare for?" In other words, building motivation for treatment and building the supports to sustain change must prepare the patient for the changes that take place in treatment.

Short-Term Therapy Is Not Synonymous with Managed Care

Short-term therapy has been mistakenly believed to be synonymous with managed care (the limiting of treatment by insurance company protocols), but the two in fact were not connected in their origins. My colleagues and I began doing research on short-term approaches to treatment in the late 1970s, because we were interested in learning how to make therapy as efficient and effective as possible. David Malan, Peter Sifneos, Franz Alexander, and others were developing brief forms of treatment for decades before. At that time, the term *managed care* did not exist.

Short-term treatment evolved over the past century because of the work of many groups of deeply concerned therapists, who worked together— often in their own time, at their own expense, and under much opposition— to develop methods of treatment that were effective in the shortest amount of time for the greatest number of patients. Finances were only part of the resources that would be conserved. Time spent in suffering was the original target for reduction, and it continues to be the concern. It has been only in the past 5 years that most managed-care facilities have begun to draw on the knowledge of short-term therapies to help meet their economic objectives. Today, the goals of managed care and this form of short-term therapy overlap in setting out to maintain a clear focus, high therapist activity, and time consciousness.

Currently, however, the ultimate goals of managed care and short-term dynamic therapy are different. Managed care, because it is business-based, necessarily tends to limit the goals in treatment according to the time and money allotted. In contrast, the treatment approach described in this book ultimately seeks the *resolution of the underlying character structure* and, whenever possible, advocates that time be taken (but as efficiently as possible) to see that achievement of this goal is stably under way before therapy is ended. At present, this goal most often is accomplished, as it has been historically, by patient payment, not insurance payment. When time, money, or both are so restricted that the goal of character change cannot be achieved, clear steps toward that goal can be identified and made clear to the patient, and a prescription for continued work outside of therapy can be laid out. Some of these steps can be employed in some managed-care settings but certainly not in all. It is hoped that, someday, comprehensive coverage (therapy for characterological as well as symptomatic impairment) may be made available to the widest possible range of people.

Much criticism has been leveled at insurance companies and health care providers for putting the "bottom line" above human values. It is the responsibility of clinicians and researchers, however, to continue to develop time-conscious, effective, and cost-efficient treatments. When effective treatment modalities are well established, we must educate not only the insurance companies but also the public at large that a comprehensive therapeutic approach can profoundly benefit both the patient and the company providing the service. The bottom line and our value system then can be in agreement.

Historical Evolution of Short-Term Therapy

James Gustafson, in *The Complex Secret of Brief Psychotherapy* (1986), has provided a comprehensive review of the work of the pioneers in short-term psychotherapy. I address only the major trends that have influenced the development of this model. Jeffrey Magnavita (1993) identified three "waves" in the evolution of brief treatment that culminate in the model presented in this book. The first wave began with Sigmund Freud's few brief treatments, for example, his well-known cure of the impotency of the composer Gustav Mahler in one afternoon's walk. Later, Rank and Ferenczi, concerned that analysis was becoming interminable, attempted to explore more active forms of treatment and struggled with the issue of gratification versus "abstinence." However, Ferenczi admitted that his "grand experiment" of actively gratifying all his patient's wishes had failed, because his patient was only minimally better after several years. Alexander and French continued the study of short-term treatment in the 1940s, providing patients with a "corrective emotional experience," in part through behaving in a manner "opposite to the parents."[4]

In the early 1950s, at the Tavistock Clinic in London, Michael and Enid Balint, David Malan, and several others established a research group to study short-term therapy. Michael Balint was also interested in the issue of gratification, but through understanding. Malan put their position succinctly: "The aim of therapy is not to make up to patients for the love that they have missed, but to help them work through their feelings about not having it" (1979, p. 141).

The second wave of brief psychotherapy pioneers can be characterized by a stronger focus on management of the defenses. Certainly Wilhelm Reich's *Character Analysis* (1949) must have had an impact on these thinkers, because the idea of "breaking through" character armor, or the defensive barrier, is predominant in these models of treatment.

Another factor that was influential was identified after the occurrence of a tragic fire at the Coconut Grove restaurant in Boston in 1942, in which customers, rushing to escape, found the exit doors locked. The survivors of this fire, who had seen friends and loved ones die beside them, were rushed to Massachusetts General Hospital, where Erich Lindemann and his staff provided treatment. Lindemann was surprised to find that these "survivor victims" showed greater improvement in 6 weeks than his regular patients had shown in years of psychotherapy. He surmised that the crisis raised anxiety levels, which resulted in their defenses being more responsive to intervention. Two of Lindemann's residents, Peter Sifneos and Habib Davanloo, went on to develop major forms of short-term "anxiety-provoking" therapy (Sifneos, 1972, 1979; Davanloo, 1978, 1980). Also in Boston at that time, James Mann developed a model for a 12-session time-limited treatment focusing on grief and loss (Mann, 1973).[5]

---

[4]Unfortunately, Alexander and French were strongly criticized by the analytic establishment because there was active "manipulation of the transference." In practice, however, the transference is inadvertently "manipulated" by whatever therapists do and no less so when neutrality or passivity is maintained in the analytic technique. The point is that we must acknowledge and specify whatever therapeutic maneuvers are being employed (and what "manipulation" or impact is desired) so that the effects can be experimentally examined.

[5]Of the three, it was only Davanloo's model that was consciously inspired by Lindemann. When Davanloo asked what he should do if there was no crisis, Lindemann responded, "Well ... create one then!" (H. Davanloo, personal communication,

There is a remarkable similarity in the ways each of these men put *well-intentioned pressure on their patients to face, bear, and resolve long-standing conflicts.* In England, Malan was working in a similar vein, although he did not aim to provoke anxiety intentionally but to deepen the affect. Malan's often-quoted standard, that "the aim of every moment of every session is to put the patient in touch with as much of his true feeling as he can *bear*" (1979, p. 74), implies the necessity of modulating the degree of anxiety that is provoked. Malan's impressive body of research spanning 4 decades (e.g., 1976, 1979; Malan & Osimo, 1992) is testimony to the validity of brief dynamic psychotherapy.

The third wave of brief psychotherapy included research my colleagues and I conducted at Beth Israel Medical Center in New York. The integrative model that evolved from this research was influenced by Gustafson's fundamental mechanisms of brief psychotherapy (1984); its principles may be summarized as follows:

1. *Focal inquiry:* focusing on a core theme that is hypothesized to underlie the current problem
2. *Managing the resistance:* helping the patient with the reluctance to change the focal problem, that is, the defenses against change
3. *Supplying the missing capability:* before altering or removing behaviors that have sustained the individual, helping the patient to build new skills, resources, and relationships

By focusing first on defenses (the resistance) and then on adaptive affects and sense of self and others (the missing capabilities), this model incorporates Gustafson's three basic components.

PRINCIPLES OF SHORT-TERM DYNAMIC TREATMENT: MALAN'S TWO TRIANGLES

Malan (1979, chapter 10) depicted two triangles that together provide the foundation for the specific objectives of the short-term model that forms the basis of this book (Figure 1.1). For the past 15 years, this simple conceptual schema has guided much of my clinical and research work; therefore, I describe it in considerable detail. With each passing year, I become more appreciative of Malan's clarity of thought.

The Triangle of Conflict (Ezriel, 1952) is derived from Freudian structural theory and focuses on the patient's defensive behavior patterns that block impulses or feelings owing to the experience of anxiety (or guilt, shame, or pain). The Triangle of Person, based on Karl Menninger's (1958) Triangle of

---

1985). Davanloo went on to do so. Sifneos was more inspired by well-adjusted mothers in a Wellesley clinic who were able to respond effectively to rapid and deep interpretations. Mann decided on 12 sessions by dividing the number of patients on a waiting list by the number of therapists available. He wished to provide help for as many individuals as possible.

Insight, focuses on how these maladaptive patterns of responding originated in past relationships and how the same patterns can be seen in the relationship to the therapist and in relationships with current persons. Malan's
genius was in recognizing that by putting these two triangles together, the
constructs represented what he termed the "universal principle of psychodynamic psychotherapy" (see Figure 1.1):

> The aim of most dynamic psychotherapy is to reach beneath the de-
> fense and anxiety, to the hidden feeling, and then to trace this feeling
> back from the present to its origins in the past, usually in relation to the
> parents. . . . The importance of these two triangles is that between them
> they can be used to represent almost every intervention that a therapist
> makes and that much of a therapist's skill consists of knowing which
> parts of which triangle to include at any given moment. (1979, p. 80)

These principles of psychodynamic technique can be applicable to either a
long- or a short-term model. I have intentionally presented these triangles in
three-dimensional form to represent the perspective of the self and the other
in each. From the vantage point at the top of the pyramid, the self observes
and is observed by others.

FIGURE 1.1
**Malan's two triangles demonstrate the universal principle
of psychodynamic psychotherapy.**

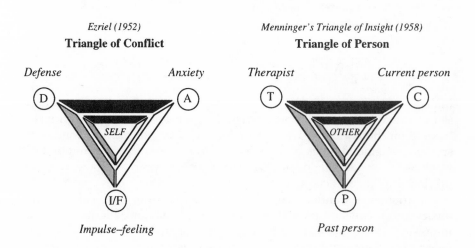

In the Triangle of Conflict, the defense pole signifies patient behaviors that
serve as a means of avoiding the awareness or experience of a hypothesized
unpleasant thought or feeling. The therapist addresses the defensive behavior: *Do you notice that you look away and change the subject* [D, defensive be-
havior] *when I mention your sadness* [I/F, the conflicted affect] *over your*

father's death? Are you feeling some discomfort in facing this painful topic [A, inquiring about anxiety, guilt, shame, or pain]?

In another example, focusing on the impulse–feeling pole, the dialogue might go something like this:

THERAPIST: Can we look at your anger here with me? [*Focus on the impulse in the patient–therapist relationship*]
PATIENT [*Haltingly*]: I don't know what to say. [*Defensive avoidance of the anger*]
THERAPIST: What's the most difficult part of having negative feelings toward me? [*Exploring anxiety*]

In contrast to earlier, anxiety-provoking models of short-term dynamic psychotherapy (e.g., Davanloo, 1980), this model of short-term anxiety-regulating psychotherapy gently clarifies defenses while emphasizing the exploration of the inhibitory feelings that give rise to, as well as maintain, the defensive behavior.

The Triangle of Person provides a structure for noting patterns of responding originating in past relationships and the similarity of those past patterns to the patterns in the patient–therapist relationship and other current relationships (including the relationship to the self, which is discussed later in the chapter). It is these long-standing patterns of responding that make up character styles and, in patients, character disorders. By changing the long-standing and repetitive "transferring" of the patient's maladaptive past patterns onto current relationships, we are changing character. *Can you see that your quiet, withdrawn response with me* [T, therapist] *is the same way that you respond now to your wife* [C, current person], *and this pattern seems to come from how you reacted, as a boy, toward your father as well* [P, past person]?

In this manner, a therapist links or distinguishes defensive patterns of behavior following the Triangle of Conflict schema. These responses always must be connected with specific people in the present and past following the Triangle of Person schema. In short-term dynamic treatment, the therapist is active in identifying each of the conceptual poles in the two triangles and the repetitive pattern across different relationships. Until recently, however, a major aspect of intrapsychic and interpersonal functioning—the self—was not explicitly represented in this schema. After considerable deliberation,[6] I have made the role of the self explicit by representing the two triangles in three-dimensional form in Figure 1.1. The perspective of self-concept, therefore, is represented at the top of the pyramid; it is the observing or observed sense of self. In addressing these issues regarding the self and the self in relation to others, the therapist might say any of the following: *How do you feel about yourself when you are angry?* (S, exploring self-concept) *How do you think*

---

[6]A discussion with members of the Trondheim Short-Term Psychotherapy Research Group resulted in placing the concept of the self into the two triangles. The participants were Martin Svartberg, Ronnaug Leland, Ottar Hummelsund, Tore Johnsen, and myself (March 17, 1994, Trondheim, Norway).

I feel about you? (S, exploring self-image with others) What is your sense of me (or others)? (S, exploring self-perspective of others)

PRINCIPLES THAT DISTINGUISH THIS MODEL FROM ITS SHORT-TERM PRECURSORS

This integrative and anxiety-regulating model of short-term dynamic psychotherapy uses an empathic and collaborative relationship for restructuring defenses and anxieties that block feelings toward self and others. The model retains many of the fundamental components of its short-term dynamic therapy precursors (Davanloo, 1980; Malan, 1976, 1979; Mann, 1973; Sifneos, 1972, 1979). On the basis of extensive research, however, it substantially modifies these approaches in several important ways:

1. Defenses are more often clarified than confronted.
2. Anxiety is regulated rather than provoked.
3. There is connection rather than "collision" in the patient–therapist relationship that provides a "continuous, graded corrective emotional experience."[7]
4. Treatment objectives are specified, and outcomes are quantified.

Defenses Are Clarified Rather than Confronted

In some of the earlier models of short-term dynamic psychotherapy, the therapist attempted to elicit deep feelings by provoking a patient's anxiety in a number of ways: by challenge and pressure (e.g., Davanloo, 1980), by setting and enforcing strict time limits (Mann, 1973), or by rapidly offering deep interpretations (e.g., Sifneos, 1972, 1979). There are problems encountered with these more confrontive and anxiety-provoking approaches, however, which the present approach avoids. First, strong confrontation can be a difficult process for the patient to endure, and second, many patients are not *optimally* responsive to this type of treatment. On one hand, if handled masterfully, confrontation sometimes can be quite effective. On the other hand, intense confrontation sometimes can be perceived as a wounding, traumatic experience. Some patients feel not only unhelped, but harmed by the experience.[8]

The first goal in treatment should be to do no harm. Therapists using this

[7]Martin Svartberg, personal communication, 1995.

[8]In the Beth Israel Research Study, 4 out of 64 patients who completed treatment (6.6%) were deeply disturbed by the confrontive procedures. Two additional patients dropped out after the initial evaluation. These patients had been carefully selected and were informed of the confrontive methods in advance; they were offered another, more supportive form of treatment afterward. As research director, I spent many hours with each of these upset individuals, hearing their complaints and trying to make amends. None of these patients deteriorated; however, each one refused other treatments, and the two dropouts refused any further participation in the research. In fact, 3 of the 4 patients who complained grudgingly admitted that treatment had helped them but felt that the ends did not justify the means. Experiences such as these caused me great concern and were influential in the eventual modification of the treatment model.

anxiety-regulating model gently point out defensive behaviors but, at the same time, provide a "holding environment" to help the patient manage whatever anxiety or unpleasant feeling emerges. As a result, patients often give up defensive behavior just as readily (and sometimes more easily and sooner) than in a confrontive model. Another problem with the strongly confrontive models is that they are both difficult for therapists to master and painful to employ, owing to the degree of stress one must place on the patient. Certainly, if intense confrontation were the only path to character change, it would be essential to master these techniques; however, gentler, effective alternatives are available. Note the difference in the following two approaches:

Confrontation and challenge: *You are avoiding my eyes right now as I ask about your feelings. And now you're drumming your fingers on the table. This silence erects a barrier between us. What will happen if you continue to evade these issues in treatment?*

Clarification and support: *As I ask you about your feelings, you often look away and become silent. Are you aware that this is happening? Is this topic painful for you to look at? Is there some way that I can help you make it more bearable to face?*

Treatment Is Anxiety Regulating Rather than Anxiety Provoking

The earlier methods of short-term therapy attempted to *provoke* anxiety to break through defenses by using various forms of confrontation without support. In contrast, the "regulation of anxiety" in this model is designed to help the highly defended patient face the painful and difficult process of defense analysis in dosages that are bearable and not overwhelming. Even with empathy and support provided, the constant focus on defenses invariably elicits some degree of anxiety, guilt, shame, or pain. In this model, therefore, anxiety is repeatedly elicited but then regulated, or brought within manageable limits as soon as it emerges.[9] It is explored and resolved before the therapy moves forward.

The anxiety-regulating process is often similar to the cognitive therapy approach, in which one asks, "What is the worst thing that would happen?" or "Why would that be so frightening or shameful?" This model is unlike purely supportive therapies, however, because anxieties are not simply reduced.[10] The process involves both the eliciting of anxiety-provoking material and the immediate resolving of those anxieties, in a step-by-step manner. At the first emergence of maladaptive inhibitory responses, the therapist

[9]Many theorists have debated this distinction regarding how to work with defensive resistance. On one hand, there are those who advocate the "adversarial" approach to the character armor (e.g., Reich, 1949), a method involving challenge to and pressure on the defenses (Davanloo, 1980), or a confrontation of the defenses (Kernberg, 1983). On the other hand, there are those who advocate a more "affirmative approach" (e.g., Schafer, 1959, 1983), a "holding environment" (e.g., Winnicott, 1965), or empathy (e.g., Bollas, 1983, 1986, 1995; Kohut, 1971, 1977).

[10]The distinction between anxiety reduction and anxiety regulation was made clear to me by David Malan.

shifts to anxiety-regulating procedures that help the patient master whatever anxiety conflict or inhibition is elicited when the defenses are made conscious. A holding environment is established in a supportive and empathic relationship with the therapist to encourage and assist the patient in the painful exploration of aversive modes of responding.

The regulation of anxiety has similarities to the approach developed by Joseph Weiss and his colleagues: "The therapist's noncritical attitude and the pledge of confidentiality create an atmosphere of security. Patients therefore may conclude *unconsciously* that they can safely bring to consciousness certain repressed material" (Weiss, 1990, p. 105; italics added). In contrast, in the technique described in this book, an atmosphere of security is *consciously and intentionally developed* throughout treatment as in the following example.

EXAMPLE: ENHANCING SAFETY BY CONSCIOUSLY ADDRESSING ANXIETIES

THERAPIST: What is so frightening to you about exploring your sad feelings here with me?

PATIENT: I don't know. . . . My mother was depressed her whole life. I guess, if I look at my feelings, I might get depressed like my mother was [*pausing*]. But come to think of it, if my mother *hadn't* examined her feelings, she would have been even *more* depressed.

This patient, like many others, began coping with her anxieties about looking at feelings the very moment she realized what the fear was. She then demonstrated her mastery of her anxiety by moving to examining her emotional life. Other patients are less able to do this on their own and need support and encouragement from the therapist to restructure cognitively the maladaptive belief that holds the anxiety in place.

PATIENT: If I look at my feelings, I might get depressed like my mother was . . . and that terrifies me!

THERAPIST: Can we look at how you imagine you would be? How depressed would you become?

PATIENT: I wouldn't be able to get out of bed. I wouldn't go to work. It's terrifying to even talk about.

THERAPIST: It's often more terrifying when fears are avoided. So, here together, let's imagine what you might do then, while lying in bed. How might you manage it so that this prospect no longer frightens you so? How long would you lie there?

PATIENT: Days.

THERAPIST: Really? You mean you wouldn't get up at all?

PATIENT [*Smiling slightly*]: I guess I would get up after a while, wouldn't I?

The therapist continues to explore the fears until the patient generates a greater capacity to cope with the imagined situation. In more impaired cases, the therapist and patient work together until coping skills are built that are adequate to manage the situation.

This approach also has similarities to that of Joseph Lichtenberg and his colleagues, who maintained that "we do not actively apply the concept of optimal frustration (Kohut, 1971, 1977), but rather are guided by an attempt to be optimally responsive (Bacal, 1985) to the patient's developmental needs, and the patient's exploratory-assertive motivation" (Lichtenberg, Lachmann, & Fosshage, 1992, p. 123). In other words, instead of intentionally frustrating the patient through abstinence in order to provoke anxiety or permit it to build, this treatment approach requires responding in a way that regulates anxiety to an optimal level (which requires optimal responsivity by the short-term therapist).

There are two main ways people learn and, therefore, change: by the stick (avoidance of a punisher, or respondent conditioning) or by the carrot (reinforcement, or operant conditioning). Both work, and both should be considered. Life is often frustrating, and patients must learn to master it. In the acquisition of new behaviors, however, this model gives more emphasis to the carrot of responsivity than to the stick of frustration.

Primary Focus Is on Affects and Attachment

One of the reasons for the use of confrontation, challenge, and anxiety-provoking techniques was that Davanloo's therapy focused on the "sadistic organization," holding that sadistic and aggressive impulses are the primary source of pathology for many patients and are highly defended against. For Davanloo, breaking through the resistance to underlying murderous impulses and the accompanying intense guilt and grief required strong confrontation (Davanloo, 1987). In contrast, the primary focus (and the primary pathogen) of this model is the inhibition of the full range of affects (positive and negative), but fundamentally, it is the natural longing for nurturant and protective attachment, which gives rise to grief and anger when deprived.

Both Davanloo's approach and mine deal with grief, anger, and closeness. The difference is in what affects are seen as primary and the interventions used to access them. In my treatment approach, to help the patient experience affects linked to the desire for attachment requires more clarification or affirmation than confrontation, more of a therapist-as-ally than therapist-as-challenger. My intentionally gentler focus is similar to, and has grown and developed hand in hand with, the model of Michael Alpert (1992), Diana Fosha (1992), Isabel Sklar, and their colleagues at the Short-Term Dynamic Psychotherapy Institute in New York and New Jersey. In their model, called accelerated empathic therapy (AET), the grief and pain around longing are the predominant focus.[11] Indeed, my emphasis on issues of attachment was most influenced, not by the writings of Heinz Kohut, who was one of the pioneers of this perspective, but by the powerful videotape demonstrations of AET therapists empathically exploring closeness in the real relationship between patient and therapist.[12]

[11]See Fosha (1992) for an excellent discussion contrasting the focus on sadism to the focus on grief and closeness.

[12]Annual conferences are held in New York and New Jersey by the Short-Term Dynamic Psychotherapy Institute; Michael Alpert, MD, Director; 333 East 30th Street, #15J; New York, NY 10016.

In summary, the primary focus of treatment is on the natural, human longings for connection with others, which give rise to grief and anger when disappointed and joy and tenderness when met. Certainly the focus varies across patients: Some have a circumscribed problem with anger, others with grief. But for the vast majority of patients, the primary pathogen is the unmet longing for human connection, that is, what is wanted and not wanted from the self and others that is too painful, shameful, or anxiety-laden to bear. Anxiety regulation refers to the modulation of defenses and conflicts around the functioning of the impulse–feeling pole of the Triangle of Conflict, involving not just fear but *the range of affective reactions:* anger, grief, tenderness, excitement, and joy, and their association with attachment. *This holistic focus on affects and attachment has not been adequately addressed as a source of pathology in either traditional psychodynamic theory or cognitive theory.*

A Healing Connection Rather than a Head-on Collision

Davanloo (1980) advocated an approach involving a "head-on collision" in the transference using continued confrontation and challenge because of the need to break through the sadistic organization to put the patient in touch with the range of feelings associated with warded-off rage. My model offers an alternative, a "healing connection," which focuses on tenderness and feelings of closeness and often brings a patient to tears. This totally different pathway generates emotional responses equal to the intensity of the confrontational approach but of a different quality. The deep tenderness felt by the patient is typically accompanied by intense grief and pain because the warmth and involvement of the therapist stand in such stark contrast to the patient's earlier relationships. The point is that there are many pathways and that the focus on anger, although often important, is only one method and is not necessarily the most basic. (Fosha, 1992, provides a detailed discussion of these issues.)

One of Aesop's fables can serve to illustrate this distinction between the more confrontive short-term approaches and the empathic model offered herein:

> The Sun and the Wind decided to have a contest to see which one of them could make a man, walking down the road, take off his coat. The Wind began by blowing forcefully. The man responded by pulling his coat around him more and more tightly. The Wind continued to blow so fiercely that the man, though almost blown away, was still clutching the coat tight around him. At this point, the Sun said, "Let me have a turn." Then, as the Sun shone brightly, the day became increasingly warmer. As he walked, the man began to perspire and loosen his garments. And before long, as we might expect, he took off his coat.

THE CONTINUOUS, GRADED, CORRECTIVE EMOTIONAL EXPERIENCE

The mode of constant empathic therapeutic responding provides a *continuous, graded, corrective emotional experience* for the patient.[13] Therapists working in this model do not remain neutral in regard to the patient's suffering but use their own emotional reactions to guide them in interacting with patients. The therapist is permitted the *wish to help patients* surmount the obstacles to their growth and development. This must be done in an enlightened manner, however, with the therapist neither too involved nor too distant. It is a transcendent professional position that encompasses the most healing qualities of involvement and the necessary professional distance and clear boundaries to enable the patient to emerge autonomous.

Self-psychological techniques (Baker & Baker, 1987; Kohut, 1971, 1977) are drawn on throughout treatment to enhance the therapeutic alliance and to provide support, encouragement, and reassurance for the difficult tasks undertaken by the patient. For example, the therapist strives to be as near as possible to the patient's experience of the problem by inviting the patient's assistance in a mutual construction of the core conflict formulation. The anxiety-regulating relational therapist might perceive the patient as too afraid to show anger, too ashamed to cry, or feeling too unlovable to ask for needs to be met, but he or she would collaboratively go about defining or revising the problem on the basis of patient input. As Malan has said, "No one, however experienced, can be sufficiently sure of what he is saying not to need constant feedback from the patient" (1979, p. 103). *What's the most uncomfortable thing about crying here with me? You need to feel safe before you open up, and there is probably a legitimate reason why you hesitate.*

In contrast, the anxiety-provoking therapist perceives patients as behaving in a victimized, helpless, or walled-off manner and challenges them to do otherwise: *You repeatedly hold back from crying here. This is taking a distant, walled-off stance with me. Do you see how you stay isolated and locked inside your prison doors? What do you want to do about that right now?*

Although I am distinguishing this model from its precursors, I am wary of setting up needless polarities. Both forms of dealing with resistance against feelings can have merit (confrontation versus clarification and empathy; anger versus grief or closeness). Both approaches are responded to by some patients under certain conditions. Sometimes rage is the primary pathogen and strong confrontation a useful tool. It is wise for therapists to have both sets of skills in their therapeutic armamentarium: optimal frustration as well as optimal responsivity. Indeed, in the process of anxiety regulation, there is rapid pointing out of defenses (by clarification or mild confrontation, which does in fact elicit anxiety), but then immediately (often in the same state-

---

[13]This concept was identified and the term coined by Martin Svartberg, Director of the Short-Term Therapy Research Project in Trondheim, Norway. It is drawn from Alexander and French's (1946) term "corrective emotional experience" but extends its meaning from the more general "offering the patient a new ending" to the literal focus on and modification of emotional responding in the relationship through exposure to a more adaptive (and less aversive) relationship. A gradual desensitization of fears about relationship is the result. This aspect is discussed further in chapter 6.

ment), support and validation are given, which brings the anxiety level down. Anxiety regulation can be viewed, therefore, not as one technique pitted against another, but as a blend of supportive and challenging techniques that are more widely applicable, easier for patients to bear, and easier for therapists to learn than the more confrontive alternative.

Objectives Are Specified and Results Are Quantified

The fundamental goal of psychodynamic therapy, the analysis of defenses that ward off conflicted emotion, has been broken down into specific behavioral objectives that permit scientific examination (McCullough Vaillant, 1994; see Figure 1.2).

FIGURE 1.2
Short-term treatment objectives.

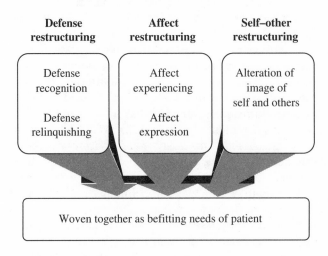

Defense restructuring consists of two components. First, the defensive behavior must be recognized by the patient, and second, it must be felt as undesirable. *Affect restructuring* also consists of two objectives. First, conflicted feelings are contained and experienced with the therapist, and then they are expressed appropriately in interpersonal relationships. *Self–other restructuring* includes two main foci: alteration of the inner representations of self and of others.[14] These objectives offer a flexible, but not rigid, data-oriented approach for working with the two triangles. The bulk of this book is devoted to teaching these treatment components, including how to assess them. The Achievement of Therapeutic Objectives Scale (ATOS; McCullough Vaillant, Meyer, & Cui, 1996) has been developed to rate the degree to which the pa-

---

[14]These objectives are related to Gustafson's (1984) three principles as follows: The defense restructuring is a set of techniques to "manage the resistance," whereas the affect restructuring and the self–other restructuring "foster the missing capabilities" (i.e., experiencing the affect and reorganizing intra- and interpersonal experience). Focal inquiry is underscored with the active delineation of the treatment objectives.

tient achieves each of these objectives. In addition, this model involves having patients rate the severity of their presenting problems throughout the treatment process to evaluate whether meeting these objectives is leading to improvement. The ultimate objectives in this scientist–practitioner approach are to (a) resolve the problem for which the patient came to treatment and (b) identify the effective treatment mechanisms. (In-session treatment evaluation is discussed in chapter 10; research methods are described in chapter 12.)

RETAINING THERAPIST INDIVIDUALITY IN A STRUCTURED TREATMENT

At the same time that I endorse this degree of standardization in treatment, I hold that it is essential for therapists to remain flexible and to retain their own personal style. Therapists are tremendously creative and idiosyncratic in the way they work, and they often vary their style for each patient being seen. Many writers on psychodynamic technique have chosen to limit structuring of treatment and specification of procedures owing to the valid concern about hampering therapist activity and rigidifying the treatment process.

The solution to this problem emerged from reviewing of videotapes with research therapists. In the struggle to develop a treatment model that was sufficiently standardized to allow research examination but permitted therapists flexibility, I began to look for points of agreement among the research therapists. The greatest consensus among the research therapists occurred regarding points at which the therapy became "stuck." I reasoned that if therapists could agree to focus on a few primary objectives (i.e., getting patients through agreed-on obstacles), they could be free to use their own particular style or their intuition to achieve the specified objectives. This provided sufficient structure for a research model and the flexibility so crucial to the therapist–patient interaction. As long as the patients were recognizing defenses and becoming less conflicted about their feelings and themselves, the therapists could decide how to accomplish the goals.

Indeed, therapist creativity is the most valued and discovery-oriented component of our research; a wide range of methods for healing can be generated, studied, and refined on the basis of this creativity. There are, and must always be, many roads to the top of this mountain. As Malan (1979) said,

> Once more it needs to be emphasized that all this is only a rough guide, which helps the therapist to find his way through the maze of the patient's material, but which will certainly be a treacherous guide if followed slavishly. (p. 93)

Rationale for Treatment: Obstacles That Became Objectives

The objectives in Figure 1.2 represent points at which therapists and patients have become bogged down in short-term treatment. These pitfalls concern problems in the resolution of defenses, affects, and relationships. The rationale and description for each objective are given in the following sections:

Obstacle 1: Inability to Recognize Defenses

While reviewing videotapes, my colleagues and I noticed that patients persistently "defended" against anger, grief, or longing for closeness by behaving in a variety of stereotypic detached or avoidant ways. The patients had no idea of what they were doing. The therapist, in the face of such behaviors, often remained silent, saying nothing that brought these avoidant or defensive behaviors into the patient's consciousness. That was the first obstacle of treatment. How can people stop being passive–aggressive or stop intellectualizing if they have no idea that they are acting in those manners? The resolution to this problem was to make the recognition of the defenses an explicit objective. The therapist could point out the defensive behavior and then empathically (not critically) help the patient to recognize it as well.

EXAMPLE OF INTERVENTIONS FOR DEFENSE RECOGNITION

I wonder if refusing to respond is an indirect way of showing anger toward your wife? What do you think?

Right now, you have begun talking rapidly and very abstractly. Do you notice yourself doing that? [Patient replies, Yeah, now that you say it.] *Could that be keeping you away from your feelings?*

Obstacle 2: Inability to Relinquish Defensive Behaviors

The second obstacle in treatment was observed when patients gained insight into their defensive avoidance but lacked the motivation to give it up. Therapists would not know what to do at this point and typically became quite frustrated. Treatment would often become stalemated. Progress would stop. The lack of motivation to give up defensive behavior is probably the biggest obstacle in psychodynamic treatment. Many levels of "reinforcement" hold such defenses in place. But if the therapist can remain focused on the idea that defenses need to be relinquished, the search can be maintained for ways to assist the patient to begin to change.

EXAMPLE OF INTERVENTION FOR DEFENSE RELINQUISHING: THE MAN WHO LOVED ICE SKATING

This 38-year-old medic and father came to treatment for marital problems. His wife refused to come to therapy.

PATIENT: Yeah, I can see now how I've been passive–aggressive with my wife. And I'm not very proud of it when I catch myself doing it. But how can I change? If I am direct, she becomes angry. What's the use? She'll never change!

THERAPIST: Well, it makes sense that no one wants to stop doing something when change would make it worse. But let's look a little closer at the pros and cons of telling your wife when you feel angry rather than staying silent in a vengeful way. You tell me that she refuses to join you and the kids on outings—like ice skating—and sometimes the two of you do not speak for days on end.

PATIENT: Yeah, I hate that.

THERAPIST: And you have been complaining that your sexual relationship suffers enormously from this "cold war" going on.

PATIENT: Yeah, it's true.

THERAPIST: It sounds pretty unpleasant.

PATIENT: It is. It's hell to live like this. I just try not to think about it.

The more ego-dystonic the defenses (i.e., the behaviors are considered distasteful and not reflecting the patient's sense of self), the easier they are to abandon. It is quite satisfying to be able to point out the harmfulness of a defensive pattern and have the patient immediately take the ball and run with it. Such cases are less frequent, but they do occur: *I never realized how I inwardly criticized myself until you pointed it out! I was stunned to see I was doing to myself just what my mother did to me! And I hated it when she did it. I never want to do that to myself again!*

Indeed, this patient did stop a large proportion of her masochistic responding just through recognizing it and wanting to stop it. But there was still emotional work to be done in regard to her angry feelings toward her mother, her grief about her painful childhood, and her longing for better treatment. This discussion leads to the next set of obstacles in treatment, which involve the experiencing of conflicted emotion and the interpersonal expression of that emotion.

OBSTACLE 3: INABILITY TO EXPERIENCE ADAPTIVE EMOTIONS

The third obstacle that was routinely noted was the phobiclike inhibition[15] of adaptive emotional responding. If patients are unable to express or even identify their basic wants and needs, they are crippled in their ability to respond in the ways necessary for adaptive living. If they cannot set limits when intruded on or grieve when there is a loss, they emit less adaptive responses to soothe or protect themselves. If they cannot ask for what they want or say *no* when undesired requests are made, how do the wants and needs become expressed?

In psychodynamic terms, such emotional inhibition is seen as the warding off of unconscious conflicts. In behavioral terms, it can be reframed as a phobic avoidance of the capacity to feel. Phobias are often associated with avoidance of external stimuli like bridges, elevators, or snakes. But phobic reactions can also occur in response to conflict-laden internal stimuli, like thoughts, feelings, or images. Phobic reactions to conflict-laden internal responses give rise to defensive reactions. One can think of such reactions as "internal phobias" or "affect phobias." It is often frustrating and perplexing

---

[15]Such inhibition is hypothesized to occur as a result of linkages of the inhibitory affects (anxiety, guilt, shame, and pain) with the adaptive affective response, possibly through a process similar to sensitization in a respondent-conditioning paradigm. Adaptive affects (e.g., assertion, grief) become sensitized by association with aversive stimuli (e.g., anxiety, shame) and are thus avoided.

to therapists to see patients recognize their defenses, want to give them up, and still be left with a phobic avoidance of feeling,[16] yet this is often the case. The experiencing of conflict and its link to the adaptive emotion, therefore, became the third objective. This objective is the sine qua non of character change (the change in procedural memory); its achievement leads to a better, fuller, and less inhibited life, a life more deeply felt from moment to moment.[17]

EXAMPLE OF INTERVENTION FOR EMOTIONAL EXPERIENCING: THE MAN WHO LOVED ICE SKATING

PATIENT: Okay, I can see that responding differently to my wife might actually help. But when I even think about speaking up or disagreeing, I just get paralyzed and freeze right up.

THERAPIST: But you say you feel angry. What's the most uncomfortable part of speaking up?

PATIENT: I have no idea.

THERAPIST: See if you can stay with that thought for a moment and discover what it might be.

PATIENT [*Long pause*]: Well, I guess it's one of two things. My mother taught me *never* to be angry with a woman. Women are delicate and can't take it. I'd feel like a horrible person.

THERAPIST: Okay, let's start by just imagining how you were feeling at a specific moment with her and how horrible you'd feel if you said what you wanted to say. Let's examine your feelings in fantasy, here where there are no consequences. Later, we can help you prepare to actually speak with her. But let's not jump to that point until you are comfortable and clear about what you feel.

In this manner, the therapist actively continues to focus on the pure experience of feeling (in this case, anger). Only after the feeling is comfortable and clear will the therapist move to the interpersonal expression of that feeling.

OBSTACLE 4: INABILITY TO EXPRESS EMOTIONS INTERPERSONALLY

Traditional dynamic therapists often have assumed that all the therapy work was done in the transference and that the benefit would automatically generalize to the patient's current life. Yet patients repeatedly demonstrate much difficulty in taking the work of therapy and effectively using it in their lives. This underscores the need for specific therapeutic intervention aimed toward that goal.

---

[16]People do not spring from the womb conflicted about crying. The 2-year-old is not initially conflicted about saying *no*. We learn to become so.

[17]This point was clarified by Lee Birk, M.D.

EXAMPLE OF INTERVENTION FOR AFFECT EXPRESSION: THE MAN WHO
LOVED ICE SKATING

PATIENT: Okay. I can see that it would be a good idea to let my wife know
when I dislike something. At least I can find out how she would respond.
But what would I say? I have never done this in my life. How does one do
it?

THERAPIST: Well, let's explore that. What would you feel like saying in the situation you mentioned earlier?

PATIENT: You mean at breakfast? Oh, yeah, let's see. Maybe I'd like to say that
I really hate it that she never joins me and the kids on our outings—even
just to watch. Since there's nothing I can do, I really want to tune it out.

THERAPIST: How could you say that to her in a way that would make it easiest for her to hear you and respond differently?

PATIENT: I guess I could tell her I was worried about her, and us, and I
wanted to talk about a problem.

THERAPIST: How would she respond to that?

PATIENT: I think, okay.

THERAPIST: All right, how would you want to say it then?

OBSTACLES 5 AND 6: MALADAPTIVE PERCEPTION OF SELF AND OTHERS

Traditional psychodynamic therapy did not target the self as a primary
therapeutic focus. However, many contemporary psychodynamic theorists
now see the negative sense of self and the negative manner in which one is
viewed by and views others to be a fundamental cause of psychopathology
(e.g., Kohut, 1977; Lichtenberg, 1983; Mann, 1973; Mitchell, 1988; Stern,
1985). The maladaptive inner representations of self and others constitute a
major obstacle to healing. *The regulation of defensive behavior patterns and affective responding goes hand in hand with improving the patient's intellectual and
experiential sense of self and others.* From this premise, the last set of objectives
emerged. As defenses are altered and affects are reorganized, the therapist
must be vigilant for opportunities to assist in shifts in negative sense of self
and maladaptive views of others.

In stably functioning individuals, self–other representations might be
minimally impaired and thus able to be rapidly altered so that the central
therapeutic focus can be on defenses and unconscious affects. In more impaired patients, the therapy work might have to involve much exploration
of conscious (rather than unconscious) affects to build a more adaptive perception of self and others. For the passive–aggressive man in the preceding
examples, learning to speak assertively to his wife about his concerns led to
shifts in his sense of himself and of her: *You know, my wife can be a much nicer
person than I thought. And* [laughing] *so can I!*

The preceding set of specific objectives provides some basic therapeutic
guidelines, analogous to learning the basic notes of the musical scale or the
basic ballet steps. Only after basic skills are acquired can one proceed to the
complexity of the symphony or Swan Lake or flow freely as in jazz or
modern dance. In like manner, after therapists acquire the basic treatment

skills, they can, with experience, proceed more and more deftly, creatively, and intuitively. Overviews of completed cases are given at the end of the chapter to demonstrate the variation in the application of these objectives.

Part 2: Terms, Theoretical Integration, and Examples

DEFINITIONS OF TERMS: SAYING
WHAT WE DO AND DOING WHAT WE SAY

At this point, I return to the poles of the two triangles and carefully lay out the mechanisms important to the treatment process I am describing. Throughout this book, I endeavor to clearly define what I do and what my terms mean. In my workshops, theory is constantly demonstrated by video-taped examples. In this book, theory is demonstrated by explicit definitions and transcripted segments of sessions. In the following sections, terms that are crucial to this treatment are defined with regard to their specific operations in the therapy setting: defenses, anxieties, emotions, affects, feelings, restructuring, Freudian structural theory, conflict–deficit, solution focus, and so on.

Defenses and Maladaptive Behavior

Defenses, as originally described by Freud, are unconscious mental mechanisms (e.g., projection, sublimation, suppression). Because defenses are intrapsychic and unseen, we can only infer their existence through manifest behaviors (McCullough, 1992; Vaillant, 1977, 1993). These include overt, observable behaviors, including verbal behavior, as well as covert behaviors such as thoughts, feelings, and images. Malan's defense pole, as operationalized in this model, refers to defensive or coping behaviors that fall on a continuum from adaptive to maladaptive in function. Indeed, many defensive responses that present as maladaptive and bring people to therapy might initially have been quite adaptive in the situation in which they were learned or first elicited. Such defensive behaviors become maladaptive only when individuals are faced with situations that require different responses from those they have been prepared to give. Therefore, defensive behaviors should be regarded as *the best ways the patient knew how to cope in the past*.

Defensive behaviors are important, if not essential, to human functioning. George Vaillant (1977, 1993) described a hierarchy ranging from mature defenses (e.g., sublimation, humor, suppression, altruism) that enrich the individual's life to immature defenses (e.g., projection, dissociation, passive–aggression) that may be protective in the short run but, in the long run, are destructive and often tragic for the self and others. When I discuss defensive or coping behaviors on the defense pole, therefore, I refer to this full, hierarchical continuum ranging from maladaptive responses (which severely inhibit adaptive responding and cause harm to self or others) to adaptive responses (which reduce stimulation but can be helpful to self and others) and including adaptive coping skills.[18] In therapy, we focus primarily on alteration of the inappropriate defenses responses, but we should not lose sight of the mature defenses that signal adaptive functioning.

Although the underlying mental mechanisms are biologically prepared, the ways they are behaviorally implemented are acquired. Defensive behavior patterns, to the extent that they have been learned, can be unlearned. For the portions that are biologically driven (through anxious, depressive, or obsessive temperaments), new learning can help the person to manage the maladaptive response better and to acquire alternative responses.

There are many ways of working with defenses. Figure 1.3 offers some examples. If we turn the Triangle of Conflict on its side and conceptualize the defense–anxiety face as a barrier (a brick wall in Figure 1.3), treatment interventions can be thought of metaphorically as ways to get over, under, around, or through the brick wall to work with the unconscious, adaptive impulses or feelings that are blocked or thwarted. Behaviorists have used flooding or implosion to go "over the top" of the defensive barrier (Stamfl & Levis, 1967). Hypnotists work with defenses, but they sneak under them or slip by them with the use of poetry, simile, or metaphor. Psychoanalytic therapists use free association to make the defenses vivid and noticeable to the patient. Free association also can extinguish conflicted experiences eventually through repeated exposure (although that was not the conscious intention).

In short-term dynamic treatments, two ways have been used to permeate the defensive barrier rapidly: anxiety-provoking and anxiety-regulating techniques. In the former, the defenses are confronted and challenged to be given up. In the latter approach, described in a subsequent section on defense restructuring, the defensive behaviors are gently and collaboratively pointed out and clarified, and the patient is encouraged and invited to relinquish them. Each approach has its merit, and each should be kept in mind.

Anxiety: The Driving Force Behind Psychopathology

On the Triangle of Conflict, the anxiety pole represents the inhibitory affects that signal conflict and lead to defensiveness, including anxiety, guilt, shame, and pain. These inhibitory affects are part of our biological endowment for response to stress and avoidance of aversive situations and, as such, overlap with Freud's "signal anxiety," which "allows us to defend against or prepare for the danger before it occurs" (Brenner, 1957, p. 121). These inhibitory reactions sometimes arise with little outside stimulus owing to biological predisposition.[19]

---

[18]See Vaillant (1977, 1992) for full descriptions of and research on defense mechanisms. Vaillant's hierarchy of defenses is more fully described in chapter 4.

[19]Research on inhibited versus uninhibited responders (e.g., Kagan, 1992, 1994) and on temperament (e.g., Whybrow, Akiskal, & McKinney, 1984) must always be taken into consideration to remain aware of the biological boundaries or limitations on learning (as discussed in Seligman & Hager, 1972).

FIGURE 1.3
Different methods for handling defenses.

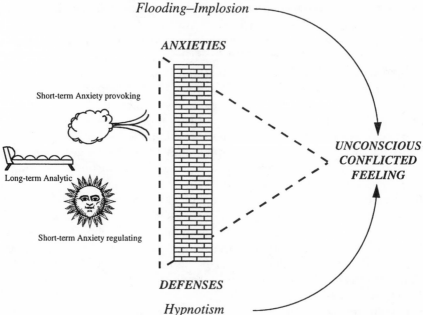

The anxieties also can become attached to various experiences through the teachings of our caretakers and our society. Optimally, such teaching helps to guide and direct the self in the process of self-protection or obtaining of wants or needs. Anxiety can tell people when they are proceeding in a direction that might be hurtful. Guilt signals that some rule or law is being transgressed. Shame signals that one has behaved in a manner unacceptable to one's deepest sense of self. Pain, referring to emotional pain, signals that some experience is distressing or unbearable. These natural inhibitory responses are essential to our well-being, therefore, and they signal danger to ourselves and to others. They can become our own worst enemies, however. When our caretakers or society (often unintentionally) teaches excessive levels of guilt, shame, pain, and anxiety, these feelings, originally helpful signals, begin to thwart the expression of wants or needs. The extreme versions can go beyond mere signals and even lead to self-attacking or self-abusive behavior (a form of traumatic anxiety). Signal anxiety can become traumatic and paralyzing inhibition; guilt can become self-attack and self-hate; shame can become humiliation or self-degradation; and emotional pain can become unbearable anguish.[20] These severely aversive reactions are not the

---

[20]On the anxiety pole, signal anxiety should be distinguished from traumatic or primary anxiety, in which the psyche is overwhelmed by an influx of anxiety that is too great to master (Brenner, 1957). Signal anxiety (i.e., conflict) generates defensiveness that blocks alternative and more adaptive responding. Traumatic anxiety, as Freud used the term, represents the *absence* of higher level defensiveness such as in-

optimal forms of the inhibitory affects but the generators of psychopathology; therefore, the restructuring of the learned component of inhibitory reactions is a major factor in psychotherapeutic change. In summary, *the driving force behind much psychopathology is the maladaptive level of the affects at the anxiety pole and the related cognitions and beliefs.*

Relation of Affects to Emotions, Drives, and Feelings

Emotions in this model are not limited to the Freudian dual-drive concept of sex and aggression but include the full range of emotional reactions in our biological repertoire. There is a growing body of empirical research supporting the basic motivational qualities of affects (e.g., Emde, 1992; Stern, 1985), which underscores the fact that Freud's dual-drive model needs reconsideration. Both Silvan Tomkins and Daniel Stern, as well as others, tell us that the observed infant presents a different picture from the one Freud originally predicted; there are multiple affect-based motivational systems demonstrable in infancy, such as attachment and curiosity. Stern concluded that "it is of no help to imagine that all of these are derivatives of a single unitary motivational system" (1985, p. 238). The view emerging from neurological research on affect responses (e.g., MacLean, 1972, 1985) and the functioning of the amygdala in lower mammals (Insel, 1992; LeDoux, 1992) and humans (Damasio, 1994; Halgren, 1992) suggests that emotional and cognitive systems become more highly interwoven the more complex the brain but that affective processing has strong impact on motivation of behavior.

Silvan Tomkins's affect theory (1962, 1963, 1991, 1992) elegantly and simply comes the closest to my understanding of clinical reality and is more fully described in chapter 6. Here, I give a brief overview. The term *emotion* in this model is used as Tomkins uses it, as a global category for inner bodily experience, which includes three biologically endowed systems: drives, affects, and pain.[21] *Affect* is a subtype of emotion, therefore. *Feeling* is a more general, more conversational term that I use for the felt experience of all these emotions, which are (whether we are aware of it or not) always there with us, to a greater or lesser degree, every moment of our lives.[22]

Drives signal a primary bodily need that requires transport of something

---

termediate or even immature defenses. In this case, the overwhelming anxiety reaction is paralyzing to the self and is an example of extreme self-assault. Defenses no longer are able to operate to avoid the anxiety–conflict. However, the traumatic anxiety that floods the system can be seen to *function as a primitive and masochistic defense in that it blocks the expression of other adaptive responses.* I label such reactions as *defensive feelings.*

[21]Basch (1976) defined *affects* as discrete but unconscious categories of biological experience, *feelings* as consciously felt experience, and *emotions* as feelings associated with memories (also conscious). Because discrete affects as well as complex emotions can be both conscious and unconscious, I do not find Basch's distinction about consciousness a useful one. I have chosen to retain Tomkins's more grounded definitions.

[22]We may not be consciously aware that we are sad, or sexually aroused, or ashamed, or angry until the emotional signal becomes strong enough, or unconfused enough, to be labeled. But until feelings are made conscious, these vague, subliminal, but ever-present wants and needs drag us hither and yon.

in and out of the body. These include breathing, eating, drinking, bladder and bowel functions, sexual behavior, and attachment, or social responsivity. It is clear what each of these drives transports, except possibly for social responsivity; however, research on mammals has clarified attachment behaviors, for example, caretaking of offspring, breast feeding, and cuddling (e.g., Insel, 1992).[23] Such research lends support to the existence of a "drive" for "affectional bonding" noted by John Bowlby (1982).[24] The point is that the drives have specific behaviors and targets. Tomkins noted that we rarely confuse hunger with thirst or the need for air with the urge to defecate. Sexual desire is also a distinct experience from the other drives. Drives tend to be unambiguous, unconditioned responses (e.g., hunger) linked to unconditioned stimuli (e.g., food).

Affects, in contrast, have not been so easily defined or distinguished. Although everyone knows one is hungry in the mouth or stomach and aroused in the genital area, it is much less clear where in the body one is afraid, angry, sad, or excited. Tomkins noted that "it is not altogether clear what [the affects] are, how many there are, how different one is from another or even 'where' they are" (1992, p. 171).

A critical point in understanding the functioning of affects in mental health or illness is that because these *affective associations* (not the affects themselves but what they come to be attached to) are learned, they can be unlearned. Drives are not learned, nor is what they transport learned; therefore, *drives are far less malleable than the affects.* We breathe air, and we cannot learn to breathe anything else. According to Tomkins, however, we can learn and thus relearn what gives us joy or excitement versus what gives us shame or distress. Thus, the affects can impact on the drives. We can learn to breathe with ease or pain, to eat with shame or enjoyment, to have sex angrily or excitedly, and to be attached to others fearfully or joyfully. Affects impact on other affects as well. If guilt or anxiety becomes associated with the expression of anger, sorrow, or attachment, that expression will be inhibited as well as confused and difficult to label or identify. *Affects, not drives, are the stuff of psychotherapeutic change and the focus of this treatment.*

Tomkins devoted his life to clarifying issues concerning affects on a mild–strong continuum.[25] His research identified nine categories of affects, two positive (interest–excitement and enjoyment–joy), one neutral (surprise–startle), and six negative (anger–rage,[26] distress–anguish, shame–

---

[23]Insel (1992) demonstrated the differences in limbic structures underlying such attachment behavior in the prairie vole ("cuddlers") compared to the montane vole ("noncuddlers").

[24]Tomkins noted that we "stay in touch" through the eyes and the smile when physically separate. And it is through imagery and memory that we stay attached when out of sight.

[25]See Tomkins (1981) for a compelling account of his lifelong struggle to bring affective responding to the attention of clinical psychology and the neurosciences.

[26]To clarify confusion about aggression and anger, Tomkins noted that anger is not a drive but an affect, because it does not serve to transport anything in or out of the body; it does not demonstrate the periodicity of the other drives; and it does not have a specific target. Unlike eating food or breathing air, anger is a more general signal

humiliation, fear–terror, contempt–disgust, and dissmell, i.e., the unpleasant experience of smelling spoiled food). Each of these categories is identified by (a) a particular pattern and density of neural firing in response to inner or outer stimuli, (b) an inner bodily sensation, and most important for Tomkins, (c) a specific facial expression. Subsequent research by Paul Ekman (1984, 1992b) and Carroll Izard (1990) on facial expression has found consistent cross-cultural convergence in recognition and labeling of five affects (anger, fear, sadness, enjoyment, and disgust), supporting the innateness and the universality of most of these affect categories. There is less consistent evidence cross culturally for surprise–startle, contempt, and shame–guilt (Ekman & Davidson, 1994, p. 413).

Each of the basic affects is not a single affective state but "a family of related states," and each affect family "can be considered to constitute a theme and variations" (Ekman, 1992b, p. 172). For example, the "affect family" represented by Tomkins's continuum called distress–anguish includes sorrow, sadness, grief, despair, woe, and so on. The affect family referred to as anger–rage includes related affects such as irritation, annoyance, assertion, and fury, to name only a few. The affect family referred to as interest–excitement encompasses curiosity, enthusiasm, and attraction. Robert Plutchik, who studies the evolutionary significance of affects, pointed out that emotions are like primary colors that can be mixed to yield a wide range of variation (1984, p. 200). The variations around the basic affect family themes are discussed in chapter 7.

Equally important to what affect categories *are* is what affect is *used for*. One of Tomkins's major contributions to the understanding of psychopathology is his recognition that drives are not the powerful forces psychotherapists think them to be. *Rather, Tomkins cited abundant evidence that we are far more controlled by our affects than our drives.* He pointed out that our sexual drive, which seems so strong, can easily become quite "finicky" when associated with shame or anxiety. Similarly, the drive for attachment can be thwarted by conflict, an ever-present problem in therapy.

> Affects constitute the primary motivational system not only because the drives necessarily require amplification from the affects, but because the affects are sufficient motivators in the absence of drives. . . . We are therefore confronted at the outset with the paradox that what is of secondary motivational significance for man is clear and well known [the drives] but what is of primary motivational significance [the affects] is less clear and less certain both to everyman and to students of motivation.
>
> The specificity of the drive system is such that it instructs and motivates concerning *where* and *when* to do *what*, to *what*—lending the drive

---

that negatively amplifies *any* experience it becomes associated with. Furthermore, aggression is only one possible consequence of anger. Adaptive assertion is an equally probable response. In like manner, joy positively amplifies whatever experience it becomes linked with. Anger is discussed further in chapters 6 and 7.

its peculiar visibility. An affect is inherently more general in structure. This increased generality greatly reduces the visibility and the distinctness of the affect. (Tomkins, 1992, pp. 171–172)

This confusion about our basic motivational systems presents a major problem for the study of psychopathology and of human nature in general. Social science has for too long ignored the functions of the limbic cortex (the seat of the affects as well as the attachment drive) in favor of the drives governed by the hypothalamus (e.g., hunger, thirst, sexual functioning). "A world experienced without any affect would be a pallid, meaningless world. We would know *that* things happened, but we could not care whether they did or not" (Tomkins, 1978, p. 203). Furthermore, because affects are more malleable than drives, they offer the practicing clinician a way to have an impact on environmentally based psychopathology.

We learn to fear or enjoy certain things and, depending on our experience, we learn not to fear or not to enjoy other things. Although some fears (e.g., spiders, heights) are more biologically prepared than others, the majority of fears arise from or can be impacted on by current experience. A toddler will avoid crawling over what appears to be a drop-off unless the mother's face is smiling and reassuring, in which case, the toddler "learns" that it is safe (and possibly enjoyable) to proceed. We may learn to enjoy sports but not to enjoy dancing, or vice versa. The affects are so flexible because the evolving human species required just such a flexible motivational system to permit adaptation to a wide variety of experience. Because these environmentally acquired associations are learned, they also are responsive to the new learning offered in psychotherapy. Because affects are our *primary motivators* and are *responsive to learning*, the treatment approach in this manual focuses on the restructuring of affective experience and the learned affect associations that undergird psychopathology.

Finally, to restructure affective experience appropriately, it is crucial to understand how affects are used, that is, the adaptive and maladaptive functions they serve. The action tendencies of affects are fundamentally soothing, protective, exploratory, care soliciting, and caregiving. The growing body of mother–infant research suggests that human nature at the core is essentially benign and relationship-oriented, unless the individual is deprived or attacked (e.g., Lichtenberg, 1983, 1989; Shapiro & Emde, 1992; Stern, 1985). Affects have evolved to guide and direct our behavior *toward adaptive ends*, that is, to cry when sad, to assert limits when intruded on, to laugh when happy, to seek out what is interesting, to withdraw from what is threatening, and to feel calmness and joy when all goes well.

The assumption that our basic nature is benign is at odds with the Freudian position that we have primitive, bestial urges that have to be controlled. Jay Greenberg and Stephen Mitchell found these two views of human nature irreconcilable, because they viewed drive theory (i.e., that "social organization is . . . purchased at the price of massive instinctual renunciation"; 1983 p. 402) as basically incompatible with relational theories (i.e., that "human fulfillment is sought in the establishment and maintenance of relationships with others"; Mitchell, 1988, p. 403).[27]

A solution to this "irreconcilable" dichotomy can be found in Tomkins's affect theory. If Freud's dual-drive model is broadened to include the full range of drives as well as affective responding, according to Tomkins, then social responsivity becomes one of the drives, and affect is the soil that attachment grows in. We spring from the womb socially responsive (the infant tracks the human face and smiles). The affect that becomes associated with attachment creates the bridge, or the gulf, between self and others. Positive affective connections build closeness, security, and trust; negative affective connections build interpersonal barriers. Again, affects, not drives, are the primary focus of psychotherapeutic intervention.[28] Expressed somewhat differently and in part metaphorically, "hypothalamic" drives have increasingly evolved to take a backseat to the "limbic" affects and attachment. Affect bridges the gap between intrapsychic and interpersonal orientations and has the power to make or break relational bonds.

When bestial or evil behavior emerges, therefore, it does not arise only from primitive instinctual urges or biologically endowed impulses; it arises also, and probably more often, from inhumane treatment from others. In other words, most destructive human responses can be seen, at least in part, as *defensive* in function. Certainly, we must take into consideration the heritability of antisocial traits (e.g., twin studies of Jary & Stewart, 1985). Nevertheless, such criminal individuals constitute a very small percentage of the human population. Without such biological impairment, does the newborn

[27]Mitchell (1988) struggled with an integration of relational theories and drive theory. He felt comfortable with Stern's description of human development as "a continuous unfolding of an intrinsically determined social nature" (Stern, 1985, p. 234). Yet Mitchell asked, "Is it meaningful to speak of an innate drive toward relation? . . . as soon as one establishes a motive as innate, one ironically closes it off somewhat from analytic inquiry" (1988, p. 62). Mitchell preferred to use the "notion of the relational matrix" in a "broad paradigmatic sense" including "many different forms of connection . . . including innate wiring . . . , motivational intent . . . , self-definition, etc." (p. 62). I agree with this problem of innateness not being open to analytic inquiry. But the affects that are associated with attachment *are* open to inquiry (e.g., joy vs. shame): associations that psychotherapeutic learning can have an impact on.

[28]Many theorists have been converging on an affect-related view of human functioning. Kernberg, Kohut, and others have addressed the affect-relational issues but without a specific theory of emotion. Greenson (1967), Basch (1976), Nathanson (1992, 1996), and Lichtenberg (1983) have suggested that a broader range of affects replace the dual-drive model. (Basch and Nathanson specifically have endorsed Tomkins's model.) More recently, Benjamin (1993b) has emphasized that attachment is fundamental in psychopathology, although she does not incorporate an affect theory explicitly in her model. Nathanson (1992, 1996) has been one of the strongest proponents of Tomkins's affect theory in psychotherapy but does not incorporate attachment as a drive. Lichtenberg (1983) proposed five affect-based motivational systems to replace the dual-drive model. But for the past 30 years, Malan has included the full range of emotion (i.e., impulse/feeling) in his model, and always in relation to closeness to others. Therefore, his thinking is most compatible with this model.

infant spring from the womb a rapist, a murderer, a child abuser? Research on mother–infant interaction suggests not.

Stern holds that classical libido theory has not proved to be operationalizable nor of great heuristic value for the observed infant. He suggested that the concept of motivation be "reconceptualized in terms of many discrete but interrelated, motivational systems such as attachment competence-mastery, curiosity and others" (1985, p. 238). The theoretical Kleinian baby, bursting with primitive rage, seems mysteriously missing from the research laboratories, where infants cry when frustrated but when not frustrated seek the mother's gaze and reach out and smile. Could it be that rage-filled criminals are more often "made" than "born"? And conversely, is it not possible for the environment to cause even highly prepared (i.e., biologically innate) reactions (either positive or negative) to be amplified, minimized, or nullified by positive or negative affective reactions? The model in this book is dedicated to the amelioration of the *learned component of socially aversive or destructive behavior,* despite the inevitable biological contributions.

The inclusion of Tomkins's affect theory in this model also provides the needed connection between affect and attachment. I concur with Tomkins that (a) the action tendencies of affects are primary motivators in human functioning; (b) the affects associated with social responsivity are fundamental to human interaction; (c) because affects become associated with various experiences through learning, these affect associations, when maladaptive, can be altered or unlearned in psychotherapy; and (d) when destructive behavior occurs, it is probably generated to a large degree as a result of inhumane treatment (i.e., shame) from others.

The Self and Its Role in Psychopathology

While no one can agree on exactly what the self is, we have a sense of self that permeates daily . . . experience. . . . There is the sense of a self that is a single, distinct, integrated body; there is the agent of actions, the experiencer of feelings, the maker of intentions, the architect of plans, the transposer of experience into language, the communicator and sharer of personal knowledge.

Even though the nature of the self may forever elude the behavioral sciences, the sense of self stands as an important subjective reality. . . . How we experience *ourselves in relation to others* [italics added] provides a basic organizing perspective for all interpersonal events. (Stern, 1985, pp. 5–6)

The aspects of the self that this model focuses on in promoting character change are represented by the poles of the Triangle of Conflict (defenses, anxieties, and the full range of feelings) in the context of its relationship to the categories of the Triangle of Person. First, and most fundamental to self-knowledge, is knowing our affects (i.e., our motives on the I/F pole). Knowing what one likes and dislikes, knowing what one wants or does not want, is to know oneself as the experiencer of feelings. Understanding our inhibitions or conflicts (i.e., the inhibiting or sometimes self-attacking affects at the A pole) tells us to what degree we are or are not the "maker of our intentions." Finally, understanding our defensive and coping behaviors tells us how and when we are or are not the agents of our actions and the architect of our plans. The Triangle of Conflict offers the therapist and patient a structure within which to organize, and reorganize, a stable sense of self.

This self-knowledge is learned (and relearned) in relation to others, however, and must be communicated and shared. The age-old dichotomy of individuality versus relatedness can be transcended through knowledge of the interwoven nature of the two triangles, similar to the "self-in-relation" presented in the work of Judy Jordan and her colleagues (Jordan, Kaplan, Miller, Stiver, & Stiver, 1991). Sense of self represented by the Triangle of Conflict originates, and can only be changed, in this relational context: the interpersonal environment of the Triangle of Person (as the book cover illustrates), which is paramount in the relationship with the therapist and extends to current persons and past persons. A stable and compassionate sense of self can occur only within a matrix of caring relationships. (For an excellent review, see Guisinger & Blatt, 1994.)

Restructuring
There are two main forms of restructuring: (a) altering the severity of inhibitory, aversive, or potentially self-attacking affects (anxiety, guilt, shame, pain, and so on) that have become associated with various forms of adaptive affect-based responding along with the acquisition of new capabilities in the procedural memory trace and (b) building new insights or concepts in the declarative memory trace. Restructuring of procedures is primarily achieved through an extinction process similar to desensitization, in which the patient is exposed to these inhibitory feelings and their associated experiences until they are brought within normal limits, that is, either sensitized or desensitized. This can be done in some clinical situations through imagined scenes (imaginal desensitization) or through the positive, healing relationship with the therapist ("in vivo" desensitization), so that the memory trace, or the procedural structure, is altered. The corrective relationship with the therapist replaces with positive affects the inhibitory emotion previously associated with attachment. Restructuring of concepts requires education or modeling to alter the declarative memory.

Freud's term for the change agent in psychoanalysis was *Nachtraglichkeit*, "the retranscription of the memory trace."[29] Modell pointed out that through this dynamic reconstruction *the present can alter the past* (1990, p. 128). Restructuring can be thought of as reorganizing the way we view, experience, and remember the world, and the worldview held in memory is not cast in stone but *constructed and reconstructed over time* (e.g., neural Darwinism; Edelman, 1992). Therapy is an optimal occasion to restructure these

[29]Modell (1990) highlighted this concept throughout his book. He pointed out that memory is a dynamic reconstruction and cited Freud using words such as "the remodeling," "rearrangement," or "reconstruction" of memories (pp. 16–17).

affect-laden memories and, by doing so, heal the long-standing pain of character pathology. In each of the three main treatment objectives, *regulation of anxiety through exposure to the conflicted feelings* is the fundamental change agent in the restructuring process.

This process of exposure has extensive theoretical and research support, such as reflected in the following words of Barlow:

> For years, therapists of all persuasions have agreed that a necessary step in the treatment of clinical phobia is to encourage contact with the feared object or situation. The well-known statement of Freud on the necessity of having phobic patients eventually face their fears has often been used to support exposure-based treatments: "One can hardly ever master a phobia if one waits till the patient lets the analysis influence him to give it up ... one succeeds only when one can induce them through the influence of the analysis ... to go about alone and struggle with the anxiety while they make the attempt" (Freud, 1919/1959, pp. 165–166). In fact, exposure to feared situations has become the sine qua non of any therapeutic approach to phobia. (Barlow, 1988, p. 311)

Because this model considers the basis of psychopathology to be affect phobias, effective restructuring in short-term treatment must include some component of exposure. The following paragraphs describe how restructuring occurs in the main treatment objectives.

Defense restructuring means both building new concepts (identifying patterns) and altering the association between the inhibitory affects and the maladaptive or defensive behavior until the behavior is no longer necessary. Psychodynamic theory posits that defenses occur because of anxieties or conflict. In behavioral terms, then, defensive or maladaptive behaviors have become associated with aversive affect, and defensive behavior will not be given up until it is less aversive to do so, that is, less anxiety-connected.[30] For example, passivity will not be given up until there is less shame or fear in assertion; numbing of feeling will not be given up until there is less pain involved in reexperiencing ungrieved events or memories. In defense restructuring, the therapist moves back and forth, first pointing out defensive patterns (declarative knowledge) and then pointing out destructive levels of anxiety, guilt, shame, or pain, until the associations between the anxieties and the defensive patterns are reduced (procedural knowledge); see Figure 1.4a: *Do you see how you numb yourself* (defensive–maladaptive response) *when you feel sad* (affect being avoided) *because you're afraid of how painful* (anxiety–conflict) *it would be? Can we explore your memories of how painful it was until you feel more able to bear it?*

The goal of defense restructuring is first to identify and then to regulate the anxieties (i.e., the anxiety- or conflict-laden memory or appraisal) to a level at which the maladaptive defenses are no longer necessary (i.e., when

---

[30]Lichtenberg (1989) similarly maintained that defenses are the result of an "aversive motivational system."

thought about, the situation is viewed less aversively). As a result, more adaptive coping behaviors may be employed. For most people, defensive behaviors leave a lot of room for improvement, and restructuring of defenses offers a valuable treatment intervention.

Affect restructuring means reducing the anxieties or conflicts (the inhibitory affects on the A pole) that have become associated with primary adaptive responses, feelings, wants, or needs by identification and then exposure. Put differently, the potentially adaptive, self-soothing affects are often experienced just milliseconds before the inhibitory response is elicited. Exploration in imagery helps the patient become aware of the adaptive feeling, and repeated exposure in imagery helps the warded-off affect become more familiar (less aversive or anxiety provoking and thus desensitized). As a result, inhibition is no longer so necessary or desired, and it becomes replaced by positive affect (i.e., "retranscribing" the feelings and images in the memory trace).

FIGURE 1.4a
Defense restructuring.
Defense recognition
Defense relinquishing

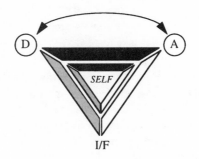

Primary focus:
Identification and regulation of anxieties
associated with defensive behaviors
Underlying affects are pointed out but not explored in depth

In restructuring of affect, the therapist moves back and forth between the I/F pole (adaptive feeling) and the A pole (inhibitory affects), first making distinctions among the affective processes and then exposing the patient to specific emotional memories (current or past) and the associated anxiety, guilt, shame, or pain until the adaptive feeling is experienced comfortably and the expression is appropriately freed up (see Figure 1.4b): *Whenever I ask you about your father's death, you skip away. I wonder if we can look at what is the most painful part to remember. How was it for you to visit him in the hospital?*

In affect restructuring, imaginal desensitization and in vivo desensitization are the same. It is through imagery that affective experience is elicited, and it is during imagery that the patient is exposed to the actual inner experience of the affect.

FIGURE 1.4b
Affect restructuring.

Affect experiencing
Affect expression

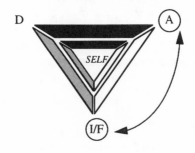

Primary focus:
Exposure to and regulation of anxieties
associated with experience and expression of affects
Defenses are always present to some degree but need not be focused
on in depth unless they block the affective experience

Restructuring of self–other representations means that the therapist helps the patient regulate the degree of aversiveness or inhibition that has been associated with attachment, that is, the experience of self, others, or both. An adaptive "attachment to self" is a much overlooked concept, but it is a crucial one for self-care, self-compassion, and self-esteem. To restructure the sense of self, the therapist helps to identify the patient's perception of the ideal self and optimal relations to others. Then the associated aversive images of the self (i.e., anxious, shameful, painful, or guilt-laden memories; images represented on the A pole) are regulated (see Figure 1.4c): *Why do you think of yourself as a shameful child because you overate? Weren't you desperately hungry for attention? Didn't you feel soothed by eating something?*

In clinical work, these three objectives are not dealt with sequentially but are parallel strands to be woven together as needed throughout the treatment process. Some patients can recognize and give up their defenses readily but remain blocked to feelings of closeness to others or carry an entrenched negative sense of self. Other patients have mixed capacities in each of the objectives, so that the therapist has to move back and forth among them, identifying concepts and encouraging exposure to the anxiety-laden experiences.

Relation Between Freudian Structural Theory and Malan's Two Triangles
Because the two triangles, according to Malan, represent the "universal principle of psychodynamic psychotherapy" (1979, p. 94), the three poles on

the Triangle of Conflict are often mistakenly considered to be synonymous with Freud's structural theory: The defense pole is sometimes seen as synonymous with the ego, the anxiety pole with the superego, and the impulse pole with the id. Referring back to Figure 1.1, the I/F pole could be mistaken as representing the "uncivilized" impulses of sex and aggression that need to be held in check or controlled by civilizing influences, which are represented by the anxiety pole (the superego). Following this line of thinking, the defense pole represents various compromises between internal and external reality: the price we pay for civilization. Although there are large areas of overlap between the traditional view and the model in this book, these definitions now require updating and revision on the basis of recent research.

FIGURE 1.4c
Self–other restructuring.

Alteration of inner representation of self
Alteration of inner representations of others

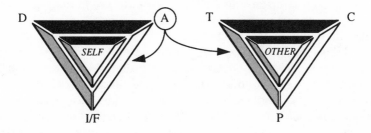

Primary focus:
Regulation of anxieties
associated with the sense of self and perception of others
In more severely impaired patients this focus may precede
defense and affect restructuring

The superego is, indeed, encompassed in the functions of the anxiety pole. (*Superego* is defined as the inner representation of society, i.e., conscience or morality, and includes the ideal as well as the negative sense of self and others [Hinsie & Campbell, 1960].) Our conscience is needed to guide us. An adaptive superego and sense of self should signal dangerous, taboo, or harmful responses. Red traffic lights mean *stop*, and they help to save lives. When our social learning is sufficiently severe to inhibit or even attack the self, however, it can become a source of psychopathology. In such cases, the overly harsh superego and the resulting negative images of self and others are more like an electrical shock, ranging in response from a mild punishment to a masochistic assault to annihilation through suicide.

In short-term anxiety-regulating psychotherapy, a typical goal is to restructure actively, or regulate, these harsh reactions (negative–punitive conceptions of self or others) into an adaptive set of images that guides and protects the individual, rather than one that attacks, belittles, or destroys. (Conversely, insufficient guilt or shame leads some people to misuse anger and contempt; insufficient anxiety can lead to lack of impulse control; and so on.)

Similarly, the defense pole certainly does represent one facet of ego functioning. (*Ego functioning* is defined as responses that mediate between and adapt to inner and outer reality [Hinsie & Campbell, 1960].) But such functioning can range from adaptive to maladaptive reactions. In this model, the defense pole is focused on primarily when it is malfunctioning. Consider the analogy of an immune response. Immune mechanisms and white cell manufacture require treatment only when they malfunction. If ego functioning is put on a maladaptive-to-adaptive continuum, the maladaptive defensive reactions are those most at odds with the adaptive emotions on the impulse–feeling pole. Adaptive defensive reactions are those most integrated with the impulse–feeling pole, which is the new version of the id, including the full range of adaptive drives and affects. Altruism, sublimation, and other ingenious coping strategies all facilitate some degree of adaptive gratification of our wants and needs.

Again, the Freudian construct of the id, "part of the energy system of the psyche" (Hinsie & Campbell, 1960), is only partially represented by the impulse–feeling pole and requires the greatest alteration in this model. The view that the id consists of bestial impulses (sex and aggression) needing to be controlled by the superego and repressed through the ego defenses needs reevaluation in light of recent research. As mentioned earlier, the dual-drive model emphasizes hypothalamic function and downplays or ignores the limbic cortex. Researchers and theorists of affect (Ekman & Davidson, 1993; Plutchik, 1984; Tomkins, 1962) and of mother and infant (e.g., Emde, 1992; Shapiro & Emde, 1992; Stern, 1985, 1995) have amply described emotional or "attuned" interactions that, far from being bestial, are self-soothing, self-protective responses that are our biological endowment. Far from holding these in check, we need to learn how to mature so that our affects evolve into well-guided expression. Many contemporary "post-Freudian" analysts endorse similar themes (e.g., Balint, 1968; Basch, 1976, 1985; Bollas, 1986, 1989, 1995; Lichtenberg, 1983, 1989; Lichtenberg, Lachmann, & Fosshage, 1992; Malan, 1979; Pine, 1990; Stolorow & Atwood, 1992; Stolorow & Lachmann, 1980; Winnicott, 1965).

This affect–relational interpretation of the Triangle of Conflict posits that at our core are a range of adaptive emotions that reflect our basic wants and needs. These emotions are represented by the impulse–feeling pole at the bottom of the triangle. At the top of the triangle are responses, which have been learned in our environment (defense and conflicts poles), that either guide and direct or thwart and abuse our emotionally based responding. Of course, we must always be mindful that our biological endowment, or temperament, shapes our responding to some degree. But our defensive responses and coping abilities become associated with our experience largely through learning. Rather than being the necessary compromise of civilization, these learned associations can range from the most freeing and mature forms of guidance and self-help for the individual to the most destructive and crushing forms of self-abuse that deny individuals the expression of their emotional birthright. The tragedy of civilization is that the biologically prepared responses of the impulse–feeling pole, which have the potential to motivate us toward obtaining adaptive and necessary wants and needs, are the very responses that are so often annihilated by the destructive inhibition of anxiety, shame, and pain, so often originating (whether intentionally or not) with caretakers and society.

If our basic emotional endowment is seen as adaptive, where does one place the uncontrolled or destructive impulses on the Triangle of Conflict? Where resides the traditional Freudian id, our bestial impulses? (We know we have them!) They certainly cannot reside on the I/F pole because, as noted previously, that pole is defined as representing adaptive emotional functioning. Because each pole of the triangle is defined in terms of its function, I put maladaptive emotional responses on the destructive end of the defense pole continuum; any form of behavior (including affects or any emotion) that is destructive or maladaptive goes there. Put differently, maladaptive emotional responding (along with all other forms of maladaptive responding) also occurs at the maladaptive end of the defense pole continuum, owing to conflict at the anxiety pole. I call such emotions "defensive emotions," a concept that will be a crucial factor in understanding and changing pathology throughout this book.

Organic deficits, attention-deficit disorder, and intoxication (like abuse in childhood) make affect hard to pull up into consciousness and even harder for an individual to guide or control. As a result, biologically impaired individuals more frequently replace healthy affects like grief, longing, and assertion with affects such as extreme frustration, perverse or dependent attachment, or self-attack. But the latter affects are defensive in function; they are neither primary nor adaptive. Although emotions start off being adaptive, they can become perverted and destructive through environmental learning, abuse, neglect, or frustration from organic deficit. In such cases, the originally adaptively designed emotions become "bestial" only when perverted by the environment, society, caretakers, or brain pathology.

Freud wrote, "Where id was there ego shall be" (1930, p. 73). If the concept of the id is to be updated with the current research on affect, Freud's maxim needs rewording: Where defensive or self-attacking responses are, there adaptive self-soothing responses shall be. Where want and need are, there shall we strive toward more optimal expression of wants and needs (see Figure 1.5).

FIGURE 1.5
Two views of human nature using Malan's two triangles.

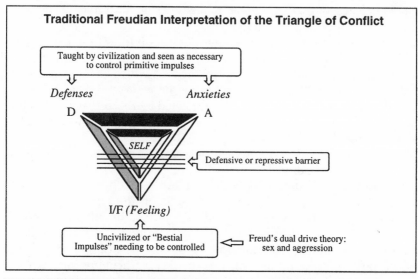

Traditional Freudian Interpretation of the Triangle of Conflict

Taught by civilization and seen as necessary to control primitive impulses

Defenses   *Anxieties*

D   A

SELF

Defensive or repressive barrier

I/F *(Feeling)*

Uncivilized or "Bestial Impulses" needing to be controlled ← Freud's dual drive theory: sex and aggression

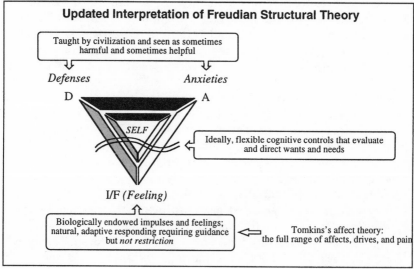

Updated Interpretation of Freudian Structural Theory

Taught by civilization and seen as sometimes harmful and sometimes helpful

Defenses   *Anxieties*

D   A

SELF

Ideally, flexible cognitive controls that evaluate and direct wants and needs

I/F *(Feeling)*

Biologically endowed impulses and feelings; natural, adaptive responding requiring guidance but *not restriction* ← Tomkins's affect theory: the full range of affects, drives, and pain

Conflict Versus Deficit Pathology:
The Building and Renovation of Psychic Structures

For many years, theoreticians have seen conflict and deficit as separate forms of pathology. One can be inept at dancing because one never was given lessons (a deficit) or because of anxiety resulting from harsh instruction (conflict). Modern writers such as Glen Gabbard (1994), Arnold Modell (1990), and Hans Thoma and Horsh Kachele (1985) have tried to avoid such a polarity, because most patients have pathology in both areas. Nevertheless, there are distinctions that must be made, and for the short-term therapist, there must be ready guides for action. For this reason, I identify some simple rules of thumb. First, we need to be aware that with each patient there are some structures that need to be "built from the ground up," and other structures, built not wisely but too well, that require renovation. Frank Lachmann (1988) suggested that we view these two forms of pathology as "figure–ground" distinctions.

Much of the prior discussion has referred to the conflict, or renovation, process, assuming a basically sound individual needing restructuring of defenses and affects. (Short-term therapy was not developed for criminals or abandoned children.) However, some patients have an absence of knowledge of the self or of others that the therapist has to help remedy through exploration, validation, or affirmation of the patient's experience. The difference between conflict and deficit pathology lies in their etiologies and in the interventions that are needed. The issue is whether different models of pathology are necessary to guide treatment or whether one model may suffice. In the following discussion, the functions of Malan's Triangle of Conflict and Triangle of Person demonstrate my position that both deficit and conflict forms of pathology may be explained by the structures in this single model.

Conflict pathology (also referred to as "oedipal" conflicts, or "triangular" conflicts such as competition for a parent or rivalry with siblings) has typically referred to responses seated on the anxiety pole, the inhibitory, aversive, or even self-attacking feelings that ward off more adaptive responses (i.e., the superego). Freudian theory suggests that conflict arises in response to rivalry with a parent or sibling for the other parent. The resulting competitive and aggressive impulses are met with feelings of guilt or shame and thus become conflicted. In conflict pathology, one may not assert oneself (or openly grieve, or love tenderly and passionately) because one has a conflict about doing so (e.g., anxiety, guilt, shame, or pain). This can result from the caretakers, society, or culture being overly restrictive or not properly attuned to the child's needs. Conflict also can result from an overly sensitive or impaired temperament that needed special handling.

Whatever the origin, such individuals often have been taught, or have learned indirectly, that to express certain affects is bad. Or they simply may not have been taught how to channel the full adaptive repertoire of emotions. Those burdened with conflict pathology typically have been well taught what they must do to win acceptance or approval but not taught how to identify and value their own wants and needs. All societies put some degree of restriction on emotional responding, so this problem is ubiquitous. In any case, such individuals can be seen as having been overly or improperly socialized before they were allowed to discover their own humanity. This usually means either *too much involvement* or *inappropriate involvement* with others.

The term *deficit* generates more confusion. Theoretically, this form of pathology typically refers to preoedipal or early life trauma that occurs in a deficient dyadic relationship; generally, the relationship is between the mother and child, but the deficiency can also occur from lack of responsivity in others at any age. Kohut's (1977) definition of *deficit* is a "structural lack due to empathic failures."[31] This deficit can be seen as "undersocialization" (neglect or abuse) in children who are not guided toward discovering their own humanity. This means there were deficits in relationships: too little involvement or abusive involvement from others. Sometimes the result is the absence of an appropriate sense of self or others, or the lack of a superego, or conscience (i.e., intrapsychic structures), but at other times the result is conflict about self-in-relation: an enormously anguished sense of self or others. Children whose cries, wishes, or joys are ignored can experience such neglect as profoundly emotionally shameful and painful. Such individuals have learned that interpersonal closeness is hopeless or aversive.[32]

The present model views two types of deficits:[33] (a) a lack of adaptive social responses from others (resulting in lack of sound inner models of others and lack of sense of self) and (b) abusive responses from others, leading to conflict about attachment; for example, the patient is too afraid of closeness, too ashamed of vulnerability or tenderness, too frightened to trust, too hurt to grieve.

In addition, patients with deficit pathology often, although not always, present with a lack of impulse control, which makes them appear quite different from overly controlled neurotic patients. Lack of impulse control leads to acting out of *defensive emotion*. The most typical example is the "borderline rage," which hides enormous sorrow over unmet, and natural, longings for validation of experience. Such underlying longing generally is not expressed directly for at least two reasons: (a) the need or affective experience has not been organized into a concept that the individual knows how to use or (b) the pain of experiencing what has been denied would be unbearable. Just as affects are inhibited in the conflict model, in deficit pathology, the natural desire for closeness is inhibited by pain, shame, or terror of abandonment.

Consequently, both conflict and deficit pathology result either in an overinhibition of adaptive emotions or an inability to deploy emotions because they have not been identified or integrated into the structure of the personality. In either case, there is restriction or inability in the experience or expression of emotion, which is our basic motivational system. The difference

[31]Often this has been seen as a basic, incurable flaw in the individual. Indeed, there are severe biological deficits (e.g., temporal lobe epilepsy, biologically driven antisocial behavior) for which short-term therapy may be contraindicated or have only limited usefulness. Even though temperament always plays a role to some degree, deficit pathology often arises from predominantly *learned* responses.

[32]To the degree that the child is temperamentally lucky, such interpersonal deficits may "roll off," or have less severe effects. To the extent that the child is temperamentally "sensitive," or hyperresponsive, the environmental deficits may lead to disorders of the self.

[33]Jon Monsen, of the University of Oslo, Norway, strongly encouraged me to give equal attention to the lack of socialization in deficit pathology, along with the conflict associated with attachment I have mentioned. The remainder of this discussion was influenced by his comments of January 1996, which balanced my perspective.

is partly in *which* emotions are involved (affects or attachments) or the presence or absence of internal models. The difference is also in the rapidity with which the conflicts and the deficits can be resolved. Davanloo (1980) said that with severe character pathology, one has to build the Triangle of Conflict. To the extent that there is a lack of structure rather than of defense recognition, the patient needs help with affect and self-concept recognition. This type of approach was Kohut's great contribution.

To the extent that disorders involve conflicts, the inhibition around *expression of specific affects* is predominant. Treatment always involves the adaptive disinhibition and management of those affects. To the extent that disorders involve deficits in caretaking or socialization, there is inhibition in regard to affects associated with attachment or social responsivity. Treatment must also build adaptive attachments (generally beginning with the therapist) and more adaptive inner representations of others (an inner model of a caring other). Often the therapist is first; subsequently, the work is generalized to others in the immediate environment. This process is accomplished by reducing the anxiety, guilt, shame, or pain associated with attachment-related feelings.

If defensive feelings are uncontrolled or acted out, the patient needs help with identification, desensitization, and containment of the affects associated with attachment. Cognitive and behavioral techniques are useful for teaching impulse control. Little character change is possible unless the underlying and human longings for adaptive and validating attachments (to others and to the self) are worked through.

As noted previously, it is important to remember that these two forms of pathology rarely exist in isolation. Many patients have a blend of conflicts about specific affects together with deficits in relationships (with self and others) that has resulted in conflicts about attachment, care, tenderness, or devotion. Furthermore, deficit pathology is not restricted to severely impaired individuals. *Many high-functioning individuals experience conflict about attachment feelings, and deficits in necessary (sometimes vital) validating experiences from others can occur throughout life.* Until there are adequate assessment methods for evaluating the degree of conflict versus deficit pathology for each patient, there is no way to know in advance. According to Killingmo, with any given patient, the therapist "has to be in a state of constant receptivity to *oscillate* between the two strategic positions . . . from one of unveiling meaning, to one of [affirming or constructing meaning]" (1989, p. 77; see Figure 1.6). From a cognitive science perspective, there is also a continual oscillation between building procedural and declarative knowledge structures.

However much is *lacking* in deficit pathology, there are *conflicts about attachment* inherent in this disorder that are often overlooked. Even though deficit pathology may be acquired through lack of responsivity of others and lack of something important happening (and a subsequent lack of formation of internal models of self and others), this lack invariably results in negative feelings about the self, predominantly shame, which then generates intrapsychic conflict about self and others. "In the end all psychopathology is based on intrapsychic conflict" (Killingmo, 1989, p. 65; see this reference for an excellent discussion of these issues). In contrast, Kohut's theoretical formulation (1971, 1977) states that all pathology has to be conceptualized in terms of deficient self-structure.

FIGURE 1.6
The yin and yang of conflict and deficit pathology.

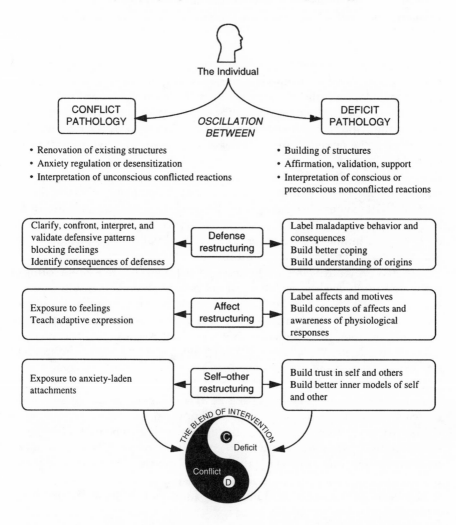

One need not choose. In this model, both conflict and deficit pathology are conceptualized as involving aspects *not only of deficient self-structure but also of intrapsychic conflict.* These must be figure–ground considerations with each patient. Defenses, affects, and sense of self and others sometimes must be built and sometimes renovated. Conflict pathology requires more interpretation of unconscious conflicts around affects and less, but still some degree of, building of new inner models and structures or parts of structures. Deficit pathology may require more reparative, validating, and affirming interventions and more focus on the therapeutic relationship to build new inner models (of affects, sense of self and others, and so on), as well as more interpretation (i.e., explanation) of conscious or preconscious (less conflicted) experience. But deficit pathology ultimately requires the restructuring of conflicts associated with affects and attachment to self and others. Each patient has some degree of conflict in both areas.

In summary, the structures of Malan's two triangles may be used to (a) integrate both conflict and deficit pathologies, (b) guide the building of intrapsychic structures necessary for a sense of self in relation to others, and (c) work through conflicts about affects or attachments. Of course, interventions necessarily vary according to patient needs. In both forms of pathology, the *inhibitory affects block innate human adaptive responses and result in maladaptive defensive responding.* Healing in both these forms occurs in part through the regulation of the anxieties around affects and attachment and in part through the building of missing structures or components. The structures of the two triangles (defenses, anxieties, feelings; relations with the therapist and current and past persons) are sufficient to guide the continual oscillation between building (identifying and integrating) and renovating (regulating anxieties) structures, in the inevitable "yin and yang" of conflict and deficit.

Character Change: Restructuring with a Solution Focus

Basic to this model of psychotherapy is the restructuring of defenses (D pole) and affect expression (I/F pole) by the regulation of the inhibitory affects (i.e., anxieties and conflicts, or A pole). This means that the therapist and patient work together to *change the maladaptive behaviors that compose major aspects of character, that is, long-standing, repetitive, and inappropriate forms of responding.* Specifically, character change in this model means that defensive responding is not only increased (when deficient) or reduced (when excessive) but also qualitatively changed from a more maladaptive, immature level of response to a more adaptive, mature response. Sometimes this task requires anxiety regulation, and other times, affirmation and validation of experience. Anxieties are not simply reduced or removed but are altered so that they guide rather than attack the individual. Another way to understand the process of restructuring, therefore, is to consider the change in the character structure (i.e., the adaptive solution) that is desired and focused on.

Instead of thinking of defenses as a fixed category of behaviors at a "point" on the Triangle of Conflict, one can think of defensive behaviors as a range of possible responses that can fall along a continuum from the most maladaptive (either too much or too little) to the most adaptive. Anxieties can be thought of in the same way: not as a static set of responses but as a range of responses that fall on a continuum ranging from insufficient or excessive guidance or signaling to the optimal amount of guidance and protective responses. The adaptive levels of the defenses and the anxieties would work in harmony *with* the affects (on the I/F pole) instead of fighting *against* the experience or expression of adaptive affects.

In this model, the I/F pole is conceptualized as a blend of biologically prepared and socially learned "adaptive responding." Adaptive self-responding means that defenses and coping skills, as well as inhibitory affects, must operate in concordance with the activating affects so that they may be expressed in the most constructive and appropriate fashion possible, but also as fully as possible in relation to self and others. Such deep structural changes in the behaviors represented by the Triangle of Conflict inevitably change the way people experience themselves and others, thus restructuring the inner models of self and others. In short, the former, maladaptive Triangle of Conflict becomes a new, more adaptively functioning psyche and self, in an interpersonal context of the Triangle of Person. This shift, in effect, represents character change (change in repetitive and inappropriate long-standing maladaptive responses), the optimal goal of the work. Robert Clyman (1992) pointed out that at base, character change is a change in procedural knowledge.

INTEGRATED TREATMENT APPROACHES
FROM MULTIPLE THEORETICAL ORIENTATIONS

As noted in Figure 1.3, there are various approaches to altering defenses. Similarly, there are many techniques that could be employed to achieve each of the objectives in this model, and therapists are always encouraged to be creative in their ways of doing so. The suggestions to be given are not intended to be rigid or exclusive, therefore, but are a sampling of approaches frequently observed or empirically demonstrated to be helpful in working with concepts represented by the Triangle of Conflict. These recommendations offer a memory key, or prompt, to assist the therapist during a complex and fast-moving session (see Figure 1.7).

When attempting to help patients identify defensive or maladaptive behavior patterns, therapists can derive simple and straightforward techniques from behavioral methods. A well-conducted defense analysis can also be seen as a well-conducted behavioral analysis of defensive behavior. Students of behavior therapy are taught to remember the ABC analysis: Problematic *behaviors* are examined in regard to their *antecedents* and *consequences*. In this model, defensive behavior patterns are examined in the same way.

For the purposes of this model, the problematic, maladaptive, and defensive behavior patterns do not fundamentally differ from each other. The main difference between the two models is that the psychodynamic perspective hypothesizes an internal emotionally based state: a conflicted feeling that gives rise to the problematic or defensive behavior. The behavioral model focuses on *environmental* reinforcers and punishers. This integrative–psychodynamic model examines both internal and external (i.e., intrapsychic and environmental) *behaviors*, as well as their internal and external antecedents and consequences, or sources of reinforcement and punishment.

Many examples of this integration of psychodynamic and cognitive–behavioral forms of treatment are given in the following chapters; put simply, patients' inner thoughts, feelings, and fantasies can be used in maladaptive ways and can cause problematic or defensive responding, just as adverse environmental conditions can. Each of these components must be vividly described to patients, on both a cognitive and an emotional level, until patients can clearly recognize and report what they are doing: *Can you see that when I asked you about feelings of sadness about your father's death, you changed the subject both times?*

FIGURE 1.7
Different theoretical perspectives integrated by the Triangle of Conflict.

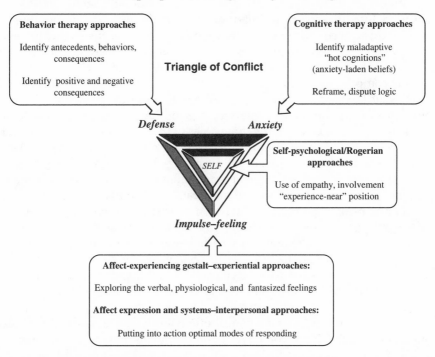

When working on the regulation of the anxieties (the A pole of the triangle), some interventions used to achieve this objective are drawn in large part from cognitive therapy, assisted by self-psychological techniques. The therapist must identify the anxieties (as well as guilt, shame, and pain) that maintain the defensive behaviors and assist patients in coming to see the lack of logic in their fears. This process looks similar to that of a cognitive therapist identifying maladaptive cognitions, then encouraging the patient to examine the reality of the fears and disputing the logic: *What would be the worst thing that would happen if you let yourself feel sadness about his death?*

When the objective is experiencing of affects (the impulse–feeling pole of the Triangle of Conflict), the techniques in the short-term approach reflect some departure from psychodynamic technique (although not from the theory). The focus remains the eliciting of warded-off affect. Instead of using the traditional dynamic methods of free association and regression into the transference neurosis, however, short-term techniques often are drawn from gestalt or experiential therapy; an example is guided imagery with close attention to the physiological concomitants of emotion to heighten the experiencing process. In addition, the process is assisted by the support of self-psychological techniques: *Can we look at how you experience the sadness? How does your body feel? What are the images that come up?*

When working on the expression of affects (again, on the impulse–feeling pole), the focus is on adaptive interpersonal expression of wants and needs. The newly experienced feelings from the Triangle of Conflict are now expressed in each of the relationships represented by the Triangle of Person. Traditional psychodynamic therapy often does not sufficiently emphasize the need for direct work on interpersonal communication. Techniques to achieve this objective are drawn predominantly from behavior therapy and interpersonal therapy: *What do you want to say to your father when you see him tomorrow? What is in your heart that you have tended to hold back?*

To encompass some important aspects of self psychology, as mentioned previously, the triangle evolved into a three-dimensional pyramid. From the pinnacle of the pyramid, the observing ego, or the "self as an organizing capacity," has a perspective of the three poles of the Triangle of Conflict as well as the Triangle of Person. As the self-attacking anxieties are altered in treatment, this self-organizing perspective is changed: one's inner representation of oneself—one's defenses, anxieties, and emotions—as well as one's representation of others. These inner representations of self and others (the final set of objectives in this model) also become restructured while defenses and affects are restructured. Furthermore, self-psychological methods are used by the therapist in the maintenance of an empathic stance throughout treatment: *So now we can see that you have taken a protective position for yourself of not feeling strong emotions, because you had no real support to help you through them. It is not that you were flawed or lacking, but rather that you needed more emotional support than your parents were able to provide.*

I have pointed out the main contributions from several major theoretical orientations: behavioral, cognitive, gestalt, systems–interpersonal theories, and self-psychology/object relations theory. The last theoretical orientation to be mentioned, the fundamental one, is psychodynamic. Remember that Malan's triangles represent (functionally) the universal principle of psychodynamic psychotherapy—the working through of defenses that ward off conflicted emotions. Therefore, this model remains fundamentally psychodynamic in orientation. The problem with the psychodynamic orientation, and the reason for inclusion of the time-efficient techniques, is that when the focus changes from neuroses (milder, more malleable conflicts) to character pathology (long-standing maladaptive behavior patterns that are highly resistant to change), the defenses are ego-syntonic (i.e., behaviors are seen as part of the individual's identity, or self) and thus not easily given up. Before ego-syntonic defenses, psychoanalysis, alas, sometimes must lay down its arms. Free association and an absence of therapist activity can lead to an interminable psychotherapeutic process. Hence the need for the technology of behavior change as well as the integration of interventions from other theoretical orientations, all brought to bear on the fundamentally psychodynamic objectives of the restructuring of character pathology to be done in the shortest possible amount of time.

AN INTEGRATIVE MODEL OF
SHORT-TERM PSYCHODYNAMIC PSYCHOTHERAPY

My model is highly integrative, through a combination of intention, intuition, and empiricism. Although theories have guided me well, I follow Isaac Newton's recommendation to take our theories lightly. My allegiance is ultimately to "what works." The treatment objectives and many interventions emerged from practical attempts to resolve obstacles in a short-term psychodynamic treatment. In the original research conducted at Beth Israel Medical Center in New York, there was not an intentional incorporation of different theoretical interventions. My colleagues and I were closely following psychodynamic principles represented by the two triangles, which remains the basic framework today. Later, the "emergent techniques" (Lazarus & Messer, 1991) that evolved were often intuitively generated in response to trying to achieve the general psychodynamic objectives in a short-term framework (i.e., restructuring of defenses, affects, and sense of self and others).

As mentioned previously, the process of recognizing defensive behavior patterns shares some fundamental similarities with behavior therapy, and identifying the maladaptive aspects of the anxiety responses is similar to cognitive therapy.[34] As we attempted to restructure affects in a desensitization format by exposing patients to deep feelings, I was surprised, in retrospect, to find that we sounded like gestalt or experiential therapists. At another point, one of my graduate students told me that I was a self psychologist and did not know it.[35] He was right. I had not thought of myself as employing "experience-near techniques."[36] I called such interventions *supportive*. Empathic statements that affirmed and validated the patient's experience had been incorporated because they were essential in helping the patient to manage the anxiety that is engendered by the rapid uncovering in the short-term treatment. Since then, I have been told many times that I am incorporating Rogerian, or client-centered, techniques, as well.

In each of the preceding instances, it was clinical intuition and striving to overcome repetitive and frustrating treatment obstacles that gave rise to in-

[34]It was several years before I realized the words on the videotape were almost identical to those of Aaron Beck (1976), and indeed, the objective was the same as Beck's as well.

[35]Judd Bortner, personal communication, 1988.

[36]*Experience-near* techniques involve statements by the therapist that attempt to reflect a position as near as possible to the patient's experience. This is in contrast to *experience-far* responses.

terventions with strong similarities to those of different orientations. The principal force that shaped this model was not intuition, however, but empiricism. In the Beth Israel program and since, at the program at Harvard Medical School, therapy hours have been videotaped and reviewed, and many were coded by a research team. Although many of the integrative techniques came initially from intuitive inspiration, they were retained in the model only if the result of objective video replays demonstrated effectiveness.[37]

The one intentional integration was that of learning theory and psychodynamic theory (see McCullough, 1991a). I was initially inspired by the work of Paul Wachtel (1977), in which he demonstrated the commonalities in the functions of behavior therapy and psychodynamic therapy. I was also inspired by Joseph Cautela's principles of covert conditioning (e.g., Cautela, 1966, 1973; Cautela & McCullough, 1978), in which learning theory was applied to thoughts, feelings, and behaviors. If principles of reinforcement can apply to both overt and covert behavior, it took only one more intuitive step to posit that learning principles can also apply to the representational behavior of intrapsychic functioning.[38] Not only can *behavior, thoughts, and feelings* be reinforced, punished, and extinguished, but so can their intrapsychic *models* and their *meanings*. Defenses and anxieties exist because of meanings associated with affects and attachments. Throughout this book, I demonstrate techniques for reinforcing adaptive meanings and extinguishing maladaptive meanings. The deepest level of integration in this model occurs in the application of learning theory principles not only to external behavior but also to the *psychodynamic experience and meanings* of the two triangles. Behavioral principles (reinforcement, extinction, desensitization, and so on) provide the general mechanisms by which the intrapsychic workings of the mind are altered.

Recently, there have been two intentional points of integration that resulted from theoretical formulations that seemed to describe accurately what was being seen on the clinical videotapes. I selected Tomkins's affect theory, the finest descriptive and explanatory theory for impulse and feelings in the Triangle of Conflict. This work is in line with much of the post-Freudian position that the dual-drive theory is outdated, and I intentionally chose Tomkins's work as an alternative.[39] What emerged later was uninten-

[37]A detailed discussion of the research studies and how they built this model, step by step, is presented in chapter 10.

[38]*Intrapsychic functioning* is defined in this model as either simple covert behaviors (thoughts, feelings, and images) or *symbolic* covert behaviors (thoughts, feelings, and images that stand for or represent something else). These intrapsychic, or covert, behaviors follow the same principles of learning (reinforcement, punishment, extinction) as overt behaviors (Cautela, 1966). Elsewhere, I have discussed in detail how principles of reinforcement can be applied to a precursor to this model (McCullough, 1991a).

[39]For many years, I searched for the theory of emotion that best fit the Triangle of Conflict representation of human emotional functioning. Tomkins's model was, to me, nothing short of brilliant. I first heard about Tomkins from colleagues in Norway.

tional, but exciting. Tomkins's understanding of the interaction of attachment and affect provided a bridge between psychodynamics and attachment theory: between affects and relation. The self–other objectives that were the last components added (at the urging of my Norwegian colleagues) further blend facets of object relations theory with psychodynamic theory. It is not that we added new techniques; we added to the theoretical structure a category to describe a set of relational interventions that we had been doing for many years but not explicitly addressing. I have named this model *anxiety-regulating therapy* to highlight the major change agent in psychodynamic theory. But an additional descriptor could be *affect–relational* because of the integration of affect theory, attachment theory, and object relations theory to enhance the efficacy of psychodynamic theory.

Basically, this model seeks to achieve psychodynamic goals through behavioral principles; character change is achieved through alteration of defensive functioning and unconflicted expression of feeling with self and others. But multitheoretical methods are used to extend and achieve those goals in a time-efficient manner. This anxiety-regulating and affect–relational model also could be seen as an intensified post-Freudian analytic process, not only as a short-term process.[40] The integrative process is probably closest to those described by both Lazarus's technical eclecticism and Messer's evolutionary or assimilative integration, which advocate a "predominant, even traditional, theoretical framework within which to incorporate attitudes or techniques from other therapies" (Lazarus & Messer, 1991, p. 153).

In conclusion, it is now widely recognized that seemingly diverse theoretical orientations address vital components of human functioning, all of which need to be taken into consideration. This model is based on a psychodynamic premise and draws from learning theory, behavior and cognitive therapy, and experiential, object relations, and self-psychological theories to achieve the psychodynamic objectives. I am repeatedly told by practicing clinicians in my workshops on short-term therapy that they, too, draw from the full range of theoretical constructs, sometimes intentionally, sometimes intuitively, in trying to do what works. What is done out there on the front lines of clinical practice represents an amalgam of theories that begs to be

---

[40]The reader is referred to three excellent articles for discussion of, in various combinations, four types of psychotherapy integration. Technical eclecticism is espoused by Lazarus, and evolutionary or assimilative integration is presented by Messer (both in Lazarus & Messer, 1991); common factors and theoretical integration are described by Arkowitz (1989) and Norcross and Grencavage (1989). The model in this book includes components of each of those four but particularly those of technical eclecticism and evolutionary integration. Techniques similar in form and spirit to a range of other theoretical orientations have been incorporated to speed up the treatment process and achieve treatment goals in a time-efficient format. In this regard, the model can be seen as *technically eclectic* because it focuses on what works, within a traditional theoretical framework but freely employing interventions on the basis of what is effective. The model also emphasizes *common factors*, because the change mechanisms of desensitization and exposure are incorporated, and mastery and change in sense of self are subgoals in this short-term framework.

formalized and studied. This model is one attempt to provide a structured and coherent framework for such grassroots integration that can continue to grow and evolve through empirical examination.

OVERVIEWS OF COMPLETED CASES

A few brief examples are included to describe the range of effects that are possible in short-term treatment. Each case is described in terms of the major treatment objectives (i.e., defense, affect, and self–other restructuring), some of the primary change mechanisms, and how these methods can vary and be interwoven throughout the flow of treatment. More detailed examples of these cases are presented throughout the book. Each patient has maintained and improved on the reported gains according to a 3- to 5-year follow-up.

The Machine Builder: One 3-Hour Evaluation and Three Sessions

This 26-year-old female graduate student in mechanical engineering (i.e., machine building) came to treatment with a speaking phobia that threatened her professional functioning. The initial evaluation focused on her general avoidance of showing feelings, the strongest example of which was inability to grieve her father's death, in which she resolved a 10-year pathological mourning. She was vividly aware that she defended against these feelings (defense recognition) but was quite afraid to experience the painfulness of it. The treatment focus in this first session constantly oscillated between affect experiencing (to desensitize her grief-laden feeling about her father) and defense relinquishing (anxiety regulation for giving up the avoidant response to grief). This initial session reduced symptoms of anxiety by one-third, feelings that she felt had been bottled up for 10 years. Self–other restructuring helped her to recognize that the therapist was supportive and that others might feel concerned on her behalf. Her sense of others was fairly good to begin with, however, so that intervention in this area was not extensive.

During the next session, defense restructuring and a little self–other restructuring were employed to help her see that her social anxiety (fear of public speaking) was in part due to her projection onto others that they would make fun of her or ridicule her. The remaining therapy time was spent in affect experiencing and expression, focusing solely on desensitization of anger and assertion, through exposure in imagery and anxiety regulation around anxiety-provoking situations. At the end of Session 4, she said she felt much more comfortable about public speaking. The following week she presented a proposal to her class with almost no anxiety. She was exhilarated by the freedom she felt, but she knew she had to keep working on the issues.

The Man Who Loved Ice Skating: Five Sessions

To resolve this 38-year-old man's conflict about assertion with his wife, treatment focused solely on restructuring affects around anger. However, a constant and energetic defense restructuring was required during the first session (to help him to recognize his avoidance of assertion and to build the desire to respond differently by emphasizing the negative consequences), because his "gentlemanly" behavior was so ego-syntonic that he forbade himself to be even mildly assertive with women. (He interacted comfortably with men.) Confrontation by the female therapist helped him speak up to her in the therapy situation, and his defensiveness decreased as he realized that he would not destroy her.

The remaining four sessions focused solely on restructuring of affects (exposure in imagery to desensitize his experience of angry impulses toward his wife (affect experiencing), followed by exposure in imagery to desensitize his fears about assertion with his wife, as well as role-playing and learning new communication skills. His marital conflicts markedly abated with his increased ability to state his needs and set his limits kindly but firmly with his wife. A second focus then emerged concerning his deep sadness that his wife could not be more of a partner to him, which seemed to have resulted from her apparent and inexplicable resentment about having children. She consistently refused any form of treatment. He was much less defended about sharing sad feelings and only needed brief exposure to resolve this issue, at least for the time being. He decided that he would not spend his life in such a relationship but that, because of his children, he would not leave at that time.

The Unforgiven Teenager: First Block, 15 Sessions

(After the 3-hour evaluation session, this patient had 9 sessions 1 week apart and 6 booster sessions spaced over the next 7 months. One year later, she had 20 additional sessions.)

This 36-year-old single businesswoman felt such a degree of self-hate that she imagined God hating her and punishing her. However, she said initially that she wanted to focus on her anger at her father. When affect experiencing was attempted (exposure in imagery to violent impulses toward her father), her masochistic and paranoid reactions were so self-punitive (she believed herself to be evil for having such thoughts, and her self-hate increased) that treatment shifted to restructuring her defenses and her extremely poor sense of self, particularly in relation to the therapist and to God. Five sessions of repeated focus on defense recognition were needed before she could clearly see how she painfully attacked herself. (Prior to this time, she felt she just deserved to be punished.) Defense relinquishing was achieved simultaneously as she realized how she hated treating herself in such an abusive manner. Sessions 6 through 10 repeatedly focused on the recurrence of her masochistic defensive pattern, as well as on self–other restructuring around the enormous shame she carried. (This included how the therapist, her friends, and God felt about her.)

Her major depressive disorder was no longer present at Session 10, and her problem with poor self-esteem was greatly improved. Frequency of treatment dropped to one session every 4–6 weeks (as needed), in which we monitored her improvement, which she was able to continue. She let herself develop friendships and a social life for the first time in many years, because she now felt likable.

She returned to therapy the following year because she realized that her enmeshed relationship with her abusive father still dominated her and prevented her from ever having had a sustained, intimate relationship with a man. It was still difficult to proceed with affect restructuring around anger, so treatment focused on grief about loneliness and neglect in her childhood. Because she was resistant to affect experiencing, much defense restructuring was needed throughout. Self–other restructuring was necessary as well to build her sense of compassion and help her see her parents in a different light. After 20 more sessions, she made significant steps toward the difficult emotional separation from her father, but she still did not totally resolve the problem. At that time, I did not focus sufficiently on what she might have longed for from her father, and this might have deepened her experience of loss. A job transfer to another city interrupted treatment, but she continues therapy there with a highly experienced therapist.

The Ferryman: 35 Sessions

This 36-year-old hospice worker came to treatment because of low self-esteem, passive behavior, and a divorce. Although his defense of passivity was strong, he was highly motivated and had a strong ability to trust and connect with others, which permitted rapid changes. Treatment primarily involved affect restructuring around experiencing of anger and strong resistance to feeling anger, with frequent pointing out of defensive avoidance to help him proceed. (He often said of his angry feelings, "I'm not that kind of guy.")

A second topic that emerged concerned grieving the death of his grandfather, whose love he had almost entirely forgotten. Yet he had chosen to work with the dying because he had been so grieved about the poor care his grandfather had received at his death. This deeply sensitive patient saw himself as the ferryman in Dante's *Inferno*, helping to carry the dying across the river Styx. This reawakening of the "lost love" within the first 20 sessions gave him a new sense of self. "I'm growing a new person inside," he said. A 20-year dysthymic diagnosis was resolved during this time. Little defense restructuring was needed for the grief process because his barriers against grieving were not strong, and his trust in the therapist was sound. As he became more comfortable with this side of himself, his perception of himself as a man dramatically changed. (As his remembrance of his grandfather changed to include his grandfather's love for him, the Ferryman's sense of self improved tremendously.)

The Girl Who Danced in Blood: 44 Sessions

This 20-year-old female college student made a suicidal gesture (pouring out pills in her hand and then blacking out from anxiety) owing to an intense fight and fear of breakup with her boyfriend. During the first five sessions, defense restructuring and self–other restructuring were used to help her see that her suicidal feelings were linked to her anger at her boyfriend, which she turned on herself (i.e., "I'm no good, I'm not worth anything").

She learned how she sought dependency on her boyfriend to bolster her self-esteem because she could not bear to be alone (i.e., to soothe, comfort, or care for herself). In the next 10 sessions, she saw that her poor self-esteem came from her harsh and demanding father, whom she loved and admired, nonetheless. Becoming aware that she treated herself like her father treated her, harshly and judgmentally, although in some ways idealizing him (i.e., alteration of images of self and other), resulted in a strong wish not to continue doing so. The suicidal feelings ceased after a few sessions and have not returned.

Her manner of responding to her boyfriend then shifted, and the relationship improved. After 17 sessions she said, "I'm learning a whole new personality. My friends tell me I'm completely different." But the work was only half done.

The difficult part of treatment (Sessions 20 through 35) involved prolonged experiencing of the difficult, anger-laden feelings directed primarily toward her father and secondarily toward her mother. Defense recognition and relinquishing had to be heavily interwoven with affect restructuring until the angry feelings were sufficiently freed up for her to protect herself in her father's presence. She also needed help to feel the strong positive feelings for him. This work led to her eventually building a more loving relationship with both her father and her mother.

This case is reminiscent of Malan's case the Almoner (1979, pp. 97–98), another young woman whose relationship with her parents dramatically improved after she faced her angry feelings in treatment and learning constructive self-assertion.

The Woman with Butterfly Feelings: 90 Sessions

This was a far more difficult case, requiring extended sessions. It is included to emphasize that short-term methods can be useful in severe and long-standing personality disorder. Although this treatment was not short, it may have approached the "shortest time possible." The therapist was active throughout, and the patient seemed to handle as much pain as she could bear during most sessions.

This 57-year-old teacher and divorced mother of two adult sons came to the first session dressed in a man's shirt and tie. She reported that she had been "dead from the neck down" for most of her life. The first 8 months of treatment were devoid of feeling and focused solely on identifying and giving up massive defenses. The most rigid defense was autistic fantasy: She lived a constant romantic drama in her head that consumed hours each day, in which she was a famous actress swept away by a famous actor. Although the fantasy seriously impaired her accomplishment of tasks, she had no desire to give it up, for she could not envision any real-life alternatives. _Months_ were required for her to (a) begin to relinquish this 40- to 50-year-long defensive fantasy pattern, because so much was needed to replace what would be given up, and (b) restructure her sense of self (as well as view of the world around her) enough to permit her to give up her lifelong emotional deadness and find some pleasure in reality. (She did so by joining a theater group and a choral group, which she had never before dared to try.)

Only in the second year of treatment, when she had acquired some capacity for coping with and enjoying real life, was she able to address conflicted feeling. We then focused on the full range of feelings and the masochistic role she took in her family. Treatment oscillated between affect and defense restructuring. Her entrenched patterns shifted slowly and arduously with the emotional separation from an overly idealized, rigidly religious mother, who had forbidden all emotional responses, and a father who had encouraged her dependency on him. After about 18 months of treatment, she had acquired the ability to cry when sad, stand up for herself for the first time in her life, and express tenderness to her children and granddaughter. The changes, although at first shocking to her family, were enormously comforting to her, and she reported further improvement at the 3-year follow-up.

The Bickering Daughter: One 3-Hour Evaluation Session

This well-adjusted, well-respected 47-year-old married midwife and mother had only one focal problem: Over the years she had often found herself bickering with her father (now aging), and she wanted to stop doing so. She did not understand why this happened because they had a basically loving relationship. This one long session focused on exposing her to her feelings toward her father. Affect restructuring uncovered defensive sexual and aggressive feelings toward him, but these appeared to be warding off even stronger guilt over closeness to her father owing to her (now deceased) mother's jealousy. When asked to explore these feelings in depth, she was initially resistant. However, with some work on anxiety regulation and a little encouragement, she was able to do so. Following this session, she went to visit her father. They had a long conversation about their difficulty being close, which brought them both relief and tender feelings, and the bickering stopped.

This case is a much milder variant of Malan's case called the Director's Daughter, in which the woman's oedipal rivalry and conflict about tender feelings led to more defensive anger and sexual feelings (not just bickering) toward her father, which generalized to all men as well as the therapist. Malan's case required a much longer time (1979, pp. 46–51).

Changes as rapid as those undergone by the Bickering Daughter happen infrequently, but just as we need to be mindful that unraveling massive defenses can take a year or two (as with the Woman with Butterfly Feelings), we need also remember that there are people with less severe inhibitions and better interpersonal relationships who can make major changes in a short time.

SUMMARY

Part 1 of this chapter presents an overview of the basic principles of short-term anxiety-regulating psychotherapy, including principles that distinguish this model from its precursors, the centrality of affect in this model, and the healing connection of the therapist–patient relationship. Three main objectives (each with two subgoals) are presented that guide and focus the treatment: defense restructuring (defense recognition and defense relinquishing), affect restructuring (affect experiencing and affect expression and reconnection), and self–other restructuring (alteration of the inner representations of self and others).

In Part 2, terms are operationally defined, the contributions of various theoretical orientations to this integrative psychodynamic model is discussed, and examples of overviews of completed cases are presented.

CHAPTER 2

Assessment and Treatment on the Basis of Patient Level of Functioning

PATIENT-SPECIFIC TREATMENT

In the initial interview, therapists are immediately confronted with the task of determining where the patient falls in the range of psychopathology and what types of treatment might be most suitable for the patient's problems. To answer these questions requires obtaining a tremendous amount of data as rapidly as possible and evaluating the data in light of recent research regarding what works best for whom. This chapter describes an efficient, short-term approach to assessment and patient-specific treatment using level of functioning (Axis V of the DSM-IV) to assist in determining general treatment requirements.

The treatment interventions described in this manual were originally developed for and, for the most part, tested with patients with Axis II personality disorders, who demonstrate a level of functioning that is moderately impaired but not severely impaired or incapacitating.[1] Active and rapidly uncovering interventions could be too overwhelming for patients already burdened with severe impairment unless much support or structure is provided. With modifications to this model (as well as the addition of support and structure, to be discussed subsequently), findings from numerous single case studies suggest that this model may be used effectively with a much broader range of patients than was initially anticipated. Indeed, because of wide variation in strengths and vulnerabilities across patients, there is always a need to tailor treatment interventions to the individual, as pioneered by Allen Frances, John Clarkin, and Samuel Perry (1984) in their work on "the art and science of treatment selection" or "differential therapeutics."

---

[1]The short-term dynamic psychotherapy tested at Beth Israel Medical Center in New York gave rise to the current model of treatment. The successful results of this treatment are described in chapter 12.

This approach to selection of short-term treatment has been guided in part also by the "functional process diagnosis" method recommended by Greenberg and his colleagues to help differentially select treatment interventions according to different patient processes and levels of functioning (e.g., Greenberg, 1986, 1991; Greenberg, Rice, & Elliott, 1994). General recommendations for short-term patient-specific treatment according to global range of functioning are presented here, and further tailoring of treatments according to levels of individual patient processes (i.e., defensive, affective, and self–other responding) is discussed in chapters 3 through 9. Chapter 11 presents a discussion of differential interventions according to specific diagnoses or disorders.

Historical Selection Criteria for Short-Term Treatment

The pioneers in brief psychotherapy gave much thought to identifying the patient characteristics that permitted a rapid uncovering of feelings in a short-term manner, fitting their particular models. Sifneos's (1979) method of rapid interpretation for well-functioning individuals called for selection criteria that included the following:

1. A circumscribed chief complaint
2. One meaningful, give-and-take relationship during childhood
3. Ability to express feelings freely and interact flexibly with the evaluator
4. "Psychological-mindedness," or psychological sophistication
5. Adequate motivation for change as opposed to symptom relief

On the basis of extensive clinical and research experience, Malan (1976) offered a broader set of criteria for planned brief psychotherapy, which could allow more resistant patients to be treated if able to respond effectively when interacting with the therapist. The first three of his four criteria were based on the patient's functioning in the initial evaluation:

1. The patient's life problem can be clearly identified and offers a clear-cut *focus* for therapy.
2. The patient has responded to interpretations related to this focus.
3. The patient clearly has the motivation to work with this focus.
4. Possible dangers of brief psychotherapy have been considered, and either none can be seen or it seems reasonable to suppose that they can be overcome or avoided (e.g., potential psychosis, organicity, poor impulse control, and severe suicidality).[2]

Davanloo's criteria are similar to those of Malan. Indeed, Malan wrote the chapter on patient selection for Davanloo's (1980) edited book. By offering

---

[2] I would add to these possible dangers, severe impairment in daily functioning.

methods for working with rigid defenses, Malan and Davanloo's models can serve a much wider range of patients than can Sifneos's model.

Mann (1973) suggested that, despite significant defects in mothering and the absence of an early predictable environment, there are many patients who enjoy a resilience that allows this rapid affective engagement and disengagement with the therapist. Both Malan and Mann anticipated the selection of treatment by level of patient functioning, and both realized that looking at the contraindications reflected by the patients' weaknesses without assessing strengths gives a lopsided picture of individuals' capacities.

How does a beginning therapist keep these lists of indications and contraindications in mind to make a determination that short-term treatment is advisable? How do experienced therapists check to see if their intuition conforms with standard short-term practice? On the basis of the aforementioned studies of progress in short-term psychotherapy treatment and recommendations by Greenberg, Elliott, and their colleagues, I propose that therapists use level of patient functioning to guide (not dictate) selection of *interventions*. Fortunately, there is a simple and widely used scale that takes into consideration many of the factors necessary in determining suitability of a wide range of interventions for short-term treatment as well as many other forms of therapy; it is the Global Assessment of Functioning (GAF) Scale (Endicott, Spitzer, Fleiss, & Cohen, 1976), which is Axis V of the DSM-IV. Following are a description of this rating scale and a discussion of how it can be used to guide treatment decisions.

Assessment of Level of Functioning

The Global Assessment of Functioning Scale involves a rating of from 1 to 100 of "global," or composite, level of functioning, which takes into consideration individuals' strengths as well as vulnerabilities in social, occupational, and psychological functioning. Two ratings are given: one for current level of functioning, and one for the highest level achieved in the past year. This scale was developed as a diagnosis-free way of characterizing the degree of function–dysfunction exhibited by psychiatric patients irrespective of the form or content of dysfunction exhibited. Its original format was the Health–Sickness Rating Scale (HSRS) developed by Lester Luborsky (1962) for the Menninger Psychotherapy Project. The HSRS had eight subscales related to different facets of functioning (e.g., social, occupational, symptoms, global). The GAF collapsed these subscales into one scale, which is anchored at each 10-point interval with descriptions of *psychological, occupational,* and *social functioning* at that level (see Figure 2.1). *The GAF rating reflects the lowest rating of any of the three categories of functioning.* "The GAF was an attempt to improve on the HSRS by providing more anchor points and more behaviorally oriented descriptors, and by eliminating its diagnostic constraints" (Endicott et al., 1976, p. 771).

Briefly, the 81–100 range represents good-to-excellent functioning with only mild or transient symptoms and with traits of "positive mental health, such as superior functioning, a wide range of interests, social effectiveness, warmth, and integrity" (Endicott et al., 1976, p. 766). The next level (71–80) describes individuals with minimal or no psychopathology but without the positive traits described in the higher ranges.[3] "Although some individuals rated above 70 may seek some form of assistance for psychological problems, the vast majority of individuals in treatment will be rated between 1 and 70. Most outpatients will be rated 31–70, and most inpatients between 1 and 40" (Endicott et al., 1976, p. 766).

When evaluating patients' level of functioning for suitability of short-term interventions (as opposed to cognitive, supportive, or long-term dynamic interventions), the following questions can be considered:

Psychological functioning. Where on the range of severity are the patient's symptoms (incapacitating versus absent or minimal)? Is an absence of symptoms owing to the presence of medication or other supports? *Symptom severity can provide a barometer for assessing the individual's capacity for coping under stress.* Prior hospitalizations, psychosis, organicity, or severe suicidality are indicators of vulnerability.

Social functioning. Does the patient have at least one close, give-and-take, interpersonal relationship? Is there evidence of being able to interact flexibly and freely with the interviewer? Or is the patient isolated, with only superficial associations and no close confidants? These factors shed light on the patient's capacity for basic trust, which is crucial for an active, short-term exploratory process.

Occupational involvement. What level of satisfaction is obtained from occupation (school, work, or home)? Is there interest and enthusiasm, or is there boredom and lack of interest? Is impairment so severe that there have been repeated firings, conflicts, or serious difficulty obtaining or maintaining employment or completing tasks?

An additional criterion for short-term treatment that the GAF takes into consideration more implicitly than explicitly is the patient's *impulse control.* Impulse control disorders (substance abuse, acting out, eating disorders, aggressive outbursts, and so on), generally place the individual below 50 on the GAF. Because patients often minimize or deny problems related to substance abuse, however, the therapist should assess such areas more carefully when making the GAF rating. Also, some higher functioning patients act out when stressed. Rapid uncovering of strong feelings can lead to an increase in substance abuse or acting out of damaging behaviors. I do not recommend intensive short-term psychotherapy for patients with impulse control disorders until the impulsive behaviors are *well under control,* nor do I treat substance abusers until they have been abstinent for at least 1 year. Seasoned alcohol counselors who are also trained in short-term methods tell me that it is possible to use active uncovering techniques in treating substance abuse

[3]Complete instructions for the GAF will be in the DSM-IV User's Guide currently in preparation. Mimi Gibbon (Biometrics Research Department, New York State Psychiatric Institute, New York City), personal communication, 1996.

but that there must be a skillful blending of a great deal of structure and support (e.g., use of Antabuse, rehabilitation, an inpatient setting) provided along with the exploratory treatment.[4]

Finally, there are criteria for short-term treatment that are not encompassed by the GAF and should be included in an initial evaluation; these include motivation, current stressors (e.g., Axis III or IV of the DSM-IV), psychological-mindedness, and response to treatment.

Motivation. Absence of patient motivation is not a contraindication in itself but a call for work to be done to increase the patient's desire to become involved in change. Consideration of the patient's readiness for change is important. Did the individual seek out treatment or was the impetus pressure from others or the law? Is there recognition that there is a problem? Is there interest in changing the problem? If a patient lacks motivation for change, either treatment should not be attempted or the only focus should be eliciting or enhancing motivation. Many suggestions for increasing motivation are provided in chapter 5.

Current life stressors can contraindicate a rapid uncovering process. These include medical problems (Axis III) such as multiple sclerosis or ulcerative colitis, which call for much more support and a gradual exploratory process. Environmental stressors (Axis IV) such as a pending courtroom trial *may* suggest the need for a supportive milieu rather than exploration. There are environmental stressors such as death of a child or loss of a job, however, that may indicate the need for short-term interventions provided the patient demonstrates the capacity to tolerate the emotional uncovering.

Lack of psychological-mindedness makes this treatment difficult, but it is not always a contraindication. If the patient has some motivation to look beneath the surface and grasp the emotional meanings of the maladaptive behavior, this capacity might be acquired. The patient's response to interpretation is a way of assessing the capacity. Does the patient respond emotionally and add new material following an interpretation? Or is there a bland or cynical view of the psychodynamic formulation, with a preference for tangible or biological reasons for problem behavior (diet, sleep, genes)?[5] When psychological-mindedness is neither present nor desired, other forms of treatment such as the educative and training procedures of cognitive or interpersonal therapy are excellent alternatives.

---

[4]According to Jeffrey Foote (Director of Research, Smithers Alcohol Treatment Center, New York City; personal communication, 1995), if one does either too little of the uncovering work or too much, one loses the substance abuse patient. He finds that a careful blend of structure, support, and psychodynamic uncovering is optimal.

[5]It is important for the therapist to assess and either rule out or take into consideration biological causation. However, this manual focuses primarily on treatment of functional or learned disorders.

FIGURE 2.1
Global Assessment of Functioning Scale.

Global Assessment of Functioning (GAF) Scale

Consider psychological, social, and occupational functioning on a hypothetical continuum of mental health–illness. Do not include impairment in functioning due to physical (or environmental) limitations.

Code (**Note:** Use intermediate codes when appropriate, e.g., 45, 68, 72.)

100 | **Superior functioning in a wide range of activities, life's problems never seem to get out of hand, is sought out by others because of his or her many positive qualities. No**
91 | **symptoms.**

90 | **Absent or minimal symptoms** (e.g., mild anxiety before an exam), **good functioning in all areas, interested and involved in a wide range of activities, socially effective, generally satisfied with life, no more than everyday problems or concerns** (e.g., an occasional argument with
81 | family members).

80 | **If symptoms are present, they are transient and expectable reactions to psychosocial stressors** (e.g., difficulty concentrating after family argument); **no more than slight impairment
71 | in social, occupational, or school functioning** (e.g., temporarily falling behind in schoolwork).

70 | **Some mild symptoms** (e.g., depressed mood and mild insomnia) **OR some difficulty in social, occupational, or school functioning** (e.g., occasional truancy, or theft within the household), **but
61 | generally functioning pretty well, has some meaningful interpersonal relationships.**

60 | **Moderate symptoms** (e.g., flat affect and circumstantial speech, occasional panic attacks) **OR moderate difficulty in social, occupational, or school functioning** (e.g., few friends, conflicts
51 | with peers or co-workers).

50 | **Serious symptoms** (e.g., suicidal ideation, severe obsessional rituals, frequent shoplifting) **OR any serious impairment in social, occupational, or school functioning** (e.g., no friends, unable to
41 | keep a job).

40 | **Some impairment in reality testing or communication** (e.g., speech is at times illogical, obscure, or irrelevant) **OR major impairment in several areas, such as work or school, family relations, judgment, thinking, or mood** (e.g., depressed man avoids friends, neglects family, and is unable
31 | to work; child frequently beats up younger children, is defiant at home, and is failing at school).

30 | **Behavior is considerably influenced by delusions or hallucinations OR serious impairment in communication or judgment** (e.g., sometimes incoherent, acts grossly inappropriately, suicidal preoccupation) **OR inability to function in almost all areas** (e.g., stays in bed all day; no job,
21 | home, or friends).

20 | **Some danger of hurting self or others** (e.g., suicide attempts without clear expectation of death; frequently violent; manic excitement) **OR occasionally fails to maintain minimal personal hygiene** (e.g., smears feces) **OR gross impairment in communication** (e.g., largely incoherent
11 | or mute).

10 | **Persistent danger of severely hurting self or others** (e.g., recurrent violence) **OR persistent inability to maintain minimal personal hygiene OR serious suicidal act with clear expecta-
1 | tion of death.**

0 | Inadequate information.

The rating of overall psychological functioning on a scale of 0–100 was operationalized by Luborsky in the Health-Sickness Rating Scale (Luborsky L: "Clinicians' Judgments of Mental Health." *Archives of General Psychiatry* 7:407–417, 1962). Spitzer and colleagues developed a revision of the Health-Sickness Rating Scale called the Global Assessment Scale (GAS) (Endicott J, Spitzer RL, Fleiss JL, Cohen J: "The Global Assessment Scale: A Procedure for Measuring Overall Severity of Psychiatric Disturbance." *Archives of General Psychiatry* 33:766–771, 1976). A modified version of the GAS was included in DSM-III-R as the Global Assessment of Functioning (GAF) Scale.

Patient response to treatment. The patient's ability to respond construc-
tively to confrontation was one of the most important indicators for
short-term treatment reported by Malan (1979) and Davanloo (1980). If
a patient became flooded with anxiety, this signaled a contraindication
for short-term interventions. This criterion is less salient with an anxiety-regulating approach because the treatment is altered according to
the patient's level of anxiety. However, there are patients who are not
receptive to any active, change-oriented short-term methods. If resistance to uncovering is strong and persistent after attempts at anxiety
regulation, the therapist should consider other treatment approaches.

Once a GAF score has been derived, it is necessary to consider it in yet a
broader context. The assessor must consider whether the level of functioning had been stable for the past year and what are the lowest and highest
levels of functioning the patient has ever reached. If symptomatic functioning is poor, is it balanced by good social and occupational functioning? Has
the individual had long periods of symptom-free and satisfying functioning? This information provides a broader perspective of the strengths versus
the vulnerabilities of the patient and the stability of the GAF score.

Using the GAF-MAPP to Inform Treatment Decisions

The rating of overall level of functioning generated by the GAF encapsu-
lates many of the criteria for short-term treatment. The GAF, along with assessment of *motivation, Axis* III or IV stressors, *psychological-mindedness,*
and *patient's* response to treatment, provides such an evaluation. The
acronym GAF-MAPP provides a pragmatic way to assist the therapist in remembering these criteria.

*The top half of the spectrum, or above 50 on the GAF Scale, provides an approxi-
mate cutoff point applicable to most patients for whom one would consider the active
change interventions of short-term treatment.* Such patients function moderately well, have a moderate degree of impulse control and a few friends, and
a moderate degree of occupational satisfaction. These are the patients for
whom this short-term treatment was initially designed.[6]

My clinical experience has also demonstrated that through the incorporation of support, validation, and understanding of defensive behavior, a
much broader range of patients can tolerate the uncovering process. Treatment can be tailored to manage the specific patient's anxieties about the material that comes up by modifying or slowing down the uncovering process
until the conflicts and anxieties are regulated. A typical example follows:

PATIENT: I have been in so much pain in the 3 weeks since coming here that I
can hardly bear it. I'm having frightening dreams, and I'm so distracted at
work that I'm not getting my tasks done.

---

[6]An improvement of 1 standard deviation on many outcome measures was
demonstrated in patients with personality disorders who had an average intake GAF
score of 55 (Winston et al., 1991). This study is discussed in chapter 12.

THERAPIST: Then we need to slow down what we're doing so that it doesn't interfere too seriously with your daily living. Therapy can be painful and difficult at times, but it need not cause you this degree of stress. Tell me what were the most difficult parts of the past weeks, and let's see if we can work together to help you feel stabilized.

Subsequently, my own experience and that of therapists treating substance abuse and eating disorders taught me that a modified version of this model (with the focus on defenses and issues of self but not on conflicted affect) can be helpful to some patients in the 40–50 range of functioning. For patients with ratings below 40, rapid uncovering work is recommended only in a structured and supportive environment such as an inpatient setting with a highly trained staff. These disorder-specific applications of the model are discussed in detail in chapter 11.

In summary, the level of functioning rating on the GAF plus the MAPP considerations provide a rough guideline to determine *whether* rapid uncovering short-term interventions might be employed, and if so, how rapidly and aggressively one might proceed in uncovering hidden feelings, as well as what degree of support might be needed in doing so. It is not always a question of *whether* short-term techniques are appropriate; there can be a question of *when and how* they are appropriate and what form of additional support is needed. In all cases, uncovering should not be attempted unless sufficient supports are available.

To date, little controlled research has been done on selection criteria, and none that I am aware of has looked at the interaction effects of patient characteristics and treatment intervention. Malan's (1976) research demonstrating that his selection criteria were linked to improvement has provided some empirical support for the recommendations presented in this chapter. However, Binder, Henry, and Strupp's (1987) study did not replicate Malan's findings except for the variable of alliance. Much carefully designed research is now needed to increase understanding of the complex relationship of patient characteristics to outcome as well as to specific interventions. This chapter offers recommendations for *patient-specific interventions* on the basis of confirming clinical evidence from videotaped sessions.

Controversy Concerning the Usefulness of the GAF

Sometimes students become frustrated in making a GAF rating saying, "My patient is all over this scale!" Reminders are needed to rate psychological, social, and occupational functioning separately. The GAF score, the *lowest* of those three ratings, can alert the therapist to the "weakest link in the chain."

Criticisms of the GAF Scale also have come from a few researchers who complain that the GAF has only 3 or 4 points that are frequently used (e.g., 40, 50, 60, and 70). Many researchers have not made this complaint, however, and overall reliability and validity ratings on the GAF have been high (Endicott et al., 1976). Furthermore, to complain of restriction of range, one has to be looking at only one population (e.g., only outpatients). Inpatients fall between 0 and 40, outpatients between 30 and 70, and the nonpatient population generally falls between 60 or 70 and 100. Clearly, it is important for researchers to identify where their patient population falls within this wide range of functioning. As is discussed later, the GAF rating also has important implications for what treatment should be considered. Finally, as treatment methods improve, the change in the GAF rating will be an important indicator of the efficacy of interventions in moving patients toward healthier functioning. It provides a standardized scale on which people from any patient or nonpatient population can be placed. Rather than throw out such a clinically useful scale, we should consider further improving the manner in which ratings are made.

GAF LEVEL OF FUNCTIONING AS A GUIDELINE FOR TREATMENT

The Supportive–Expressive Continuum as a Guide for Patient-Specific Treatment

The supportive–expressive form of psychoanalytic psychotherapy was originally developed at the Menninger Foundation in Topeka, Kansas, and further developed by Luborsky (1984). The term *supportive* refers to the techniques aimed at directly maintaining the patient's level of functioning. The term *expressive* refers to the techniques aimed at facilitating the patient's expressions about problems and conflicts and their understanding. In a review of supportive treatment (Winston, Pinsker, & McCullough, 1986), the techniques identified were reassurance, praise, encouragement, providing information, direction, advice, and teaching. In contrast, exploratory techniques included questioning, confrontation, clarification, interpretation, and exposure to warded-off feelings. Both classes of techniques may be used, to some degree, with all patients. The lower the patient's level of functioning on the GAF, the greater the need for supportive techniques. The higher the patient's level of functioning on the GAF, the greater the indication for expressive or exploratory interventions. In the midrange of functioning, a more balanced combination of supportive and expressive techniques can be used. Figure 2.2 provides some general guidelines regarding what types of treatments are typically *considered* (i.e., not dictated) on this supportive–expressive continuum at various ranges of functioning. These forms of treatment are described in the following paragraphs.

Well-Functioning Patients: GAF of 71 and Above

Patients in this range of functioning exhibit mild or transient symptoms and good interpersonal and occupational adjustment. They have many personal strengths to draw on to sustain a deep exploration into intrapsychic matters. Sifneos's (1979) short-term anxiety-provoking psychotherapy was designed for people who were high functioning and not highly defended, and it is still a viable resource in short-term treatment. He discovered that such patients had the ego strength not only to tolerate but also to use "deep"

FIGURE 2.2
Supportive–expressive continuum for patient-specific treatment.

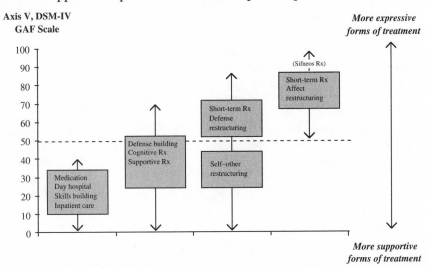

interpretations[7] without being overwhelmed by conflicts. Sifneos's model thus can skip over the defense restructuring referred to in this book, and treatment can move immediately to affect restructuring. Patients in this high-functioning category can experience and express conflicted feelings, often with the help of such interpretations. The therapist can rely on the patient's well-developed sense of self and alliance with others to help the therapy process move along rapidly. Such cases, although only a small percentage of the typical outpatient population, can result in major resolution of the core psychodynamic conflicts in a few sessions. It is important that therapists be able to recognize which patients could be responsive to rapid and deep interpretations because major changes of the core conflicts can occur rapidly, making extensive therapy unnecessary. The Bickering Daughter presented in chapter 1 is such an example; she was able to resolve a lifelong focal problem in two sessions.

In this category, an ongoing crisis (Axis IV) or medical illness (Axis III) may suggest contraindication for or caution in proceeding with short-term treatment. In addition, not all people in this group are psychologically minded.

Moderately Impaired Patients: GAF 51–70
The 51–70 range of the GAF represents mild-to-moderate impairment in functioning or a mild-to-moderate level of symptoms. These are the patients

[7]*Deep interpretations* are defined here as explanatory statements about feelings and relationships largely outside of the patient's awareness, such as "I think you avoid your father because of your discomfort over sexual feelings for him."

for whom the treatment described in this book was originally designed: individuals with moderate but long-standing character pathology and a moderate level of impairment in social and occupational functioning. At intake to the Beth Israel Medical Center (New York City) study, 64 patients averaged 55 on the intake GAF. Both Malan and Davanloo focused their treatment efforts on working with defensive behaviors of patients in this range of functioning. Patients with GAF scores above 50 who are psychologically minded and demonstrate good impulse control can generally handle some version of the short-term defense, affect, and self–other restructuring. Of course, the closer the score is to 50, the more supportive interventions are called for and the greater the need for careful restructuring of the defensive patterns. The higher the GAF score, the more rapidly the therapist can offer deep interpretations and address conflicted emotions.

In this range of functioning, medication may or may not be provided. If symptoms are moderate, use of medication generally depends on the Axis I diagnoses and whether or not the patient wants to take medication. Clearly, one should not attempt exploratory, uncovering psychotherapy if the symptoms are so stressful that functioning may become impaired. In such cases, it is the responsibility of the clinician to recommend the appropriate medication or a medication consultation.

As noted previously, if an individual is functioning with moderate impairment *and is burdened with an impulse control disorder* (e.g., active substance abuse), the full repertoire of short-term techniques is contraindicated unless additional support or structure is provided because of the danger of further loss of control. In such cases, cognitive therapy is an excellent outpatient alternative to help build control.

Severely Impaired Patients: GAF 41–50

The 41–50 range of the GAF represents severe impairment and severe symptoms but generally the ability to maintain outpatient status. Scores below 50 on the GAF reflect a rapidly descending gradient of pathology, and the recommended treatments and interventions take a sharp turn to more supportive ego- or skills-building approaches (as described in the section on deficit pathology in chapter 1) in contrast to the rapid uncovering and removal of defenses of the short-term procedures. In patients with scores below 50, the length of treatment also tends to increase. Marsha Linehan (1993a) developed her cognitive–behavioral treatment for patients in this range with borderline personality disorder. Linehan's patients' GAF scores were in the low 40s at intake and low-to-middle 50s at follow-up. Judith Herman (1992) developed treatment techniques for severely impaired trauma victims at this level of functioning. Her interventions include providing support and teaching daily living skills. In addition to the acting-out borderline personality disorders with impairment in identity as well as lack of impulse control, this category includes bingeing alcoholics, anorexic patients, severe trauma victims, and many nonhospitalized patients with schizophrenia.

The treatment methods in this book were not intended originally to be applicable to people at this impaired level of functioning, but my perspective was changed by a visit to the Renfrew Center in Philadelphia. When first invited to speak there, I declined, believing that my methods were not appropriate for their population of inpatients with anorexia. To my surprise, they repeated their invitation, saying that two of their staff had attended my conferences and were employing some of my techniques. The visit was most instructive, and taught me that modified versions of defense restructuring (e.g., empathically helping patients see and give up self-destructive or masochistic behaviors) and self–other restructuring (e.g., helping them build a better inner representation of self and others) can be helpful with more impaired patient groups.

Clearly, medication should be considered in this severe range of functioning; many of the Axis I disorders (e.g., bipolar illness, schizophrenia, severe attention disorder) are more responsive to pharmacological intervention than to psychotherapy.

Patients Requiring Custodial Care: GAF 40 and Below

A rating of 40 or below on the GAF represents a level of impairment with incapacitating symptoms that often requires hospitalization or custodial care. The average GAF score for psychiatric inpatients at admission is between 35 and 40 (e.g., Longabaugh, Stout, Kriebal, McCullough, & Bishop, 1986). Patients at this level of functioning are incapacitated and require support as well as structure. Medication and inpatient or day hospitalization are usually the treatments of choice. Interventions to consider include teaching daily living skills and providing social interaction groups. At hospital discharge, the GAF rating averages 55 (e.g., Longabaugh et al., 1986), which places many patients in the moderately impaired group. However, these patients typically are not appropriate for outpatient short-term treatment because of their recent instability in functioning and vulnerability under stress.

THREE APPROACHES TO ASSESSMENT OF FUNCTIONING

Typical Assessment Package in Research Settings

For many years, I have been administering assessment materials to participants in research projects. In a typical research study, this may involve a lengthy battery of instruments often requiring 6 hours or more to complete, including a patient self-report and a personal interview with a diagnostician. The resulting stack of paper is generally many inches thick. Furthermore, this entire process should be repeated several times during a study. Recommendations for such a battery can be found in a chapter I wrote (McCullough, 1993a), which contains the basic assessment package used by the Center for Psychotherapy Research at the University of Pennsylvania.[8]

---

[8]These instruments were chosen in part from the most commonly used outcome-assessment instruments found in studies in the *Journal of Clinical and Consulting Psychology* and the *Archives of General Psychiatry* between 1980 and 1990.

The battery of instruments included idiographic (patient-specific) measures such as a listing of target problems (Battle, Imber, Hoehn-Saric et al., 1966), nomothetic (standardized) measures such as the Beck Depression Inventory, and standard diagnostic measures (e.g., the Structured Clinical Interview for the DSM-IV, Axis I [SCID I] and Axis II [SCID II]; Spitzer, Williams, Gibbon, & First, 1988). Although researchers such as Michael Lambert (1994) are striving to reconceptualize and improve the assessment process as a whole, this battery reflects the state of the art up to 1990.

Unfortunately, this extensive assessment is not practical or even possible for clinicians in practice, especially when the number of sessions is limited by insurance company requirements. Not only is such research assessment too lengthy to be incorporated into the typical clinical setting, but each separate instrument is copyrighted, often involving a high initial fee plus additional costs for each set of instruments that is ordered (typically 25). The use of these tests becomes prohibitive not only in time but also in cost for the independent clinician. After many years of extended assessments of research patients, I found myself needing an abridged version of this assessment package in my clinical practice. Ideally, I would like to see assessment laboratories developed, just as we have laboratories for biochemical tests for medical treatment. Until such a service is available for psychotherapeutic assessment, however, the clinician is left with increasing demands for provision of diagnoses without proper assessment tools.

Time-Efficient Assessment Methods

A standardized assessment package, reasonably priced for the practicing clinician, although greatly needed, has not been widely available because the field of psychotherapy assessment is still in its developmental stage. Even the research community varies in use of assessment packages, because different studies have different requirements. Recently, popular writers in the field of psychotherapy have recognized the clinician's need for assessment tools and have begun to offer various methods at a practical cost. David Burns (1989) offers a package of instruments tailored to his model of cognitive therapy for depression, and Linehan offers a workbook (1993b) as a companion to her cognitive–behavioral therapy manual for borderline personality disorders (1993a). Both Burns and Linehan charge a onetime fee, which permits the buyer to photocopy the instruments for their professional use.[9]

In addition, two instruments have recently been developed by Robert Spitzer and his colleagues. First, an abridged version of the structured interview for the DSM-IV (Axis I) has been developed for the clinician.[10] Al-

---

[9]Linehan's *Skills Training Manual* for treating borderline personality disorder can be obtained from Guilford Publications, Inc., 72 Spring Street, New York, NY.

[10]The clinician version of the SCID for Axis I can be obtained for a small fee from Biometrics Research Department, New York State Psychiatric Institute, Department of Psychiatry, Columbia University, New York, NY, or from American Psychiatric Press, Washington, DC.

though it can take an hour or more to complete, it is an improvement over the longer research forms. This will be of much assistance to clinicians faced with demands to provide an accurate DSM-IV diagnosis. The second one is the PRIME-MD, a short, greatly condensed, and extremely convenient method for rapid overview of major psychiatric problem areas: anxiety, mood, alcohol, somatization. Unfortunately, this instrument is not for sale, but it is available from Pfizer Corporation.

Someday there may be a standardized and comprehensive package of instruments for the clinician and assessment laboratories to administer them. Like the initial diversity in computer software, many different versions of assessment batteries will necessarily evolve before a standard battery is widely used.

In response to requests from hundreds of workshop participants, I plan to make available the comprehensive self-report assessment device that I have derived from my research battery.[11] This Psychotherapy Assessment Checklist (PAC) Forms includes a shorter, simpler set of items than is found in the full research battery and provides an overview of patients' demographics, diagnoses, and problem areas. Personal data and demographics are assessed, including description of main presenting problems rated for severity; major medical conditions to assist determination of Axis III (in addition to the frequency of medical visits, sick days, psychotherapy visits, cigarettes and alcoholic drinks per day, number of family members with alcohol problems or mental illness, and so on). Patients are asked to report current stressors to assess Axis IV, and respond to many questions on life functioning to assist in rating Axis V, the Global Assessment of Functioning scale (GAF; 1–100 rating). In addition, the PAC Forms contain a checklist of items that are criteria for the major Axis I and Axis II diagnoses. These forms *do not generate a diagnosis*, but can assist the clinician in following the DSM-IV guidelines for diagnostic assessment. Therefore, if the patient answers "yes" the therapist will need to further assess this category using the DSM-IV manual. If the patient responds "no" the therapist may accept the diagnosis as not present, unless clinical judgment suggests otherwise (e.g., if the patient says she is not depressed, but reports lack of interests or lack of sleep, and so on). Time is saved by being able to rule out the "no" responses. *This checklist is not a replacement for a careful clinical evaluation and diagnosis*, but it is an efficient summary of a large amount of important clinical information that has helped reduce the time required for determining DSM diagnoses in my private practice.

Similar to the checklists of physical symptoms (e.g., allergies, diarrhea) and medical history (e.g., measles, mumps, operations) that are filled out before a medical visit with a physician, this checklist is designed to *assist* the psychotherapist in taking a comprehensive history and in the determination

[11]My Psychotherapy Assessment Checklist Forms (PAC Forms), which may be photocopied for clinical use, may be obtained for $35 from The Short-Term Therapy Research Program, P.O. Box 466, Dedham, MA 02026. All proceeds will be used to further research in short-term psychotherapy.

of DSM-IV diagnoses. After the first phone contact, the checklist is mailed to the patient with instructions to complete it (the time required is about 1 hour) and bring it to the first session. The completed checklist can be scanned by the therapist in a few minutes and highlights a broad spectrum of clinical problem areas that may or may not need further assessment. When checked items reflect the possibility of a diagnosis or even the presence of a symptom the therapist wishes to evaluate further, the therapist is referred to the DSM-IV or to the SCID to assess the disorder in an in-depth manner.

Useful Questions to Determine Level of Functioning

In the absence of any of the assessment batteries mentioned, there are four specific questions (in addition to those of the GAF) that therapists can ask to obtain a broad perspective of patients' levels of functioning. According to Malan's "fundamental law of psychotherapeutic forecasting," one should expect to revisit the worst states the patient has known. He also reminds us that we need to know the best, "the depth of feeling in the best relationship the patient has ever known" (Gustafson, 1984, p. 941). These excellent points are encompassed in the following four questions (and also included in the aforementioned PAC Forms):

1. What were the worst times in your life?
2. Who helped during those times?
3. What were the best times in your life (the times you were most proud of)?
4. Whom did you share those times with?

These four questions rapidly summarize the lifelong overview of severity of symptoms (e.g., hospitalizations, suicide attempts) as well as the highest level of functioning that was achieved. Asking about the people involved provides a perspective on the relatedness of the patient. Was there no one in the patient's environment who offered support or congratulations? Was there at least one person who was helpful during the troubled times or pleased with the successes? Furthermore, was the patient able to reach out and ask for help or receive the help that was offered? Was the help not what the patient wanted? Did the patient go through the crisis or the success alone? Could the patient receive congratulations comfortably? Gustafson (1984) suggested asking the patient to describe an instance when something was given up for someone who was loved.

If the worst times "brought about dangerous actions" or "required more support than the patient's present environment can provide" (Gustafson, 1984, p. 941), a much more supportive or graded approach should be provided. A rapid uncovering process would risk reactivating the patient's vulnerabilities. Just as the GAF-MAPP questions summarize much detail about recent and current functioning, so do these four questions help to summarize many years of detail about lifelong functioning.

SUMMARY

A patient's level of functioning on the GAF can be helpful in determining what type of treatment to provide along the supportive-to-expressive continuum. The acronym GAF-MAPP summarizes these points for determining suitability of short-term treatment: a GAF rating above 50 plus *m*otivation, a low *A*xis IV stress score, *p*sychological-mindedness, and favorable *p*atient response to treatment.

Practice Examples to Determine GAF Ratings

The following cases (some presented earlier and some new) are presented to give the reader an opportunity to practice rating patients' levels of functioning on the Global Assessment of Functioning Scale. A brief synopsis of GAF procedures is as follows: Refer to the examples on the GAF rating scale in Figure 2.1 and locate a verbal description that accurately portrays the individual in terms of psychological or social–occupational functioning. Select a number in that range that best represents the patient's lowest level of functioning. The GAF rating represents the weakest or most vulnerable area of functioning.

Some patients fall squarely within a 10-point range on both psychological and social–occupational functioning. When this is the case, the rating can be done fairly easily. Difficulty in making a GAF rating is increased when individuals present a more varied range of severity across these areas of functioning. Some individuals have much distress but good functioning (e.g., the "worried well"), and some have high occupational functioning with poor or false social functioning (e.g., the successful narcissist). When making a rating, one should examine the adjacent intervals to evaluate where the patient falls within the 10-point interval. For example, if symptoms appear to be moderate (50–59) but there are some factors reflective of the category below (severe impairment), the score could be between 50 and 53. If the symptoms fall closer to the category of mild impairment, the score would be between 57 and 59. If symptoms are pretty much in the middle of the category, the score would fall approximately within the 54–56 range, depending on the clinician's judgment of the patient's presentation. For consideration of short-term psychotherapy, however, I have therapists also consider an *average* of these scores to be mindful of the patients' relative degree of strength versus vulnerability reflected in their functioning. With one notable exception (the narcissistic personality),[12] very high functioning in one area or an *average GAF score above 50* can indicate sufficient personal strength for short-term psychotherapy. As an additional check, one should compare this numerical average to one's clinical impression of the case. If clinical judgment

---

[12]Patients with narcissistic personality disorder are exceptions because they may have high occupational functioning and apparent absence of symptoms, yet the serious deficits in interpersonal functioning (although not always immediately apparent) make the active, uncovering techniques of short-term psychotherapy difficult if not impossible to employ. Their deficits in authentic interpersonal relating necessitate longer-term work to build identity and relatedness.

does not concur with the rating, each of the ratings should be rechecked carefully.

Rate each of the following examples on the GAF Scale, and identify the candidates for short-term psychotherapy versus those who would require other treatments. Consensus GAF ratings and explanations are given in Appendix A.

The Man Who Loved Ice Skating

A 38-year-old married man and father of two children ages 5 and 7 came to treatment because of marital problems. His wife had refused to go for marriage counseling. He loved his work as a medic and was a highly respected member of the team. He had many friends in the community and several people he could confide in. He was caring and devoted to his children. He described with joy the trips they took and the fun they had ice skating on a local pond. His only symptoms were occasional increased irritation (and feelings troubled by his relationship with his wife), which caused him to lose his temper and yell at his children rather than his wife. Although loss of temper happened only rarely, it upset him and the children quite a bit. He also behaved in a passive–aggressive way, refusing to respond to his wife, because he felt unable to stand up to her. This behavior made his wife madder. She was often in a bad mood, was very harsh with the children and with him, and always refused to join them on their outings.

The Unforgiven Teenager

This woman had had a history of alcohol abuse and promiscuity (as a teenager) that made her feel unforgiven by God ever since her teenage years. An explosive drunken episode following a break up with a man friend brought this now 36-year-old, unmarried businesswoman to treatment. She had been sober for the previous 3 years and felt confident that she would not return to drinking, but she wanted help with her poor self-esteem and her history of choosing abusive partners. She met more than the minimum criteria for major depressive disorder, which had lasted for 3 weeks, but she did not want to take medication. She was functioning well at work and was valued as a manager of a large department (though her symptoms had recently made it more difficult), and she had some conflicts with her boss and coworkers. Her evenings and weekends were spent depressed and alone. She did not have friends whom she met socially on any regular basis, and she had never had a close love relationship that lasted more than a few months. But she had one close confidante—her sister, with whom she spoke on the phone weekly.

The Personal Ads Man

This 37-year-old unmarried man requested brief psychotherapy, but he was unable to identify a problem that he wanted help with. He demonstrated flatness of affect throughout the interview punctuated with occasional dry witty remarks that seeming fitting to his academic milieu. However, he felt that his life was a facade, he had no one he felt close to, and he was constantly worried that he would be found out to be a fake. He felt inadequate both at work and socially. He regularly placed personal ads in the newspaper, to which many women responded. Almost every day he would meet a woman for breakfast, lunch, or dinner, but he rarely saw anyone twice. He functioned sufficiently well to stay employed as a college English teacher, but he was bored with his work and found little satisfaction in it. He was witty and congenial, if inauthentic, with his coworkers. He had never felt truly happy, and he had been mildly depressed most of his life.

The Wife with a Soul Mate

A chance meeting and subsequent brief affair the year before with her previous lover, Tim, brought this 26-year-old married woman to treatment. She felt desperate. She was married to a solid, stable, but distant man, with whom she does not communicate. In contrast, Tim had felt like a "soul mate" to her, but he had been so unreliable that she had married her husband on the rebound of one of many breakups. Tim had not asked her to be with him, but she yearned to leave the marriage to be with him anyway. Her reality testing (under questioning by the interviewer) proved within normal limits. She felt that she had always been overly dependent on others and needed to "get away from everyone and find herself." But her mood, judgment, and decision making were unstable to the extent that some days she felt in danger of impulsively acting out (which is why she sought treatment). She was in constant distress from depressed mood. She was functioning with difficulty as a housewife forcing herself to get up and do things. She had some superficial friendships and described her mother as caring, but she had spoken to no one about this dilemma. In fact, she had suffered in silence because of shame of the affair—for the entire year.

The Machine Builder

This 26-year-old female graduate student requested treatment because she was experiencing "panic attacks" concerning public speaking. She did not meet diagnostic criteria for any type of panic disorder, but she did for social phobia. She was completing a degree in mechanical engineering, which she was excited about. Although she was a good student, she was feeling overwhelmed by the prospect of having to present her thesis orally and give presentations for job interviews. Her fear was so severe that she was seriously considering dropping out of school. She had a boyfriend whom she confided in a little, but no other close friends or confidants. She got along with schoolmates in her classes, but declined parties because she was so nervous in front of people and would not eat in the school cafeteria because she was phobic of eating in public.

The Nailbiter

A 34-year-old divorced woman was overwhelmed by the task of raising two children. Her husband had left her for another woman because, in addition to holding a full-time job, he had been required to do much of the domestic work, including cooking all the meals, shopping, and cleaning. Although now she was cooking meals, keeping house, and taking care of her children more than she had done before, her anxiety symptoms were severe and functioning required enormous effort on her part. Her house was messy and cluttered. She felt that her 2-year-old daughter controlled her and would hound her for the next 20 years. (She realized this was absurd, but she felt out of control.) Her children woke her repeatedly in the middle of the night, and because of fatigue and desperation, she frequently screamed at them at the top of her lungs; this grieved her enormously, because she longed to give her children a better childhood than she had had but felt flawed and inadequate as a person and was unable to change. She bit her fingernails so obsessively that her fingers and arms ached, but she was unable to stop. She spoke almost daily to her mother, who frequently pointed out her faults and discouraged her attempts at autonomy. She was close to her sister but had never been in love, and wondered how she would know if she were in love. She was highly motivated for treatment but felt despairing that she could truly overcome these problems.

The Ferryman

This 36-year-old hospice worker came to treatment because of difficulty concerning his divorce. His wife had been having an affair and was so demeaning of him that she would have the lover in the house when the man returned from work. He had always been a passive man and afraid of conflict, and he had been mildly depressed as long as he could remember. (He met criteria for dysthemia.) However, his functioning was stable, he had good friends he confided in (indeed, he frequently asked for advice and direction), and he was very caring with his daughter as well as with clients facing death. Though a responsible worker, his job review stated that he had trouble taking criticism, and he had occasional conflicts with coworkers.

The Artist with Jaw Pain

A 23-year-old single woman came to treatment because she was overwhelmed by recent events. She had had difficulty with sexual relationships and was very confused about her sexual identity. She had dropped out of college the previous semester because of a breakup with a boyfriend that led her to be depressed and frightened. She had firmly believed that he was listening to her conversations (he lived in the apartment directly below her) and spying on her. She also suffered from chronic, severe jaw pain, as did her father, which did not respond to medical intervention. She was articulate and creative and had been studying art. She planned to return to school the next semester. She was presently working at a health food restaurant, which she liked; however, there was a man who worked there whom she feared was following her, and during the session she spoke softly because she worried that he might be listening outside the office door. She said she had dropped out of therapy before, because the therapist learned too much about her too soon. When her female therapist said that it might be important to go slower this time and not divulge too much too quickly, the patient answered that she was worried that she might have sexual feelings toward the therapist.

The Stalker

This 36-year-old, never-married college graduate had worked only a few years before having a psychotic break. Medication stabilized him, but he often refused to take it and became delusional. He had been living on his own for several years but had become unable to maintain his apartment, so his landlord was evicting him. He had no friends. He was planning to return to his parents' home to live, as he had done for most of his life. There was a woman he was infatuated with who lived in the neighborhood and whom he wanted to marry. She had explained that she was already married, but this did not dissuade him. He would pace back and forth in front of her home during the night, trying to see her. One evening, he noticed the front door had been left slightly ajar, so he entered the home, frightening the woman and her family but leaving when asked. As a result of this incident, he had been brought to the hospital for treatment by his parents.

The Bickering Daughter

This happily married 47-year-old midwife came to treatment because of concern about her relationship with her aging father. She loved him, but every visit was difficult, with the two of them ending up bickering. She longed to be closer to him before he died. Her relationship with her husband and teenage daughters was excellent. She had many friends and a lively sense of humor. She had a few enemies because she was willing to take a stand on important issues, but she was greatly respected for this in her community. She loved her work and was sought after as a teacher and supervisor in her field. She had no symptoms other than this occasional irritation with her father.

CHAPTER 3

Determination of the Core Psychodynamic Conflict Formulation and Its Resolution

I came to explore the wreck. . . .
I came to see the damage that was done
and the treasures that prevail. . . .
the wreck and not the story of the wreck
the thing itself and not the myth. . . .
We circle silently
about the wreck
we dive into the hold.
I am she; I am he . . .
We are, I am, you are
by cowardice or courage
the one who find our way
back to this scene . . .
in which
our names do not appear.

                              Adrienne Rich,
                              Diving into the Wreck (1973)

THE PSYCHODYNAMIC JOURNEY

Each new patient challenges the therapist with enormously complex and conflicting material that must be organized into a coherent format. Cognitive and behavior therapists have the advantage of focusing in on maladaptive cognitions, "automatic thoughts," or observable behaviors. There is an immense clarity in doing so, and the research results for these approaches support the efficacy of such clear-cut objectives. The task of such therapists is to make the patient's muddled story as simple and as unambiguous as a fourth grade primer.

The psychodynamic therapist is more encumbered. Because we choose, prefer, or cannot avoid the more elaborate psychodynamic view of human nature, we bear the burden of making sense of hidden meanings. The dynamic therapist is often confronted with a barrage of "meaningful" details, as is the reader of a sonnet or of Adrienne Rich, and the struggle for clarity is more difficult. Nevertheless, it seems crucial for those of us who are theoretically wedded to the concept of the dynamic unconscious to learn to decipher it. The challenge is to understand the core message of a sonnet as clearly as we understand faulty attributions or maladaptive behaviors.

The psychodynamic therapist must examine not only the symptoms, but also the *meaning* of the symptoms. We must look "through" the manifest behaviors or automatic thoughts to their hidden meanings, and then "below," to the underlying, or latent, feelings. In undertaking such a journey, in diving into the wreck, a dynamic therapist must have a well-detailed plan of how to proceed. Clarity of focus means so much. Such journeys down into the psyche have already been charted, sometimes in tremendous detail, by myriad psychoanalytic writers. But such guidelines, although brilliant, are intuitively based and often quite hard to follow. Each writer uses different metaphors.

Furthermore, traditional dynamic procedure typically has recommended "tolerance of ambiguity." Even though it can be healing to "sit with" a patient during a grief process, however, it is no service to the patient to be overly tolerant of unclear aspects. At times, what parades as a virtue is more a defense: passivity in the face of conflict, confusion, or intense passion. In short, the therapist's silence can represent passivity in the face of confusion. In time-conscious treatment, tolerance of ambiguity is encouraged only when one is, at the same time, actively seeking solutions but coming up empty-handed. The capacity to tolerate rather than become frustrated or active to no purpose provides the energy for tenacity and persistence. Our long-range goal should be intolerance of the ambiguity of pathology and intolerance of human suffering. It is crucial in the formulation of a core dynamic conflict to play with ambiguity: to study it, deconstruct it, and not be defeated by it. Our patients desperately need us to do this. They have been the unwilling victims of ambiguity for too long.

How can the psychodynamically informed therapist catch sight and feeling of the submerged living core of a human being in the murky depths and find the way back up to the surface? How can we acquire the clarity of focus enjoyed by the cognitive or behavioral therapist when, even with such active measures taken, sometimes after 5 or 10 sessions (or alas, a year) the once-clear focus becomes vague? The dynamic therapist is once again floundering and wondering, "Now where *are* we, and what are we supposed to be doing?"

> *And now: it is easy to forget*
> *what I came for . . .*
> *and besides*
> *you breathe differently down here.*[1]

[1]From Adrienne Rich, *Diving into the Wreck* (1973).

Oh how marvelous to be a cognitive therapist at such times! Indeed, other therapies would do well to follow suit in such clear specification of objectives. Traditional psychodynamic therapy has been slowest to achieve such clarity, but impressive research efforts (to be discussed) have begun the task of systematically identifying the dynamic focus.

> The use of the focus is the single most decisive and active alteration of psychodynamic technique introduced by brief therapists, with the exception of the use of time limits. A treatment which is focused . . . implies an endpoint [which] intensifies motivation to tackle the focal problem." (DeLaCour, 1986, p. 133)

The methods described in this chapter are intended to carry forward this focus on affect by incorporating Tomkins's affect theory within Malan's two triangles. Tomkins's script theory (1978) says that affects are organized in *scenes* (patients' narratives with at least one affect and one object) that have underlying *scripts.*

> In my script theory, the scene, a happening with a perceived beginning and end, is the basic unit of analysis. The whole connected set of scenes lived in sequence is called the plot of a life. The script, in contrast, does not deal with all the scenes or the plot of a life, but rather with the individual's rules for predicting, interpreting, responding to and controlling a magnified set of scenes. (Tomkins, 1978, p. 217)

Lichtenberg, Lachmann, and Fosshage (1992) call these scripts "model scenes" that represent the "larger picture" contained in the patient's narrative (p. 217). Although this model uses the research-based term *core psychodynamic conflict formulation,* or *core conflict,* the reader should be aware that the psychodynamic formulation as used in this approach is similar to Tomkins's *nuclear scripts* (maladaptive, repetitive, and magnified affect patterns); both represent the underlying and affect-based organization in the stories our patients tell us. According to Tomkins, nuclear scripts are formed in part because affects become "magnified." "Scenes are magnified, not by repetition, but repetition with a difference" (Tomkins, 1978, p. 219). The repetition of affect magnification across many varied scenes results in our capacity to generalize from one experience to another and provides us with great flexibility and adaptability in responding. There is equally great potential, however, for mistaken overgeneralization. Adaptive nuclear scripts can be seen in the eternally optimistic or resilient personality who sees the world through rose-colored glasses. In contrast, maladaptive nuclear scripts are the result of painful or negative overgeneralization, for example, people in the present are misperceived to be as threatening as were people in the past, expression of feeling is felt as shameful now as it was then, and so on. These scripts, whether constructive or destructive, sensitize us to scan for certain possibilities and respond in repetitive ways. "The number and variety of such scripts is an important part of the total personality structure" (Tomkins, 1978, p. 278).

SEARCHING FOR THE CORE OF
MEANING IN THE WEB OF CONFUSION

The task of the dynamic therapist is to discern the patient's main maladaptive nuclear scripts or core psychodynamic conflicts. (But keep in mind that patients also have adaptive nuclear scripts that guide their lives.) Converting a patient's often rambling and unstructured narrative into a psychodynamic formulation can be rapidly achieved if the patient's main problems can be identified and then deconstructed into Malan's components of defenses (i.e., symptoms), meanings–conflicts, and feelings in relationship to self and others.

The first of these components, the symptoms, are generally conscious, evident, and clear. But how does one know the primary affective needs underlying those symptoms? How do you discern, as Karl Menninger (1963) suggested, what is behind the symptom? The answer is, you don't at first. But questioning can begin concerning these highly probable affective responses, the people to whom they are attached, and the person's basic sense of self that has resulted. Specifically, questioning can focus on the wishes and desires that support and enhance the adaptive experience of self, in contrast to the ways the wishes and desires have been blunted by a negative sense of self. What is wanted and not wanted, although astounding in multiplicity, springs from a small group of affects represented at the bottom of the Triangle of Conflict. This can be viewed as the "solution focus" (e.g., Walter & Peller, 1992) or the resolution to the problem: how one might feel or be motivated to act to satisfy or solve whatever need or dilemma is at hand.

In addition, when one reviews a video of the first 3–5 minutes of the first session for most patients, embedded in the description of the presenting problem are sufficient data to begin to decipher the defenses, anxieties, and adaptive affective solution to the problem, so that a working hypothesis can be constructed.[2] This formulation does not have to be final, but it can be provisional.

Just as cognitive therapy focuses on maladaptive cognitions and behavior therapy on maladaptive behavior, this model focuses on maladaptively handled affects. Taking both thought and behavior into consideration, the dynamic therapist assists the patient toward adaptive (rather than defensive or maladaptive) expression of *basic wants and needs*. If we see personality simply as the individual's variegated attempts at adaptation—attempts to express a certain affect or set of emotions, which defenses and anxieties block (or, put another way, which are blocked by a conflict and result in symptoms)—we begin to have the kind of clarity enjoyed by cognitive or be-

[2]Hannah Levenson noted the same phenomena in her book on time-limited therapy (1995).

havior therapists. If adaptive emotions can be expressed without conflict, the patient is relieved of the quirky symptoms and the defensive depression or anxiety that led them to seek help in the first place. Both Tomkins and Lichtenberg and their colleagues advocated a view of psychodynamics that places affects or fundamental motivators at the core of human experience.[3]

The focus on affective responding brings one closer to observable reality than did previous perspectives.[4] By operationalizing the *unconscious* as "unlabeled inner experience" and verbally labeling previously unnamed affects, we no longer have to grapple with an amorphous hypothetical construct. Furthermore, operationalizing the term *neurosis* as "conflicts about feelings" refers us to the functions of the anxiety pole, where we find an amalgam of *beliefs and "self-inhibiting or self-attacking" responses that block adaptive responding.* Again, this construct is much more tangible than *neurotic conflict.* A well-operationalized, *affect-based psychodynamics* can reduce the confusion.

In each of the following examples, the focus is primarily on affects and secondarily on the cognitions that hold those affects in place. Although cognition, like a director, guides and directs the affects, affect functions more like the producer. Although it may seem that the director is running the show, there would be nothing to direct if the producer did not provide the power or motivation to act. Put differently, cognitions can be thought of as the steering wheel, whereas affect is the motor that drives the car. Both affect and cognition are essential components of functioning and both can malfunction and need repair, but affect in this model is the fundamental motivator and thus a primary source of psychological disorder.

The Machine Builder: Hidden Feelings

This female graduate student came for treatment of phobias of speaking and eating in public, which threatened her professional functioning. A cognitive therapist would have focused on her conscious maladaptive cognitions regarding her belief that she would look foolish if she showed any emotion interpersonally. The integrative dynamic therapist would look at those cognitions as well but would attempt to relate them to underlying, and blocked, motivations. Question: How is the dynamic therapist to discover her basic wants and needs when they are not expressed?

---

[3]Lichtenberg and his colleagues chose to focus on five "motivational systems," whereas Tomkins identified discrete categories of drives and affects. I have much respect for both models, and they have large areas of overlap. I have selected Tomkins's theory over Lichtenberg's because of Tomkins's greater conceptual clarity. Tomkins clearly distinguishes between drives and affects, whereas Lichtenberg's motivational systems combine drives and affects (e.g., Category 5, "sensual enjoyment and sexual excitement," does not adequately distinguish joy, the affect, from sexual desire, a drive). I find these to be important distinctions, clinically; the two are quite different experiences, and they need to be handled differently in clinical work. In chapter 7, in the discussion of specific affects, I demonstrate how such distinctions may be made.

[4]Research by Tomkins (1962, 1963, 1991, 1992), Ekman (1984, 1992a, 1992b), and Izard (1990) has brought the study of affect into the realm of science.

THE FERRYMAN: HIDDEN FEELINGS

This 36-year-old male hospice worker came to treatment for chronic low self-esteem and passivity. He met criteria for dysthymia, which had lasted many years. Maladaptive cognitions were prominent (e.g., I don't feel good about myself. I can't do anything right. I need a lot of reassurance from others that I'm doing okay). The cognitive therapist would work on restructuring the maladaptive cognitions. The dynamic therapist would seek to alter the maladaptive cognitions by relating these cognitions to underlying motivations or needs. Question: How would the therapist discover the crucial affects underlying his poor self-esteem, when the patient did not have conscious awareness of these feelings?

The "Fingerprint of Personality": The Idiosyncratic Relationship Between Symptoms and Underlying Affects

The challenge in a dynamic formulation (without ignoring biochemistry) is to discover the idiosyncratic connection between the manifest behaviors and the underlying wants and needs that give rise to them. The same symptom picture can have quite different psychodynamic causes in different people, and similar causes can generate quite different symptoms. Like fingerprints, no personality is identical to another. Both depression and anxiety can be symptoms of many underlying wants and needs, like fever and elevated blood pressure can be symptoms of many underlying diseases. But neither the aspirin that takes down the fever nor the medication that reduces high blood pressure addresses the underlying pathophysiology, which is potentially both biological and environmental in origin. Clearly, the core psychodynamic formulation addresses the *learned or environmental sources of suffering*, but the *biological or temperamental source of the symptoms* must be considered as well and is discussed later in this chapter. Because each personality is a unique blend of responses to conflicting forces (an idiosyncratic set of compromises between inner needs, predispositions, and the constraints of reality), we must not oversimplify or we lose perspective of the whole person.

Just as similarities in fingerprints can be categorized across certain dimensions to permit classification, so individuals can be classified along dimensions of personality. For a psychodynamic formulation in this model, these dimensions include a few basic activating and inhibiting affects, a larger number of resulting symptom syndromes, coping mechanisms, or defenses, which manifest themselves in a seemingly infinite array of individual and idiosyncratic personalities. Despite consistent, repetitive patterns in human responding, therefore, it is the rare individual who fits neatly into one category. Typically, each individual has an idiosyncratic blend of several styles or traits. We might consider "personality" as a complex molecule that must be broken down into its elements: basic wants and needs (motivations) and the ways that those are or are not obtained (coping and/or defensive behavior) due to the degree of anxiety-laden inhibitory responses. Thus, figure begins to separate from ground, and an organized set of response categories begins to emerge that can help unravel the meaning behind the symptoms.

Unfortunately, the human personality all too often does not directly reveal its learned motivational components, as the coming examples demonstrate. Because of fears, conflicts, or cultural mores, we often learn to act "as if" things were otherwise or "other than" the way we really feel like acting. We may put on a smile when we are angry. Other times when we are angry, we may weep or become silent, frightened, or busy. Still other times, we might display angry behavior when we are feeling sad or even tender. The ways we can inauthentically hide our true motivations (to ourselves as well as to others) are myriad. Even more problematic is that much of the time these "coverups" of basic motivations are largely or entirely outside of our awareness.[5] The therapist seeking the psychodynamic conflict must find the adaptive but hidden motivation disguised in the defensive behaviors. Following are examples of patterns encountered in clinical work to help in discerning different causes of the same symptoms and similar causes of different symptoms.

THE MACHINE BUILDER: POSSIBLE MOTIVATIONS

This young woman with anxiety over public speaking could be using the anxiety to block any of the basic emotional responses. We might hypothesize that her interpersonal anxiety (a) helped her avoid being *assertive* owing to her discomfort over interpersonal conflict, (b) reflected *a wish to be accepted* (i.e., positive feelings attached to self-in-relation to others) and a fear that she would not be, or (c) represented her fear of breaking down or showing vulnerability to others owing to the *grief* she was fending off. Can you think of other possible hypotheses? Do you think there could be more than one pattern in operation?

THE FERRYMAN: POSSIBLE MOTIVATIONS

This man had symptoms of dysthymia for 20 years, which might be hypothesized to result from (a) the inability to express *angry feelings* appropriately to an unfaithful spouse, (b) the blocked *grief* of the loss of someone who was dearly loved and desperately needed, or (c) poor self-esteem (lack of positive feeling associated with sense of self). Can you think of other possible hypotheses? Are more than one in operation?

THE MACHINE BUILDER: POSSIBLE DEFENSIVE REACTIONS

The Machine Builder openly stated in the first interview that she did not want to grieve her father's death because it would be unbearable to her. As a result, she dissociated, or refused to think about her loss. Others block the experience of sorrow by (a) intellectualizing or minimizing the emotional experience, (b) an exaggerated buoyancy or "Pollyanna" style, or (c) various forms of depression, or numbing of experience Do any other ways of avoid-

---

[5]Such responses are often referred to in dynamic language as "unconscious" or "preconscious." In behavioral terminology, these are covert, or inner, experiences (thoughts, feelings, images, or behaviors) that *have not acquired verbal labels*.

ing sorrow come to mind? It is important to remember that the same affect–conflicts can present in a wide range of defenses.

THE FERRYMAN: POSSIBLE DEFENSIVE REACTIONS

The Ferryman had some obvious problems with anger that he dealt with by being passive and devaluing himself. Others block anger in a variety of ways such as (a) repression (I can't remember what the disagreement was about), (b) reaction formation (When I'm mad, I always find something nice to say), and (c) acting out (I didn't even think, I just threw the cup across the room!). Can you think of other ways people avoid showing anger? Also in the preceding cases, can there be more than one affective response pattern that is being avoided? Might there be other underlying wants and needs of which the Machine Builder or the Ferryman is not aware?

Can you think of other responses (or defensive behaviors) that might be used to block or avoid the appropriate expression of tenderness, anger, sadness, or joy? What other patients do you have who have defended in ways different from these? Can someone use more than one defense to avoid feeling?

Tender feelings can be frightening because one feels so vulnerable. One individual can hide these feelings by indifference (playing it cool), another through irritability (picking fights at moments of closeness), and another through dissociation into work or other activities (being "too busy" for a great deal of close time together).

The preceding examples demonstrated some ways that symptoms manage or compensate for underlying affects. The problem now becomes the correct linking of affects to symptoms and how to be optimally responsive to the patient's vulnerabilities in doing so.

PREPARATION FOR FORMULATING THE CORE PSYCHODYNAMIC CONFLICT

The set of procedures that follows outlines the management and identification of the core psychodynamic conflict formulation. First, the therapist needs to understand the issues that arise in the formulation process regarding the transference, the countertransference, and the real therapeutic relationship. Second, the therapist needs to know how to regulate the patient's anxieties in the uncovering process. After a discussion of this preparatory work, the steps in the formulation process are described in detail.

Therapist Stance in Formulation of the Core Psychodynamic Conflict;
Transference, Countertransference, and the Real Therapeutic Relationship

Throughout this book, I highlight aspects of the "real" relationship versus the transferential relationship between the therapist and patient, as well as the countertransference issues. Psychoanalysis and long-term psychotherapy have focused predominantly on the transference relationship. Anna Freud (1936) defined *transference phenomena*, in part, as defensive reactions caused by the painfulness of wishes or longings. Ralph Greenson (1967) added that the patient's projection onto the therapist must be a *repetition of the past* and must be *inappropriate to the present*.

Some early analytic authors have considered the real relationship, or the "working alliance," of major importance in healing as well as in the understanding of the transference phenomena (Greenson, 1967; Szasz, 1963; Zetzel, 1956). "If there were no real relationship, this idea of the distorting influences would make no sense (A. Freud, 1954). Greenson and Milton Wexler wrote that "we should *leave room somewhere* [italics added] for the realization that the analyst and patient are two real people of equal adult status, in a real personal relationship to each other" (1969, p. 27). Greenson and Wexler lamented that in analytic circles it is "highly suspect to do anything which resembles being kind to the patient" (1969, p. 37).

Indeed, short-term dynamic therapies focus to a large extent on the real, relatively "transference-free," relationship between the therapist and patient, because it is the major agent in resolving transference issues. One of the main distinctions between long- and short-term approaches is this difference in handling transference distortions within the real relationship. In short-term dynamic therapy, transferential responses are viewed as defensive projections that are quickly pointed out and clarified. The patient is asked to recognize, examine, and give up the feelings involved with the distorted image of the therapist, rather than becoming immersed in these projections. The iatrogenic "transference neurosis," therefore, which is essential to the analytic process, is prevented from occurring in short-term dynamic treatment.

The major change agent in short-term therapy is the healing connection of the real relationship, which allows the distorted transferential views to be given up.[6] I call this the "real therapeutic relationship" to underscore the professional context that must be maintained. The relationship between the patient and the therapist is not personal, nor is it a friendship, but it is entirely human. It is a relationship between caring, feeling individuals of equal adult status who are emotionally involved with each other in a way that promotes the patient's healing. Almost 3 decades ago, Greenson and Wexler (1969) beautifully described the relationship of humanitarian concern and respect that this model aspires to today in the following instructions:

- Explain every new or strange procedure to the patient so he understands why we work in a certain way.
- Dosage interpretations so that patients will not be forced to deal on their own with new and painful insights for long periods, for example, over the holidays.

---

[6]It is my understanding that there is great power in both the long- and short-term approaches. Research is greatly needed to determine which patients require an "immersion" into the transference neurosis to tap the affective component necessary for character change in contrast to those patients who can reach these underlying feelings in a short-term mode, without the lengthy process involved in the development of the transference neurosis.

- Try to accommodate to special circumstances in the patient's life as long as it is not [hurtful or counterproductive].
- [Do] not dismiss the patient at the end of the hour in silence or with a remote interpretation.
- Encourage the patient to do some of the interpretive work to promote feelings of participation and achievement.
- *Frankly admit any and all errors of technique* whether due to countertransference reactions, faulty interpretations, or shortcomings in the therapist's personality or technique, as long as the patient is given ample opportunity to (1) discover the mistake himself, (2) explore fantasies about the mistake, and (3) explore the feelings in reaction to the mistake. (Greenson & Wexler, 1969, pp. 36–37)

Also essential in this discussion are the countertransference responses of the therapist: reactions, feelings, images, defenses, and so on, from the therapist's past experience that are transferred (or generalized) onto the patient. Sometimes therapists react personally and defensively to patients' transferential projections, resulting in "projective identification" (see Gabbard, 1994; Gabbard & Wilkinson, 1994). In other cases, the countertransference reactions can be in reaction to the real relationship (e.g., the patient correctly points out a therapist's failing, which the therapist then becomes defensive about). Fortunately, the understanding of how to view and manage these reactions has evolved. Countertransference used to be regarded as a pathological response (A. Reich, 1951, 1960) or as something dangerous or hazardous to be avoided or controlled (e.g., Schafer, 1983).[7] If countertransference reactions occurred (e.g., the therapist becoming angry at the patient), it was considered that the therapist had not been successfully or sufficiently analyzed. Now there is a more compassionate and realistic view of such therapist responses. Countertransference reactions are increasingly seen as ubiquitous, and although they should not be indulged or abrogated, they are viewed as potentially contributing to the understanding of the therapeutic process generally and the patient's impact on others specifically (e.g., Bollas, 1986, 1995; Feiner, 1979; Winnicott, 1965). Now let us examine the real relationship, transference issues, and countertransference issues as each impacts on the psychodynamic formulation process.

THE REAL THERAPEUTIC RELATIONSHIP

The active and involved short-term therapist takes the role of a private investigator who, in collaboration with the patient, acts as a companion sleuth to discover what is secret or hidden. Ideally, this is an egalitarian relationship of mutual respect that acknowledges the areas of expertise of each of the participants. The therapist is expert at discerning conflicted psychodynamic patterns. Patients are expert regarding their own life experience.

---

[7]Also see Burke and Tansey (1991) or Epstein and Feiner (1979) for excellent reviews of the evolution of thought on countertransference.

Nothing the therapist says can be considered valid until the patient corroborates it or adds more data in support of the hypothesis. The therapist must be careful not to impose or force an interpretation on a reluctant patient.

In this model, interpretations are generated immediately and *tentatively*. This process is intentional and has many merits. Collaborative construction of the dynamic formulation serves to draw the patient into the discovery process from the start. Furthermore, it teaches the patient how to analyze his or her behavior from a psychodynamic perspective. From the outset, therefore, the tools of the therapist are gradually transferred to the hands of the patient.

The problem with rapid interpretation is prematurity. If it is done tentatively, however, no harm should come of such speculation. If a patient does not agree, the therapist does not have to feel stupid. The error in interpretation may be more than compensated for by the therapist's satisfaction with being collaborative, hardworking, and willing to risk a tentative hypothesis. In this process, the therapist loses some of the mystique of the distant and idealized figure. The replacement, a compassionate and involved human being, seems a favorable one. As with all approaches, one must remain mindful regarding which patients need the more abstinent approach versus those who can benefit from active interaction.

This aspect of the "continuous, graded, corrective emotional experience" pertains to the therapist's ability to provide a holding environment sufficient to permit patients to face what they have typically spent their entire lifetime avoiding.

TRANSFERENCE ISSUES

At each moment of the evaluation session, the therapist must be vigilant for patterns in the patient's responding that might be carried over, or transferred, from past relationships. The therapist must pay careful attention to behaviors that do not seem to fit the current situation or the current relationship. How is the patient responding that may be similar to how he or she responded to the mother or father? How is the therapist seen from moment to moment? What figure from the past is evoked? These transferred responses are metaphors that hold clues to the core psychodynamic conflicts.

COUNTERTRANSFERENCE ISSUES

The therapist has to be mindful that the core conflict may hold patterns that elicit painful personal issues. Therapists may become aware of these possibilities through the nonjudgmental examination of their own reactions to the patient (I feel furious now, or suddenly sad, or exhilarated, or uncomfortable, or sexually aroused). What does this reaction mean about the patient's core issue? How can this response be used to heal the patient, but not get in the way? It is prudent for therapists to consider obtaining therapy or supervision for themselves if the issues being identified seem to interfere with providing treatment.[8] In a broader sense, however, all uncovering work will have its impact on the therapist. It is crucial to be mindful of these constant influences and one's minute-to-minute reactions to them so that this information can be a *contribution* rather than an impediment to the treatment.

Anxiety Regulation in Formulation of the Core Psychodynamic Conflict

Before identifying the psychodynamic conflict, the therapist needs to have a clear sense of how to protect the patient from too strong a distress as a result of the rapid uncovering of unconscious patterns. The main issue in identification of the core conflict is that the awareness of the pattern can be painful, and the patient invariably needs assistance in modulating that pain. First, it has to be determined whether the patient has the strengths to proceed in a rapid uncovering form of treatment. Next, it has to be determined whether the patient has a level of current life stress that would make a rapid uncovering difficult without a lot of support. Both issues were addressed in chapter 2. If the patient demonstrates functioning above 50 on the Global Assessment of Functioning (GAF) Scale, is not overwhelmed with crisis, and is motivated for dynamic treatment, short-term exploratory treatment may proceed. The pain that may be generated by the procedure must be carefully monitored.

Rapid uncovering of the emotional conflicts can leave patients psychologically naked. The pain may come from shame or any number of self-attacking responses. Furthermore, the resulting grief from the dawning awareness of the waste that it has caused in the patient's life can be agonizing. Many patients in this treatment have said they were in continuous pain for weeks at the beginning of therapy because so much was uncovered. When the pain is too great, I recommend that the patient and I slow down a bit. This is done by regulation of the conflicts and anxieties: Attention is given to the most painful aspect of the awareness and what can be done to ease that pain to a manageable level before continuing exploratory work. No new uncovering or offering of interpretations should be done until the pain is bearable. Supportive interventions that assist in integration of the new vision should be employed until the patient feels stabilized.

THERAPIST: It sounds like you've really been jolted this week by seeing [*patient's pattern of behavior*]. What has been the worst part of this realization?

[8]I strongly recommend that therapists have their own therapy so that they may experience having their defensive behaviors and warded-off feelings pointed out and explored. People have evolved, at least initially, to be unaware of how defenses are deployed; that is how, for example, repression works. Therapists must have had their defenses pointed out not only to have an experiential knowledge of the process, but also to have resolved at least some of their conflicted feeling. In addition, I think it is essential for therapists to have experiential understanding of the mechanisms of behavior change and to have employed and felt the impact on other organisms (i.e., humans or animals) of the principles of reinforcement, extinction, and so on. I do not see how one can be an effective short-term dynamic therapist without these two experiences.

PATIENT: Oh, it's been the amount of suffering it's caused me!

THERAPIST: So let's not keep uncovering anything new until you've digested this part. We can take this at a pace that is tolerable for you. Can you tell me about the suffering that's been so hard for you to have to see.

PATIENT: It's the messes I've made of so many relationships!

THERAPIST [*After some discussion of the issues*]: But you didn't realize what you were doing. [*Intentionally offering support to reduce the shame*]

PATIENT: No, I didn't. Not at all. [*Sighing deeply*]

THERAPIST: So how could you possibly have done anything different? You were not even aware of responding this way until just recently.

PATIENT: That's true. It was a total shock to me what I was doing.

The therapist monitors the patient to see if there is a genuine sense of self-compassion. In this case there seems to be. The shame about the awareness is somewhat modulated, therefore, and the therapist can proceed to the next step: the regrets about the behavior (i.e., the pain of the awareness): *What do you regret the most in those memories?*

On the other hand, if the patient had replied, "But I should have seen what I was doing! I hate myself for it," the therapist would need to stay focused on the regulation of the shame to an adaptive level so that the patient could indicate compassion for his or her limitations without severe self-attack or self-abuse. Only after this could the therapist proceed to the regret (or move back and forth between the two). If regret is focused on first, patients sometimes use it to castigate themselves further. In the preceding case, however, it was appropriate to move to the regret.

The objective is to regulate the anxieties before proceeding to uncover further aspects of the core conflict. This process should continue until the patient feels an appropriate level of regret about the past, *not* unbearable shame or pain.

With consideration for the therapist stance (a supportive and collaborative relationship, or holding environment) and the anxiety-regulation stance (modulating pain as it emerges), one can direct attention to the specific interventions for the identification of the core psychodynamic formulation and its resolution.

INTERVENTIONS

The following reductionist view is not intended to be a thorough representation of clinical reality. These steps are general principles to guide the therapist in sorting out complex clinical material as rapidly as possible. The core psychodynamic conflict can be generated by focusing on and answering four questions in regard to each of the presenting problems (focal inquiry):

1. How is the patient defending against feeling (identification of the defensive or maladaptive response)?
2. What feeling is the patient defending against (the key to the adaptive resolution to the problem)?

3. Why is the patient defending against feeling (the reason for the problem)?
4. Whom does the defense address (person with whom the problem started)?

Although the preceding steps are stated in the singular, there may be, and often are, more than one wish or feeling and more than one pattern involved.

Focus on the Presenting Problem

The formulation process begins with the presenting problem. Gustafson (1984, 1986) emphasized the "sacred" nature of the first session and how important it is for the therapist to address what brought the patient to treatment. Often the first minutes of the therapy session are key. The presenting problem is elicited by the therapist, who begins the session by asking the following two questions: What problems do you want help with in treatment? Can you give me a specific example?[9]

Focusing on the presenting problems identifies what *the patient wants help with in therapy and therefore what the patient is motivated to work on.* Furthermore, the complaint that brings someone to treatment is usually a condensation of events representing the most conscious and recent evidence of the most salient areas of distress. The presenting "problem behavior" can represent the tip of the iceberg of a complex patterning of intrapsychic conflicts that the psychodynamic conflict formulation seeks to unravel. The use of the presenting problem or chief complaint as a focus is an expeditious way to reduce this complexity. Asking patients what problems they want help with in treatment rapidly narrows the focus. The therapist also needs to ask the patient *to provide a specific example,* because it is in specific behaviors that the underlying patterns can be best seen.

Each problem area should be discussed in detail in an attempt to understand the "Triangle of Conflict pattern" (i.e., defensive behaviors, anxieties, and underlying feelings) contained within the problem. In the two examples that follow, the Machine Builder should talk about her specific fears with the therapist. The Ferryman should outline the exact incident he refers to, that is, how he reacted to each interchange with the coworker. During this description of the incident, the therapist can begin to hypothesize about the primary motivating affects as well as defenses and anxieties in regard to self and others.

THE MACHINE BUILDER: PRESENTING PROBLEM
THERAPIST: What problems would you like help with in treatment?
PATIENT: This anxiety . . . uh . . . it's really getting to me. [*Lowers head*]

---

[9]This method differs from Strupp and Binder (1989) and Luborsky's (1977) approaches to determining the core formulation. Luborsky uses "relationship episodes" throughout the treatment session to determine the core conflict. The present approach uses specific examples of the patient's presenting problems.

THERAPIST: Can you give me a specific example?

PATIENT: Well, it's like, coming here today. [*Voice quivering*] I thought . . . it would take just a scratch, and it would be all over. I would start . . . [*Choking up and unable to continue*]

THE FERRYMAN: PRESENTING PROBLEM

THERAPIST: What problems would you like help with in treatment?

PATIENT: This divorce, it's really been hard. And my work situation is bad too.

THERAPIST: Can you give me a specific example of one of these?

PATIENT: My wife is so critical of me that I am losing my self-confidence everywhere.

THERAPIST: When is a time that your self-confidence has been the worst lately?

PATIENT: At work. There was an incident with a coworker, and I didn't know who was right or wrong.

Identify Maladaptive, Defensive Behaviors: How Is the Patient Defending?

The symptom groups that have been categorized and recategorized over many years and employed worldwide are the American DSM-IV (Axis I and Axis II) and the international version of diagnostic codes, the ICD–10. Although these categories are neither perfect nor final, they provide a common language and are becoming increasingly well operationalized. There is a finite set of symptoms that have been put into syndrome categories, therefore, and one can refer to these categories, although they need exploring and changing. These symptoms and syndromes are a large part of what is on the defense pole of the Triangle of Conflict, the pole that refers to maladaptive behaviors, defensive strategies, and coping abilities, as is discussed subsequently.

Despite these aids, it is often difficult to separate figure from ground and astutely "pick out" defensive behavior from the unstructured and rapid-fire communication that is typically thrown at the therapist as a patient tries to tell what is the matter. For years, I found it necessary to sit silently for 20 minutes or more (not often advised in short-term treatment) before I had a clue how to begin identifying defenses.[10] Following are some simple guidelines to assist the beleaguered therapist. In the quest for defensive behavior, cast a wide net. Listen to the patient's stories for what sounds "off." *Every maladaptive behavior or symptom that is troublesome, "odd," or downright peculiar can be initially considered as a form of defensive behavior.* Whatever the patient says or does that is self-destructive, self-attacking, self-punitive, or just not in his or her best interests can be put (mentally) in the "D" corner of the Triangle of Conflict. Such defensive behavior avoids some other, more adaptive way of responding because of some conflict. Listening in this way is a simple method to "get on the intrapsychic map" of the Triangle of Conflict and to begin to generate working hypotheses.

[10]One important solution is to watch yourself working on videotape as often as possible. This book is the result of thousands of hours of videotape review.

Although it makes use of an exceedingly liberal use of the term *defense*, this procedure helps the therapist to reduce the complexity into a simple psychodynamic framework and to generate a working hypothesis. The therapist does not have to immediately decipher the specific intrapsychic mechanisms defined by Anna Freud (1936), George Vaillant (1977), or others (e.g., reaction formation, dissociation). The clinician need only focus initially on the problematic behaviors that these mental mechanisms *give rise to*.[11] In that way, one can more easily begin to hypothesize what is being defended against and why. The benefits of this dynamic reframing are tremendous. The costs or losses appear to be few, if one keeps in mind that the hypotheses must remain flexible and open to alteration. In addition, it is useful to use different ways of phrasing the mental questions in deconstructing behaviors into their dynamic components:

- What defensive responses or strategies are causing difficulty (the D pole)?
- What is the maladaptive behavior?
- How is the response self-protective?
- What is the maladaptive compromise or symptom in relation to self or others?

THE MACHINE BUILDER: IDENTIFYING DEFENSIVE BEHAVIORS

THERAPIST: You know, your voice is quivering [D] as you speak. Was it difficult [A] coming here today?

PATIENT: No more so than going anywhere. It's just that I feel nervous [A] when I talk about feelings [I/F].

Later in the session:

THERAPIST: So the thought of painful things makes you nervous [A]?

PATIENT: Yeah, I try to control myself, so I won't show feelings [D].

THERAPIST: What things did you do to control yourself before coming here today? [*The therapist is intentionally narrowing the focus so that the pattern does not stay on a general or abstract level.*]

PATIENT: I usually don't think about anything [D] that would remind me of how sad I feel [I/F]. But I knew that would be difficult coming here today, because I could not avoid it. So I just got anxious [A].

This is an example of an attempt to use the defense mechanism of repression. But in a situation in which repression no longer worked for her, the anxious feelings flooded in. In such cases, the anxiety functions as a defense to avoid some other conflicted feeling. The therapist does not point out these theoretical constructs but reflects back the behaviors.

---

[11]Judy Freedman brought to my attention that Brenner came to the same conclusion in *The Mind in Conflict* (1982).

THERAPIST: So you avoid the upsetting thoughts when you can [D] and when you can't, you become anxious [A]. [*Next, the therapist identifies a specific example of this pattern.*] I did notice that every time the subject of your father's death came up, you tended to skip off to other topics [D]. [*Before proceeding, the therapist wants to make sure that the patient can see this pattern in the same way.*] Did you notice yourself doing that?

PATIENT: No, not really. I didn't notice I was doing that. [*Pausing to consider it*] But I can believe I was. I never want to talk about my father's death. It makes sense, doesn't it? People want to protect themselves from the pain.

THERAPIST: Sure, this is how we comfort ourselves when there's no better alternative.

Later in the session, other defenses appear:

THERAPIST: You seem to believe that people will laugh at you or ridicule you [D] if you get up to speak or if you show feeling [I/F]; yet is there any example of this happening?

PATIENT: No, not really.

THERAPIST: So where does this thought come from?

PATIENT: You mean from me? [*Pauses*] I guess it does come from me.

This, of course, is an example of the defense mechanism *projection*. Again, the therapist does not use this label but describes it in terms of behaviors.

THERAPIST: So you tend to imagine criticism coming from others, although it is generally not the case. And you can see that these thoughts originate in you.

PATIENT: Yeah, I can see what you're saying. But it's amazing how it *seems* like it's coming from them, until I stop to think about it.

THERAPIST: Sure, it does seem real, doesn't it? [*Validating the defensive response*] But that's why we are taking a step back to look at it more objectively.

The patient has begun to recognize what she is doing that is hurtful to herself.

THE FERRYMAN: IDENTIFYING DEFENSIVE BEHAVIORS

THERAPIST: You're telling me that you're angry [I/F] at your mother [PP], yet your eyes are full of tears [D].

PATIENT: It's not easy for me to get angry.

THERAPIST: So you seem to go to sad feelings [D] when you are angry [I/F]. Does this sound right?

PATIENT: Oh yeah, it's much easier for me to be sad.

Identify the Functions of the Defenses: Developmental Blocks

In addition to identifying the structure and content of the defensive behaviors, it is equally important to identify their function: what the defensive behaviors are used for. Defensive behaviors can be used for a number of "hidden agendas," which include the following:[12]

1. Avoidance of specific feelings
2. Avoidance of closeness
3. Avoidance of interpersonal authenticity (false or impaired self)
4. Avoidance of therapeutic change (sabotage of the growth process or ambivalent motivation for change)
5. Defeat of the therapeutic process (absence of real motivation for change)

Evidence of these defensive functions or hidden agendas can be found in patients with entrenched and long-standing maladaptive relationship styles that block the therapeutic alliance or that suggest serious lack of motivation for change. The more severe the function of the defense, the earlier or more severe the developmental deficits: poor object relations or lack of trust, initiative, or autonomy, and so on (e.g., Erikson, 1978). In each case, the function of the defenses must be identified by the therapist (although not necessarily interpreted to the patient) to make an adequate core formulation. A detailed discussion of these defensive functions is presented in chapter 4; however, a brief overview of some of the behavioral indicators of the defensive functions is given here to assist the therapist in making as thorough a core conflict formulation as possible. Following is a list of behaviors that signal the possibility of defensive functions or developmental deficits:

- Severe shyness or withdrawal
- Chronic lateness
- Help-rejecting complaining
- Acting out
- Extended silences or extensive internal "editing" before speaking
- A high level of interpersonal distrust
- A personality style that suggests an inauthentic mask, or a false self
- A presentation that is too "nice," too "smooth," or too "compliant" with the therapist
- Great difficulty confiding in people (i.e., no close friends)
- Repeated failures of relationships or chronic job problems
- No intimate relationship of long duration
- Lack of eye contact
- Vagueness, circumstantiality, or inability to delineate a focus in treatment
- Evidence of lack of readiness or lack of motivation for treatment

Some questions for the therapist to consider that can help determine the functions of the defenses include the following:

[12]These categories were, in part, suggested by Davanloo (1980).

- How is the response self-protective?
- How else does it benefit the patient?
- What would the patient lose if the defensive behavior were given up?

The behaviors described can signal the therapist to consider developmental impairment or secondary gain of the defenses; *secondary gain* refers to the reinforcing value of the defensive behavior. Some of these examples were used as exclusion criteria in earlier forms of short-term therapy. Now they can signal the therapist to proceed *cautiously* but *actively* to restructure the defensive patterns, as well as to build requisite supports and coping skills.

In discussing the presenting problem, the Machine Builder said, "It would just take a scratch, and it would be all over." Her defensive behavior is not blocking a specific feeling or two, but it is creating an interpersonal distance. Because she felt great discomfort about showing others, even her therapist, *any* emotion, she avoided people and personal discussion. Indeed, she met criteria for avoidant personality disorder (Axis II) and social phobia (Axis I). The issue of fear of closeness (or the creation of interpersonal distance to hide her true feelings) reflected a degree of lack of trust in others. The therapist began to make the defensive function of the behavior vividly clear by pointing out how she avoided being open with others.

The Ferryman did not reveal any defensive functions beyond his discomfort with specific feelings. When asked about feelings of anger, he repeatedly said, "I'm not that kind of guy." But he openly confided in friends, and he did not mind sharing personal or emotional material. The Ferryman was authentic in responding, and the Machine Builder was far more shy and withdrawn than she was, presenting a false picture to others. Neither the Machine Builder nor the Ferryman demonstrated any of the more severe defensive functions, such as showing a "false self," trying to sabotage treatment, or refusing responsibility for change in treatment. Both patients were capable of making rapid changes.

Identify the Adaptive Solution: What Feeling Is Being Avoided?

Looking at the Triangle of Conflict from a different perspective (from the bottom of the triangle up), the therapist needs to consider what emotional motivation is necessary for the patient *to do what he or she is not able to do.* The warded-off affect is the heart of the psychodynamic conflict formulation. The relationship between symptoms and affects (the defense pole on the Triangle of Conflict versus the impulse–feeling pole) is metaphorically presented to us in the poetry of the patient's personality. Figuring out this layering of the personality is indeed like uncovering the hidden meanings or metaphors in a poem. It is the task of the dynamic therapist, with the patient's help, to discover those metaphors as rapidly as possible and thus to help the patient begin to understand *the meaning behind the symptoms.*

On studying the defensive behavior, the dynamic therapist can begin to speculate, with the patient's help, on which of Tomkins's affect-based responses might be more desirable than the destructive defenses. The responses I focus on primarily are (a) grief, (b) anger, and (c) affects associated with attachment or closeness to self and others, because these are seen again and again as fundamental issues in treatment. After conflicts with these feelings are resolved, according to the patient's needs, I focus on (a) interest–excitement (b) enjoyment–joy, or (c) affects associated with sexual desire.[13] The therapist and patient speculate together on what is most deeply wanted in each of the problematic situations and then work together to determine the optimal adaptive emotional responses (the impulse–feeling pole) as well as what affect might be inhibiting that response (the anxiety pole). Many, if not most, problems in people's lives could be either adaptively resolved or maturely accepted if there were not blocks to normal, mature expression of the preceding feelings. Following are some useful questions that the therapist can reflect on in determining what might be the hidden feelings:

- What would be an adaptive solution to the problem?
- What feelings are being avoided by the defensive behavior?
- What response would be more self-caring and self-soothing than the defensive response?
- What would be the response of the patient's ideal self?
- What would be an activating, energizing, or motivating emotional response?
- What does the patient wish he or she had been able to do?

For example, the Machine Builder's presenting problem was a fear of public speaking. What emotion does she avoid? On one hand, her avoided affect could be the joy or pride in self-expression, blocked by shame. On the other hand, she might feel unable to protect herself when criticized because of a conflict over assertion or the adaptive use of anger (e.g., fear of rejection or guilt). The problem could also be longing for closeness and feeling ashamed of openness. Following is a discussion of the feelings involved in the cases under consideration.

THE MACHINE BUILDER: IDENTIFYING HIDDEN FEELINGS

This young woman was filled with fear (A) about public speaking. One must consider what motivating or activating affect would replace such fear or what affect the fear is blocking. The reader already may have generated some hypotheses about what feelings (I/F) the patient might be concealing. Anger is one possibility, but other possibilities might be the desire for acceptance from others or closeness, or grief. Each of these feelings needs to be explored to ascertain which are the most contributory to her symptoms. Following are some of the possibilities:

---

[13]For those familiar with the affect theory of Tomkins, these clinically observed affects are not always discrete affect categories but an amalgam of affects and drives, or "affect families." Grief, for example, is a combination of distress–anguish at the loss, desire for attachment, tenderness–enjoyment of the loved one, and various adaptive coping responses to assist in the acceptance of the loss. Nevertheless, the more the therapist can isolate and expose the patient to the most fundamental and conflicted affects, the more effective the treatment tends to be.

1: *Blocked anger* in response to criticism. She did not have access to her anger to defend herself in the event of criticism, thus giving rise to anxiety.

2: *Unexpressed grief* over the death of her father, which left her unprotected. She was enormously aware of her grief, because it was unbearable and took constant energy to suppress. (Suppression is conscious or intentional blocking of feeling; repression is automatic or reflexive avoidance of the feeling.) Because of shame over showing emotion, she would have to "tighten" and restrain herself in public, lest her intense feelings showed.

3: *Wish or longing for care and protection* from both her parents. She had no awareness of this issue prior to therapy, but the feeling became evident once she was able to grieve her losses. This lack could contribute to a speaking phobia, because she would not have the inner sense of others protecting or caring for her. Indeed, she had just the opposite sense: that others would abandon or attack her in her time of need.

As these hypotheses about feelings are generated, they must be explored with the patient to determine which feels most salient.

THE FERRYMAN: IDENTIFYING HIDDEN FEELINGS

This man showed a clear *inability to assert himself* interpersonally, which could be due to any of the following:

1. *Angry feelings*, which he could not tolerate in himself
2. *Unexpressed grief* over the death of his grandfather, of which he was totally unaware
3. *The unacknowledged love* of his grandfather on which, it later emerged, his positive sense of self had been based

The Ferryman denied that his grandfather had played an important role in his life and described him as a gruff old man. The therapist thought to examine this relationship because of one statement:

PATIENT: I never cried until my grandfather died.
THERAPIST: He must have meant a lot to you.
PATIENT: No, not really. He was a gruff old man. I don't think he had much love for us.

The therapist remained puzzled by the contradiction that the grandfather was not seen as loving, yet his death caused the only grief in the man's youth. This inconsistency led to continued questioning concerning the topic and eventually opened up feelings of which the man was unaware. Such hunches about contradictions do not always yield conflictual material, but they represent one pathway to the unconscious that generally needs to be explored.

Once the underlying feelings have been identified, the next step is to determine how the problem could be resolved. What might the individual be doing that he or she is not? From the first session, the therapist must begin to conceptualize what might be the adaptive solution for the patient. Why is the patient doing something destructive, when a more constructive and adaptive solution can easily be seen? What are reasonable alternatives to the patient's defenses? The answer to this question can be a challenge. Why did the Machine Builder become anxious rather than proud, assertive, self-confident, or self-accepting? Why did the Ferryman become passive rather than assertive and become depressed rather than grieve? Often the adaptive solution seems more evident to the therapist than the patient. Why is it that patients have difficulty considering alternative responses? Much of the work of psychotherapy is encouraging patients to explore alternative ways of responding and assisting them in finding the response best suited to their personality style.[14]

Identification of the Anxieties or Conflicts: Why Is the Patient Defending Against Adaptive Feelings?

It can be hypothesized that if the Machine Builder were more comfortable with her performance, she might have less trouble speaking publicly. If she could feel joy, pride, or excitement about getting up to speak, without terror or shame, she might be eager to do so. Furthermore, if she had a ready and robust sense of self-protection (the ability to defend herself) or if she could set limits when criticized (the healthy ability to feel anger, contain it, and use it in her best interests), she might be less likely to shrink from the opportunity to speak in public. She must have had discomfort of some sort around one or both of these feelings: anxiety about angry expression owing to fear of attack, or shame over being a show-off, which diminishes a robust desire to demonstrate accomplishment. There could be pain or anguish over past rejections, so that the event became traumatic.

The questioning is simple and straightforward: Why is the feeling blocked? What are the anxieties, guilt, shame, or pain that result in suppression of feeling by defensive behavior? Why are the underlying feelings of joy or pride in self being avoided? Again, there are few primary sources to consider: anxiety, guilt, shame, or pain. These are the inhibitory affects that have been so magnified that they have become self-attacking. These aversive and punitive reactions are the reasons for the existence of the defenses.[15]

---

[14]Clarissa Bullitt made this point to me.

[15]Initially, the only way to make sense of things was to think through the session afterward, talk it over with a colleague, or better still, study the videotape. My colleagues and I often noted how astute we were when we reviewed a videotape of a session, freed from the task of simultaneously interacting and doing therapy with the patient. Such vision is analogous to watching athletic events replayed in slow motion, when errors made become so obvious. But it is quite a different ballgame when you are out there, live, on the playing field. Videotaping psychotherapy sessions becomes essential to this technique, therefore, and allows one to have the luxury of the "Monday morning quarterback."

The Machine Builder tells the therapist that she is *afraid* to speak up, although at this point we do not know the idiosyncratic meanings of her fear. The therapist and patient need to work together as allies to discover what could be the specific reasons, as outlined in the foregoing questions.

THE MACHINE BUILDER: REASONS FOR DEFENSIVE BEHAVIOR

During the first 15 minutes of the first therapy session, when questioned by the therapist, this woman gave an abundance of reasons why she was afraid of having or showing feelings. The therapist asked her what was the most frightening aspect of showing her feelings. She replied that she would feel weak if she let herself show emotions. People would laugh at her and think she were foolish. Emotions were an illness to her and unbearable to feel. If she started crying, she felt she would never stop, and *the pain would be overwhelming.* She worried she might be too emotional, more so than most people.

THE FERRYMAN: REASONS FOR DEFENSIVE BEHAVIOR

When asked why he had such a hard time standing up for himself, this man was more succinct. He said, "I don't get angry. I'm not that kind of guy." Later, he told the therapist that he was afraid he might lose control of his anger. At this point, we don't know exactly what the link might be to the grandfather. But the idea should be held in the therapist's mind to explore later. One might hypothesize at this point that his poor sense of self leaves him unable to feel entitled to stand up for himself. Remembering his grandfather's love might improve his healthy sense of self and allow him to better protect himself.

Identification of the Maladaptive Aspects of Relationships: The Pattern Occurs in Regard to Whom?

The aforementioned patterns of behavior must always be related to a specific person. Affect is always attached to oneself or to others. Even when affect is attached to a place or a thing (a house, the city where one grew up, a favorite car or possession), the therapist should consider what this thing means about the self or about other people who were connected to these affect-laden objects or who were replaced by them.

People in the patient's history are as important as feelings. The Triangle of Person is crucial to the core formulation. Some questions that can be helpful in determining the relationship of the core patterns to self and others are as follows:

- In what relationship did the patient originally learn this pattern?
- What is the resulting negative (and positive) sense of self and/or others?
- In what current relationships is this past pattern continuing?
- How might this pattern play out in the therapy relationship?

THE MACHINE BUILDER: SENSE OF SELF AND OTHERS
THERAPIST: Where did you learn this pattern?
PATIENT: I'm not sure. Well, in my country, showing emotion is thought of as weak. My whole family—everyone—was like that. [*She was from Germany.*]

THE FERRYMAN: SENSE OF SELF AND OTHERS
THERAPIST: What could have happened that you lost the capacity to fight back or defend yourself?
PATIENT: Oh, it was my mother! She dominated all of us.
THERAPIST: How did this affect you?
PATIENT: Her constant demeaning of me made me feel that I could never do anything right.

Develop a Working Hypothesis: Identify an Affect Focus
As the hidden feeling becomes clear and an adaptive solution to the problem takes form, the *affect-based solution* should become the treatment goal. This formulation does not have to be rigid but can constitute a flexible "working hypothesis" that can be sharpened and refined as it is observed across many different situations. When a core formulation (the defenses and anxieties that block a *core affect*) is identified and mutually agreed on by both the therapist and the patient, the therapist's interventions should, for the most part, address the major patterns that have been delineated. The therapist should try to spend as much time as possible linking specific behaviors to the main formulations and should be vigilant to the patient's digressions from central issues. This should never be done in a rigid or demanding way but rather by allowing some digression to occur, then gently inquiring about the patient's possible resistance to exploring major topics. In fact, "relinquishing the focus . . . is probably the most frequent reason for failure of brief therapy" (DeLaCour, 1986, p. 133). The following examples demonstrate therapists presenting psychodynamic conflict formulations to patients and then proceeding to focus closely.

THE MACHINE BUILDER: PRESENTING AND FOCUSING ON A
PSYCHODYNAMIC FORMULATION INTERPRETATION
THERAPIST: It seems that you spend a great deal of energy reining in your intense emotions so that you can hide them from others [D] and that it burdens you enormously in your interpersonal relations. [*Negative consequences of the defenses*] One of the strongest feelings that we have identified is the grief over your father's death [I/F] that you have been avoiding [D] for the past 10 years. Does this seem accurate to you?
PATIENT: Yes, I know I do that.
THERAPIST: I wonder if we can stay focused on those feelings for a while so that with my help you can begin to face the grief [I/F] that you have feared [A] for so long.
PATIENT [*Pauses and puts her head in her hands. The therapist carefully watches her*

response to the interpretation and the gentle challenge to proceed. If the response is too defensive, it might indicate that more work needs to be done with the regulating of anxiety before proceeding. If the response is open and affect-laden, it is a marker to proceed.]

THERAPIST [*Concerned about the silence*]: Does that sound like something you don't want to do?

PATIENT: No, I'm just trying to think of what I haven't let myself think of yet. [*This response was not highly defensive, yet it was not a highly emotionally laden reaction either. Her words did convey sufficient motivation to proceed.*]

THE FERRYMAN: PRESENTATION OF A PSYCHODYNAMIC FORMULATION

INTERPRETATION

THERAPIST: You've felt terrible about yourself as a result of your mother's criticism. You took it as a true statement of your worth and were not able to believe in yourself and discount what she said.

PATIENT [*Putting his face in his hands, and sobbing*]: I never felt loved or special.

Although it was not apparent at the time, this was a communication of one of the main conflict patterns: dysthemia *(D)* resulting from inhibition caused by the pain *(A)* of the longing for the lost love *(I/F)* of the grandfather. The other pattern was the passivity about anger. The therapist said it this way:

THERAPIST: We have seen how you remain passive and leave yourself to be taken advantage of by others. And this happens because you have such mixed feelings—anxiety, shame, guilt—about letting yourself become angry, either with your parents, or your wife, or your colleagues. Can you see yourself doing this?

PATIENT: Yeah, I do. But I remember that once when I was in grade school, I stood up to a bully who was beating me up every day at the bus stop. One day, I finally let him have it. And that put an end to it once and for all! [*Again the patient confirmed the interpretation and added new and significant material.*]

Patient Response to Interpretation of Psychodynamic Conflict

Patients' responses to the interpretations are a crucial indicator of the working alliance. Are they with the therapist in the uncovering process, or are they blocking the process? Malan (1976), Elsa Marziali (1984), and I (McCullough et al., 1991) have demonstrated that the patient's affective response to interpretation is an indicator of improvement at outcome and previously was an indicator of suitability for short-term treatment. Research on patient–therapist interaction is discussed further in chapter 12.

In this model, response to interpretation is often used as an indicator of the degree of preparatory work that needs to be done to proceed. The Machine Builder was struggling a bit, but she indicated a desire to focus on the painful topic. The Ferryman was much more involved; he immediately went to an example of when he had been assertive, with good results. Both of these patients showed the therapist sufficient willingness to proceed. Later chapters provide much detail regarding how to handle situations when patients are not able to proceed comfortably.

Repetition of Core Conflict Pattern Across Relationships

Many examples of problem behavior should be examined and reexamined a number of times, across a number of different relationships, until a central theme or themes become clear. As noted by William Henry, Hans Strupp, Thomas Schacht, and Louise Gaston (1994), the frequency of occurrence should not be the only criterion. The severity, duration, and pervasiveness of the core conflict in the patient's life are major factors to consider. Does the Machine Builder become anxious with everyone, and how crippling is that anxiety? Is she more comfortable, or less, speaking with older people, children, the opposite sex? Are there places where she might feel more confident than others? Has she always been this way, or is this avoidance of speaking up caused by a depression? "Making the connection between past and present from the beginning calls direct attention to the repetitive nature of the transference reactions, and encourages attention to them in this light" (Winoker et al., 1981, cited by DeLaCour, 1986).

How does the patient react to the therapist? Is there any potential for the maladaptive response to be acted out in the therapy setting? As a rule of thumb, the therapist should consider variation in the core problem across (a) time, (b) relationships, (c) settings (school, work, home), and (d) mood shifts, as well as in crisis or under stress. Finally, the Triangle of Conflict pattern is generated from the interpersonal environment. The way we employ defenses, anxieties, and affects represents the effects of our socialization. The therapist should assess the patient's sense of self and sense of others that result from the core conflict pattern.

In the delineation of the core conflict, it is necessary to identify what is happening, why it is happening, and what might be a desirable affective alternative. This is charting a map of the therapeutic territory that should guide and direct most of the subsequent treatment interventions. Change mechanisms are discussed in the chapters that follow.

SPECIAL PROBLEMS IN THE
FORMULATION OF THE PSYCHODYNAMIC CONFLICT

The main problems encountered in the identification of the psychodynamic conflict include (a) accuracy of the formulation, (b) painfulness of the process, and (c) lack of readiness for the insight.

Accuracy Versus Efficacy of the Psychodynamic Formulation

In the rapid identification of the dynamic formulation, there is a danger of too rapidly drawing conclusions and thus not accurately understanding the patient. Such empathic failures can and must be guarded against by offering the interpretations or clarifications of the defensive behavior *tentatively* so that a "discovery-oriented" frame of mind is maintained. This mode also allows the patient to be actively collaborative. Any hypothesis can be discarded, of course.

There are two ways that I assess the "accuracy" or usefulness of a formulation. The first, as noted previously, is the patient's response to it. I look for a strong and heartfelt "Yes! That's exactly the way I am. You've hit the nail on the head" or "You really understand how I operate." When I am mistaken, I may hear, "No, that's *not* the way I am ... but here is how I'm different." My evaluation requires that both the patient and I feel strongly that the formulation fits the information that we have. However, therapists can never be certain that our "most plausible reconstruction" is the one most consonant with reality. All we can do is (a) stay close to the data and (b) collaborate with the patient for a consensual opinion.

Second, because one can never know with assurance the veracity of the formulation, the most robust test of the worth (if not the truth) is the *efficacy of the formulation*. Does the resolution of this conflict have *the power to effect change* and move the patient beyond the maladaptive conditioning of the past? Malan also reported using this approach (based on the deductions similar to Koch's postulates) for judging whether an explanation for a particular symptom is correct. He concluded that what was one of the most important indicators was that the explanation "results in the disappearance of the symptom" (1979, p. 107).

In healthy patients, explanation or insight alone may be sufficient to effect change. In most patients, however, change comes through restructuring defenses, affects, and sense of self and others, as determined by the pattern in the core formulation.

Painfulness of the Process

Sometimes the recognition of the pattern can be overwhelming or devastating. If a patient becomes overwhelmed with anxiety or pain, these self-attacking responses need to be worked with until they are no longer overwhelming. This is what I call "anxiety regulation."

PATIENT: I've been in constant pain since the last session. I'm seeing my life and all the waste in it as I have never seen it before.
THERAPIST: What's the worst thing about seeing this? [*Usually, it is some form of self-attack, or separation from a figure the patient is dependent on.*] What would help you now? Let's not proceed any further until you have resolved what is so painful [*or frightening or shameful*].

Some patients need to gain a sense of regulation and control by slowing down the treatment process through not being clear or direct—by not feeling too much—possibly, for long periods. One cannot and should not force someone to face what they do not want to face. But sometimes patients push themselves too hard, or open themselves too compliantly, and they can become overwhelmed. Again, this is when the anxiety-regulating approach can be most helpful. The therapist and patient can explore the "overwhelmed" experience to understand what is too much to bear. Of course, exploratory work around hidden feelings should not proceed until the patient feels able to cope with whatever has been overwhelming.

If the anxiety is so intense that the patient becomes confused or experiences cognitive disruption during the session, this is a signal that the anxiety is becoming overwhelming and that adaptive coping mechanisms need to be built to regulate the anxieties. Anxiety regulation is particularly helpful in working within a short-term model in an efficient manner. Therapists can assist patients in preparing for growth: *We do not have to face these things until you are ready. But can you tell me what your fears are about facing them?*

In this manner, the therapist can assist the patient in facing difficult issues much sooner than if they were left on their own to do so.

Readiness of the Patient for This Degree of Insight

The patient may not be ready for change, as Prochaska and his colleagues have pointed out (Prochaska, Norcross, & DiClemente, 1994). Sometimes the rapid acquisition of insight is harmful to the patient. A trauma might be uncovered that the patient cannot handle, or a great deal of pain could be generated that impairs the patient's functioning. In such cases, the therapist should move immediately to supportive measures that calm, reassure, offer support, or build coping responses (adaptive defenses or coping skills) until the patient is stabilized.

SPECIAL ISSUES IN PSYCHODYNAMIC CONFLICT FORMULATION

Relationship of DSM-IV Diagnoses to Psychodynamic Formulation

A standing controversy in the field of differential psychiatric diagnosis has been the identification of a reliable dynamic formulation. The multiple architects of DSM-III and -IV (Spitzer, Frances, and their colleagues) deserve credit for holding the standard for the operationalization of symptoms into psychiatric syndromes. Even though this chapter advocates a return to a Meyerian view (that symptoms have multiple dynamic etiologies), the DSM approach is, at the same time, equally useful and valid on two counts:

1: The DSM categorization is the most reliable formulation that our field has been able to generate thus far. Until recently, there has been no satisfactory alternative for psychodynamic diagnosis. There had been no way to operationalize neurosis or the unconscious. By creating syndromes, psychiatrists' "objective was to have an agreed-upon language for naming what they saw" (Wilson, 1993, p. 408).

2: Abundant psychopharmacological research has demonstrated that there is validity to DSM-IV categories, which relate more to biological than to psychological bases of behavior. In other words, the current DSM-IV formulations tell us much about how people respond to stress with regard to their symptomatic responding and how severe the biological contribution may be. This is essential, but only part of the picture. In contrast to the medical model, the psychodynamic formulation suggests *why* the symptom picture is emerging and what can be done environmentally (e.g., therapeutically) to contribute to its resolution. As Gabbard noted, "one unfortunate consequence of the deliberate effort to be atheoretical in the development of the DSM-III, DSM-III-R and DSM-IV nosology is the sacrifice of . . . the psychodynamic model of symptom formation" (Gabbard, 1994, p. 250).

As Mitchell Wilson concluded in his historical review of the development of the DSM system, although the shift to the research-based medical model of descriptive psychiatry had positive consequences for the profession, it represented "a significant narrowing of psychiatry's clinical gaze" (Wilson 1993, p. 407). Wilson noted that in 1977, "Spitzer suggested the development of an additional diagnostic axis for etiology.[16] This, he said, would allow clinicians to express their psychodynamic formulation of a case" (1993, p. 407). Unfortunately, Spitzer's proposal was not adopted, and today, 2 decades later, it seems long overdue. Today, both nature (DSM) and nurture (the psychodynamic formulation) need to be considered (see Figure 3.1). It is heartening to note that Henry, Strupp, Schacht, and Gaston (1994) advocated that a psychodynamic formulation be provided alongside a DSM diagnosis. Yet the problem remains: How does one make a reliable dynamic formulation?

FIGURE 3.1
The relationship between DSM-IV diagnoses and psychodynamic formulation.

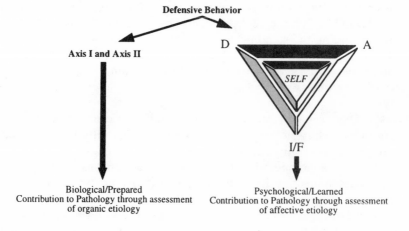

Defensive Behavior

Axis I and Axis II

Biological/Prepared
Contribution to Pathology through assessment
of organic etiology

Psychological/Learned
Contribution to Pathology through assessment
of affective etiology

[16]Spitzer made this recommendation in a memorandum to the Task Force on Nomenclature and Statistics, March 28, 1977 (Wilson, 1993).

Relationship of Personality Categories to Psychodynamic Formulations

Many different systems have been developed for the categorization of "personality" patterns. They include Luborsky's Core Conflictual Relationship Theme (CCRT; 1977), Paul Costa and Robert McCrea's Five Factor Model (1990), the personality disorders of Axis II–DSM-IV (American Psychiatric Association, 1994), the Millon Clinical Multiaxial Inventory (MCMI; Millon, 1987), Chris Perry's Idiographic Conflict Formulation method (1994), Lorna Benjamin's Structural Analysis of Social Behavior model (SAS-B; Benjamin, 1974; Schacht & Henry, 1994), Mardi Horowitz's Configurational Analysis (CA; 1994), Hartvig Dahl and Virginia Teller's FRAMES method (1994), the Plan Formulation method (Curtis, Silberschatz, Sampson, & Weiss, 1994), the Consensual Response Psychodynamic Formulation (Horowitz & Rosenberg, 1994), and others.

Each of these approaches offers valid methods to assess personality, although most are more interpersonal than dynamic in orientation. My approach developed in part from one of the most popular methods: Luborsky's CCRT.

COMPARING PSYCHODYNAMIC FORMULATIONS

The CCRT method provides a way for researchers to formulate patients' central relationship patterns from interpersonal episode narratives told in psychotherapy sessions (Luborsky & Crits-Christoph, 1990). Three components of the relationship themes are identified: (a) the patient's main wishes, needs, or intentions toward the other person in the narrative; (b) the responses of the other person; and (c) the responses of the self. The "core theme" is determined by identifying the most commonly occurring wishes and self–other responses across all the relationship episodes. The CCRT is a valuable contribution and widely used, but its format does not provide a full *psychodynamic* formulation, because it does not distinguish defensive behavior.[17] (This is also true for Strupp's model and for Horowitz's Configurational Analysis.)

It is useful to compare Malan's Two Triangle (i.e., DAI/TCP) schema to Luborsky's CCRT to demonstrate the similarities and differences. The first CCRT category, "responses of self," does not distinguish two primary psychodynamic functions, the defensive behaviors, on one hand, and the anxiety responses or conflicts, which Malan clearly separates. The second CCRT category, "wishes of self" is similar to Malan's impulse–feeling pole except that it does not distinguish *adaptive* from *maladaptive* wishes. In the DAI/TCP model, maladaptive wishes or feelings are categorized with be-

---

[17]First, Soldz (1993) pointed out in his review that the only CCRT component that is truly taken from Freudian theory is the wish. Second, defenses are not addressed at all; they are a crucial component of Freudian structural theory. Indeed, Luborsky acknowledges that the CCRT has been criticized for not including defenses. Last, although the name of the CCRT includes the word *conflictual*, none of the three components addresses conflicts per se. As Soldz noted, "the idea of conflicts between wishes is proposed but it is never systematically discussed. This absence weakens the fealty of CCRT concepts to commonly understood clinical reality" (1993, p. 69).

haviors on the defense pole. The third CCRT category, "responses of the other," combines the three components of Malan's Triangle of Person: the therapist, the past person, and current person. The DAI/TCP provides a more distinct framework for a psychodynamically based core conflict formulation than does the CCRT or other, similar measures. The model in this book is based, therefore, on Malan's psychodynamic formulation of defenses, anxieties, and feelings (see Figure 3.2).

The DAI/TCP instrument needs to be psychometrically validated for research purposes. Fortunately, a review of the existing systems[18] reveals that there are well-operationalized research methodologies already developed that closely adhere to psychodynamic formulation. One is Chris Perry's Idiographic Conflict Formulation (ICF; Perry, Augusto, & Cooper, 1989), and the other is Jon Monsen's Affect Consciousness Interview (ACI; Monsen, Eilersten, Melgaard, & Aadegaad, 1996). These instruments are compared with the DAI/TCP and the CCRT in Figure 3.2.

Like Malan's Triangle of Conflict, Perry's ICF can be seen as representing the tripartite model of Freudian structural theory:

> The Wishes and Fears components delineate the dynamic motives involved in conflict, while the Resultant component describes the surface manifestations of conflict (both symptoms and avoidants). The importance given to motives is what most clearly distinguishes dynamic from other systems of personality assessment. (Perry, 1994, p. 240)

Wishes and fears are similar to the anxiety and impulse–feeling poles of the triangle, and the category that Perry labeled *resultants* refers to defensive behavior. Perry's model also encompasses Erik Erikson's stages so that developmental deficits may be assessed. The components in my model are similar.[19]

The Affect Consciousness Interview (ACI), developed by Jon Monsen and his colleagues (Monsen, Eilersten, Melgaard, & Aadegaad, 1996) at the University of Oslo in Norway, is the other promising research method for dynamic formulation; it is directly compatible with the method in this book and, in fact, was derived from Tomkins's affect and script theory. This interview, like the approach described in this book, focuses on patient descriptions of affective "scenes" to identify the predominant affective "scripts" (or

---

[18]As noted earlier, many systems of formulation are interpersonal in structure: Luborsky's CCRT (1977), Horowitz's CA (1994), and Benjamin's SAS-B (1974) focus on self and others, not on dynamic conflict. The Plan Formulation method (Curtis et al., 1994) approximates a dynamic formulation. Anxiety and conflict are referred to as "obstructions," defensive behavior as "tests," and wishes (both thoughts and feelings) as "goals." This schema is creative and useful clinically but does not closely adhere to the structural theory. Horowitz and Rosenberg (1994) subscribe to a psychodynamic formulation, but their constructs are not operationally defined.

[19]There are two differences between my model and Perry's. My model uses Tomkins's affect categories rather than Perry's "wish list," and it distinguishes between defensive and adaptive wishes. Perry calls them "wish–wish conflicts."

FIGURE 3.2
Comparison of methods for psychodynamic formulation.

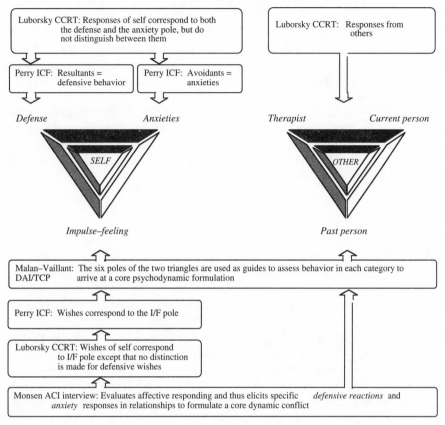

CCRT: Core Conflictual Relationship Theme. ICF: Idiographic Conflict Formulation. ACI: Affect Consciousness Interview. DAI/TCP: Defenses, Anxieties, Impulse–Feeling: therapist, current, and past persons

core schemas) and conflicts and the defenses that underlie psychopathology. Research by Monsen and his colleagues (Monsen et al., 1995) on the treatment of patients with severe disorders with an affect-focused long-term model has shown significant improvement in personality disorders as well as improvement in affect consciousness (on the ACI) at 5-year follow-up. A comparison across cases of the types of formulations generated by the ICF, the ACI, and the DAI/TCP would have potential for furthering understanding of core formulation.

COMBINING THE DSM-IV CATEGORIES AND PSYCHODYNAMIC FORMULATION

As a reliable and valid psychodynamic formulation becomes possible, it can and should become a companion to the DSM-IV diagnoses. The dynamic formulation describes the patient's *learned* response pattern to conflict. The DSM symptom diagnosis describes the *biological* component of the response and permits the patient to be classified for purposes of insurance reimbursement and pharmacological and biological research.

Furthermore, the psychodynamic formulation and the DSM diagnoses have an important point of overlap. The DSM diagnoses can be seen as representing some of the same symptoms that are conceptualized as "defensive behaviors." Conceptualizing symptoms as both diagnoses and defensive strategies encourages therapists and researchers to consider the contributions to symptom formation made by both biology and the environment.

Recently, an optional DSM axis has been included for defenses, which is only one component of a psychodynamic formulation. To broaden psychiatry's gaze, the defense axis could evolve into a complete psychodynamic formulation permitting experimental examination, with warded-off affects as the central focus and with linkages to defenses and anxieties. Spitzer's suggestion could finally come to fruition.

SUMMARY

Defenses can be thought of as any behaviors, overt or covert (including thoughts, feelings, images, and mental mechanisms), that protect the individual by avoiding what is painful or unpleasant. The warded-off adaptive feelings would be soothing, nurturing, or caring for the self if the anxieties did not inhibit their expression. The goal of formulating the core psychodynamic conflict, therefore, is identifying the main patterns of conflicted affects, not unlike constructing a well-thought-out interpretation in psychoanalysis. The difference is that in a short-term approach, formulation is done actively and collaboratively by the patient and therapist and in the first few sessions.

This deconstruction of the presenting problem into its dynamic components, as suggested by Malan's Triangle of Conflict (D-A-I), points the way to a solution focus. I have recommended that diagnostic formulations be accompanied by a psychodynamic formulation for a complete diagnostic picture of the individual. A summary for generating the dynamic formulation follows:

1. The patient describes the presenting problem.
2. The therapist identifies the maladaptive behavior within that problem (the defenses).
3. The therapist and patient then speculate on what the adaptive response might be (the warded-off feelings).
4. The therapist and patient explore the reasons that the adaptive response is difficult or avoided (the anxieties or conflicts).
5. The therapist and patient identify the interpersonal origin of the maladaptive pattern and the negative sense of self that has ensued (whom the problem originated with, and with what effects on the self).
6. The therapist empathically sums up the pattern and presents it to the

patient, focusing on conflicted affect as the central theme to be worked on.

7. The patient's response to the interpretation of the pattern is considered and the formulation process continues until the pattern is mutually agreed upon.
8. The patient's relationships are reviewed for the recurrence of the conflict pattern.
9. The mutually agreed-on formulations become a guide for treatment intervention.

Practice Examples to Determine the Core Conflict Formulation

Before reading these examples, it would be useful to get a pen and paper and jot down the Triangle of Conflict (DAI/TCP) formulation. Two of the three patients in the following examples have been presented at the end of chapter 2 as practice examples for GAF ratings, and that information may be reviewed first. For each of these examples, the presenting problems are given along with a specific example of each problem. The reader may practice making a core conflict formulation and possible resolutions to that conflict. The answers may be compared to the formulations presented in Appendix B. It should be kept in mind that these formulations are working hypotheses, not cast-in-stone truth.

THE MAN WHO LOVED ICE SKATING

This well-liked and respected man enjoyed his job, his coworkers, and activities with his children. His concern was about his marriage; however, when he was asked to describe the conflict with his wife, he found it difficult to do so, fearing he would not represent his wife's perspective fairly. (His wife had refused marriage counseling.) When asked why he was so overly protective of his wife, he said that his mother had taught him that women were fragile and that he should never under any circumstances be angry with them. He reported that he had talked, reasoned, and even begged his wife to stop her constant yelling and to join him and the children on their outings. She always refused, and he had given up trying. When asked how he responded to his wife's frequent temper outbursts, he reported that most often he was compliant and pleasing, but sometimes he would refuse to respond, which made her even madder. Her resulting frustration, he admitted with a little guilt, gave him pleasure.

His second problem was his temper outbursts at the children, with whom he was typically tender and gentle and spent a great deal of time. He was aware that he was actually angry at his wife. He also reported that whenever he became angry he had diarrhea, and he knew it was directly linked to the turmoil he felt within.

THE GIRL WHO DANCED IN BLOOD

This woman's presenting problem was described as "problems in her relationship with her boyfriend," to which she gave the most severe rating of

"13." She was referred to treatment because of a suicidal gesture following a critical remark from her boyfriend that led to a screaming fight. She poured pills into her hand and then blacked out; after that, she called her parents and sought treatment. She felt strongly that she did not want to kill herself, but she became so upset the suicidal thoughts frightened her. When asked to describe some of these painful episodes, a pattern emerged. She never revealed how sad or hurt she felt about her boyfriend's critical remarks but instead would attack him or herself. In fact, she never told anyone that she felt sad, lonely, or tenderly because her father had taught her it was humiliating to show weakness. She always remained guarded and tried to out-perform others out of fear of being looked down on or disliked. Nevertheless, she had good friends and was respected at work.

THE UNFORGIVEN TEENAGER

This woman sought treatment for her shame and poor self-esteem, which she respectively rated "11" and "12" (very severe). She hated herself and believed God was punishing her on a daily basis for being a terrible teenager. (She had used alcohol liberally and had sexual encounters during adolescence.) She was deeply religious, and she could not forgive herself because she strongly believed that she should have known better. She also distrusted people at work and believed that they talked about her behind her back because she was such an unlikable person. If she received a compliment or kind word she did not believe it. She spent most of her free time in her apartment in despair and loneliness. She even turned down invitations to do things with others because she felt so undeserving.

Her other complaint was her hurt and hostility concerning her parents, which she rated "11" (severe). She was the sibling selected to care for aging and self-absorbed parents. Although she visited several times a week and did errands for them, they showed absolutely no interest in her. They did not know where she worked, what friends she had, or anything about her life, but they were controlling and demanding of her time. When she brought up something about herself, they became uninterested. She was terrified to decrease her involvement with them or to ask them to pay more attention to her. She was close to her sister, but she had never had a long-term relationship with a man.

CHAPTER 4

First Major Objective of Defense Restructuring: Defense Recognition

There will be time, there will be time
To prepare a face to meet the faces that you meet . . .
And indeed there will be time
To wonder, . . .
Do I dare
Disturb the universe?
Should I, after tea and cakes and ices,
Have the strength to force the moment to its crisis?
I grow old . . . I grow old . . .
I shall wear the bottoms of my trousers rolled.
Shall I part my hair behind? Do I dare eat a peach?
. . . I have heard the mermaids singing, each to each
I do not think that they will sing to me.
                    T. S. Eliot, "The Love Song of
                    J. Alfred Prufrock" (1917)

INTRODUCTION TO DEFENSE RESTRUCTURING

This chapter focuses on how to identify and undo socialization that has gone too far. As we become socialized, we learn much that is valuable; however, we also learn a range of defensive reactions. On the positive side, we learn how to perform socially acceptable responses such as saying "please" when making a request and "thank you" when the request is granted. Politeness, in its normal usage, does not constitute defensiveness, but rather a form of adaptive coping that is likely to enhance the probability that a person receiving a request will want to grant it. On the negative side, socialization can be harmful.

All societies place some degree of restriction on expression of feeling. Instead of helping a child direct a wish or express a need in a manner that will

113

aid the child in receiving the desired response, the process of socialization often tends to tone down the expression or even lead to restriction or severe blunting of the wish or need itself. Instead of being taught to say *no* politely, many children are taught that saying *no* itself is bad, not allowed, or forbidden. In such cases, the expression of the need becomes diminished. The child swallows the *no* and either gives up the desire (with a loss to the self), substitutes another behavior in its place, or associates the bad *no* with his or her own consequently flawed identity.

There are many variations on this theme. A child can respond by giving up saying the *no* altogether, resulting in a lack of boundaries or an inability to set limits, which we label as taking the victim role, performing self-defeating behaviors, or having borderline personality disorder. Instead of saying *no*, the inhibited child may act out the *no* with uncontrollable temper tantrums or by becoming passively resistant or stubborn.

It is not only saying *no* that is targeted as unacceptable. Sometimes it is the expression "I want" or "I need" that is punished. Other times, "I'm excited," "I'm angry," "I'm sad," "I'm proud," or "I love you" is the unacceptable affect. The responses of the parent, which can range from a benign turning away of the head to outright corporal punishment, can begin the conditioning process that *with sufficient repetition or intensity* will set a pattern for a lifetime of restriction of feeling; the extreme forms result in personality disorder.[1]

Sometimes the caretaker inhibits curiosity and exploratory behavior by saying, "No, no, don't touch," rather than assisting the child in examining the object of interest. Similarly, the child might be told, "No, no, don't climb up there, you might fall"—rather than guiding and assisting the climbing or trusting the natural ability of the child. The caregiver may say, "Nice children don't touch themselves," rather than teaching where and when touching the body is appropriate. Even laughter does not escape the wand of inhibition. I am repeatedly dismayed by the number of patients who, chronically flat in affect and unable to feel, tell me that they have been told, "Don't laugh, or you'll soon cry," or cautioned, "The ax will soon fall," instead of having their caretaker share in the joy of the moment. Another source of restriction of joy evolves in families with alcoholism, in which good times are quickly followed by bad. All too often in our culture, and in cultures around the globe, children's spontaneous, adaptive reactions are inappropriately, and often unintentionally, blunted. All too seldom is the child's reaction affirmed or jointly shared or the child, when necessary, guided toward a more socially acceptable or adaptive expression.

Caretakers in many of our "first-world" countries frequently overly burden children with social acceptability long before the children are allowed to discover their own particular, idiosyncratic form of humanity. As soon as children express what they like (Gimme or I wanna!) or what they

---

[1]Vaillant and Perry (1984) demonstrated how the immature defenses underlie the Axis II personality disorders.

do not like (No), they are taught that such reactions are bad or unacceptable rather than how best to make the request. This practice can strongly diminish not only the child's affective expression, but also the child's internal experience of wanting or not wanting. The child learns that frank interpersonal expression is often forbidden, but so is even thinking or feeling the desire (whether positive or negative). The temperamentally luckier ones may do something useful or creative with the feeling. The less temperamentally lucky may simply become blunted and restricted in living. Such is the parched earth from which defenses emerge, like cacti from the desert: dense, thick, and prickly. Prickly defenses are, nonetheless, the best responses the person has been able to muster given the often thwarting conditions of anxiety, guilt, shame, and pain in which they were raised.

In the most benign of circumstances, the socialization process can emphasize certain ways of responding and extinguish others. Caretakers might attend in an affirming way to some reactions and not attend to others. In such cases, the child does not necessarily behave defensively but simply responds to what is taught. Conflict might arise only at later points in life when situations occur that require a totally different way of responding than the familiar one (Stern, 1995).

Hierarchy of Defenses

What are the alternatives when adaptive expression is blocked or suppressed? George Vaillant described a hierarchy of defenses that occurs in such instances. He categorized 18 mental mechanisms of defense as representing the most adaptive (mature), moderately adaptive (intermediate), and least adaptive (immature and psychotic) ways of responding (Vaillant, 1977, 1993; see Table 4.1). These defensive responses represent the biologically endowed responses that help us avoid what is unpleasant. The "defensive behaviors" that result are formed through environmental learning.[2] For example, one may act "as if" one did not have the desire and behave in the ways dictated by one's caretakers. Whether the caretakers are dead or alive, the lessons so carefully and repeatedly taught direct us from within. Some of us alter the way we look at the world through intellectualization—"I'm not mad (or sad or glad), I'm just confused (or perturbed)"; through repression—"I can't even remember what the fight was about"; or through reaction formation—"I'm not angry, I really love my wife." Others behave in ways that are destructive to themselves and their relationships, by deploying immature defenses. Anger can be acted out (through poorly directed

---

[2]Lichtenberg, Lachmann, and Fosshage (1992) see defense as an aversive motivational system, which is a view that I agree with. From my perspective, the defensive or aversive motivational system is the result of inhibitory affects that, when associated with basic wants and needs, give rise to conflict. Inhibitory affects are motivators that decrease any responding they are paired with. However, Lichtenberg et al. do not see defenses arising from conflict owing to tensions between the id, ego, and superego, because they do not use the Freudian tripartite model (p. 159). My model retains the valuable and viable aspects of the tripartite model by updating the operational definitions of id, ego, and superego on the basis of current research on affect.

TABLE 4.1

Examples of the Hierarchy of Defenses

Contrasting ways of altering the conscious representation of a conflict

Defense	Conscious representation of idea, feeling, or behavior		DSM-III Phenomenological diagnosis[a]
No defense	I hate (!) my father.	309.9	Adjustment reaction with atypical features
Psychotic defense			
Denial	I was born without a father.	298.8	Brief reactive psychosis
Immature defenses			
Projection	My father hates (!) me.	301.0	Paranoid personality disorder
Passive–aggression	I hate (!) myself (suicide attempt).	300.4	Dysthymic disorder
Acting out	Without reflection, I hit 12 policemen.	301.7	Antisocial personality disorder
Fantasy	I daydream of killing giants.	301.2	Schizoid personality disorder
Neurotic (intermediate) defenses			
Dissociation	I tell my father jokes.	300.15	Atypical dissociative disorder
Displacement	I hate (!) my father's dog.	300.29	Simple phobia
Isolation (or intellectualization)	I disapprove of my father's behavior.	300.3	Obsessive–compulsive disorder
Repression	I do not know why I feel so hot and bothered.	300.02	Generalized anxiety disorder
Reaction formation	I love (!) my father or I hate (!) my father's enemies.	—	
Mature defenses			
Suppression	I am cross at my father but will not tell him.	—	
Sublimation	I beat my father at tennis.	—	
Altruism	I comfort father haters.	—	

Note. From Vaillant, 1993.

[a]Diagnosis assumes that conscious representation of the conflict was carried to pathological extremes and that the other criteria for the diagnosis were met.

temper outbursts, rather than contained, planned responses), and grief can be acted out through indiscriminate wailing and moaning. Anger could be cloaked in some self-defeating but infuriating behavior (passive–aggression) or divided between two people, one hated or devalued and the other, often a relative stranger, loved or idealized (splitting). Examples and definitions for each of these defense mechanisms can be found in Vaillant (1977, 1993).

When defenses break down, anxiety and depression are often the result: *the symptom becomes the defense.* For example, if we cannot assertively change or defensively ignore a bad situation, we might become either depressed or overwhelmed by anxiety, panic attacks, phobias, or shame. Indeed, the whole range of Axis I symptoms can be conceptualized as unpleasant defensive alternatives to the modulation of wants and needs (e.g., learned helplessness results in depression; Seligman, 1975). I do not diminish the influence of biological contributions here: Although this book focuses predominantly on the *learned component of defensive behaviors*, the person who has a strong family history of depression is not going to "unlearn" that response. In such cases, medication must be considered, and psychotherapy is but one of the means for *modulation* of the biological condition. Just as a polio victim can be assisted by physical therapy, so can a person with a mood disorder learn to improve management of stressors that might otherwise exacerbate a biologically vulnerable condition.

Preparation for Defense Recognition

A number of methods have been developed to accomplish the recognition of defensive behaviors. Some of the procedures are similar to those of the core conflict formulation, except in this chapter the focus is on the identification and management of defensive behavior. Several interventions designed to facilitate defense recognition are described in the sections that follow, with examples given for each.

- Maintain a collaborative therapist stance.
- Regulate anxieties by teaching self-compassion.
- Identify the *structure* of defenses: *how* the patient is avoiding feelings.
- Identify the *hidden impulse or feeling:* what emotion the patient is avoiding.
- Identify the *conflicts*—anxiety, guilt, shame, or pain: the *reason* the defenses occur.
- Generate a working hypothesis about the preceding patterns, and note the patient's response to it.
- Identify these patterns as they are repeated across relationships.
- Use this formulation to guide treatment interventions.

THERAPIST STANCE IN DEFENSE RECOGNITION: COLLABORATION

THE REAL THERAPEUTIC RELATIONSHIP

In the short-term therapy process of defense recognition, the therapist is an ally who helps point out problematic responses that are unseen by the patient. This is similar to the "companion in discovery" stance that was taken in the identification of the core conflict formulation. The process of mutually identifying patterns that have been confusing or unclear can be painful and embarrassing, so it is crucial that the therapist be empathic and sensitive to the patient's discomfort or distrust. Because a major goal of short-term treatment is to put therapeutic tools into the patient's hands as soon as possible, the therapist also acts as a guide in the exploration of response patterns. The active collaboration with the therapist in the recognition of defensive responses is practice for the patient's more autonomous role of continuing the work of therapy between sessions (i.e., catching defensive responses), as well as when therapy is completed. Throughout treatment, a collaborative and empathic relationship should be maintained.

The confrontations and interpretations are intentionally put in tentative form to enlist the patient's involvement in the confirmation or disconfirmation of what the therapist is presenting. Nothing should be considered valid until it rings true to the patient. The hypothesis may *seem* absolutely accurate to the therapist, and the therapist may ultimately be proved correct. But the point of the tentative approach is to allow the patient either to *catch up with the therapist's insight* and confirm it or to *disconfirm the therapist's insight with meaningful examples*, which teaches both the patient and the therapist a new way of viewing the problem. I cannot emphasize enough how important it is for the therapist to stay flexible and open in regard to the patient's revision of the therapist's interpretations. When I say to patients that I might be wrong in my interpretation of their behavior, I am not playing games. It happens with a dependable regularity that the way I view the patient's situation is *off the mark* to a greater or lesser degree from how the patient experiences it. If a patient does not strongly confirm my interpretation, I repeatedly encourage correction.

EXAMPLE: A PATIENT REVISING AN INTERPRETATION

THERAPIST: From what you are telling me, it seems like you are quite compliant with your husband.

PATIENT: No. I'm not compliant! That's not it.

THERAPIST: Then maybe I don't see it exactly right. How would you describe it?

PATIENT: It's more . . . I don't know . . . let me think. [*Pausing*] Why am I quiet with him? I'm not being compliant . . . I know that, because I've disagreed with him a lot. I guess I've just given up [*tears come to her eyes*] that's it . . . I haven't been aware of it, but it's resignation. I've tried to get through to him, over and over, but it never works. So I've just given up.

THERAPIST [*Remains quiet for a while as the emotion wells up in the patient; then, as the patient raises her head*]: Compliant wasn't the right description. You seem to feel more hopeless.

PATIENT: Oh yes, exactly! Why bother anymore?

Although the patient and therapist began by seeing the situation differently, their active collaboration brought them to a strong sense of agreement.

When the patient continues to disconfirm a suggested hypothesis, it is the therapist's task to explore the areas of disagreement. If the patient and therapist are seeing the world in fundamentally different ways, the sooner this is examined and (if possible) resolved, the better the therapy will proceed. On the other hand, if such pockets of disagreement are *not* made explicit and resolved, it is unlikely that treatment will proceed effectively. In this process, patients learn quickly that their opinion is valued and that disagreement is encouraged; *the patient's authenticity is valued over compliance or submission.* Patients are respected collaborators in the narrative reconstruction of their lives. From the start, malignant dependency on the therapist is avoided.[3] The therapist's procedures are actively taught, and the patient is encouraged to use them throughout the therapy process, in session as well as between sessions.

EXAMPLES: COLLABORATIVELY POINTING OUT DEFENSES

THERAPIST: Do you notice that you [*description of the defensive behavior pattern*]?

PATIENT: Yes, I hear what you say, but I disagree.

THERAPIST: Well, it's not valid unless it rings true to you. Can you tell me how *you* see this?

Alternatively, the intervention might go like this:

THERAPIST: Can you see that (*description of defensive behavior pattern*)?

PATIENT: No. I don't.

THERAPIST: Well, I may not be describing it quite right, and what I'm saying has to feel right to you. But sometimes people do shift attention away from painful topics. Can we watch for this pattern together and continue to explore it until we both can see it the same way?

TRANSFERENCE ISSUES

The therapist must stay constantly vigilant for defensive behaviors (or the core conflict pattern) as they occur in the therapist–patient relationship. Using the transference is as important in integrative psychodynamics as it is in psychoanalytic psychotherapy. The therapist must also be aware of whom the therapist might be representing to the patient. (Who are we, and how are we being constructed in our patients' minds?) A constant issue in the process of defense recognition is patients' reluctance to be seen. They may want the therapist to back off, to be less intrusive. At one moment, the therapist may seem to the patient to be the distant and judgmental but caring father, whereas at the next moment the therapist may seem more like the in-

---

[3]Dependency on the therapist may be a crucial part of treatment if it supplies an emotional experience that the patient has never had (i.e., the adaptive capacity to be vulnerable and trust another person), but this learning mode must be time-limited and continued only long enough for the patient to first acquire this new skill with the therapist and then generalize this ability to other people in his or her life.

trusive and domineering mother. There are innumerable idiosyncratic patterns of defensive responding that the therapist must be vigilant for. Just as Michelangelo filed his fingernails down to the nailbed so that by lightly dragging his raw fingertips over his highly polished statues he could catch the smallest degree of "roughness," so do therapists through years of experience need to continue sharpening their sensitivities to these nuances of the transferential patterns.

COUNTERTRANSFERENCE ISSUES

Therapists need to develop a heightened receptivity to their own affective reactions that suggest their own accumulated psychodynamic conflicts: emotional baggage on one hand and human responsivity on the other. This is a subtle thread that runs throughout the treatment process that can be an enormously important source of information or cause difficulty in treatment. As the therapist scans the patient's reactions, a parallel scanning of his or her own reactions can provide enlightening data.

Do the patient's defenses anger or irritate the therapist? This is often an indicator that the patient is distancing or avoiding the therapist's actions. Does the patient's reluctance to recognize the defensive pattern anger or hurt the therapist or induce the therapist to become competitive or attacking? Is the patient provocative in a way that elicits a projective identification in the therapist–patient relationship? (An example of projective identification would be a patient blaming the therapist for being cold and unfeeling, provoking the typically empathic therapist to act in a cold and unfeeling way, thereby "identifying with the projection.") Does the therapist feel some vague discomfort that may suggest that the patient's dynamics are in some way impacting on the therapist's dynamics? Does the therapist use this discomfort appropriately to intensify the exploratory process or move to understanding the reasons for the blockage (i.e., anxiety regulation), or does he or she act out the irritation or become depressed because treatment is not proceeding effectively? Some countertransference issues are always present, but therapists need to be as aware as possible of their own issues so that they can be guided to inform rather than derail the treatment.

Regulation of Anxieties in Defense Recognition: Teaching Compassion for Self

The goal of anxiety regulation in defense recognition is to guide the patient toward a compassionate self-appraisal and the desire for constructive action. The main issue in acknowledging defenses is the same as described in chapter 3 for the core conflict formulation: The shame and pain must be regulated if the patient is to face difficult personal patterns. When we scrutinize our defenses too closely, it often generates unbearable feelings. It is like taking off our overcoat on a freezing mountain peak. Although painful issues need to be recognized, the self-critical feelings must rapidly be brought within normal limits. Instead of feeling stupid, incompetent, or bad for their pattern of responding, patients need to be helped toward understanding the reasons for their behavior and seeing that it was the best way they knew to cope in the past. I tell patients not to "add insult to injury" by punishing themselves for defenses that were protecting a vulnerable part of themselves. Self-compassion comes to replace the inevitable self-criticism patients feel for having the defensive behavior. Patients need to be helped to accept that the anxiety that they feel without their protective overcoat is legitimately painful.

It is often counterproductive to push patients too hard on recognizing their defenses and to open them up too rapidly. Provoking too much conflict is like taking a canoe over "white water": The canoe is easily capsized, and the passenger is likely to be lost. With anxiety-regulating techniques, one can get to the same goal in a smoother fashion with most patients, without the dangers inherent in the more confrontive technique. In summary, regulation of anxieties in defense recognition means management of the self-attacking feelings (anxiety, guilt, shame, and pain) that unavoidably occur in the identification of defensive behavior. The following sections describe two interventions that are particularly useful in helping to mitigate such anxieties: validation of the defensive pattern and pointing out of personal strengths.

VALIDATION OF DEFENSIVE PATTERN

This intervention has been a cornerstone of the collaborative defense analysis in the short-term anxiety-regulating model. Validating defensive behavior helps patients to bear the unbearable feelings of ignorance and shame that result from too close scrutiny. The process of validating affirms rather than criticizes patients and helps them to begin to take a compassionate view of their behavior. This comforting and comfortable neutrality, or unconditional acceptance, helps the defense analysis move along more rapidly because it reduces the guilt and shame associated with the use of destructive defenses. Some prototypic interventions follow, but individual therapists create a repertoire of approaches that represent their own style for helping patients see something difficult about themselves. I have found the following ones useful:

1: *Of course you reacted in these ways. What other choice did you have as a child? What would have become of you if you hadn't?*
2: *It makes sense that you became withdrawn and passive when you felt angry. Your parents were not comfortable with your anger, and you wanted so to please them.*
3: *I can see why you lash out spitefully rather than feel the tremendous pain underneath. In the past, it seemed there was no one to bear it with you.*

The eventual response sought from the patient that would signal that self-compassion was emerging might be, "Oh, I see now, it could have been no other way!"

IDENTIFICATION OF STRENGTHS TO COMBAT MALADAPTIVE DEFENSES

In addition to addressing our patients' weaknesses and destructive capacities, it is essential to point out their strengths and adaptive coping abilities that can help to alter long-standing character patterns. Pointing out strong points is another way of helping patients more easily face the less complimentary and more painful truths about themselves. In *The Complex Secret of Brief Psychotherapy*, James Gustafson (1986) recommended that the therapist "ride the main current, but also ride the opposing current." In this model, Gustafson's maxim could be interpreted to mean that one should identify both the problematic behavior and the adaptive tendencies that counteract the problem.[4] Recognizing both strengths and weaknesses seems to foster rapid movement in the defense-restructuring process.

EXAMPLE: POINTING OUT STRENGTHS ALONG WITH DEFENSES

THERAPIST: You keep saying you have such trouble with closeness, and we will need to look at that. Yet you have told me several stories which suggest that you are a much loved and valued friend and father.

PATIENT: I lose sight of that, because I've had such bad luck with women.

THERAPIST: So we'll examine why you have more difficulty in those kinds of relationships. But while doing so, let's keep in mind that you have close friends and confidants who have told you that you are generous and considerate. Also, it seems quite special that each of your grown children has lived with you at different times, and you really enjoyed each of them.

It was much easier for this patient to bear facing his negative qualities when he had a vivid awareness of his basic decency and kindness. These of course should not be vague "compliments" by the therapist but the clear identification of specific behaviors that indicate adaptive skills.

In the following, more severe example, the patient cannot trust his own judgment and the data confirm it. The therapist needs to acknowledge the deficit honestly but to put it in the context of whatever strengths can be found.

EXAMPLE: POINTING OUT STRENGTHS THAT ARE ACCEPTED VERSUS DENIED

THERAPIST: We can see that you have had destructive patterns throughout your life, yet you have continued to function reasonably well in spite of the burdens you have carried. That takes a great deal of self-discipline and stoicism, doesn't it? Can you see this?

PATIENT: Yes . . . sometimes I wonder how I keep going, but I do.

THERAPIST: It's something to respect about yourself, isn't it?

PATIENT: You know, it is! Thanks for pointing it out. I take it so much for granted.

The patient might respond differently:

---

[4]Marsha Linehan (1993a) expresses the same philosophy in her approach, dialectical behavior therapy.

THERAPIST: Can you see how you've kept going during hard times?

PATIENT: No, I don't. I've completely collapsed sometimes and made a real mess of things.

THERAPIST: Well, you haven't told me about those times. But you have told me about how you've handled some tough situations quite well. Remember the time in college for example . . . and that time when the woman was drowning . . . ?

PATIENT: Yeah, sometimes I do okay.

THERAPIST: But you also want me to be mindful that sometimes you don't do okay. Why don't we look at both good and bad times to see when your strengths come out and when they don't? Maybe we can help you have more control that way and a clearer picture of yourself.

In more impaired patients, there may be little that can be pointed out as strengths. Such patients usually function at a level below 50 on the Global Assessment of Functioning (GAF) Scale (as discussed in chapter 2), so that issues of relationships and identity as well as functioning may be sufficiently impaired to contraindicate a rapid uncovering process. (Supportive therapy, cognitive therapy, or self–other restructuring should be considered.) Still, the more severely ill the patient, the greater the need to recognize and build on strengths. The therapist must scan the patient's history, as it is being told, for evidence of the few times or even the one time that the patient coped well with something difficult or demonstrated good judgment. There may be few strong points, but it is terribly important to find them. A workshop participant offered a helpful suggestion for such cases: "I tell them it takes strength just to have gotten themselves to therapy!" This is true, and it needs to be said. Sometimes we take the fact of seeking treatment too much for granted.

After the therapist has become aware of the optimal stance to be taken and is equipped with methods for the regulation of anxieties, the challenging process of the identification of defensive behavior can be safely undertaken.

Specific Interventions to Assist in the Recognition of Defensive Patterns
IDENTIFYING STRUCTURE OF THE DEFENSES:
HOW DOES THE PATIENT AVOID EMOTION?

The process of identifying defenses resembles a careful behavioral analysis: *One always notes the core dynamic conflicts underlying the presenting problems and the relationships in which they occur.* In describing the structure of the defenses, it is important to depict the specific defensive behaviors in vivid images. Imagine trying to paint a picture for the patient that will demonstrate with the greatest impact the form of the defensive behaviors and the context in which they are enacted. Also, whenever one is examining defensive patterns, one must always be asking (with the core dynamic formulation[s] in mind) whether each defensive pattern corroborates the core formulation, calls for a revision, or implies a new one altogether. The therapist keeps a broad perspective, to avoid getting lost in detail, but constantly links the behavior-based scenes to the "scripted patterns" in the core formulations.

In searching for defensive behavior, one must cast a wide net. *Find out what behavior is problematic, and think of it as defensive.* Defenses used by patients are not delivered in the discrete categories of Vaillant's hierarchy; in therapy, one sees complex combinations. Many different "mental mechanisms" (such as reaction formation, intellectualization, and dissociation) can be combined to form a response. Indeed, any single symptom or action can be the condensation or "tip of the iceberg" of an enormous amount of material. It is not the task of the therapist to deconstruct these defense complexes during a therapy session; that can be left to the research coders. It is simply necessary to note problematic, disguised, or avoidant responses and bring them into the patient's awareness.

Just as in the formulation of the psychodynamic conflict, in the defense-recognition phase, three main questions must be answered:

1. How is the patient behaving maladaptively? (usually, a defensive behavior pattern)
2. What would be a more adaptive response? (a feeling-guided response motivated by the patient's real needs)
3. Why is the patient behaving maladaptively rather than adaptively? (probably conflict around the adaptive response)

Recall the example of the Machine Builder. How did she behave maladaptively? She became flooded with anxiety and avoided situations. What would have been a more adaptive response? It would have been adaptive for her to assert herself and experience feelings of self-worth and self-confidence. Why did she become anxious rather than assertive and confident? She had a great deal of fear and shame about showing any emotion in public.

Phrasing the questions somewhat differently provides another way of deciphering the meanings of the problem behavior:

1. How is the patient avoiding conflict? (usually by using defensive behavior patterns)
2. What is the patient avoiding? (usually a more adaptive, feeling-guided response; the question of what is avoided also provides a solution focus. If one knows what the patient might better be feeling and expressing, one knows where to go.)
3. Why is the patient avoiding a preferable response? (usually anxiety, shame, or pain)

The same questions may be looked at from yet a third slant. Each slightly different perspective can serve to illuminate the problem further.

1. How is the patient disguising or compromising the true need or wish? (How is the problem presenting itself?)

2. What emotion does the patient need to employ to meet the real underlying need? (What is the real motive?)
3. Why does the patient disguise the deeper wish or need? (What is the reason for the inhibition of the real motive?)

To help the patient begin to recognize defenses, the patient's defensive behavior is gently but continually pointed out as it occurs throughout the session.

THERAPIST: Can you see how stubbornly you resist doing what your boss requests [D]? Even as you tell me, you're clenching your fists and tightening your jaw. [*Nonverbal examples of I/F*]
PATIENT: Geez. [*Looking down at his fists in surprise*] I guess I am! I didn't realize how mad [*I/F*] I was.

Then, the defensive behavior must be linked both to the associated anxiety and to the adaptive emotion-based reactions that the defenses are employed to avoid: *Do you think you have a lot of discomfort* [A] *with your feelings of annoyance* [I/F] *at your boss, so this leads you to shut down* [D] *rather than speak up?* [Adaptive expression of I/F]

Next, the defensive behavior must be distinguished from nondefensive behavior: *I wonder what else you might have done?* [Solution focus, I/F] Subsequently, one identifies the behavior in many other contexts to determine whether it is a major and repetitive pattern making up one of the core dynamic patterns: *Are there other relationships in which this pattern occurs?*

It is also important in the recognition of defensive behaviors to examine the antecedents and consequences: what happens just before the defensive behavior occurs and what happens afterward. What happened in the moments just before the response that might elicit defenselike or problematic behavior? This model suggests that a major antecedent condition causing the defensive behavior is the aversive experience of the adaptive feelings: the anxiety, guilt, shame, or pain that have come to be associated with basic wants and needs. These aversive feelings act as "punishers" by suppressing or inhibiting the adaptive feeling to a greater or lesser degree. Even when conflicts are not in the patient's awareness, antecedent events can be examined for the possible conflicts that they engender (i.e., anxiety, guilt, shame, or pain).

In a similar manner, it is important to consider what happens in the moments just after the defensive behavior occurs. There are typically some positive consequences that need to be explored. Is something altered outside or inside the individual? Is there something being avoided (i.e., the conflicts about feelings or emotional separation from a longed-for parent) that would otherwise have to be faced? Is there a sense of inner relief that reinforces the avoidance? Is there some form of satisfaction obtained as a result of the defensive behavior? In the consequent events that follow the defensive behaviors, the reinforcement or secondary gain that maintains the defensive behavior can be found. Even when pain or suffering is the result of the defensive behavior, one can ask whether this pain is easier to bear than some other, more intense pain. Again, the process of pointing out the form of defenses is, in effect, a thorough behavioral analysis of defensive behavior.

EXAMPLE 1: POINTING OUT DEFENSES

THERAPIST: Do you notice that you repeatedly look away [D] when we begin to discuss your mother? [*Antecedent condition*] Is that a way to avoid the discomfort [*A, the aversiveness*] of your feelings toward her?

PATIENT: I don't know. I've never thought about it. [*D, or just selective inattention*]

THERAPIST: Well, can we explore that possibility? It's not valid until it rings true to you. [*Invitation for collaboration*]

EXAMPLE 2: POINTING OUT DEFENSES

THERAPIST: Can you see that you begin speaking quite rapidly [D] just as soon as you begin to feel sad [I/F] about your father's [P] illness? [*Aversive antecedent condition*]

PATIENT: No, did I really?

THERAPIST: It certainly seemed so. Why don't I point it out the next time it happens, and we can look at it together to see if there is some relationship to the topic. [*Collaboration rather than pronouncement*]

EXAMPLE 3: POINTING OUT DEFENSES

THERAPIST: Did you realize you just smiled [D] as you were telling me quite a sad story about how you and your brother didn't get along? [*Aversive antecedent condition*]

PATIENT: I can tell I'm doing it now but only because you pointed it out.

THERAPIST: What would happen *if you didn't smile* here with me? What might you feel in its place? [*Inquiring about the aversiveness of the conflicted feeling — the anxiety*]

PATIENT: It lightens the sad feeling. It really does ... it feels a lot better to smile. [*The patient instead points out the positive consequences of the defensive behavior.*]

THERAPIST: There's some comfort in smiling. [*Validating the defensive behavior*]

PATIENT: Yeah, there really is.

THERAPIST: The sadness is something to get away from, then. [*Noting the aversiveness of the feeling*]

PATIENT: I'll say.

THERAPIST: What's the worst part of the sadness? What hurts the most? [*Exploring and learning to cope with the conflict or aversiveness that leads to the defensive behavior will eventually help the patient begin to experience the painful feelings.*]

In this fashion, the defenses are vividly pointed out to the patient, as rapidly as the patient can tolerate facing them. Of course, this tolerance varies widely across patients, and the therapist must be vigilant to keep anxieties within bearable limits as they emerge. Some examples of ways to regulate the anxieties during the analysis of the defensive behaviors follow.

EXAMPLES OF REGULATING ANXIETIES

The therapist must acknowledge the difficulties the patient has in facing the defenses:

It must be very difficult to talk about such painful things with me.
It can be so painful to face problems in therapy.

The therapist needs to validate the defensive behavior:

Of course, you responded this way. There was little else you could do.
There are reasons for defenses. People don't spring from the womb this way.
You had to learn this.

The defensive behavior needs to be normalized for the patient:

Looking at sexual feelings can be one of the most uncomfortable parts of therapy.
Anger is a difficult emotion for many people.
Defenses serve an important purpose. We need to decrease the amount of stimulation that life confronts us with daily.

The adaptive components of the defensive behavior need pointing out:

You were clever, weren't you, to devise this means of protecting yourself from your parents' temper?
How necessary that you learned to numb yourself and stop crying when your mother turned away. Otherwise, you might have been overwhelmed by longing to be comforted when no one was there. It takes a lot of strength to put the feelings away and just go on.

The forms that this process can take are many and varied, and therapists find their own intuition helpful in guiding such responses. The preceding examples do not happen in isolation, of course. Each technique is blended into the treatment process according to the therapist's judgment and intuition.

THERAPIST: Can you see that you often make a joke [D] whenever we begin talking about your feelings of anger? [I/F]
PATIENT: Yeah, I guess I do.
THERAPIST: What do you think the joking is doing? [*The purpose of the defense*]
PATIENT: Trying to keep things pleasant, I guess. [*The positive consequence of the defense*]
THERAPIST: I wonder why you need to keep things pleasant with me when you're talking about anger? There's probably a good reason for it. What do you think that might be? [*Exploring A*]

Another way to demonstrate defensive behavior to patients is to have them watch themselves on videotape or listen on audiotape. These are powerful tools to help patients recognize how they respond during sessions. My colleagues and I have begun giving our patients either audio- or videotapes to take home and review. In addition, the therapist must make sure that patients are simultaneously creating their own internal "videotape" to help them autonomously monitor and guide themselves toward adaptive responding.

THE DEVELOPMENTAL FUNCTIONS OF THE DEFENSES: HIDDEN AGENDAS

Equally important to identifying the *structure* of the defenses is identifying their *function*. Relinquishing long-standing defensive patterns, which may be the greatest challenge faced in therapy, is the focus of the next chapter. The relinquishing of defenses depends on knowing how defenses are used, however. Defensive behavior patterns are employed to *avoid something*, for some reason, but if the therapist is not aware of these hidden agendas, defense restructuring can become hopelessly bogged down. In this chapter, the categories of defensive functions are described in detail because defenses cannot be fully recognized or understood if it is not clear *what the defensive pattern is being used for*. This is another aspect of the "scripts" (the broader patterns) that direct the patient's actions: the fundamental reasons or motivations for the defensive behavior that have their origins in developmental impairments or arrests resulting from early-life problems in relationships.

Until now, I have discussed the most general reason defenses are employed: for the avoidance of conflicted feelings. However, the deeper levels of resistance (meaning less available to the awareness) are employed regularly. These defensive functions, or "hidden agendas," are highly repetitive patterns of behavior (scripts), largely outside of consciousness, that avoid the experience of massive levels of anxiety, guilt, shame, or pain and thus ensure preservation of sameness. Davanloo (1980) delineated four of these levels: avoidance of emotion, avoidance of closeness, sabotage of treatment, and self-defeat. I have added another category, disorders of self, which refers to the false self (narcissistic disorders) and the impaired or fragmented self (borderline disorders). These levels of defensive function are presented in Figure 4.1, arranged with the least severe functions toward the top and the most severe toward the bottom.

The list in Figure 4.1 is not intended to represent an exhaustive compilation of all defensive functions; it includes a selection of some that have been repeatedly observed in clinical work. Erik Erikson's (1978) developmental stages can be useful in understanding some of the issues that contribute to defensive functions, although there does not appear to be a direct linear relationship between his stages and the level of defensive function.[5] The point is that the therapist should be vigilant for the various and often complex reasons, purposes, or functions served by the defenses that suggest developmental impairment, that is, lack of basic trust, fear of autonomy, excessive

---

[5]Much research needs to be done to assess the number and range of possible defensive functions, as well as the developmental impairments that form them.

FIGURE 4.1
Developmental functions of the defenses.

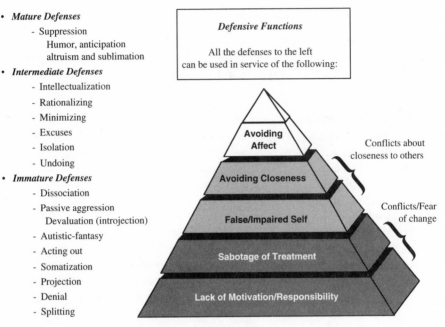

- *Mature Defenses*
  - Suppression
    Humor, anticipation
    altruism and sublimation
- *Intermediate Defenses*
  - Intellectualization
  - Rationalizing
  - Minimizing
  - Excuses
  - Isolation
  - Undoing
- *Immature Defenses*
  - Dissociation
  - Passive aggression
    Devaluation (introjection)
  - Autistic-fantasy
  - Acting out
  - Somatization
  - Projection
  - Denial
  - Splitting

Defensive Functions

All the defenses to the left
can be used in service of the following:

Avoiding
Affect

Avoiding Closeness

False/Impaired Self

Sabotage of Treatment

Lack of Motivation/Responsibility

Conflicts about
closeness to others

Conflicts/Fear
of change

The lower on the pyramid the defensive function:
- the greater the severity
- the greater the pervasiveness of the problem in the
  person's life
- the earlier or more severe the developmental impairment

shame about the self, lack of initiative, inability to achieve intimacy, and so on. Furthermore, any of the defenses at any level of the hierarchy listed to the left in Figure 4.1 (i.e., mature, intermediate, immature or psychotic) can be used in service of *any* of the defensive functions. A patient might use intellectualization, an intermediate defense (e.g., I'm not angry, I'm just a little perturbed, that's all) to avoid underlying feelings, to avoid closeness to the therapist, or to defeat change in the treatment process. Where the defense falls on the hierarchy of defenses does not tell how it might be used in terms of the hierarchy of defensive functions. That can only be deduced from assessing the patient's hidden agendas or unresolved developmental issues as discussed in the following sections.

A review of the defensive functions will highlight the main obstacles to treatment and the degree of the patient's readiness or unreadiness to change. Until these defensive functions are made *clear and aversive* (and often, *replaceable*), patients tend to maintain their lifelong character patterns. I have found it useful to think of defensive functions hierarchically ordered according to at least two factors: (a) the degree of interpersonal closeness or distance (probably a function of the severity of shame) and (b) the degree of motivation for change or desire to preserve sameness (possibly a function of the severity of pain involved in facing feelings). In other words, the more severe or rigid the defensive functions, the poorer the alliance and the poorer the motivation for change and the earlier and more extensive were the developmental impairments, traumas, or deficits. In addition, the more severe the defensive function, the less ready the patient is for the action-oriented short-term approach, and the more time the therapist will have to spend with the patient in preparation for change. This often requires more extensive work in defense restructuring or self–other restructuring.

AVOIDANCE OF A SPECIFIC AFFECT

The least problematic level of defensive functioning is simply the avoidance of the experience or expression of a specific affect or feeling, often due to inhibition or lack of models during development. For example, an otherwise well-functioning person has difficulty being sufficiently assertive. Another individual might need to be helped with grieving. The examples used earlier in this book have dealt mostly with the simple defensive warding off of such specific conflicted feelings. When avoidance of one or two specific affects is the only issue, treatment can often move along quite rapidly, because there is a focus unencumbered by other sources of resistance. When avoidance of a specific affect is the sole function of the defense, this generally means that the patient has good interpersonal relations, will form a ready and strong alliance, and is motivated to do the work of therapy to make a change. Alliance, motivation, and ego strength are usually sound enough to permit the therapist to confront the patient in an empathic but fairly direct manner. Also, gentle and repeated clarification of the Triangle of Conflict (D-A-I/F) pattern with current or past persons is generally sufficient. The following example of avoidance of affect repeats the style of intervening that has been presented thus far in the book.

THERAPIST: Do you notice that your mind seemed to wander [D] just as I was asking you about angry feelings [I/F] toward your mother [P]? Your eyes were staring out the window, and you seemed miles away. [*Further description of the defensive avoidance*]

PATIENT: Yeah, I really phased out [D]! This is what I always do!

THERAPIST: It must be really hard for you [A] to feel mad at her. Do you think these ways of tuning out might be ways of avoiding looking at these angry feelings? [*Defensive function: avoidance of feeling*]

PATIENT: Yes, I'm sure it is.

THERAPIST: What is the hardest part of it for you? [*Exploring the anxiety that causes the avoidance*]

PATIENT: She's so helpless. I feel sorry for her.

THERAPIST: So I wonder if there's some feeling of guilt [A].

PATIENT: Oh. Tons of it!

AVOIDANCE OF CLOSENESS

In the second level of defensive functions, patients not only wish to avoid conflicted feelings, they also wish to avoid closeness to others (this suggests developmental impairment in the interpersonal openness of expression of any feelings, wants, or needs). It is a useless endeavor for a therapist to point out defenses against specific feelings, if the person wants to avoid closeness altogether. Indeed, people who are shy and withdrawn want to avoid showing *most* emotions. These defenses are used to avoid letting others (or oneself) see what one is feeling or thinking. There is a global hiding of what is going on inside. To dislodge this defense, the therapist must point out the sadness, isolation, and loneliness that is created by the defensive "walling off." There are mild-to-serious developmental deficits in attachments that contribute to this barrier to expression.

If the major defensive function is to avoid closeness, it is imperative to describe the Triangle of Conflict (defenses, anxieties, and feelings) in the patient–therapist relationship and the function it is serving (i.e., distancing). When there are problems with closeness, the therapist–patient relationship becomes more crucial as a vehicle for change: It is important for the patient to see the distancing mechanisms, experience the feelings with the therapist, and to open up and become more vulnerable. If the patient does not trust or feel close to people, no real change is possible unless the patient first resolves this problem of interpersonal closeness with the therapist.

> *It must be very painful* [A] *for you to share these feelings* [I/F]*, because each time I bring up the subject of* _____*, you pull back.*
>
> *Isn't it sad that you come for help with issues that are deeply painful and then feel that you cannot open up* [D] *with me* [T]*?*
>
> *Could you be putting up barriers* [defensive function: avoidance of closeness] *here with me* [T] *by staying silent* [D]*?*

EXAMPLE: THE EMOTIONALLY DISTANT BUSINESSWOMAN

PATIENT: I just don't want to cry here [D].

THERAPIST: What would you fear [A] the most if you did? What would you imagine that I [T] might be feeling if you were crying?

PATIENT: Oh, you're a doctor. You'd be cool and clinical. You'd do your job [D].

THERAPIST: Is that so? Do I feel cool and clinical to you? Is doing my job being cool and clinical?

PATIENT: Well, no. I guess not . . . oh, I don't know [D]!

THERAPIST: I wonder if there is some other response you could imagine me having [T]?

PATIENT: I guess you could feel sad for me. But I don't believe you [T] really would.

THERAPIST: Well, it would feel awful to open up and cry in front of someone "cool and clinical." [A, *validating her fears*] There must be some really uncomfortable feelings [A] here, because each time we get on a sad topic [I/F] you quickly shut down. [*Defensive function: avoidance of closeness*] I watch you compose yourself [D] and purse your lips [D], like you have probably done that all your life.

PATIENT: Yeah, I have.

THERAPIST: Well, it takes strength to contain emotion that much [*pointing out strengths*] . . . but now it's doing you no service. [*Negative consequences*] Isn't it sad that you come here needing to pour out the grief [I/F] you've been carrying, but you don't feel free [D] to do so?

Patient: Yeah, I know . . . but I don't feel free [D]. I feel uncomfortable [A] letting anyone close or crying [I/F] with anyone [T?]. [*Note that a core pattern or script is becoming evident.*]

THERAPIST: So why don't we work on your getting comfortable [*anxiety regulation*] here with me [T] first? The most important thing now is for you to see whether I am actually cool and clinical, or whether that's your perception of me [D].

PATIENT: You think *I'm* doing this? [*D, some denial is involved here.*]

THERAPIST: Well, where does the thought come from that I'm cool and clinical?

PATIENT: From me? Well, I guess . . . but it seems real.

THERAPIST: You've been here for a number of sessions. How have I seemed to you?

PATIENT: Well [*thinking*] . . . you *have* seemed concerned [*pausing*] . . . so maybe I am doing it.

THERAPIST: Let's take some time and see. You seem to understand this intellectually, but it's even more important for you to feel deeply comfortable here with me before proceeding.

The therapist does not push for the immediate experiencing of sadness but focuses on the therapist–patient relationship to reduce anxiety and build trust and a sense of safety and comfort. But this does not have to take months or years; in many cases the level of safety and trust can be significantly improved in a few focused sessions.

DISORDERS OF SELF: THE FALSE OR IMPAIRED SELF
False Self
At an even more problematic developmental level are those who, like those who avoid closeness, do not want to expose themselves. At this more severe level of avoidance, however, they go a step beyond mere withdrawal to generate an even greater form of avoidance of closeness: a "false self" to hide behind. Although there is some degree of interpersonal authenticity in the person who presents as shy and withdrawn, "false self" individuals have twisted their interpersonal responding into something or "someone" that they are not. The deeply hurt and angry child can force herself to be a chronically smiling and compliant do-gooder to disguise her aggressive and grief-laden urges. The child badly traumatized through shame can put on a mask of coolness or suaveness to hide overwhelming anxiety. The deeply

shamed child can become the distant authoritarian figure who never lets anyone close. If a child feels utterly worthless, for any reason, it often can be overwhelming to feel the pain of such a poor sense of self at such a vulnerable age. The more protective response could be to fake it and act as if one were very special.

These defenses, which are part of the responses seen in deficit pathology, protect an enormously fragile sense of self and often have to be handled with exquisite gentleness, affirmation, and acceptance. Anxiety-regulating interventions are helpful and can decrease the time it takes to *build* a more robust sense of self. However, this building or rebuilding of the self-image, and the building of the alliance (i.e., the building of new models of others), generally requires months rather than weeks. (This process is discussed in chapter 9). Defense restructuring typically is too anxiety provoking for patients with this level of pathology and must be put off until their sense of self is stronger. Following are examples of a therapist validating defenses with the false self.

How good that you bring this problem up in here.

It takes a lot of courage to open up and reveal yourself for the first time.

It seems that it has been very difficult for you to open up to anyone and just be yourself. And I can see why staying closed off might have been a reasonable thing to do.

Impaired Sense of Self

In this category of defensive function, there is a serious disturbance in the development of the identity: the sense of self. These patients do not know "who they are," what their values are, or who they want as friends or lovers. They often feel empty or bored inside.[6] Again, such responses are examples of deficit pathology. Such people are often labeled as having borderline personality disorders or posttraumatic stress disorders. Whatever the diagnosis, the defensive behaviors are deployed to compensate in various ways for the confusion about the self and the resulting inability to respond in the most optimal way to satisfy legitimate wants or needs. As explained in chapter 2, like schizoid patients, patients with severe cases of this disorder are often not suitable for short-term uncovering treatment. But some aspects of defense restructuring (pointing out how their behavior hurts them), self–other restructuring (building a more positive sense of self and others), and affect restructuring (identifying what they are feeling) can save a year or two of time in treatment.

In addition, many well-functioning individuals have aspects of impairment of self. I call these "borderline pockets" or limited identity disturbances in otherwise well-adjusted individuals. It is for such people that the short-term therapist can be particularly helpful. Ways of working with dis-

---

[6]These behaviors form some of the criteria used in the diagnosis of borderline personality disorder.

orders of self are further discussed in chapters 9 and 11. Following is a brief example of a more disordered patient with an impairment of the self involving the inability to avoid pain:

THERAPIST: It seems like you get confused about what kind of people are good for you [D] and what kind aren't, so you end up in relationships that really cause you misery [D]. Does it seem so to you?

PATIENT: It's all I think about. But it keeps happening.

THERAPIST: Can we take some time to examine which relationships have been comforting to you and which ones have not? [*First the therapist will build better inner models of adaptive relationships. Later the therapist will also explore the comforting versus uncomfortable aspects of the therapist–patient relationship, as well as why the patient might avoid people who would treat her better.*]

The focus here is on building a capacity that is absent or lacking in the patient: the ability to discern and avoid destructive relationships. Some identification of the patient's emotional responses in these relationships would be important, as is done in the defense-restructuring phase. However, it would be incorrect to move to affect restructuring by eliciting the depth of the conflicted emotion because of impairment in impulse control.

SABOTAGE OF TREATMENT: AMBIVALENT MOTIVATION FOR CHANGE AND PRESERVATION OF SAMENESS

Self-destructive or therapy-destructive defensive functioning can extend beyond withdrawal from others or disorders of self to another, even more difficult form of self-destructive behavior: taking a few steps toward change and then undoing it. Such individuals demonstrate all the defensive functions mentioned previously—they don't want to look at their feelings, they don't want to be close to others—and in addition have the desire to stay in the familiar beaten, helpless, dependent, or childlike position. It may also be true that they want to avoid affects or closeness as well, but even more fundamentally, there is conflict and resistance about change and growth. Indeed, there can be a lot of secondary gain in self-sabotage. Sometimes the rewards for staying in a dependent or regressive position are compelling. For example, one can avoid the terrors of adult responsibility. If the therapist does not identify this position, much time can be wasted in focusing on the avoidance of a specific affect, when much stronger defensive forces are operative. Identifying such patterns involves taking a step back and looking at the broader perspective (the context in which the defenses are occurring) to see the most comprehensive script that makes up the core psychodynamic focus. Developmentally, this level of defensive function can suggest impairment in initiative or autonomy.

Some patients who behave in a self-sabotaging manner seem to dabble with change (after all, they have sought therapy). Some change may occur, only to be followed by a relapse into the old, destructive patterns. Some patients appear to work hard in the therapy session but forget everything that was said as soon as they walk out. Other patients stay "stuck" but at least consciously appear to want to do something about it. Davanloo highlighted this phenomenon and emphasized the need to bring it to the individual's consciousness as soon as possible. The manner in which this is brought into awareness in the present system is quite different from Davanloo's challenge and pressure: "If you continue to behave in this way, therapy will fail!" (Davanloo, 1980, p. 2). In contrast, the approach in this book provides a supportive exploration of the impediments. Following are two examples of therapist interventions in this situation:

> *Do you notice how between sessions you forget the work we have done* [D] *and continue in the same harmful patterns* [D]? [The patient must first concur. If the patient does not agree, the discrepancy in viewpoints needs to be resolved before the therapist proceeds with the intervention.]
>
> *There must be something not just frightening, but really terrifying* [A] *about giving up these patterns of behavior* [D]. *Could we look at the fears* [A] *that might be holding you back if you responded differently?*

LACK OF MOTIVATION FOR CHANGE

Other patients have no motivation for the work of therapy but come to treatment hoping the therapist will effect a magical cure. It is useless to point out the less severe defensive operations (e.g., avoidance of emotion) if they are present if the patient does not wish to engage in treatment. Such patients frequently complain: *This isn't helping me. I don't feel any better* [D].

In other words, the patient is saying, "What are *you* going to do about it?" Such comments challenge therapists to examine whether their work has been adequate; however, if active, involved interventions have been made and destructive patterns pointed out, the therapist needs to reflect on the patient's resistance to change.

EXAMPLE: PATIENT WANTS TO BE TOLD WHAT TO DO

THERAPIST: Let's review what we've done. There seem to be a number of patterns we've identified that have been hurtful to you.

PATIENT: Yeah, but what use is that? I just feel worse. You haven't told me what to do [D].

THERAPIST: No, but we have been considering what you might want to do in each of these situations [I/F].

PATIENT: That's no help. Why won't you just tell me? [*This blaming is at least in part a form of projection.*]

THERAPIST: It seems hard for you to imagine that the answers could come from you [D].

PATIENT: Why should I? They never have before. And I wouldn't trust it anyway. [*Defensive function: seeking the magical cure*]

THERAPIST: That sounds demoralizing. Let's see if I can help you find answers for yourself.

EXAMPLE: MILDER LACK OF MOTIVATION

The following is a milder example of lack of motivation in a man who began by complaining about coming to therapy, although he had chosen to do so. No treatment could begin until his ambivalence about therapy was resolved.

PATIENT: Do you know how long it took to get here? Forty-five minutes! And the traffic was a nightmare. I had a terrible time parking, and I hate hospitals [D]. [*Complaining is a common defensive behavior and is an example of displacement.*][7]

THERAPIST: You seem unsure about how much you want to come here [D].

PATIENT: Yes and no . . . yes and no [D].

THERAPIST: So part of you wonders if it's going to be worth it to come here with all this hassle. [*In this example, the therapist addresses the lack of motivation for treatment, because it is the more destructive function of the defense, rather than confront defenses against the feelings of anger.*]

PATIENT: Yeah, that's for sure. Hospitals mean pain for me [A], and I have some doubts about how much I want to do that [I/F], but I guess it's the best thing for me. [*This disclosure about feelings and taking responsibility reflects some mature coping and is a good prognostic sign.*]

THERAPIST: Well, let's look at the pros and cons and see if it seems worth the effort to continue.

Lack of motivation can be conscious or unconscious. We want to get out of bed in the morning, but instead, we turn off the alarm. When lack of motivation is conscious, it is often the case that the patient is coming to therapy because someone else is insisting on it. Sometimes it is a spouse or parent; also, court-mandated treatment for abuse or drug-related offenses is becoming more frequent. To overcome this serious treatment obstacle, the therapist must help the patient find some genuinely motivating reason for coming to treatment, or the whole process will be a sham and no therapeutic change can be expected.

Lack of motivation may be unconscious in the case of patients who bring themselves to treatment but seek a magical cure. This level of defensiveness suggests a serious lack of motivation to participate in the therapeutic process. Developmentally, this can suggest problems in initiative, autonomy, basic trust, and so on. If there is any willingness of the patient to be there, it is due to a yearning for the therapist to do the work and the longing to be in the position of a dependent child who is totally looked after and on whom no demands are placed. This type of behavior has been referred to as the "golden fantasy" (Brenner, 1957). Unless the problem with motivation is addressed, there will be no significant movement in psychotherapy. This de-

---

[7]On the basis of a review of hundreds of hours of videotaped therapy, complaining seems to be a major aspect of what patients do in psychotherapy. It can give momentary relief, but it does not lead to change unless the patient is assisted to confront and alter what is being complained about.

fensive function has to be confronted as do all the others, but with strong empathic accompaniments.

EXAMPLE: RESPONSE TO THE WISH FOR THE MAGICAL CURE

THERAPIST: You seem to long for me to be able to flip a switch and take your pain away [D].

PATIENT: Yeah, well, aren't you the expert? Aren't you supposed to have the answers [D]? [*Note that this is an example of intellectualization used in the service of sabotaging treatment.*]

THERAPIST: You know, *I wish I could do that*, and in fact, if that were possible, and I had such power, I'm sure I would! But the reality is that therapy doesn't work that way. I have no capacity to help you unless you work along with me. [*Empathizing but also presenting reality*]

PATIENT: You mean I'm supposed to do the work! I didn't come here for that [D]!

THERAPIST: What's the most difficult part of it for you—if *you* did the work [A]?

EXAMPLE: MANDATED TREATMENT

In an example of even greater resistance, the patient is mandated to come for treatment by the court:

THERAPIST: Look, you probably wouldn't be here if it were up to you, right?

PATIENT: You bet! I've got better things to do. I never thought therapy did any good anyway.

THERAPIST: Well, it's a waste of time to just go through the motions. Why don't we try to find some reason that you might want to be here so you get something out of this that matters to you? [*Then, starting with the negative consequences of the problematic behavior*]: You've been having a lot of trouble lately, and it doesn't sound like it's been very pleasant. I wonder how it could have been better?

Some patients engage at this point, focusing on how they can make their lives better, but other patients do not. The following is an example of how to handle an even more severe level of resistance:

PATIENT: So, whadyawant from me?

THERAPIST: Maybe we can start by looking at what an effort this seems to be for you. It must be a real drag to realize that no one can do it for you (or no one will be able to make you better or no one will get you out of this mess but you).

PATIENT: It sure the hell is!

THERAPIST: So let's look at the worst parts of nobody doing anything for you.

This focus on the pain is an anxiety-reducing maneuver that attempts to build motivation. When all else fails, there may need to be sessions concentrated on relationship building. The therapist should monitor whether there is a growing motivation for change, because such therapy can become custodial rather than change-oriented. Sometimes, custodial work is the best that can be done, but one should not have illusions that therapeutic work is occurring when it is not.

IDENTIFICATION OF HIDDEN IMPULSE OR FEELING

Along with recognition of defensive behaviors and functions, the patient must be assisted to identify the inner affective experience that is being avoided by the defensive behaviors. Affects must be carefully described, linked to and distinguished from defensive behaviors and anxieties, and they always must be identified in an interpersonal context. This identification of feeling differs from the in-depth exploration of the affect-restructuring objectives. The purpose here is not full experiencing of the feeling (desensitization through exposure) but *recognition* of what the hidden feeling is and a start toward placing the feeling in its proper context (i.e., how it might be defended against; how it might be best expressed).

The first step in identifying affective feeling is for the patient to give the internal experience a verbal label, or name. It is common in our society for individuals to confuse the internal experience of anger with that of anxiety or the internal experience of stomach pain with sadness and simply to be unclear or confused about whatever is being felt. Individuals often do not correctly identify what is going on inside. Because confusion in the labeling of feeling is ubiquitous in our society, clinicians *cannot take for granted that patients know what they mean when they use an affect word.* They may be labeling an entirely different internal response than we think they are. Patients need to learn to identify the bodily or physiological concomitants of various affects to ensure that their internal responses have a commonly agreed-on verbal label. Each separate affect must be assessed for the patient's ability to label, experience, and express it appropriately. Following are some examples of labeling affect experience associated with defenses.

> *I wonder what the looking away* [D] *is avoiding. Do you suppose there are some sad feelings* [I/F] *that you don't want to show me?* [Defensive function: avoiding closeness] *The story you tell is a sad one.*
>
> *The rapid way that you are speaking* [D] *probably helps you stay away from the tender feelings* [I/F] *that you seem to be having here with me right now. What do you think?*

As presented in chapter 3 concerning the core psychodynamic pattern, it is not a difficult task to begin to hypothesize what adaptive feelings might need to be dealt with; the choices are few. For a rough guideline, I have categorized into three clusters the most frequently addressed affects in therapy. The first two clusters each contain affects that have a more activating function (predominantly those on the impulse–feeling pole), and in the third cluster are inhibitory affects (predominantly those on the anxiety pole). The first cluster, which contains the feelings most frequently dealt with in therapy, involves those I call the regulatory affects: anger–assertion, sadness–

grief, and the affects associated with closeness or attachment. The second group of affects, which are less frequently dealt with but no less important, contains the pleasure-giving emotions: interest–excitement, enjoyment–joy, and the affects associated with sexual desire. The third group of affects, ubiquitous in therapy work, involves the inhibitory affects: anxiety–fear, guilt–shame, and emotional pain. The methods of restructuring affects in treatment are discussed in much detail in chapters 6, 7, and 8. Again, the goal for defense recognition is simply to identify these feelings clearly. The correct identification of the function of the affects is crucial for the recognition of the defensive pattern, specifically, and for mental health, generally. Our affects and how they are associated with experience provide us with a major component of our sense of self and guide our responding, and they have been too long ignored in traditional psychotherapy.

During the process of identifying which affect is being defended against, it is not uncommon for patients to shift automatically from describing the affect to imagining what they would like to do: the "action tendency." This exploration of the desire to act is part of another, often later, part of treatment: affect restructuring. Unless there are strong contraindications (a history of acting out, poor impulse control, current impairment in functioning), however, the therapist may follow the patient's lead and move directly to affect restructuring. As noted earlier, these objectives for restructuring of defenses and affects are not rigidly separated but represent parallel categories from which the therapist can select the appropriate intervention as the patient's needs and motivations indicate.

IDENTIFICATION OF SPECIFIC ANXIETY, GUILT, SHAME, OR PAIN

As the defenses and the probable warded-off affects are identified, the inquiry proceeds to exploring *why* the defenses are taking the place of the more adaptive possibilities. Part of the task of the therapist is to encourage the curiosity of the patient in this inquiry: *Why would defensive avoidance be happening when we have seen the destructiveness that it entails? There must be a valid reason. I wonder what this could be?*

For patients to want to proceed in this inquiry, their embarrassment over such investigation must be relatively low. This task requires an empathic stance by the therapist, which must be kept in the forefront of the therapist's mind.

The original evolutionary function of the inhibitory affects was for self-guidance or self-control, but when pathology occurs, these reactions represent feelings and associated beliefs that have been intensified beyond the bounds of adaptive control into some degree of self-inhibition, self-thwarting, or in extreme cases, punitive self-attack. This sometimes results from inadequate caretaking and sometimes from unknown causes. Whatever the reasons, *the unnaturally exaggerated inhibitory or self-attacking affects are a major cause of defensive behavior and thus a major cause of environmentally based psychopathology.* Furthermore, the lower the degree of anxiety, guilt, shame, or pain, the less the need for the thwarting defensive patterns and the greater the capacity for emotional expression. Of course, we need adaptive levels of anxiety, shame, or pain to guide our actions and set appropriate limits on our behavior. A reasonable degree of self-control is essential to optimal adaptation. The point is that when these reactions leave the realm of self-guidance and become sufficiently intense that they function as self-thwarting or inhibiting, therapeutic intervention is necessary to reduce that intensity of inhibition to more adaptive levels. The "self-attacking feelings" described in this section represent intensities of anxiety, shame, and pain that no longer guide, but inhibit or even assault, the self. These are severe forms of self-attack that must be reduced if healing is to occur. Once these aversive feelings are made conscious, they can be disputed; reality can be presented; and the patient can slowly begin to put fear, guilt, shame, or anguish into a realistic perspective.

In the model presented in this book, anxiety refers to *exaggerated or unrealistic* fear, guilt, shame, pain, hurt, or anguish. Much has been written about the distinction between guilt, regarding feelings about breaking external rules or laws, and shame, concerning feelings of being personally inadequate, inferior, or unworthy. These distinctions can be helpful in the development of interpretations, but for the following discussion, anxiety, guilt, shame, and pain are addressed as a group because the goal of clinical intervention is similar for each, that is, to be brought within an adaptive range of intensity. Each of these feelings is seen as harmful to the self when it no longer is used to guide the individual but rather to terrify, punish, condemn, or torment the self.

EXAMPLES OF ANXIETY REGULATION: POINTING OUT SELF-DESTRUCTIVE REACTIONS

What could have happened to you to cause you to respond in this manner with authority figures like your boss? There seems to be a lot of discomfort.

When you bite your fingernails so much that your arm aches, can you see how this is an assault on yourself? [Patient says, How do you mean?] *Well, you are doing something that causes yourself pain, rather than soothing yourself.*

It seems that when you have difficulty accomplishing what you need to do, rather than feel forgiving toward yourself, you insult yourself by calling yourself stupid (or foolish or a jerk). Can you see how that makes a bad situation worse for yourself?

Whenever you start to feel angry, do you notice that you then feel guilty or ashamed, as though you did not have a right to your feelings?

Whenever you start to feel sad, do you notice that you immediately feel embarrassed, as though there were something wrong with having that feeling?

Whenever you start to feel enjoyment, do you notice that you become frightened, as though something terrible were going to happen?

GENERATING A TENTATIVE PSYCHODYNAMIC FORMULATION TO GUIDE TREATMENT

The formulation requires information on what affect is avoided or disguised, how it is being avoided or disguised, and why this is happening.

Making the defensive pattern clear to the patient is a crucial part of summing up a session. The therapist needs to organize the data in a coherent format and collaborate with the patient to see if the psychodynamic formulation rings true. These scripts or formulations are presented intentionally as tentative suggestions, or inexact, interpretations, in contrast to "exact interpretations" as defined by Edward Glover (1931) to foster patient participation in their construction.

As the various functions of the defensive behaviors are determined, the relationship of the defensive behavior to the other poles on the Triangle of Conflict needs to be made vividly clear, that is, the relationship of the defenses to the hidden feeling, and how the anxiety, guilt, shame, or pain causes this response. As quickly as possible, the therapist should generate some working hypotheses for the avoidant, defensive behavior that takes the place of more adaptive responses: *Why* is the patient avoiding, *what* is being avoided (i.e., wished for, desired, wanted, or not wanted), and with *whom*. With repetition and reexamination of many examples of problematic behavior, the defensive patterns become clearer; figure separates from ground. According to Tomkins's script theory, this step means seeing the scripts or cohesive structures underlying the patient's narrative scenes. According to Malan's schema, these scripts follow the format in the two triangles (i.e., defenses, anxieties, and feelings across relationships). This process, as described in chapter 3, leads to the formulation of the core psychodynamic patterns.

EXAMPLES: SUMMING UP THE DEFENSIVE PATTERN
IN THE CORE FORMULATION

Can you see how you [D, careful description of the defensive behavior] *every time we get to the subject of* [I/F, the specific feeling in question] *toward* [T, C, or P, the specific current or past person]?

There seems to be some difficulty with this. What do you think might be stopping you? [Anxiety, guilt, shame, or pain involved in the expression]

Do you think there might be anxiety [or guilt, shame, or pain, A] *around expressing this feeling? Which seems to be the stronger influence in this case?*

In other situations, the therapist can point out the defense in relation to the emotion being avoided:

Can you see how you tend to do (D, the defensive behavior)?

Whenever you are talking about [T, C, or P, a specific person], *you seem reluctant to experience* [I/F, a specific feeling], *but tend to avoid it by* [D, another careful description of the behaviors that represent the defenses].

I wonder if there's some discomfort [A, inhibition such as anxiety] *in relation to your feelings with this person?* [Then, to enhance the collaborative relationship, the formulation is presented tentatively]: *How does this sound? Does this seem to fit your understanding of what you're doing?*

EXAMPLES: INTERPRETATIONS OF MAIN DEFENSIVE PATTERNS

It seems now that looking away [D] *helps you to avoid the anxiety* [A, inhibitory feeling] *you feel about closeness* [I/F] *to me* [the person being responded to]. *Can you see this?*

You have told me about a great deal of loneliness in your early life [D; behaviors reflecting loneliness such as staying isolated rather than reaching out can be seen as defensive or at least less than optimally adaptive]. *There must be a lot of pain* [A] *for you whenever you long for someone* [I/F, the wish for attachment, as well as the sadness of unmet longings] *and that causes you to close off* [D], *as you closed off to your mother* [PP] *at such a young age. Carol* [CP] *is one striking example. It seems like it would be extremely painful for you to tell Carol what you feel. Does it seem this way to you?* [Patient says, Yes, you are exactly right.] *Then, the inability to express* [D] *your desire for her* [I/F] *must put you in tremendous turmoil! What would be the most painful thing* [A] *that might happen if you were to let Carol know the depth of your feelings for her?*

When hypotheses are suggested to the patient, as the preceding examples show, the patient should be encouraged to confirm or disconfirm them until one of two things happens: (a) the patient adds new information that disconfirms the hypothesis or (b) the patient comes to see the suggested relationship and confirms it by providing further examples. One can never know if the narrative reconstruction is absolutely accurate, or even partially accurate, but one can increase the meaningfulness of the formulation by constructing it collaboratively with the patient. *The accuracy of the interpretation can be assessed only by the efficacy of the formulation to bring about change. Patient improvement is the only test we have of the value of any interpretation.*

REPEATED PRESENTATION OF THE TRIANGLE OF CONFLICT PATTERN

Once the defensive pattern has been made clear, the therapist should not assume that the patient knows it as thoroughly as the therapist does. Typically, therapists have had thousands of opportunities for observing psychodynamic patterns and have had many exposures to examples of defensive behavior. Patients usually have such issues brought to their consciousness only a few times, and even then the significance of the pattern can be easily forgotten or denied. Consequently, the defensive pattern needs to be identified in the patient's narrative over and over again.

Each time the pattern is identified, the therapist should encourage the patient to put it into his or her own words. As this process continues, patients should also be encouraged to catch themselves in the defensive behavior outside of the session. This process is emphasized until patients become acutely conscious of their defensive patterns, rapidly noticing them whenever they occur. The goal of this stage of treatment is to help patients monitor their own defenses both in and outside the session. The therapist should be vigilant to hear patients' reports of catching themselves in defensive behavior as well as to hear patients elaborating on the causes of the defenses and the purposes served. We need to hear the same thing over and over before it becomes well integrated into the psyche and able to be used fluently. Our patients are learning an entirely new language, and it necessitates practice and repetition.

FURTHER DISTINCTIONS

In the preceding discussion, I outlined the basic steps of defense recognition in a simple and straightforward manner. There are a number of crucial, and often subtle, distinctions of which the therapist must be aware, however.

Distinguishing Adaptive from Inhibitory Affects

It is common for patients to confuse the expressive and adaptive forms of affect (the impulse–feeling pole) with the inhibiting or self-attacking forms of affect (the anxiety pole). At first pass, it might seem unlikely for this confusion to occur. Yet this distinction is one of the major confusions we have about our affective lives. It is ubiquitous in our society. In contrast to the energized experience produced by the adaptive emotions, the self-attacking affects make us feel immobilized, paralyzed, or stuck. Instead of the freely flowing, inner-to-outer direction of adaptive affect, self-attacking or inhibitory affective responses are generally represented by a pulling in, a cowering, a shrinking, a withdrawing, a gaze aversion. Some patients readily make this distinction, but the vast majority of patients (and therapists) confuse these different feeling states. For example, when asked how anger feels, they may say it is a "tightening in my stomach, cold clammy hands, difficulty breathing." I then ask, "Is that anger?" Sometimes that is sufficient to bring them to the awareness that they are describing being flooded with anxiety. More often, the distinction is not clear, and a careful exploration of emotional responses must occur before the therapy process continues. When there is difficulty in distinguishing inhibitory reactions from more activating emotional responses, the therapist can model the different reactions to accentuate the difference and help the patient see the distinction.

EXAMPLE: IDENTIFYING AFFECTIVE INHIBITION VERSUS ACTIVATION

THERAPIST [*Crossing arms in front of face and chest*]: Do you feel frightened and withdrawn, like this?

PATIENT: Yes, exactly! My stomach is in knots. [*Or the chest, or throat, or shoulders; D*]

THERAPIST: Do you feel as if you are pulling yourself back or reining yourself in rather than energized or ready to act?

PATIENT: Oh yes, definitely.

THERAPIST: So which feeling is predominating when you are tight, tense, or withdrawn?

PATIENT: I guess it would be anxiety [*A*]. I never thought about it before.

THERAPIST: And if you are feeling mostly anxiety [*A*], how do you know you are angry [*I/F*]? Can you see how the anxiety would diminish the assertive response? This signals that you are burdened with too much anxiety when you need to have access to feeling that could energize you.

The preceding technique, used by the active, short-term therapist, involves making a tentative suggestion about the impulse or feeling that seems to be avoided. The classical stance is that this would be "leading" the patient. As in so many aspects of life, there are both constructive and destructive ways of making these suggestions. Before making suggestions to patients with the intent of focusing the discussion and speeding up the therapy, it is beneficial to use Socratic dialogue to explore the patient's feelings: *I wonder what you were feeling toward John right at that moment?* When exploration yields nothing, suggestion can be considered, but the suggestion can be made tentatively to draw out the patient's involvement in the process: *Could you have been feeling angry? Does that seem to fit with your experience?*

Another issue to consider is compliance. Analysts so often are concerned that patients will passively go along with them. If an atmosphere is established at the outset that encourages active collaboration of the patient and the therapist in the generation of interpretations, patients will readily disagree with a hypothesis that does not feel right. *It does not have to be destructive to lead the patient if one has a relationship that encourages the patient to lead or dispute also.* Rather than being harmful, this atmosphere can strongly support autonomous functioning by encouraging disagreement with the therapist when the interpretations do not feel right.

Distinguishing Between Defensive and Inhibitory Affects

Another crucial distinction that must be made is the difference between the affective responses that are *defensive* in nature versus those that are *inhibitory* in nature. Sometimes they look similar, but the distinction lies in their function. It is the difference between the defensive maladaptive responses (the defense pole of the Triangle of Conflict) and the reason for the maladaptive response (the inhibitory affects on the anxiety pole of the Triangle of Conflict). Affects can be used adaptively or they can be used defensively to inhibit or even attack the self. Affects can be used at any pole of the Triangle of Conflict: as defenses, as inhibition, or as adaptive motivation. Defensive affects are one form of maladaptive defensive responding. Examples include anger used to disguise grief, weeping used to mask anger, and "putting on a happy face" or using an exaggerated joy to hide pain.

The self-attacking or inhibiting affective responses represent the *reasons* for the maladaptive responses and are often experienced internally rather than directly expressed. The behavioral manifestations of these inhibitory feelings are often not seen unless the defenses break down; otherwise, only the defenses are apparent. The problem in differentiation comes when the same emotion is used in more than one way. In that case, the only way to make the distinction is to evaluate how the affect is used. *Assess the affect by the function it serves.* Affect used to cover up, hide, or avoid something else is defensive emotion; affect used to attack or inhibit responses of the self is self-attacking; and affect used to express wants or needs in an appropriate manner is adaptive and self-soothing or nurturant. Severe forms of both anxiety and depression, for example, attack or severely inhibit the self as well as defensively block the expression of adaptive wants and needs.

EXAMPLES: AFFECTS USED DEFENSIVELY

Anxiety can be used defensively. When defenses (such as repression or dissociation) do not work, anxiety can flood the individual and function like a "radar jam" to block thoughts of anger. The anxiety *functions as a defense*, because anger is blocked.

Shame can function as a defense when the defenses fail to sufficiently ward off conflicts. In such cases, the embarrassment, or even humiliation, can be overwhelming.

Weepiness (defensive teariness) can be used to cover up angry reactions, because the *pain* (conflict) of the threatened separation might be unbearable.

Other Defensive Feelings That Are Self-Attacking

Patient responses such as masochism, jealousy, envy, and resentment pose problems in treatment. By viewing the extreme and destructive aspects of these responses as defensive, the therapist can begin speculating about what responses might be more adaptive for the patient. For example, masochism can be seen as defensive self-attack (D pole) because of shame (or guilt, anxiety, or pain; A pole) about assertion of wants or needs (I/F pole).

Jealousy, in its extreme and pathological manifestations, can also be conceptualized as a defensive response. Maladaptive jealousy is in large part the result of shame or self-hate. Functionally, jealousy can be seen as a defense. Why do we become jealous? We might speculate that it is because we feel (a) too afraid to compete, (b) in too much pain to show how much we care, or (c) too ashamed to feel deserving of love. In contrast, consider the optimal responses. If one cares for and respects oneself, rather than being devastated that another person is loved more, there are at least three adaptive responses that could occur: (a) one could feel secure enough to compete for the desired person (adaptive longing or desire); (b) one could find fault in the individual who lacked loyalty (i.e., anger), thus feeling less desire for the individual; or (c) one could acknowledge and grieve the loss of the desired person, which frees one to seek other relationships. There is an adaptive and a maladaptive version of most things in life. An adaptive form of jealousy might be competition, if the loss is retrievable. Grief and replacement of the loss is the appropriate response if the loss is not.

Envy, resentment, or bitterness can be worked with in similar ways in the therapeutic setting. It can be helpful to think of such reactions as defensive reactions to the pain, grief, or anger of self-deprivation or self-devaluation. If one feels joy and a mature pride in accomplishments, as well as the security that one can obtain much of what is desired, one is freed up to enjoy the successes of others. The more emotionally at peace one is, the less one is likely to begrudge others what they have. From this perspective, destructive envy or resentment can be thought of as arising from the *pain or anguish of not having*, rather than not having itself. One possible resolution for envy might involve appreciation, gratitude, or thankfulness for one's own blessings, whatever they may be. Before this is possible, however, the individual has to come to terms with the conflicts that give rise to envy. There may be many defensive obstacles to overcome (barriers to grief over loss, anger, or closeness) before a sense of grace can be achieved. In the final analysis, the capacity for one's own joy may be the ultimate antidote for envy.

Distinguishing the Person Who Is the Object of Conflict: Linking the Triangle of Conflict to the Triangle of Person

With every interpretation of the Triangle of Conflict, the therapist must be vigilant to identify the *interpersonal focus* in which the behavior occurs. This should go on simultaneously with pointing out the behavioral pattern. In the examples in this chapter, a specific person was identified. Following are statements the therapist might make:

> *It seems difficult for you to cry—with your wife.*
> *Saying what you think is hard for you to do—with your boss.*
> *Is it difficult for you to be honest about your feelings—here with me?*

The defensive pattern also needs to be identified in the current and past relationships. It is not sufficient to work only in the therapist–patient relationship. Patients need to become aware of how they interact in all current relationships and how they learned to interact, typically from their past relationships. The awareness of repetitive patterns across a wide range of people and times slowly reveals a core psychodynamic conflict pattern.

Noting the Defensive Pattern When It Occurs with the Therapist

The therapist should also be vigilant to catch any occurrence of the defensive pattern in the patient–therapist relationship, because the opportunity for learning, feeling, and experiencing the defensive behaviors is more vivid than in any other context. Whatever patterns of behavior are seen in other relationships in the patient's life, the therapist must immediately consider that they will potentially occur in the therapeutic relationship, and vice versa. If the main psychodynamic patterns are not occurring with the therapist, there should be clear reasons why they are not.

Many patterns inevitably emerge in the patient–therapist relationship, and they should be watched for. If the patient has a history of becoming close to people but then dropping them, or sabotaging ventures just as they become successful, or using passive aggression to express anger in other relationships, each of these should be flagged to watch for, because it is highly probable that it will also be acted out in treatment.

EXAMPLE: ANTICIPATING POTENTIAL FOR DROPOUT

THERAPIST: You've just told me that you've dropped out of therapy [D] three times before when things got too difficult [A]. Then it's probably a good chance that some similar feelings could come up in here [T], do you think . . . ?

PATIENT: Yeah, I suppose so.

THERAPIST: Let's see if we can watch for those feelings to come up in here, so we can talk about it first, before it happens. Does that seem reasonable to you?

PATIENT: Oh yes. It feels like a relief. I am always afraid of getting out of control and running [D].

THERAPIST: Then we'll both watch for it. It sounds like you run [D] because things get too overwhelming [A] for you.

PATIENT: Yeah, that's true.

THERAPIST: So if you and I are mindful of that, then we can work at a pace that is bearable for you, okay?

SUMMARY

This chapter focuses on the interventions that can be useful in assisting patients in the recognition of defensive patterns. With a collaborative therapist stance, anxieties are regulated as defenses are pointed out. Interventions include the following:

Identification of defenses, anxieties, and adaptive feelings in the Triangle of Conflict

Identification of the costs and benefits of the defensive pattern

Validation of the defensive pattern

Pointing out strengths to balance vulnerabilities

Identification of the range of functions of the defensive pattern

Generation of a tentative hypothesis of the core psychodynamic patterns

Repetition until the pattern is clear to the patient

CHAPTER 5

Second Major Objective of Defense Restructuring: Relinquishing of Defenses

> To be, or not to be, . . .
> Whether 'tis nobler in the mind to suffer
> The slings and arrows of outrageous fortune, . . .
> Or, . . . by opposing end them?
>
> Shakespeare, *Hamlet* (3.1)

The fundamental question presented in this chapter is whether to suffer or not to suffer and to what extent suffering will go. It is the question of whether to live or not to live and how full that living will be. Whereas the preceding chapter focused on the cognitive aspects of change—the insight into or recognition of destructive behaviors—this chapter addresses how to put an end to those behaviors. Stories are frequently heard of patients who have acquired insight but who do not change. Hence, the riddle asking how many therapists it takes to change a light bulb—only one, but the light bulb must *really want to change*. How should therapists proceed when patients see what they are doing with defenses but nevertheless continue the suffering that results from the now-conscious destructive behavior patterns? What are therapists to do when insight and awareness are simply not enough, as is too often the case?

The second objective in the defense-restructuring phase is devoted to the resolution of the obstructions that prevent patients from putting an end to their suffering. The techniques have evolved primarily from years of working with research therapists and colleagues in examining videotapes. After long hours of close and careful scrutiny, we developed approaches that offered promise in working through entrenched defensive "barriers," or behavior patterns that were resistant to change. The new approaches were tried, the tapes viewed and reviewed again, and the interventions further refined. We discovered that the behavior change that took place resulted from the application not only of psychodynamic principles but also of principles of reinforcement and operant conditioning, self psychology, and object relations theory. When all of these theoretical perspectives are brought to bear on entrenched defenses in a psychodynamic formulation, it seems increasingly possible to bring about change in defensive behaviors. The research basis for these changes is discussed in chapter 12.

From a psychodynamic perspective, I have hypothesized that recognizing the defensive pattern is the first but not the only step toward change. This factor is the "insight" that psychodynamics is both famous and infamous for. The adage "insight is all" or "awareness is all" simply has not been borne out by practical experience. Too many patients have had the experience of knowing why they do something but being unable to change the behavior. For many cases of character change, much more than insight is needed. Because psychodynamic theory does not offer a formula for what causes defenses to be given up, we had to look elsewhere.

From a learning theory perspective, it appeared that identification of negative consequences helps to decrease the motivation for the continuation of the maladaptive behavior. Identification of positive consequences of the defensive patterns offers patients an understanding of what they are getting out of it (the secondary gain); the patient learns that what is obtained from the maladaptive defensive behaviors might be obtained in other, less destructive ways.

From a self-psychological perspective, the absence of a positive and compassionate sense of self seemed to be a major stumbling block to adaptive change. When identified, focused on, and actively encouraged, self-compassion has been observed time and again to be a major change agent. The more patients care for and feel positively about themselves, the less they wish to behave destructively.

From an object relations or interpersonal perspective, if the early caretakers were critical and punitive, so will be the relationship of the self to both the self and others. When destructive internalized relationships are identified and new and more affirming ones are either identified from the past (the recovery of lost loves) or built anew (in the current life or in the therapeutic relationship), the capacity for character change is enormously enhanced. These change mechanisms warrant greater detail, because the alteration of entrenched, long-standing defensive patterns is the nuts and bolts of character change.

The problematic behaviors (defensive responses and maladaptive coping) must be identified in many contexts so that patients can clearly recognize their harmful as well as helpful response patterns. Only then can the next question be fully addressed: Why am I behaving in this way? What is maintaining my behavior pattern?

To decrease these avoidant defensive behaviors, the inhibitory feelings that cause the avoidance must be reduced (anxiety regulation). This is the first step in the change process, which can be greatly assisted by an analysis of the antecedents and consequences of the defensive behaviors. Antecedents are typically less conscious (more difficult to describe verbally) than consequences. Inference, intuition, and therapist training can be quite useful in the discovery of these behaviors. Why is the person doing what he or she is doing? What are the conditions that *cause* or *elicit* the problematic response?[1] In addition, the consequences of the problematic behavior need to become clear to the patient as well as the therapist. Both must discover how such behaviors help and how they hurt. (What are the pros and cons, or the cost–benefit analysis, of the defensive behavior?)

The punishing or negative consequences of the defenses must be acknowledged as well as deeply felt. (This can be conceptualized as not only seeing but also, maybe for the first time, *feeling* the punishing aspects of the behavior).[2] One may ask why this is necessary. If patients understand what they are doing, why does there need to be an accompanying emotional response?

My answer encompasses three perspectives. First, we learn on more than one level. Intellectual learning is different from emotional learning. Although there is increasing evidence from research that cognition and affect are interwoven in experience, each influencing the other (e.g., Halgren, 1992; Panskepp, 1982), it appears that these modes of responding need to be addressed separately for change to occur. Put another way, when one alters beliefs or attitudes, the accompanying feelings do not always alter accordingly, which obstructs a full behavior change. When one focuses only on feelings, the beliefs are not always sufficiently altered, so that a full behavioral change is obstructed.

Second, affects make up our basic motivational system. To change behavior, we must change what motivates that behavior. Although cognition, beliefs, and attitudes are crucial factors influencing motivation, in this model affect is the fundamental mechanism of motivation. Third, drawing from reinforcement principles, positive affects have the potential to reward behavior and negative affects to inhibit or punish behavior. To effect change we need to keep in mind these principles of behavior change: how the defensive behavior is reinforced by the underlying affects, how it is punished, and how the behavior can be extinguished.[3]

---

[1] Conditions that *cause* behavior versus *elicit* behavior can represent the two ends of the continuum from "learned" to "prepared" responses, but any single response probably involves contributions from both nature and nurture.

[2] This change mechanism was first identified for me by Davanloo (1980).

[3] Some readers may remember the book *A Clockwork Orange* by Anthony Burgess, and the subsequent movie, which provides a classic example of the gross misapplication of behavioral principles. The manifest behavior of a young criminal is "punished" by having him watch films with his eyes forced open. Any sophisticated behaviorist knows that punishment serves only to suppress behavior temporarily. Lasting change requires reinforcement of successive approximations to more adaptive behavior. This man's basic motivations were not addressed. The behavior therapy, not surprisingly, was a complete failure, and he returned to his violent ways

It can be painful and terrifying to stop responding in ways that represent one's identity. Such behavior is like an old shoe: It may be worn out and have problems, but it feels familiar and to some degree comforting. It can be soothing, at least to some degree, to continue responding in ways that were accepted by those to whom one was most deeply attached. It can be gut-wrenching at first to stop doing so. The therapist must be acutely aware of the painfulness of this process of character change and of the courage and fortitude it takes for the patient to go through it. On the other hand, continuing such patterns can perpetuate suffering. These alternatives have to be put squarely before patients.

Change in the "how" of defense restructuring occurs as a result of an application of principles I shall call "psychodynamic behaviorism." We do not wish merely to punish or extinguish the *manifest defensive behavior* and reinforce an alternative behavior as we would in a patient with an elevator phobia. Rather, we wish to attend to the whole person, which must include unconscious motives, intrapsychic meanings, as well as cognitive and affective responses. From a behavioral perspective, Joseph Cautela (e.g., 1966) was one of the first to extend the principles of reinforcement beyond the overt behaviors of Skinnerian behaviorism. Cautela went beyond manifest, observable responses into the "black box" to address responses that he called *covert behaviors* (i.e., internal, unseen responses such as thoughts, feelings, and images).

In similar fashion, to achieve behavior change from a psychodynamic perspective, I have extended the principles of reinforcement further yet into the black box to a category I refer to as *symbolic behaviors*. When any response *stands for something else*, or *represents some other person, place, or thing*, I think of it as symbolic, or representational. Our capacity to symbolize makes even observable, manifest behavior more complex; therefore, to attend to the reinforcement contingencies (reward, punishment, extinction) only on the manifest level is not a sufficient analysis for behavior change. *If there are factors that motivate or inhibit unconscious, covert, or symbolic responding, they must be taken into consideration.* We must attend to the antecedents and consequences of *unstated needs*, *unlabeled motivations*, and the *metaphorical meanings of behaviors* in order to change them. This is not so mysterious: Sometimes our perception of a cigar does, indeed, represent something other than a cigar. Sometimes a cigar is just a cigar, but sometimes, even often, it is something more.

To help patients give up patterns, we also need to keep in mind what is maintaining the *symbolic behavior*, just as we need to know what is maintaining the *covert and overt behaviors*. How is the symbolic behavior being reinforced? Put another way, why are these destructive symbolic behaviors so rewarding? And why are their punishing qualities so ignored? How could some other, more adaptive response become more rewarding to the patient? These are the mechanisms of change in this model.

---

with gusto. The story is an excellent example of how not to go about behavior change.

In the case of the Machine Builder, covert behaviors would be her thoughts, feelings, and images that relate to the problem at hand. For example, *I don't want them to see me looking nervous. I have more feelings than most people. Emotions are an illness. They would laugh at me if they knew how I felt.*

Symbolic behaviors are in our conscious awareness to a lesser extent. For the Machine Builder, her perception of her classmates as potentially attacking her was symbolic of her relationship with her cousins who had teased her unmercifully as a child while her mother sat by, doing nothing to help. Her classmates felt similar to, or "represented," these people from early-life relationships. Her overt behavior, motivated by symbolic meaning, was to avoid speaking in front of them, as though this was going to protect her when in fact it was endangering her career.

In the following examples, the meaning of the responses was completely unconscious before therapy. The insights that were achieved by each individual are not direct quotations in this case but have been put into a sentence structure that demonstrates the underlying pattern of change. Note that there is both a cognitive appraisal and an emotional component to the new learning.

EXAMPLES OF UNCONSCIOUS MEANINGS OF RESPONSES

- Never crying . . . *means that I am a person that my father respected.* [The Machine Builder]
- Staying distant and detached, rather than enthusiastic and involved, *means that I am safe from others devaluing me.* [The Machine Builder]
- My low self-esteem . . . *meant that I had forgotten the love that my grandfather had for me.* [The Ferryman; feeling loved by his grandfather allowed him to feel like a lovable, worthwhile person]
- My feeling that God hated me . . . *meant that I imagined God to be as unforgiving as my father.* [The Unforgiven Teenager]

Try to hypothesize possible meanings for the following statements or thoughts:

- I must do every job perfectly.
- Why don't they realize how great I am?
- I absolutely must look my best.
- Those people are talking about me.

Behaviors can have a symbolic component. Ask yourself what might be the reason for the following behaviors:

- Excessive collecting of things
- Needing others to start tasks
- Inability to throw things away
- Kicking the dog
- Sarcasm or cynicism
- Stinginess

In psychodynamic psychotherapy, we not only change behavior but also change the symbolic *meaning of behavior*. To do this, we need to understand the underlying and usually not-so-conscious motives and desires. If we do not think of change as occurring on a symbolic level, we will not achieve alteration in intrapsychic structure.

Giving up comforting responses such as perfectionism, stinginess, sarcasm, or the hypervigilance of paranoia means that some other more mature response, *equally valuable*, has to occur in its place. Other behaviors or values that are equally reinforcing have to be acquired. For example, patients need to come to deep, self-affirming realizations such as described in the following report of a patient: *I can see now that never getting angry (or grief-stricken or enthusiastic) is not the kind of person I want to be. It is no longer what I respect. And it grieves me that my mother (or father or caretaker) could not see this. But now it's only me keeping it going.*

- *I don't have to feel so afraid* [A] *to trust someone* [I/F].
- *People can stand up for themselves* [I/F] *without having to feel guilty for it* [A].
- *Just because some people will devalue my enthusiasm* [A, embarrassment] *doesn't mean I have to stop feeling excited about things* [I/F].

Antecedents to more adaptive behavior need to become more conscious so that free choice is enhanced: *My stomach is hurting* [D], *which generally means that I am mad* [I/F] *but not acting on it as I should* [adaptive solution]. *What do I need to look at more closely?*

Consequences to adaptive behavior need to become more reinforcing: *If I don't speak up* [adaptive solution] *here, I'm going to be stewing* [D] *all weekend, and nothing will change at work.*

In all defensive functions, secondary gain is the linchpin that holds the behavior pattern in place. The greater the resistance in the therapy process, the more the therapist needs to be on the lookout for the hidden agendas that are *reinforcing the defensive behaviors*. Why does someone stay closed rather than open? Why does someone put on a mask and pretend to be someone he is not? Why does someone create havoc for herself or sabotage a treatment that she is paying for? The simple answer is that *whatever these patients are doing must be preferable to the alternative*. At one time in their life, that choice made sense. By the time they have come to therapy, it probably makes less sense than it did. The cost–benefit analysis of their choices has shifted, but they may not know it yet. Anxiety, guilt, shame, and pain are the underlying affects attached to these reasons for maintaining sameness, but what are the self-attacking emotions linked to? We are back to the question of why the patient is avoiding and how that is symbolically represented in the maladaptive behavior.

PREPARATION FOR THE RELINQUISHING OF DEFENSES

The following list contains suggestions regarding therapist stance and anxiety regulation that are important in preparation for the relinquishing of defenses:

- Take a stance that is active and involved.
- Offer an outline of methods for achieving regulation of anxieties involved in relinquishing defenses.
- Point out the negative consequences of the defenses.
- Distinguish the origin from the maintenance of the defensive behavior.
- Seek the expression of grief over losses caused by the defensive pattern.
- Assess and replace secondary gain of the defensive pattern.
- If there is no grief, assess the degree of self-compassion: Why doesn't the patient care?
- If there is no self-compassion, assess and build alternative relationships to replace the destructive relationships that are being given up.

The following sections discuss each method and intervention in detail.

Therapist Stance in Relinquishing Defenses: The Catalyst
THE REAL THERAPEUTIC RELATIONSHIP

In helping a patient give up defensive behaviors, the short-term therapist must be active and involved to *catalyze* change. This is a dramatic departure from the traditional analytic stance of abstinence or neutrality. In contrast, the attitude in short-term therapy is one of "enlightened involvement": at once extremely involved, yet not overly involved and not uninvolved. How does one accomplish such a feat? Although it requires enormous skill as well as personal development on the part of the therapist, it should not feel daunting. There are good models for coaching artistic development (e.g., singing, gymnastics, figure skating) from which one can draw inspiration in coaching in human development. A good coach knows when to intervene and when to back off and let what is natural emerge.

The therapist must *care* that the suffering be reduced or eliminated. This attitude can be constant across patients and problems even though certain interventions may be varied according to different patients' needs for closeness or distance or for more or less involvement. Patients come to therapy for help with problems, and in this model, the therapist is permitted to provide such help, in a professional manner, of course. When patients' defensive behavior patterns remain entrenched, I tell my supervisees that they must "wrestle with the defenses," that is, point out the defenses actively, put energy into the endeavor, and put themselves into it. Emphasize the negative effects of the defenses. Crawl into the foxhole where the patient is hiding and try to understand *why* he is doing what he is doing. At the same time, I tell them to be vigilant for the sadness of the plight. Demonstrate concern. Dramatize what is at stake, and highlight the patient's indifference. Sometimes it is the very "lending of concern" that ignites the patient to change. But one should always be attuned to when the encouragement is meeting with resistance, so that it does not take on the tone of badgering. In the following examples, the therapist is showing appropriate concern and involvement in response to the patient's resistance.

EXAMPLES: ENLIGHTENED INVOLVEMENT

It is really upsetting to see you suffer [D] *week after week. How can you bear to continue behaving in ways that bring you so much pain?* [Highlighting the negative consequences of the defensive behavior] *I am just an outside observer listening to the story, and it seems so sad to me.* [Modeling the adaptive response] *But you are living it!*

Can you see how you keep this going [D]! *What could have happened that would lead you to care so little for yourself* [D]? *I have no power to stop you, but at least I can point it out until you are better able to see how destructive it is for you.* [Pointing out the negative consequences]

In both cases, the therapist is at once involved but maintaining appropriate distance. "I am just an outside observer" and "I have no power to stop you" underscore that the locus of control and responsibility resides in the patient.

Such heightened activity and involvement invariably bring up a variety of responses in the patient. On the positive side, there are often tears from the pain of feeling what previously has been so absent in the patient's life: another person's concern. This is a major component of the healing connection. This affect should be gently focused on until the patient can comfortably receive the gift that is being given. On the negative side, there can be, and typically is, resistance in the transference.

TRANSFERENCE ISSUES

It is common for patients to be unable to respond to the therapist's active, involved interventions. Distancing or deadening the connection with the therapist needs to be pointed out and worked through. Many patients feel that the therapist is taking something from them that is crucial to their survival, and they become stubborn and resistant. Other patients devalue the therapist precisely because of his or her show of concern. Patients may also externalize their motivation to change by wanting the therapist to do the "worrying" or even sabotage the therapist's efforts to help them. These are only a few of the many reactions that might arise. The therapist must be vigilant regarding how the patients are receiving or rejecting the involvement. This is grist for the therapeutic mill.

EXAMPLE: THE UNFORGIVEN TEENAGER AND
SELF–OTHER RESTRUCTURING

PATIENT [*Offhandedly*]: I didn't know why you seemed concerned about me last week.

THERAPIST: How did my show of concern feel to you?

PATIENT: I didn't know how to take it [D].

THERAPIST: Is it hard for you to let yourself feel cared for?

PATIENT: Yeah, I don't believe it [D].

THERAPIST: So it's hard to believe that I would have concern for you. [*Note that the therapist does not protest how much he cares but puts responsibility on the patient for not accepting the caring.*]

PATIENT: It's hard to believe [D] anyone would have concern [I/F] for me.

THERAPIST: What makes it difficult [A] for you to believe it here with me [T]?

PATIENT: My parents never did [P].

THERAPIST: So does that mean that I can't [T]?

PATIENT: If they didn't find me worthwhile, why should anyone else [D]?

THERAPIST: That sounds so painful [A] that I can imagine it would be hard to believe [D] in others.

The therapist continued to explore the inhibition of the receptive capacity until the patient was more able to allow such feelings into her experience. In chapter 9, on self and other, the issues of expressive and receptive capacities are discussed in much detail, and examples are provided.

COUNTERTRANSFERENCE ISSUES

The active and involved position can bring up a range of intense reactions in the therapist. Indeed, in my psychodynamic training, I was taught that I should not try to "do" anything but to explore and understand. More than one supervisor was inspired to say to me, "Leigh, why is it that you feel that you must *do* something for the patient?" These "superego voices" are still with me, so that I have some level of discomfort in writing this section. There is a degree of wisdom in those words, cautioning us not to become harridans who mercilessly hound and badger patients, nor to put our needs and desires before theirs. Yet, I retain valuable remnants of my behavior therapy training, in which behavior change *is* paramount and seen as a legitimate goal to be accomplished with skill, dignity, and humanity.

Therapists must be mindful that patients often do not respond as desired and that this can bring up feelings of frustration and anger in the therapist. Patients' opposition or noncompliance can spoil therapists' cherished fantasies of omnipotence that they will be the patient's savior. One antidote for the therapist is to remember (and to remind the patient, as well) that therapists have no power to make patients change. Therapy is not like surgery; it requires the patient's full participation. It is the patient's choice, and the patient's life. That does not mean that the therapist does not care about patients' choices or their suffering. This position of "involved acceptance" is one that *necessitates* that therapists accept that some people will hang on to their misery much longer than the therapists would like. But it is not the patient's fault. Patients are doing the best they can at the moment, given the circumstances of their lives. Ultimately, when the patient is not changing, it is the responsibility of the therapist to figure out why and to put those issues before the patient in as helpful a manner as possible.

It is much easier and safer, in some respects, to hide behind the mask of neutrality or, on a deeper level, to affectively numb oneself to the feeling of concern for the patient. Detachment does not put the therapist on the line. Emotional involvement can be painful, and with some patients it is more painful that with others. It can be painful to acknowledge that one is simply not coming up with the needed combination of factors to motivate patients to reduce their suffering. It can be painful and frustrating when patients choose to remain defended even when the issues are largely clear. Some therapists may fear that involvement allows patients to torture therapists by intentionally failing. But patients do not have the power to torture therapists; they can only try to do so. Therapists cannot become tortured, destroyed, or miserable unless they permit themselves to become so. Such reactive forms of involvement have been called *codependency* or *projective-identification,* and they happen regularly in treatment.

Furthermore, therapists must never blame patients for not yielding or not complying. To be angry that patients are not giving up their defensive behaviors is to lose the compassionate position. On the other hand, it is inevitable that the compassionate position will be lost from time to time, and therapists need to be aware of such reactions and ready to take action when they occur (e.g., consultation or supervision). In such cases, Winnicott's classic article "Hate in the Countertransference" (1949) can offer solace as well as humor to help therapists get back on track.

There are many ways of staying involved but also appropriately autonomous and affectively centered. Therapists can point out to the patient that their caring has appropriate limits that do not extend to masochistic self-attack if the patient does not improve. The following examples demonstrate ways a therapist might integrate concern with appropriate distance.

EXAMPLES: INTEGRATING CONCERN AND DISTANCE

To express a modulated concern, the therapist might say the following to a patient: *I will feel sad if I am not able to help you resolve these conflicts. However, I know that I cannot always succeed, and I would not be doing you a service if I had to have you succeed for my self-esteem. The change in here has to be for you, when you are ready and able to do it.*

The following dialogue presents another example of the necessary blend: The therapist is deeply and openly involved but not codependent or needy of patient performance to ensure professional competence.

THERAPIST: We have seen the destructive patterns [D] quite clearly, and it is really sad [*negative consequences*] to see you continuing them. Does it seem sad to you?

PATIENT: Not really. Isn't life like this for everybody [D]?

THERAPIST: I'm not so sure. It seems that you have a lot of suffering the way things are. Do you think everyone should just put up with so much unhappiness?

PATIENT: What else can you do [D]?

THERAPIST: That's what you're here for, isn't it!

PATIENT: Yeah, I guess. But I don't really believe that anything will work [D].
THERAPIST: So I will hold the hope for you, until you can feel it yourself. [*Pause*] Can we see what feels most impossible for you . . . what's the most hopeless part . . . what makes it seem unchangeable [A]?

The principles of anxiety regulation discussed previously are invoked here. The therapist "holding the hope" offers some easing of the pain of having faced things alone and without success. The exploration of the hopelessness allows the patient to identify and work through the fears that she cannot be healed, the shame that she does not deserve to find relief, and so on. This process constitutes the resolution of the conflict, that is, the regulation of the inhibitory emotion related to self-care. The therapist is working to reduce the self-attacking feelings on the anxiety pole and encouraging the emergence of the adaptive feelings on the impulse–feeling pole of the Triangle of Conflict.

As the destructive, wasteful patterns become more and more evident, patients should begin to experience and express a sense of care and concern for themselves. When this is absent in the patient's experience, it generally implies that there was not a strongly compassionate person in the patient's life. As a result, such patients lack a compassionate introject, or a compassionate inner representation of another person. The therapist's empathic sharing of the experience of the pain or sorrow is a means of "lending ego," as Fred Pine (1984) has suggested, as well as "supplying the missing capability," suggested by Gustafson (1984). The therapist must represent a model of caring while the patient builds a new inner capacity for a compassionate sense of self. (This process is discussed further later in this chapter and in chapter 10.)

Continual Assessment of Change

The constant question in the therapist's mind, before, during, and after every session, should be, "Is there change, and if not, why not?" The techniques described in the section on interventions are powerful in their potential to promote behavioral change. If maladaptive behavior is not shifting, *something is not being attended to*. It bears repeating that the patient should *never be badgered about changing*. The responsibility to understand why change is not happening belongs to the *therapist*, whose job it is to analyze the resistance, the anxieties, and the secondary gain. It is, of course, ultimately up to patients to determine whether they have the necessary motivation to make the desired changes. Even here, it is the responsibility of the therapist to try to understand the reasons motivation is lacking and to put the issues clearly before the patient. As mentioned many times earlier, it is not the responsibility of the therapist to *make* things happen but to catalyze them (Bennett, 1989).

THERAPIST: How are you doing with the problem we've been focusing on?
PATIENT: I'm no better. I still do the same old thing, like a broken record [D].
THERAPIST: So let's look at it again and again, until we get to the core of it.

There must be strong forces holding it in place. We know you intellectually want to change it, but emotionally you seem to fall back in the same patterns. [*Validation, empathy*]

PATIENT: Damn right!

THERAPIST: Can we look at what's the hardest thing about giving it up? What'll you lose [*A*]?

With entrenched defenses, there is a great deal to lose. Sometimes what will be lost is the only relationship that the person has ever known, albeit a destructive one. Other times what will be lost is the person's total identity or sense of himself. Such fundamental components of the self cannot be given up unless something equally sustaining or more sustaining replaces it.

Sometimes, after a therapist has strenuously and repeatedly addressed an issue, a patient may indicate that she does not wish to deal with that issue at that time. Even if the therapist's judgment indicates that the issue should be addressed, one must remember that therapy is for problems that the *patient* wants help with. Therapists can encourage patients to keep important issues in mind to explore at another period in their lives. When patients insist that they do not want to work on a topic the therapist has flagged, that decision must be respected. Therapists' suggestions and encouragement (given gently and respectfully) can be like planting seeds that someday may come to fruition. Here is the optimal stance of caring yet letting go. The therapist deeply cares that patients *at some point* do what is best for them yet understands that people have their own timetable and pace at which they can grow. Patients often hold these suggestions within themselves until there is an appropriate time and space to grow.

EXAMPLES: VALIDATING DIFFERENCES OF OPINION WITH PATIENTS

To express and validate a difference of opinion, a therapist might say something like this: *I think that this is an important issue in your life, but this may not be the time for you to address it. People have their own ways and own times for sorting things out. We both should trust your judgment that this is not the time for you.*

Patients have both agreed and disagreed strongly with statements of this sort. Such statements can be highly motivating to patients who are holding back, and they insist that they want to proceed. Those who are not ready to make the change may be relieved. The therapist can push to a certain degree but must always respect the patient's position. The following two examples demonstrate patients who were very resistant to change.

An accountant with marital conflict sought psychotherapy but refused to face issues of anger in his marriage of 4 years. (He and his wife were already in couples treatment, which was not helping, and his wife had been in analysis for 24 years.) He said they were "therapy junkies." The subterranean anger between him and his wife was enormous, but he refused to focus on angry feelings. He felt, with some justification, that doing so would end the marriage, and because he was in his 60s and divorced once before, he felt too vulnerable to be alone. I offered to help him build his motivation and decrease his fears and, in fact, urged him to face these feelings. He finally said he would drop out of treatment rather than focus on anger. Reluctantly, I shifted the focus to cognitive therapy for marital problems, and I learned quite a lot from doing so. Indeed, his marriage did improve and stabilize, and he worked quite hard to improve his share of the relationship. I came to respect that his pathway was a legitimate one and that different individuals have different, but equally valid, ways to solve problems.

A young woman college student living at home was in constant conflict with her mother and in much distress. When I suggested that we might examine her angry feelings toward her mother, she became uncomfortable and abruptly decided to stop treatment. Although I was enormously frustrated with her, I reined in my reaction and I told her, in as accepting a manner as I could muster, that it was all right if she chose not to face these issues just now but that some day she might find it helpful to do so. A year passed, and I received a lovely letter from her. She had moved to another city and was doing well. She had entered therapy and was beginning to understand why she and her mother had been so angry with each other. She told me that my focus had been right but she had not been able to face it when she was living at home. The physical separation allowed her to face issues that had felt overwhelming the year before. Her letter has made it easier for me to trust my patients' timing needs in facing particular issues.

Anxiety Regulation in Defense Relinquishing

Nowhere is the need for anxiety regulation greater than in the giving up of defensive behaviors. When patients give up a manner of responding that has been a source of soothing or protection or that allows them to hide, one should expect an adverse reaction to letting it go. Yet let it go is what one hopes they will do. The task of the therapist is to assist actively in managing the fears, conflicts, and losses that inevitably arise in the attempt to alter lifelong character patterns.

On the deepest level, it is the positive consequences of entrenched defenses that hold them in place. *No defense will be given up unless something preferable seems likely to occur in its place.* Following are some examples of how a therapist might help to regulate a patient's anxieties to assist in the giving up of defensive patterns.

PROTOTYPIC INTERVENTIONS FOR REGULATION OF ANXIETIES

> *Giving up lifelong patterns of behavior can be difficult and frightening. Does it feel so when you think of stopping?* [Defensive pattern]
>
> *I wonder if we can look at the worst part of it . . . what would be the most overwhelming (or painful or shameful) thing* [A] *if you no longer did* (the defensive pattern)?
>
> *What would help you give it up?*
>
> *What would be the best part of altering this pattern?* [Positive consequences of change]
>
> *How can I help you in making some changes in this way of responding?* [Collaboration]

Can we do this in stages that are not overwhelming for you? You do not have to ramrod yourself through change. [Successive or graded approximations to the desired response]

I have found that the last intervention in the list actually facilitates changing. It is comforting to be told not to pressure oneself, whereas pushing oneself to do something that one is conflicted about often is fruitless effort.

EXAMPLES: RELINQUISHING ENTRENCHED DEFENSES OF PERFECTIONISM

A 28-year-old woman was so dominated by her mother that she never allowed herself to explore her own wants and needs. When she began treatment, she sat stiffly with a frozen smile on her face. It took her months to relax. The following excerpt is from the fifth session:

THERAPIST: Being the "perfect daughter" [D, *defensive pattern*] has been a tremendous burden all your life. [*Negative consequences*] Yet you derived so much pride and satisfaction from doing it, because you were indeed a super performer. [*Positive consequences–secondary gain*]

PATIENT: That's right. We were such good kids!

THERAPIST: We might expect it would be terrifying [A] for you to begin to take down that enormous scaffolding [*metaphor for the defensive behaviors*] that has held it all in place.

PATIENT: I can't even imagine it [D].

THERAPIST: Can I help you anticipate what might be the most frightening and difficult parts [A] of it? [*Again, anxiety about giving up the defensive behavior*]

PATIENT: Oh! I wouldn't be perfect.

THERAPIST: What might it be like to be a little less than perfect? [*Beginning to focus on an alternative solution that might begin to replace the perfectionism*]

PATIENT: I wouldn't know how to recognize myself. It seems terrifying *not* to constantly try to be perfect. [*Negative consequence of change: She will lose her sense of self!*] We *had* to be perfect. We *had* to be . . . my mother demanded it! It's like I wouldn't exist if I ever did the smallest thing wrong . . . even though, as I say it, it seems like it would be a relief to stop. [*Patient can begin to imagine some relief in relaxing.*]

THERAPIST: But if it is so terrifying that you wouldn't recognize yourself, we should go at a pace that isn't overwhelming to you. [*Anxiety regulation*]

PATIENT: [*Sighs and nods, but remains silent*]

THERAPIST: I wonder if we could start, here with me, just *imagining* what it would be like for you to be slightly not-so-perfect. [*Small exposure to the anxiety-provoking experience of being spontaneous, relaxed, authentic*] Nothing has to change until you feel comfortable to do so. [*The minimal exposure is accompanied by anxiety regulation.*] But just imagining something never hurt anyone. [*Anxiety regulation*] What might you *imagine* yourself doing that would not be perfect? [*Again, exposure; then, intentionally using humor to decrease the terror*] What would be the best part of it? What would be the most fun in not being perfect? [*Beginning to build alternative responses*]

PATIENT: Oh! I've always wanted to be messy. [*Laughter, shared by both*]

This patient began the unraveling process by giving herself permission to leave magazines on the floor of her impeccably clean apartment. One year later, she was tearing down and rebuilding the psychological structure that had guided her entire life. She was so terrified of being "out there unprotected in the universe" that the memory of her terror remains palpable to me. Yet she courageously took risks and moved out of a dead-end job into a challenging position in her profession. Without strong encouragement and active involvement of the therapist to catalyze this process, this enormous restructuring of the character would never have taken place. Without continual regulation of the anxieties, she would have been overwhelmed.

When a defensive pattern supports the positive sense of self, the removal of that pattern requires a change in identity: a change in basic sense of relatedness to self and others and a change in fundamental values and worldview. This is a large undertaking and clearly does not resolve as rapidly as less global issues. Yet the process does not have to take years. If identity, relatedness, and worldview are held as the major focus, much change can occur in a few months.

Teaching and Providing Information

Although many therapists trained in dynamic therapy have been taught to maintain neutrality and to provide no information, we have begun to recognize that we can facilitate movement through the treatment process by providing information to the patient when appropriate. The analyst John Gedo (1979) agrees and described this process as "beyond interpretation." Behavior therapists have known it for a long time as well. Often, more damage can been done by the therapist's withholding than the therapist's gratifying the patient's need for information or providing something that is missing, as long as the patient is not infantilized, and unconstructive dependency is not elicited.

ASCERTAINING WHAT INFORMATION IS NEEDED

The kind of information that can speed up the process of giving up defenses often is about the treatment process itself. Information should be provided when the patient asks for it or when progress in treatment is blocked because of the lack of information, although it does not have to be given immediately. The *reasons for the question* and *the capacity of the patient to answer the question* should generally be explored first. *I'll be glad to answer your questions and give you that information at the end of the session. But first can we examine why you have asked and what your thoughts might be? There may be important meanings for you in those questions that would be helpful to understand. And also, can we see if you have tried to answer them for yourself?*

After such exploration, the question often is answered or it is no longer an issue. When the question remains, a collaborative, problem-solving approach can be taken. It is important to teach only what patients do not know or could not know through their own experience. Consequently, teaching about their inner experience (the patients' own feelings, attitudes, or opinions) is inappropriate; in those areas, Socratic dialogue and collaborative exploration are crucial. However, short-term treatment approaches attempt to give patients the tools to allow them eventually to become their own therapist; it is these tools concerning therapeutic rationales and mechanisms that must be taught when they are not readily apparent to patients. They must have a cognitive map to guide them when therapy is over. Indeed, this book is a cognitive map of the territory. A few examples follow.

NORMALIZING

Providing information to patients about others having similar problems can make their burden easier to bear or put it in better perspective. Many patients have been isolated in their fears and conflicts, and a human perspective is immediately reassuring. This is not sufficient to remove the problem altogether, but it is a mechanism to reduce the patient's anxiety. It allows attention to be focused on the underlying issues rather than patients' unnecessary panic that they might be bizarre or weird.

BUILDING A COGNITIVE MAP OF THE TREATMENT PROCESS

My colleagues and I have repeatedly been told by patients that it is helpful when the theory of the two triangles is explained to them so that they can understand the treatment focus. The same principle applies for teaching the difference between the origins versus the maintenance of behavior, the importance of replacing losses, or any of the treatment mechanisms described in this book. Patients proceed more smoothly through the therapeutic stages when they understand the treatment rationale as well as we do. It is crucial to provide the patient with a cognitive map of the psychological territory. At the same time, much didactic work (imparting of knowledge) can be done by Socratic questioning, in which the patient is led through a process of discovery.

The regulation of anxiety is a process to be maintained particularly acutely in this objective. Anxiety-regulating considerations are woven throughout the following interventions. Examining negative consequences and the origin versus the maintenance of the behavior allows the development of a more objective (rather than self-blaming) appraisal of the patterns. The eliciting of grief, the building of compassion, and the restructuring of sense of self and others each provide a capability that is essential to the restructuring of the defensive pattern. In other words, as behaviors are "taken away," new, more adaptive capacities need to be built to replace them. The anxiety that results from such changes in character is regulated by each of these successive interventions.

INTERVENTIONS FOR THE RELINQUISHING OF DEFENSES

With an involved therapeutic stance and some methods for regulating anxiety, the therapist begins to impact strongly on the defensive behavior pattern so that change occurs. As discussed earlier, it is unfortunately all too common for patients to see what they are doing but remain entrenched in the old defensive patterns. Resistance to change can vary widely; this section discusses interventions that deal with mildly to severely resistant defensive patterns.

Giving up of defensive patterns is not, in and of itself, the fundamental change agent. The process of reawakening the emotional capacities that support adaptive functioning is the basis of character change. Nevertheless, the relinquishing of defenses represents *the removal of the character pathology and greatest obstacles to adaptive functioning.*

The process of relinquishing entrenched defensive behaviors is often the most difficult part of treatment. Nothing is more taxing to the therapist's patience nor more challenging to the therapist's skill. The therapist must employ diligence, tenacity, and persistence to "do battle" with the defenses and become active and involved in helping to replace the losses incurred when the defenses are given up. The goal of this section is to suggest interventions that assist in the removal of such obstruction to growth and change. I start with the simpler and more direct methods and move to the more intense or stronger procedures.

Identify Negative Consequences of the Defenses

Identifying the negative consequences of the defenses assists the patient in giving up defensive behavior by *highlighting the costs involved.* This process needs to occur on two levels: The patient needs to see the costs intellectually and to feel the costs emotionally as negative and hurtful to the self.

EXAMPLES: POINTING OUT THE COSTS OF DEFENSES

> Although it was not your fault, there have been significant costs to you that you are now in a position to do something about.
>
> Can you see the years of loneliness that have resulted from your anxious avoidance of social situations?
>
> What will happen if you continue to respond in this way? There have been tremendous losses and waste to you as a result of this behavior.
>
> It's tragic to see that you have lost raises, promotions, and even jobs throughout the years because of your conflicts with authority figures.
>
> We can see this is a way to try to get love, but the price you're paying seems so high. I wonder if it is worth it?

Eliciting Grief Concerning Losses Caused by Defenses

It is hypothesized that the patient will not be fully prepared for affective restructuring unless the negative effects of the defensive pattern can be fully understood and *strongly felt* (Davanloo, 1980; McCullough, 1991b). It is only when the defenses are truly grieved that the patient wants to relinquish them. Therapists need to be persistent in guiding patients toward the emotional awareness of the negative consequences of their behavior. If patients fully feel the loss in their life, they are *often*, although not always, more ready and able to move on to exploring the warded-off, conflictual feelings.

PROTOTYPIC INTERVENTION: FOCUSING ON
CONSEQUENCES OF THE DEFENSES

The therapist might make a statement such as this: *So all these losses, such as (the specific losses), have added up over the years and have cost you an enormous amount. Can you see the damage caused by this behavior pattern?*

The following are examples of typical patient responses, accompanied by a nonverbal indicator that sorrow is being experienced:

> *It all seems like such a waste. So many wasted years!* [Tears begin to flow along with the full affective experience of grief over the losses due to the defenses.]
> *It's hard to believe* [voice quivering] *that I haven't been able to see what I've been doing to myself.*
> *I never want to do this to myself again.* [Tears welling up and voice breaking]
> *Oh . . . all those wasted years.* [Sighing hard and pausing] *My life could have been so different. It didn't have to be like that.* [Crying]

These reactions are common in a successful restructuring of defensive patterns. It is crucial that this intervention is done in as uncritical a manner as possible and that the patients do not blame themselves. Sometimes patients go into depressive or self-attacking weeping that must be differentiated from an adaptive grief process (see chapters 6, 7, and 8).

When patients are flooded with the sadness of their situation and a robust grief response, it is a sign that the defensive behaviors are becoming ego-dystonic (i.e., not desirable to the sense of self). Such patients have sufficient motivation to proceed to the experiencing of the underlying emotions. Treatment does not always proceed so smoothly, however, that patients recognize the costs of their defenses, grieve them, and relinquish them in a simple linear progression. The real world of therapy is filled with patients who get stuck at this stage and to some degree fight the therapist's attempts to help them proceed any further.

When Grief Does Not Emerge

Too often therapists are faced with apathy and "la belle indifference." Therapy becomes stuck, with neither therapist nor patient knowing how to proceed effectively in dislodging entrenched defensive patterns. When one does everything one can to put patients in touch with the destructiveness of their behavior, it is disheartening to hear the patient say, "Yeah, I know. So what?"

Again, psychotherapy is unlike abdominal surgery; it requires the effort of both parties. Seemingly intractable patients present an enormous challenge. Even after I have presented the preceding techniques, I see frustration on faces of workshop participants and supervisees. I see the "yes, buts..." forming in their minds. "*Yes*, I can see that these techniques would be useful in many cases, *but* I have a patient (or two, or more) that I have tried much of this with, and *still* there is no change!"

It is this kind of patient that the following methods are intended to reach. My colleagues and I often sit for long periods and brainstorm what it might take to mobilize such entrenched patients; it is a fascinating process. It generally requires increased involvement on many levels. Therapists can turn to other therapists for consultation and advice. They can focus on the patient's motivation, because strong motivation is needed to shift the patterns. Finally, the therapist has to care (in a professional manner) that the behavior will change and has to put in personal effort (within professional limits) to see that change happens.

On the other hand, the most effective path to change sometimes is *being tolerant and understanding when the patient does not change for some time*. Rather than doing so passively, however, the therapist can actively explore the fears, shame, and pain that would be involved in change so that the path is prepared. In the most severe cases, the building of compassion in relationship to self and others is an essential ingredient for change.

EXAMPLE: PATIENTS WHO DO NOT CRY

The following example portrays an intellectual distancing from the subject matter followed by strong resistance to grieving in a young male carpenter who had been mildly depressed his whole life. His family urged him to come to therapy and wanted him to "get on with his life."

PATIENT: But everyone tells me to put the past behind me [D].

THERAPIST: It looks like you've been trying to do that a long time without much success.

PATIENT: That's for sure.

THERAPIST: Of course in the long run, our goal here is for you to put the past behind you in the sense that it no longer causes you anguish. [A, *unbearable pain*] But at present you are still being affected by behavior patterns [D] that originated long ago. Sometimes the past has to be dug up to see why it's still hanging around. Sometimes the only way out is through. What do you think? [*Teaching and encouragement to continue working*]

PATIENT: I suppose you're right. What you say makes sense. But I just don't want to look back.

THERAPIST: What is the most difficult part of looking back for you? [*By now this should be a familiar refrain; if a patient is resisting exploring the past, anxiety regulation about that resistance is called for: What would be so difficult about exploring the past?*]

PATIENT: Oh, a lot of people had it worse than I did [D].

THERAPIST: Does that make your suffering any less? [*Validation*]

PATIENT: I guess not . . . but I don't want to feel sorry for myself when so many people have suffered so much more. [D; *many patients confuse self-pity with self-compassion.*]

THERAPIST: There will always be those who have suffered more, and those who have suffered less. I wonder why you feel you don't deserve concern for what suffering you have endured?

PATIENT: I don't know. I just don't [D].

THERAPIST: It's upsetting to see how you let yourself fall through the cracks, isn't it? [*Both pointing out and modeling the negative feelings associated with these defenses*]

PATIENT: Yeah, I guess so.

THERAPIST: I wonder why your attention is on the suffering of the rest of humanity rather than your own. This is your therapy. Isn't this the place just for you?

Here the therapist begins the work of building compassion for self, which is more fully discussed later. To readers who feel that one *should* be focused on the rest on humanity *rather* than oneself, I state that I, too, believe that ideally we should be focused on *all* of humanity *but that we should include ourselves as part of humanity.* Care for self does not have to compete with care for others, when there is so often a path that takes both self and other into consideration. Too many people struggle with caring for others when they themselves are neglected, so that their caring for others eventually becomes resentful, obligatory, or draining. In meeting needs, people may have to take turns, but optimally, no one should be sacrificed. In addition, the more one's emotional conflicts are resolved, the more one can be truly charitable toward others. If one is truly selfless, one is worthless to humanity; if one is selfish in a mature way (i.e., having enlightened self-interest) and thus able to grow in love and wisdom, one can serve the world well. The goal of this therapy is neither self-absorption to the exclusion of others nor self-denial in service to others; it is the balanced and overarching ability to care for self and others.

EXAMPLE: EMOTIONAL DISTANCING FROM THE SADNESS OF THE PAST

This 38-year-old, tough male lawyer acknowledged that his situation was not optimal, but he strongly resisted feeling sad.

PATIENT: Yeah, it wasn't so great, I can see that, Doc. [*Small laugh, D*]

THERAPIST: What causes you to laugh at such a time?

PATIENT: Oh, it just seems ironic [*D*].

THERAPIST: But what might you be feeling if you didn't laugh [*I/F*]?

PATIENT: I guess I wouldn't like it very much [*some acknowledgment of I/F*] ... but I think it's better to laugh. What else can ya do? The past is the past [*D*].

THERAPIST: Yes, but where in your body are you feeling the past, right now [*I/F*]?

PATIENT: Oh, it's in there all right. I just don't like it when you make me pay attention to it.

THERAPIST: Well, let's see if we can. What's the most uncomfortable part [*A*]? [*Later, other questions are asked.*] How would you describe the feeling? What memories are coming up [*I/F*]?

When defenses remain in place and the patient resists giving them up, there are several interventions that can be helpful in undoing the seemingly intractable pattern: (a) distinguishing the origin from the maintenance of the defensive pattern, (b) an analysis of possible secondary gains from the defenses, (c) an assessment of the degree of self-compassion (or lack thereof), and (d) an examination and replacement of the destructive inner representations of self and others. Each of these is discussed in the following sections.

Distinguishing Origin from Maintenance of Defensive Patterns

The main thrust of this intervention is to provide patients with an objective rather than subjective view of their behavior. It is also tremendously helpful in reducing the shame involved in "owning" or acknowledging defensive behavior patterns. The *origin* of the defensive pattern needs to be pointed out by identifying what was learned in *past circumstances and past relationships* that led to the patient's defensive behavior. Although the defensive behavior pattern originated with people and circumstances beyond the patient's control, it is the patient, and only the patient, who maintains that destructive pattern in the current time.

This distinction between the origin and the maintenance of defenses is not to be misunderstood by the therapist, nor conveyed to the patient, as *assigning blame or absolving the patient of the proper sense of responsibility*. This process is *not the assignment of blame to anyone!* The healing mechanism is in assisting the patient to recognize objectively and honestly how destructive patterns of behavior originated (more often than not, *without bad intentions* on the part of the caretakers) but all the while encouraging the patient to accept full responsibility for maintaining these patterns in the present. The ultimate goal to be reached is for patients to hold a compassionate and responsible view of what happened to them, as well as a compassionate view toward those with whom the behaviors originated.

Patients are never encouraged to feel sorry for themselves in a pathetic or regressive sense, nor to blame others for victimizing them. This would not constitute mature or adaptive functioning but rather a maladaptive, defensive position. Patients are encouraged to face the sad or tragic fact of life that to a greater or lesser degree most of us have had less than optimal caretaking or less than optimal circumstances. It is the deficits in these circumstances or in the *caretaking* (i.e., the *behaviors* of the caretakers rather than the caretakers themselves) that have caused problems that need correcting. The early-life caretakers can do nothing in the present time to resolve the habits patients maintain within. It is the sole responsibility of the patient, with the therapist's help, to alter the patterns. The goal of this procedure, therefore, is to help the patient face (a) the grief that comes with the true acknowledgment of the painful or traumatic life events and relationships and (b) the self-compassion that causes the motivation to change.

When patients strongly blame themselves for maladaptive patterns (e.g., I'm just stupid, I was a bad kid, I should have known better), the following interventions can be helpful.

PROTOTYPIC INTERVENTIONS: ORIGIN VERSUS MAINTENANCE OF DEFENSES
THERAPIST: Your parents, probably without realizing it, set up certain pat-

terns of interactions that might not have been the best for you. [*Environmental origins*] Of course you may have reacted to them in your particular style and temperament. . . . We know you are and were high-spirited (or anxious, sensitive, very active: *biological origins*). And your parents did not appear to know the best way of responding to you. So the problem resulted from the interaction of your temperament and theirs.

PATIENT (the Ferryman): Yeah, but that means it was my fault.

THERAPIST: How can a child take responsibility for what the parents do? Children are totally dependent. Anyway, some parents really enjoy high-spirited or active kids. Other parents naturally soothe the anxious or sensitive child. So the parent sets up certain patterns of responding. Can you see what I am saying? [*Statements like this convey the assignment of responsibility to the people and circumstances that were present when the habit pattern originated.*]

PATIENT: I'm beginning to.

THERAPIST: Okay, but even though it was not your fault that the pattern started, only you are now responsible for changing it. In fact, no one else but you can do anything about it. There have been costs to you, but now, as an adult, you are in a position to do something about it. [*The therapist conveys the assignment of responsibility for the maintenance of the behavior to the patient.*]

Two other ways of saying the same thing include the following:

> *You didn't ask to be taught this way of responding; it just occurred because this was the only way you could have managed in the chaotic situation that surrounded you. Children are enormously dependent on their caretakers. Now you automatically respond in the way you learned to respond.*
>
> *You didn't spring from the womb unable to cry or be angry. The infant naturally cries. The toddler naturally stamps his or her foot and says "no" with gusto. You had to be taught to tone down your feelings to this extent. The sad thing is that now there is only you to correct it.*

When the Unforgiven Teenager heard the latter statement, the following dialogue took place:

PATIENT: But what if I was just a bad kid [D]?

THERAPIST: What kid at 3 or 4 is bad? Aren't children who are called "bad" really in pain [A]? [*My experience is that many patients with personality disorders resist taking a compassionate view of themselves. This patient's self-hate was particularly strong.*]

PATIENT: I don't know. I think I was a bad kid. I probably drove my mother crazy [D].

When this happens, the therapist must persist patiently to dispute the logic of blaming the victimized child. A typical intervention might be something like the following:

THERAPIST: You seem to be forgetting how unbearably sad and lonely you re-membered feeling every day on the school playground [*I/F*]. [*This had to be repeated many times before the Unforgiven Teenager could respond as follows:*]

PATIENT: Yeah [*thoughtfully*] . . . yeah, you're right. I *was* in pain. Geez, I was in so much pain. [*Both anxiety owing to conflict about longing for care and grief about loneliness*]

THE INNER CHILD VERSUS THE INNER ADULT

I was supervising a bright psychology intern,[4] when she became frus-trated and said, "I'm so sick of hearing all this talk about the inner child! Why don't people talk about the inner adult!" The term *inner adult* is a clever way to convey mature, well-modulated, and disciplined responding. Her point struck me as excellent. To stay entirely focused on the inner child is not a mature adaptive position. My only warning is that we not seek the inner adult to the exclusion of the inner child. We need to have compassion for where we have been to guide where we are going. Although we need to have access to the spontaneous feelings that we were born with (the inner child), the focus of this book is on how to shape those motives and desires in the most adaptive manner possible, which might be thought of as seeking the inner adult.

Assessment and Replacement of Secondary Gain

All too often patients who are brought to the point of grieving the de-structiveness of their defenses are not able to go on to relinquish them. People may hate the situation they are in but maintain it nonetheless, be-cause it seems better than any alternative. There often are subtle forces that are sufficiently reinforcing that even an aversive response pattern continues. Even more important for behavior change than the negative consequences of the defenses are these *beneficial consequences of the defensive behaviors*.

Let us backtrack for a moment to put this pattern into perspective. The primary reason the defensive behavior occurs is to *avoid* some conflict (e.g., anxiety, guilt, shame, or pain associated with a want or need). The first reason for or the primary gain of the defensive avoidance, therefore, is that the *conflict constitutes a form of punishment that decreases the probability that the avoided behavior (some emotional response) will occur*. The second reason for or secondary gain of the defensive avoidance is *the reward, or gain in comfort, that occurs*. This other layer of reinforcement increases the probability that the defenses will continue. As one middle-aged man told me as he was be-coming painfully aware of his defensive patterns, "Oh, for the *blessed safety* of repression!" If there were not some gain to it, or some comfort in it, the defensive behaviors would be less alluring. Repression occurs to avoid painful memories, but that avoidance also provides a peaceful sanctuary. The more severe the conflict, the more substantial the benefit in avoiding

[4]Sherrie Fitts, personal communication, Beth Israel Hospital, Boston, 1994.

that conflict. Both reward and punishment contribute to the defensive behaviors being maintained, therefore, and the therapist has to be skilled at identifying and altering both in order for defensive behaviors to be relinquished. Because behavioral research has demonstrated repeatedly that reinforcement exerts a much stronger control over behavior than does punishment, it is crucial, in changing defensive behaviors, to examine and alter the *secondary gain* (i.e., the reinforcers).

The more ego-syntonic the defenses, the greater the secondary gain. In patients who want desperately to change their identity, the defenses are ego-dystonic (not congruent with their sense of self): *I hate being passive; I long to be a strong, assertive individual. I have been numb too long; I want to be able to feel!*

In patients whose identity is bound up in the defensive pattern, the pattern is ego-syntonic, or synonymous with the sense of the self. If defensive behavior is syntonic with or highly correlated with one's identity, the secondary gain of the defenses is enormous. The defensive pattern defines the person. Even if it is not optimal, it is familiar and highly cathected; one is attached to one's identity. To alter the defensive pattern would be to alter the sense of self. Changing it can feel devastating, whereas maintaining it is familiar and, in many respects, comforting. The unemotional lawyer mentioned earlier said the following: *I like being the kind of guy who keeps cool. I'm no wimp. What is all this fuss about being able to cry? I was raised tough! I bite the bullet, and I'm proud of it!*

The secondary gain is great when defenses are synonymous with the identity. This means the person's view of the world or of himself has to be restructured before any motivation to change occurs.

EXAMPLE: SECONDARY GAIN AND SELF-SABOTAGE

A 36-year-old married woman sobbed hard and long over the grief [I/F] of not being able to have a child. She genuinely expressed her want and need for a family, but her husband was not open to adoption or in vitro fertilization. Even though their relationship was not great, she clung to her partner, with whom she had intermittent explosive fights [D], hoping he would change his mind. Biologically, time was running out for her, and her continued ambivalent and angry attachment [D] to someone who resisted helping her realize her dream suggested her own wish not to realize her dream [D]. With some probing, the patient came to acknowledge her own deep fears [A] of becoming a mother. She greatly feared her own sense of inadequacy [A, shame] *as a parent*, and staying with her husband allowed her to blame him [D] rather than herself [the secondary gain].

When these fears [A] became conscious, and her insecurities about motherhood [A] were explored until she could see that she could cope, she became less ambivalent [I/F, more able to say what she wanted] about having a child. She also realized that she had never really talked to her husband about her longing for a child [I/F] but had picked fights [D, defensive anger] and blamed him [D] for his reluctance in a manner that never led to their coming to a decision. This realization freed up her ability to assert herself [I/F] with her husband, and fortunately, after more heartfelt urging [I/F] by her, he saw how much it meant to her and became responsive to her requests to try to become pregnant.

If there is some expression of grief but no rapid move toward change, it is important to reassess secondary gain of the defensive behavior. A person may truly long to have a family and even experience grief over not having one but, on an unconscious level, long far more to remain in a child position or, in the preceding case, a childless position. When it is difficult to determine secondary gain or other unconscious motives, exploration of dreams or free association can often be helpful in eliciting meaningful connections.[5]

Assessing and Building Self-Compassion

With secondary gain, the motivation may be strong to change, but the patient feels somehow stuck, and the glue is the positive consequence, or the rewarding quality of the defensive behavior. Treatment can become stuck even when the defensive pattern and the secondary gain are seen quite fully but there is still no motivation to replace the destructive behaviors with more adaptive ones. In such cases, two factors require attention: (a) the absence of grief over the destructiveness of the defenses and (b) the lack of concern, or lack of compassion for self, that is a major obstacle to healing.

If compassion and grief are not present, the therapist must ask the patient why there seems to be no emotional response to seeing these sad and often tragic patterns.

EXAMPLES: EMPATHICALLY POINTING OUT TRAGIC PATTERNS

Following are examples of words I hear myself saying repeatedly. After a few gentle repetitions, they begin to sink in, and I see care for self begin to sprout, like a leaf through parched earth. These interventions should be made most empathically. Exploration of the patient's capacity to care for him- or herself must be handled sensitively by the therapist.

> *Can you see how little compassion you have for yourself? I wonder why that is? Does your life mean so little to you?*
> *Isn't it striking that you have been telling me one painful story after another, and yet you seem to have no feeling about it? Can you see how sad it is that you have so little concern for yourself?*
> *Isn't it astonishing that an outsider—me—listening to your story, feels sad for you? But I am not living it. It is you who have lived it, and yet you feel nothing!*

Often these words have an impact on patients who were impervious to other interventions, although it rarely happens in a dramatic way. The effect seems to take time to "percolate." But days or weeks following such inter-

---

[5]Judy Freedman pointed out that secondary gain and other unconscious motives often can be arrived at through free association or an exploration of dreams. (Personal communication, 1995.)

ventions, many patients have responded as follows: *Last week, suddenly it hit me. I couldn't help remembering that you were more concerned about me than I was. It shouldn't be that way. It made me feel sad for myself.*

This is the beginning expression of self-compassion. It is not self-pity, which is a "poor me," helpless, and hopeless victimized role. It is, rather, a deeply felt sense of caring for self that acknowledges the sorrow of bad things that have happened and the willingness to work for things to change.

I want to underscore that these interventions rarely produce results at the moment they are given. Indeed, such words seem to fall completely flat at the time. The power in compassionate statements emerges from *gentle repetition*. Like seeds planted, they need time and warmth to come to blossom. Many times I have repeated the preceding phrases to a patient a few times per session for three to six sessions before the thought "sunk in." But when it does finally register, typically outside of therapy, patients suddenly experience a wave of sorrow for themselves that they did not care for themselves as much as I did. This sadness signals the beginning of the growth of self-compassion.

EXAMPLE: HEIGHTENING COMPASSION BY CHANGING PERSPECTIVE

This excerpt is from the Unforgiven Teenager. It took many, many repetitions of such statements to alter her harsh and uncompassionate view of herself.

THERAPIST: What would another person feel hearing this story?
PATIENT: They'd be sad, I guess.
THERAPIST: What would *you* feel if *you* heard this story from another person?
PATIENT: I'd feel terrible for them.
THERAPIST: Isn't it shocking, then, that you have such a diminished concern for yourself? How could this happen? Why would you come to care less for yourself than for someone else?
PATIENT: Yeah . . . I don't know why it's that way . . . but it is.
THERAPIST: It's a sad thing to see, isn't it?
PATIENT: I suppose so [*blandly and without feeling*], but I've always been this way.

At points such as this, the therapist can back off until the next opportunity arises to address lack of compassion. The point has been made, and it will need some time to percolate within the patient. With a moderately impaired patient such as this one, this means weeks, not months. Ten weeks of treatment with this focus led to dramatic improvement in self-care for the Unforgiven Teenager. With more severely impaired patients, one should strive for such change in months, not years!

When Compassion Is Absent: Assessing and Building Relationships and Identity

There are many instances of patients who cannot easily be brought to a sense of self-compassion. When this is the case, it indicates either the harshness of the inner representations of self and others or simply the absence of compassionate others. Sometimes there is just an "empty space where a compassionate self should be."[6] The patient and therapist have to work together to make *alterations* or *additions* to these inner representations before significant change can occur. This is a process of supplying the missing capabilities by building new and more adaptive inner representations. It can be a complex and difficult process and, for these reasons, often becomes drawn out.

Building what is missing also can become drawn out because of therapist abstinence, when the therapist takes a stance of neutrality, avoiding a stand on issues, and not bearing witness. There are times when therapist openness is crucial in helping to rebuild the memory trace, that is, to begin to build memories of caring and involved people. If a patient has a poor identity or sense of self and believes that others hold the same poor impression, this view is not easily relinquished. It constitutes the patient's worldview and personal identity, which have been established over several decades. Such a long-standing *weltanshauung* requires therapist involvement, active presence, and sometimes a degree of self-disclosure to dislodge. An abstinent therapist can reinforce the entrenched inner view that the patient is not worthwhile.

The rebuilding of relationships is a complex process involving working on two fronts at the same time.[7] First, the patient needs to build a new "sense of self" by identifying with and "internalizing" the caring and compassionate therapist. Second, the patient must simultaneously relinquish (analytically speaking) the inner representations of the uncompassionate early-life caretakers (the introject). In behavioral terms, this is the relinquishing of the way of responding that was learned with the caretaker. To give up deeply entrenched and maladaptive defenses, one must identify *maladaptive relationships* and relinquish them as well. The defenses that hold such maladaptive patterns in place are the defensive functions against closeness, authenticity, and change. These may have begun to be addressed in treatment. New relationships must be built, however, before the old relationships can be given up. Because of the tenacity of early attachments (i.e., one has only one set of parents), it is typically no small matter to accomplish these decathexes and recathexes (emotional disconnections and reconnections). *It is only when a new identity is being developed and is feeling steady that the old identity can be let go. Only when new, more adaptive coping responses are learned and fairly well established can the old ways of coping be relinquished.*

This process can be extremely difficult. Acquiring a new sense of self and a new sense of one's early-life relationships seems to be one of the most difficult tasks to accomplish in a time-limited manner. The emotions that are being warded off are primitive, overwhelming, and terrifying: generally, the deepest rage, grief, and longing for care. Certainly, many patients appear to require *months* rather than *weeks* to accomplish this process. The fact that this

[6]Martin Svartberg, personal communication, 1995.
[7]This point was brought to my attention by Judy Freedman (personal communication, 1995).

process is difficult, however, does not mean that it needs to ramble on and become protracted. *Indeed, precisely because of the depth and complexity of the problem, we need to be as focused and clear as possible about our objectives and how to achieve them.*

There are interventions we are just beginning to become aware of that can greatly hasten these goals. As mentioned earlier, building a new internalized relationship can be achieved more rapidly than otherwise with the use of the *real relationship with the therapist.* Therapist involvement can cause tremendous strides to be made; in contrast, *neutrality might draw treatment out much longer than necessary.* Therapist neutrality is a powerful tool for eliciting patient projections and allowing regression into the transference neurosis, during which, optimally, the patient relives the emotional trauma of the past and "works it through" until it is resolved. This process can be lengthy and unpredictable.

In short-term therapy, it is not necessary to allow the full transference neurosis to evolve to be able to determine the underlying trauma. As discussed in chapter 3, concerning the formulation of the core dynamic pattern, these relationships can be determined relatively early by analysis of the defenses, anxieties, and impulses. Subsequently, the patterns in the psychodynamic formulation can be predicted to occur between the therapist and patient. In short-term treatment, the pattern can be predicted and vigilantly watched for in the patient–therapist relationship, so that each small occurrence of the transferential distortion can be brought up and worked through rapidly. What is sacrificed in not allowing the transference neurosis to develop is that particular method of reaching the emotional intensity of the relationship, because it is possible to reach this intensity by other pathways. What is gained is the intensity in the real relationship as well as saving a great deal of time.

Building New Attachments: Emotional Connections with Significant Others

At this point, the defense relinquishing can proceed no further without active work in affect restructuring and self–other restructuring. At this point, the treatment objectives merge. There are many points when the therapist works with both defenses and affects, on the basis of patients' needs; however, when identity and attachments are seriously impaired, the therapist has to work largely, if not exclusively, on the emotional relationship between the patient and the therapist and between the patient and others. To effect deep change, this means working compassionately with the full range of feelings between patient and therapist, as well as attending actively to the sense of self and sense of others. These issues are dealt with in detail, with many examples, in chapters 6 through 9.

Optimal Frustration and the Limits of the Compassionate Position

Finally, it must be acknowledged that no therapist is going to be perfectly empathic and compassionate all the time. Far from representing a failure on our parts, it may be the right and only way. Optimal frustration can result from empathic failures on the part of the otherwise mostly empathic therapist. Such failures are unavoidable, and the therapist should be vigilant concerning their occurrence. For patients with impairment in sense of self, working through episodes of empathic failures by the therapist can help to build a more gentle and benign inner representation of the world. Occasional failures on the part of the therapist allow the patient to integrate negative experiences with positive ones; it is hoped that the balance will be more favorable than it was in the past. The capacity to tolerate such letdowns should be enhanced. Examples of this process are given in chapter 9 concerning the restructuring of the self and others.

SPECIAL PROBLEMS IN DEFENSE RELINQUISHING: MULTIPLE SECONDARY GAIN

In the case of severely entrenched defenses, the primary reason for the resistance to change appears to be the secondary gain involved. For some reason or set of reasons, the rewards of maintaining the defense are greater than the rewards of giving it up. The more resistant the defense, *the more beneficial it must be to the patient.* There may be one major reason that the person needs to cling to it. If the defensive behavior is holding the person's false self or whole identity in place (e.g., If I'm not a smiling compliant good girl, I will no longer exist), careful building of adaptive capacities has to be done before any change will transpire. In such cases, a new identity has to be built before the old foundation can be pulled away.

In some cases, the defensive behavior pattern is rewarding many times over. There may be three, four, or five strong reasons that an individual wants to maintain a behavior pattern. In one case, a capable, highly respected professional man could not let himself be assertive. He played the role of the caretaker or the giver in every relationship he had, even when it cost him a great deal. He was unable to set limits or ask for things to enable his needs to be met in his personal life; he undercharged his clients; and his friends took advantage of him. Because he was greatly loved and quite competent, he got by. But he suffered in silence. This pattern was largely ego-dystonic in that he wanted desperately to change. It was *more* ego-syntonic, however, because he was reluctant to acquire the behaviors that were necessary for change.

After careful analysis, it became clear that there were multiple reasons (or reinforcers) maintaining his pattern. Each few sessions, we unearthed another important issue. In the meantime, this intelligent, hardworking man was engaging in a difficult struggle; he was not getting significantly better. After about 20 double sessions (two sessions back-to-back), he complained, "I thought this was short-term treatment!" I thought so too. The man had many strengths, but I was overwhelmed with all the resistance to change that his background presented. If I was overwhelmed as the therapist, one can only imagine what he must have felt like!

At one point, I had to put all the reasons on a list, because I could not hold them in my mind and keep them straight. One week we worked on one issue of secondary gain, and the next week on another. It seemed that we were going in circles. We would go over and over the same five or six issues and seem to make headway, except that the behavior pattern hung on like a loose tooth that hangs on by a thread. The following list is only a partial representation of all the issues he had facing him:

1: He would destroy his father's fragile self-esteem if he did not stay submissive.
2: He would disobey his mother's strong command that he be thoughtful and considerate of everyone, especially his father, who was chronically ill. She had raised her son to be his father's caretaker and to change that would be to give up his identity.
3: If he asserted himself, he would be selfish, and he had been taught that he was "bad for wanting." Selfishness was anathema.
4: If he took his father's role, he might have to face libidinal feelings toward his mother; she was an attractive woman who had been inappropriately seductive toward him. He had maintained enormous restraint in response to her but, as a result, had massive resistance to allowing himself to become completely free sexually.
5: There had been tremendous performance demands on him as a boy, as the preceding indicate, and if he asserted himself fully in manhood, there would be two additional things that would cause him problems: (a) He would have to give up being the boy, to the extent that he maintained this role, and (b) he would have even more demands on him, and he felt that he could not live up to the expectations of the world. He felt deep down that he was really a fraud, because he had never performed for himself, only for others.

In addition to the preceding list, there were subcategories that added to the maintenance of the defensive pattern. During one session he realized that he did not stand up to his overbearing father because he was, unconsciously, trying to hold on to the possibility of inheriting his father's fortune. It was not that he needed money or was even that money-oriented. He made a good living. It was that the inheritance represented all that his father had provided: financial security. Once he realized this, he was able to let it go. This was probably the least resistant of the secondary gain issues but the last to emerge. At about session 30, he was able to feel significant anger at his father for the first time and to throw off the terrible burden that had been placed on him as a boy. Afterward, he and his father were able to become much closer.

In this manner, the therapist and patient need to work diligently to discover all the reasons that hold defensive patterns in place. It appears that the greater the number and intensity of secondary gains, the more time will be needed in treatment to address each one in depth and find something more adaptive to replace it.

It is not always the case, but often the greater the secondary gain, the more syntonic the defense. One cannot take away defensive behavior patterns that are psychologically sustaining to the patient. The therapist has to assess what has to be built before the defenses can be taken away. What would be more rewarding than the pattern of behavior that the patient clings to? Can a positive sense of self be maintained (or improved) if the secondary gain is taken away?

TIME REQUIREMENTS IN DEFENSE RESTRUCTURING

The potential for rapid restructuring of defenses is great in the short-term anxiety-regulating model. In many cases of patients who are suitable for this treatment, defense restructuring of the core dynamic formulation is possible in a few sessions. In the research project at the University of Trondheim, Norway, the research therapists were given the goal of achieving the defense-restructuring objectives within the first 10 sessions. This sometimes was achieved, but even when not fully accomplished, there was often improvement as a result of the process. Many patients whose functioning is moderate or better (i.e., above 50 on the Global Assessment of Functioning Scale) are able to face their defensive pattern squarely in 3 to 5 sessions.

With more severe levels of pathology, the process of defense restructuring may require a longer time: months rather than weeks. The time required depends on the degree of ego-syntonicity and of secondary gain the defenses provide, as well as the object-relatedness of the patient and the cleverness of the therapist. Furthermore, the treatment interventions are dramatically different in cases of severe pathology. Such patients are not able to tolerate an exploration of their defensive patterns in the way described previously. Instead, they need to be assisted to learn who they are by an empathic exploration of their feelings.

THREE CASE EXAMPLES: LONGER VIGNETTES

I provide examples of treatments for more and less malleable defensive styles so that the reader can get a sense of the range. The first example, The Girl in Danger of Not Graduating, is of a young woman who saw her defenses rather rapidly; the second woman, The Falling Acrobat, did so with some difficulty; and the third, The Woman Who Hated Doctors, could not work with the active, focused technique.

CASE EXAMPLE: THE GIRL IN DANGER OF NOT GRADUATING

This business-college student came to treatment a few months before graduation. She was in a crisis because she was not able to complete her assignments, and she was in serious danger of not graduating. Although her functioning level had always been extremely high, she had not been able to go to class or finish an assignment for weeks. She was overwrought and exhausted from hounding herself to perform but not doing so. She had partial insight into the problem, but that had not changed it. A single evaluation session (3 hours in length) put her in touch with the underlying issues and allowed her eventually to return to classes. The following are a few excerpts from that session:

PATIENT: Instead of doing it in my own time, I feel like I haven't done anything, so therefore at this point I feel like I'm not doing what I want to be
doing and so that's part of the problem.

THERAPIST: You sound like you were a good little performer all your life.

PATIENT: Yeah.

THERAPIST: And now you're not performing so well anymore.

PATIENT: Part of it is because—I was talking to my parents about this—my
parents really put very little direct pressure on me and they never have,
but they are both very successful now. [*She describes their remarkable accomplishments and business successes.*]

THERAPIST: What an act to have to follow!

PATIENT: Yeah, and I'm studying business too.

As I listened to her story, I started pointing out defenses. See if you can
pick up the defensive responses in this next paragraph, before I discuss
them.

PATIENT: So, there is a lot of pressure there, and I don't think it's that much of
a coincidence that it's here too, in business school. For the last year and a
half I have had a really hard time handing in a paper on time. I mean I just
blank out. I can't sit down and write. I mean it just does not get done and
so . . . so what happens is I come up with excuses all the time, you know,
to the point where I just feel like I'm lying all the time. And it started with
little things . . . you know, I was sick. [*Her speech was pressured, and she was
smiling as she spoke.*]

As she spoke, I scanned her behavior for defensiveness. During the session, I picked up three things: She mentioned procrastination, a defensive
behavior in her current life; she spoke very rapidly, in an intellectual way
with no feeling; and she was smiling. As I go over this paragraph, I also note
she says she blanks out, makes excuses, has lied, and so on. All of these behaviors signal the probability that defensive avoidance is occurring.

PATIENT: And I didn't do a good job then. But now it's happening all the
time, and I just don't even do anything. So I'll say to myself, "Okay, I'm
not going to do this anymore! This is ridiculous." I'm aware of it every
time, but I still do it!

THERAPIST: It's clear that your heart isn't in it. Your head says you should get
your work in on time. But your behavior shows us something different.

PATIENT: Yeah, and it can be different every time.

THERAPIST: So you just criticize yourself instead of giving in to it. You say,
well, I'm gonna get better.

PATIENT: Right, right.

THERAPIST: There's a strong resistance in you to being the way you've always
been . . . so perfect, and getting everything done when you're supposed
to.

PATIENT: Right, right. [*Cutting me off and speaking very rapidly*] And a lot of it is . . . I can feel the rebellion. I sit in class and I've constantly been comparing my teachers to my parents.

In my previous statement to her, I noted the way she pressured herself, but she interrupted, as though she could hardly bear to hear that. I had intended to go on and point out to her how hard she was on herself, but she just ran immediately away. There was a strong intellectual defense going on there.

PATIENT: And I'll walk into my teacher's office, and I can . . . I can, I can almost feel it, and I'm saying silently to the teacher, "I'm not going to hand this in, and I'm gonna see if you still think I'm smart enough." So I do that now with my work and with my relationships, and I know what it is but it doesn't change! [*She ends almost breathlessly.*]

It is important to note that this patient sees her defensive behavior fairly clearly, and she wants to change it. This means that part of the initial work has already been done on her own. However, her considerable insight and even the large degree to which her defensive behavior is ego-dystonic are not sufficient to change her behavior. She continues to be out of control and to threaten seriously her chances to graduate. She does not understand why she is behaving this way, nor what the underlying need or warded-off feeling is.

The reader is encouraged to formulate a dynamic hypothesis to explain why the patient is behaving this way and what might be the emotional experience she is yearning for but not giving herself. Also, in a short-term model, one needs to ask what experience the therapist needs to provide the patient so that she has a distinctly better grip on the problem when she leaves the session. (It may not always be possible to achieve this goal, but it should always be strived for.) My goal here is, first, to make these unconscious aspects of the defensive behavior conscious and, later, to move to the alternative emotional experience that she needs to be able to resolve this problem.

THERAPIST: That sounds so difficult. But you know, you're being so intellectual about all of this.
PATIENT: Yeah, I know.
THERAPIST: You may not be completely aware of all the feelings involved, so maybe we can look at that today. In fact, you're smiling as you're telling me about this. [*She laughs.*] Is it actually pleasurable to think about?
PATIENT: No.
THERAPIST: Or do you think you're lightening up?

In this last statement, I am leading her—not the optimal approach. A preferable comment would have been, "What do you think the smile is doing?" This would have provided the patient the opportunity to attend more closely to the defensive behavior and to generate within herself the reasons for it. When her response indicated that she was not following my lead, I went back to the preferable Socratic approach.

PATIENT: No.
THERAPIST: Then what do you think this smile might be doing?
PATIENT: I guess it's just because I've been thinking about this now for like 2 or 3 years.
THERAPIST: Uh huh.

This is a good place to describe the difference between the anxiety-provoking and the anxiety-regulating approach. If I were to confront her now in an anxiety-provoking mode, I might say, "Look, you're racing right now. I point out something, and you don't even pause. There's no feeling here. Do you see how intellectualized you are?" She might react a bit, but if I kept on "holding on the defenses" as Davanloo teaches, she might have become more regressive and said something like, "Well, why are you picking on me?" This would elicit iatrogenic anger in the transference. Because she is not comfortable with expressing her anger, this confrontation would definitely drive the anxiety level up. If I had continued the confrontation, there would have been a burst of feeling during the session. She would have cried and felt attacked, and she would have felt anger closer to the surface.

This type of episode can be dramatic, and it is sometimes successful. We can imagine that if I continued pushing her, she would feel the same kind of demands and pressure that she had felt from her parents. She might have blurted out, "You're just like all of them. You keep pushing me to do more and do it right!" Of course, she would be right. I would have been putting pressure on her, and I would have been taking a role similar to that of her parents. Although this is a difficult path to follow, it can be healing. She would have become viscerally aware of the anger toward her parents, her teachers, and me! If her burst of anger was accepted by me and understood, she also would have been more desensitized and more able to stand up for herself in the future.

I was initially drawn to the anxiety-provoking approaches because there is great potential for change in the affect-laden confrontation. But there are also problems. First, not everyone can open in the face of such confrontation. Second, some people burst open in the first session but close up and are resistant in the second session. They do not like the openness that they are forced into. Third, some do not come back. Because first we must not do harm, I began to have deep concerns with the anxiety-provoking route.

In an anxiety-regulating approach, I still point out the defenses, as described, but I do so in a more collaborative manner. I continually ask her if she can see what I am pointing out. If she does not agree, we explore our differences. If she agrees but feels it is painful or difficult to face, we explore her fears. We do not proceed until we are in agreement and her anxiety is at a bearable level. I do not confront the defenses as much as I clarify them. The process is gentler but still very focused, and we rapidly get to the sadness.

PATIENT: I'm probably trying to take this lightly, I don't know, I'm unaware that I'm even smiling about it except now I am. I guess I'm trying to take it lightly or I'm trying to say, Okay. . . . [*Again, racing speech, but she does corroborate the lightening up.*]
THERAPIST: If you did not smile right now, what would you be feeling?
PATIENT: Probably less control.
THERAPIST: Less control isn't a feeling, though. You see? What would be the emotion? [*Pause*] Think about struggling with this for 3 years and always testing everybody.
PATIENT [*Pausing*]: I can feel it. It feels heavy.
THERAPIST: What would be the feeling that goes along with the heaviness?
PATIENT: I can't really tell. It doesn't feel like fear even though I—sometimes I know that I feel panic.

At this point, I was truly surprised that she was unable to label her feeling of what appeared to be sadness. I then had sadness dawning in me with the realization that no one had attended to her sad feelings.

PATIENT: It's hard for me to control now. A lot of times it's like the alphabet's wrong and it isn't. [*She continues to speak in a frantically fast way.*]
THERAPIST: Let me stop you a moment. Did you notice how you attempt to run away from the heavy feeling?
PATIENT: Yes, yes.
THERAPIST: You quickly ran into thoughts and very fast speech.

Although my technique is active, this is anxiety regulating, not anxiety provoking. The difference lies in not demanding that the patient face the underlying feeling but merely questioning about it. Just helping her notice the feeling seemed to build the alliance.

THERAPIST: That heaviness is what happens when you slow down. But still you don't know what it is.
PATIENT: No I, I don't, I can't. I'll say it doesn't seem like fear. No, it doesn't feel, I . . . just immediately when I, when I felt it, it didn't . . . feel like a fear in terms of being tense . . . like part of a panic. You know, just, um, and, um, it probably feels more like I'm . . . gonna cry. [*Here, she finally is able to identify that she feels sorrow. I slow down and speak gently.*]
THERAPIST: Mmm. Yeah. That's how your eyes look when you slow down, like there's a wave of sadness that wells up in you.
PATIENT: Yeah. [*Eyes now full of tears, but struggling to contain herself and to restrain a smile*]
THERAPIST: I know you're struggling. You don't need to hide the smile in here, but just to pay attention to how much as your eyes water, you fight it by putting on a smile . . . when you really are feeling so much pain.

PATIENT: Yeah. It's really hard for me, I mean not to try to smile, and when I'm smiling it's a feeling of control. It stops the sadness. It puts it aside and . . . [*Pausing*]

THERAPIST: That's right. When there's nothing to be done about the pain or you are frightened of it, it's very resourceful isn't it to go on to smiling or laughing?

The last sentence attempts to reduce her shame by validation of her need to smile. But it must be simultaneously pointed out that it is difficult to understand the deepest troubles if they are lightened up. I have found this combination approach (confrontation and validation) most helpful in enabling patients to explore the warded-off feeling.

The next intervention is designed to begin to encourage the patient to give up the defensive position by pointing out the negative consequences.

THERAPIST: But, what you just got through telling me is nothing is changing. It's just the same things all over again. You must be so exhausted.

PATIENT: Yeah . . . yeah. [*Still fighting tears*]

THERAPIST: So let's see what brings the tears now. It may not be on the tip of your tongue, but let's see if you can stay in the sorrow you've run from so frantically.

PATIENT: Well, a lot of it is feeling that I'm not doing what I should be doing, and I guess I'm not doing what I could be doing.

THERAPIST: I'm guessing now that you're not doing the kinds of performances that you told your parents you were doing.

PATIENT: Right.

THERAPIST: What's that like for you to have to try to be a superstar like your parents?

PATIENT: Well, it . . .

She hesitated, and I should have waited to see what she would say. One of the occupational hazards of short-term therapy is that the therapist becomes so activated that time is not allowed for reflection. The short-term therapist must learn to shift gears fast: to intervene actively, and then to be able to hold back at a moment's notice.

THERAPIST: What's it like to have parents who are so successful? It must be awfully hard.

PATIENT: Yeah, it's a little bit strange. [*By saying "it's strange," she stays on an intellectual level and doesn't go into the feeling.*] Because it's hard, I mean I, I, I can get upset very, very easily, but then I try, my parents, especially my mother, is always trying to reassure me, you know, they were coming from a completely different place. They *had* to do it.

THERAPIST: But you're not reassured?

PATIENT: No.

THERAPIST: So, your mother's words didn't help. What's important is what is the feeling in you. What is the most painful aspect of the fact that you're not like them?

PATIENT: Well, probably that I just don't feel good enough. And it's not so much that I, I see a lot of what I've done is kind of like sabotaging what I *could* do. I know I'm underachieving.

THERAPIST: So there's a feeling of not being good enough.

PATIENT: Yeah. And I try to not judge it. And I say, okay, it's a behavioral thing.

I had invited her to explore the sad feelings, but she is talking at a tremendous speed. She's not with me emotionally, and that means we have to go back to defense restructuring. She needs to see how she's racing away from the feeling and terrified to face the pain. Until these two things are conscious, she's not going to have much control over it.

THERAPIST: Do you realize the speed in which you speak?

PATIENT: No, but I've been told.

THERAPIST: It's remarkable, isn't it? It's like you're racing all the time. And do you notice now you don't feel as heavy or as sad?

PATIENT: No, I don't. [*Chuckling*]

THERAPIST: Right, the smile and the fast talking helped you run from the feeling again. When I stopped you for a moment, we saw very quickly what came right out on the surface, a lot of pain about not being good enough. [*I immediately refocus her on the sadness.*] Can you give an example of when you've felt the most inadequate, or not good enough?

PATIENT: When it ended up that I had to take an incomplete in one class, and I was so stressed about it, um [*pauses, and looks sad*] that I . . .

THERAPIST: Are you getting sad now when you think about it? Because you hesitated a little bit there.

PATIENT: A little bit.

THERAPIST: Yeah. What happened that you fight the sadness in here?

PATIENT: It's just that, the problem is as soon as I start feeling it, I do have this urge to really laugh, or really run, you know, and that's not appropriate. [*She is catching herself.*]

THERAPIST: Yeah. There must be a great deal of anxiety around sad feelings.

PATIENT: Yeah. Yeah. [*Now her defensive style is becoming conscious to her. So I focus on the anxieties in order to reduce her fears about experiencing her sadness.*]

THERAPIST: Let's put the other thing on hold a minute [*I am referring to her sadness itself*], and let's look at what anxiety is there. What is the most frightening part of being sad here with me?

PATIENT: That I'm going to be found out to some extent. At this point, I avoid my professors. Even the ones I am not having a hard time with I avoid [*laughs*] like I don't want to see them.

THERAPIST: So, you fear people are going to find you out. That's one of the fears, but even the wave of feeling makes you rush into laughter. So I wonder what is threatening about this feeling.

PATIENT: Um, probably that it's going to be too much, I think. The pain will be too much.

THERAPIST: The pain will be too much. So there must be a huge well of pain you want to avoid.

PATIENT: Probably, yeah.

At this point, I shift from pointing out the defenses [*the racing voice, the laughter*]. The sole focus becomes all the things she's afraid of, to help her calm down. The process is more cognitive, to help her develop some control over her fears, which, being outside of her awareness, automatically control her responding. She will not need to run away from the feelings if she is less afraid of them.

THERAPIST: Yeah. And, and what would happen to you? If you were to let go, for example, to let yourself let down and feel here with me all that sorrow that you contained?

PATIENT: Yeah. Probably I would see it as a sign of weakness. [*Here is the reason for the defenses and for the avoidance of the sadness. She would be ashamed of crying in front of me.*]

THERAPIST: You would be criticizing yourself if you really broke down and cried here with me?

PATIENT: Yeah. Uh huh.

THERAPIST: How sad that when you feel the pain deeply, you also fear there will be criticism. [*Acknowledging this shame immediately brings an association to how she acquired the shame.*]

PATIENT: Yeah, yeah, I think that's true. I'm very close to my father, but one of the things that my father always said is, that you should be able to control yourself all the time, 'cause if you lose control, you let somebody else know how you feel. He's always said you shouldn't do that, and he's always really been critical of a real display of emotion.

As we discussed her father, there was a change in this patient's perception of herself. When she saw for the first time how her father's high standards resulted in her feeling shame over not being disciplined enough, compassion for herself began to grow. She began to see how she had stuffed down her wants and needs for far too long and how the constant pressure had hurt her. We worked out a plan that she would take a 2-week break from classes and catch up on her sleep. I spoke to her professors to approve her absence.

After this session, she came back and reported that "my symptoms are half gone! I'm catching myself a lot of the time, and treating myself better. The other half, well, I'm still doing it, but at least I know I'm doing it and I'm able to do something about it." She got back on her feet, completed her course work, and graduated with her class.

This one evaluation session was able to alter one aspect of the character structure, the harsh, demanding inner model of the father, so that she was able to get through the graduation crisis. However, this was not her only issue. Her relationships had always involved performing for other people. I underscored this for her and recommended that if she found herself having trouble in the future in this area, she might want to consider therapy to become more comfortable with interpersonal authenticity and closeness.

CASE EXAMPLE: THE FALLING ACROBAT

This woman's defenses were more entrenched than those of the preceding woman, and she provided a fascinating example of denial. She had a boyfriend who was moving to California and had told her he did not want her to come along; however, she continued to deny that they were breaking up. Throughout her life, she had looked at the optimistic side and refused to face the truth. She had been a gymnast in a group that toured and put on demonstrations. There had been a routine in which she had to demonstrate an error in procedure by faking a fall on her hip. She did this so zealously that falling so hard night after night severely damaged her back, yet she had denied the physical pain in the same way that she currently denied the emotional pain.

THERAPIST: You've told me that the man doesn't care that much, in fact, told you not to move to California with him. Yet you keep making excuses for him. It's hard to see why you cut him so much slack.

PATIENT: Uh huh. [*Blankly*]

THERAPIST: It seems like you're still keeping all of your feelings numbed over by saying you think you can work it out. And you seem to think he really wants to work it out even when there's evidence to the contrary that is very clear. Didn't you tell me that he said he didn't want to work it out? Do I have it right? Or did I misunderstand you? Am I in error? [*By this time, I was confused because I was hearing two completely different stories.*]

PATIENT: No, you're right. [*Pausing*] I'm thinking about what you are saying.

THERAPIST: I think this must be very difficult for you to hear. I said the same thing to you last week, and you heard me last time, too. But maybe when you went out of here, the longing for him came up so strong that it got in your way. You start to forget, and you make excuses for him.

PATIENT: Um, yeah, I think I know what you're saying in a sense, but it's hard for me to see that. I don't know why.

THERAPIST: It's hard for you to see what? How coldly he's treating you? What's the hardest part?

PATIENT: Yeah. How coldly he's treating me. It's hard to see.

THERAPIST: So his behavior doesn't *feel* cold to you?

PATIENT: No! He just seems very confused. I think he's very confused.

There are two things going on here. We are talking about her behavior with this man but also with me. As I confront her defensiveness, she dissociates a little bit in the session by becoming confused and disoriented. She later reported that this was a painful session, but it did help her to eventually let go of the boyfriend emotionally.

PATIENT: I'm confused, but maybe it's just that I have trouble seeing what you're saying. It must be that I have this thing in my head where I create a real ideal situation. It's very hard for me to see that it's not true.

THERAPIST: What's the ideal situation?

PATIENT: Um, that this is the right person, that we'll get married, have kids, and all these bad things are not really happening.

THERAPIST: Yeah, the real situation is just the opposite. And for some reason, you can't bear to see it.

PATIENT: Yeah, for some reason I have a lot of trouble. I had the same trouble with Eric when we broke up. I had a really lot of trouble accepting it. I don't know what that is, why that is.

THERAPIST: Yeah. You seem to want it so very much. In your heart, it's like you're clinging to these relationships despite evidence that would suggest they are over, or not good for you.

PATIENT: Right.

This is the process of defense recognition: helping her see that she longs for something so much she cannot bear to face that she is not going to get it. I have not focused on anxieties yet. What might be the reasons that a person so fiercely distorts and denies reality?

THERAPIST: In both cases, it seems like you were getting hurt and you denied it.

PATIENT: Uh huh.

THERAPIST: Evidence that the effort you were putting in wasn't giving you back what it should have.

I also pointed out this pattern occurring in other relationships in her life and in her gymnastics routine. Through repetition, she began to see it and how the pattern generalized.

PATIENT [*After a long pause*]: I've been taking a long time to think about it because it's really, it's a very hard thing for me. I can just very easily walk out of here and totally ignore this whole discussion. I could just forget that we had it.

THERAPIST: It would be so much less painful wouldn't it, at least in the short run? [*Validating and accepting the soothing capacity of the defensiveness*]

PATIENT: Yeah. And I know I can do it. I am capable of a lot of denial.

THERAPIST: Yeah, it seemed to be how you soothed yourself from pain, by forgetting.

PATIENT: I have a lot . . . of pain. I've had chronic back pain for a long time. And I used to just deny it. I wouldn't even tell people there was anything wrong, and that took a lot of energy.

THERAPIST: Oh! It must have taken tremendous discipline to keep all that to yourself.

PATIENT: And I don't know where I learned to deny things this way.

THERAPIST: Maybe there was no one to share your pain with?

PATIENT: No, I wouldn't even tell. [*She doesn't say who.*] No, I would just ignore it.

THERAPIST: When did you learn not to share your pain? What would have happened if you did?

PATIENT: Oh, nothing would have happened. My mother would have pretended I didn't say anything. My mother just wouldn't hear it . . . like my words never happened.

This was such a poignant session that it lives vividly in my memory today, years later. I was astonished at the amount of physical and emotional deprivation this woman could sustain, while at the same time having so much resilience, stoicism, and personal strength. The pain of her mother ignoring her must have been tremendous. In the absence of the nurturance she needed, she simply learned to shut down and not feel anything.

At any rate, she did not forget the session. She remembered it and later told me how painful it was to do so. She even skipped a few sessions after this, because the emotional work was so difficult that she needed some time to titrate the information she had to face. But face it she did, courageously. After 12 sessions, the major depressive disorder that brought her to therapy was no longer present. She was transferred to another city shortly afterward, but we met by accident in a store when she returned for a visit. She looked wonderful and spoke happily: "Dr. McCullough, I'm doing great now. And I want you to know, I don't get involved with abusive men anymore!"

CASE EXAMPLE: THE WOMAN WHO HATED DOCTORS

This 28-year-old female bank teller was brought to treatment by her much older man friend, who was concerned with the degree of anxiety she was having. She was unable to define a problem to work on in therapy, but twice in the first 15 minutes of the initial interview, she mentioned that her parents had put her sister through college and not her.

THERAPIST: Can we go back to how hard it must have been for you to have your parents put your sister through college and not you?

PATIENT: That was then, that's not now.

THERAPIST: Can you see that you try to push me away when I ask about things that seem to be quite sad ones or angry ones, and you don't seem to want to go there. Does it seem so to you?

PATIENT: Yeah. [*Chewing her gum*] Yeah. Look, I just don't know where you want me to go with my feelings. I've told you, I'm very angry. I don't know what more I can do than that.

THERAPIST: Hmm. I wonder if there's more to it than just anger?

PATIENT: I don't understand why we're focusing on this.

THERAPIST: It seems like it's very hard for you to examine feelings.

PATIENT: I can't see how much deeper you can get. [*Still chewing her gum*]

THERAPIST: [*I gently tried to see if I could make any human contact with her or reach any agreement.*] How is it being with doctors?

PATIENT: Oh, I hate doctors. They're so arrogant. They poke you, they prod you. You know, I was at this doctor's when I had these bruises all over my body, and they didn't care about me.

THERAPIST: So I must feel like I'm poking and prodding, and like I don't care.

PATIENT: Oh, I don't know. [*Then, in a moment of insight*] You can see I screw around, ya know.

THERAPIST: Yeah, you seem to want to dance away, like a rock skipping over the water. [*I thought she had begun to see her defensiveness, but my direct response just angered her.*]

PATIENT: I don't know what you want of me. And I don't know why you focus on these little insignificant things like my parents' sending my sister to college instead of me.

I dropped the interpretative approach and switched to support. I asked about her bruises, which she said had appeared all over her body "with no explanation" (suggesting dissociative episodes). But we went no further because she dropped out after this session.

A few months later, I got a phone call from her about an insurance form. She needed money badly because she had been to many medical doctors since she had seen me. I asked her if she would speak with me for a moment. I said, "You know, I felt bad about our session, because I felt you didn't get the help you wanted." She replied, "Oh, no, no, no. I just thought you were dealing with these little details, and I just needed a general picture. I was so confused. I just couldn't understand where you were taking me." I responded, "No, I think it was *I* who didn't give you what you needed. It's our responsibility, the therapist's responsibility, to provide the kind of help that you can use."

She seemed surprised and appreciative of this. I wished her well, and we ended on a warm note. I was trying to do some reparative work because I was so concerned about her. Today, I would be much less active and more focused on building a bond during the initial session. When I did switch to supportive interventions, it was too late, and I was not able to engage her. Not only were the defenses not relinquished, the case was lost. There are some people who cannot respond to active focused techniques. This woman was one. She needed help first to build an alliance and to define a problem on her terms.

SUMMARY

This chapter focuses on the interventions that can assist patients in relinquishing defensive patterns. With an active and involved therapist stance, anxieties are regulated as defenses are given up and replaced by more adaptive responses. The interventions include the following:

- Identification of the negative consequences of the defenses
- Identification of the secondary gain of the defensive pattern
- Identification of the origin versus the maintenance of the defensive pattern
- Eliciting grief over the losses caused by the defensive pattern
- If no grief, assessing and building self-compassion
- If no self-compassion, assessing and building relationship and identity
- Repetition until the pattern is clear to the patient

CHAPTER 6

First Major Objective of Affect Restructuring: Affect Experiencing

I can wade Grief
Whole Pools of it
I'm used to that
But the least push of Joy
Breaks up my feet—
and I tip—drunken—
Let no Pebble—smile—
'Twas the New Liquor—
That was all!
　　　　　　Emily Dickinson

INTRODUCTION TO AFFECT RESTRUCTURING

People have a terrible time understanding and handling emotion. Some, like Emily Dickinson, can "wade grief" but are uneasy with joy. Others can allow a certain level of joy in their lives but remain strangers to grief; they attend funerals with dry eyes or avoid them altogether. Still others are completely blocked to the experience of any emotion and exist like the living dead, cut off from the richness of their feeling life. It is the goal of this stage of the therapy process to give patients a taste of this "new liquor," unbalancing or overwhelming as it may feel at first, so that they may begin to live more fully.

We did not begin our life so inhibited. The newborn cries lustily when something is desired and continues the wailing as the mother tries out a variety of things until she gets it right. At birth we have the full capacity to let people know when something is wanted. We also naturally scream in protest when something does not suit us. How is it that so many adults cannot find their voice? As infants, we spontaneously smiled and reached out to our caretakers. We naturally gazed deep into the eyes of those who held us and cooed. How tragic it is that so many of us have had that natural openness twisted into shyness, withdrawal, or closing off of the depths of ourselves to others. Toddlers are enormously curious, inquisitive, and exploratory of the world around them. Small children play during most of their waking hours. What happens to that joy and excitement? How is it that initiative is so often destroyed? Two-year-olds spontaneously stomp their feet and say *no*. They have definite limits and feelings about things. Why do so many adults have difficulty with limit setting? How do people learn so thoroughly to feel ashamed of saying "that's exciting" or "no, I don't want to"?

The first major objective of affect restructuring is to alter what is in essence maladaptive social learning by helping patients become comfortable with the experience of their full range of adaptive emotions. As crucial as it is, however, the process of reawakening our feeling life is one of the most confusing, confounding, and amorphous subjects facing human beings. Affect is at the core of our being and our daily functioning. Affects are our motivators; our actions are based largely on what we feel. Yet affects are misunderstood, poorly described, and ill-managed. The result is that, all too often, we do not control our feelings; they control us.

The heart of this short-term affect-regulating model is the alteration of the emotional responding that underlies pathology. *Nothing is more central to psychotherapeutic process than the modulation of affects and drives.* Certainly, cognition plays a vital role and shares the stage, but affects have been too long ignored and devalued as a source of change. Our field is just beginning to understand how to work with these long-neglected phenomena.

Whereas the defense-restructuring stage focuses primarily on the intellectual task of identifying behavior patterns and serves only to identify and label affect, the affect-restructuring stage involves exposing patients to specific feelings and to increase their experience of affect. This step is followed by a facilitation of the integration of cognitive and affective understanding to guide interpersonal expressions and wants and needs. Affect restructuring is the process of separating the negative *self-inhibiting* or *self-attacking affects* from the experience and expression of *adaptive, activating affects*. This chapter focuses on the first step, which is the experiencing of affect.

Affect experiencing refers to the full experiencing of hidden feelings in their pure form in fantasy (i.e., the use of emotionally laden mental imagery to allow a sublimated and contained form of catharsis). The goal is to desensitize the *conflicted feelings*, which are the conditioned inhibitory affects (e.g., anxiety, guilt, shame, pain) that have become associated with the experiencing of adaptively oriented drives and affects. I have discussed elsewhere that this objective can be understood as a phobic avoidance paradigm; we might think of these reactions as "internal affect phobias." Such affect phobias require repeated imaginal exposures to the avoided inner affective response until that experience of feeling is desensitized, that is, until that affect can be experienced without fear, guilt, or shame (McCullough, 1991b). Affect restructuring begins with the patient experiencing previously avoided feeling to discover *why* the feelings are avoided and to provide exposure to what was avoided.

The experiencing of affect gives patients a chance to come into greater contact with themselves: to find out what they feel about things, what they like and dislike, and what they want and don't want. One extreme example is a woman who had had no awareness of feeling in her body for 57 years: the Woman with Butterfly Feelings. When I asked her to attend to her body and attempt to identify emotional reactions, she was at a complete loss for many weeks. She insisted that she was "dead from the neck down." Then, during one session she suddenly blurted out, "I have a little flutter in my stomach, like a butterfly flapping its wings. Is that a feeling?" That was the first opening into her awareness of bodily responses! Although her process was slow by some standards, after 20 months of treatment, with laborious work on the restructuring of numerous rigid and lifelong defenses, she was able to feel angry and to stand up for herself for the first time in her life. She also was able to feel sad and cry, as well as to find some sources of joy in her life, experiences she had not had since early childhood.

The feelings we encounter most frequently in clinical work are grief, anger, affects associated with attachment (including the wish for closeness and the ability to be open and vulnerable with another person), affects associated with sexual desire and excitement (enthusiasm), and joy. (These families of emotions are presented in much detail in chapter 7.) Desensitization of the phobic inhibition of feeling involves freeing the adaptive and activating affects from the constraints of debilitating self-attack, inhibition, or restraint.

In each core conflict, the therapist needs to consider, not one isolated feeling that is inhibited, but how one or a combination of several blocked affects contributes to the problem. A range of feelings needs examination to see if the patient is able to express them appropriately and comfortably (without self-attack or inhibition of anxiety, guilt, or shame). This model explicitly focuses on the freeing up and reintegration of *each of the major categories of affects*. This task calls for a comprehensive theory of affects or emotions in which to place these clinical phenomena and to guide interventions for affect restructuring.

The ego psychologists Ruben Blanck and Gertrude Blanck (1974) also emphasized the need for a comprehensive theory of emotion. They were dismayed that "even at the end, Freud... said that the aggressive drive was considered ... as hostility or rage, with *destructive* aims only" (p. 33). Blanck and Blanck summarized their view as follows:

> Psychoanalysis does not yet have an internally consistent drive theory. Clarification of drive theory promises to pave the way toward evolution of an adequate affect theory as well as toward clarification of energic concepts. Certainly drive theory is ripe for reconsideration. (1974, p. 31)

In my quest for a theory that offered clarity to human emotional functioning, I reviewed, in addition to Tomkins's work, the work of other emotion theorists in some detail, including Richard Lazarus (1991), Dahl (1978, 1991), Plutchik (1962, 1984), Jeremy Safran and Leslie Greenberg (1991), Ekman (1984, 1992a, 1992b), and Izard (1990). All make specific valuable contributions to the understanding of affective life and overlap in reassuring ways; each also sheds light in different areas of the darkness. Tomkins's model is the most comprehensive, however, and makes several distinctions that I consider to be crucial. Following Darwin's "The Expression of the Emotions in Man and Animals" (1920), Tomkins sees the evolutionary significance of emotion, as do many others, *as a basic motivational system.* Tomkins also describes in detail *the relationship of drives to affects,* the magnification of affects and its contribution to pathology (i.e., script theory), and *defensive versus adaptive use of affects.*[1]

First, Tomkins's affect theory carefully explains the motivational contributions of and relationships between drives, affect, and pain. Second, although Tomkins does not use the term *defensive,* he does discuss what he calls "pseudo-emotions" or "backed-up affects" that "stand in" for other emotions (e.g., 1962, 1978). He provides countless examples of destructive "nuclear scripts" (or core conflict formulations) in which affect is used defensively (e.g., 1978).

In this book, I incorporate Tomkins's affect theory into Malan's model for the functioning of the impulse–feeling pole of the Triangle of Conflict. Tomkins provides an exhaustive analysis of each category of affect plus a detailed theory about the psychological role of each affect. In addition, Tomkins sees the role of affect as shaping personality and culture. Tomkins's description of the interplay of the drives and affects (described in this chapter) is the most accurate representation of human emotional functioning, from healthy to pathological, that I have encountered.

THE AFFECT THEORY OF SILVAN TOMKINS

Tomkins has been described by Donald Nathanson as "the American Einstein, that sort of genius whose work was so far ahead of its time that it simply could not be understood when it first appeared." Nathanson (1992) explained that although Tomkins's affect theory has influenced thinkers worldwide, Tomkins wrote in a "dense prose style requiring far deeper study and an attention span far longer than that usually required by even the most difficult theoretical work" (p. 28). As described in chapter 1 of this book, Tomkins posits three systems of emotion: pain, drives, and affects (see Table 6.1). Pain is a signal system for danger. Drives are innate programs for transport in and out of the body (breathing, eating, bladder and bowel function, sexual drive, and to some extent, social responsivity). Affects are biologically endowed mechanisms to analogically amplify or inhibit the drives.

---

[1]Greenberg and Safran (1987) also acknowledge defensive use of emotion, but they do not give it a central role in pathology or therapeutic change.

To oversimplify, all but one of the drives arise in the hypothalamus in both mammals and reptiles. Affects and the one remaining drive (social responsivity, or the propensity for attachment) arise in the subcortical limbic system, a facet of brain organization found only in mammals. For locus of attachment behavior, see Thomas Insel (1992) and Edward Halgren (1992). For locus of affects, see Halgren (1992), Michael George and his colleagues (1995), and LeDoux (1992).

Within the affect system, Tomkins identified two positive affects (interest–excitement and enjoyment–joy), one neutral (surprise–startle), and six negative affects (fear–terror, anger–rage, distress–anguish, shame–humiliation, contempt–disgust, and dissmell).[2] Indeed, the major theorists of emotion (e.g., Ekman, 1992a; Izard, 1990; Lazarus, 1991; Plutchik 1962, 1984) show a reassuring overlap in five or six of these major categories of emotion. "There is robust, consistent evidence of a universal facial expression for anger, fear, enjoyment, sadness, and disgust" (Ekman, 1992b, p. 176). With the addition of pain and the drives, which include sexual desire and attachment, Tomkins's model provides a comprehensive and widely corroborated categorization of the range of human emotional responding.[3]

TABLE 6.1
Tomkins's Three-System Model of Emotion

Pain (Signal system)	Drives (Transport system)	Affects (Motivational system)
Pain (danger)	Breathing	Interest–excitement
	Eating	Enjoyment–joy
	Drinking	(surprise–startle)[a]
	Urination	Fear–terror
	Defecation	Distress–anguish (grief, sadness)
	Sexual desire	Anger–rage
	(Social responsivity	Shame–humiliation
	or attachment)	Contempt–disgust
		Dissmell[b]

Note. Where is love? According to Tomkins, interest–excitement is the affect in romantic love and in the choosing of a career. This affect supports attraction. Enjoyment–joy is the affect in committed love, supporting bonding and satisfaction. It also supports long-term career satisfaction.
[a]Determined by Ekman to be a reflex.
[b]Recent research by Tomkins distinguished this affect from contempt and disgust, but in the clinical setting, this distinction is not as salient as in other settings.

[2]When one considers the ratio of our endowment of negative to positive affects (i.e., about 3:1), we can see what we are up against. Evolution has prepared us to be responsive in twice as many negative as positive ways. We therapists have our work cut out for us. As one Mets fan said, there's more Mets than Yankees in all of us; maybe that's why the very human and chronically losing baseball team had such appeal.

[3]Tomkins's affect theory has been somewhat revised and updated by both Izard

The Interaction of Drives and Affects

An even greater contribution than the itemized categories of affect is Tomkins's description of *the manner in which these three systems of emotion (affects, drives, pain) interact,* providing a powerful explanatory system for the basis of psychopathology. Tomkins (1962, 1963) postulated that affects constitute the primary motivational system. Affects provide our experiences with their positive or negative valence, forming our preferences. Furthermore, the connections that are learned through experience can be the basis of healthy adaptive functioning or of pathology. *The theory of change in the present therapy is based on Tomkins's premise that affective connections undergird both adaptive functioning and psychopathology.* If affects are our primary motivational system, psychotherapy must impact the full range of affective associations so that maladaptive responding can be replaced by more adaptive responding. Let us consider how that might work clinically.

If we study Table 6.1, we may begin to imagine how such maladaptive and adaptive reactions develop. If the affect interest–excitement or enjoyment–joy becomes associated with sexual desire, sexual desire is amplified. But if the affect shame–humiliation becomes associated with sexual desire, the desire is diminished. If the affect anger–rage becomes associated with sexual desire, there may even be a perversion of the desire into some defensive form of sexualized aggression. Consider the person who has been raped or sexually abused. We can imagine that several negative affects may have become associated with sexual responding, all with potentially deleterious effects. The memory of such situations could elicit pain, fear–terror, anger–rage, shame–humiliation, disgust–contempt, or distress–anguish. In short, every negatively valenced affect could potentially become associated with sexual arousal under sufficiently adverse circumstances. In this model, a blunted sexual response would need to be desensitized (i.e., each of the negatively valenced affects needs to become *disassociated* from the sexual response, and positive affective associations need to replace them). In extreme cases, this task requires a lot of work. The model provides a pathway of how to work, however, which is highly focused and can be submitted to empirical examination.

Consider how the affects might become further associated with the drives. If the drive for breathing becomes associated with fear, it can contribute to an inhibited response such as hyperventilation (e.g., Fensterheim, 1994). Relaxation training and associating positive feelings with the intake of oxygen can replace or reciprocally inhibit the association of breathing with anxiety.

(1990) and Ekman (1992a, 1992b), but it remains essentially intact. My presentation in Table 6.1 includes modifications on the basis of more recent research. These modifications have to do with two controversial categories of emotion. First is the surprise–startle response, which Ekman's research now suggests is more of an orienting reflex than an affect. This is consonant with my clinical experience as well, and I have chosen not to use surprise–startle as one of the major affect categories to focus on in clinical work. Second is the distinction between contempt, disgust, and dissmell, which at this writing is less necessary for therapeutic work. It seems sufficient to recognize the "shaming" affects that are directed toward others as opposed to the self.

Eating behavior shows similar patterns. If eating becomes associated with shame or fear, it can contribute to the emergence of an eating disorder. Although there is a genetic contribution to alcoholism, the association of enjoyment–joy with the ingestion of alcohol certainly is an additional reinforcer that is learned and relearned over time. The attempt by alcohol counselors to break that affectively positive association and inhibit drinking by increasing the association to distress–anguish is one of the greatest challenges of the field. At present, this is not easily achieved in alcoholism treatment. The clinician must stand by, often watching several relapses occur. Eventually, the natural environment may provide sufficient distress–anguish in the form of "hitting bottom" that some alcoholics are able to learn to inhibit their drinking. Parenthetically, hitting bottom can be thought of as the influence of nurture (learning) on nature (biologically based addiction).

On the most fundamental level, therapists constantly deal with the affects associated with attachment to self and others. Whether we think about it explicitly or not, therapy attempts to alter the association of the negative affects (pain, anger, distress, fear, shame) with attachment and increase both interest and enjoyment in self and others. Reducing shame and embarrassment associated with tender feelings (or even with the word *tender*) becomes basic to enhancing adaptive interpersonal functioning. Affect is the medium through which the bonds of attachment are either enhanced or stultified. Affect is the soil in which the bonds of attachment to self or others either grow or die.

Tomkins emphasized that the affects are more powerful forces than the drives. He argued that drives are far less powerful than we believed. For example, he pointed out how anxiety can make the sexual drive a finicky "paper tiger" (1981, p. 322). Although at first this statement may seem counterintuitive, after a moment of reflection, it makes sense. Think of the number of sexual problems encountered in society when the "inhibiting" affect of anxiety, shame–guilt, or pain becomes associated with sexual feelings. This so-called powerful drive can be astonishingly easily inhibited. The same is true of aggression. Freud posited this as the other "bestial" impulse that we need to restrain through civilization. But when shame or fear becomes associated with the voicing of wants or needs, how easily human wishes can become inhibited and that voice silenced. Drives, Tomkins said, only appear to cause us trouble. It is the "magnified affects" attached to the drives that propel them in a positive or negative direction.

Freud suggested that all such primitive intense emotion made human nature bestial. In contrast, I suggest that only some variants of human nature are bestial and are caused by genetic vulnerability and/or aberrant socialization, resulting in the anguish of disconnection (e.g., the rapist, the mass murderer). Certainly, primitive emotion is not our natural adaptive state when things go relatively well for us genetically or developmentally. For such anguished individuals who spread their enormous pain to others, this bestial potential likely was acquired either as a result of harsh demands imposed by caretakers (abuse) or the lack of sufficient or appropriate forms of human contact (neglect–abandonment) when basic needs were not met.[4] *To the extent that such characteristics are acquired through learning,* these hyperbolic emotions are not our endowment for meeting adaptive wants and needs, but rather the perversion that happens *when adaptive wants and needs are not met.* Rather than reflecting "human nature," they represent an extreme perversion of human nature—often as a result of inhuman treatment from others. For patients who are otherwise moderately well functioning (above 50 on the GAF), the extremely intense and maladaptive forms of affect should be immediately considered as candidates for defense-based behaviors, or *defensive emotions,* which I describe in detail in chapter 7.

Under certain conditions, defensive affects can know no bounds. As Tomkins says, there can be unlimited "magnification" when traumatic circumstances are repeated, even in otherwise well-functioning individuals (1978). We all have our breaking points. When anger or the pain of longing becomes associated with the blunting of wants and needs, how perverted and sometimes sadistic we can become in our strivings! Under normal circumstances, these behaviors are not human nature at all; they are the angry and anguished (defensive) representations of our desperately unmet longing for love or recapitulations of old trauma. Hell hath no fury like the adult child who was once scorned and abused. Sometimes such anguished and enraged individuals have not had the experiences in human connectedness necessary to temper their primitive emotion. When torment and anguish give rise to rage in a person lacking a component of human compassion or reflective thought, the rage can flare into sadistic and boundless acting out.

Other examples of human "emotion gone wrong" in daily psychotherapy practice include the rages of patients with borderline personality disorder. Is such rage to be categorized as adaptive assertion? Hardly! The rage is in large part defensive against grief and longing. We are becoming increasingly more sophisticated in the field of psychology in recognizing in such individuals the syndromes of posttraumatic stress disorder or devastating neglect. Pain, anguish, and distress give rise to an acting out that may look like anger but is really a defensive combination of negative emotions including unbearable distress and longings of "love gone hungry." These people are wild in their pain, and the angry screams originate in anguish. Borderline personality disorder is a severe but often treatable condition involving many defensive affects; such interpersonally distancing expressions of rage often conceal longing or grief that cannot be borne.

These emotional themes are portrayed in a hauntingly beautiful Norwegian film, *The Pathfinder,* which describes an ancient saga passed down for over 1,000 years. The story depicts the warmth and closeness of a small family that was destroyed when savagely attacked by a bloodthirsty, nomadic tribe that the character called the Old Pathfinder describes as having

[4]When human contact is not available as a source of comfort, the substitutes can be many and varied. In extreme examples, the inflicting of pain on others, and the thrill of power it engenders, can be the only source of comfort available.

"left the bonds of humanity." Both extremes of the affective continuum can be seen in this film: human devotion and tenderness and worse-than-bestial violence and brutality. The extremes of human connectedness and human alienation are also poignantly portrayed. The young hero, the Pathfinder-to-be, must overcome his own rage and pain over the brutal murder of his family to preserve his human connectedness and not repeat the acting out of the inhuman nomadic tribe. Today, Palestine and Israel struggle with the same issues of how to separate healthy assertion from defensive rage.

To a greater or lesser degree, it is precisely the "leaving the bonds of humanity" that we struggle with in the depths of psychopathology. The more severe the pathology, the greater the damage to trust and human connectedness. The main goal of this affect-focused treatment, therefore, is to reintegrate the emotions into harmony with each other and, ultimately, to bring each individual into harmony with the therapist and others in their world: to draw them closer within the bonds of humanity. *Human relatedness is a major focus of the interventions that assist in affect experiencing.* Affect has the power to build or break those bonds.

The Crucial Distinction Between Defensive and Adaptive Functions of the Affects

Before time and energy in therapy are spent on the desensitization of a phobia concerning a particular affect, it is crucial that primary, or adaptive, affective experience be distinguished from defensive affect. This topic is discussed in earlier chapters, but it is of such importance that it bears mentioning again. Tomkins (1962) discussed how one feeling can "stand in" for another and how "pseudo-affect," or backed-up affect, is *most of the affect we see expressed interpersonally.* But apart from the work of these and a few other authors, defensive feelings have largely been overlooked. Yet defensive feeling makes up much of what we call psychopathology.

Defensive affect is affect used to avoid something else, such as thoughts or other, more conflicted feelings. Familiar examples are the adolescent who angrily acts out anger to conceal grief, the abused wife who weeps piteously to conceal rage, and the grumpy and irritable man who thus avoids tenderness. Of course, there are many occasions in life when one is not allowed to express oneself openly, and defensive action is appropriate or useful. Not all defensive uses of affect are destructive. An exasperated homeroom teacher may bring an unruly class to order more rapidly by bursting into tears than by yelling at them. Each defensive behavior (whether thoughts, emotions, or actions) is an attempt to cope with some difficult aspect of the environment. The issue is whether the defensive action is constructive or destructive to the individual and whether the individual has an appropriate outlet for the underlying emotion that is aroused. If the person does not, the thwarted motivational response can find outlet in symptoms, if only mild or transitory depression, anxiety, or insomnia.

The therapist must carefully discern, for every emotion that is presented, whether it is a primary drive or affect (in the service of an adaptive goal) or a defensive drive or affect, which is a form of avoidance. Some affects are used to amplify experience (I/F pole), some to temper or inhibit experience (A pole), and some to disguise experience (D pole). Drives can be used defensively as well. How common it is for sexual behavior to disguise a longing for closeness, or for eating or sleeping to be used to avoid feelings of grief. If such basic distinctions are not made, how can we effectively treat our patients? Chapter 8 describes defensive versions of each emotion in detail.

PREPARATION FOR AFFECT EXPERIENCING

Therapist's Stance in Affect Experiencing: Shared Experience
THE REAL THERAPEUTIC RELATIONSHIP

In contrast to defense restructuring, in which the therapist points out the patient's defenses, in affect experiencing there is greater personal intimacy and greater emotional challenge to the therapist. Although much skill is required in defense restructuring, the therapist is not as personally on the line. The therapist's own defenses are part of the process, but affect emitted by the patient can be contagious. In the process of coaching a patient in affect experiencing, the therapist, unless massively defended, inevitably experiences some degree of the affect as well.

The more in touch, involved, and evolved the therapist, the better, as long as it is enlightened involvement rather than overinvolvement for the therapist's personal gratification. The involvement must be empathic rather than sympathetic. It must always be the patient's "turn." Therapists often are drawn to the field of psychotherapy because of pain, and as we learn to become therapists, we may struggle to find our own needs and cures. We, too, need "turns," but not from our patients. Once we have made some sense of our own suffering, we may be better able to guide our patients. Our own journeys toward self-understanding should never be at the patient's expense.

SHARING FEELING WITH THE PATIENT

One goal of affect experiencing is to share the patient's experience. If the patient tells about an infuriating (or heartbreaking or wonderful) incident, the therapist should try to feel how infuriating or sad or thrilling the experience might be. These shared emotions may or may not be made explicit, depending on the needs of the patient, but they heighten the empathic understanding. Some patients can resonate to and deeply feel an unspoken but strongly empathic experience. Other patients strenuously ward off this type of therapist response. In the latter case, it is important to explore the patient's capacity to acknowledge any shared feelings and the patient's defenses against experiencing them.

There must be interactive growth in emotional connectedness between the therapist and the patient. This process involves the emotional touching of one person by another. The therapist must be involved enough to be real (especially when the early-life caretakers were distant or uninvolved) and distant enough for the patient to feel safe and to allow autonomy to develop. How does one transcend this dichotomy to find the optimal blend? One rule of thumb is to acknowledge the shared feelings, while sometimes in the same sentence, making explicit the boundaries or the limits in the relationship:

> *As you speak, it brings up sadness in me as well, but my sadness must be only a small representation of what you must feel.*
>
> *We have both worked hard to reduce the suffering in your life, and there are strong positive feelings on both sides. Therapy is a safe place to discuss our feelings, positive as well as negative, for as you know, there are clear boundaries. We use only words here.*

TRANSFERENCE ISSUES

The predominant issue in affect experiencing is the conflict involved in being so open and vulnerable. In some patients, this elicits tremendous shame. They feel foolish, stupid, "jerky": a range of pejorative terms. Patients are afraid that their openness will elicit ridicule, devaluation, or humiliation from the therapist, which inevitably leads to a struggle between opening up and distancing. Some patients feel annihilation anxiety: that being so exposed and so vulnerable will lead to their being destroyed in some unfathomable way. For many patients, closeness is a metaphor for psychological death. The terror that is experienced by such patients as they open to the therapist gives the impression of a life-or-death struggle. The budding feelings of trust, long ago destroyed, are once again trying to emerge from the parched earth like tiny sprouts reaching for the sun. The empathic connection is crucial to permitting such timid (if not terrorized) reactions a safe and protected place to grow. At such moments, I often feel that a birth—or a rebirth—is taking place, as life struggles to push itself through the obstacles and the pain.

COUNTERTRANSFERENCE ISSUES

Therapists' reactions to the experiencing of deep feeling in patients are a large part of what was meant by the traditional notion of countertransference. Sharing of affect inevitably touches the therapist's own issues. Affect is contagious, and as intense emotions are generated, the therapist is emotionally challenged in many ways. There can be a tendency to identify too strongly with the patient's reactions. When therapists find themselves empathizing too strongly, that is a possible signal of dynamic issues rearing their head. There is danger that therapists will lose the objective position and will intervene on the basis of their needs more than those of the patient. On the other hand, the contagion of the patient's issues can lead the therapist to lighten up or move away from the deep experiencing of emotion.

This is one of the more common therapist responses my research group has found when examining videotaped sessions. At the moment when the patient is approaching a groundswell of deep feeling, the therapist is observed saying something that leads the patient into intellectualization. In the next moment, the affective richness is lost.

It is not realistic to expect therapists to have all their affective conflicts resolved. Our issues inevitably impact on our patients. In the best of circumstances, however, we should be able to recognize and control our reactions so that they do not adversely control us or our patients.

Anxiety Regulation in Affect Experiencing: Desensitization of Conflicted Feelings

The main goal of anxiety regulation during affect experiencing is the desensitization of adaptive feeling. Desensitization does not mean the reduction of the adaptive affects but rather the reduction of the *anxieties associated with* those adaptive affects. Desensitization is the breaking of the conditioned association between the self-thwarting emotions and the adaptive emotions: the hold of shame on sexuality or assertion; the inhibiting effects of anxiety on joy or excitement; the crushing effects of anxiety, pain, or anguish on the experience of attachment. Desensitization requires exposure, and it will be described further.

A secondary goal of anxiety regulation is to keep the patient's moment-to-moment experience of the conflict within manageable limits so that the exposure to the feeling can continue. As long as the experiencing of conflicted affect is proceeding (i.e., the patient is proceeding through memories or reflections that are affect-laden and somewhat anxiety-laden), the exposure process is under way. It is when patients cannot continue and complain that it is too difficult or that they feel that they have gone dead that anxiety regulation is necessary. The therapist must step in to explore the conflicts (anxieties, shame, pain) until the patient has more control and is able to go back to the affect experience.

THERAPIST: You've just pulled away from the joy (or sadness or anger or tenderness) that you were feeling as you described (that situation) with (that specific person). Can you sense that?
PATIENT: Yes, now that you mention it . . . I guess I did.
THERAPIST: What is the most uncomfortable part of that for you?

This gentle process of exploring anxieties constitutes a "graded exposure" to the feelings. The model presented in this book is analogous to Wolpe's (1958) graded hierarchy of "successive approximations." In this type of behavior therapy, instead of putting the patient directly on the elevator, the patient is encouraged first to think about being on an elevator, until the anxiety subsides. Next, the patient might stand 100 yards away from an elevator, until the anxiety subsides. Slowly, the phobia decreases. In successive approximations to affect experiencing, the patient is exposed to graded degrees of a specific affect until the anxiety subsides. Then, a little more affect experiencing is encouraged. I think of the process as successive approximations to the ability to feel once again.[5]

INTERVENTIONS TO ASSIST IN THE EXPERIENCING OF AFFECT

This section describes interventions that can be helpful in assisting the patient to experience previously warded-off emotions. This list of interventions is not intended to be exhaustive but to spur therapists' imaginations in helping patients to achieve these objectives.

- Verbally labeling emotions
- Describing the physiological experience of the emotion
- Guided imagery: accessing emotion in fantasy
- Desensitization: regulation of anxieties by graded exposure to feeling
- Containment of affective experience in fantasy: avoidance of acting out the impulse
- Repetition of scenes until desensitization is accomplished

Verbally Labeling Emotions

First, the affect must be labeled verbally (e.g., I feel angry, sad, aroused, joyful, loving). The patient must be able to give the inner experience a clear, unambiguous label and to distinguish one feeling from the other. This can be accomplished by repeatedly pointing out the experience and helping the patient to put a label on it.

THERAPIST: You have made two fists with your hands. What do you think you might be feeling?
PATIENT: Anger? Is it anger? Yes . . . it is. I'm angry at him! [*Many people have trouble labeling anger correctly.*]
THERAPIST: Your face looks somewhat different now. What are you feeling inside?
PATIENT: I don't know.
THERAPIST: Well, take a minute to see if you can become aware of even a small bit of emotion.
PATIENT: Huh . . . now that I think about it, I do feel a little sad.

In more severe cases, patients have great difficulty discerning any form of inner emotional experience. Presumably, as children such people had no one to notice or label their sadness or to acknowledge anger, tenderness, or joy. Such individuals are tragically out of contact with themselves and with

---

[5]Laws of learning have been demonstrated to hold for internal stimuli as well as for external behavioral stimuli (for which desensitization has typically been empirically examined). Cautela (1966) originated the application of such principles to internal, or covert, processes. Continuing systematic research is needed to examine further this apparent similarity.

others, as well, for is it not through shared feeling that we make contact with one another? The resulting degree of loneliness and confusion is often enormous. In such cases, the therapist may need to label the experience, in a tentative manner, so that the patient has some guidance in exploring his or her inner life. In the case of the Woman with Butterfly Feelings, in the following example, the therapist repeatedly had to point out, inquire, and encourage her to label her experience.

EXAMPLE OF DIFFICULTY IDENTIFYING AFFECTS:
THE WOMAN WITH BUTTERFLY FEELINGS

THERAPIST: Can you tell me what you are experiencing right now?

PATIENT: No, I'm not feeling anything.

THERAPIST: Your face looked sad. Do you have any awareness of that?

PATIENT: No, none at all.

THERAPIST: Well, that was a sad topic you were discussing. I wonder if you might be feeling sad?

PATIENT: Yeah, it was, but I don't feel it.

THERAPIST: Isn't it poignant that your words convey sadness, and your face conveys sadness, but you have no sensation of feeling?

PATIENT: Yeah! I feel so dead inside.

THERAPIST: So I will continue to point out when you show certain emotions on your face, and we'll work together to help you become aware of your inner experience. Are you feeling something right now?

PATIENT: No.

THERAPIST: Your voice sounded angry. Do you think you might be irritated at me?

PATIENT: If I am, I'm just barely aware of it.

THERAPIST: Okay, so let's keep looking at this, so that your awareness of it can increase; you have told me you have real trouble knowing what you are feeling.

After several repetitions of this type of intervention, patients often begin to attend better to their inner experience. If there is one angry (or grief-laden or joyful) incident in a patient's life, the therapist can use this to help reacquaint the patient with his or her emotional responses.

EXAMPLE OF REMEMBERING GRIEF:
THE WOMAN WITH BUTTERFLY FEELINGS

THERAPIST: It may be difficult to pinpoint sad feelings now, but have you ever been extremely sad, or have you ever cried really hard about losing someone?

PATIENT: Oh, yes, but when I was much younger.

THERAPIST: Could you tell me about one of those times? Who comes to mind right now? And can we pay special attention to how your body felt when the sadness was strong, so that you will be able to identify it easier in the future?

PATIENT: I can remember when my grandmother died. I was sobbing so hard,

I had to gulp to get air. And my chest was heaving. I haven't had feelings like that for over 50 years!

EXAMPLE OF USING PAST FEELINGS TO IDENTIFY CURRENT FEELINGS: THE FERRYMAN

This excerpt is from the first session, when this patient was unable to feel anger at his mother.

THERAPIST: So you don't feel angry at all now? Have you *ever* had an incident in your life when you were really furious at someone?

PATIENT: Only once, when I was 10 years old. But I remember it like it was yesterday. I stood up to the class bully and we got in a fight. He had been picking on me all year, and I finally had enough. I really let him have it!

THERAPIST: Do you remember how your body felt when you were the maddest at him?

PATIENT: I sure do! I was exploding inside. Boiling! Full of energy! I wanted to throttle him!

If the patient cannot remember experiencing the emotion consciously, a description of how the emotion feels in others can be a starting point, along with some teaching of what can be looked for and a *constant exploration and amplification of the patient's internal response to situations in which strong emotional responding is indicated.*

Physiological Experience of the Emotion

The patient needs to describe the experience of the feeling physiologically, in terms of bodily reactions and sensations. Although facial expression is a major way to distinguish the different emotions, one generally cannot see one's own face, and we have to rely on inner signals. One of the major problems in emotional experiencing is *mislabeling of one's inner experience.* If asked to describe anger, patients say "butterflies in my stomach" or "a knot in my chest." Neither of these is correctly labeled anger, but anxiety. The therapist must be clear about what labels tend to go with what specific emotions. Although individuals vary somewhat in their idiosyncratic experience, there are some general guidelines for responding. The internal experience that can signal an adaptive affect is typically an energized flowing from inside to outside the body. For example, anger might be described as a buildup of energy or a wish to punch, lash out, set limits, or act in some way. Grief is often described as a welling up of tears or a desire to pour off the sad feelings through crying. Interest or excitement is the motivation to reach out and explore. Fear prompts us to run away or freeze. Joy is the gentle flowing of calm throughout the torso and out toward the limbs.

Tomkins refers to the drive system as a "transport system" that goes in and out of the body. It is interesting that adaptive drives also reflect this energized flowing. Some drives are represented by a flow from inside to outside the body: urination, defecation, orgasmic release. Other drives are represented by an energized flow from outside to inside the body: inhaling, drinking, eating. Attachment behavior may be a flow in both directions: reaching out to others as well as being cuddled and held close; the mother giving the breast milk, and the infant receiving it; the caretaking and being cared for. The drive for connection (to hold and be held, to give and receive) may be the most bidirectional of the drives. These are emotions on the I/F pole.

In contrast, anxiety-based and inhibitory reactions tend to have a pulling inward response, a withdrawal, or a tightening. The form of the response is not an outward flowing of energy but a tightening and constricting. Of course, the immobilizing paralysis of fear is a response that can be adaptive; however, this inwardly constricting reaction can become so pervasive and destructive that it thwarts adaptive functioning. One example follows, but the entire next chapter is devoted to detailed guidelines for the manifestations of each specific emotion. These inhibitory affects are represented on the A pole.

EXAMPLE OF DISTINGUISHING SADNESS FROM INHIBITION: THE MACHINE BUILDER

THERAPIST: How do you experience the sad feelings right now?

PATIENT: My throat is tight.

THERAPIST: Is that sadness or is it something else?

PATIENT: I guess that's me fighting the sadness.

THERAPIST: What would happen if you didn't tighten your throat?

PATIENT [*Pausing*]: I'd cry . . . so I guess I'm squeezing down the sadness.

THERAPIST: Can you pay attention to those sad feelings that the tightness is fighting?

PATIENT: Yeah, now I can feel it. Like waves through my body. I feel the pressure of the tears behind my eyes.

THERAPIST: Is there anything else you notice?

PATIENT: A feeling of heaviness in my chest, and, I just noticed this, the corners of my mouth feel pulled down. [*Tears begin to flow.*]

Here the therapist ideally should become silent to allow the patient to explore the new experience of sorrow. But if the patient has difficulty moving ahead, the therapist can encourage the patient to explore the images that emerge: *What images come with the sad feelings?*

Guided Imagery: Accessing Affect Through Fantasy

Experiential therapies have long used guided imagery procedures to enhance the experience of emotion. The present approach uses a form of guided imagery similar to Hanskarl Leuner's "guided affective imagery" (Leuner, 1969, 1977, 1978), in which specific scenes of interpersonal episodes and associated affects are imagined in the session. Particular attention should be paid to the quality, mode, and degree of emotional arousal that is felt during the imagery process to enhance the experience of the feeling in terms of the action tendencies. The patient is encouraged to fantasize how the feeling would be behaviorally expressed in the specific interpersonal relationship, while simultaneously experiencing as strong a physiological response as possible. Often the intense levels of experiencing are not possible at first, but even low levels of arousal in imagery can be effective in beginning behavioral changes. Subsequently, the therapist and patient can practice imaginal scenes with graded and increasing emotional intensity. Ultimately, the more exposures to the affective arousal, the freer the individual will be to function optimally, that is, to identify feelings and to reflect on the best course of action.

EXAMPLE: USING GUIDED IMAGERY TO INTENSIFY SORROW

THERAPIST: Are there any thoughts or images that come with that sorrow? Say whatever comes to mind.

PATIENT: Oh, it's my brother, Tommy. I remember the day he died.

THERAPIST: Where were you when you heard the news?

PATIENT: I was at home. I got a phone call. Oh, it's so painful to remember.

THERAPIST: What's the most painful part of that memory?

PATIENT: It's that he was always so reckless. He was driving too fast.

THERAPIST: How do you imagine him driving that night?

PATIENT: Gripping the wheel. Intense . . . pushing it . . . always pushing the needle too far into the red!

THERAPIST: I know you loved him very much. But it sounds like there is some anger too.

PATIENT: There's so much feeling I want to scream. I've never known what to do with it all. Why did he have to be so reckless!

THERAPIST: What would you want to say to him if he were here right now?

PATIENT: Why did you do it! Why didn't you take better care of yourself!

THERAPIST: You needed him to take care of himself for you!

PATIENT [*Crying*]: I did! I did!

BENIGN REGRESSION FACILITATED THROUGH GUIDED IMAGERY

Regression means to go back to an earlier or less mature level of functioning. One might wonder why we should encourage our patients to do that, but in fact it carries potential for healing. Balint (1968) helped distinguish between constructive and destructive forms of the process. *Malignant regression* leads to acting out of the impulse. In contrast, *benign regression* is a healing process because it can permit the patient "to go back to something primitive—to a point before the faulty development started, and discover a new better-suited way to respond" (p. 132). He called this process "regression for the sake of progression."

Balint gave an example of an emotionally constricted woman who had always wanted to do a somersault but had never dared to. "Why don't you try one?" he suggested. "Right here? Now?" she asked. "Of course," he replied. And so she did! On the floor of his office (p. 185). As Balint described it, this spontaneous, in vivo expression of feeling, accepted and shared with the therapist, led to her opening up emotionally and becoming increasingly more comfortable in her relationships. When sharing of feeling is possible, it is a major pathway to healing.

Not all such fantasized wishes are so easily gratified in therapy, however. The therapist and patient need to have a means of working with desires that cannot be safely acted out. Indeed, Balint generally discouraged regression that was acted out and, instead, advised that patients be gratified chiefly by understanding or recognition of their needs (1968, p. 187).

In long-term psychotherapy or psychoanalysis, regression occurs as a result of the patient's free association, which, coupled with the therapist's neutral stance, allows the patient increasingly to project or "transfer" onto the therapist certain aspects of the parents or significant others. Through the analysis of this "transference neurosis," the patient's original, conflicted defensive patterns can be seen. In behavioral terms, "stimulus generalization" occurs: The therapist is seen as similar to past figures. Also, "response generalization" occurs: The patient responds the same way to the therapist as to the past figures. Regression can be seen, therefore, as a response "overgeneralization" from past stimuli to present stimuli and makes possible the observation of behaviors that the patient might not be sufficiently aware of to describe. This is one path into the "unconscious" functioning or to the interpersonal "learning history" of the patient. Given that much of our behavior is motivated by circumstances that are long forgotten or outside of our awareness, regression can be a useful method to tap this important material.

The manner in which regression is elicited and handled differs in short-term dynamic psychotherapy, in which benign forms of regression are *actively encouraged* as well as facilitated by the patient's immersion into the experience with guided imagery. Such "passion recollected in tranquillity," is in service of the ego, or the growth of the self. The key distinction is that benign regression is analogous to a child psychiatrist's play therapy in which desires are sublimated in fantasy. In contrast, malignant regression is analogous to loss of control, to infantilization, and to enabling a patient to become too dependent on the therapist.

In short-term therapy, guided imagery provides a holding environment for any wish to be safely gratified while being shared by the therapist. This process resolves the Freud–Ferenczi controversy regarding how much gratification of the patient should be allowed by transcending the dichotomy of gratification versus abstinence. These active techniques permit *complete self-gratification, but contained in the patient's imagery.* Allowing regression to occur in this safe manner exposes a patient to more intense and primitive levels of emotion, which probably originated at an earlier and often preverbal developmental level. By actively guiding the patient to explore the images that emerge more deeply and affectively, the experience of early-thwarted wants and needs can be reawakened. The deepest needs and longings can be identified, validated, and experienced as fully as possible on an affective level. Abusive authority figures can be mercilessly murdered; one's lust can be fulfilled with whomever one pleases, however one pleases; and in fantasy, one can be held and caressed tenderly and lovingly by whomever and for as long as one wishes.

Of course, such imaginal experiences are *not ends in themselves.* (The goal is not to create schizoid disorders, with patients lost in autistic fantasy!) The use of imagery, although indeed gratifying in itself, is employed as a *means to an end*. It is vital for people to be conscious of such inner experiences, for we all have them. Feelings come unbidden as reactions to living. The more conscious we are of them, the more in control we are. These feelings and images help us recognize our deepest needs, desires, and frustrations. We need to acknowledge such desires, bear them, and learn how to respond to, and, as much as possible, fulfill them in realistic and adaptive ways.

Passion recollected in tranquillity provides the time and place to sort things out and decide on the proper course of action. For example, if one is furious at one's spouse or boss, it might be both relieving and clarifying to allow oneself to feel the full extent of rage that was elicited by the interaction. To experience that fury inwardly, under full control, provides the sanctuary to become fully conscious of what is most needed and to determine how best to correct the situation. In another situation, if one is intensely sexually aroused by someone other than one's partner, allowing the full exploration of that desire in fantasy can both provide some relief, at least in the short run, and lead to greater understanding about what might be missed, and longed for, in the partner. The fantasy of the desire itself is somewhat relieving, but the real relief results from the identification and implementation of a plan of appropriate action that will either achieve the best possible resolution or lead to acceptance that what is desired is not possible. In the short-term model, it is only after the affects are labeled and fully experienced physiologically and in fantasy (and well under control) that the therapist joins with the patient to generate a plan for action. (This step is further discussed in chapter 8.)

Long-term therapists are concerned that activity on the part of the short-term therapist limits the depth and quality of the regression: that the regression brought on early is not sufficient to heal as completely as the longer term version. In the practice of short-term treatment, however, a little regression can go a long way. Low levels of affective experiencing appear to have significant impacts on behavior. On the other hand, long-term approaches, in allowing deep regression, seem more likely than short-term approaches to elicit maladaptive dependency and *malignant* regression. Much research is needed on both methods to determine what forms of regression are the most healing for patients.

Mindless catharsis of emotion, venting, or acting out is never encouraged. It has been said that the emotional context is a dangerous context. Although this *can* be the case, emotional experiencing is dangerous only if it cannot be contained. If emotions are well contained (e.g., experienced in fantasy), this experience is the pathway to healing. Learning how to bear and contain the painful affects requires the dyad. To heal patients, therapists must be able to travel this road mindfully and skillfully.

Mere ventilation of feeling is not the point. Although there may be some relief that results in the short run from venting or complaining, this rarely resolves problems. The point of affective experience is to contain it long enough to understand the real need and decide on *a proper course of action* in real life.

Desensitization: Regulation of Anxieties by Graded Exposure to Primary Affect

Desensitization means exposing the patient to previously warded-off emotions (drives or affects) until there is no longer maladaptive conflict or self-attack (i.e., anxiety, guilt, shame, or pain) involved in the experiencing of these feelings. Psychodynamic theory has long talked about warded-off feelings, but little guidance was given to the clinician in terms of mechanisms for eradicating the warding-off process. Research on behavior therapy provides a useful model. The treatment for a phobic response is desensitization: exposure to the phobic stimulus *until the anxiety is altered in form or reduced* to normal limits. In behavior therapy treatments, the phobic stimulus could be snakes, taking tests, or driving across bridges. In the psychodynamic approach, the phobic stimulus is *internal* rather than *external*. The stimulus that is feared is *one's own emotional response*, not some external object or event. Patients often dread feeling (or expressing) anger, grief, tenderness, sexual desire, and as Emily Dickinson tells us, even joy. Affect experiencing has as its goal the process of desensitization and follows the same behavioral principles that can be observed in desensitization experiments.

After affective awareness has been enhanced, either through in vivo sharing of feelings with the therapist or through imagery procedures, it must be sustained long enough for desensitization to take place. The therapeutic interventions that promote desensitization involve moving back and forth from the experience of affects or drives (the impulse–feeling pole) to the thoughts and feelings that too severely inhibit those experiences (the anxiety pole). The goal is to regulate the level of inhibition, which means, by the process of desensitization, to *reduce the self-attacking anxieties* that have been associated with healthy emotional experience. This process constitutes a desensitization of adaptive feeling—a relearning of the patterns we were born with—and thus a recovering of the capacity to feel spontaneously.

Although individuals may attain insight into their passive responses to conflict through defense restructuring and even gain some motivation to change those defensive patterns, a "phobic avoidance" of affective responding is common, with the affect phobias or internal phobias maintained. The first major objective of affect restructuring is to alter what is, in essence, maladaptive social learning. The capacity for shame or guilt may be inborn, but what it becomes associated with is taught, to a large degree, by caretakers. When this social learning becomes restrictive, new, more adaptive learning needs to replace it.

Treatment techniques to accomplish desensitization of these affect phobias can take several forms. In the form called *flooding,* the phobic affective stimulus is presented in large doses until anxiety subsides (used in behavioral implosion procedures or anxiety-provoking confrontive approaches). In contrast, in this model the desensitization of anxiety attached to affect is not attempted in one massive dose, but rather by "reinforcing successive approximations" to feeling as in Wolpe's model. As a result of the defense analysis and the work linking and distinguishing the three poles of the Triangle of Conflict, the patient should also have some idea *why the affects are blocked* and *how harmful this is.* The cognitive groundwork has been laid, which should facilitate affect restructuring. In the anxiety-regulating form of short-term dynamic psychotherapy, *exposure to feeling is titrated* by the presentation of emotional images in small, manageable, but increasingly larger dosages that the patient can bear.

To begin the desensitization process of affect experiencing, the therapist should simply ask the patient to explore the feelings (i.e., relive the emotions in fantasy) related to a problematic situation as vividly and as intensely as the patient can bear at that time. The therapist can assess the process, encourage it, intensify it, and guide the patient toward a freeing of the adaptive emotional experience. Exposure is graded, rather than precipitous. The patient is given the time to integrate and metabolize the new experience before moving on. Ultimately, the greater the regression into the experience, the greater will be the intensity as well as the potential for desensitizing the affective experience (i.e., learning how to experience the primary feeling without the associated anxiety, guilt, shame, or pain). At each minute of the therapy session, Malan taught, the therapist should facilitate the experiencing of *as much feeling as the patient can bear*—and assimilate—without being overwhelmed. Research and repeated clinical experience have underscored that experiencing even small amounts of affect can have significant and beneficial effects.

EXAMPLE: CONFLICTS ABOUT COMPETITIVE FEELINGS

This 40-year-old married man was a competent professional, but feared dominance.

THERAPIST: Now that we know how you tend to become frozen in any competitive situation, and how unfrozen you want to be, let's look at a specific example when that happened and explore all the feelings that come up.

PATIENT: Well, I threw my last tennis game, and I knew I could win. Why did I do that?

THERAPIST: Why do you think? Must be a lot of conflict about winning.

PATIENT: Must be, but I don't know what it is.

THERAPIST: Can you go back to a moment in the game when you played less well than you could have. Let's go over that carefully.

PATIENT: There was one time when I hit my opponent a long, low shot, just out of his reach.

THERAPIST: What did you feel at that moment?

PATIENT: I just had a sinking feeling in the pit of my stomach.

THERAPIST: A sinking feeling? But did you have some other reaction as well?

PATIENT: Yeah. I was damn pleased with my shot.

THERAPIST: Part of you was proud of your shot.

PATIENT: Well, I wouldn't say proud. I felt awful immediately.

THERAPIST: What's the hardest part there, of hitting the ball well to your tennis partner?

PATIENT: It's that I don't want to humiliate him. I am a better tennis player.

THERAPIST: So it's hard for you to cut loose and take pleasure in your own power. You seem to think that showing your full capacity is destructive to others.

PATIENT: Oh yes, absolutely!

THERAPIST: Then, can we go over that again, and *let yourself imagine playing aggressively.* [*This is the specific desensitization scene in which the patient will be exposed in imagery to the conflicted feeling until he is no longer uncomfortable with it.*] Let's see if you can imagine those awful feelings you get when you compete, and let us explore them further.

EXAMPLE OF CONFLICTS AROUND SORROW: THE MACHINE BUILDER

This patient, the Machine Builder, had been depressed since her father's death, but she could not bear to discuss him or even think of him.

PATIENT: For so many years now I've been deadened. No feelings at all. I haven't thought of my father at all.
THERAPIST: What would be the worst part of thinking about your father? [*Exploring the anxieties*]
PATIENT: It's just so painful to think about. [*Eyes welling up with tears*]

The therapist had planned to explore the painfulness of exploring her sadness here, but the fact that the patient was so full of feeling suggested that the feeling might be more available than she realized. Exploring the pain now could pull the patient away from the tears into a more cognitive process. So the therapist decided first to offer encouragement and support to see if that would suffice to get the patient over the hump of resistance.

THERAPIST: I know it's painful, but can you stay with these sad feelings about your father for a few more minutes? Can you take me with you so it might be easier to bear? What images of him come up with this sorrow?
PATIENT: Going to the hospital and trying to get him to eat.
THERAPIST: That must have been so hard for you.

It has become a rule of thumb for me that every time I hear a patient say, "I could never do X," I reply (a) "What are the fears of doing X?" and (b) "Can you imagine doing X here with my help?"

EXAMPLE: CONFLICTS ABOUT JOY

Sadness and anger are not the only emotions that are blocked by defensive responses. People are remarkably uncomfortable with positive emotions as well. This middle-aged businesswoman was terrified to slow down her frantic pace.

THERAPIST: So you were about to lay back and relax for the first time in weeks. Sounds wonderful, What stopped you?
PATIENT: Oh! I thought . . . therapy is gonna make me into a wuss! Without my drive, I'm nothing! I thought I was gonna lose my anger, my irritation, my fury, what really gets me going!
THERAPIST: I'm gonna rob you of all your power! [*Both laugh heartily at this point, because much work has been done, and the patient has some intellectual distance on this issue.*]

THERAPIST: But by now you know that isn't so, don't you? [*Using encouragement to move beyond this defended place*]

PATIENT: Yes and no. No. Yes! I know better . . . it just still is so scary not to stay on the treadmill.

THERAPIST: Yeah, I can imagine. You've been in a state of perpetual motion. It must be like, well, being another person to be calm. [*Addressing the fears of calmness and joy*]

PATIENT: It's *not me* at all. It really is like being in another person's body to just let myself go down. I feel just certain that the ax is going to fall—something terrible would happen!

THERAPIST: What would be the most terrible thing about letting down and relaxing?

In cases such as this, the therapist should relentlessly explore the fears until the patient shows signs of beginning to cope with those fears in an adaptive way: *Can you imagine really relaxing and enjoying yourself, here with my help?* [To prompt some images]: *What would you be feeling inside? What would you be doing?*

The typical pattern is for patients to begin to feel a specific affect but become blocked in further exploration in fantasy, just as they do in the actual situation. At this point, instead of confronting the resistance and challenging the patient to experience the full emotion (e.g., the anxiety-provoking approach), this model takes the more graded approach by asking the patient to explore what fears are present. (Depending on the situation, the fears could be guilt, shame, jealousy, pain, hurt, and so on.) Embedded in the following cases is a series of useful affect-focused anxiety-regulating questions.

EXAMPLE: ANXIETY REGULATION AROUND ASSERTION

This female graduate student felt hurt rather than appropriately angry:

THERAPIST: So you hesitated to open up to your friend and tell him how disappointed you were that he canceled your theater date at the last minute. Can we look at why that would have been so difficult? What would have been the worst part of it?

PATIENT: I dunno . . . I'd just feel weird.

THERAPIST: How would you have felt if he had realized how bad you felt?

PATIENT: Oh, I'd feel terrible! I can't bear to make someone feel bad.

THERAPIST: So how would he have felt if you had let him know?

PATIENT: Well, I guess he'd feel pretty bad that he let me down.

THERAPIST: What's so bad about that?

PATIENT: I guess it wouldn't be so terrible, and he might be more considerate the next time.

Other patients might need a great deal more anxiety regulation to reach an adaptive level of coping. In such cases, the therapist must spend a longer time exploring the anxieties, disputing their logic, and building coping responses that replace the defensive pattern. The time required for this process often is proportional to the severity of the anxiety, the degree that it is ego-syntonic, and the strength of the secondary gain.

EXAMPLE: GREATER RESISTANCE ABOUT ASSERTION

Many times during the therapy of the Unforgiven Teenager, it was necessary to change perspectives to help undo her strong resistance to adaptive responding. She would feel more than just hurt; she would feel anguished for days. Yet she was far more resistant to responding differently than the woman described in the preceding section.

THERAPIST: What would be so bad about telling your friend Steve he did something inconsiderate by not calling you to let you know about the meeting?

PATIENT: I just could never do that to anyone! I'm sorry! I'm not that kind of person. [*Her defensive pattern is highly ego-syntonic.*]

THERAPIST: Well, let's look at this. What kind of person tells another person when they've been inconsiderate? [*This is taking a cognitive therapy approach, identifying the maladaptive cognitions and disputing their logic.*]

PATIENT: I think it would be a mean thing to do.

THERAPIST: Has anyone ever told you when you've been inconsiderate?

PATIENT: Well, my sister-in-law was upset when I didn't offer to go to the hospital with her for her checkup after her operation.

THERAPIST: How did you feel when she told you?

PATIENT: I felt terrible!

THERAPIST: What did you do?

PATIENT: Oh, I apologized like crazy, and I went with her the next time. I felt awful that I forgot.

THERAPIST: How long did it take for you to get over it?

PATIENT: I felt bad for a few days, but I felt better that I went with her the next time.

THERAPIST: What if she hadn't told you?

PATIENT: Oh, I would have wanted to know, or she would have stayed angry at me.

THERAPIST: So can you imagine that your friend might also want to know how you feel?

PATIENT: Yeah, I guess, but I wouldn't want to hurt his feelings.

The therapist should be vigilant here to check for secondary gain; in this case, the patient might be maintaining a compliant, masochistic stance to hold on to a less than desirable relationship. When people are overly concerned about hurting others, they are often also concerned about losing the relationship. If her behavior did not change after this session, more work on the secondary gain would be necessary.

THERAPIST: Are you worried he won't be your friend anymore?

PATIENT: Yeah, a little. But now that we've talked about it, it seems like I can say something to him. I shouldn't be that worried.

THERAPIST: So how could you tell him in a way that was careful about his feelings, but also let him know about yours? [*Here, the therapist moves into affect expression; the interaction with the friend will be role-played in fantasy to reduce the conflict around speaking with him.*]

The preceding questions represent only a few samples of the type of inquiry that elicits the anxieties related to the feeling. Following this step, the consequences of those anxieties are explored in enormous and relentless detail. Focusing on a person's fears, guilt, shame, and pain allows both the patient and the therapist to problem-solve. It is reassuring as well as surprising how quickly and easily many anxieties *dissolve* when they are brought into the light. Fears are often far more powerful when they remain *outside of the patient's awareness*. When they are examined in minute detail with a supportive and encouraging therapist, many blocks to feeling lose their potency. Merely discussing and scrutinizing self-attacking feelings lead to resolution or better coping. These repressed fears are like adult nightmares that haunt us until brought out into the light of day, where they often lose their power.

Standard Method for Regulation of Anxieties
As the preceding examples illustrate, one should follow a pattern of oscillating between affect and anxieties as follows:

1: Focus on feeling, using guided imagery and careful monitoring of the physiological concomitants of feeling (until anxiety emerges).
2: Explore with the patient what anxieties exist until the patient gains some perspective on the fears and begins to take some steps toward coping. This coping comes with some calming or as a sense of mastery over the anxieties.
3: Refocus on exposure to the specific feeling, and note whether or not the experience is more fluid than before. Maintain the exposure by exploring the experience in fantasy. If this is not possible, go back to the anxieties or defenses to unravel the resistance.

A cyclical process occurs, therefore, in which the therapist oscillates back and forth between exposure to affects and anxieties until the affect can be experienced and expressed comfortably and freely. It is an integrated set of feelings and an integrated set of cognitions playing in concert that we strive for.

Containment of Experience in Fantasy
In any exposure to feeling, care always must be taken to ensure the *containment of feeling in fantasy* so that acting out does not occur. The practicing of experiencing emotions in fantasy, in graded steps, builds the capacity to reflect on feelings without having to act on them. This teaches the patient a new way to handle emotional experience. Rather than just reacting, the patient learns emotionally guided action. This is the heart of the skill of

"having emotions without emotions having you." Emotional intelligence is really the art of living.

I am often asked if it is helpful to have patients hit a pillow if they are angry or use body movement to intensify or express the feeling. The answer depends on the needs of the patient. My colleagues and I have found that, in most cases, the greater intensity of feeling is experienced *when the body is still. It is somewhat distracting to the inner experience, and probably also relieving of the feeling, to act it out.* If a patient has the capacity to experience a particular feeling even slightly, therefore, it is generally advisable to process this experience in imagery. If a patient is *not able to experience feeling at all,* however, the acting out of the impulse (by the self or others) can "jump start" the process. One patient who was completely incapable of feeling anger was able to retrieve the inner sensation of rage by angrily wringing a washcloth. Once she had accessed these feelings, we were able to move to fantasy to work them through further. Another patient who was "alexithymic" (incapable of labeling feeling experience) attended a weekend experiential group workshop. She did not participate in the emotion-exploring activities, but she *watched others do so.* In watching two group members fight with each other (a very intense few minutes, she recalled), she became aware of what anger feels like. She then was able to access feeling better in imagery in individual therapy, which she had been completely unable to do before attending the workshop.

On the other hand, when a patient has a prior history of impulse-control problems, intensification of the experiencing of affect must either be avoided or done *cautiously until self-control is ensured.* This process will be described further in the section "Acting Out."

Repeated Exposure Until the Patient Can Continue Independently

Exposure in imagery must be repeated until desensitization of the conflicted feeling occurs, that is, until the patient is able to monitor, control, and guide the appropriate expression of the feeling. One or two presentations of the conflictual scenes are not enough to eradicate a long-standing conditioned pairing of anxiety and feeling. These patterns of responding have been developed over the course of a lifetime. The therapist must go over and over the significant imagery with multiple repetitions to effect change. In addition, patients should be encouraged to practice such scenes between sessions, both in imagery and in personal interaction, as soon as they feel ready to do so.

MAJOR PROBLEMS IN ELICITING AFFECT

Even with support and encouragement, people have a difficult time facing feelings. Often they say, "My family tells me to just get on with my life. Put it behind me. Forget the past." Yet so often, the only way out is through. Doing therapy effectively truly *is* the way to get on with life. It is disturbing that there is so much encouragement to forget the past, when so much of healing involves remembering and reintegrating how the past has impacted on current functioning. So much illness occurs because important aspects of the past have been consciously "forgotten" but are unconsciously experienced and thus are still controlling us, although outside of our control.

The reason for society's advice to "get on with it" is probably the observation that a lot of people become stuck in chronic rumination, bitterness, blaming, and complaining of past people and events. Certainly, such venting or complaining behavior is nothing more than a *defensive position:* a maladaptive avoidance of the more basic underlying emotions that would, if faced, resolve the past problems or put them to rest. Such defensive responding must be distinguished from adaptive functioning so that exploring of past experience is *constructive* rather than destructive. If the past is totally avoided because of fears of becoming stuck in it, however, healing will be obstructed. Bowlby reminds us that a child's first human relationship is the "foundation stone of his personality" (1969, p. 177). How can the foundation stone of our personality be ignored or lightly "put away"?

Even though it is crucial to work through underlying feelings, it is just as crucial to handle appropriately the pitfalls inherent in doing so, so that "spinning of wheels," or worse, becoming a "chronic victim," can be carefully avoided. This section addresses the following topics related to the task of encouraging patients to reopen old cans of worms for new growth:

- Confusing defensive emotions with adaptive emotions
- The danger of acting out: Eliciting feeling too quickly may lead to loss of control
- The danger of acting in: Eliciting feeling too quickly may lead to self-attack
- The danger of going too slowly in the experiencing of emotions
- The overwhelming quality of emotions
- The fear that emotions will do terrible things to us
- Therapists' fears in the eliciting of feelings

Confusing Defensive Emotions with Adaptive Emotions

The term *emotion* encompasses affects, drives, and pain. The word *feeling* refers to the felt experience of the emotions. I often use the more generic term *emotions* when the topic includes both affects and drives. The subject of defensive emotion provides one such instance: The drive sexual desire can be used defensively, as can the affects joy, anger, and sadness.

Because of its importance to adaptive functioning, the distinction between defensive and adaptive feelings has been discussed at length in earlier chapters and is discussed in detail in chapter 7. Nevertheless, defensive expression of emotion is sufficiently destructive to bear mentioning briefly once again. One of the main dangers in the experiencing of feelings is that the therapist may elicit defensive feeling and then think, "Oh, I'm really doing a great job!" One of my supervisees told me how stunned she was, after clearly learning this distinction, to think back to all the times that patients were crying in a helpless, victimized way that did them no good because she had mistaken the defensive affect for significant therapeutic work. Similarly, patients can rage and scream, but if it is in a helpless or victimized way, it will not lead to change. This process is no better than spinning wheels that dig a bigger rut. The one guideline to hold in mind when affect is flowing is to assess whether the quality of the affect will or will not lead to an adaptive resolution of the problem at hand.

Acting Out Caused by Eliciting Feelings Too Quickly

An assessment of the degree of impulse control must precede any exploration of affect. If the individual has a history of problems with acting out of anger inappropriately, or has been so passive that anger has never been expressed and much abuse has been taken, there is a danger of lashing out inappropriately as the angry feelings emerge into consciousness. Similarly, if patients have been incapacitated by feelings of grief, it is of utmost importance to ensure that there is sufficient self-control to experience the feeling without acting out or loss of impulse control. Lack of control of impulses is a contraindication for the affect-experiencing stage of short-term therapy. If insufficient impulse control is a problem, cognitive work or defense building and restructuring must precede desensitization of affect, as described in chapter 4.

With defenses lowered, the patient may feel like exploding to get relief. But if the exploding or venting ultimately leads to loss of self-esteem or distancing of others, it clearly is not beneficial. If the venting occurs so rapidly that the patient cannot pull the feelings up into the mind and apprehend them, the catharsis is for naught. A highly graded exposure approach is helpful in such cases because it permits the step-by-step building of cognitive skills along with emotional skills to help the patient identify the emergence of affect and either control, guide, or stop it. In such cases, patients are guided through emotionally bland images with just the *thought* of an emotion, so patterns of acting out can be recognized. Patients are then helped to identify and control the earliest physiological signs of emotion, such as minor irritations that precede temper outbursts or small disappointments that build to pain-based impulsivity. Subsequently, the intensity of the fantasized affect is successively increased, but *only to the extent that the patient feels in control.*

Let's imagine, in a very calm way, the moment when you were angry at your neighbor. Can you tell me how you might imagine that it would play out: first in a positive way, and then in a negative way. Let's use the fantasy to explore the options you have available.

Over many repetitions, the emotional component of the fantasy should be titrated from bland to intense, only as the patient demonstrates the capacity to control the expression outside the session. Patients should be told that the feeling should be experienced in small doses until they are comfortable with their ability to control it: *Can you go over that scene with your neighbor again, but this time, at the moment that he insults you, can you let yourself begin to feel a small amount of anger? Then describe what it feels like to you, in your body, and how you would guide its expression.* The patient is given exercises, or "emotional pushups." There is repeated practice until mastery is achieved.

There are several significant points to keep in mind. First, patients often have less trust in their control of impulses than is warranted. My experience is that most overly controlled patients will not fully act out an impulse but will attenuate it somehow so that it is in essence harmless. They often do not have faith in themselves, however, that their behavior will be harmless. I have assisted patients in portraying anger only to have them feel extremely anxious in the subsequent week about their ability to contain that feeling. In the subsequent session, I point out to the patient many examples of emotional control that have been discussed previously. This issue is discussed further in the section entitled "The Danger of Going Too Slowly in Eliciting Feeling."

Second, if a therapist is genuinely concerned with the possibility of acting out, therapeutic maneuvers to elicit affect should be minimized or should proceed in small steps until the therapist is secure with the patient's ability to contain the emotion. Eliciting of affective responses should never be avoided but should be worked through at a comfortable pace. It is negligent to fail to attend to patients' needs to defend themselves.

A third concern is that even a well-controlled patient may have a tendency to act out in small ways (e.g., yelling) after an intense session. The solution is always to *anticipate* this possibility and alert the patient before the end of the session that he or she may feel more mobilized in regard to the feeling that has been elicited. This process provides some cognitive control for the individual: *Look, you have just experienced fully how angry you are at your wife. Be aware that you may have a tendency to act out during the coming week. At such times, stop and think of what you need to do or say.*

A review of patients' capacity to restrain themselves in the face of newly emerging emotions is a process of building an awareness of their coping ability and increases self-confidence and self-esteem. Nevertheless, it is frightening and painful for patients to handle prolonged periods of uncertainty; it is helpful to move slowly and methodically through emotional experiencing (taking several weeks) when patients are unsure of their capacity to control the emotion. Control of impulses is one of the main criteria for patient suitability for rapid exploratory treatment. If a patient has a history of trouble containing emotion or overwhelming anxiety concerning the imaging of certain feeling states, other forms of treatment should be considered (e.g., cognitive, behavioral, interpersonal).

Because all human beings have defenses against conflicted affect, presumably anyone, given the correct instruction and experiences in therapy, would be able to work through the issues as outlined in this manual. "Going too fast" means pushing someone to face emotional issues while the anxiety, guilt, shame, or pain is still too great to bear. The anxiety-regulating approach is designed to help patients proceed in experiencing warded-off emotions only to the extent that they are able to bear the unbearable feelings without defensively blocking the process.

Acting In Caused by Eliciting Feelings Too Quickly

A major signal that affect restructuring is premature is when eliciting strong feeling brings with it a hurtful amount of the associated anxiety, guilt, shame, or pain. Patients become, even more than before, the target of their own internal battle. As in real battles, where soldiers are tragically but inadvertently killed by the "friendly fire" of their comrades behind, the more masochistic the patient, the more he is in danger of causing himself a fair amount of suffering through his own boomeranging rage.

EXAMPLE OF SELF-INJURIOUS BEHAVIOR: THE LITTLE SOLDIER

This case concerns a 24-year-old male musician who was living his life on the basis of his mother's demanding and unrealistic ideals. When he began to see the damage that this had caused him in his life, his grief was enormous. He retained some of his self-blaming and self-attacking response patterns, however, so that the following incident occurred.

After a therapy session, this young man was in such pain that he went home and cut himself in the side. The cut was tiny, only about an eighth of an inch in length, but it was sufficient to draw blood. It symbolized the degree to which he felt "crucified" by reliving what he was experiencing in therapy. When he called me, in great pain, to tell me what he had done, I reacted strongly. I spoke with him for some time until he was calm. (The focus of my intervention, of course, was to reduce the degree of shame and pain he was suffering and to help him gain control over the desire to hurt himself.) I scheduled an additional appointment for him for the next day. (If the cutting had been greater, I would have seen him immediately to assess further the degree of self-destructive impulses and the need for hospitalization.) As it happened, he assured me that he was in control and would not cut himself again.

The next day, we went over what happened, and I helped him see his massive pattern of turning negative feelings on himself. It became clear that the cutting was the symbolic enactment of the lancing of a boil of pain that resulted from his having fully seen that he had been forced to be his mother's little soldier all his life. Following this realization and the management of the negative affects, he truly healed during the next months. He never hurt himself again, and at his 3-year follow-up he was doing extremely well.

The main techniques involve a two-pronged approach for handling the self-attack: (a) holding back on the experiencing of conflicted affects until masochistic responses are reduced or brought under control and (b) working on directing that affect experience toward the appropriate person (in imagery, of course, until it is mastered). One of the statements I made to this man was as follows: *Can you see how you're attacking yourself when you're really angry at your mother? Can we focus on the anger you feel toward her, rather than your anger at you?*

The Danger of Going Too Slowly in Eliciting Feelings

Although emotions can be frightening and hard to manage, when therapists avoid a patient's emotional issue, it is generally not just because we are protecting the patient. If we are to be honest, it is because we are also protecting ourselves. All too often, while watching videotapes, I have seen myself, a colleague, or a supervisee lightening up or avoiding an important issue with a patient. Sometimes, this was an issue that caused the therapist personal pain. Sometimes, it was just reflexive social conditioning. We can prolong the suffering of our patients by being so "protective" and "concerned" about upsetting or criticizing them that we do not alleviate their pain. This book describes a number of anxiety-regulating and shame-reducing interventions to help patients bear painful feelings so they do not remain plagued by chronic and far worse symptoms.

The Overwhelming Quality of Emotional Experience

Probably the greatest barrier encountered in the eliciting of feeling is the fear that whatever feeling is experienced will take complete control of the individual and destroy everything. The sensation of being overcome with feeling is like being sucked up into a tornado. When one is angry, the fear is that the anger will destroy a relationship or turn the individual into a violent monster. One also feels that one will never *not* be angry. If the experience is grief, we feel that the sorrow will never end and we will never stop crying. When one is grieving, the world seems empty, and it seems that happiness never will be experienced again. If the issue is vulnerability, there is fear of appearing either foolish or disgusting and thus being abandoned or of becoming forever entrapped, engulfed, or dependent. In the fever pitch of sexual desire, one c.n fear becoming uncontrollably promiscuous, perverted, or wanton. With joy, fears are that "the ax will soon fall," the person will "burst," or some kind of punishment will be given. Following are some examples, together with the therapist's response.

PATIENT: I just don't want to cry. If I start, I'll never stop.

THERAPIST: It's very common for people to feel this way: Standing on the edge of an ocean of pain that has always been avoided. The problem is that many people just stick their toe in and jump back and run off. The solution is to jump in or wade in slowly but to stay with the experience long enough to get through it, which means becoming able to bear it. Can I help you do that?

The therapist in this case used teaching and support to encourage emotional experiencing. Another helpful approach to the patient's comment is to present reality: *What is the longest you ever cried? Was it 30 minutes? Or as long as 2 hours? What did you do then? Were you alone? Maybe you needed someone with you to make it bearable.* [Reality testing, reassurance, and support] Alternatively, the therapist can be encouraging with words such as these: *It may feel like you will never come through it, but you will. You won't be swallowed up. In fact, the real difficulty is to stay with the sadness so that it can be worked through. The problem is that it feels so horrible that most people want to run from it rather than stay with it.* These statements demonstrate the use of encouragement, reassurance, and teaching to assist the grief process.

One colleague told me she often uses a dash of humor along with presenting reality: *I know it feels like you'll never stop crying. But the truth is, you'll eventually get hungry or have to go to the bathroom!*

In summary, the therapist can err on the side of conservatism and leave the patient suffering. On the other hand, the therapist can also err on the side of too much zeal and traumatize the patient with excess pain. With patients who have experienced severe trauma, this possibility has to be carefully assessed. The affects need to be faced, but they need to be faced in "successive approximations," step-by-step. Therapists have to find their own style for encouraging patients to begin the process of immersion into the experiencing of deep affect, influenced of course by the type of patient and related circumstances. The point is to work toward the specific objectives guided by one's intuition and experience, while being mindful of maintaining a careful balance between too much exposure and too little.

The goal is to help patients make peace with all that is within them. Instead of shutting it out or sealing it over, patients must be encouraged to face honestly and come to understand whatever they feel or think. If individuals have compassion for the rage and pain and longing that they experience, this will allow them to better understand their needs and decide upon constructive action. They will be more empathic with such feelings in others as well.

Fears That Emotions Will Do Terrible Things

A cognitive therapist I know claims that one should never trust that "feeling in our gut." The example he gives is that the gut feeling makes us uncomfortable when driving on the left-hand side of the road when in England rather than the familiar right-hand side in France or the United States. He uses this information to illustrate the virtues of being guided by cognition over feeling. This case certainly argues for logic over intuition, but there seemed to be a fallacy in it. I came to see that to dismiss the feeling in one's gut (the inhibitory affects) as *not reliable across the board* is to overgeneralize. That gut feeling (anxiety) about driving was learned back home, in familiar circumstances of everyday life, and can be lifesaving. When in another country, the traffic rules change and heightened cognitive processing is needed for guidance, *but only during the adjustment period.* (Affects are not as quick to change as thoughts. One must learn to be anxious about different conditions.) With time and practice, the anxious feeling in the gut shifts to become compatible with the different road conditions. Consequently, if one followed the guidance of the cognitive therapist and *never* trusted the gut feeling, one would constantly require a cumbersome logical process to make decisions. Life always would feel like driving in a foreign country! In fact, after one has become adapted to new situations (through use of cognitive processing), one can, literally or figuratively, drive "on automatic pilot" and let one's gut be one's main guide for standard and recurring conditions. (Although cognition is essential too for noting variations in common themes.)

How does one know whether that gut feeling is authentic, defensive, or *inappropriate to the situation*? The answer is, one does not always know immediately. Logic sometimes needs to be applied; this therapy model repeatedly emphasizes the necessity of *cognitive guidance of affect.* When patients tell me they cannot trust their feelings because they do not know if the feelings are "justified" or "correct" or "right," I emphasize that their feelings—their gut feelings in particular (rational or irrational)—carry extremely important information that needs to be considered, along with all the other data at hand. To dismiss "feeling information" is cutting off an essential part of the self (or others). What needs to be done is to consider the question, What are my feelings telling me? The logic goes like this: What would be the optimal thing for me to do? What hurts me and my relationship to others? What helps me, as well as my relationship to others? Even if the affect is defensive, destructive, or self-attacking, *it does not create a problem if it is not acted on.* That is why so much effort in this approach is put into pulling feelings up in fantasy so that they can be cognitively sorted out. The feeling in the gut however crazy it may seem is a valid signal that tells you that something needs to be attended to. The reason emotion needs to be contained and processed cognitively is so that the meaning of the affect can be sorted out and the best course of action can be taken. After this is done a number of times, and courses of action are arrived at, one can successively shift back on automatic pilot. Indeed, much of our living is done on automatic pilot, such as driving and social behavior.

Therapists' Fears in Eliciting Feeling

It is not only patients who have fears about experiencing feeling, but therapists as well. How does the therapist know whether the anger unleashed will be acted out destructively, even in the session? One resident said anxiously, after watching me push a patient to explore anger, "How will I know he won't hit me?" How does the therapist know for sure that the patient will ever stop crying, especially by the end of the session? If the therapist is pushing to explore grief-laden material, how can he or she be sure patients can tolerate facing the depth of their hopelessness or despair at that time? Likewise, if therapists have not fully experienced the depth of their grief (or anger or sexuality), it is difficult for them to tolerate experiencing it in others or to know what form it will take. Therapists need to have navigated the emotional waters first.

With therapists who are not emotionally experienced, there tends to be a turning away, lightening up, or deintensifying of the patient's material. Such avoidance by the therapist should be watched for and dealt with. Optimally, we should not stand in the way of the patient. Nevertheless, *the therapist's struggle with emotion should be treated with the same compassion as the patient's.*

QUESTIONS ABOUT AFFECT EXPERIENCING

The following categories of questions are addressed in this section:

- What feelings does the therapist focus on first?
- How does one intensify the affective experience?
- Why intensify the affective experience?

- How does one lighten up the intensity of the affect and why?
- Can you stop the pain?

What Feelings Do You Focus on First?

Grief, anger, and the affects associated with attachment to self and others are generally the first issues that need to be dealt with in psychotherapy. When an unmourned loss has occurred in the person's life, even years before, grief is typically the initial focus. Often other therapeutic work is hampered unless grief has been resolved. Most of our patients have suffered losses, if not of people, then of caring, of attention, or of some unmet hope or dream that has been longed for and needs to be grieved. At the same time, all grief is a form of unmet longing—so these two foci may be fundamental to the healing process.

There are times, however, when anger takes precedence, as when a patient's current life is being seriously impaired by lack of ability to express anger or assertion in an adaptive way. In one case of this sort, a man was in danger of being fired as a result of his unconscious passive–aggressive behavior. He met criteria for major depression, and his anhedonia threatened his ability to go to work. Confrontation of anger in his case resolved the major depressive symptoms that very week, and mobilized enough assertion for him to successfully negotiate a probation period. In a few more sessions we worked on blocked anger and adaptive expression, with a successful resolution that has been maintained for 3 years. After he was functioning well and his job was stable, we worked on grieving. The grief had to do with how beaten down he was by his mother. This led back to feelings of anger and longing for closeness.

Blanck & Blanck (1974) made a cogent argument for not dealing with anger prematurely. "Although these affects [e.g., anger] do indeed exist, to elicit them too soon would serve only to sever connection" (p. 185). They feel that such affects should be addressed only after a "sufficient reservoir" of positive feelings has been established (both with the therapist, and toward the past figures) so that rage can be tolerated without fear of destroying the relationships that are so longed for (p. 185). Some patients have the capacity to make a good alliance, however, and Davanloo has successfully confronted anger early on with many patients. At the same time, many patients are so poorly connected interpersonally, that pushing for negative affect too soon (i.e., emotional "separation") can be terrifying for them.

It is often difficult to determine the affective focus and these are but rough guidelines. Sometimes it is optimal to simply follow the patient's affective lead, or ask the patient which feelings are closest to the surface.

Intensifying Affect Experience

The objective in affect experiencing is the increasingly full experience of feeling until the inhibitory affects are brought within normal limits. This is the process of exposure that leads to desensitization of internal experience. In the early years of the development of this treatment approach, my colleagues and I often found ourselves floundering during the therapy session with the problem of blandly expressed emotion. We would do a thorough defense analysis and be clear about the feeling to be explored, but we would be frustrated by the flatness or lifelessness of what was being expressed by the patient. Often we would ask each other, "How should I help the patient intensify the experience?" We are now aware of many techniques that can assist with this problem. Gestalt and experiential therapies provide a number of techniques that are useful.

The use of imagery is particularly helpful. The patient is encouraged to describe vividly the expression of the feeling in relation to another person. This means painting a vivid picture in fantasy of the thoughts, feelings, and behaviors that would occur if anger, or closeness, or sexual feeling were expressed. In the case of grief or longing, the patient is asked to describe the sad images thoroughly. The more vivid the imagery, the more connections there are to affective experiencing. There are structures in the brain that suggest the close connection of affect and memory. The amygdala, the conductor of many affective and attachment responses (e.g., Aggleton, 1992; Halgren, 1992; Kling & Brothers, 1992), is located near and heavily interconnected with the hippocampus, the seat of declarative memory (e.g., LeDoux, 1992). Activating one of these areas activates neuronal networks in the other.

EXAMPLE: USING IMAGERY AND MEMORY TO ELICIT AFFECTS
A 60-year-old man was haunted all his life by feelings that he was "bad." In this excerpt, he explores in memory the source of that bad feeling.

THERAPIST: Where were you in the house when you spoke with him?
PATIENT: I guess I was in the hall.
THERAPIST: What do you remember the hall looking like? [*Sometimes the setting or the specific location, carefully described, can elicit emotional memories.*]
PATIENT: Dark, foreboding. For some reason, I remember the floor was painted green.
THERAPIST: Maybe you were looking down?
PATIENT: I sure was. I didn't want to look at my father's face.
THERAPIST: What do you imagine you would have seen if you had looked up? [*Here is an example of encouraging the patient to do what is, or had been, avoided.*]
PATIENT: I don't know. I never wanted to look straight at him.
THERAPIST: Well, can you take a moment? You know your father well. What look would his face take on that you most dreaded to see?
PATIENT: Oh, that curling of his lips. He sneered when he got real mad.
THERAPIST: Can you imagine seeing his lips curled like that?
PATIENT: Yeah, but I hate it. I don't want to imagine it.

The therapist persists in encouraging the patient to face the image and desensitize the painful associations.

THERAPIST: How does it make you feel, seeing that image?
PATIENT: Like a nothing. Like a rotten, no good, nothing. [*Shivering in his seat*]

THERAPIST: That sounds terrible. His anger was enormously painful for you.
PATIENT: I was devastated by it.
THERAPIST: What would you have longed to see on his face? Can you imagine the eyes you longed to see? [*Beginning to build a replacement image*]
PATIENT [*After a silence*]: Proud. Pride. I wanted him to be proud of me! [*Tears come with these words.*]

The therapist exposes the patient to the warded-off feelings by using specific images. The focus is on the father's eyes, not on their dialogue.

Encouraging Affect Experience

Affect should be drawn out by empathizing in the most emotionally connected way. This is mainly a process of clarifying, which means restating what the patient has said. But this restatement should contain an emotional sharing that is as deep or deeper than what the patient has been able to do. Examples include:

- You long to sob.
- You seem to want to explode.
- You've carried this pain so long.
- It sounds horrible.
- It feels as though your father is here with you now.

At all costs, one should avoid at such points asking questions that might pull the patient into cognition or intellectualization. The cognitive understanding can be built after the affect is sustained.

Once a patient is deep into the process of experiencing feeling, the therapist must shift from active facilitation to attentive listening. It is hard to know ahead of time when words will facilitate or impede the experiencing process. Each patient is different. Once patients are caught up with emotions, however, continued talking can divert their attention away from their inner experience. Often the merest empathic sound is sufficient: "Mmmm." The only way to know is to try something and be vigilant in regard to the patient's response. Empathic statements often cause affect to deepen, although not for everyone. In one case, I said, "That sounds terrible, you must be in so much pain," and the patient yelled at me, "Will you shut up already, you're distracting me from what I am trying to feel!" (I took his advice.)

If done sparingly, attenuated but shared experiencing of affect can be extremely powerful. Immersion in the experience by both the patient and therapist deepens the affect. Therapists should try to put themselves in the position of the patient to assist in the working through. Therapists must separate affect that belongs to their own experiences from affect that is synchronous to the patient's experience. Mindful of what belongs to both, the therapist can share what is happening internally in a free-associative manner. This is the active use of real relationship to intensify the experience.

Handling Resistance That Blocks Intensity

When affect is present, it is important to continue to focus on it and to keep deepening the experience. The therapist should not be overly concerned by the presence of *some* defensiveness, because *defense is always there to some degree.* The issue is whether the defenses thoroughly *block or terminate the process* or just *titrate it* so that the patient can bear it.

If continuing defensiveness blocks or impedes the experience of the feeling, the therapist should note it and encourage the patient to "put it aside" if possible.

THERAPIST: Can you see that you're daydreaming and going off the subject as we approach this difficult topic for you, yet you agreed that you wanted to pursue this. Is that still the case?

PATIENT: Oh yes, definitely.

THERAPIST: Well, can you try to concentrate a bit more on this topic so that we can continue?

PATIENT: Sure, I'm not consciously trying to avoid this.

The self-attack must be rapidly pointed out and reduced or eliminated before further experiencing is done.

EXAMPLE OF CONFLICTS ABOUT ANGER: THE UNFORGIVEN TEENAGER

PATIENT: The more we talk about my anger at my father, the worse I feel about myself! I shouldn't have these feelings toward a parent.

THERAPIST: If you're feeling worse about yourself, then we need to work on that before we go further. We are not here to increase your attack on yourself! Let's stop and look at what's the worst part for you of having these angry feelings toward him.

The focus will then be on the feelings of anxiety, guilt, shame, or pain. Therapy should not proceed with exposure to the angry feelings until the self-attacking responses are eliminated, that is, until shame, guilt, fear, or pain is brought to adaptive levels that guide rather than abuse the self. In other, less severe cases, therapy can move along with the defenses pointed out and set aside.

THERAPIST: Do you notice that you are criticizing yourself pretty badly as we begin to look at these painful feelings? Can you get some distance on that?

PATIENT: Yeah, I think so.

THERAPIST: We've looked at how hurtful it has been for you to do this to yourself, so can you try to proceed without being so hard on yourself?

PATIENT: Yeah, I don't want to keep doing that, and I really don't feel it as strongly as I used to. It's just a habit. I'll watch it.

Subsequently, the therapist must be vigilant to determine whether the affect deepens or lightens and whether the patient is able to maintain a compassionate stance toward the self.

Sometimes reminders and gentle encouragement such as in the preceding example are sufficient to keep the patient on track. Because this is the most direct path and requires the least effort, it should be tried first. Many patients cannot put their defensive actions and self-attacking feeling aside, however, and remedial work must be done. When this is the case, the therapist should return to the defense-restructuring stage and work through the anxiety pole feelings until the approach to feeling is not so blocked. The less the inhibitory affects, the more the affect can flow freely.

EXAMPLE OF AVOIDING ANGER: THE HARD-DRIVING BUSINESSWOMAN

THERAPIST: You are dodging my questions constantly this morning, yet you said you wanted me to focus on your anger. You seem to be having a hard time staying on focus so we can explore this topic.

PATIENT: Yeah, but I don't know why. I know I said I wanted to look at my anger, but I dreaded coming here today. I almost canceled.

THERAPIST: Okay, something's still blocking you from proceeding, and "dread" sounds really uncomfortable. Let's *not* explore the angry feelings right now. Why don't we just look at what's so difficult for you, until looking at the anger feels more bearable?

As soon as the conflicts are brought out and some coping responses are made, it is time to return to the exploration of feeling. If the patient still resists the intensification of feelings, the therapist can ask, "Are we on the right theme?" It is important to determine whether the patient is going through the motions to try to please the therapist. If one is not sure, one can ask the patient directly. One can share the concern, and let it be a collaborative problem. Does the patient not share the goal of experiencing emotions intensely? If not, a resolution will have to be reached or a new goal agreed on, as in the case of the man who would not face his anger toward his wife but who worked well in a cognitive treatment.

Why Deepen the Affect Experience?

The more the patient is able to experience the affect on a physiological level, the more thorough the desensitization process will be. This does not mean that intense levels of affect are required; one aims for as much feeling as the patient can bear, as Malan wrote. Mild-to-moderate "felt experience" is often sufficient for change to occur. The point is that the affect needs to be felt, not just thought about or talked about. If the patient has had sufficient "practice" feeling a particular affect without being beset by some inhibitory affect, it is more likely that the affect will be freely experienced in life. I call these repetitions "emotional push-ups," and I tell patients that they need to develop "emotional muscle." It may sound trite, but the analogy is an apt one. As each new wave of feeling swells, the patient should be encouraged to stay with it and not run away. As a general rule, the therapist can stay focused on the feeling unless the defenses or anxieties totally block the experiencing. The presence of some affect emerging signals the therapist to avoid getting hung up in defense restructuring. There are always some defenses present, but when at least some degree of affect is being experienced, the desensitization process can proceed.

When to Lighten the Emotional Intensity

Just as important as deepening the emotional experience is to be able to "lighten up" and control the flow of emotion. It is necessary to teach patients to *open and close the door on emotion* so they are able to control emotions rather than have emotions control them. But the control needs to be flexible, not rigid. One needs to cry when sad and stop crying when there are legitimate reasons to stop. One needs to be angry when the situation calls for it and stop being angry when appropriate. Cognitive techniques are useful for teaching the appropriate use of some of the intermediate-level defenses that we all use to help us get through the day, such as distraction, rationalization, and minimization. The use of mature defenses such as humor, sublimation, suppression, and altruism also can help control and guide feelings.

Can One Stop the Pain?

Although many therapists feel pessimistic about this question, my experience, and that of many colleagues, is that pain from the past *can be* significantly decreased, discontinued, or metamorphosized into constructive action. "Stopping the pain" in such cases literally means that the sting (the pain, the anguish, the misery, the hurt of the anxiety pole) can be removed from the sad or traumatic memory and replaced with more proactive or constructive affects. There may always be some sadness for the way it was, but it is hurtful to the self to maintain unremitting anguish about the past. Those who stay enraged at the unfairness of life are inadvertently maintaining a defensively angry and blaming position that is neither nurturant nor self-soothing. It is a chronic feeling of "I'm screwed."

In the case of traumatized or abused individuals, there may forever be a profound sorrow that certain events occurred, but the bitterness and sting of misery need not be carried into the future. When memories are no longer traumatizing and no longer control the patient, he or she has control over them. The goal of therapy should be to become in control of the painful memories by removing the personal shame or anguish and replacing these self-attacking responses with adaptive emotions. *Grief* must be encouraged to permit resolution and acceptance of the sometimes horrible aspects of life. *Anger* should be sufficiently freed up so that the individual feels less vulnerable to being easily victimized. Finally, the eliciting of a strong healthy *outrage* is particularly adaptive for replacing the anguish of trauma or inhuman atrocities. Outrage, used maturely and generatively, can promote constructive action that helps to prevent further abuse or traumatic incidents from being committed. The world is helped by the constructive outrage that promotes action taken against rape, childhood abuse, and senseless violence.

Additionally, we must not forget the positive emotions. *Interest, joy, caring attachment, and sexual desire* need to be enhanced so that new and pleasure-giving ways of living can replace old ones. *We can't change the past, but we can change our reaction to the past—and we can, and must, work toward changing the future.*

SUMMARY

This chapter focuses on the interventions that can be useful in assisting patients in experiencing previously warded-off affects. Through an empathic sharing of feeling with the therapist, anxieties that have been associated with adaptive affects are regulated. Interventions include:

- Identification of the verbal, physiological, and action tendencies of the affects
- Use of guided imagery to explore and contain action tendencies
- Desensitization through exposure to affects in fantasy and regulation of anxieties
- Repetition until the affect can be comfortably experienced and contained

CHAPTER 7

Specific Affects in Clinical Work

The previous chapter focused on general *interventions* for use in encouraging affect experiencing. Because of the enormous confusion surrounding what affect is, what affect does, and how affects are used and misused by everyone, specific attention to each affect "family" is warranted. In addition, the way specific affects are used must be carefully analyzed, because each affect can be used for different, and often opposing, functions. First, adaptive and activating affects (represented on the impulse-feeling pole) must be distinguished from affects used to inhibit responding (represented on the anxiety pole). Second, each of the affects in these two categories can also be used defensively (and thus represented by responses on the defense pole).

For desensitization of conflicted affect to take place, the adaptive, activating affect must be experienced *exclusively* to alter the connection to the inhibitory affects. Only after the individual has become comfortable with the experience of each conflicted affect can the range of affects be integrated to allow appropriate interpersonal expression.[1]

Many, if not most, people and most cultures operate within a narrow band of feeling. Although this restriction can lead to a lack of richness in life and may cause suffering, restriction of affect can be a somewhat adaptive compromise. Inappropriate and defensive emotional outbursts are both frightening and destructive. It is these defensive variants rather than adaptive expressions of affect that have led to fear and suppression of emotions. Unfortunately, the baby may be thrown out with the bathwater. *It is not our emotions, themselves, that are destructive; it is the misuse of our emotions that is harmful.* We must learn to tell the difference in affect functions in order to use

[1]"Regulation of state lies at the heart of our theory" (Lichtenberg, Lachmann, & Fosshage, 1992, p. 162). Regulation of affects lies at the heart of this model. The concept of "state" is an affect-based motivational system for Lichtenberg and his colleagues. There is, therefore, a reassuring convergence in the ways we view change processes in treatment.

our emotions wisely rather than misuse them. Nathanson said the following of affect-guided treatment:

> Watch your patients perk up when you teach them how to partition their emotional discomfort into easily recognizable categories that permit highly specific systems of solace. And smile with contentment as the work of psychotherapy is made just a little bit easier by this new approach. (1992, p. 19)

Before I discuss specific affects in detail, I address two general themes: first, the level of affective intensity needed for change, and second, for a closer look, the distinction between adaptive and maladaptive forms of affect.

THE INTENSITY OF THE FELT
EXPERIENCE NEEDED FOR CHANGE

There has been some confusion about the intensity of affect needed to effect change. Stern (1985) pointed out that psychodynamic theory focused too exclusively on intense affective experiences. Indeed, in our early research on short-term dynamic therapy, my colleagues and I sought tremendous affective intensity, believing that it was essential for change. As the Beth Israel research study evolved, we discovered that lower levels of affect experiencing resulted in distinct behavioral change, even in characterological shifts, despite our belief to the contrary. We also noticed that intense levels of affect were often disruptive to cognitive functioning, so that interpretations could not be absorbed, and sufficiently unsettling that some patients dropped out of treatment. Repeated clinical review of videotapes of short-term psychotherapy has led Alpert (1992) to the same conclusion. Research from Stern's laboratory lends support to the impact of low levels of affect: "Rather ordinary and very moderate affective experiences can be well remembered one week later" (MacKain et al., 1985). Stern (1985) noted that infants learned a great deal about themselves when there were *not* pressing physiological or external needs, that is, when they were alone or in equilibrium. Research from Emde's laboratory also has demonstrated the value of moderate levels of affect in the facilitation of learning (Emde, 1992).

One might hypothesize that psychotherapy patients also learn better in milder, or at least titrated, affect states. At times intense levels of affect may be necessary for certain types of change. But intense affect states may have been *overrated* as the only change agent, whereas milder affective arousal may have been *underrated* for its potential for organizing experience or as a change agent. My colleagues and I have made repeated clinical observations suggesting that small, successively increasing "doses" of affect may help "metabolize" stepwise changes, which may in turn promote more stable and lasting changes. Much more research is needed to establish the frequency, intensity, dosage, and duration of the various affective states needed to achieve lasting behavioral change.

DISTINCTIONS BETWEEN ADAPTIVE AND
MALADAPTIVE AFFECT

My colleagues and I spent many years in concentrated study to determine whether patients' affect was being used adaptively or not. Affect researchers have found that facial expression can reliably distinguish different affect states for the observer. To identify their own feelings, however, patients need to acquire the ability to read their ongoing inner physiological sensations, and inner sensation, unfortunately, is fraught with confusion. So often these sensations are outside of awareness, and patients need careful instruction in how to bring these sensations into awareness and how to make sense of their bodily responses. Furthermore, in addition to learning the simple labeling of affects, patients and therapists must come to understand the distinction between defensive (maladaptive) and adaptive forms of these affects.

Through repeated videotape analysis, as well as clinical scrutiny with the assistance of hundreds of patients, my research team has begun to identify rules of thumb that can help distinguish adaptive from maladaptive affective responding. My colleagues and I found that there are physiological patterns that patients can learn to identify that can signal adaptive emotional responding.

Characteristics of Adaptive Affects

When affects are used adaptively, they often are experienced as either *a surge of energy* or *a gentle flowing sensation that moves from the area of the torso toward the extremities, out from the body.* For example, with anger there is a rush of energy and an action tendency to lash out. With sadness, there is a welling up to cry with tears pouring forth. With interest and excitement, there is a surge of curiosity and an exploratory tendency. With joy, there is the flowing of warmth and comfort and a tendency to become calm. (This appears to be a function of increased blood flow to the extremities owing to the relaxing of muscles.) This *surge* or *flow* generates an *action tendency*, which if applied adaptively is an appropriate *reaction* to an event, leading to a sense of *relief* or *satisfaction*. In some circumstances, such as with grief or assertion, such reactions can lead to the resolution of an issue.

In short, the characteristics of the regulatory or pleasure-giving emotions used adaptively are as follows:

1. An outward *surging, flowing,* or *resonating* of some form of energy
2. Generation of an *action tendency*
3. An interpersonally adaptive *reaction* (toward the self or others)
4. Relief

The adaptive forms of the inhibitory affects should also guide behavior in a way that brings relief. For example, patients often voice relief that they restrained themselves when affectively aroused and did not say hurtful things. The inhibitory affects have the opposite physiological manifestations of the activating affects, that is, restriction or inhibition of flow of energy and inhibition of the action tendency. When used adaptively, however, moderate levels of inhibition can improve relationships and bring relief.

Shock is a common reaction to my criteria of "relief" following adaptive expression of affect. I am often asked, "How can anger be relieving? How can grief be relieving?" The answer is in the adaptive application of these emotions—and indeed, that is what they were *designed to do* through evolution (see Plutchik, 1962, 1984, for discussion of the evolutionary significance of affects). When anger is well guided and well applied, relief should result from setting right a bad experience. Grieving should result in the feeling of loss becoming more bearable.

Therapists need to remain sensitive, however, to individual, gender, social, and cultural differences when assessing affective experiencing. As we grow in our understanding of adaptive affective responding, these guidelines will become more finely honed.

Characteristics of Maladaptive Affect

When relief does not follow the experiencing of emotions, then two issues need to be considered: (a) excessive inhibitory affects and (b) excessive defensive use of affects may be *following* (sometimes only by milliseconds) the experience of the adaptive affect. For example, a patient might say, *When I say no, I feel guilty,* or *When I cry, I feel ashamed.*

In more extreme instances, inhibitory or self-attacking feelings may function as a defense to totally block the experience of the affect: *When he yelled at me, I became overwhelmed with anxiety,* or *After his death, I was consumed with guilt.* In the first statement, the anxiety appears to be completely replacing the anger, and in the second, guilt seems to completely stop the grief.

The physiological description of the maladaptively used affects presents quite the opposite picture to that of the adaptive affects. Instead of a sense of vitality and integration of experience, maladaptive use of affect can take the form of (a) higher intensity of expression due to insufficient inhibition (e.g., raging, yelling, bellowing, affect magnification) or (b) higher constriction of expression due to excessive intensities of inhibition.

The characteristics of the maladaptive use of affects include either:

1. the outward *acting out* or *an intense rush* of some form of energy;
2. the generation of a heightened or *urgent action tendency;*

or:

1. the inner direction of energy (constriction, withdrawal, inhibition);
2. the generation of excessively thwarting or self-attacking inhibition of action.

The result is:

1. short-term or momentary *relief* for the patient if acted out and increased frustration if not;
2. a *maladaptive reaction* in its interpersonal application (toward the self or others);
3. greater conflict or problems.

SPECIFIC AFFECTS IN CLINICALLY RELEVANT CLUSTERS: ACTIVATING AND INHIBITORY

Each of the specific affects is presented in three different groups. The first and second clusters are "activating": The regulatory affects act on relationships to regulate the experience of separation, boundary violations, or closeness–attachment; and the pleasure-giving affects act on the body to promote interest, comfort, or sexual desire. The third cluster is the inhibitory affects, which act in a way that restricts or limits responding. Although these labels are based on repeated clinical examination of videotapes, this is not the only possible grouping; affects and drives can be categorized in a number of ways depending on the purpose for doing so. Affects can be separated into positive versus negative clusters (e.g., Watson & Clark, 1992), or into those that protect the species versus those that support procreation, and so forth (e.g., Plutchik, 1984). This particular clustering of activating versus inhibiting emotions represents a useful distinction in the psychotherapeutic process. A description of these categories follows.

CLUSTER 1: ACTIVATING–REGULATORY AFFECTS
1. Distress–anguish (including sadness, sorrow, and grief)
2. Anger–rage (which leads to constructive self-assertion)
3. Affects associated with attachment (e.g., excitement and enjoyment, which lead to attraction, tenderness, devotion, etc.)
4. Fear–terror (i.e., the flight response)
5. Contempt–disgust (when appropriately directed at unacceptable behavior of others)

CLUSTER 2: ACTIVATING–PLEASURE-GIVING AFFECTS
1. Interest–excitement (including enthusiasm, curiosity, thrill, awe)
2. Enjoyment–joy (including serenity, tranquillity, peace)
3. Affects associated with sexual desire (e.g., excitement and enjoyment that generate passion)

CLUSTER 3: INHIBITORY OR AVERSIVE AFFECTS
1. Fear–terror (i.e., inhibition or paralysis of response, including anxiety)
2. Shame–guilt–humiliation (including shyness, embarrassment)
3. Pain (a blend of many affects, including intense levels of fear, shame, and anguish)
4. Contempt–disgust (directed at one's own unacceptable behavior)

As noted in chapter 1, these labels are not single affective states but families of related states that constitute "a theme and variations" (Ekman, 1992b, pp. 172–173). The affect clusters (both activating and inhibitory) are presented as a mnemonic device to aid the clinician in sorting out the complexity of patients' emotional communications.

The First Activating Cluster: Regulatory Emotions

Often the healthiest patients present with just one or two specific feelings that need sorting out (e.g., sorrow or anger). These patients, a relatively small percentage, otherwise function well socially and occupationally, and they can be helped to be more comfortable with their angry or grief-laden feelings in a relatively few sessions. Most patients, however, have difficulty not only with grief and anger, but also with the affects associated with attachment or closeness to others. Almost 20 years ago, Malan pointed out what has not been adequately realized in the field: the degree to which the combination of unfulfilled love, unexpressed grief, and anger about loss and deprivation plays a part in neurotic illness of all kinds (1979, p. 193). This first cluster of affects (desire for closeness, grief, and anger), therefore, is the most frequently dealt with in therapy. (Fear, as in flight, and contempt play a less frequent role here than they do as inhibitory affects.)

Sorrow, anger, and the affects associated with attachment can be seen as having the regulatory function of setting things right when they go wrong. To borrow from the laws of physics, for every life event or environmental *action*, there appears to have evolved a biologically prepared, *equal, and analogous* emotional *reaction* (e.g., Plutchik, 1984; Tomkins, 1962). Sorrow regulates loss; anger regulates intrusion, wanting, and not wanting; and fear (as in flight) regulates threat. Affects associated with attachment regulate closeness or distance to others and form the basis of social bonds and human development. This chapter presents examples of these affective reactions in both their adaptive and maladaptive versions. Sorrow, anger, and desire for attachment are focused on predominantly because of their frequent contribution to pathology. Fear, which both regulates distance and freezes action, is focused on briefly here and more extensively in the category of inhibitory affects. Clinical interventions that are useful with each specific category of feeling are discussed.

Distress–Anguish: Sadness, Sorrow, and Grief

Tomkins labeled this affect category "distress/anguish," and its basis is the separation cry of the infant (e.g., Panskepp, 1982; Tomkins, 1984):

> The distress cry of the infant subjects the mother to the same kind of punishment the infant is experiencing, since the cry as heard will activate the cry in anyone who hears it. In addition to the cry as a motive urging both the infant and the mother to "do" something, there is the positive reward of the shared smile which will make it more likely that, after the crisis . . . is past, the mother will continue to interact with . . . the child. (Tomkins, 1962, pp. 398–399)

Other affects in this affect family are sadness, sorrow, and grief, all of which are natural reactions to various types of losses or unmet needs.

BEHAVIORAL MANIFESTATIONS OF SORROW

The experience of sadness should involve some welling up of sorrowful feeling accompanied by a wish to cry or sob. Patients may feel tears in their eyes, their chest heaving or becoming heavy, or quivering in the lips. The therapist must stay vigilant for comments like "I feel tense. My throat feels tight. I feel a knot in my stomach or chest. I feel numb." The tight sensation typically represents a defensive reaction: a way of fighting down or holding back the expression of the grief. If the patient acknowledges a holding back, the therapist should move to the defense-restructuring procedures of exploring the anxiety (or guilt, shame, or pain) in the transference: *What would it be like for you to share the depth of your sadness with me right now?*

More often than not, people carry shame or embarrassment about being that open or vulnerable with anyone, even a therapist they trust. Discussing the possibility allows the patient to practice, in imagery, so that the fear is desensitized. Often patients are more able to allow sorrow to flow after a quiet examination of their fears about letting go.

THE PROCESS OF GRIEF

An important aspect of dynamic therapy is helping patients to bear the grief that has been previously warded off. Grief is not one specific affect; it is an adaptive coping process for adjusting to loss that involves the working through of many affects, memories, and beliefs. In full grieving, the heaving sobs release a tidal wave of sorrow with each gulp. The effect is like putting a heavy burden down, or letting something go to regain one's equilibrium. The need to release the energy of grief can be like the *opposite* of a strong thirst, in which water is gulped down an open and receptive throat. In full and unfettered grieving, the throat is similarly open, but expressive, with sobs feeling as though they flow from inside the body outward, with relief.

Grief is largely composed of sadness but also encompasses the full range of affect in relation to the loss. Tenderness and love are crucial components (e.g., *I'll miss him so, his patience and gentle nature*). Anger needs to be addressed as well, because if one does not easily integrate positive with negative feelings, the resolution of the grief is impeded. Therefore, anger and unmet longings must be sorted through and made peace with, in "putting love away."

In the grief process, the previously existing image has to be transformed into a new inner representation that is in line with current reality, whether the loss is of a person, a job, a place, a thing, a hope, or a dream. All the memories—or hopes for the future—need to be stored in a way that comfort rather than torment the individual.

According to George Vaillant, "grief work leads to remembering, not forgetting; it is a process of internalizing, not extruding. Attachment, if properly treated, provides us strength forever" (1988, p. 158).

Mature defenses are also employed in a healthy grief process. Suppression is needed to modulate the overall affect so that it does not become overwhelming. Sublimation is essential to be able to process the range of positive and negative affective memories in fantasy until they are well integrated. Patients need to be taught that grief comes in waves and will ebb and flow over weeks and months. Again, the patient must be made aware of the distinction between adaptive forms of mourning and melancholic depression. This differentiation is presented in Table 7.1.

If pathological mourning is present, many clinicians have recommended that this affect must be attended to first or at least be *considered* first in treatment. In a sense, unresolved mourning always is a factor in psychotherapy. It has been said that *all sorrow is unmet longing*.[2] What therapy problem does *not* concern unmet longings? The vast majority of patients wanted *something* they did not get. Even when something was given that was not wanted (e.g., abuse, overprotection, or overindulgence that elicited dependency), there still remain the longings for support, protection, or encouragement that were not given.

To assist the grief process, therapists should use guided imagery to gently expose the patient to the most vivid of the sad memories: *Did you have a last good-bye? What more would you like to have said? What do you remember about the funeral? When was the last time you saw him? What did her face look like when last you visited? How would it have been to hold his hand? What regrets do you have? What were the feelings inside you that you were unable to share? What words were in your heart that remained unsaid? What would you have wanted most to hear said to you?*

The therapist's job is to try, step-by-step, to work through and expose the patients to all the conflicted aspects of the grief. One may ask patients whether they feel they have reached the point at which nothing more is held back, so there is a sense of resolution or peace about the loss. If this is not the case, the therapist should be mindful of this and return to the same subject in later sessions. In chapter 10, there is an example of grief work with the Machine Builder.

CONFLICTS ABOUT EXPERIENCING SORROW

Most common fears about sorrow are expressed as follows: *I'll never stop crying. I'll look foolish. You'll think I'm weak or stupid.* Many of these issues have been addressed earlier; the main point is to regulate the anxieties around the fears until grief is experienced.

DEFENSIVE FORMS OF SORROW

Sorrow and weepiness often disguise other feelings, typically anger or disgust. In addition, many genuine expressions of sadness also include a portion of defensive sorrow. The maladaptive components can be easily identified, however, because they always involve some form of *inhibition, self-pity, taking a victim role,* or *complaining: Boo hoo. Poor me. Why does it always happen to me? Nothing will ever get better.* In *Mourning and Melancholia*

[2]Jonathan Crist, M.D., Providence, R.I., personal communication, 1994.

(1917/1955), Freud noted that the "fall in self-esteem" is the major distinguishing feature:

> Mourning is regularly the reaction to the loss of a loved person, or to the loss of some abstraction which has taken the place of one, such as fatherland, liberty, and ideal. . . .
>
> The distinguishing mental features of melancholia are a profoundly painful dejection, abrogation of interest in the outside world, loss of the capacity to love, inhibition of all activity, and a lowering of the self-regarding feeling to a degree that finds utterance in self-reproaches and self-reviling, and culminates in a delusional expectation of punishment. . . . With one exception, the same traits are met with in grief. The fall in self-esteem is absent in grief. (p. 157)

The Axis I disorder major depression is, in some cases, an example of defensive sorrow, or melancholia, in which negative affects have become associated with the sense of self (hence the fall in self-esteem). Defensive melancholia may avoid an adaptive grief reaction, avoid anger or conflict (as in anger turned inward), or avoid the pain of longing. Table 7.1 presents examples of both adaptive and maladaptive forms of the emotion sorrow.

TABLE 7.1
Adaptive Versus Defensive Forms of Sorrow

Adaptive sorrow (mourning)	Defensive sorrow (melancholia)
Compassion for self	Self-blame, self-pity, self-attack
Relief follows	Frustration follows—hopelessness
Good memories integrated with bad	Bad memories predominate
Hopeful about future	Bleak, hopeless about future
Feels close to others	Feels more distant
Listener feels deep compassion	Listener feels attacked or helpless

However important grief work is, therapy will be lopsided if this is the sole focus. Patients can become overly sensitized to the chronic pain and suffering in the world: not an optimal resolution of any psychic dilemma. In addition to being able to grieve, we need to be able to assert ourselves, feel close enough to others to ask for what we want, say *no* to what we do not want, and feel enthusiasm, joy, and sexual desire. The other emotions are reviewed with that context in mind.

ANGER–RAGE AND ASSERTION

If feelings of grief, or defenses against it, provide a frequent starting point in therapy, anger is not far behind and must also be attended to. The capacity to handle one's own emotional power is a complex and frightening skill but one of the most important capacities we can teach our patients. Our angry feelings represent our emotional boundaries and our personal strength. Anger allows us to set limits and to say *no*.

Angry feelings have evolved as responses to our need to prevent intrusions, to right wrongs, or to obtain something that is lacked. If patients are not able to set limits when attacked, give voice to what is wanted or not wanted, feel deserving of things desired, or walk into a room with their head high and feel a right to be there, they have missed a huge component of healthy adaptive functioning. Anger can and does lead to a range of potential responses. Anger can make bad things *better* for oneself (by making it *worse* for transgressors) if one knows how to direct it properly. As Tomkins (1991) made clear, anger *motivates* us to act, but aggressive *action* is not synonymous with *angry feeling*. Assertion, for example, can be another, more adaptive way of responding. Depression can be the response when anger is not expressed but directed toward the self.

Tomkins repeatedly underscores that anger is an affect rather than a drive. Angry behavior obeys none of the rules common to other instinctive forces. Unlike drives, anger has no intrinsic periodicity; there are no metabolic changes produced by the absence of anger (as when an organism is deprived of food, water, or air); and animals do not need to attack unless provoked. Furthermore, Nathanson noted that the extensive study of affect in infancy and early childhood has been so damaging to classical psychoanalytic theory that many eminent scholars have had to rethink the old system (1992, p. 119). Tomkins wrote the following:

> Anger need not result in aggression or destruction if the stimulus is brief. It may result in no more than a brief howl or growl and a flailing of arms and legs, or a banging of a fist on the table. . . . If intensity of stimulus and anger is prolonged, however, the probability of aggressive, destructive motor action is increased if there is any action at all. . . . I am *not* supposing that anger necessarily leads to aggressive behavior, since clearly such behavior may be inhibited by fear of consequences, by shame or guilt, or be aggressive but turned against the self in self-mutilation or suicide. . . .
>
> As the duration of such intensity increases, the difficulty of control also increases, and a person is both less able to turn anger off and less able and less willing to control or inhibit explosive aggressive behavior. In this respect, anger is not unlike any intense affect, but it is more so because its combined intensity and duration potential is higher than is the case for any other affect. (1991, p. 121)

The reader is referred to Tomkins's chapter "Anger and Its Innate Activation" (1991, pp. 111–171).

BEHAVIORAL MANIFESTATIONS OF ANGER

The physiological responses that most often go along with anger are a building up of energy and an urge to lash out. The sensations have been described as a rush, a sense of energy swirling up through the body, a feeling of empowerment, and a desire to move or to act. One patient said she felt energy in her legs, as though she wanted to lunge. Many patients describe energy filling their arms, resulting in a desire to hit or push. Others want to yell. One should carefully scan the patient's body for such signs: a clenching of fists, pursing of lips, flexing of muscles, setting of the jaw, kicking of the foot, and so forth. Such behaviors are pointed out to bring the sensations in the various areas of the body into the patient's consciousness. It is also important to be vigilant for signs of inhibition. If the patient reports something like tenseness in the chest, arms, stomach, or elsewhere, this suggests holding back or fighting the emotion. Often, this is the only sensation that the patient is aware of. Indeed, anxiety can so flood the system at the first emergence of anger that in many individuals no visceral sensation of anger is felt at all. The therapist can inquire whether it is anger that is being experienced or something else going on. It is useful to let patients have a few minutes to ponder this question and come to their own conclusions. This may be the first time that the patient has recognized any physiological manifestation of an affect, so there often is a need to reflect on it. *Emotional processing moves much slower than cognitive processing.* The goal is to bring patients to a vivid awareness of their own internal responses so that the next time they are angry (outside of the session), they can at least identify what is happening to them: whether they are becoming pumped up with the energy of anger or allowing themselves to be flooded with anxiety.

THERAPIST: You seem filled with feeling right now toward your boss. Can you tell me what it is?
PATIENT: I feel so angry at him!
THERAPIST: How does that feel in your body?
PATIENT: I don't really know. I never thought about it.
THERAPIST: Well, these things aren't generally on the tip of the tongue. Take a moment and see if you can tell how your body signals you that you are angry.
PATIENT: I guess I feel energized . . . and there's tingling in my arms.
THERAPIST: Do you notice that you are clenching your fists?
PATIENT: Oh! I guess I am.
THERAPIST: What would you want to do if you were to put that energy into action, in fantasy of course?
PATIENT: I'd want to *punch* him.
THERAPIST: Let's look at how hard, and how often. We are not talking about acting on this of course, but we are looking honestly at what you feel.

This process allows patients to explore the angry feelings in their pure and irrational form. We are hard-wired to have this sort of responding potential, so we must make peace with it as it stirs within and know how to guide and control it as well. This is just the first step in the process of affect restructuring, however. The ultimate goal is to help build the capacity for assertion: a combination affect of anger and positive feeling. If one moves directly to teaching assertive expression, patients are in danger of trying to behave appropriately while still struggling with their own inner conflict about their "undesirable" angry feelings.

Therapists often have difficulty with any strong affect, but anger may be one of the most difficult (and controversial) of all. In helping a patient to feel violent or murderous feelings, therapists often feel they are doing something that conflicts with one of their values, that is, *that patients should not be encouraged toward violent behavior of any form.* Of course, I could not agree more, but this thinking reflects a confusion between the *inner experience* and the *outward behavioral expressions* of anger. One workshop participant wrote a note to me saying "I valued your presentation tremendously, except for your encouraging of the man to imagine beating up his mother! Please do not ever show this tape again!"

I could dismiss this comment as coming from someone who is not at peace with angry feelings toward parents, but in fact, many people are uncomfortable with this process, and their voices need to be heard. It often feels unpleasant to both the therapist and the patient to explore angry feelings. My rationale for continuing to amplify affective responses, including anger, is that *what happens inside our bodies need not be harmful or immoral.* Only our behavior should come under moral law. If our patients are ridden with guilt or shame at the arousal of anger, they will be crippled in the tasks of setting limits, asserting themselves, or defending themselves. Anger is not always a pleasant emotion, but it can be a most effective one. Repeated observations of dramatic improvement following desensitization of anger have underscored the value of doing so.

I present the example of the intentional amplification of angry feelings in a passive and beaten-down man (the example the woman in the workshop found so distressing). The patient was berated by his mother, his wife, and his bosses. He desperately needed to regain access to angry feelings. The following process was one way of helping him do so.

EXAMPLE: THE FERRYMAN'S ANGER AT HIS MOTHER

THERAPIST: You've told me several incidences of your mother standing over you and screaming. How did you feel toward her when she did that?

PATIENT: Oh, I didn't feel angry. I'm not that kind of guy.

THERAPIST: No? Look at the two fists that you just pulled up in front of you!

PATIENT: Oh! I didn't realize I did that! Well, I do get kinda mad. But that's as far as it goes.

THERAPIST: Can we see what you would feel if you let it go further, in your fantasy, of course.

PATIENT [*Laughing*]: Guess I'd want to punch her. [*Pausing*] Yes, I would, I'd knock her down!

THERAPIST: You say that blandly. Are you experiencing anything inside?

PATIENT: Yeah. [*Becoming animated*] I *do* feel angry, when I let myself. [*Holding up his fists*]

THERAPIST (*Continuing the imagery*): If you imagine knocking her down, what's the impulse now?

PATIENT: I'd want to knock her down . . . and kick her—in the feet!

THERAPIST: In the feet? [*I was confused by this; the head or stomach is much more common.*]

PATIENT: Yeah, 'cause then, she couldn't get up and yell at me anymore! [*Very energized*]

This was a relatively mild angry scene, yet it was offensive to people in several audiences. The imagery was enormously helpful to the Ferryman in standing up to his mother, and his relationship with his mother improved.

In 15 years of working with such images, my colleagues and I repeatedly have seen relationships get better when people *acknowledged (but of course, did not act out) their angry feelings*. Malan's (1979) case of the Almoner provides another example of constructive assertion improving a relationship. Mothers feel much more tenderness for their infants (and compassion for themselves) when they accept that they can feel murderous toward their children at times. A minister said to a friend of mine years ago, shortly after her daughter was born, "Have you had any child-abuse fantasies yet?" She just laughed, but the inner relief his comment provided was profound. She had been awakened four times one night and had a demanding schedule the next day. She had been hating herself and thinking she was a bad mother for having fantasies of wanting to throw the child against the wall! The minister's comment drew to her attention that such fantasies were a common reaction, and she calmed down. In like manner, adult children and their parents become closer when angry feelings are acknowledged openly but not with hostility. Typically, parents are defensive at first, but I have been touched by the large number of parents who work hard to see their children's point of view and learn to respond more considerately.

If therapists are uncomfortable in dealing with violent images, however, they should consider other methods. There are many roads to the top of the mountain. The objective that is crucial is to help patients feel angry without shame or acting out and to comfortably assert themselves whenever necessary. If a therapist accomplishes this goal without the use of violent images, so be it. As our treatment interventions evolve, we may learn new and different ways of eliciting healthy protective assertion in nonviolent ways. However this task is done, patients need to become at ease with their angry and even murderous responses, which are inevitable in living.

There is another viable pathway that I discovered accidentally: After patients experience deep grief and awaken a sense of compassion for themselves, a self-protective anger bubbles up within them naturally. One severely impaired man, who had gone through a lengthy grief process and grew enormously in his compassion for himself, came into therapy one day shaking his fist and saying quietly but passionately: *I will never again let anyone treat me the way my mother treated me. Never!*

His anger erupted naturally and fully without a minute of focus on anger in the treatment. Hitherto, he had been completely unable even to consider anger at his mother. At 7-year follow-up, this man was remarkably improved. In trying to locate him after a move, I spoke with his father, who said, "We just had a wonderful visit. He is totally cured." Given the severity of this man's dysfunction, his father's statement seemed too good to be true. But he is living happily with his wife, from whom he had been estranged for many years, and he does seem to be functioning fairly well.

ASSERTION

Assertion is an optimal adaptive use of the affect anger–rage. Assertion, like grief, is an adaptive coping response. Just as grief is a complex combination of sadness, other affects, and cognitive coping skills, so assertion is a complex combination of affects as well as cognitive appraisal and guidance. Assertion is based on not liking something that is happening (the need to set limits) or needing something to happen that is not (the need to ask for things). Anger is one major component of assertion but not the only one. To be assertive, one must integrate the positive feelings with the negative ones so that aggression is tempered. Inhibition must be reduced so that shame and fear do not predominate. Cognitive coping skills must be employed so that actions are guided toward adaptive resolution. This includes a conscious use of suppression to temper one's response. Many ego capacities such as judgment and insight can be used to guide assertive action. Of course, in treatment, pure forms of anger (e.g., fury, murderous rage) must be explored in imagery and desensitized. The goal of such desensitization is to become sufficiently comfortable with angry feelings that anger can be integrated with other affects and cognition and used in a balanced, well-guided assertion.

CONFLICTS ABOUT EXPERIENCING ANGER

Some of the typical pathogenic beliefs (or maladaptive cognitions) regarding anger include the following: anxiety (I'll lose control and hurt someone; I'll be rejected by the people I need); shame–guilt (I'll feel like a terrible person; I was taught never to be angry; I don't know if I'm justified in getting angry); and pain (I can't bear to make someone else feel bad). Therapists need to be vigilant for the many conflicts about anger that vary widely across patients.

DEFENSIVE FORMS OF ANGER

Carol Tavris wrote a book entitled *Anger: The Misunderstood Emotion* (1982) in which she correctly pointed out the destructive purposes that anger can be put to. However, Tavris's arguments against anger addressed the *defensive* form of anger, which are inappropriate. She noted the uselessness of "venting," "catharsis," and "letting your anger out." As Lorna Benjamin (1993a) noted, such defensive anger plays a role in several Axis II personality disorders, such as borderline, antisocial, and paranoid disorders.

There is a danger, however, of "throwing the baby out with the bathwater" by devaluing or shaming a vital aspect of our emotional life. Anger, well-managed, can serve the individual and the culture through establishing clear boundaries. Good fences make good neighbors. Anger provides us our power, our boundaries, and our protection, and we desperately need it in our lives. On the other hand, defensive anger can be used destructively, and this is what Tavris argued against. Defensive anger differs from adaptive anger because it is destructive rather than constructive, is often louder, involves more frustration, and results in interpersonal closure rather than resolution (see Table 7.2).

At the other end of the anger continuum, there are therapists who are strong proponents of the idea that it is okay to be mad across the board. They indulge patients' acting out or displacement of defensive anger, thinking that their patients are doing something therapeutic by showing feelings. But cathartic and defensive bursts of anger are impotent in their impact, and are ultimately destructive. This form of anger leaves the individual in a helpless, frustrated position and does not resolve the problem at hand. It is far more useful to help patients see what might be underneath the anger—generally, hurt feelings, pain, and unmet longings—to appreciate its intensity and to transmute *consciously* the legitimate anger into assertion, grief, and longings for closeness.

PATIENT: You are 20 minutes late, and I have to leave immediately after the session . . . and I really needed to see you today. A lot has happened. I'm real upset, and now, on top of that, I'm furious with you!

THERAPIST: I don't blame you for being angry. Just when you really needed me, I wasn't available.

PATIENT: No!

THERAPIST: It must be agonizing to have so much to say and not be able to do so.

PATIENT: Yeah, you bastard. You doctors only care about yourselves.

THERAPIST: That's a painful, lonely feeling to have . . . that I might not care.

The therapist gently moves the focus from anger to the pain of longing, not because anger should not be explored, but because grief and longing are even more fundamental here.

TABLE 7.2
Adaptive Versus Defensive Forms of Anger

Adaptive use of anger (Assertion)	Defensive use of anger (Aggression)
Conscious containment of angry feelings	Unreflective venting of angry feelings
Quiet, firm, clear statements of wishes	Loud tone, swearing, bluster covering pain
Anger integrated with positive feelings	Anger split from positive feelings
Planning of best course of action	Little or no forethought of action
Relationships often improved	Relationships often damaged

AFFECTS ASSOCIATED WITH ATTACHMENT–SOCIAL RESPONSIVITY
(CLOSENESS–CONTACT)

As difficult as it is to talk about anger in therapy, it may be even more un-comfortable to explore tender feelings; however, nothing is as important. Therapists historically have had little instruction concerning management of positive feelings in the therapeutic relationship. The traditional psycho-dynamic dictum was: "Interpret negative transference; ignore positive trans-ference." Yet doing so ignores the most valuable part of living—closeness, tenderness, care, and devotion—vital areas of functioning that are most often impaired in patients. "It may cause problems, so ignore it," is not an adequate solution. Therapists need extensive instruction on how to manage both positive and negative feelings. Chapter 9 on self–other restructuring discusses this topic of closeness in great detail.

Harry Harlow (1958) taught us about the drive for social contact through his famous experiments demonstrating that orphaned baby monkeys sought a terrycloth "mother" to cling to (even when fed milk by a wire "mother"). Harlow argued, therefore, that affectional bonding is not a drive that is sec-ondary to the hunger drive but an independent drive clearly requiring "con-tact comfort." Tomkins, considering the relationship between social respon-sivity and the sexual drive, believed that the sexual drive, although a "powerful amplifier of social responsiveness," did not by itself provide "suf-ficient or enduring enough interest in others" to produce the social sensitiv-ity necessary for human development (Tomkins, 1962, p. 400). Harlow's ex-periments lent support to Tomkins's premise by demonstrating that deprivation of "contact comfort" had profound and deleterious effects on socialization in animals (e.g., Harlow, 1958; Harlow & Harlow, 1962; Harlow & Zimmermann, 1959).

Bowlby believed that attachment behavior (affectional bonding) was as important to mating as it was to parenting behavior (1969, p. 179). Today, much neurological research is accumulating to support Bowlby's theories (e.g., Insel, 1992; Kling & Brothers, 1992; and Panskepp, 1982). For Bowlby, attachment consisted of several specific categories of behaviors. There were primary behaviors of sucking and clinging and the gratification of physio-logical needs (e.g., hunger, warmth) from the mother (1982, p. 178).[3] Bowlby also noted the classic work by Spitz and Wolf (1946) demonstrating that the human face is a powerful elicitor of an infant's smiles (Bowlby, 1982, p. 285). Today, neurological research (e.g., Insel, 1992) has demonstrated that attach-ment behaviors (parenting, breast feeding, mating, cuddling) are under-girded by the neuropeptide oxytocin.

---

[3]Along with sucking, clinging, and gratification, Bowlby added an additional pri-mary drive: the "return-to-womb" drive. I have omitted it from this discussion be-cause it is the most highly inferential of the four; the others are based on easily ob-servable behaviors. To the extent that on bad days we might want to collapse into someone's arms or crawl into bed and pull the covers over our head, it may not be totally without substance. However, the human behaviors of cuddling and clinging satisfy "sanctuary needs," and those responses can subsume this fuzzier construct.

In addition, the work of Stern (1985) and other infant researchers has extended awareness of the richness of the mutuality of the mother–infant interaction. Stern pointed out that attachment theory makes the achievement of a basic sense of human connectedness "the end point, not the starting point, of a long, active developmental course" (1985, p. 241). Pervasive feelings of connectedness and interpersonal well-being occur between 2 and 7 months of age and serve as an emotional reservoir of human connectedness. One of Stern's more important contributions was his demonstration that the attachment process (as well as the development of the self) is not passive but results from the infant's *active contraction of representations of interactions with self-regulating others* (1985, p. 241). In contrast to those who suggest that connectedness is the result of a failure in differentiation, Stern sees attachment as a developmental and interpersonal success (1985, p. 241). The explanation for these conflicting viewpoints is that *defensive connectedness* is the result of a failure of differentiation: the desperate clinging demonstrated by those who have never been secure enough to separate. In contrast, the adaptive drive or propensity for attachment or affectional bonds makes the infant reach out to the mother and draws people together at times of sorrow, loneliness, or happiness, but it also allows for enough security in those attachments to support independence and autonomy.

Tomkins has further extended the understanding of attachment by emphasizing the connection between the biological drive that he calls "social responsiveness" and the affect system (1962, chapter 12). Attachment and affects are long overdue for being seen as inextricably intertwined phenomena. Furthermore, neurological research increasingly points to the interconnectedness of attachment and affect responses in the amygdala and related structures (e.g., Brothers, 1990; Kling & Brothers, 1992). One cannot and should not be studied without the other, because social bonds grow in the fertile soil of joy, die in the poisonous atmosphere of shame or contempt, and suffer in the face of conflict. In contrast, interest–excitement paired with the drive for attachment results in eagerness to make social contacts, attraction, or romantic love. Enjoyment–joy paired with the drive for attachment is the basis of social bonds and committed love.

Tomkins noted that the smile of joy does not require body contact: it extends the range of the social bond by providing mutual satisfaction and reward at a distance, mediated through eye contact. Indeed, Tomkins said, one of the prime ways in later life for adults to recapture this type of communion is by "the mutual awareness of each other's smile"; these are the conditions that allow falling in love (1962, p. 398). In therapy, the importance of human contact through the meeting of the eyes and the smile of joy cannot be underestimated. If the therapist's face remains neutral, the patient's capacity for attachment may be missed or never encouraged.

EXAMPLE OF FEAR OF CLOSENESS: THE UNFORGIVEN TEENAGER
THERAPIST: You seem to have a difficult time looking into my eyes.
PATIENT: Oh, that would be impossible . . . I couldn't.

THERAPIST: What would be so impossible about it? What would be the worst part?

PATIENT: I don't know. [*Still looking away and now beginning to fidget*]

THERAPIST: Can we explore that together? You seem so uncomfortable. What makes you the most uncomfortable when you think of looking at me?

PATIENT: I couldn't bear it if you didn't feel as I did. I'd feel so alone I'd want to die.

THERAPIST: Well, no wonder you avoid my eyes! You want to feel close to me. And not being close would feel so devastating.

PATIENT: Yeah.

THERAPIST: Let's consider this more. Does it really seem that I am an adversary, or against you in some way?

PATIENT: No. I know you're not.

THERAPIST: Okay, do you think you could let yourself trust me enough to look at me for a moment?

PATIENT [*Glancing up, hesitantly*]: Oh . . . this is so hard to do!

THERAPIST: There are a lot of nervous feelings there.

PATIENT: Oh, yes!

THERAPIST: Can we look at what some of those fears might be?

PATIENT: It's been so long since I let myself feel compassion from anyone. It's been such a long time since I've . . . I've [*struggling to speak*] I've let myself feel it.

In this way, the therapist gently exposes the patient to the feelings (the closeness and the anxiety about it) in the patient–therapist relationship.

Many therapists feel uncomfortable with the sexual feelings that may be aroused by directly focusing on feelings of closeness. This is probably one of the reasons neutrality and abstinence have felt so safe. But it is incumbent on therapists to learn to handle these strong emotions wisely. They are the stuff that robust and healthy attachment is made of. We need to provide adequate teaching for therapists-in-training as well. (The handling of sexual feelings is discussed later in the chapter, and issues of closeness are described with examples in chapter 9.)

EXAMPLE: A WOMAN WHO BEGINS TO OPEN UP

This middle-aged businesswoman has decided to let herself be more vulnerable:

PATIENT: Time has come for me to not be so tightly wrapped. [*It took 6 months of hard work to bring this withdrawn and intellectual individual to this point. I felt joy at hearing her words, and I said so. She felt embarrassed by my saying so.*]

THERAPIST: What is your embarrassment about?

PATIENT: Not wanting to look too pleased. Not wanting to lap up your praise . . . not wanting to feel foolish or look foolish in my eyes for too naively taking in my praise. [*This implied that I would turn on her if she let herself feel pleasure in my positive remark.*]

THERAPIST: Isn't it sad that you still have such a struggle trusting me? But I can tell that you have some distance on the struggle, just by your telling me about it. So can we feel joy together right now . . . about you and the important work you have done? [*She smiled and nodded and tears filled her eyes.*]

CHARACTERISTICS OF ADAPTIVE FORMS OF ATTACHMENT

Adaptive attachment means that a person can distinguish friend from foe, and can appropriately approach a caring person as well as manage or avoid uncaring persons. These capacities require the full range of adaptive affects.

In positive affects, most patients report an experience of warmth, softness, or gentle waves of a pleasant sensation in the chest area when thinking about or being with the cared-for other. This is the affect Tomkins (1962) called enjoyment–joy that, experienced interpersonally, is a calmness and sense of peace with others. Along with these feelings is generally a longing to touch, hold, caress, and so forth. In defensive or immature forms of attachment, calmness is often incorrectly confused with boredom, or lack of interest. The adaptive calmness presented in this discussion entails an extremely low level of any form of anxiety (i.e., openness, vulnerability), and it allows the deepest sense of delight or pleasure in the interpersonal experience.

Tenderness, devotion, and emotional openness, like grief and assertion, represent complex adaptive functioning involving a range of feelings. To allow the vulnerability of tenderness, one must be able to defend oneself if attacked (assertion) and risk bearing the loss (grief). *The capacities for maintaining boundaries and bearing losses are essential prerequisites for sustained intimacy.* If patients have not acquired these capacities, they should not be encouraged to make themselves vulnerable. It would be like sending a lamb to the slaughter.

The therapist should be aware that this sense of openness and vulnerability is often terrifying and can be strenuously defended against. For example, many people (of both sexes) are not comfortable with feelings of tenderness, so they move quickly to sexuality. Other patients move quickly to devaluation of others to avoid tender feelings. Defensive sexuality and devaluation are all too common, and both disguise the longing for closeness.

DEFENSIVE FORMS OF ATTACHMENT OR CLOSENESS

The defensive or maladaptive variants of the affects associated with attachment are the subject of songs about unrequited love, much romantic poetry, and most soap opera plots. It is "love gone hungry." Benjamin's position that "every pathology is a gift of love" (1993a) is a way of alerting us to the ubiquitous crying out for love, affirmation, and approval that underlies all the personality disorders. In some of these disorders, this defensive longing can be conscious and excessive (e.g., borderline, dependent, depressive, and histrionic disorders), whereas in others, the longing is overly avoided or defended against (e.g., avoidant, obsessive, narcissistic, paranoid, schizoid, and schizotypal disorders). In most personality disorders, therefore, the ability to be close to others, in healthy give-and-take interactions, is seriously impaired and warrants attention in treatment.

Longing is an ambiguous term that can have both adaptive and defensive variants. Up to a point, it is healthy, normal, and biologically predispositioned to wish, desire, or long for another. However, an excessive degree of longing—*defensive longing* or desperate desire—avoids *the grief and the anger of what one has not received*. If one continues to long passively for someone who is unresponsive or abusive, one has never truly said good-bye, never truly emotionally separated. This is what Michael Alpert[4] has called "pathological hope." Such need-filled longing or craving is not adaptive excitement that fuels enthusiasm and promotes involvement; it reflects anxious desperation. *Such "desire" is not a loving joy that cherishes and values; it is grasping need.* It is crucial that this distinction be made, for defensive *need* (e.g., addiction, codependence) all too often has been mistaken for *love* (i.e., valuing, cherishing, caring, holding dear), with tragic results. Of all our affects, love is the most confused and misunderstood.

This defensive and needy "loving" reflects three main factors: (a) an *excess of defensive longing*; (b) a *deficit of anger, contempt or disgust, or grief (for defensive or nonresponsive others)*; and (c) a *deficit of self-compassion*. Each patient who yearns desperately for an abusive or neglectful partner is experiencing *defensive longing*—not the satisfaction and comfort of adaptive loving. In contrast, defensive attachment is an *addiction* or *maladaptive need*. Adaptive loving involves some degree of enjoyment or joy, as well as care giving and care soliciting. Adaptive loving does not persist long in the face of abuse; however, if one has never experienced adaptive forms of loving, it is easy to accept abuse or neglect in its place (see Table 7.3).

TABLE 7.3
Adaptive Versus Defensive Attachment

Adaptive attachment (Love, care)	Defensive attachment (Need)
Care for self and others	Need, dependency; addictive attachment
Grateful hugging, holding	Angry, needy, clinging, codependent
Gratitude	Envy
Eye contact sustained and comforting	Anxious eye contact, gaze averting
Active desire for closeness	Passive or demanding longing
Closeness grows slowly over time	Urgent, rapid moves toward closeness
Need satisfaction is negotiated	Need satisfaction is demanded
Autonomy–separation is respected; other's growth encouraged	Autonomy–separation is frightening; other's growth feared
Empathy is felt for the other	Self-absorption blocks empathy
I–thou relationship; the other is cherished	I–it relationship; the other is used or ignored

[4]Michael Alpert, M.D., personal communication, 1993.

CONFLICTS ABOUT EXPERIENCING ADAPTIVE FORMS OF ATTACHMENT

Stories about conflicts concerning attachment and closeness could fill volumes. Indeed, it is the basis of all pathology, the dilemma of civilization. As industrialized societies grow, so grows interpersonal estrangement. We are born exquisitely socially responsive, but our responsivity is threatened, if not deadened, by inhibiting reactions from others: anxiety (I'll be betrayed or rejected), guilt (I don't deserve to be loved), shame (I'm just not lovable, I'm disgusting and pathetic), and pain (I never want to be hurt that much again). The fundamental task of the dynamic therapist is to find the conflicts or inhibitory affects associated with attachments and replace them with positive feeling and nurturant inner models of others.

THE REGULATORY FUNCTION OF FEAR AND CONTEMPT OR DISGUST

A brief discussion of the activating, regulatory function of fear and contempt or disgust is included here because these affects are fundamentally adaptive but are less frequently dealt with in treatment.

One of the functions of fear, its evolutionary function, is to promote flight: to put distance between us and a threatening object. (The other, sometimes life-saving, function of fear is to freeze, which can be both maladaptive and adaptive and is discussed in the later section on inhibitory affects.) In this section I focus only briefly on *insufficient* fear (i.e., when the adaptive flight response is blocked or thwarted) because this response is lower in frequency in clinical work. In contrast to the high frequency of occurrence of the restriction of sadness, anger, or closeness, it is less common for pathology to be a result of insufficient fear. It does occur, however, when people place themselves in or do not remove themselves from dangerous situations by denying the danger. People can be insufficiently vigilant or "care-less" about themselves and thus vulnerable to harm. "Thrill-seekers" or battered wives can be seen as having insufficient fear or insufficient self-care, thereby placing themselves in potentially dangerous or destructive situations. (There may be shame or pain of longing inhibiting the fear response.) Certainly, therapists need to be aware of this problem and be prepared to work with it using processes similar to those described for working with other affects. The more common problem in pathology, however, is maladaptive high levels of fear and anxiety, which are discussed in the sections on inhibitory affects.

The regulatory function of contempt or disgust is similar to that of anger; to put distance between the individual and the offensive person or behavior, or to inhibit the offensive behavior. Excessive contempt or disgust of others creates destructive barriers to closeness. Insufficient contempt or disgust may reflect deficient self-protection mechanisms and permit an individual to stay connected with harmful others. Defensive forms of contempt or disgust may be seen in arrogance, social cruelty, or disdain that cover insecurity and poor self-esteem. In psychotherapy, I suspect that contempt or disgust is often labeled as anger, yet there are subtle differences that need to be better understood. Research is needed on this set of affects because little attention has been given them.

The Second Activating Cluster: Pleasure-Giving Emotions

> Dynamic psychology has tended to limit itself to the ramifications of the affects of fear and anger and the biological drives of sex and hunger. Yet it is clear that one does not understand a human being unless one knows what interests him and what he enjoys and how this came to be. (Tomkins, 1962, p. 396)

The second cluster of feelings (interest–excitement, enjoyment–joy, and sexual desire) is less frequently dealt with in treatment, yet it is as important as the first cluster. The importance of these emotions became salient as my patients resolved their conflicts concerning grief, anger, and closeness and felt freer to consider more positive aspects of life. We need to help build pleasurable, life-enhancing experiences for patients, as we work to reduce the occurrence of unpleasurable experience.

INTEREST–EXCITEMENT

In therapy, interest–excitement may be the most overlooked of all the affects, and it is rarely mentioned when therapeutic interventions are considered, with a few exceptions from the gestalt–experiential school (e.g., Polster & Polster, 1973; Zinker, 1977).[5] Yet we deal with the inverse form of interest–excitement with most of our patients, most of the time. *Anhedonia* (the lack of interest in things), along with blue mood, is one of the two primary indicators of depression and remarkably frequent in occurrence. Only rarely have I heard therapists discussing the adaptive alternatives of interest or excitement or even curiosity or enthusiasm as a treatment focus. In my training, I received not one word of supervision on this topic. Yet what could be more crucial to an active, healthy, involved life? Where are we without our interests? How desperately flat and dull must be a life without enthusiasm. Tomkins pointed out that interest is a necessary condition for the infant's formation of the perceptual world and for support of long-term physiological exertion. "Excitement lends more than spice to life," Tomkins said. "Without zest, long-term effort and commitment cannot be sustained, either physiologically or psychologically" (1984, p. 173). Furthermore, excitement is a fundamental component of creativity, and the heightening of attention and the pull to explore, to reach out, to examine (1962, p. 352). Excitement and, therefore, some forms of creativity are greatly influenced by and interact with the degree of enjoyment in affectional bonds.

Harlow's monkeys who were reared without benefit of the affection and solace of a terrycloth mother ran in terror from a frightening object. Those who had enjoyed the benefits of a comforting mother ran to her for protection and, shortly after experiencing the reassuring contact, turned to explore and do battle with the object that had a moment before frightened them (Tomkins, 1991, p. 530).

[5]My thanks to Clifford Mahler of Buffalo, NY, for bringing these authors to my attention (personal communication, May 1995).

CHARACTERISTICS OF INTEREST–EXCITEMENT

Interest–excitement is demonstrated behaviorally by attention, curiosity, exploration, and energy. The individual's attention is drawn to that which is interesting, which could be a person, place, or thing. Interest–excitement is the affect that underlies much of romantic attraction, the choice of career, and vacation destination. Enthusiasm is another affect word whose meaning overlaps with that of excitement. Think of toddlers crawling around touching things and putting things in their mouths. Think about the active, exploring curiosity of children. Museums are now set up to allow children to touch and examine the exhibits in many different ways. "Look but do not touch" may be necessary in some situations, but when it is too frequent, curiosity can be hampered.

Examples of Interest–Excitement and Its Lack

I loved the course so much that I couldn't stop reading. I gulped down the assignments.

I was fascinated by him. He was one of the most interesting people I had ever met, and I could have talked to him all day.

The following example presents a patient who does not feel entitled to be interested or excited:

PATIENT: I have no desire to do my schoolwork. I used to force myself, but now it just doesn't work.

THERAPIST: What's the part that is most aversive?

PATIENT: There is nothing I am interested in.

THERAPIST: Well, then, no wonder you are having a difficult time pursuing your schoolwork. How can you expect to keep your attention on something if you are not interested in it?

PATIENT: Well, I *should* be interested in it.

THERAPIST: Who says so?

PATIENT: My parents. They want me to go into the family business.

THERAPIST: But what do you want to do?

PATIENT: I have no idea. I never had a choice in the matter.

THERAPIST: What courses did you find the most interesting?

PATIENT: Oh, I really liked my history courses. I even thought of teaching history. But my parents wouldn't hear of it.

THERAPIST: So it looks like there are some conflicts about pursuing things that interest you. Can we look at what some of those conflicts might be?

The next example is one in which a young man came to a grinding halt in his life in terms of involvement in work and love. His shame was excruciating.

PATIENT: I don't care about much. Nothing really turns me on.

THERAPIST: What would happen if you did get turned on to something? Can you think of a time when you were more interested in something?

PATIENT: Well, whatever I try just gets shot down. Once I really got into a science project at school. I made this exhibit, and I was going to put it in the Science Fair. But people just made fun of it. After that, I just felt, why bother. People just dump on you.

THERAPIST: That sounds so painful. Tell me more about it—the worst parts for you.

PATIENT: I never want to give anyone the satisfaction of dumping on me again.

THERAPIST: It must have hurt enormously for you to shut down so completely, but look at what you lose as a result.

In both of the preceding cases, the therapist will work with regulating the anxiety, guilt, shame, and pain associated with the experience of excitement until that energy is freer. Also, related affects of anger at parents and assertion of wants and needs will be important.

CONFLICTS ABOUT EXPERIENCING INTEREST–EXCITEMENT

Conflicts around interest–excitement are tragically common in our society. It is highly rewarded to act cool and detached. Shame is all too rapidly leveled at the individual who is filled with ebullience. (You're too damned enthusiastic!) The natural human response of curiosity can be drummed out of a child before grade school, and the rest of life becomes a dull shade of gray.

The lack of interest–excitement, or what we call laziness, can be thought of as resulting from its restriction. If one takes a compassionate view of human nature, there is *no such thing as laziness,* in the pejorative sense that we have come to think of it. In this model, *laziness is a defensive response* to initiative that is blunted or paralyzed by fear, shame, or pain. There is only learned helplessness, learned hopelessness, and lack of self-love. We do not spring from the womb lazy. Small children are seldom lazy unless ill. The young of all species play almost all the time. People who are not interested or excited in things have been taught to shrink back from active and involved participation in living. As therapists, our task is to regulate the anxieties around interest and excitement and help expose the patient to the full experience of this vital and life-enhancing affect.

DEFENSIVE FORMS OF INTEREST–EXCITEMENT

Therapists need to be vigilant for defensive forms of interest, because it may represent either histrionic dissociation or compulsive isolation of a more adaptive affective response. The Axis I diagnosis of mania is a maladaptive magnification of excitement. Patients with bipolar I disorders (the full cycling of both manic and depressive syndromes, which have a stronger biological component) thus are less responsive to psychotherapy and more responsive to medication. But bipolar II disorders (less extreme cycling, without the full manic syndrome) are more environmentally based, and patients can be responsive to psychotherapy. For such patients, attention to the emotional needs underlying the manic symptoms can be a useful approach. Another form of maladaptive "interest" is the compulsive attention to cleanliness and order of the Axis I obsessive–compulsive disorder. Recent research has shown a strong biological component, however, thus calling for treatment with medication and behavior therapy.

Fabricated interest can avoid other underlying and painful affects, and many people lose themselves in their interests. Many examples of creativity are the anguished dissociations and sublimations into art (e.g., van Gogh) or music (e.g., Beethoven, Mozart) that make more bearable the underlying grief and pain. Certainly, these are more adaptive forms of defensive behaviors, but they are largely (although not entirely) defensive, nonetheless. In contrast, creativity can also emerge directly from excitement and joy rather than from the defensive sublimation of grief or anger (e.g., the gentle paintings of Monet or the playful sculpture of Calder).

There are many examples in clinical work of defensive dissociation into interests. An individual can dissociate from grief by skydiving and isolate from affect with an interest in coin or stamp collecting. (See Table 7.4 for adaptive versus defensive forms of interest–excitement.)

One patient was a bundle of excitement about skiing, tennis, squash, volleyball, and a variety of other diversions that kept her constantly distant from her chronic underlying fears that she was not capable of loving or being loved. She was happy a great deal of the time, but it required constant effort. Although her addiction to recreational pursuits was far more adaptive than promiscuity or drug addiction would be, it kept her from being able to relax and feel comfort in relationships either with herself, when she was alone, or with others. In fact, her relationships tended to be with people who were equally busy, involved in many activities, and sports-oriented. To be calm or quiet with another person was most uncomfortable, thus close relationships were often excruciatingly uncomfortable for her. In therapy she had to face the extremely painful feelings of being unlovable (to her mother) and grieve that experience before she could allow herself to calm down with those she might love.

Another patient was a successful man, the classic "workaholic," but one who had found much to interest him in that arena. He could dissociate into pleasant feelings while on the job, but his personal life suffered, as is so often the case. In this case, as in the case of the woman just described, the defensive use of interest helped avoid the fears and shame surrounding the experience of closeness.

TABLE 7.4
Adaptive Versus Defensive Forms of Interest–Excitement

Adaptive interest–excitement	Defensive interest–excitement
A cared-about person or product	A compulsive attraction, endeavor or repetitive ritual
Relaxed but deep involvement	Intense and driven involvement
Energizing, vitalizing	Ultimately tiring, draining
Deeply satisfying and lasting	Excessive repetition is required for satisfaction

ENJOYMENT–JOY

Enjoyment–joy is the other positive affect family that is largely overlooked in treatment, although attention to it has been increasing in recent years. For example, much has been said about the smile of joy and its role in building social bonds. Indeed it is difficult to separate the affect joy from attachment bonding in the descriptions herein. Unfortunately, all too often patients do *not* have joyful affects associated with attachment either to the self or to others.

In contrast to interest–excitement, which stimulates and draws attention, joy gives comfort and satisfaction over time. Whereas interest–excitement is a function of an increase in the density and frequency of neural firing, enjoyment–joy reflects a decrease in stimulation (Tomkins, 1991). Tomkins pointed out that we are a species whose individual survival, group reproduction, and developmental learning rest heavily on social responsiveness and the mutual enjoyment of each other's presence. He wrote that we "will require motivational systems which punish alienation and isolation" (1962, p. 399).

CHARACTERISTICS OF JOY

Enjoyment in regard to the self can be reflected in healthy pride in oneself or in creative, spontaneous expression in what one does. It can be demonstrated in the pleasure and gratification obtained in one's job or hobbies. Enjoyment experienced with others is the stuff of which positive attachment is built and might be thought of as what affectional bonds are made of. Tomkins wrote that "joy *is* the social bond" (1962, p. 396). Enjoyment–joy is the affect that makes gratifying commitments possible—to a career or to a marriage.

There is a gentle energy that seeks expression when one feels joy: the calmness of things going well, the sense of peace and contentment at other times, the gentle smile of feeling safe and good. The person experiencing joy is relaxed, at ease, and at peace. Such individuals are easy to be around.

CONFLICTS ABOUT EXPERIENCING JOY

As conflicts about grief and anger (or other affects) become resolved, patients report better interpersonal relating, a freeing up of energy, and often, a new experience of joy. The problem for so many people is that so much anxiety is paired with joy that their hypervigilance can never be let down and joy is stifled. Along with the experience of joy comes anxiety (this will never last) or guilt (I don't deserve to be this happy). In many of us, there is a huge resistance to pleasure. Few of us were taught to sustain good feelings and to let ourselves fully experience joy. There are so many social injunctions that pair anxiety with enjoyment: Don't laugh, or you'll soon cry! Things are too good; something bad is bound to happen next. To help patients fully experience joy, the associated anxiety or conflicts must be desensitized. After sustaining a bitter loss of a loved one, some people feel pain with the sudden, new joy of tenderness with another. Closing off to the tenderness also helps avoid unbearably painful memories that the tenderness brings. Others have shame paired with joy and feel they do not deserve happiness. Many pleasurable situations are paired with pain that needs to be eliminated from the experience of joy.

When people have received far too little love, care, or attention in the past, it can be extraordinarily difficult for them to receive it. Each opening to the new pleasure is like prying open the lid on the pain of the awareness of how much and how long one has done without. Like giving too much food to a starving person, sudden joy can be agonizing. Joy, like the other affects and drives, often needs to be desensitized.

As feelings of joy emerge as treatment progresses, there are concomitant fears to be alert for. Some people fear they will never again do anything productive or worthwhile and sit around doing nothing. Many patients, as we have seen before, find joy a frightening prospect. But with the regulation of anxiety, joy becomes more bearable. The therapist must examine the fears around positive affects one by one, put them into perspective, and encourage patients to have such experiences more and more until what was unfamiliar slowly becomes more natural.

Another reason pleasure seems dangerous is that each opening to pleasure is prying open the lid on the years of pain. There is a tidal wave of "look at all I have missed!" that seems unbearable at the first pass. With each opening to joy, there is often a burst of awareness of the sharp contrast to all the times when the joy was absent and when there was only pain.

Sometimes therapists have fears of joy, and that includes myself. When the Ferryman had grieved his grandfather's death, he was able to recapture the positive sense of self that he had lost 20 years before. Not surprisingly, he came to a session feeling joyful and wanting to tell me about it, but after a minute or two I began feeling uncomfortable. I was worried inside that if I just sat there feeling good, I would not be helping him! I needed to *focus the session*, to help him get back to work on his anger at his father or some other problem, and I said so:

PATIENT: I had an incredible week. My life has changed. The memories of my grandfather keep coming up, and for the first time in 20 years, I can remember being loved by someone!

THERAPIST: What a blessing that must be for you.

PATIENT: It certainly is. I just love to think about him.

THERAPIST: What memories come up?

PATIENT: Oh, just how I would sit on the couch beside him. He was so big . . . and still . . . and quiet. It was so soothing.

THERAPIST: Did you sense that he liked having you there?

PATIENT: Yes, very much. [*Tearing up*] I had no doubt about it. There was a quiet, unspoken sense that he was proud of me, and pleased to have me next to him. [*Savoring this memory*] It was the one place in my life that I felt safe and accepted. But you know . . . very few words were said. He didn't say much. He didn't need to.

I listened for a few more minutes, but then mistakenly became concerned that no work would get done that session if pleasant memories were all that were attended to:

THERAPIST: The memories of your grandfather are lovely, but let's not forget that you have a lot of unresolved conflict with your father. Can we move to those issues?

PATIENT: For God sakes! Will you let me have my joy, already! [*Laughing, but quite firm*] You know I will work on my father. I've worked hard in this treatment. But right now I want to remember my grandfather and savor those memories. I'll get to my father next week.

THERAPIST [*Stunned*]: Of course you can have your joy! I was way off base on that suggestion!

Here the patient was quite comfortable with joy, but the therapist was not. Fortunately, this patient, who was passive, successfully confronted the therapist!

DEFENSIVE FORMS OF JOY

The defensive use of joy is difficult to find on Axis I or II. Joy is calmer than excitement and thus does not present like mania. When enjoyment–joy is used to cover other, more painful experiences, it simply does not look like psychopathology and might be one of the more adaptive ways to defend oneself. Indeed, in 1987, our research diagnostician could not determine whether an elderly female patient applicant met criteria for major depression. When asked about each of the criteria (blue mood, loss of interest in things, feeling hopeless), she emphatically stated that she *would* feel those things if she let herself. However, she got up every morning, made herself go out, enjoyed her friends, visited her grandchildren, and did volunteer work. She kept busy with things she enjoyed and did not give in to the depression. The enjoyment she felt was in part adaptive and in part defensive; she was certain that if she did not keep involved in such activities, she would become depressed.[6]

Defensive use of joy can also be seen in those who addictively seek "peak experiences," "encounters," or "miracles." Although such experiences can provide real joy, often they represent a dissociation into joy that moves the person away from the shame of grieving or the pain of loneliness. One way to distinguish the two ends of this defensive versus authentic continuum (because all reactions are blends of things) is to assess the degree of addictiveness of the joy. Did the joy soothe, comfort, and leave the sense that it *can* and *will* happen again? Or is the person a "joy-junkie" longing for another "hit" (see Table 7.5)?

---

[6]We consulted with Spitzer and his colleagues (developers of the DSM-III and III-R) to determine the correct diagnosis. The verdict was that the woman's *behavior* did not meet criteria for major depression, because she was able to cope effectively with the symptoms (Mimi Gibbon, personal communication, 1987).

TABLE 7.5
Adaptive Versus Defensive Joy

Adaptive enjoyment–joy	Defensive enjoyment–joy
Calming, soothing	Exhilarating
Quiet	Loud or dramatic, must be talked about
Experienced deeply within	Experiencing dependent on external source
Lasting, satisfying	Satisfaction is fleeting

I once knew a beautiful woman who always had a look of absolute contentment on her face, giving the impression that she was utterly at peace with herself and with the world. After getting to know her better, I found that she was miserable in her marriage, having an affair, and resentful in many ways. Her facial expression was a mask of joy, not the true representation of the emotion. She had adopted the look of tranquillity to disguise the less than beautiful feelings that she constantly carried. She often participated in encounter groups, during which she would experience a moment of intimacy with a group member, whom she would never see again. She told me of several of these "exquisite" experiences that she clung to in her memory, and in telling me, she showed an enormous intensity. I do not doubt the truth of her experience of the joy of attachment at those fleeting moments. The tragedy was that she had never been able to incorporate that capacity and find those intimate moments with the ongoing relationships in her daily life. Her "joy" defended her from facing enormous pain and loneliness.

I do not mean to trivialize the quest for peak experiences in life but to point out occasions when this way of responding is *primarily used to avoid something else*. Like interest and excitement, this is one of the most benign and constructive ways to defend oneself; there are far more destructive alternatives. It is even more freeing, however, to work through the grief or longing and be able to relax without being on a compulsive quest or addictive pursuit to stop the pain.

Nathanson (1992), in discussing shame and pride, described a form of defensive joy but used the term *disguise* rather than *defense*. He studied adults whose character structure was based on an apparent decision to hide shame through the false and highly exaggerated display of both interest–excitement and enjoyment–joy:

> Everything, everybody interests them; anybody, any situation can provide an opportunity for the mutualization of laughter. Woe to the unwary other who fails to accept such a brittle and artificial demand for mutualization, for such refusal of attunement is greeted by suspicion and anger quite resembling a paranoid display. (1992, p. 148)

SEXUAL FEELINGS

There is much we do not know about the relationship of sexuality to our affective life. Unlike the other drives such as hunger and thirst, and as distressing as sexual deprivation might be, "no one has ever died of sexual deprivation" (Tomkins, 1992, p. 123). What kills is the pain of lack of love or human connection, so often masked by sex. Also, in contrast to the painful urgency of hunger or thirst, the activation of sexual desire can be exciting and rewarding.

Unless one has specialized in sex therapy, therapists are given drastically insufficient supervision concerning how to handle sexual desire in the therapeutic setting, whether it be desire for others, desire for the therapist, or the therapist's desire for the patient. Guided imagery around sexual behavior is extremely difficult for both the patient and the therapist, yet it can be crucial to healing. The skilled handling of sexual material takes much experience and as much supervision as can be elicited from supervisors, who all too often avoid the topic because of lack of proper supervision given to them. It is not possible in this context to give the topic of sexuality in therapy the attention it needs and deserves. (The reader is referred to the work of Gabbard, 1994, for an excellent discussion of these issues.) I attempt here to identify main themes regarding sexual feelings in short-term treatment as well as obstacles and conflicts that are frequently encountered in patients and therapists.

BEHAVIORAL MANIFESTATIONS OF SEXUAL DESIRE

Sexual feelings, like other feelings, should be described verbally, physiologically, and in imagery. The physiological responses that signal sexual arousal include a general overall feeling of warmth, excitation in the torso, and stirring in the genital area. Discussing such responses is a difficult endeavor for both therapist and patient. To conduct such a sensitive evaluation in a graceful and professional manner requires that therapists be comfortable with themselves, with their sexuality, and with inquiring about that of others. Few therapists start off this way. Optimally, we need extensive videotaped sessions for teaching that portray appropriate handling of this sensitive topic.

The thorough exploration of the sexual experience and expression in imagery should occur if there is a *distinct problem related to sexual functioning or identity*. The therapist should make sure that behavioral and medical causes of the problem have been ruled out. When sexual feelings are the source of the conflict, the therapist needs to *make boundaries very clear* and provide a safe place for the patient to learn to understand the defenses and anxieties related to sexual expression. Many sexual problems or issues are in fact issues concerning closeness or intimacy. If the therapist feels uncomfortable about dealing with sexual feelings in treatment, peer supervision or consultation with a senior therapist or sex therapist should be sought.

EXAMPLE: SHAME AND SELF-ATTACK CONCERNING CONFUSING SEXUAL FEELINGS

This single young woman felt humiliated by her sexual fantasy:

PATIENT: I feel terrible that I have these perverse sexual desires. What's wrong with me?

THERAPIST: Why do *feelings* have to make you terrible? There must be some legitimate reason for feeling the way you do and important needs that aren't being met. Let's see if we can discover what that might be. Can you describe a specific example of a sexual response that you feel particularly uncomfortable about?

PATIENT: I hate to even say this, but I have really weird sexual fantasies that really turn me on.

THERAPIST: Can you describe one?

Patients report a variety of shameful desires that include having sexual activity with "inappropriate" persons or things or in inappropriate places or ways. The variety is undoubtedly limitless, and the therapist needs to be prepared to hear anything with equanimity and to help the patient come to understand the hidden meanings and motivations in the metaphor contained in the sexual fantasy.

Inappropriate people who are sexually desired can be those seen as bad or evil (e.g., Saddam Hussein) or can be relatives, spouses of friends or siblings, or the therapist. One should consider who the individual represents to the patient, what is desired from that person in addition to sexual contact, and what it means about the patient's sense of self.

Inappropriate ways of eliciting sexual desire can involve forcefully subduing or being subdued, exhibiting oneself, or being watched. One should consider the needs for attention and approval in these cases. Behaving or fantasizing about sexual acts that break taboos can be a way to express anger. Behaving in ways that are humiliating or degrading can be using sexual imagery or behavior to turn anger on the self rather than someone else.

It is the task of the therapist to help the patient discover the underlying pattern, or script, in the sexual responding that suggests what the alternative response is that would be ultimately more fulfilling. By considering the functions of the Triangle of Conflict, one should ask whether the sexual response is genuine and solely for sexual expression or stands in as a defensive way of obtaining something else the patient wants but does not feel he or she can obtain any other way.

When explicit sexual material is being discussed, the patient should be asked if there is an awareness of some experience of arousal (especially if the person has difficulties in this area). If not, the therapist should inquire whether a deadness, numbness, or dissociation is occurring. Such defensive responding could indicate shame in sharing the information with the therapist or a broader inhibition. Some degree of embarrassment is generally expectable, but if a patient is blocked in the full discussion of sexual feelings, this should be dealt with as other resistances to feelings are dealt with: by examining the specific anxiety, guilt, shame, or pain that is associated with the discussion of sexual material or the issues of closeness that might be involved.

CONFLICTS ABOUT EXPERIENCING SEXUAL FEELINGS IN A SAFE THERAPEUTIC ENVIRONMENT

During my entire training as a psychologist, I received only 1 minute of supervision on how to handle sexual feeling, but it was enormously useful to me over the years. My supervisor said, "Be explicit. Be clear, and set firm limits. When necessary, say 'I don't sleep with my patients.'" These words gave me some basic guidelines. Sometimes, I have used his words exactly (thanking him quietly within). At other times, I varied what I said, for example: *Sexual feelings need to be explored. Especially if you are having trouble with them. But you need a safe place to do that. This is a place where we explore feelings but we do not act on them.*

Often, examination of sexual issues comes up after much work has been done on other feelings such as grief and anger. When this is the case, I use humor to lighten the tension, reminding the patient how we sublimated the experience of anger in imagery: *You know how we have explored murderous rage in fantasy, but no one is murdered.*

Because sexual feelings that come up in the therapy session often are defensive, this aspect of the behavior should be assessed first. Are the sexual reactions used as a way of diverting the conversation from some other topic? Or are sexual feelings being used in the place of closeness? Sexual feelings in the relationship between the patient and therapist *are often defensive in nature.* Even if the sexual feelings toward the therapist are genuine, they may be brought up to avoid other, more frightening issues such as closeness or vulnerability. If a patient has no sexual problems in his or her personal life but behaves seductively or brings up sexual topics, it can indicate a defensive distancing of the relationship with the therapist or a sabotage of treatment. (See the examples concerning this topic and additional guidelines for therapist behavior in chapter 8.)

Helen Singer Kaplan (1974) pointed out that sexual problems may have behavioral or psychodynamic origins, or both. The simpler and more straightforward behavioral treatment can rapidly clear up many sexual behavior disorders. For the behavioral treatment of sexual dysfunction, excellent guides have been developed by Kaplan (1974, 1983) and Joseph LoPiccolo and Leslie LoPiccolo (1978). Psychodynamic approaches need be tried only if the behavioral interventions do not work and areas of intrapsychic conflict are discovered. The model in this book provides one method for assessing and working through such psychodynamic issues.

DEFENSIVE FORMS OF SEXUALITY

When a patient is unable to control the acting out of the sexual impulses (in contrast to being troubled only by the fantasies), a behavioral therapy or medication is more effective than psychotherapy *to bring the impulse under control.* Many of the sexual disorders of Axis I, however, to the extent that they do not have a strong biological component and are not straightforward behaviorally based disorders, may reflect defensive sexual responding. Some of the paraphilias such as exhibitionism, fetishism. pedophilia, masochism, sadism, and voyeurism suggest defensive expression of underlying feelings. If the behavior is under control, it may be possible to analyze the underlying meanings of the desires.

At base, most defensive sexuality is some form of unexpressed grief or anger concerning unmet longings for attachment or connection. This can be the case when sex is used angrily or violently, because the pain of longing is so often defended against by anger. The following are some examples of how sexual feeling can be used defensively. This is not meant to be an exhaustive list but to alert therapists to a range of possibilities of how sexual feeling might be "misused" and to provide a few suggestions concerning why it is so.

- Sex for power or dominance (longing for self-worth or fear of being adversely controlled)
- Sex for mothering, care, or attention; promiscuity (longing for closeness)
- Sex to demean oneself (turning anger or disgust toward oneself, rather than someone else)
- Sex to hurt someone else (defending against anger or closeness)
- Sexual addiction (displacing intense longing for closeness)
- Sexual perversion (displacing longing for closeness)

Other examples of confused emotional responding involve "inappropriate" feelings that emerge unbidden. For example, some patients experience a burst of aggressive or violent images when sexually aroused and find this terrifying or even disgusting. Yet such imagery can convey important information about the dynamic structure of the patient. It may be information that is painful or embarrassing until it is fully understood (Oh my God, I must be some kind of a pervert!). But in tracing the source of such emotions, one repeatedly finds the *hurting, longing, pained inner self* that has been disavowed. If patients (or their therapists) ignore these inner sensations because they seem shameful, some important aspect of the self is left unattended to and remains unintegrated. In the following general example, a woman came to the treatment with a complaint of promiscuity. I explored her sexual behavior as follows:

PATIENT: I hate myself. I feel like a no-good whore. All I seem to want is sex.
THERAPIST: Tell me what it is that you like most about the sexual contact. [*Sometimes it is with one particular partner or particular types of partners, and sometimes it is a general theme.*]
PATIENT: I just like the touching.
THERAPIST: What kind of touching? Genital touching, for example?
PATIENT: No. The holding. Being in someone's arms. Being special to someone. You know.
THERAPIST: What about the orgasm . . . the sexual arousal. Do you enjoy that?

In this type of questioning, the therapist intentionally tries to distinguish the affective and attachment desires from the sexual desires.

PATIENT: I don't ever have an orgasm. I don't even get very aroused.

THERAPIST: So what is it you really want then? Can you see?

PATIENT: Yeah, what is it that I want? I never really thought about it. I guess I want somebody to care about me.

THERAPIST: It seems like you are yearning for affection more than for sex. Can you see this?

PATIENT: Oh! [*Pausing*] Do you really think so?

THERAPIST: Well, let's explore it. What do you think?

PATIENT: It seems like it, doesn't it? I've never liked the sex part. I just put up with it. [*Tearing up*]

It is generally worthwhile to focus on this dawning awareness until it is valid to the patient. When, in other cases, the sexual interaction is very much enjoyed, I ask what is most wanted, the affection or the sex. Almost invariably in such women, it is the affectional component. In such cases, I offer the following interpretation: *Could it be that you are wanting something that we all want, that is, human care and affection? But you are going about getting it in ways that aren't the best for you, and you end up feeling bad about yourself? Can you see how sad that is for you?*

The preceding is an abbreviated example. It sometimes takes much more exploring to tease out the differences, as well as building of alliance and trust beforehand. But realizations such as this one are often both shocking and tremendously soothing to such patients, and they decrease the feelings of shame. Also, I have seen a number of patients in whom this awareness, coupled with newly awakened compassion for self, totally stopped the promiscuity. By caring more for themselves and receiving compassionate interpretations from the therapist, the desperate urgency for sexuality as a vehicle of "care" subsided.

With these themes in mind, and staying open to other possible hidden motives, the therapist should trace the sexual feelings to their *most gratifying component* to find what is being disguised. Just as we always ask what is the worst thing that could happen when anxiety is the issue, we also need to explore what is most stimulating in the particular sexual act. I provide three examples to give the reader a sense of how this is done; of course, each patient has an idiosyncratic presentation.

EXAMPLE: THE MAN WITHOUT A SEXUAL PROBLEM

A high-functioning man brought up sexual feeling toward me in treatment. This was a happily married man with a satisfying sexual life, so I did not pursue the sexual feelings. My countertransference response was to feel somewhat offended, but I did not explore his or my response further. I was concerned that he wanted to play out a fantasy, when he was in therapy for problems concerning his actualization in his work. I felt I could help him by focusing on other issues.

At 2-year follow-up, he told me his treatment was only partially successful. There were issues that he had not been helped with in treatment, and he had returned to therapy. He felt that he needed longer term treatment, and he may have been right. But I was reminded of the sexual comments he had made. In retrospect, this man had the strength and the interpersonal connection to be able to talk about the meaning of his sexual feelings as well as my response to them. If I had trusted that, it might have been *one way (although no doubt there were many ways)* I could have reached more depth around the issues we did not resolve: emotional separation from his mother, his identification with his father, and his difficulty seeing himself as a strong, capable man. I cannot be sure that I could have tapped into these issues in a short-term framework, but I regretted missing this "pocket" of disorder that he genuinely needed my help with.

EXAMPLE: THE DOMINANCE AND CONTROL GUY

This 46-year-old single man had a series of broken relationships, and he could not understand why. He was particularly attracted to successful and strong-minded women. The relationships tended to end badly, and the only complaints he had gotten were of the unpleasantness of his sexual style. This confused him enormously because he considered himself a good lover. I asked him to describe his favorite masturbatory fantasy. He told of ripping a woman's clothing off and throwing her on the floor. He then would penetrate her and forcefully have intercourse.

THERAPIST: What is the most exciting thing about this fantasy. The part that would bring you to orgasm? [*Although it was not immediately clear to him, with some exploration of his sexual behavior, he began to see what he most wanted.*]

PATIENT: Oh, it's the power and the domination. The most exciting thought to me is that I'm in *total* control and she has no control over me at that moment. In fact, she is out of control, and I'm on top.

THERAPIST: So this is not exactly a tender and affectionate interaction. It sounds more like a battle to the death! You must feel like there is a fight going on between you and them, or at least a competition!

PATIENT: Yeah. I do! I have to be on top! She can't have the control.

THERAPIST: Is it any easier, now, to see why a woman might not like that, as a steady diet?

PATIENT [*Perplexed at first, but after being thoughtful for several moments*]: Yeah . . . I can see how it could be a turnoff.

This insight was not sufficient to alter his behavior with women. He had to do more work in therapy around his fears of closeness to women, his dread of being vulnerable, and so on. But he did do so. His outcome was an interesting one. He lost interest in the more dramatic women he had always dated and became involved with a less attractive, less commanding, but warm, motherly woman. With her, he could allow himself to be open and tender, and with the help of marital counseling, they built a solid relationship. Two years later, I received a wonderful picture of him, his wife, and their new son, and a note saying how happy he was.

EXAMPLE: THE MAN WHO WANTED MOTHERING INSTEAD OF SEX

A strikingly handsome entrepreneur came to see me for problems with impotence. He had been to a sex therapist who had not been able to cure him with traditional behavioral methods and referred him for work with the underlying dynamics. He was able to masturbate to orgasm but could not function with his wife. Because the dynamics were not clear, I asked him to bring his wife in for one session. She was even more beautiful than he was handsome; she could have been on the cover of a magazine. She acknowledged that he was warm and generous to her, but she showed virtually no capacity for warmth or empathy toward him. Nothing that I said could penetrate her self-absorption, nor draw her attention to her husband's plight. She was annoyed by his impotence because it reflected on her sense of attractiveness.

After a few more sessions, he revealed that he had sexual feelings for me. I was inwardly quite upset by this because I did not want to deal with sexual feelings with such an attractive man. I proceeded as follows, trying not to show my nervousness:

THERAPIST: How would you want to act on those feelings, if we explore them in fantasy?

PATIENT: I would imagine gently undressing you and making love to you.

THERAPIST: And how would you imagine that would play out?

PATIENT: Well, just as I imagine that I would penetrate you, I imagine myself becoming impotent.

THERAPIST: What do you think my reaction would be to your impotence? [*I expected him to be ashamed and humiliated and that he would imagine that I would look down on him as his wife did.*]

PATIENT: Oh, you would be very understanding. You would hold me and comfort me and tell me it didn't matter. I actually imagine myself curled up with your arms around me.

THERAPIST [*Because I was a fairly novice therapist at this point in my career, I inwardly felt quite surprised*]: So, can you see what you are *really* wanting in this fantasy?

PATIENT: What do you mean?

THERAPIST: It seems to me that you could make your fantasy go any way it wanted, but instead of completing the sexual act, there was something you seemed to want more.

PATIENT: Oh, I see. I want to be held and taken care of.

THERAPIST: And the way you described yourself curled up, what images does that bring to mind?

PATIENT: Mothering. [*Pausing*] I want you to be my mother. Yeah ... that's right. I want my wife to hold me, mother me. [*Becoming very sad and speaking very softly*] I crave it. I've even asked her for that.

THERAPIST: I wonder if the impotency has been a way that, without realizing it, you are crying out to her to hold you and comfort you. And given what you've told me about the coldness of your mother, it might not surprise us that you would want that from your wife.

PATIENT: Oh God, that's it. That's it.

It was a profound moment. We sat in stunned silence and stared at each other in sad recognition of the truth. His impotence resolved itself shortly thereafter. In later sessions, we dealt with the sadness of his wife's incapacity to give him empathic understanding. The grief for what he was missing was strong. He ultimately decided to remain with his wife, but with great awareness, as well as acceptance, of her limitations.

The preceding examples happen to be of male patients with a female therapist, but patients often experience sexual attraction to their same-sex therapist, whether they are homosexual or heterosexual in orientation. These are important areas that should not be overlooked. A few general themes include the following: (a) identifying the true sexual orientation, (b) looking for the deeper need that the sexual response may be masking, and (c) examining whether the sexual response is a way to sabotage treatment or to avoid a much more uncomfortable issue.

When the patient's sexual orientation is confused or unclear, I repeatedly examine sexual or masturbatory fantasy to find out *what gives the patient the greatest joy or satisfaction*. This tells me to whom the patient is most drawn or motivated. Sometimes this is clear and unambiguous; other times it is less clear. The following is the most difficult case I have encountered in this regard.

EXAMPLE: CONFUSION CONCERNING SEXUAL IDENTITY

A 40-year-old man came to treatment because he had never had a strong sexual identity. He had always lived alone, was extremely lonely, and wanted to resolve his dilemma. He was so ashamed of his homosexual feelings that he could not allow himself to have pleasure even in fantasy. On the other hand, he was so terrified of closeness to women that he could not bear to have sexual contact with them, although he could fantasize about women with pleasure. This led me, initially, to think he was heterosexual in orientation. Because of his ambivalence toward both sexes, however, we examined sexual fantasy repeatedly. He seemed to have some degree of attraction to both sexes and a great deal of conflict around both; therefore, we worked to reduce both the shame of his homosexual desires and his fears of closeness to women. I reasoned that, with the conflicts reduced, he would be freer to choose a partner. The fear of closeness to women was far more resistant to change. This was not a short-term treatment. It required months for him to build sufficient trust in me, a woman, to be able to explore such issues. Also, he needed to build the capacity for closeness in all his relationships. After 3 years of treatment, he became comfortable and satisfied with a homosexual relationship. Table 7.6 lists some indicators of adaptive versus defensive sexual responses.

TABLE 7.6
Adaptive Versus Defensive Sexual Desire

Adaptive sexual feeling	*Defensive sexual feeling*
Deeply satisfying	Addictive
Comfortable arousal	Compulsive arousal
Sex is mixed with interest and enjoyment	Sex is paired with anger, grief, longing
Deepens closeness	Does not enhance closeness
Desire paired with love or care	Lust that objectifies the partner

The Inhibitory Cluster: Aversive Affects

Throughout this book, there has been continual focus on the inhibitory affects. Almost every example has included some attempt to identify, evaluate, or remove some degree of anxiety, guilt, shame, or pain. Because of their importance in clinical work and the confusion surrounding them, however, each specific inhibitory affect deserves detailed discussion. Nathanson (1992) referred to these affects as the "attenuators" of the drives and other affects, acting to limit these functions once they have been turned on (p. 120).[7]

FEAR–TERROR–ANXIETY

Almost as confusing as attempts at defining the self are the attempts at categorizing anxiety. Tomkins, Nathanson, and other affect theorists and researchers have pointed out, however, that regardless of distinctions such as primary versus signal anxiety, "at the level of innate affect it does not matter what triggered fear—all fearful emotion is, at its core, merely fear" (Nathanson, 1992, p. 93).

> The familiar distinction between fear and anxiety, in which fear is differentiated from anxiety on the basis of the presence or absence of an "object" or on the basis of consciousness or unconsciousness of its object, is, we think, inadvisable ... *because it makes one distinction when many need to be made* and because *the distinction properly applies to combinations of affect ... rather than to the affects themselves.* [Italics added]
>
> The fear which is experienced as a single affect will appear to be quite different when it is experienced concurrently with [other affects].
>
> One must not confuse the component of fear or terror with other components, perceptual, cognitive, and motoric, with which it is coassembled. (Tomkins, 1991, p. 503)

The reader is also referred to chapter 17 of Tomkins's (1991) book, from which these quotations were taken.

---

[7]Nathanson's (1992) discussion of these affects includes an interesting view concerning their etiology (pp. 121–149).

CHARACTERISTICS OF FEAR–ANXIETY

Anxiety seems to be a coassembly of many factors (fear or terror being only one major component), and its presentation is altered depending on what it is associated with. Tomkins (1991) reminded us that "fear is different when it is experienced concurrently with anger or shame or contempt or distress" (p. 503) and that "how fearful anyone may be depends critically on how much excitement and enjoyment is magnified" (p. 509). Anxiety can be associated with anger to yield a frustrated worry, with grief to yield a hopeless or helpless anxiety, or with excitement–joy to yield a hypomanic reaction. Cognitive and biological contributions to the manifestations of anxiety are also significant. Although some anxiety disorders, such as panic, appear to have a greater biological loading than others, such as phobias, one needs to consider *both* psychodynamic and DSM diagnoses.

What is most important in this discussion of the dynamic function of fear or anxiety is the ultimate goal: *the alteration of severe inhibition of adaptive responding.* For this purpose, one does not have to tear apart the various distinctions within fear and anxiety. Like the variations in defenses, one can clinically alter their avoidant functions without having to code their specific variations. Likewise, one can make an impact on the severely inhibiting functions of anxiety or fear without knowing all their finer gradations. Fortunately, there are some fairly simple mechanisms that can be identified that can be of assistance in bringing maladaptive levels of inhibition within normal limits. It is also important to assess to what extent the fear reaction is appropriate or whether there is some other, more adaptive response that would resolve the problem at hand.

Fear elicits the well-known flight (urgency to run away) or fright (reaction of paralysis) response. Fear is experienced in a wide variety of ways: weakness in the knees, trembling all over, stiffening of muscles, sweating, quivering lips, racing heart, constriction of the throat, butterflies in the stomach, cold and clammy hands, tension, and so forth. In general, when assessing the degree of fear or anxiety present in a response, one should note whether the patient's thoughts or behaviors involve avoidance of the situation (flight) or paralysis and inaction (fright, or inhibition).

CONFLICTS ABOUT EXPERIENCING FEAR

Individuals are commonly afraid, ashamed, or in dread (pain) about feeling fear. Fear can be experienced as weak, inadequate, vulnerable, unmanly, shameful, foolish, and so forth. Patients typically need assistance and encouragement to be allowed to have the fear reactions without shame. That may be the first step toward regulating the fear or anxiety to normal levels.

Regulating the Anxieties by Cognitive Restructuring

There are many effective ways to reduce the way people inhibit themselves, and clinicians should remain open to a variety of methods. Some techniques that I have found quite effective in regulating anxiety, guilt, shame, and pain are similar, if not identical, to cognitive therapy approaches such as procedures developed by Beck and his colleagues (Beck, 1976; Beck et al., 1979), Barlow (1988, 1993), and Clark (1989). One of the main techniques brings maladaptive beliefs into awareness, and through discussion and disputation the logic or illogic of the belief is made conscious.

It is noteworthy that the disconfirmation of "pathogenic beliefs" is also the identified change agent in analytic psychotherapy as described by Joseph Weiss and his colleagues (Weiss, 1990; Weiss et al., 1986). Both major theoretical schools (psychodynamic and cognitive) agree, therefore, on the crucial involvement of restructuring beliefs for cure. This short-term anxiety-regulating model also sees pathogenic, affect-laden beliefs ("hot cognition" is the term used by some) as the linchpin or the cause of pathology. The focus in this model, however, is largely (although not exclusively) on the affective component of those beliefs, what I call the *inhibitory affects*. Regardless of the variation in emphasis on affect or cognition, there is a reassuring overlap between the cognitive approach and the dynamic approach in their focus on maladaptive cognitoaffective reactions. In both orientations, the alteration of these *affects and their associated beliefs* is a major component of the resolution of pathology. The therapist must dispute and restructure the way patients experience and understand their fears: *What is the worst thing that could happen? Is it true that you would be a terrible person if . . . ?*

EXAMPLES: DISPUTING ANXIETY-LADEN BELIEFS

THERAPIST: From your description, you seem quite afraid to stand up to your father. What is the worst thing that could happen if you did?

PATIENT: Well, he would think badly of me.

THERAPIST: So what would happen if he thought badly of you? [*Or if it is not a realistic fear*] Why do you think he would feel badly about you for that?

The exploration continues until the patient has unearthed all the fears and can at least envision and begin to employ alternative methods of coping. At other times, the inhibiting emotions step in to take the place of the adaptive feelings:

PATIENT: I was standing in my kitchen thinking how happy I was. Everything is going so much better between Ken and I. The kids are happy. And I felt so blessed. But just as I thought that, I felt panicked and started to tremble.

THERAPIST: Can we look more closely at what made you so panicky at that moment?

PATIENT: Oh, it's so new. And I'm too scared to trust it. It might go away.

THERAPIST: So it's hard to relax and just let yourself experience the joy of the moment. It makes sense, 'cause it's been a long time coming. But then again, this is exactly what you've been working toward, isn't it?

PATIENT: Yeah, and I've gotta let myself get used to it, don't I!

EXAMPLES: EXPLORING ANXIETIES BLOCKING RESPONDING

The therapist might say something like the following:

You seem to be worrying about looking foolish so that you stay silently think-
   ing to yourself for minutes at a time. [Defenses]
I wonder what you would fear if you said whatever came to your mind? Could
   you be frightened of some reaction of mine? What might that be? [Anxiety]
What reaction would you be wishing to have from me instead? [Wish, hidden
   feelings of desire for closeness]

DEFENSIVE FORMS OF FEAR–TERROR

When one considers how fear may be used defensively, one may refer to
the Axis I anxiety disorders or the Axis II, Cluster C, anxiety-prone personality disorders. Of course, anxiety plays a major role in all pathology (as reflected on the anxiety pole of the Triangle of Conflict), but these disorders reflect anxiety functioning as a *defense.* Although one must always take into
consideration the biological contribution, the dynamic contribution plays a
strong role as well. These symptoms can be seen as defensive responses
masking a more uncomfortable affective experience, owing to some conflict
(composed of anxiety, guilt, shame, or pain).[8] Sometimes it may be beneficial
to behave fearfully rather than assertively or excitedly, because such behavior serves to deflect another person's anger. Such responses might reflect
conscious manipulation as well as unconscious defensive maneuvers (see
Table 7.7).

TABLE 7.7
Adaptive Versus Defensive Fear

Adaptive fear (signal anxiety)	*Defensive fear (traumatic anxiety)*
Protective of the self	Attacking, thwarting of the self
Able to run, cry for help, or freeze (when necessary, but not forced)	Blocked desire to run; unable to cry out; paralysis of action tendencies
Appropriate to fear stimulus	Inappropriate to fear stimulus, exaggerated
Allows general functioning to continue	Impairs general functioning

SHAME–GUILT–HUMILIATION

It is now widely recognized that shame arises earlier than guilt developmentally and is related to one's sense of self. Guilt is related to the breaking
of parental or societal rules or laws. The underlying affect that contributes to
both experiences is the affect family of shame–humiliation. Tomkins (1962,
1963) proposed that any experience that partially decreases but does not
eliminate interest–excitement or enjoyment may activate shame. In contrast,
situations that completely eliminate interest or excitement are not shaming,

[8]See the excellent discussion by Gabbard (1994) of anxiety disorders (chapter 9, pp.
249–289).

because the attention is diverted or the pleasure is eliminated. Other interruptions may briefly reduce the pleasure, but if the desire is strong enough, the interest will not waver. When an experience "rains on one's parade," however, shame plays a fundamental role in that response. When one considers how common it is to have what one is interested in or enjoying partially reduced or dampened, Tomkins noted, one can imagine that shame must be a frequent experience of the preverbal child. "No, no, don't touch. Don't do this, don't do that. Stop that. Be quiet. Don't be so loud." Another, more benign example is the happy, excited child running with arms open to the parent to share an experience, only to meet a distracted response.

"Shame," said Tomkins, "strikes deepest into the heart of man." Twice Nathanson quoted the Talmud on human response to shame: "Humiliation is worse than physical pain" and "shaming another in public is like shedding blood." Nathanson concluded that "some have gone so far as to say that there would be no unconscious were it not for shame!" (1992, pp. 148–149). "Soul murder" (Shengold, 1989) is, at base, shame. Shame is one way that we can control others without killing them, but the effects, nonetheless, can be deadly. Shame carries the greatest potential to damage the sense of self and must be attacked most vigorously in the healing of psychopathology.

Tomkins maintains that shame and guilt, as well as shyness and discouragement, reflect the same innate program of inhibition but are experienced differently because of separate coassemblies of causes and consequences, that is, different cognitive associations. Shame is associated with feelings of inferiority. Guilt is the sense of committing a moral transgression. Nathanson (1992) suggested that guilt is shame coassembled with fear of reprisal based on memories of prior punishment. Shame is associated with the self, and guilt arises from rules one learns from society or caretakers.

CHARACTERISTICS OF SHAME

Shame and guilt (and the related affects) need to be made conscious and distinct from other emotions. The physiological sensation of shame is often reported to be a drenching feeling of humiliation, a diminishment of energy, and a sickening feeling inside. When shame is intense, it is important to help the patient to identify shame-based behaviors. This can be the lowering of the head, inability to look in the other's eyes, shrinking away from contact, or wishing to be out of sight. Individuals who are unable to "flirt" or be socially effective are typically laden with shame and cannot bear the horror of meeting the possibly rejecting or disinterested eyes of someone whom they would desperately long to have show interest. The most prominent nonverbal indication of shame is the lowering of the head, with averting of the eyes. But the unpleasant, sickening inner sensations associated with shame or guilt must be carefully detailed with each patient so they can identify these feelings whenever they occur.

CONFLICTS ABOUT EXPERIENCING SHAME

We seem to be a shame-addicted species. There have been many times when I wished that my patients would have more conflict about feeling shame, yet they seem awash in it, pouring it over themselves. Inner conflicts about shame and guilt seem to be fewer than with other affects. The most common conflict about shame may be about revealing shame interpersonally. People are generally resistant to show or reveal to others their shame, for fear of being seen as bad, weak, immoral, and so on. This pattern underlies the excessive pride or stubbornness that inhibits a more adaptive response.

METHODS FOR REGULATING SHAME OR GUILT

There should be a vivid portrayal of the shameful acts on verbal, physiological, and action-tendency levels. The patient often feels wide open, naked, unprotected, and extremely vulnerable, so that the therapist must assess the degree of anxiety, shame, or pain over having shared the experience, that is, how the therapist feels about hearing about the shameful behaviors. It is crucial to bring the shame within bearable limits before the session ends, or there is danger that the patient will not be able to return.

EXAMPLE: REDUCING SHAME IN A PATIENT WHO HAS REVEALED A SHAMEFUL ACT

Several things the therapist might say are as follows:

How do you feel having told me?
When you walk out of here today, how will you feel about my having heard this?
How do you imagine me thinking and feeling about you?

When the patient's response lacks self-compassion, the therapist should work to build a more compassionate view:

THERAPIST: How sad it is that you create a hostile (or bleak, uncaring, critical, or judgmental) world around you. Can you see how, in your mind, you make me into a critical and judgmental figure or parent? Is there anything that I have done to make you feel this way?

PATIENT: No. But still . . .

THERAPIST: It sounds like you know intellectually that I don't have negative feelings for you, but emotionally, the feeling of doubt still lingers.

PATIENT: Yes, that's right.

THERAPIST: You know, we learn on different levels, and many times we can see things intellectually but we still feel quite differently inside. Let's continue to talk about this until both your thoughts and your feelings are in agreement. Tell me, what are you most worried that I might be thinking? What have you told me that would make you the most uncomfortable?

PATIENT: I've told you about the mess I've made of my life and the bad things I've done. I don't see how you'd have any respect for me.

THERAPIST: So you come to me asking for help with tremendously painful problems, that you openly share with me, and your concern is that after hearing you I would sit in judgment of you or condemn you inwardly.

That's a terribly uncomfortable situation to be in, isn't it? What kind of therapist would I be if I did that? *I* would be uncomfortable *too* if that happened to me. Don't you think you deserve to have a therapist who would help you find a way to resolve these things rather than to sit in judgment of you?

In other instances, the patient may have done something that was truly harmful or unfair to another person, and shame can be legitimate. The goal in such cases is to have the patient grieve what he or she did that was hurtful to another. It is the grief that will alter the pattern of behavior, not more shame. This is discussed further under the topic of capacity for regret.

When the therapist is afraid the patient will leave the session and do something destructive, he or she should predict it during the session:

> *I think you might get home tonight and feel terrible for having told me this. What do you think?*
>
> *You have told me many painful things today. It would not be surprising if you find after you leave this session that you feel like never coming back. If that is a possibility, let's discuss it before you go, so you are not burdened with those kinds of feelings when you are alone.*

THE ANTIDOTE FOR GUILT OR SHAME: SELF-COMPASSION AND THE CAPACITY FOR REGRET

When people act in less than optimal ways, shame and guilt are appropriate. Guilt, shame, and pain are internal forms of punishment, and when impulses are strongly in conflict, the punishing capacity is only a *temporary suppressor* of the behavior. The inhibitory feelings do not automatically elicit more adaptive responses, they only temporarily inhibit the undesired response. "Guilt means you'll do it again" (Smothermon, 1980).

The only effective way to stop guilt- or shame-inducing responses from recurring is through helping the patient *regret what was done* and *grieve the past circumstances that caused it*. Guilt and shame elicit self-recrimination (What a jerk I am!), making us feel bad about ourselves and thus avoid the grief of the situation. To have the capacity for regret, one must also have the capacity for self-compassion, or the regret will turn into depression or self-attack. Grieving or regretting the shameful behavior means facing and taking responsibility for the worst parts of it, experiencing the fervent wish that it could have been done differently, and doing so with compassion for oneself. The capacity for regret builds the desire to replace the loss (of one's self-esteem or the pain or esteem of others) by engendering the hope and desire to do it differently the next time. The grief of regret carries with it a compassionate stance that can heal by offering an alternative *that the individual feels capable of achieving.*

EXAMPLE: HEALING LEGITIMATE GUILT OR SHAME WITH REGRET

A 28-year-old single male musician was constantly worrying about many things, one of which was the welfare of his younger brother. It was eventually revealed that a large part of his feeling of shame, guilt, and hate for himself was caused by early sexual abuse (fondling of genitals) of his brother. Through detailed discussion of the abusive situations and the longings that gave rise to them, the patient began to see his own desperate cravings for human touch, arising from a seductive but neglectful mother, which he then acted out on his 5-year-old brother. He then could truly grieve, not only for what he had done to his brother, but also for himself and his desperate loneliness and longing. He was eventually able to talk with his brother and convey the depth of sorrow he felt over what had happened. This was a fortunate case in which the brother was well adjusted and felt the sexual play had not been harmful to him. Indeed, the brother revealed, to the patient's astonishment, that the patient had taken the place of both mother and father for him and had done far more good than harm.

Except for these incidents with his brother when he was 9, there was no sexual contact until later, with women his age. However, these relationships were driven and needy. As he increasingly recognized the source of his neediness, he became less compulsively driven by these feelings. He learned to act in ways to meet his own needs and eventually chose a woman who was a good partner for him.

DEFENSIVE FORMS OF SHAME OR GUILT

Shame probably plays a role in all the Axis I and II disorders. Shame is obvious in depressive disorders: "feelings of worthlessness or guilt" is one criterion. But shame and guilt also can be found in the eating disorders, the sexual disorders, borderline personality disorder, and others.

Tomkins described mechanisms that *disguise* or *stand in* for shame. Rather than appear ashamed, some people strenuously avoid lowering the eyelids or averting the gaze; instead they force a direct stare at others, with the head tipped back and chin jutted forward, and adopting a disdainful look. This response is not "defensive shame" but the use of contempt–disgust to disguise feelings of shame (1963, p. 146). It is a common reaction in snobbishness, arrogance, false pride, and narcissistic personality disorder.

Defensive shame or guilt might also play a role in many of the exaggerated claims of *mea culpa*. "Oh, it's my fault, I feel terrible, please forgive me" stands in for or disguises the more authentic emotion of longing for acceptance or the desire to deflect anger (see Table 7.8).

TABLE 7.8
Adaptive Versus Defensive Shame or Guilt

Adaptive shame–guilt	*Defensive shame–guilt*
Quietly expressed	Loudly expressed
Experienced deeply within	Experienced in the external relationship
Leads to genuine regret or remorse	Leads to self-recrimination
Lower probability of repetition of act	Higher probability of maladaptive response

EMOTIONAL PAIN–HURT–ANGUISH

As in the pain of touching a hot stove, adaptive emotional pain signals that there is something hurtful to the individual. In clinical usage, *pain* is an emotional response that signals hurt. This category of emotion probably is a combination of affects: possibly a magnified level of distress–anguish, contempt, disgust, or anger–rage directed at the self (self-hate). In severe pathology, pain, like shame, is a powerful inhibitor of emotional experience or expression. Emotional pain represents the sting that makes an experience unbearable. Generally, emotional isolation has made the pain unbearable, so that the connection with the therapist is paramount in healing.

CHARACTERISTICS OF EMOTIONAL PAIN

When one is emotionally anguished, the head is not necessarily dropped as in shame nor raised with the jutted chin of contempt toward others. Instead, there is a wincing of the eyes and a flinching of the body as though one were feeling pain or nausea inside. Common statements that go along such responses are, "I couldn't do that, I just couldn't," and "I can't bear the thought of that." The head is typically shaken side to side in a manner that seems to say "no, no, no!" The eyes are often shut tight and the shoulders raised as though to ward off the experience. The tongue darts out as though something is repellent. The inner physiological sensation includes stabbing, gut-wrenching, or nauseated sensations.

CONFLICTS ABOUT EXPERIENCING PAIN

Many people are burdened with the incapacity to feel pain (i.e., numbing themselves) or to show pain (I don't want to give them the satisfaction of knowing they hurt me).

There is also a shame–pain blend seen in counterdependence. When there is a tremendous reluctance to show vulnerability, the individual wants to appear strong and independent rather than needy or weak, but a disguise is worn that denies the hurt feelings because of embarrassment about them.

A most helpful mechanism for regulating the severity of emotional pain is the sharing of the pain with the therapist. The patient tells the therapist how bad it was and grieves the long years of carrying it. The sting of the pain is generally because of the loneliness in which the pain had to be borne and the inability of the patient to self-soothe. The sharing of this affect with a compassionate and supportive therapist helps with both of these factors. Because anguish is a large part of emotional pain, methods for working with pain are similar to those used in the grief process. Guided imagery is used to explore painful memories and face the unpleasant thoughts and feelings connected with them.

DEFENSIVE FORMS OF PAIN

The most prominent forms of defensive pain are the Axis I depressive disorders. Pain enacted defensively could be used to disguise or stand in for other, embarrassing or anxiety-provoking reactions. "I can't bear it" or "It's too painful for me" could cover for an angry "How dare you!" Hurt feelings, which are ubiquitous, are the *defensive use of emotional pain* and are the basis of the classic "victim role" that is seen in so many patients. Pain in its defensive form may be a major contributor to masochism, in which self-attack defends against rage or the unbearable grief of loss of the desired person. Chronic complaining is undergirded by defensive pain or hurt. Like shame, the inhibitory response of pain or anguish is undoubtedly frequent in both Axis I and Axis II disorders. The greater the developmental deficits, the greater the emotional pain and the underlying, even more unbearable, grief and longing (see Table 7.9).

TABLE 7.9
Adaptive Versus Defensive Pain

Adaptive emotional pain	Defensive emotional pain
Signal of emotional harm	Chronic harm turned on self
Should result in adaptive avoidance	Feels unavoidable (stuck in it)
Leads to grief, mourning	Leads to depression, melancholia

NOTES ON THE MANAGEMENT OF THE INHIBITORY AFFECTS AND THEIR FUNCTIONS

After the self-inhibiting affects have been carefully identified, the patient needs to learn how these responses (anxiety, guilt, shame, pain) block the expression of certain feelings and result in the problematic defensive behavior. In each case, resolution is reached by a compassionate examination of the inhibiting feelings until the patient reports that anxiety (or guilt, shame, or pain) is diminished and replaced by a more benevolent self-understanding.

Change also depends partly on making the distinction between the patient's fantasy and reality. Unconscious anxieties or conflicts can wield enormous control over functioning, but once such "hidden terrors" are identified and brought out into the light of consciousness, their control diminishes. Just putting into words "the worst thing that could happen" brings an automatic inner coping response or, at least, the conscious realization of what needs to be coped with. As Gabbard said, there is a "broadened ideational mastery of the affect" that enables the patient to control the symptoms (1990, p. 282).

There is a range of severity of these inhibiting responses that has been partly addressed earlier by the distinction between signal anxiety (on the A pole) and primary or traumatic anxiety (when the anxieties flood the individual and function defensively, the D pole). For this discussion, I describe the functions of the inhibitory affects as observed in videotaped sessions: a continuum of inhibitory responding that ranges from mild to maximum inhibition. In the mild forms, inhibition follows the response, but the discomfort is experienced later, such as in the following reactions, represented by the anxiety pole:

- Behaving assertively, but feeling guilty afterward
- Allowing oneself to cry, but feeling anxious later that the other person felt burdened by it
- Blurting out feelings of tenderness, but feeling shy or embarrassed afterward
- Expressing excitement openly, but feeling foolish later

In the moderate stages, the inhibition noticeably blunts or thwarts the expression, as in the following reactions:

- Attempting to be assertive, but succeeding only partially
- Beginning to cry, but quickly choking it down
- Expressing tenderness, but in a way that is toned down, lightened up, or dissociated
- Expressing enthusiasm, but quickly diminishing the expression

In the most severe levels of inhibition, the adaptive response virtually is not experienced. In such cases, the inhibitory emotions become so strongly associated with the adaptive feelings that the only response is the flooding of inhibition. The adaptive emotion is neither experienced nor expressed, and it is often fully outside of awareness. In these situations, the anxiety (or guilt, shame, or pain) functions as the defense, because it stands in place of the more adaptive feeling. Nothing is felt in such cases except for how helpless, terrible, or anguished one is, in one form or another. This is a major component of masochism, "turning against the self," or what I have called the "self-attacking" quality of these affects. The combination of the defense pole and the anxiety pole (i.e., the top of the Triangle of Conflict) is functioning as a solid block to the necessary feeling and is punitive to the individual and others. In such cases, wants and needs of the patient are felt as neither deserved nor worth considering. Shame is so great that no crying is close to the surface—only numbness. No tenderness or care for another is expressed, only a cool, detached facade. No anger comes into consciousness, only passivity, acting out, or helplessness. This form of extreme inhibition can be likened to the concept of primary or traumatic anxiety as represented on the defense pole when the *inhibitory affects (A pole) function as the defense.*
Following are examples of patients expressing extreme inhibition:

I couldn't think of anything to say. I was paralyzed. [Anxieties so eradicating that no assertion is experienced on any level]
I don't want anything for my birthday. No, no. Don't go to any trouble. I'd feel terrible. [Guilt so strong that all wants or needs are eliminated]
I'm a disgusting person, and I deserve to be mistreated. [Shame that devastates any compassion for self]
When he left me, I just wanted to kill myself (or him). [Pain or anguish that annihilates self-care or grief]

I don't deserve that. [Shame that blocks assertion]

If I let myself lose control, I might never stop. [Anxiety that prevents sexual expression]

I shouldn't want that; it's greedy. [Guilt that blocks the asking for needs to be met]

I'd never say what I think; I'd look like a jerk! [Shame that is devastating to self-esteem]

I couldn't bear to say a last good-bye. [Pain or anguish that blocks grieving]

It is important to note that a major confusion in distinguishing affective functions occurs when anxiety (i.e., inhibition) takes on the function of a defensive response. The top two poles of the Triangle of Conflict (the defense pole and the anxiety pole) can function as one, to defend by total inhibition. Examples are learned helplessness, environmentally based depression, and anxiety. The following examples further illustrate how these inhibitory emotions can interact with each other:

One can become *anxiety-ridden,* as in generalized anxiety disorder (defensive behavior), because one is *guilty* or *ashamed* (conflict) concerning the desire or need to voice *anger* (impulse–feeling) to an authority figure (current persons). *The anxiety-ridden behavior occurs because the defensive responses, such as rationalization or denial, are overwhelmed and no longer working.* If a patient can no longer deny a conflict with the boss, more severe anxiety is elicited, which functions as a defense. The only feeling left is the anxiety itself.

One can also become *anxious* (defensive behavior: trembling or shaking) because one is anticipating rejection or conflict about self-assertion (impulse–feeling). A patient, knowing that confrontation is inevitable, becomes flooded with behavioral manifestations of anxiety because of fear of abandonment or rejection (being fired).

One can become *anxious* (defense) because one feels too much *pain* (conflict) over the *rage (I/F) at the boss.* The thought of the conflict might be unbearable to a person who had a rageful father. Conflict may have led to beatings, the memory of which would elicit tremendous pain. The behavioral manifestation of the defensive anxiety might be trembling accompanied by the inability to speak. However, the anxious behavior of trembling is quite different from the reason for the inhibition: the painful memories.

SUMMARY

This chapter describes the three clusters of feelings frequently encountered in clinical work and provides extensive examples of their adaptive and maladaptive (or defensive) variants. These clusters include:

- The activating–regulatory emotions: grief, anger–assertion, and desire for attachment
- The activating–pleasure-giving emotions: excitement, enjoyment, and sexual desire
- The inhibitory affects: anxiety, shame–guilt, and pain

CHAPTER 8

Second Major Objective of Affect Restructuring: Affect Reintegration, Expression, and Reconnection

EMOTIONAL INTELLIGENCE: THE LAST FRONTIER

Ever since I was in high school, I have thought that there should be an EQ, or emotional quotient, that accompanied one's IQ, or intelligence quotient, because so many people of high intelligence seemed lacking in wisdom in the art of living. It has been enormously gratifying, therefore, to see current interest emerging in the area of emotional intelligence (e.g., Goleman, 1994; Salovey & Mayer, 1990). Goleman described *emotional intelligence* as a set of traits that *some might even call character* that offer preparation for reacting to the vicissitudes of life and that "matter immensely for our personal destiny" (1994, p. 285).

> Much evidence testifies that people who are emotionally adept—who know their own feelings well, and who read and deal effectively with other people's feelings—are at an advantage in any domain of life whether romance or intimate relationships . . . or organizational politics. (Goleman, 1994, p. 36)

The capacity for the adaptive expression of affect (the ultimate goal of this treatment model and an indicator of character change) is precisely what is meant by emotional intelligence. Elvin Semrad, a Harvard psychiatrist who trained a generation of psychiatrists during the 1950s and 1960s, had three rules in regard to emotion: *acknowledge, bear, put in perspective*. Semrad's guidelines for "intelligent" handling of affect overlap well with the present model. In defense restructuring, response patterns are *acknowledged*. In the experiencing stage, one learns to *bear* the previously unbearable emotions.

During the reintegration and expression of emotion, everything is put to-gether—*in perspective*.[1] The second objective in affect restructuring, there-fore, is the *reintegration and expression of the full range of affects and drives*, as well as the *reattachment or reconnection to others*.[2] Patients are assisted in de-veloping the appropriate integration, cognitive understanding, and finally, expression of feeling in relationships.

In the experiencing of affects, the intense focus on discrete feelings (e.g., the deepest grief, purest fury, most blissful joy, most passionate sexual desire) was essential for desensitization and, therefore, the regulation of overly severe inhibitions. However, *the pure experience of feeling is not the end goal of treatment*. The next step, and the focus of this chapter, is the inter-weaving of the emotional life into all other aspects of life. A holistic per-spective must be taken. Affects must become adaptively integrated with drives and other affects. Cognitive linkages to feeling must be developed to provide *balance, guidance,* and *control*. The cognitive–affective blend of re-sponding must integrate the needs not only of the person but of the person in relation to others. The adaptive expression of affect reflects the process by which patients have greater emotional contact with others and can play their newly unconflicted emotions in concert; for some, this may be a new connec-tion; for others, it is a reconnection to previous conflicted relationships. For clarity of presentation, a detailed discussion of interpersonal issues is post-poned until chapter 9, in which self–other restructuring is considered.

This chapter describes how therapists can assist their patients in acquiring emotional intelligence. Peter Salovey and John Mayer, coformulators of the theory of emotional intelligence, describe this ability as involving five do-mains: knowing one's emotions, managing emotions, motivating emotions, recognizing emotions in others, and handling relationships. The reader may note the similarity of these domains both to Semrad's guidelines and to the objectives in the present model. These domains, or objectives (as guided by the core formulation), represent the "solution focus" of this treatment.

Patients at this stage of treatment, freed up to understand, experience, and control their feelings, now can make informed decisions about what they want for and from themselves and others. In contrast to behavior therapy and cognitive therapy, which teach the appropriate expression of wants and needs, this model endorses the expression of wants and needs only *after* or *alongside* the work on defenses and internal affect responses. In this objec-tive, all the prior learning and restructuring of defenses, anxieties, and af-

[1]My thanks to Jim Sabin for passing this information on to me. Semrad didn't write; he taught.

[2]Following my 1994 Cape Cod workshop, David Levit wrote asking me to con-sider changing the mechanistic term *affect restructuring* because "it fails to convey the richness of the therapeutic process between you and your patients." Although I agree with him, the term appeals to me, and I retained it. I also appreciated Levit's alterna-tive term *affect reintegration and reconnection*, however, and wove it (along with the term *expression*) into the subtitle of the second objective of affect restructuring. Cor-rect and sensitive labeling that clearly conveys what is done is a continual challenge.

fects come together in a new way. The ultimate goal is for the defenses and anxieties to be of a quality and intensity that optimally guide and direct the most fully felt affect. The result would be "controlled excess" (i.e., fully felt but well-guided affect) for optimal richness in living.

There are rules of thumb for integrated forms of affect. Each affect has optimal forms of expression guided in part by relational considerations. Table 8.1 identifies some of these optimal forms of responding.

TABLE 8.1
Clusters of Emotions (Affects and Drives) Observed in Clincal Work

Emotion clusters (affects and drives)	Some optimal forms of expression
Regulatory emotions	
Distress–anguish	Grief, sorrow, sadness
Anger–rage	Constructive self-assertion (making requests, setting limits)
Affects associated with social responsivity–attachment[a]	Tenderness, devotion, bonding
Pleasure-giving emotions	
Interest–excitement	Involvement, curiosity, enthusiasm, spontaneity, creativity, romantic love–attraction
Enjoyment–joy	Acceptance, humor, "flow," wonder, hope, awe, spirituality, committed love, grace, peace
Affects associated with sexual arousal[a]	Sensuality, passion
Inhibitory emotions	
Fear–terror	Caution, care
Shame–humiliation (including guilt)	Remorse, regret
Pain	Grief, help seeking

[a]Optimal forms of attachment and sexual arousal necessitate a strong association with the positive affects, excitement and joy.

With these general themes in mind, we can better guide our patients toward optimal use of their emotional capacities. The following case is an example:

The Woman with Butterfly Feelings, presented in chapter 6, experienced a dramatic change in her personality structure. When this 57-year-old, long-beaten-down woman acquired the capacity of emotional expression, it was quite upsetting to her extended family, who had been most comfortable with her compliant, submissive, and self-deprecating behavior. When she stood up to an obnoxious cousin at a picnic, she drew some sharp criticism for being outspoken, but she was able to defend her position. "I had a right to tell her to stop badgering me!" she said, stomping her foot. It was only later, after the dust settled, that several family members admitted to her that the cousin had been difficult for them all. She was helped by receiving the support but thankful she had not been dependent on it to make the change. This woman, now over 60, cries freely and openly when she is sad, plays joyfully with her grandchild, and as described, is not pushed around as much anymore.

PREPARATION FOR AFFECT REINTEGRATION AND RECONNECTION

Therapist Stance in Affect Reintegration and Expression
THE REAL THERAPEUTIC RELATIONSHIP

In this objective, the therapist acts as an educator and a coach, assisting the patient in steps toward the authentic functioning that should, by now, have become quite clear. Teaching is often essential. Therapist behaviors that might have been less helpful earlier in treatment, when inner exploration was necessary, can now be performed more safely: guidance, advice, providing information, instruction, role-playing, and modeling. Standard educational tools, such as encouragement, support, and praise, are also useful. Furthermore, according to Jordan, "we have denigrated encouragement in therapy, but it is profoundly important in relationships" (1994). Indeed, at this point in short-term treatment, encouragement can be remarkably beneficial.

The pitfall in encouraging behaviors is the creation of false or compliant aspects of the self. Everything that is taught in psychotherapy must be assessed from the patient's perspective. Jordan puts this another way: "Bringing your truth into relatedness means moving out of shame and moving into the courage of talking one's own truth, and acting with integrity" (1994). It is the therapist's task, therefore, to help build courage and connection and to help patients find their true voice.

PROTOTYPIC INTERVENTION

A therapist might say something like the following: *I would like to offer a suggestion about the way many people have handled such a problem. But I also want to hear whether this suggestion fits your own personal style and beliefs. If my suggestion does not feel right to you, then we should explore other solutions.*

One might argue that many patients do not know what they want but will, if suggestions are offered, passively comply with the therapist. My experience, and that of many of my colleagues, has revealed that the therapist's early and repeated emphasis on a collaborative therapeutic relationship allows patients to feel greater freedom to voice their own perspective. This form of treatment provides a safe environment for that budding voice to emerge and, subsequently, a place to practice how to sustain that voice in the external world. By this point in treatment, the patient should have acquired a *robust ability to respond authentically to the therapist's suggestions.*

Following an interpretation of a specific defensive pattern, the therapist should be vigilant for compliant behavior and begin the encouragement of the patient's authentic participation:

THERAPIST: I may be right, or I may be wrong, but this is the way I am seeing it. Do you see it differently? Or does this fit your experience?

PATIENT: Well, I guess it does.

THERAPIST [*Listening carefully for compliance*]: You sound somewhat hesitant. I wonder if you have some other thoughts about what has been happening. You know, you are the expert on your life.

PATIENT: Well . . . I don't think it's exactly like you've said it.

THERAPIST: Oh. Let's hear your view!

PATIENT [*Sheepishly*]: You know how I tend to keep my disagreements to myself.

THERAPIST: Yeah, we've seen that in several other relationships, haven't we? And we've also seen how it ends up hurting you. What would happen to your therapy, if you do it here?

PATIENT: I guess we wouldn't be playing with a full deck, huh?

The patient proceeds to disclose her view of the situation, thus continuing a process of desensitizing herself to the shame of self-expression, beginning with the therapist.

This approach differs from the traditional analytic approach of abstinence, in which the therapist (a) withholds any suggestion or leading of the patient, (b) does not encourage behaviors in a direct manner, and (c) permits patients to arrive at decisions in their own time without direct intervention. The short-term interventions are quite different. There is an active, involved collaborative process in which both the therapist and the patient brainstorm and problem-solve, with the therapist always mindful of the patient as a separate and respected individual. The long- and short-term approaches use *different pathways but toward the same objective: authentic interpersonal responding.* The abstinent approach tends to drive up anxiety and elicit a transferential reaction (possibly, anger at lack of involvement or appreciation of the therapist's patience). The active, encouraging approach can lower anxiety and engender an entirely different form of transferential reaction (possibly, devaluation of the therapist's input or feelings of tenderness for what is being given). Each of these forms of response is grist for the therapeutic mill. Regardless of which path is taken, the capacity for inner representations of caring and concerned people is the optimal outcome.

There is another unstated, but natural, human reason that therapists and others are reluctant to direct, give advice, or make suggestions: They might be wrong. To give advice means to emerge from the safe and hidden position of the "all-knowing and omnipotent" therapist to the position of a tentative, struggling-to-learn individual, who is like everyone else. This treatment model is predicated on the therapist being an imperfect but involved and concerned human being who has the courage to try things out with the patient. When therapists repeatedly remind patients that the suggestions may not be the *only* way to view the situation, it reduces the perception of thera-pist omnipotence and invites patient autonomy and creative participation.

EXAMPLE: TENTATIVE, COLLABORATIVE SUGGESTIONS

Following is an example of a therapist offering a suggestion: *Let me offer a suggestion here. I am not telling you to do this, mind you. I am asking you to con-sider this suggestion among various possibilities that exist, so you can figure out what response would feel the most satisfying for you.*

Such interactions offer the patient a new relationship and an opportunity to build a new inner representation of how they might be treated. The en-couraging, guiding, but still respectful therapist responses are reactions that have been missing in many patients' experience.

TRANSFERENCE ISSUES

The problematic issues that arise in this area of therapeutic interaction in-clude, on one hand, patients' feelings of being intruded on, dominated, or devalued. On the other hand, directive therapist activity can inspire some patients to become passive and dependent, allowing the therapist to do all the work. In either case, therapists need not fear these reactions but should remain vigilant for them and ready to interpret them when they occur. If pa-tients become either oppositional to suggestion or overly compliant with what the therapist is offering, the therapist can be optimally responsive by backing off, as in the following examples.

EXAMPLES: OPTIMAL RESPONSIVITY TO DEFIANCE OR COMPLIANCE

PATIENT: I hate being told what to do! You and my mother think you know better than me what I want.

THERAPIST: That sounds very unpleasant—to have people close to you treat you this way. What is the worst part of this for you? [*or*] That must bring up a lot of feelings in you toward me. Could we look at that?

Alternatively, the therapist can express a position that is the opposite of the parent's: *If that's the impression I am conveying, that I know better than you, that's not very respectful of you, is it? I have my way of looking at things, but you are the expert on your life, not me. Let me back off and take your lead. What would you see as a better course of action for you?*

When the patient is all too welcoming of the therapist's involvement and lets the therapist do all the work, the therapist should back off and gently encourage the patient's involvement.

PATIENT: What would *you* do in this situation?

THERAPIST: I'll be glad to share my suggestions about what I might do. But my views might not fit at all with what is best for you. So, let's put a number of thoughts out there—yours and mine—about different courses of action, and let's see which fits you best.

These are only a few examples of possible interventions. The basic objective is the resolution of the patient's conflicts about autonomous functioning and their replacement with more adaptive responses, however that is best perceived by collaborative effort of the therapist and patient.

COUNTERTRANSFERENCE ISSUES

The countertransferential reaction of greatest concern during directive intervention is the frustration the therapist can feel when the patient does not respond as wished. Unresponsiveness by the patient can puncture therapists' omnipotent fantasies of having the right answers and their wish to be richly appreciated. Suddenly, the therapist can feel frustration or contempt toward the "stupid, ungrateful, incurable" patient for not learning the therapeutic lessons. Or the therapist can feel devalued by the patient for ignoring all the therapist's hard work. We therapists need to divest ourselves repeatedly of our inevitable narcissistic opinions that we know the right and *only* way.

The other frequent oversight by the therapist is, once again, patient overcompliance. We need to remind ourselves repeatedly that our patients' agreement may be reluctance to disagree rather than a testament to our wisdom. Such omnipotent feelings spring eternal in us, and have to be repeatedly "pruned down." Trusting patients to find their own pathway is often crucial. Indeed, one of the great strengths provided by long-term or analytic therapy is the respectful arena provided for patients to explore their own motives and desires. In the more active and interactional short-term approach, we must be extremely careful to guard against sacrificing the patient's needs to those of our own. Therapists need to be equipped with mechanisms for self-solace, comfort, and reassurance. One that has helped me enormously is the following: *I cannot possibly know for sure what would be best for you. If you are not sure, then the best course of action for you has to be collaboratively discovered between us.*

Anxiety Regulation in Affect Expression

The main issues in this objective involve the generalization of the newly acquired behavior from the therapist–patient relationship to relationships in the outside world. Hitherto, the patient has engaged in phobic avoidance of the adaptive expression of wants and needs. In moving affect expression into the external world, patients expose themselves anew to feared situations. Because affect expression (the adaptive interpersonal expression of wants and needs) will change the basic nature of the patient's interpersonal relationships, much support is needed from the therapist in "reconnecting" with others in a new and often disconcerting way. One approach is to anticipate possible reactions of current persons in the patient's life.

EXAMPLE: ANTICIPATING OTHERS' REACTIONS TO PATIENT CHANGE (THE WOMAN WITH BUTTERFLY FEELINGS)

THERAPIST: You are feeling strongly [I/F] that you want to tell your father and brother to stop telling you how to run your life. Can we consider how they might respond if you were to say something to them? [*Anticipation of consequences, either negative or positive*]

PATIENT: Oh, they will be furious with me [*A*]. I have never voiced a word of my own thoughts to them.

THERAPIST: Then we can expect them to be shocked and upset at first, because you are going to be doing something that they are totally unprepared for. [*Teaching and exposure to the feared response*]

PATIENT: You bet! And it does frighten me to think of it [*A*].

THERAPIST: So let's look at your fears in this transition [*A*] so that it might be as comfortable as possible—or maybe just as little discomfort as possible—for you as well as them.

This conversation could be followed by role-playing the interaction with both the father and the brother to provide some "stress-inoculation" for what the patient might encounter. Examples of role-playing follow.

INTERVENTIONS TO ASSIST IN AFFECT EXPRESSION

The following interventions, which are helpful in guiding the expression of emotion, are discussed in this section:

- Identifying a solution focus: collaboratively developed, optimal adaptive responding
- Assisting in the integration of opposing feelings: playing feelings "in concert"
- Assessing current interpersonal functioning, both expressive and receptive capacities
- Providing instruction and training in areas in which there are genuine deficits in knowledge or skills
- Role-playing difficult interactions
- Returning to defense and affect restructuring when maladaptive behavior persists

The Solution Focus: Optimal Responding

The ultimate goal of this therapy is the cognitively and adaptively guided expression of wants and needs—not regressive discharge. To the extent that one can make this distinction, one can guide oneself to set limits firmly when intruded on (adaptive anger or assertion), cry fully when grief is present, express tenderness and devotion openly and without shame, give and take sexual pleasure freely, and laugh or feel peace and contentment when experiencing joy. Certainly, this is the basis of self-soothing and mature, healthy functioning.

How does one guide affective responding for a patient in the most mindful way? The answer is derived from an integration of standard, recognized adaptive behaviors (e.g., mature defenses, mature affective responding) but tempered by the values or beliefs of the individual patient: values and beliefs that direct affective responding. What kind of person does the patient wish to be in relation to others? What is his ideal sense of self? What is her idea of optimal adaptive responding in regard to the problems she brought to treatment? When the ideal self is not in agreement with the conventional wisdom concerning mental health, this discrepancy can be put forward to the patient and collaboratively resolved.

THERAPIST: I have seen that you believe strongly in being kind and generous. And certainly these are important values to maintain. But I wonder if sometimes you take generosity to the point that it is hurtful to you. What do you think?

PATIENT: Yeah, I know I do that, but it's so hard to hold back.

The patient and therapist can collaborate on an optimal solution that the patient is comfortable with. Even if the therapist does not completely agree, as long as there are some adaptive steps taken, however incrementally, the therapist should respect the patient's decision as a part of an unfolding developmental process.

Such issues should always be dealt with in a noncritical and flexible manner. None of us responds optimally all the time, but if we assist our patients toward a *"good enough adaptation,"* their way of living can improve over time. The ideal self should be held as a *patient-centered* process of working toward something, never a fixed response requirement *nor a covert demand arising from the therapist's* countertransferential desires.

Assisting in the Integration of Opposing Feelings: The Optimal Emotional Blend

If emotions have been made easily discernible and available during the affect-experiencing objective, the goal in this stage is reintegration, or "playing the feelings in concert." When the deepest love can be felt *during moments of fury,* the negative feelings can be put into perspective. If tenderness can be experienced *with sexual arousal,* the lovemaking is enriched. If grief can be experienced *together with longing or anger,* the individual can bear to risk the vulnerability of loving and possible loss.

Each affect must be integrated into the whole experience of the individual and thus "tempered." Again, each feeling must be "put into perspective." The integrative component, or the weaving of the strands of pure feeling into adaptive expression, is accomplished by a blend of cognitive and affective awareness. The extremes of anger must be moderated by feelings of love, care, or at least objective compassion. Sadness needs to be tempered by other joys in life and the desire to replace losses of cherished people or things. All feelings need to be tempered by taking into consideration the feelings of others.

The experiential therapies such as gestalt or Primal Scream have encouraged affective experiencing and a cathartic form of affect expression. Their interventions can feel initially quite relieving, but once the momentary relief passes, the ubiquitous frustration inherent in human life can set in again, leaving the person lost in the morass of conflict or needing more catharsis. Defenses need to be dealt with as well, or the anxiety engendered by the intense affective experience can cause the individual to close off to further experiencing. Pure experiential approaches do not provide the cognitive–affective or affective–affective integration needed for the guidance and the maintenance of curative and adaptive long-term effects. Venting is not an end in itself, and it often is a less useful pathway to experiencing than inner-felt but well-contained affect. A little cognitive guidance, or even a lot, need not destroy a robust affective life. Quite the contrary, *it is through well-developed cognitive structures that the full intensity of our emotional life can be adaptively guided and put to the best purposes.*

Appropriate expression of feeling must integrate the whole of an individual's cognitive and emotional responding. The goal of affect-restructuring is the patient's capacity to express well-thought-out and well-integrated affect. Does the patient have feelings of anger that do not take into consideration the tenderness in the relationship? Or, from the opposite perspective, does the patient feel such excessive gratitude or need that the insensitivities or abuses of others are ignored? Guided imagery can be used to integrate affect experience just as it was used to focus on singular affects.

EXAMPLES: INTEGRATION OF OPPOSING FEELINGS

You seem much more comfortable with angry feelings now. But are there more positive sides of the relationship that need to be remembered as well, to put the anger in perspective? What touches you most about your husband?

You have come to value what your parents have given you, and that is important to hold on to. But can you also remain aware of when they become overly critical?

You have worked deeply and fully in therapy to grieve the sorrow of your early life. But now can we look at what brings you the most joy these days?

A note of warning: Some therapists have become so capable and so focused in working with grief that their patients learn only how to grieve, to the exclusion of assertion, excitement, or joy. It is as though grief becomes the focal piece of the patient's life, rather than one of many potential ways of responding to life experience.

To the extent that a balanced integration of affective experience is mastered, long-standing defensive behavior patterns (the basis of Axis II disorders, according to Vaillant & Perry, 1984) should *increasingly approach resolution.*

Assessing Current Interpersonal Functioning:
Expressive and Receptive Functions of Affect

This chapter involves affect *reintegration and reconnection* on many levels. Once the ideal problem solution is identified, the therapist needs to assess whether it encompasses an adaptive relational balance. After specific feelings have been desensitized and can be focused adaptively (spontaneously, but with integration and control), attention needs to be directed to the purposes for which these feelings are used. Just as there are specific *defensive functions*, there are also specific *affect functions* to which therapists must be

alert: in this discussion we will focus on the expressive function and the receptive function.[3] The general *expressive* function (from the self to the other)
is the most obvious way that affects are used and includes (a) self-nurtu-
rance (asking for satisfaction of wants and needs) and (b) self-protection
(saying no, or setting limits). The other, and often ignored, dimension of
affect responding is the *receptive* function (response of the self in reaction to
others), that is, the ability to respond adaptively or to resonate to affective
communications from others. What does the patient feel about communications that come from the therapist or current others?

As affect restructuring is being mastered by the patient, the therapist
needs to be evaluating how these expressive and receptive capacities are
generalizing in the patient's current interpersonal relationships. Is the patient comfortable with the expression of feeling only in the safe environment
of the therapist's office, or are there clear indications of ability to express
wants and needs in his or her current interpersonal functioning? Is the patient open and receptive to a range of emotional sharing from others? To
assess this, the therapist can consider the following questions:

1. Is the patient able to express and receive a wide range of emotions
   adaptively?
2. Is there emotional resilience in response to bad times?
3. Are the patient's relationships significantly improved or improving?
4. Is there remaining anxiety, guilt, or shame concerning the expression
   or reception of feeling that has not been sufficiently addressed?
5. Is there secondary gain that still lingers, so that the patient does not
   have the motivation to respond differently?
6. Is there insufficient knowledge or skills to allow for ease of expression?

The concern is whether the patient can experience both pleasant and unpleasant communications from others in an adaptive and connected manner.
Although this *receptive* capacity is fundamental to interpersonal relationships, it is often overlooked in treatment in favor of *expression* of feeling.

A rule of thumb is to evaluate in the current interpersonal interaction
whether patients accept and respect their own needs and those of others.
The integration of mutual sets of wants and needs is an essential component
of adaptive interpersonal expression. Certain guidelines can be helpful in
making this assessment. The therapist needs to consider whether patients'
communications have been (a) stated in a mature way without blaming or

---

[3]Dahl's (e.g., 1978, 1991) theory of emotion (specifically, his organization of the
directionality of emotion: orientation [it–me], valence [attraction–repulsion, positive–negative], and activity [to–from, active–passive]) has been helpful for me in the
development of the expressive–receptive function of affects. Dahl adapted his theory
in part from Freud's (1915/1957) three "polarities" basic to mental life:
subject–object, pleasure–unpleasure, and active–passive.

criticizing but *honestly and decently,*[4] (b) made in a manner that optimized the chance that the communication would be responded to, and (c) presented so that *both* the giver and the receiver benefited.

If communication is *honest,* it reflects authenticity and a high degree of respect for oneself. If the communication is conveyed *decently,* it is humane and shows a high degree of respect for others.

The capacity to bear interpersonal conflict must be assessed and, if lacking, further developed. "If you can't be in conflict, you can't be in authentic relatedness" (Jordan, 1994). Fear of conflict leads to the danger of being silenced or taken over by another person's truth. Jordan pointed out that to be receptive is to allow another person to make an emotional impact. She referred to this state as moving out of the power dynamics toward connection. In a popular song of the 1970s, this capacity was expressed in the words "Can you let someone else be strong?" Put another way, "Can you let another person make an impact on you?" Power is often seen as inflicted by men on women; however, men exact enormous submission from other men in the workplace and in the locker room. Women are also quite capable of misusing their power over men as well as over other women. Although there are clear gender biases in power dynamics, there are also human issues that operate in both directions. Both men and women can have tremendous difficulty being receptive (i.e., vulnerable) to others.

Because there has been insufficient attention given to the distinction between expressive and receptive capacities, in the following sections I offer therapists general guidelines for assessing their patients' interactional capacities.

The Expressive Capacity: Feelings Directed Toward Others

Most of the examples in the book so far have been of expressive forms of affect experiencing, that is, outer-directed experience of the emotion. *I feel angry at him. I want to cry over a loss of someone or something. I am afraid of him. I feel contempt for her. I am excited to meet them. I am happy to be with him.*

One important category of emotional work in therapy, therefore, has to do with what Dahl (1978, 1991) called "me–it" or "self–other" directedness of the patient's emotions. Can a patient direct affective responses toward appropriate individuals, or are they turned toward the self? A typical example of the development of the expressive capacity would look like this:

PATIENT: How can I blame my father! He's just doing the only thing he knows how to do.
THERAPIST: Of course, but you blame yourself instead.

---

[4]A highly respected teacher and friend, Ina Dinerman (now Ina Rosenthal Urey), once told me that her philosophy of life was that we owe other people only two things: honesty and decency. If we try to do more than that, she said, we are playing out some caretaking, codependent, or sadomasochistic relationship. This idea has been extremely valuable for me and many others in sorting out optimal responses.

PATIENT: Yeah, I do.

THERAPIST: Do you think you might be turning your anger on yourself that way? Can we look and see what you might feel *toward your father.* The point is not to blame but to look at what happened and examine your feelings.

PATIENT: Well . . . I *was* furious at him, but it is scary to be that mad!

In contrast to examples in the previous chapter, focused on the inner felt reaction and how it could be tolerated or contained within, in this chapter I focus on whether the emotion is integrated enough to be *shared* or *expressed interpersonally* in an adaptive fashion. There are two main categories of expressive affect that need special attention in clinical work: (a) setting limits and (b) asking for things. These capabilities are components of "constructive self assertion," which Malan has said is the easiest disturbance to correct in short-term treatment (Malan & Osimo, 1992, p. 273).

THE CAPACITY FOR SELF-PROTECTION: FEELING WHEN TO SAY NO AND SET LIMITS

It is essential for adaptive human functioning to know when one is angry, when one has been pushed too far, and when requests have been made that one does not wish to fulfill. It is important to feel justified, so that one can use these inner signals appropriately. Caring for oneself means setting limits when intruded on and saying *no* when necessary. Such responses constitute our emotional "boundaries." Many patients have no idea when these inner signals merit attention. Even when the patient can fully experience anger in the session, there remains a need to assess patients' capacity to identify, in the outer world, when their boundaries have been crossed and when they need to say *no.*

In addition, the appropriate expression of negative feelings often makes possible reconciliations whenever there are the "inevitable ruptures" (Jordan, 1994) in relationships. One must first be able to identify and feel comfortable with what one feels, especially the negative emotions, before one can reconcile with others in close relationships. So many patients have told me, with surprise, that after they were able to express some of the pent-up hostility they had carried in close relationships, they felt a sudden rush of tender feelings returning. There are data in support of the capacity of adaptively expressed negative feeling to improve interpersonal relationships (e.g., Ruben, 1992). The *adaptive* expression of anger can set things right that have felt wrong and pave the way for positive feelings to emerge once again.

THE CAPACITY FOR SELF-NURTURE: ASKING FOR WHAT ONE WANTS

Enlightened loving of oneself or caring for oneself means *knowing the reality of one's needs,* that is, being able to identify the inner signals of one's own feelings—what one wants and does not want—and *to experience these sensations as valid and worth consideration.*

In the process of learning how to ask for things, the patient needs to be able to identify the feelings that signal specific wants and needs: (a) what is exciting and interesting, (b) what is enjoyable or comforting, and (c) what the body needs (the drives); these needs include sexual release, hunger and thirst, bladder and bowel functions, sleep and relaxation, the comfort of closeness, and so on. This fact may seem basic to some readers, but many patients are so dissociated from their inner experience that they have no idea when their body is signaling an affect-motivated wish or a drive-based need. In such cases, the capacity for basic self-care is impaired.

On the other end of the self-care continuum are the patients who are overly demanding that others meet the needs that they should be meeting themselves (externalization). Either of these extremes is maladaptive: too many demands or too few.

These basically pleasure-giving responses are particularly important to recognize and draw patients' attention to. Note that the drives all yield relief when satisfied. This is the basis of the pleasure principle: Drive reduction is inherently pleasurable. Yet drive reduction can be conflicted by the association with negative or inhibitory affects. This blocked need for comfort can be overlooked in therapy, because if a patient has become numb to inner needs, *how is the therapist to know what is missing?* The therapist must be vigilant for these blunted responses, "blind spots," or the "lost voice" in the patient.

It is essential to know how to go about meeting needs (i.e., asking for things, as well as setting limits) in a manner appropriate to the interpersonal situation. Although one cannot expect to get what one asks for in every case, the more one asks, the more one gets. To keep asking reflects hope and optimizes one's chances of being responded to. The trick is to know when one's requests are falling on deaf ears and when one should seek what is desired from someone else, that is, to distinguish when one is making requests that are being registered by the other person versus when one is chronically complaining to someone unresponsive. *An adaptive request is interactional and seeks a response.* Complaints often are made as an end in themselves, with no hope for change, with such individuals continuing to knock on the same locked door. Such uninsightful complaining reflects impairment in the *reception of the negative response* that is being given. Self-nurturing affective expression requires careful assessment of the responses one is given and knowing when it is time to move on. To achieve this capacity, instead of desensitization to the pain or hurt of negative messages, the patient may have to be *sensitized* to negative messages through increasing the painfulness of being ignored—*but just until it becomes a meaningful signal.* This topic of sensitization leads directly to the following section.

THE RECEPTIVE CAPACITY: ACCEPTANCE OF FEELINGS FROM OTHERS

In addition to being able to experience feelings *toward others* and *for oneself,* patients need to learn to be receptive *in response to others.* While much of this book deals with desensitization, receptivity means being appropriately *sensitized.* There are many words for this set of skills: connectedness, openness, vulnerability, *sensitivity.* The receptive capacity is crucial in human relationships and takes the form of being able to experience, *accept,* and respond adaptively to a range of positive and negative emotions from others. One should be able to accept expressions of the regulatory emotions from others.

EXAMPLE: RECEPTIVE AFFECTIVE EXPERIENCE

She is angry at me. He cried in my arms. She needs me to respond in some way now. He wants me to do something. I can imagine how she feels. I can feel how she feels. He is frightened of me. I threaten her.

Can the patient accept and respond appropriately to the pleasure-giving emotions of others? *They really enjoy my company. She is sexually attracted to me. He really cares for me. Her joy is my joy. His interest in the subject awakens my own. He seems interested in me. She trusts me. I take delight in her enthusiasm.*

Can the patient accept and adaptively respond to the inhibitory responses of others? *He is ashamed of me. I frightened them. She feels contempt for me. I disgust her.*

Can the patient accept and respond appropriately to the *absence* of the pleasure-giving emotions? *She does not trust me. He doesn't like me. They do not seem to enjoy my company. He is not sexually attracted to me. They do not share my enthusiasm. He didn't like what I said.*

There can be many permutations of the preceding categories. The point is that the therapist needs to be alert to give-and-take responding on an affective level. Affects have evolved to be contagious, and they are transmitted primarily through facial expression, according to the research of Tomkins (1962, 1963), Ekman (1992a, 1992b), and Stern (1985). Emotions of others inevitably elicit a reaction, whether it is conscious or unconscious, in the receiver. It is important to assess whether patients' reactions are defensive and conflict-laden or adaptive in quality. Again, the receptive capacity is the substrate for vulnerability, openness, emotional connection, empathy, and intimacy.

The receptive capacity may vary for different affects. Some individuals do not perceive positive affects directed toward them, and others do not perceive negative affects. Both positive and negative affect receptivity may be impaired. If a patient cannot feel the anger, shame, guilt, or contempt that is communicated *from* others, there will not be an adaptive reaction to set things right. When significant others are basically benign, it can be adaptive to let things "roll off." But if significant others are abusive, it may be important to modify the relationship. This was the case for the Unforgiven Teenager, in the example following.

EXAMPLES: FOCUSING ON THE IMPAIRED RECEPTIVE CAPACITY

THERAPIST: It is noteworthy that you are treated so badly yet remain so detached from it.

PATIENT: What can you do? Might as well ignore it.

THERAPIST: But you're telling me your self-confidence is poor. It must have some effect on you when you're repeatedly criticized by your parents. And you do mention it often.

In another instance, a man began by being assertive, but then felt guilty about it:

PATIENT: I felt so angry inside, so I spoke up and told him that he had treated me and other members of the family unfairly, in taking action without consulting us. In the end, he made some changes, and the rest of the family were all pleased with me . . . but I felt bad anyway [D].

THERAPIST: Why did you feel bad? It sounds like it was a necessary point to make.

PATIENT: Aw, I just feel bad when I make *someone else feel bad* [A and D]. And my uncle had a sad look on his face later. [*A, a reference to what promotes the feeling of conflict*]

THERAPIST: Are you sure you *made him feel bad*, or in agreeing with your point, *did he choose to feel bad*?

For many patients, just a little teaching about emotional responsibility is sufficient to put things in proper perspective. However, this man remained conflicted:

PATIENT: It doesn't matter, I still feel bad about it [D].

THERAPIST: So you have a hard time letting someone feel the consequences of their actions [D]. What is it about your uncle's sad face that makes you feel so bad? [*Anxiety regulation*]

The therapist is building the receptive capacity for sorrow or hurt in others, just to an appropriate level of course. Angry feelings always need to be well integrated with positive feelings.

In this example, the initial affect was adaptive, but the reaction following indicated that it was difficult for the patient to cause sorrow in another. Such reactions can prevent the adaptive response from happening again or can spoil the victory. The therapist should explore and help regulate the "bad feelings": It might be that the patient was too harsh with the uncle; the therapist could explore what the patient would have liked to have said. Even if his expression of concern was given in a considerate way, he still might be concerned that the uncle took it too hard. Maybe the patient had not expressed his positive feelings for the uncle, which would have made his criticism more easily received. Finally, maybe the uncle was "guilt-tripping" the family for disagreeing with him, by acting hurt. Maybe he wanted to hurt them back and was doing so passive–aggressively. All three of these reactions are common patterns in human interactions. Therapists need to explore the data to help patients see what they have contributed to the problematic interaction and what was contributed by others.

In assessing patients' receptive capacity for affect, each pole of the Triangle of Conflict should be considered. Is the individual defending against the reception of feelings because of anxiety, guilt, shame, or pain, or can he or she resonate with the appropriate affective response? Is the patient able to stay open emotionally, accepting and receptive to current people, past relationships, and the therapist? In summary, appropriate receptivity of affect from others can be assessed with reference to the following questions:

- Can *joy* in others be joined with and shared, without having to diminish it or spoil it?
- Can *interest* or *excitement* in others be appreciated or shared, without devaluation or criticism?
- Can *grief* or *anguish* in others be tolerated and shared, without diminishment or pulling away?
- Can *anger* in others (especially when directed toward the self) be reacted to in a thoughtful, responsive, and healing manner, rather than by denial, repression, shame, or blame?
- Can *fear* in others be accepted and understood, without shame, blame, or contempt?
- Can *contempt* from others be reacted to with equanimity and limit setting if necessary, but without further attack on the self?
- Can *tenderness* or *care* from others be felt, cherished, and returned, rather than dismissed or devalued?

All the preceding questions refer to the reception of other peoples' feelings toward the self. It is just as important for patients to be able to be receptive and respond appropriately to these feeling states of the self, directed toward the self. These affective skills are as follows:

- Can one feel *joy* (healthy pride) in oneself or one's activities without shame or guilt?
- Can one feel *interested* or *excited* about various aspects of oneself?
- Can one feel *sadness* or *grief* on one's own behalf when things do not go well?
- Can one feel appropriately *angry* at oneself when one does not behave up to one's ideal standards (sufficiently to correct the error but not to punish oneself)?
- Can one feel *fear* on one's own behalf when doing something dangerous or when vulnerable to loss of control in some destructive way?
- Can one feel *shame, contempt,* or *disgust* for one's *actions rather than one's being,* when one hurts another? (In addition, can one simultaneously feel *grief* for the other's pain and *compassion* for one's failings so that the action is not repeated?)
- Can one feel *tenderness* and *care* for oneself on an equal basis with others?

These affects are our biologically endowed mechanisms to help us cope with existence. It is distressing to see the degree to which improper socialization inhibits experiences such as joy or pride in the self, excitement about one's growth or accomplishment, and care or compassion for the self. It is all too common to find a great deal of impairment of these skills in patients. There is also a great deal of resistance in society to encouraging positive feeling toward the self. Yet these positive feelings about the self are essential for mental and emotional health.

ACCEPTANCE OF THE PAST, PRESENT, AND FUTURE

Acceptance, representing one of the broadest applications of the receptive capacity in the psychological sense of the word, can be thought of as the loftiest task or function of ego: the "general synthetic function manifested in assimilation of external and internal elements, in reconciling conflict ideas, in uniting contrasts, etc." (Hinsie & Campbell, 1960, p. 246). It is the integration of the good and the bad: the ability to see and integrate the positive and negative qualities in the world. Unfortunately, many patients come to therapy with resentment and bitterness as though they were recipients of the "cosmic screw": the universe was created solely for the purpose of making them miserable. In contrast, acceptance can be thought of as the combination of the following affective capacities: (a) an enjoyment of the world and the people in it, (b) enough of a sense of one's own efficacy (joy in self) and capacity for assertion that one is not constantly feeling victimized by the vicissitudes of fortune, and (c) a capacity for grief when things do not work out well.

Many therapies and self-help books advise this view of the world; however, if patients are urged prematurely by therapists to accept this position, it can result in false compliance and a superficial and temporary appearance of change. (The result could be called "defensive joy" or false acceptance covering up unresolved conflicts.) The only authentic path to acceptance is to work through the conflicts that prevent patients from changing what they can (assertion) and accepting what they cannot change (grief) so that there can be more enjoyment in living.

SPIRITUALITY

The most profound form of acceptance of our experience of existence is the ability to feel awe or wonder for the universe and life despite the inevitable disappointments. We must not overlook this important capacity in our patients, which is fundamentally supported by the affect family *joy* in all its variations; when associated with attachment, this group includes tenderness, devotion, committed love, "flow," hope, and grace. (For a discussion of flow, see the work of Csikszentmihalyi, 1990.) The capacity to feel enjoyment or joy in regard to the world—all that is in it, and life itself—contributes to a sense of connection and, ultimately, spirituality and peace. The Unforgiven Teenager needed to feel the blessing of her sense of God in order to accept herself. *However one understands this capacity, which involves the profound and universal acceptance of and connection to oneself, others, and the world at large,* it is a crucial component of healing and therefore one for therapists to hold in mind for each and every patient.

TRANSCENDENCE

After one of my workshops, a wise-looking white-haired man came up to me and said gently, "With all your work on eliciting anger in people, do you ever think about transcendence—you know, the capacity to move beyond or rise above getting angry with people?" I smiled with pleasure at his question, and it prompted me to review how I handle this phenomenon. Do I think about transcendence? Yes, quite often. Do I deal with it in therapy? Hardly ever. Am I providing a soulless therapy? I hope not. After a moment of reflection, my response to him was as follows: Almost all my patients come with problems of severely restricted assertion, and many suffer enormously from their inability to set limits or to establish adequate boundaries. To suggest or work toward transcendence of anger before one has mastered the capacity to experience anger or to employ constructive self-assertion would be to encourage a false solution. (I would call it "defensive transcendence.") We need to meet our patients where they are. Indeed, I have not had one patient arrive at my office with feelings all mastered and integrated. It is only when one has mastery of the affective capacities and can integrate them and play them in concert that transcendence (or some approximation of it) is possible. It is only when one *feels* that one carries a big stick that one can walk softly.

That man's wonderful question has forever brought into my therapy consciousness a concept that used to be reserved for my more philosophical moments. After reviewing the cases of the Machine Builder, the Ferryman, and the Unforgiven Teenager, I realized that each had taken steps toward a more transcendent position, all spontaneously and on their own, after therapy had ended. I underscore this fact in chapter 10. No doubt many patients continue to grow and evolve after successful therapies help them sort out the nuts and bolts of life. Maybe we therapists, at our very best, offer a springboard to transcendence.

Providing Instruction, Teaching, and Skills Training

I turn now from pondering philosophical issues to a discussion of some of the nuts and bolts of therapy. In helping patients develop expressive and receptive affective skills, teaching is important. Cognitive, interpersonal, and behavioral therapists incorporate skills training into their treatment repertoire. Short-term approaches also require such interventions. Many patients have reported finding it helpful to be taught the distinction between passive, assertive, and aggressive behavior. The distinction provides an excellent model for adaptively guiding the expression of anger, yet everyone does not know it. Similarly, it is often helpful to instruct the patient in the differences among acting out, "appropriately expressed" emotion, and "appropriately suppressed" emotion. Such instructions can provide a "map of the territory" to help guide individuals in their choice of responding.

By the time patients have worked through defenses and conflicted affects, they should be better able to integrate the recommendations or instructions contained in this section or those contained in many self-help books. They also should be able to disagree with suggestions or to pick and choose among styles of responding to select what feels right for them.

EXAMPLES OF THE LEGITIMATE NEED FOR INSTRUCTION

One patient was working hard in therapy to identify defenses. He was highly motivated to change, but he cried out to his therapist that he felt entirely lost: *I know what not to do, but I don't have any idea of what to do now. I've never been angry before. How do I get angry at my father? I can see I need to stop him from running my life, but what do I say? How do I say it? Is this an appropriate time since he is having so many financial difficulties?*

Each week he virtually begged the therapist to give him some direction, which she was reluctant to do. She feared that it would result in compliance rather than "real" change. As her supervisor, I was concerned that this patient would, indeed, go through the motions without the feelings. We studied the videotapes to see if he was in touch with the angry feelings, which seemed to be the case. We then decided to go ahead with the instruction. We gave him books to read on assertion, and the therapist gave him a session on assertiveness training and encouragement and direction on how to implement the information. Once she did these things, the patient took the ball and ran with it. He said quietly, "I have never heard these things before; I have never thought them." He had done sufficient underlying work to make the expression authentic, and he just needed a map of the interpersonal territory to allow him to proceed. At 2-year follow-up, his was a most successful outcome.

Therapists often find it difficult to distinguish a true need for help from a passive–dependent defense. In such cases, the following interventions can be considered: Socratic questioning could discern whether the patient ever has exhibited the desired behavior or has a model for it. *You tell me you have no idea what to do. Have you ever seen anyone handle such a situation in a way that you admired or thought was effective?*

Also, the therapist can assess whether the underlying feelings are available or whether the patient wants to skip over them. *You want me to tell you what to do, and if it is simply guidance you need, that can be given. But I would do you no service if I did not explore all the issues around your request. Can we first see if you are comfortable with the feelings?* [For example, the anger necessary for assertion] *Otherwise, you may be asking me for a mechanism to "go through the motions" and avoid the conflicts you have with deep feeling.*

Caution is required to ensure authentic responding. Sometimes, suggestion can lead to straining to behave "as if" one feels assertive when one really does not. Sometimes, this "trying to be assertive" is desensitizing (through exposure to the feared situation) and can lead to behavior change. Sometimes, patients need repeated practice to become accustomed to responding in new ways. If the responses are becoming easier and more natural with each repetition, this is an indication that sufficient therapy work has been done, and the patient can continue the process outside of therapy. However, if fears remain, continued behavioral exposure may result in false solutions and painful attempts at assertion that are not free, adaptive expressions.

Providing information with encouragement and coaching is a fundamental method for learning and should not be forbidden in psychotherapy, although it should be applied intelligently. The rule of thumb to follow is to teach only (a) what the patient does not already know, (b) knowledge that will allow greater independence rather than greater dependence, and (c) skills that the patient is affectively prepared for.

WHY DO THEY TEACH US NOT TO TEACH?

One of my supervisees, who had been well trained in a traditional, long-term psychodynamic model, believed that the therapist stance of abstinence was the right and only way. She had been taught, either implicitly or explicitly, that providing *anything* to the patient was useless because defenses would block the patient from being able to use what was given and it would not be respectful of patients' need to discover their own truth. Although she was quite skeptical of my active, involved approach, she was nonetheless open-minded enough to try it. She was also extremely skeptical about her assignment during internship to teach an assertiveness-training course to a group of community people. One day, she came to me breathless with excitement:

SUPERVISEE: Do you know what happened? One of the women in my assertive training group reported how much the previous session had helped her stand up to her mother. I had taught her "fogging."[5] And she actually went home and did it! Every time her mother criticized her, she offered no resistance, but just reflected back what her mother said. It calmed things right down. She said it worked great, and she was thrilled! But . . . but . . . how could she be able to go home and do that after one instructional session?

LMV [*The old behavior therapist in me puffed up with pride*]: Well, a lot of times those behavioral techniques are really helpful, and people are *quite* able to take the ball and run with it.

SUPERVISEE [*Almost exploding*]: Well, why do they teach us *not* to do them, then?

I think the simplest answer to this question is that thoughtful teachers of dynamic psychotherapy have feared that such instruction would lead to false solutions. Many have been influenced by Freud's (1919 / 1955) warning about the "pure gold" of interpretation versus the plain copper of "direct suggestion." There is much evidence, however, that in practice Freud was active, directive, and quite human with his patients. Many experienced therapists across the country tell me they do the same as I do. The problem is that in training dynamic psychotherapists, how to teach patients is often ig-

---

[5]*Fogging* is a technique for handling criticism in which one assertively copes by offering no resistance and agreeing with whatever has been said. For example:
PERSON A: They told me the forms were in this office!
PERSON B [*Fogging*]: I'm sure they thought the forms were here.
PERSON A: You people sure are stupid!
PERSON B: I can see why you would think so.
This technique, plus many other assertiveness-training techniques, is described in detail in the book *When I Say No I Feel Guilty* (Smith, 1975).

nored except to discourage it. As with so many issues, polarities are not useful. It is not a question of whether to teach or not to teach, but *when* and *how* to do so.

My rule of thumb is to offer a suggestion or collaborate with a patient to determine a course of action at the point in treatment that I think there is enough affective capacity to motivate action authentically and enough cognitive capacity to control and direct it. Sometimes, this is in the first session, and other times it is much later. I encourage patients to try to implement whatever plan has been decided on, but I instruct them that if they are not able to do so, we will explore and work through the defenses and anxieties that are obstructing the desired action. The thwarted plan of action then becomes a focus of anxiety regulation in regard to defenses, affects, and relationships.

BIBLIOTHERAPY

During the past decade, self-help books have improved dramatically. Like more behavioral forms of therapy, self-help books start at the present point of this book, namely, by describing what adaptive behavior *should* be and encouraging the individual to do it. Indeed, some people are healthy enough and undefended enough to be able to take the prescriptions offered in a self-help manual and put them into action. The problem occurs when people are blocked in their capacity to perform the required behaviors and their "blockage" is outside of their awareness or maintained for very important but unconscious reasons. In either case, merely presenting the correct course of action will be limited in its usefulness.

I recommend throughout this book removing the blocks to healthy functioning before moving to teaching or encouraging the expression of feeling or adaptive behavior. Patients must be asked if there is *a continual struggle to express certain feelings that is not improving over time. They must be asked whether affective responding comes more naturally and comfortably as they practice the new behavior, or whether such expression is always forced.* If patients continually find it difficult to respond in an adaptive manner, more work may need to be done on regulation of the related anxieties or conflicts; teaching and encouragement will not be enough.

Self-help books are now taking into consideration defensiveness and anxieties concerning the enacting of desired behavior. In *The Dance of Anger* (Lerner, 1989), the author does a good job of acknowledging the obstacles to overcome and guiding the reader to adaptive functioning. Recently, compilations and reference guides for self-help books have been published (e.g., Quackenbush, 1991,[6] and Santrock, Minnett, & Campbell, 1994).

Role-Playing, Guided Interpersonal Imagery, and the Two-Chair Technique

In addition to providing information or skills training to enhance affective expression and receptivity, the therapist can employ a wide variety of experiential techniques to aid in behavior change, such as role-playing (behav-

---

[6]This was brought to my attention by David Sagula, Hammett, Michigan, 1996.

ioral or imaginal) or the two-chair technique (e.g., Greenberg, 1984). In the therapy setting, an interpersonal situation (scene) representing the core dynamic conflict (or script) can be dramatized to help *expose* the patient to the feared interaction and to practice a variety of responses until the appropriate course of action can be taken.

Role-playing is the enactment of different interpersonal roles. In a behavioral mode, the therapist might take the role of the parent, friend, spouse, or boss, and the patient might take the role of him- or herself. Alternatively, these roles can be reversed to provide the patient a different perspective on the problem. This process of practicing and exchanging different roles is similar to a recent version of the two-chair technique, in which patients enact both parts; first they sit in one chair and play themselves, and then they sit in another chair and enact the role of the other person. The switching of chairs seems to enhance the experience. In the more traditional version of the two-chair technique, patients remain seated but speak to the other person or to some aspect of themselves that is imagined to be in the other chair. For example, the therapist might say, "Put your anger in that chair. What do you want to say to it? What does your anger say to you?" In imaginal role-playing, the patient can play out the dialogue in fantasy, taking first one role and then another.

Each of these approaches provides the patient with an immersion into the experience, which research has demonstrated to be valuable in enhancing the experience. The therapist can interact as deemed necessary: with guidance, through suggestion, or by holding back and allowing the patient to explore the experience of the interaction. In both role-playing and the two-chair technique, research has shown that the patient's *experience of affect is deepened by the enactment of role* compared to simply talking about the situation (e.g., Elliott, 1983; Greenberg, 1980, 1984). The imaginal role-playing procedures can enhance exposure to the warded-off affect if the scene is constructed to contain the core dynamic conflicts. Often, some degree of anxiety is elicited through simple portrayal of the interaction, thus aiding the desensitization process. According to Greenberg and Safran (1987), the two-chair techniques lead to a "softening in the critic" that is associated with anxiety regulation and conflict resolution (p. 87).

This process is a common one in our daily lives. When we have a problem, we often talk it over with a friend and figure out what to say or do. We may play and replay interactions in our imagination until we decide what is best. Role-playing can represent a therapist-assisted enactment of the mature defense "anticipation," through which problems that may occur in the future are sorted out and prepared for in advance. Also, a variety of forms of imaginal role-playing should be implemented throughout the affect-experiencing stage, and guided imagery can help patients to anticipate what they would say, do, or feel in various interpersonal interactions.

EXAMPLE: ROLE-PLAYING TALKING TO THE BOSS

THERAPIST: Okay, you're feeling nervous about talking to your boss. Would you like to role-play this? You play yourself, and I'll play him?

PATIENT: Sure.

THERAPIST [*Playing boss*]: Yes, Joe, what would you like to talk about?

PATIENT: Mr. Smith, I would like to talk over some changes that need to be made in our department.

THERAPIST: Now, look, Joe, I've told you I'm not interested in making any changes right now.

PATIENT [*Pausing*]: Well, I'm having a real hard time with my desk out in the hall . . . .

THERAPIST: Joe, I don't want to hear it. I'm busy now.

PATIENT [*To therapist*]: Let's start over, that just doesn't sound right.

THERAPIST: Okay, what would sound better?

PATIENT [*Again role-playing*]: Mr. Smith, I have some ideas that will improve your department and help get more work done.

THERAPIST: And just what are these ideas, Joe?

PATIENT [*To therapist*]: Yeah, that's a better approach.

In this way, the difficult interactions are played out in a trial-and-error format, collaboratively. The topic does not have to be problem solving, as in the preceding case. The role-play could also involve exploring feelings in various interpersonal settings or replaying an interpersonal conflict.

EXAMPLE: THE TWO-CHAIR TECHNIQUE

PATIENT: I want to tell my husband how I'm feeling, but I just don't dare to.

THERAPIST: Would you like to play this out by sitting where you are and saying what you would want to say, and then sitting in that other chair and playing your husband's part?

PATIENT: Okay, I'll try that.

THERAPIST: Why don't you start with what you might want to say?

PATIENT: Well, I'd say, "Joe, I just don't think we communicate very well, and I want us to try to talk more." Now what do I do?

THERAPIST: Now move to the other chair and imagine how your husband would respond.

PATIENT: Now what would he say? "What's wrong with the way I communicate?" Do I move back now?

THERAPIST: Mmmhmm.

PATIENT: It's not just you, Joe. I don't mean to criticize you. I don't do very well either. We both avoid talking about things.

When the patient looks toward the therapist again for acknowledgment of the move to the other chair, he simply nods. The patient switches chairs and continues as follows:

PATIENT AS JOE: So what do you want to talk about? [*Patient switches chairs*]

PATIENT AS HERSELF: Oh . . . I guess about money, about visiting our parents, things like that. Things we fight about.

PATIENT AS JOE: Won't we just end up fighting? [*Patient switches chairs*]

PATIENT AS HERSELF: I hope not. That would defeat the purpose. I hoped we could talk things out in a way that might be calmer, so we wouldn't end up fighting.

The back and forth switching of chairs and changing roles continues until the patient feels mastery of the expression.

EXAMPLE: ROLE-PLAYING IN GUIDED IMAGERY

PATIENT: I want to talk to my mother about all the things that have come up here in therapy, but I'm not sure how I'd say it or how she'd respond.

THERAPIST: Well, would you want to play it out?

PATIENT: Okay.

THERAPIST: What would you want to say to her?

PATIENT: I'd want to tell her how lonely I was and how miserable it was for me to be the good little girl she always expected.

THERAPIST: How do you imagine that she would respond if you said those words to her?

PATIENT: I have no idea!

THERAPIST: You might have more of an idea than you realize. You lived with her for most of your life. Let's explore in fantasy what response would be most likely.

Sometimes, this much intervention is sufficient to prompt the patient to continue, but when the patient is still blocked, the therapist can ask questions as further prompts:

THERAPIST: For example, would she get mad at you for saying that?

PATIENT [*Immediate recognition*]: Oh no. That's not like her. I know what she'd do, she'd get hurt. Oh! That's what I hate. I can't tell her anything without her collapsing into tears. [*Defensive tears*]

THERAPIST: So what would you want to say to her if she broke out into tears?

PATIENT: Nothing. It's useless [*D*].

THERAPIST: Nevertheless, what would you *want* to say about the tears? [*Encouragement, I/F*]

PATIENT: Ummm . . . I don't know. . . well, I guess I'd want to say . . . [*tearing up*] I'd want to say "Mom, please listen to me. Please let me talk. Don't get so hurt!" [*Constructive self-assertion, I/F*]

THERAPIST: How would your mother respond to that?

PATIENT [*Thinking for a while*]: I think she would listen . . . yeah, I think so.

THERAPIST: So maybe it isn't as useless as you thought it would be to speak up.

PROBLEMS ENCOUNTERED IN EMOTIONAL EXPRESSION

The following topics regarding difficulties in working with emotional expression are discussed in this section:

- Superficial responding: expressing emotions without experiencing them

- Conflictual blind spots impeding progress that are not obvious to the therapist
- Compliance: living from the outside in rather than the inside out
- The pros and cons of confronting parents

Superficial Responding: Expressing Emotions Without Experiencing Them

A common problem encountered in an active, short-term therapy is the encouragement of appropriate behavior *before the patient has become in full contact with and worked through what is experienced: the underlying emotions.* When this happens, there is the potential for a superficial form of responding. Indeed, this is a common problem in patients with the histrionic personality disorder, who express feeling, which may be part defensive and part genuine, in advance of having sorted it out. Patients can be aware of what their maladaptive responses are and can be just as aware of what adaptive responding would be. There can even be strong motivation to alter the maladaptive responding. If the experience of the emotions is not desensitized, however, the patient is, in essence, hobbled in regard to freedom of expression. The problem of superficial responding has been a consideration throughout this chapter, but the issue is sufficiently important to warrant illustration with a further example.

EXAMPLE: A WOMAN'S EVOLUTION FROM MASOCHISM TO SELF-ASSERTION

A young woman was raised in a Southern state and constantly told to "be sweet, honey." She had lived 35 years with the capacity for assertion severely blunted. Indeed, she was quite masochistic: a doormat for her husband, her parents, and even her friends. She struggled so hard to please everyone that she was beset by headaches, various somatic complaints, and recurrent depressions. As time passed, however, she became increasingly impatient with how badly everyone in her life treated her and how much she was taken for granted.

When she heard about cognitive therapy, she became excited and threw herself into it. Because of her strong motivation to change, she was a model client. She easily identified the maladaptive cognitions, and the therapist did not have to work hard in disputing the logic of those cognitions. She eagerly learned the alternative responses and set out to put them to use. She memorized the words her therapist taught her: "That's entirely unfair." The next time her neighbor began sarcastically putting her down, she took a deep breath and, despite enormous anxiety about interpersonal conflict, summoned enough courage to overcome her fears and mutter hesitantly, "That's entirely unfair."

Her friend, who was accustomed to getting away with chiding this woman, was stunned. "Why, I didn't mean anything . . . I . . . I . . . was just joking . . . I hope you're not offended," she said, and she changed the subject. This response was tremendously reinforcing for the beaten-down young woman, and it demonstrated vividly how a small assertion could set up boundaries. What was even better, her friend was consistently more respectful of her thereafter. The woman went on to buy assertiveness-training books, commit them to memory, and apply the principles throughout her life. As she became more assertive, her depressions decreased.

But that's only half the story. Over the years, as this woman struggled to speak up for herself, she noticed what an effort it took. She was indeed less depressed, but the depression was exchanged for being flooded with anxiety before any assertion of her own wants and needs. This became increasingly frustrating to her, especially when she was in a difficult political situation at the elementary school where she was a teacher. A crisis at the school led her to seek therapy once again, this time from a therapist who did short-term dynamic work. "Why do I have to work so hard just to say what I want? I am nearly paralyzed, even though I know I shouldn't be. And no matter how hard I try to talk to myself, I am still overwhelmed by anxiety. The principal can destroy me with one small remark."

Her remarks demonstrated that she was painfully aware of her defensive patterns and desperately wanted to change them. She also had many strengths, however, and it was possible for her treatment to skip the defense-restructuring phase and begin with exploration of feelings of anger, of which she had little awareness. She felt only tremendous anxiety.

Within three sessions of therapy that actively confronted her feelings of anger, she touched the rage that she had carried as a result of physically and emotionally abusive parents. She said she experienced it as a rock of hate exploding inside her. Immediately after that session, she noticed a sharp decrease in the anxiety about conflict. In fact, when her boss yelled at her the next day, she surprised herself by yelling back. Although she knew she needed to temper her reactions somewhat, she was ever after more free to face anger in herself and others.

Conflictual Blind Spots Impeding Progress

The therapist needs to keep in mind that the patient may have a blunted capability of which the patient is not aware. Lack of capacity for joy and inability to ask for things are two examples that have been mentioned previously. There can be a blunted voice that the therapist also takes for granted is not blunted; the therapist may assume the patient has certain capacities that the patient does not. The list of affects and categories of expressive and receptive responding were offered to alert therapists to potentially missing capabilities. In the future, standardized assessment of emotional functioning should provide an overview of the range of impairment, but until that time, therapists have to rely on their knowledge and intuition. A session or two with a significant other present can be most helpful in providing a perspective that might not be evident to the patient and might take the therapist a long time to figure out.

IMPORTANT NEEDS OF WHICH THE PATIENT IS NOT AWARE

In obvious cases of transgression of boundaries or assault (physical or psychological), it is generally clear to the therapist that anger or assertion is in order. But how does a therapist or a patient discern that the patient *wants something* and *needs to ask for it* when the patient has long ago repressed the capacity even to identify the internal desire that needs naming? One of the most elusive problems is the patient's inability to say "I want." I call the resolution of this problem "finding one's voice." Sometimes the capacity has been shut off for so long and is so buried that the therapist has to model, encourage, and teach the patient that it is likely that something is wanted or not wanted. This is a frequently overlooked portion of emotional growth. The following example demonstrates how to work with the task of eliciting what the patient wants.

EXAMPLE: A WOMAN WHO FEARED OPPOSING HER HUSBAND

THERAPIST: You mentioned that you went downhill skiing with your husband. Didn't you tell me a few weeks ago that you hate heights? [*It was fortunate that the therapist put these two facts together and saw the inconsistency.*]

PATIENT: Yeah, but I go with him every year, and I'm scared and miserable all week!

THERAPIST: That sounds like a nightmare. Why would you do that? [*A, inquiring about it*]

PATIENT: That's what I've started asking myself lately—why do I do it [*A*]?

THERAPIST: You mentioned forcing yourself to have sex with him as well, when you don't want to. I'm beginning to wonder if you are constantly living a life of acquiescence that has gone on so long that you don't even mention it most of the time. [*Defensive pattern in several areas*]

PATIENT [*Laying her head back on the chair*]: It's been 20 years like this. I just do what I'm told. For a long time, I didn't even know what I would have wanted different. [*Costs of defenses*]

THERAPIST: Why don't we begin with the skiing? Do you have any idea what you would have rather done instead? [*Seeking the hidden wish or feeling*]

PATIENT: Oh yes, definitely! Cross-country skiing! I'd really enjoy that. [*Proudly*] I even called the cross-country ski office during our vacation just to see what they offered. It sounded wonderful. [*Her first small step at constructive self-assertion of her own wants and needs*]

THERAPIST: Good for you! Was that new for you to do? [*Encouragement and assessment*]

PATIENT: Totally. And next year maybe I'll do it [*I/F*], if I don't chicken out [*A*].

THERAPIST: Looks to me as though you have tons of courage in facing the slopes; what's so scary about facing your husband with what you want? [*Noting strengths; linking them to conflicts*]

PATIENT: I guess I just never have.

THERAPIST: So let's explore this over and over, telling your husband what you want, until you feel comfortable putting forth your wants and needs. [*Exposure to I/F*]

Compliance: Living from the Outside In Rather than from the Inside Out

The following questions can be used as a guideline for assessing which is motivating patients' behavior: their needs or the needs of others. Are they living from the "outside in" (in reaction to someone else's wants or needs) or from the "inside out" (motivated by their own needs)? Are there indications of being able to stand their ground, even if someone opposes them? Has this happened in the therapy? Is there some freeing up of patients' ability to follow their own feelings rather than react to the demands of others? Can you trust their self-report of this? Where is the locus of control? When patients say that they are able to do something, it is wise to remain skeptical until there are repeated examples from both outside and within the therapy session. Therapists do their patients no service by being overly trustful that the behavior is acquired. At the same time, damage can be done by not appreciating what was accomplished. Careful listening and asking the patient to join in the assessment can help determine the authenticity of the patient's response regarding whose feelings—the patient's or someone else's—are determining the patient's behavior.

After reviewing various responses with the therapist, some patients say, "Okay, now tell me what I should do." *This may signal a lack of personal robustness or a lingering desire for dependency that requires some degree of work on defenses, affects, or both. Here is my standard reply:*

THERAPIST: I wonder why you so doubt your ability to make this decision and elevate my capacity to decide what's best for you. Do you think you might be still inwardly putting yourself down or devaluing your own judgment?

PATIENT: Yeah, I still am doing that.

THERAPIST: Can we explore that for a while to see what is happening? How is it that you are so doubting your own capabilities?

The Pros and Cons of Confronting Parents

When working with anger and pain around early life issues many patients develop a strong desire to confront their parents or caretakers. Indeed, in recent years many therapies have emerged that deal with healing the "inner child" (e.g., Miller, 1983, 1990, 1993) and confrontation of the "toxic parent" (e.g., Forward, 1989). I often caution patients to hold back on talking to parents until they have fully worked through all aspects of their feelings, both positive and negative, and feel integrated and in relatively good control of responding. Too hurried and urgent a confrontation of parents can be defensive acting out to strike back for the pain that is coming up in treatment. It is important to keep in mind that *the ability to contain the experience of feelings should precede the expression of that feeling.* A therapist who treated older individuals including parents who were being confronted by their adult children, cautioned as follows: *I've often seen in treatment the victims of this kind of confrontation. It works in a family setting when all people have an equal degree of support. But when everyone does not have support, confrontation can be used irrationally to sacrifice a relationship to the enactment of one person's* [the adult child's] *fantasy.*

Talking with parents ultimately occurs in many of my treatments, and it is only the rare case in which there is a rupture in the relationship. There may be difficult periods while painful memories are being discussed (and almost all parents are initially defensive), but when the feelings are expressed appropriately, many parents eventually become able to grieve with their adult child or feel some degree of sorrow for the pain the child experienced. Of course, some parents are better able to accept the responsibility for the pain than others. Some parents are too proud, or too ashamed, to apologize, but they give a covert apology by changing their behavior and becoming more sensitive to their adult child's needs and boundaries. It has repeatedly touched my heart to see how relationships between parents and their adult children grow closer and warmer with the honest expression and working through of previously unspoken negative feelings. It is equally possible, even if the parents are deceased, for patients to achieve a sense of emotional resolution within themselves, but sadly, the opportunity for closeness in the relationship is gone.

WHEN AFFECTIVE EXPRESSION MEANS THE CESSATION OF A RELATIONSHIP

There are cases in which the patient is mature and appropriate, but the parent (or significant other) continues to be so defensive or vindictive that the relationship is untenable. The need to break off a close relationship comes not from *past failings* but when the parent's behavior is chronically *unacceptable* or *unbearable in present time.* If the previously abusive individual becomes more caring, more sensitive, and more respectful, the patient can safely be encouraged to forgive, even if the wisest course is not to forget— those who have been abusive can return, tragically, to that abusive behavior even when they intend not to. Vigilance on the part of the victim may always be a necessary component of an otherwise improved relationship.

On the other hand, if those who committed the abuse continue to blame, deride, or overstep the patient's boundaries, the prognosis for improved relations is not as good. The degree to which the parent's behavior is aversive depends on the sensitivity of the adult child and the degree of past trauma and abuse. Guidelines for deciding when relationships are destructive include the presence of intense somatization or of suicidal preoccupation in response to visits. A common resolution is to recommend that the frequency of visitation be inversely proportional to the degree of continuing abuse. A wise woman who had a psychotic and out-of-control mother reduced their contact to affectionate letters.

The difficult decision to break off a close relationship must be made carefully and according to the needs of the individual. This can be assisted by the therapist to ensure that acting out by the patient (i.e., nonconstructively returning the abuse) is not taking place. Has the patient actively tried to set things right? Have the issues been make clear to the significant others in a caring way? Have the parents (or others) responded? Is there no remorse from the parents for past physical, sexual, or psychological abuse? Does the parent (or significant other) insist on continuing to blame the patient?

Some parents are never able to take responsibility for the harm they perpetrated and are never able to apologize directly. For a view of such cases, the reader is referred to the book, *People of the Lie* (Peck, 1983), which vividly portrays vicious and vindictive behavior of parents toward children that is subtle but extremely psychologically damaging. The examples in Peck's book provide therapists with a portrait of the type of parental relationship that is often ultimately unworkable. He emphasized that such people can be paragons in the community and look perfectly behaved to the outside world, but they use their children as scapegoats for their own problems and commit devastating psychological abuse. Peck, who applies a theological explanation, believes that such people are unreachable except for the rare ones who permit an exorcism to be performed; he describes one such example in vivid detail. Although I do not agree with Peck's interpretation of the process, I was intrigued to discover that the "exorcism" process sounded surprisingly like a corrective emotional experience with an accepting therapist in short-term therapy. It involved caring people confronting intense emotions such as rage (or "sins"), while at the same time encircling the individual and praying for forgiveness. The underlying healing mechanisms of Peck's approach and mine might be more similar than one would realize.

A man suffering from severe irritable bowel syndrome had an exacerbation of symptoms after each visit with his harping mother. Repeated protests by him that she should respect his limits and refrain from constant criticism and intrusion were only minimally responded to by her. He eventually ceased seeing her. Several years later, he hoped that she might be more respectful of him, so he reopened the visits. Unfortunately, she returned to her previous demanding and harping self almost immediately. He became seriously ill after one exasperating Christmas day visit. He stopped seeing her once again.

Although parental relationships can be quite destructive, the cessation of such a relationship is almost always as traumatic. Because much may be lost, such as family functions and contact with siblings, a careful weighing of options must be done. To have no roots with one's family of origin is like being cut adrift in the universe. Yet, tragically, this is the only choice for some people. When such a loss is inevitable, it is important to help the patient replace this loss. What other people have been nurturant figures in the patient's life? In such cases, the real "mother" or "father" may not have been the biological one. Regardless of the patient's age, who could be mentors or role models now? Sometimes a biological family can be replaced by an "intentional family": one that the person chooses.

ADVOCACY AND BEARING WITNESS

As the therapeutic approach continues endorsing and encouraging interpersonal affective expression, the therapist needs to be prepared, when necessary, to bear witness and become an advocate on behalf of the patient in acknowledging destructive abuse from parents or significant others. When abuse has been severe and damaging, it may be necessary for the therapist to support the patient's withdrawal from the relationship, at least temporarily. This stance may have to be continued until the patient's defenses are sufficiently flexible to acknowledge and adaptive enough to withstand the parent's chronic unattenuated attacks. *However, the therapist does the patient no service by facilitating acting out, encouraging the patient to become the same kind of bully the parent was, or eliciting questionable memories by hypnosis or suggestion.* On the other hand, more damage can be done to the patient if the therapist joins the abusive, denying parents by becoming a "person of the lie" and forcing a "happy" resolution when there is none in reality. In doing so, the therapist continues the abuse.

Alice Miller described the "enlightened witness" (1990, 1993) as someone who recognizes cruelty, rejects it categorically, and advocates on behalf of the person who has been abused (1990, pp. 193–194). Miller said that this advocacy has resulted in "abundant examples of people who, with the help of an enlightened witness during childhood or later life, have become conscious of the injustice done to them, and as a result have acquired the capacity to empathize with others" (1993, p. 71).

SUMMARY

This chapter focuses on the interventions that can be useful in assisting patients in expressing affects in an adaptive manner. With encouragement, support, guidance, and teaching from the therapist, anxieties that have been associated with interpersonal expression of feeling are regulated. Interventions include the following:

- Integration of opposing emotions
- Assessment of current interpersonal functioning, both expressive and receptive capacities
- Providing information, guidance, and teaching
- Skills training
- Repetition until anxieties about affect expression are desensitized

CHAPTER 9

Restructuring the Inner Representations of Self and Others

Camus teaches us that we must learn to love that which is imperfect (and that must include ourselves and others). Before proceeding with the methods to promote change in affectively based attachments, I alert the reader to an interesting point concerning the brain centers where important facets of attachment and affective change may occur. Although attention is often drawn to the frontal lobes in discussing the integration necessary for the sense of self, there are other important areas of the brain to consider as well: the "affect and attachment" areas in the neuronal networks of the limbic cortex and related structures. It has been intriguing to me to learn that most of our drives are primarily driven from the older part of the brain: the hypothalamus and related structures. One exception is the drive for attachment, or "social responsivity," which is seated in the general limbic locations (e.g., amygdala, anterior cingulate gyrus) as are the affects (see Brothers, 1990; Kling & Brothers, 1992), suggesting close interactions between these two vital aspects of our nature.

If you put your fingertips around and above both of your ears, you will be touching the area of the skull near the limbic cortex, which is located about ½ to 1 inch inside. In the limbic cortex is a heavy concentration of the neuronal networks that represent fundamental aspects of our inner representations of self and others. It is here that affect and attachment responses appear to intermingle and percolate. Here are the neuronal networks undergirding human affect and attachment functions: in the declarative memory of the hippocampus, the experiential memory of the amygdala, and the attachment functions of the cingulate gyrus, just to name a few. In our mammalian ancestors, this was the rhinencephalon (the smell brain) that underlay the role of olfaction in governing their motivation and attachment: approach or avoidance was originally based on scent.

A growing body of research suggests that our affect-laden relationship memories may be constructed, stored, and retrieved to a large degree in these limbic structures (Aggleton, 1992; Insel, 1992; LeDoux, 1992, 1993; MacLean, 1972, 1985; Panskepp, 1982; Winslow & Insel, 1991). Such structures support not only retrieval and description of relationship memories but also the experiencing of those memories affectively. We must guard against simplistic neurogeographical concepts or attributions of mental disorder to specific brain regions (e.g., Ratey, 1995; LeDoux, 1993, pp. 2–4); however, recent research is beginning to chart the complex course of brain–behavior relationships (e.g., Andreasen et al., 1995; George et al., 1995, Gottshalk & Fronczek, 1995). One might speculate that future research on psychotherapeutic change using brain imaging technology may eventually reveal that a *complex interaction* of activity in these neuronal networks must be altered for character change to occur. Furthermore, as character change takes place, we might hypothesize concomitant structural and functional alterations in these neuronal networks.

In the meantime, we can concentrate on what the clinician might do to impact these affect–attachment responses. Issues of self and changes in representations of self and others are complicated; although one chapter is not sufficient to do justice to their richness and complexity, I identify here some of the clinical variables in the equation that carry the greatest weight and that have been observed to be involved in change in psychotherapy. A few simple guidelines are offered for active, short-term approaches to working with and rebuilding inner representations of self and others. At the same time, the reader is referred to literature in self psychology and object relations to deepen the awareness of the subtleties of interpersonal and intrapersonal experience (e.g., Baker & Baker, 1987; Benjamin, 1993a; Kernberg, 1983; Kohut, 1977; Lichtenberg, 1983, 1989; Stern, 1985, 1995), and the growing body of research on change in representations of patients and therapists (Orlinsky & Geller, 1993; Geller & Farber, 1993) and in mothers and infants (e.g., Beebe & Lachmann, 1994).

Of equal importance to the restructuring of defenses and the regulation of affect and anxiety is how the sense of the self and the sense of others are altered in brief dynamic psychotherapy. The change in how we view ourselves and others is a component of psychodynamic psychology that many say has always been there implicitly. However, restructuring of the inner representations of self and others has been more explicitly addressed by other theoretical orientations (e.g., self psychology; object relations; and client-centered, interpersonal, and modern cognitive psychology). The traditional dynamic view has been to define maturity in terms of autonomy and independence, which are achieved through the process of separation–individuation (Greenberg & Mitchell, 1983, pp. 402–403) and internalization of others (Stern, 1985, p. 243). Recently, however, Stern and other authors have attempted to encompass issues of self in relation to others on the basis of a revision of psychodynamic theory (e.g., Lichtenberg, 1983; Mitchell, 1988) or from a feminist perspective (Gilligan, 1982; Jordan et al., 1991), in which *attachment* to others, not separation, is viewed as the goal of maturity, and the need for others is seen as adaptive and legitimate not only in childhood but throughout the life span.

Like other dichotomies, separation versus attachment does not have to be an either–or proposition. The model proposed in this book encourages the capacity for both autonomy and healthy dependence. As Stern (1985) pointed out, they are opposite ends of the same continuum. For this model, autonomy and dependence go hand in hand, and optimal functioning arises from their adaptively balanced integration.

Kohut's concept of "self-object" (the way we use aspects of others to supply needs of the self) has provided a popular approach for working with issues of self across theoretical orientations.[1] Stern, however, on the basis of accumulating research, preferred to consider these relational phenomena in terms of the "memory of experiences of being with others, and the way that these memories are retrieved or stored" (1985, p. 243). Stern drew attention to the "constantly evoked companions" or "the memories of self-regulating others" (a term Stern uses as descriptive of self-object) that we all carry within us. His approach coincides with my group's work with guided imagery, retrieval of affect-laden memories of relationships, and the emotions involved in those images. Jesse Geller asks us to consider our patients' inner representations of themselves and others.[2] What images walk beside them from moment to moment, and how do they color their experience? What voices play in their heads, and how do these voices impact on their mood? What are the inner representations of the people that dominate their thoughts and feelings, and do they result in health or illness? Have these inner models been constructed from their own wants and needs, or have the models largely been imposed by others? In this therapy model, these images are the working "stuff" for restructuring of the self and others.

Throughout life, people are dependent on these memories of self-regulating others to define and structure experience and to provide a basis to guide action. Stern pointed out that these memories are not static but are constructed and reconstructed over time, depending on experience. This ongoing potential for either revision or reenactment is what permits the relationship with the therapist to be so crucial for change. *We therapists are the builders of future memories, which have the potential to undergird or alleviate pathology. We are contributors to the reconstruction of the memory trace.*

BUILDING CONCEPTS OF SELF AND OTHERS

Self–other restructuring includes the building of adaptive concepts and understanding of self and others as well as the desensitization of the associated

---

[1]The self-object relationship refers to an intrapsychic experience rather than the interpersonal relationship between the self and other. "Self-object refers to how one person may use some aspect of another person as a functional part of the self to provide a stabilizing structure against the fragmenting potential of stimulation and affect" (Stern, 1985, p. 242).

[2]Jesse Geller, Society for Psychotherapy Research, June 1995.

inhibitory affects. These processes are highly interactive and interwoven. As perceptions of self and others change, so do the associated feelings—and vice versa.

In this model the conscious understanding and adaptive use of affects is paramount. Our affective response in regard to ourselves and others is an ever-present factor in pathology and in therapeutic change, and it needs to be made explicit. Jon Monsen (1994) pointed out the following:

> According to theories of psychodynamic self-psychology [Kohut, Stern, Stolorow] affect consciousness seems to constitute an essential structural aspect of the self and determines to what degree specific affects will have an organizing or disorganizing effect on the person's capacity to relate to him/herself and others. To the extent that affect states are not integrated into the organization of self-experience, defenses against affect become necessary both to preserve the integrity of a weak self-structure, and as a way of maintaining compensatory self-esteem. (Monsen, 1994, p. 8.)

What Monsen is saying is that the more conscious one is of one's affects, the more one is likely to exhibit generally sound levels of global mental health, the capacity to experience intimacy, and the motivation to realize personal ambitions and goals (1994, pp. 8–9). Furthermore, although both expressive and receptive capacities of affect are important, it is the receptive capacity of affects in relationships that are highlighted in this chapter because of the importance of the receptive capacity in the restructuring of inner representations.

THE RECEPTIVE CAPACITY

George Vaillant asked why there is "so extensive a psychiatric literature on loss and such a scanty one on internalization" (1988, p. 150). If our patients cannot "take in" (or receive or resonate to) what we or others offer them, no revision of the pathological inner representations is possible, and little character change can occur. Conversely, if our patients have the capacity to be receptive to what is given them and appropriately expressive in response, they can achieve the objectives of psychotherapy. There are several reasons for my focus on the patient's receptive capacity: (a) This capacity has been overlooked in most treatment models in favor of expression of feeling; (b) receptive impairment represents the biggest obstacle to character change; and (c) far too much attention is placed on the study of therapist interventions and not enough on *patients' reactions* or resonance to those interventions.

One exception is the work being done at the STDP Institute at St. Clare's Hospital in Denville, New Jersey. Here, Michael Alpert, Diana Fosha, Isabel Sklar, and their colleagues have been pioneering techniques to assist patient receptivity to therapist interventions as part of their system, called accelerated empathic therapy (AET; Alpert, 1992). By continuous "reciprocal monitoring," the patient is encouraged to look for and experience the therapist's affect as well as his or her own affect. This mutual sharing of affect is referred to as "staying attuned." My close collaboration with my colleagues at the STDP Institute over the past decade has been one major contributing factor (along with insights offered by colleagues in Norway)[3] to the development of the self–other restructuring component of my model.

By changing the aspects of the maladaptive sense of self and others that impair receptive functions, patients can be helped to acquire an increasingly more open and adaptive stance in relation to others. As in defense and affect restructuring, the therapist first must help the patient to recognize these maladaptive self–other representations and the responses they give rise to; second, the therapist must help the patient to give them up; and third, the patient needs assistance to replace them with new, more adaptive perceptions that support emotionally responsive relationships with others as well as with the self. In the following example, a highly successful 35-year-old, single professional woman was struggling with problems of counterdependence in her relationship to a man named Bill, that is, desperately wanting to be cared for but rejecting care.

EXAMPLE: THE CARE-REJECTOR

THERAPIST: Can you see how you, in effect, put barriers up between yourself and him by not responding to the warmth that he offers? [*This approach can be seen as pointing out a defensive pattern but specifically addressing defenses against receptivity.*]

PATIENT: Yes, I see it, but it would be hard for me to do otherwise.

THERAPIST: What would be the most difficult part? [*Exploration of the conflicts around receptivity*]

By now the reader should be able to note the familiar pattern of pointing out defensive behaviors and exploring the conflicts around that behavior. In this chapter, the only difference is the specific focus on defenses concerning receptivity and the sense of self and others, as follows:

PATIENT: I just can't let myself act helpless. If I'm not strong and capable, even for a minute, I feel drenched with shame. So if anyone tries to do anything for me, I can't let them. It's like I am *sure* if I ask for help, or whatever, they will look at me with contempt. Just like my father did.

It is poignant that the patient reported that her boyfriend, Bill, had said he wasn't sure whether he wanted to marry her because she was so independent and did not seem to have any need for him. She was generous and caretaking of him, but she could not let him be caretaking of her in any way. She could give but she could not receive. So Bill could not "feel" the resonance from her he sought.

---

[3]Martin Svartberg, Ronnaug Leland, Jon Monsen, Ottar Hummelsund, and others.

PATIENT: Oh, I long to be married. But I just don't think it's going to happen to me. Man after man leaves me. It's like life does not have that in store for me.

THERAPIST: What is it about yourself that makes you think that Bill would want to leave?

PATIENT: I don't feel lovable–way down deep inside I just don't feel like anybody cares.

THERAPIST: I guess if you don't believe anybody cares, that would make it hard for you to ask for anything, wouldn't it? Then you would be doomed to always be alone?

PATIENT: I feel so alone.

THERAPIST: It sounds like you may be overgeneralizing from your father's behavior. Do you really think Bill would so resent giving to you or helping you?

PATIENT [*Pausing*]: I guess not—not intellectually. He does offer to do things for me. A lot in fact. But I never let him. It seems impossible to believe that Bill wouldn't feel contempt if I needed him.

THERAPIST: So you may be setting up a self-fulfilling prophecy. You may increase the likelihood of his leaving you by not allowing the relationship to grow closer—at least from your side.

PATIENT [*Pausing*]: Hmmm. I'm beginning to see that this could be my problem. I'm pushing *him* away. It seemed like it was the other way around.

THERAPIST: Well, he may back off from frustration of not being needed.

This was a capable woman who was able to shift her perception of herself and Bill fairly rapidly. Nevertheless, she needed a few more months of therapy to begin to relax her distancing behaviors and open up in a more receptive manner to others. We repeatedly worked on how she could allow herself to be cared for—something she had never tried before. We also had to prepare for the worst possibilities, while hoping for the best.

At one point, I said the following to her: *Well, it's not clear yet whether he will remain open if you become more open, but you won't find out how he'll respond unless you give it a try. Do you think you could bear it if he left?* This is the encouragement to expose the patient to the feared situations, but with the necessary supports. To bear the risk of openness in a relationship, one must be able to grieve the potential loss of that relationship and feel able to bear being alone. One uses anticipation to strengthen the courage to be open. Sometimes I say in a supportive vein: *If it doesn't work out, do you feel you could use therapy to help you grieve the loss, rather than become depressed? Maybe it wouldn't be so unbearable then.*

Another issue is the pain of her early life. Subsequent sessions focused on the grief around that loss, so that she could build compassion for herself and better face the thought of closeness and the potential it brings for loss. As it happened, as soon as she became more open, Bill responded well. They were married the following year.

Although this chapter sequentially follows chapters on defenses and affects, those aspects and the restructuring of the inner representations of self and others are *parallel strands* that are woven throughout the fabric of therapy. In well-adjusted individuals with less impairment in inner images of self and other, less work may be needed in this area. In extremely impaired individuals, restructuring or constructing of images of self and others may take precedence. In contrast to the focus on defensive *behaviors* and affective *experience,* in this chapter it is the inner *image* of the whole person in relation to others that is highlighted for restructuring. As we recognize our defenses, we increase our awareness of an important part of ourselves. As we experience our affects, we add knowledge of our wants, needs, and motivations. Important aspects of the self are brought to consciousness in these restructuring processes. But we do not change a maladaptive image by thinking about it and talking about it alone. We can change the deepest level of our inner representations of self and others only by changing the associated *feelings.*

Newer, more constructive inner representations of others have the power to undo the negative representations of abusive or neglectful caretakers. When patients take in a caring individual, they become able to remember, with warmth and tenderness, the concern and the emotional gifts given by the other person. Rather than devaluing or dismissing the caring person as foolish or needy, they slowly and painfully come to feel themselves a person *worthy of being cared for.* The word *painfully* needs emphasis. One cannot build the capacity to feel the care that has been missing for a lifetime without *at each moment of opening* being hit with the shock of the contrast to past abuse and past lack of love and, often, experiencing a torrent of grief and anger. Many patients (and other people), on finding a secure and nurturing relationship after years of being alone, find that with each welling up of tenderness in the arms of the beloved, there is a concomitant welling up and pouring out of sorrow for the years of loneliness. When the person is able to cry in the beloved's arms, the closeness is deepened and the capacity to take in more or feel greater tenderness grows. But human nature being what it is, the person often defends against the concomitant sorrow with devaluation of the care that is given or the person giving it. Tenderness, although craved in the abstract, is more often than not terrifying to experience in reality because of the intensity of the sense of vulnerability and sorrow. "The experience of closeness can evoke painful memories of times when closeness was lost or yearned for but never obtained" (Alpert, 1992, p. 142).

Patients often sabotage receiving what is given through a reflexive and subtle pulling away. At other times, when the closeness is too threatening, there may even be frank pushing away, picking of fights, or abrupt withdrawal from the loved one because the pain that comes with the tenderness cannot be borne. This chapter discusses ways to build the patient's capacity for openness and vulnerability (i.e., receptivity to experience) and for self-protection at the same time. Without the attainment of these two skills, character change will be most difficult to achieve.

THERAPIST STANCE IN SELF–OTHER RESTRUCTURING: THE HEALING CONNECTION

The therapist stance in defense and affect restructuring was presented as a precondition or an adjunct position to assist in the main therapeutic interventions. In the restructuring of the inner representations of self and others, however, *the therapist stance becomes the intervention.* The therapist stance, itself, is the healing connection. To achieve the goal in a time-efficient manner, one uses guided imagery that focuses on felt experience in the relationship and oscillates between patients' distortions (the transferential projections from their past) and patients' perceptions of the real therapeutic relationship with the therapist.

The Real Relationship: The Receptive Capacity with the Therapist

How do our patients see us? How do they carry us in their hearts and minds from moment to moment? How much are these perceptions of us distorted by past relationships? Who are we to them? How much will they open to us and allow us to impact the very intrapsychic foundations on which they stand? The capacity to hold inside the experience of the relationship with the therapist, if not already possible, must be built in treatment, or in-depth therapeutic work cannot be done. The objective, of course, is to help patients be able to respond in a positive manner to *their sense of how they are experienced by their therapist.*[4]

Franz Alexander and Thomas French (1946) and Michael Balint (1968) said therapy could change people because the relationship with the therapist offered them something different: a new ending. Gustafson (1986) suggested that short-term therapy can supply a "missing capability." This process of supplying something new occurs, in part, because the therapist reacts differently from the early-life caretakers. In the anxiety-regulating model of therapy presented in this book, the patient rapidly experiences something new that is emotionally based and "corrective." Whereas the long-term therapist lets this relationship evolve slowly over time, short-term therapists actively pursue this healing connection through encouragement, guidance, and direction. Ultimately, in either approach, the patient–therapist relationship becomes a prototype for the type of relationship that needs to be sought in the world. An example of an intervention designed to facilitate the receptive capacity of this healing connection follows.

FACILITATING THE RECEPTIVE CAPACITY
EXAMPLE: ENCOURAGING RECEPTIVITY WITH
THE UNFORGIVEN TEENAGER

PATIENT: I feel like you've seen the lack of goodness in me, and you will not think highly of me. [*This reflects the distortion caused by past relationship patterns being transferred onto the present.*]

---

[4]My awareness of this perspective has been heightened by the work of Jesse Geller and Barry Farber (1993).

THERAPIST: Is there anything I have done that gives you that impression? [*I gently began to insinuate a reality perspective to contrast with her distortion.*]

PATIENT: No, nothing I can think of. I just feel it.

THERAPIST: When you look at my face, does it seem that I think badly of you?

PATIENT: No, your face doesn't look like that at all. I guess you don't really . . . look down on me . . . but . . .

THERAPIST: Look at my face. What do I seem to be feeling right now toward you?

PATIENT [*Nervously, with her eyes darting toward mine*]: I have no idea!

THERAPIST: Maybe not, but if you let your eyes stay on my face for a moment, you might feel differently. What can you sense from me right now?

At this moment, I did not know exactly what my face looked like. I invariably feel a bit self-conscious when I draw such close attention to my responses. However, I knew I felt sad for her, and I trusted that would register on my face.

PATIENT [*Looking back at me carefully*]: Your face looks a little sad. Maybe you feel a little sad for me.

THERAPIST: Well, you have told me a sad story, haven't you?

PATIENT: Yes, I have. And I'd feel sad too, if someone had told it to me.

Only after the patient can initiate the awareness of the feeling should the therapist self-disclose or confirm the patient's perception. In the preceding instance, the therapist smiles gently and nods. If the patient continues to be unable to believe in the care or concern of the therapist, the dialogue might take the following form.

EXAMPLE: RESISTANCE TO RECEPTIVITY IN THE UNFORGIVEN TEENAGER

THERAPIST: Can you look at me again? What can you sense from me [I/F]?

PATIENT: I don't sense anything.

THERAPIST [*Persisting*]: Still, what do you suppose that I might feel?

PATIENT [*Angrily*]: How would I know! [*This frustrated defensive response is common as the therapist pushes for a close sharing of experience.*]

THERAPIST: How would you feel if someone told *you* the story you have told me? [*Changing perspective*]

PATIENT: Oh, I would feel terrible! [*This patient responds as the vast majority of patients do to the preceding statement; it is at this point that I note the discrepancy.*]

THERAPIST: Isn't it striking that you can so readily imagine yourself feeling sad for this imaginary person but that you have such difficulty imagining I might have sadness for you? Can you see how, in your mind, other people readily receive care and concern, but you—sitting here with me, telling me such painful experiences—do not let yourself imagine that *you* might be given the same degree of concern that you would give to an imaginary stranger? [*Vivifying the I/F, modeling I/F*]

PATIENT [*Pausing*]: It is striking. [*Pausing again*] But I don't.

Using the patient's own affective response as a model can vividly open the patient to the awareness of the therapist's feelings in the real relationship. The preceding interaction is a staple in my therapeutic practice. I use it again and again, in forms that vary according to the specific situation.

If this process does not immediately awaken the patient's sensibilities, the therapist should not feel discouraged, *only more resolved to persist gently over time*. Continued patient resistance signals a need for gentle repetition of such interactions as the preceding, to raise the patient's consciousness of these shared emotional experiences in a graded fashion. Initially, such interventions may do nothing more than draw patients' attention to the discrepancy in their perception and elicit some curiosity about it. But with each repetition, the therapist should be vigilant for small shifts in the patient's awareness of other people's feelings. The point is not to help patients develop empathy for therapists' feelings, but for patients to build the inner sense of being worthy of compassion and having an impact on others. Several weeks of repetitions of the preceding type of interaction typically will begin to build the new "cognitive and affective sets." For some patients, this amount of attention is sufficient to open them to the awareness of others' experience. For others, it will only begin that awareness. In the more resistant cases, the negative inner representations of others present the major obstacle to overcome.

In the most resistance of cases, the patient might respond that he or she would feel disgusted (or annoyed or nothing) toward another person telling a sad story. That response implies a more severe version of the same obstacle: a strong identification with the aggressor and a need for intensive work on separation from the harsh inner representations of early-life caretakers. (Altering the inner representation of others is discussed later in this chapter.)

The Unforgiven Teenager in the preceding examples learned to stop behaving destructively toward herself. She also learned to stop or prevent others from taking advantage of her. This change occurred through experiencing the caring relationship with the therapist. At first she could not tolerate the therapist's warmth and concern, but as this reaction was explored in the therapeutic relationship, the experience began to "metabolize," or become part of her inner experience. This meant that when she was alone, she began to respond to herself more in the way the therapist did (with care, concern, and compassion) rather than in the way she had been treated by her parents.

This change was not accomplished without the concomitant building of capacities needed to navigate relationships. She learned to become more assertive, and she stood up to a difficult boss. She also had repeated periods of grief related to the enormous loneliness in her life.

ASSESSING THE DEGREE OF EXTERNALIZATION OF NEEDS

To assess adequately the degree of receptivity in an individual, the therapist must assess the degree of externalization being used. To what extent does the patient require that the "good feelings" of care and validation come *directly* from others? The patient may be addicted to the physical presence of people for reassurance and support. Such addiction occurs because of impairment in the receptive capacity, so that affirmation and support can be experienced only on an external plane. The individual is unable to call on and *savor from within* the memories of nurturant others. When there is an inability to rely on, trust, or build a reservoir of emotional memories, one stays addicted to the physical presence of others for emotional sustenance. (I know you said you were proud of me, but I don't know if you really meant it. Do you really mean it? Will you tell me again?)

Patients often have difficulty experiencing the pleasure of others from their *own inner experience of resonance* to their memories of relating. Patients, indeed many of us, have difficulty retrieving memories and tender feelings of what others *have given* to us, experiencing the pleasure of what others *are giving*, and taking pleasure in anticipating what will *continue to be given*. Rather than holding the feeling in the heart, some individuals are dependent on the presence of others and on the repetition of their words of care, reassurance, and affirmation. Such patients have a limited receptive capacity for emotional sharing with others. Forgetting the good in relationships and remembering only the bad, they are inevitably addicted to the presence of people for affirmation. We need to help our patients hold their past loves the way an elder holds special memories of youth.

Kohut made the important observation that we all need the support and affirmation of others throughout our lives. However, there needs to be an assessment of the degree of external support necessary to transmute events into the patient's internal experience. For some people, everything remains on the surface, and nothing sinks in. The therapist needs to consider whether the patient has any feeling of self-acceptance apart from direct praise, and any experience of security, trust, or connection apart from physical presence. Clearly, as the saying goes, the therapist tries not to give patients a fish but to teach them to fish. For how long can patients savor a heartfelt emotional interaction: a minute, a month, or a lifetime? Is the memory quickly dismissed, or is it remembered in a comforting way, tenderly and repeatedly, when alone? How much can patients let the memory of others soothe them when they are alone?

EXAMPLE: THE DISTRUSTFUL SON

THERAPIST: You seem somewhat reserved at the beginning of each session.

PATIENT: Yes, I am. I haven't seen you in a week, so I have to adjust to you.

THERAPIST: How do you mean that?

PATIENT: I don't know how you're going to be. I have to see if you feel the same.

THERAPIST: Why would I feel different to you? What would change the closeness between us since last week?

PATIENT: You never know how people are going to be until you're with them. [*The transference distortion*]

THERAPIST: Really? Do you think my feelings for you could change so easily, just because of time passing? [*Beginning to explore the real relationship feelings*]

PATIENT: They might.

THERAPIST: How did it seem that I felt for you last week?

PATIENT [*Hesitantly*]: You seemed concerned about me.

THERAPIST: Why would that change?

PATIENT: 'Cause people change. Here today, gone tomorrow.

THERAPIST: So it's hard for you to trust what you feel with me will remain. I wonder where you learned that?

PATIENT: Oh, I know. It was with my mother.

The therapist would continue exploring the mother's response versus the therapist's response in a Socratic manner to raise the patient's consciousness about this distinction. The interventions in this case included the following: *Where would those feelings go in me? What would replace them? Do I seem any different now? How did your mother react? Do you think everyone else is going to be as changeable as your mother? Can you see how you distort me in a way that leaves you feeling uncomfortable and distrusting of others and that you are seeing your mother in every relationship? From what you tell me about what you were accustomed to, it's understandable that you would expect the same response from me as you did from her. But that overly programmed perception is a painful burden to carry, isn't it?*

Although we may initially need the care and affirmation of others, even their love, to eradicate self-hate, *these interactions need to become part of us: part of our memory life and part of what we use to function adaptively.* This is what Freud meant by *Nachtraglichkeit,* what Kohut (1977) meant by "transmuting internalizations," and what Modell (1990) meant by "retranscription of the memory trace." These inner representations of self and others, once adaptively restructured and metabolized, can better support our self-esteem and better guide our actions. The reservoir of tender memories needs to be carried within, together with the felt sense of a compassionate therapist (the good introject, or internalized self–object) or a memory of a person such as described by Vaillant's (1988) concept of the recovery of lost loves; these representations can make the crushing shame and self-attack dissolve "miraculously" as it did in 10 sessions with the Unforgiven Teenager.

CAPACITIES THAT SUPPORT RECEPTIVITY: GRIEF AND ASSERTION

The fundamental task of the therapist in self–other restructuring is to help the patient open to nurturant human contact rather than to shun it. The capacity to remain open emotionally to others, however, *requires the capacity to protect and defend oneself, to set limits and be able to assert, and to defend, if necessary, one's needs.* If one cannot hold one's own in a relationship (i.e., set limits and make requests), being open to others can mean becoming a receptacle for their needs: an easy target to be taken advantage of. It is a characteristic of human nature, at times, to push as far as one can go. Even the most considerate people can behave in ways that seem inconsiderate, if they are never apprised of the other's needs. We all need to be able to push back.

The capacity to be open and remain open to others also requires the capacity to experience adaptive grief. Each opening to tender feeling brings with it the impact of what was missing—the previous lack of love in one's life—and what may become missing: those who love us may develop feet of clay, leave us, or die. "The therapist's task is to reactivate mourning so that symptoms diminish and development continues" (Alpert, 1992, p. 150). Each small experience of joy inevitably brings tears of grief. This is precisely why people stay stuck in destructive, joyless patterns: the alternative anguish is unfamiliar and hard to bear. This means that the therapist needs to do whatever can be done to help patients bear the fear that comes with conflict, encourage frank assertion, and most important, endure *the pain and grief that come with tenderness*.

In previous chapters, I described a patient called the Machine Builder; this woman stopped projecting that people would attack her by coming to realize that as a child she had been attacked often by her cousins while her mother sat by without protecting her. Through the relationship with the therapist, she began to feel that someone wanted her to defend herself, to assert herself. She also remembered her father, who would have wanted the same for her but who died when she was young. Before her experience in therapy, she had walled herself off from experiencing—from grieving him. By successfully metabolizing the relationship with the therapist (and holding it in her memory) and through *remembering* the love of her father, her relationship to herself changed. Rather than becoming flooded with anxiety, she began to learn to defend herself and stand up when criticized. She viewed herself and her early-life relationships differently.

This example and the earlier example of the Unforgiven Teenager demonstrate steps taken in restructuring of the memory trace. This type of deep change takes repetition to accomplish and maintain, however. As in physiotherapy after a broken leg, intensive practice is needed to get behavior back to normal. The Unforgiven Teenager had the time for maintenance sessions and her sense of self continued to improve with time. The Machine Builder had fewer sessions and no maintenance sessions, and although she functioned well for 3 years, the anxiety returned in the fourth year in a high-pressure job.

SUPPLYING THE MISSING CAPABILITY: HOW TO GRATIFY

How do we best serve the needs of our patients? Gustafson pointed to the need to "supply the missing capability" (1986, p. 104). But how do we know what constitutes that capability? Once that is known, how best may we help patients to build the capacities that they lack? When should we gratify? When should we abstain? For some patients, this task is a major undertaking, and for others, it is as simple as helping them grieve or become assertive, that is, providing assistance with affective experience. Balint made the important distinction that a patient's needs should not be gratified but rather understood. This distinction can provide guidance to the therapist in many instances. Sometimes it is more helpful, however, for the therapist and patient to collaborate on what might be most gratifying in a holistic sense. The response depends on the patient and the problem at hand.

Baker (1991), a self psychologist and lucid interpreter of Kohut, addressed the gratification versus abstinence controversy. He offered one example in which a man received a promotion. Baker abstained from congratulating him and thus elicited material that would have not emerged otherwise (the man became hurt that he did not receive Baker's congratulations). Baker then skillfully handled this frustrating experience by helping the man see how hurt he had been by his parents, who had not been proud of his accomplishments.

Baker speculated about what would have happened if he had told the patient that he was "pleased as punch" about his promotion. Using this example, I also have predicted the result of the alternative "gratifying position" in the real relationship. Let us imagine what would have happened if Baker had indeed said spontaneously, "Congratulations!" My experience is that many patients are deeply touched by such spontaneous communications. Some are brought to tears instantaneously because of the dramatic contrast with what they are accustomed to. Joseph Lichtenberg and his colleagues (Lichtenberg et al., 1992) underscored Kohut's position that "some of the most intense experiences involving one's sense of self are triggered in the context of empathic responsiveness of others" (p. 132).[5] I would add that when empathic responsiveness touches the patient's heart and engenders a sense of validation and connection, it not only is reparative of the sense of self but also leads to affectional bonding. Sometimes abstinence cuts off the opportunity for such bonding to occur.

On the other hand, if the patient does not respond in a positive manner to a gratifying reaction, or even responds negatively, this is important information and needs to be explored. The following example reminded me of Baker's story. It is a common theme with many common responses form the patient.

EXAMPLE: THE JADED PHYSICIAN

THERAPIST: How does it feel to you to receive congratulations from me?

PATIENT [*Haughtily*]: It feels like you are too easily impressed.

THERAPIST: So there is some devaluation of the pleasure I have for you. What would it be like for you to let yourself feel my appreciation of your promotion?

PATIENT: Oh, I couldn't do that!

THERAPIST: What would stop you?

PATIENT [*Hesitating and quietly*]: I wouldn't want you to see how pleased I am that you are pleased for me.

THERAPIST: Why not? What would make you fight that?

PATIENT [*Coming to tears, but fighting it fiercely*]: Because I want it too much!

The therapist always must be attuned to whether the patient is able to receive what is being offered. How does the patient accept us? Are we being "swallowed" or "spit out"? Often, I say the following: *Can you see how, in a*

---

[5]"When empathic responsiveness ensures an experience of cohesion and vitality of the self, we designate it as a selfobject experience" (Lichtenberg et al., 1992).

manner of speaking, food is put on your plate, but you angrily throw it on the floor? Can you see how you dismiss my positive feeling for you?

Sometimes I do this with a touch of humor, to decrease the potential for feeling criticized. Other ways of intervening are as follows: *I'm sure you don't realize that you're doing it, but you're doing it nonetheless, and we need to make it conscious or it will control you. That makes me useless to you. You are in danger of spoiling the things that others try to give you.*

Baker made the point throughout his chapter that certain interventions are not called for because of intrapsychic deficits. Patients may not be able to regulate their motivation and self-esteem at the time. Baker reasoned that it would only have added insult to his patient's deficit to point out his neediness. Giving understanding without praise provided an occasion of optimal frustration, which subtly encouraged the patient to "create his own intrapsychic capabilities to perform the functions [that were missing]" (Baker, 1991, p. 304). Indeed, from this interaction, Baker's patient was able to discern some patterns in past relationships that contributed to his disappointment.

One can see why there are staunch proponents of abstinence. These advocates are understandably concerned that gratifying the patient will block a vital opportunity for growth. Certainly, therapists do not want to do such a thing. Mindless gratification that cuts off opportunities for growth in autonomous functioning only gratifies the therapist's neurotic need for being seen as empathic or, worse, omnipotent. On the other hand, mindless abstinence that cuts off opportunities for growth of closeness is equally undesirable. The skill is in the balance of both through understanding the patient's needs.

OPTIMAL GRATIFICATION AND OPTIMAL CHALLENGE

Ruben Blanck and Gertrude Blanck pointed out that "development proceeds best when there is optimal frustration as well as optimal gratification" (1974, p. 123). In a similar vein, Donald Winnicott (1965) noted the patient's needs for separation as well as for union. Patients who have had withholding caretakers can experience a well-administered gratification as a corrective emotional experience. Patients who have had no caretaker may respond as addicts do: craving care but lacking the capacity to receive it. (In general, such individuals are not ready for the active interventions of a short-term model but need preparatory work on building and resonating to relationship bonds.) Of course, it is not optimal for the therapist to gratify blindly or to abstain blindly.

Guidelines for deciding how much to gratify require an evaluation of the following:

1: To what degree does the patient need help with separation and autonomy (suggesting that the therapist should hold back) versus help with openness and vulnerability (suggesting that the therapist should be more emotionally present)?

2: Is the therapist doing for the patient what the patient cannot do for him- or herself?

3: Is the patient feeling legitimately proud (or angry or joyful) and seeking a shared experience? (In that case, a spontaneous response from the therapist might be in order.)

4: To what degree is the therapist gratifying the patient's real, adaptive need versus the patient's defensive representation of that need?

Let us explore some variations on the preceding clinical example. If the patient's information about his promotion were shared in a tentative manner and without affective response, the therapist's gratifying response could get in the way of exploring the patient's inability to feel. In such a case, one might proceed as in the following example.

EXAMPLE: THE HUMBLE PROMOTEE

THERAPIST: You're telling me about an apparently good thing, this promotion, but you are not showing pleasure in it. What are your feelings about this promotion? [*Patients have a range of inhibition in such cases.*]

PATIENT 1: I'm thrilled, but I'm embarrassed to show how proud I am. [*This response would indicate the need to reduce the shame connected with the joy of accomplishment.*]

THERAPIST: What would be the most shameful thing about showing me how thrilled you are?

The subsequent focus for this patient could be on shame about pride until the patient felt freer sharing the joy with others.

PATIENT 2: I should be pleased, but I'm not. I'm scared I won't do a good job.

THERAPIST: That sounds like a difficult position to be in. Tell me what you are most worried about.

In this case, the therapist needs to evaluate the reality basis of the fears versus the psychodynamic contributions and to respond accordingly. If the fears are real (the person is not up to the job), anticipation and problem-solving interventions are in order. In the case of unrealistic intrapsychic conflicts about performance, anxiety regulation is potentially helpful

The therapist must take into consideration the idiosyncratic response of the patient. My rule of thumb is to hold back on gratifying the patient until the issues are fully explored. I explore first and share the feelings in the real relationship second. In Baker's example, once the patient's unconscious issues were brought into awareness and resolved, the feelings between the patient and the therapist could be explored as follows:

THERAPIST: What do you think I was feeling inside when you told me about the promotion?

PATIENT [*Smiling softly*]: I, I bet you were pleased.

THERAPIST [*Smiling in return*]: Of course I was. I was pleased as punch!

After the patient has demonstrated the capacity to understand the therapist's feelings, the therapist can feel free to support that newly acquired capacity by an affirming self-disclosure. This tactic makes a vivid distinction between the transference distortion that the therapist did not care and the real relationship. Also, the interaction does not have to end here. The therapist should be vigilant for the patient's response to such a disclosure.

THERAPIST: How does it feel to hear that I was pleased?
PATIENT [*Choked up*]: I feel sad . . . but that doesn't make sense . . . [*Genuinely confused*]
THERAPIST [*Waiting silently to let the sadness well up*]
PATIENT: I feel sad because my father never said that to me.

Although this is an imaginary example, it is made up of common patterns of responding: Following the shared joy, there is often an immediate rush of sorrow. This response demonstrates the oscillating process of becoming open to experience—experiencing a little joy—and grieving what has been lost.

The approach of explore first, gratify second, can be applied to other situations, such as when the patient asks for advice. When there is often a direct request that the patient is fully capable of satisfying, it may be most gratifying (and therefore healing) not to give the advice but to respond in a manner such as the following: *I would be doing you no service if I responded directly by gratifying your request, because that would be disrespectful of your own abilities. That would imply that you were unable to do this (or get this) on your own. So instead of doing it for you, let's explore your thoughts on this matter and the strengths you have to handle it.* This intervention can also be called an example of "accurate empathy."

When a request is reasonable, my rule of thumb is to hold off responding until the patient's issues are fully explored. This is a measured application of optimal frustration, combined with the awareness that the therapist will be of assistance if needed; the therapist will be optimally responsive: *Certainly, I will be glad to answer your question (or respond to your request). But can we explore what this issue means to you before I respond? It is important to sort out what it means to you.*

The therapist needs to be aware of the patient's inhibitory responses that may be operative:

THERAPIST: Do you think you're trusting my perspective (or capability) and distrusting your own? If so, we must help you acquire a solid respect for your own capacities. Why would you doubt yourself in this regard? Why would you trust my view of things more than your own? [*This statement would lead to an exploration of the anxiety, guilt, shame, or pain concerning issues of the self.*]
PATIENT: Because when I've trusted my judgment, I've made some really stupid mistakes.

THERAPIST: So let's review some of the times when you felt your judgment was lacking.

The therapist then evaluates whether the impairment is reality-based or not: Is there really a problem with judgment, or is it the patient's perception of self? Many people feel that their judgment is bad owing to their own negative appraisal of themselves or the situation. When there are clear indications that the patient's judgment is impaired, however, the obstacles, conflicts, or blind spots need to be identified.

Optimal gratification means that therapists do only what patients cannot do for themselves or what never has been done for them. The goal must be for patients to learn to do these things for themselves or within themselves. The therapist needs to be mindful of the emergence (or lack of emergence) of new inner models demonstrating the receptive capacity. For this purpose, it is often useful to encourage patients to go beyond what they know, to stretch and take a risk rather than being told. But this is done in the therapist's office, with encouragement and support, so that mistakes can be caught before they lead to dire consequences. This method constitutes learning by the carrot: reinforcing successive approximations to the desired objective. Perhaps a better term, one that transcends the dichotomy of optimal gratification versus optimal frustration, would be *optimal challenge*.

Here are the words of a therapist who simultaneously gratifies, challenges, and conveys reality: *You want me to tell you if I think that is a good idea. In fact, it does sounds like it would be a good idea (or not such a good idea), and I am open to sharing my impressions with you. But it is important to remember that my perspective might not be the best one for you right now. I am not living your life. I don't have all the information that you do. I don't know the people involved. So if we base your response on my perspective alone, it very well might lead you astray.*

At other times, when a request is impossible to fill but represents a genuine need, it can be healing for the therapist to acknowledge the desire to supply what is missing: *I wish I could flip a switch and take the pain away, but I don't have the power to do that. Let's work together to help you become able to do what you need to do.*

Dependency, of course, can be both healthy and unhealthy (Storr, 1992). Sometimes the patient most needs the therapist to say the following: *Let me help you do this until you can do it for yourself. I will hold the hope for you until you are able to feel it for yourself. I will do you no service if I infantilize you or act in a way that overly prolongs your feelings of dependency on me. So if we enter into this relationship where you depend on me for a while, let us be aware along the way that we are helping you develop the capacity for (whatever the issue is) so you can carry our work along with you after therapy is over.*

This type of intervention allows patients to feel generously given to but also respected as potentially autonomous individuals. The preceding examples represent a few ways to balance closeness and distance as well as dependence and autonomy. When the therapist sees the possibility that the patient will become too dependent, the patient needs extra work to build an inner representation of the therapist as a guiding and nurturing figure in his or her emotional life; in this way, the patient can takes steps toward autonomy as rapidly as possible: *It will not help you to feel that I am the only one you can feel safe with or trusting with. The world has many such people. Let's work together to help you learn how to identify people you can trust and what are the steps in that process.* Often teaching is useful here.

ATTUNEMENT: THE SHARING OF AFFECT

Another form of optimal gratification is the sharing of affect between the therapist and patient. Stern called this interpersonal phenomenon *attunement;* he saw attunement responses of the mother and infant as a model for how learning of affective interaction takes place. These patterns are seen not only in infancy but also in close relationships throughout life. Just as the mother's attunement adds to the vitality of the child's affect, enhancing the sense of agency and volition, so can the therapist's attunement add to the vitality of the patient's affect. In each attunement experience during direct attachment play, Stern noted that infants initiate fully half of the responses and exercise considerable control over the patterning. I am not describing an "oceanic merger," therefore, but a combination of the patient having needs met—not usurped–and being vitalized by the therapist's attunement responses, which strengthen the patient's positive inner representations of self and others. According to Stern, differentiation is enhanced rather than lost by such experiences. According to Stern, *attunement promotes attachment.*

Like music, affects involve tempo as well as notes. Affects have qualities such as surging, fading away, fleeting, or exploding, and they involve crescendo and decrescendo. Stern (1985) called these the *vitality functions* of the affects. The therapist shares not only the type but also the vitality function of the affect. "In order for the therapist and patient to stay attuned, the affect must be at a level that can be experienced and integrated [by both parties]. It need not be intense" (Alpert, 1992, p. 149). This affective "mirroring" can convey an important message: that what the patient feels is worthwhile and valid. (It is crucial, however, to be able to distinguish adaptive from defensive affects in such situations. It is not adaptive for the therapist to be in attunement with defensive reactions, so that reactions such as victimization, helplessness, or resentment are amplified.) The therapist's attunement to the patient's adaptive motivation has the potential to add vitality to the patient's sense of self and to the intimacy in the relationship. Misattunement of the therapist's response has the potential to obstruct affirming experiences.

In chapter 8, I mentioned that when the Machine Builder sobbed over her father's death, I was moved to tears. I had to restrain myself somewhat so that I would not draw the patient's attention away from her memories. Nevertheless, I had tears running down my cheeks, and she could see them when she looked up. After a few minutes of quiet, intermittent reflecting on herself and her father—and when I felt she was ready—I drew her attention to me.

EXAMPLE: THE MACHINE BUILDER MOVES THE THERAPIST TO TEARS
THERAPIST: How does it feel to you to see my tears?

PATIENT: Good. It feels good.

THERAPIST: You don't see me as foolish? [*Earlier, she said she would feel foolish if she cried.*]

PATIENT: No! [*Her voice choking with tears*] If someone told me that story I would want to cry too, but I would be trying to hide it. [*Suddenly, racing on in a burst of intense feeling*] This is all we can get out of life, isn't it? The warmth and care of others. Touching others and letting them touch you.

EXAMPLE: THE WOMAN WHO WANTED TO STAY AT MY HOUSE

In another case, a young woman (the Nailbiter) who had been infantilized by her parents' need to keep her dependent yearned to have me for her parent. She did not say it in so many words, but the implications were clear. In the fifth session, she revealed that she had wished for a snowstorm so she could spend the night in my house. I encouraged her to explore and, in a sense, to gratify, this wish in fantasy.

THERAPIST: Can we look at that more closely—the wish to stay here overnight?

PATIENT: Oh, I didn't think about it any further than that; it was just a silly idea.

THERAPIST: But it might be important. Can we explore it a bit further?

PATIENT: Gee, I guess so . . . I don't know. What would I do? You have such a cozy house and, I guess, a nice guest room. And you'd let me stay there, and, gee, I didn't take it any further than that.

THERAPIST: But if you let your mind wander, what might you have wanted the most? [*Using guided imagery to build the exposure to the warded-off feelings*]

PATIENT: Oh, I [*Suddenly choking up*], I would want for you to talk to me and give me guidance. You'd be a healthier parent than my parents [*looking at me a little skeptically*], at least I think you would.

THERAPIST: And what do you yearn for the most from me at that point? What would you want from me then?

PATIENT [*Her head now collapses in her hands*]: I would want you to give me . . . to give me encouragement. I would want you to believe that I could do okay. [*Almost sobbing*] I'd want you to encourage me and tell me I would be a good mother!

The exploration uncovered not a malignant dependency but a tremendous craving for encouragement toward autonomy. In this way, the therapist guides the patient but does not elicit malignant dependency. Many therapists have told me that they have fears about patients becoming out of control and would avoid the preceding discussion altogether. In people with moderate or better ratings of functioning, such fears are unnecessary. Discussing anger need not lead to murder; discussing grief does not lead to helplessness or collapse; and discussing longing does not have to lead to merger. In chapter 8, the concept of *emotional intelligence* is used to convey what is sought here: well-understood, well-guided, and well-controlled but deeply felt affect. My emphasis on the need to evaluate the patient's capacity for impulse control before proceeding with emotional experiencing does not imply that full experiencing of feeling should be avoided. Poor impulse control only signals the need to proceed more slowly and cautiously, building cognitive controls while the patient experiences feelings in small doses.

Another patient could not believe anyone had positive feelings for her; when I asked her to imagine that I might, she immediately perceived me as sitting in the chair "way down the block . . . not even in the room." Positive feelings have the power to elicit defensive distancing that would otherwise go unelicited. We resolved this issue in about five sessions (spaced several weeks apart to give her time to integrate the changes) by having her imagine me sitting a little closer, and closer, until I was imagined at the door of her house. At first, she could only imagine me standing in the doorway. Later, she could bear to imagine me sitting on her couch, but when she did, she suddenly saw herself as a little girl. We followed that image and explored what she might want to do. At last she was able to imagine in her thoughts and feelings putting her head in my lap and letting me comfort her. This process of guided imagery greatly calmed her fears of closeness to me.

Another difficult issue is how to handle a patient's desire to be touched or held. Some individuals who have been severely deprived of human touch need to be touched to heal, but my impression is that individual psychotherapy is not the optimal place to provide that. One patient told me of a group therapist who put his arm around her often in the group meeting. She said it changed her from feeling alienated from the human race to feeling that she might be a part of it. I certainly give some patients a hug after an intense or difficult session or at termination. I also often shake their hands. When there is a desire to be held, however, *I "gratify" that desire in imagery and carefully assess the patient's receptive capacity.* The example that follows demonstrates how this is done.

EXAMPLE: GUIDED IMAGERY FOR THE DESIRE TO BE HELD

THERAPIST: You wish for me to hold you. Can we look at that in fantasy? How would you see me holding you?

PATIENT: This is embarrassing to talk about.

THERAPIST: Tell me what's the most embarrassing part. [*An anxiety-regulation intervention*]

PATIENT: Just that you'll think I'm weak or needy . . . but just saying that, I know you won't. [*Automatically, she begins to cope with her embarrassment and then continues.*] I've just always wanted to have you put your arm around me and me put my head on your shoulder.

THERAPIST: Let's imagine that. Would your head be here? [*I put my hand on my shoulder to make the image vivid. The patient nods.*] How would you feel to have your head there, resting on my shoulder?

PATIENT: Very peaceful. I love to think about it. [*This patient was easily able to get to the comforting feelings. Other patients need encouragement, guidance, and anxiety regulation to trace the imagery to the pleasant feelings.*]

THERAPIST: And how do you imagine that *I feel*, holding you? [*This is the process of restructuring the inner representations of self and other. I look for the patient's ability to acknowledge the care and concern of the other.*]

PATIENT: At first, I think you'd be bored. Going through the motions.

THERAPIST: Does it really seem that I would feel that detached toward you? [*When the resistance is strong, the therapist must stay on this focus until the patient can feel what the therapist feels.*]

PATIENT: Part of me wants to say yes, wants to deny that you'd care for me. But I know better. It's hard to let myself believe that you care.

THERAPIST: But it seems that another part of you *is* believing it.

PATIENT [*Smiling gently*]: Yes, I do.

THERAPIST: How does it feel to let yourself experience that?

This intervention assesses the degree of conflict concerning the positive feelings. Sometimes sexual feelings emerge and need to be dealt with (including the setting of clear therapeutic boundaries). However, sexual feelings are usually defensive in this context and are a way to diminish the more profound feelings of tenderness, closeness, and trust.

To illustrate the incorporation of relational issues in psychodynamic work (albeit psychoanalytic), Lichtenberg et al. (1992) presented the case of a woman in psychoanalysis who desperately needed to know that her analyst cared about her. Her previous analyst had stalwartly refused to respond to her repeated questions about his care for her. His abstinence had led to an impasse and the termination of the treatment. Lichtenberg described a shift in traditional analytic technique that allowed the therapist to be more of a real person. In one example, the patient was upset that the Cadillac parked out front might be the therapist's, and the therapist told her straightaway that it was not. Afterward, they went on to explore what the Cadillac meant to her. My point is that progressive psychoanalysts are also incorporating methods to help patients experience that they are a person worthy of care and concern. The particular form of such interventions can be left to the therapist's style and intuition, but making this kind of human connection in the real therapeutic relationship is increasingly being seen as healing.

Transferential Issues

In the active restructuring of self–other images, the therapist's exploration looks for pure transference: "How do perceive me?" and "How do you imagine that I feel about you?" are questions that quickly reveal whether or not the patient holds a realistic or distorted perception of the therapist. Unlike long-term or analytic treatment, which allows these transferential reactions to develop over time in response to therapist neutrality, the short-term therapist actively inquires about and explores "transference" responses beginning in the first session. After a brief exploration of the transferential issue, the therapist presents a reality perspective to see if the patient can make the distinction. The two preceding cases demonstrate this point. First, the therapist said, "If you think I would make fun of you, I can see why you wouldn't want to open up!" But shortly afterward, the therapist said, "Do I

really seem so cold and clinical?" There is an oscillation between the real relationship and the transferential relationship. Holding these two perceptions
in stark contrast to one another helps the patient to make the cognitive as
well as the emotional distinctions and can allow attunement to occur without merger or loss of boundaries.

In traditional dynamic psychotherapy, therapists were told to interpret
negative transference and ignore positive transference. This short-term approach handles transferential issues quite differently. *Both negative and positive transference reactions are identified, experientially explored, and interpreted as
soon as possible,* given the capacities of the patient. Responses that involve
idealization or devaluation (or closeness or distance) are made conscious
and linked to past relationships. It is important to note that to the degree
that there is impairment in the patient's sense of self, a period of idealized
transference may be necessary. Before I interpret a patient's idealization of
me (and thus demystify the relationship), I ask myself whether this patient
needs a period of "idealized transference" to replace a missing experience in
his or her early life. Were there people whom the patient deeply respected,
or does the patient need to learn to look up to someone? Does the patient
need to develop a sense of standards and ideal role models? This role is a
challenge for the therapist; as in issues of closeness, it can help to encourage patients to identify other people who reflect the qualities that they
admire in the therapist. The therapist can harm the patient by too readily
interrupting such a process as well as by drawing it out over too long a
time. Optimally, this process of restructuring the sense of self should be
handled in a time-efficient manner; it probably requires months, however,
rather than weeks.

Addressing both positive and negative feelings in both the real and transferential relationship "heats up" the therapy session tremendously. Many
people, patients and therapists alike, find this level of intimacy hard to tolerate. Yet this intimate level of sharing opens patients to this experience in
their current life. This is direct exposure, or "in vivo desensitization," to the
experience of deep feeling with another human being. Not all patients are
able to work with the intensity of this therapeutic modality. Someday, I hope
we will be able to ascertain which patients need the "hands off" approach of
analysis and which are able to benefit from the "hands on" approach of
short-term treatment. Some patients who have been traumatically intruded
on need the therapist to maintain a respectful distance, but not all such patients do. There are other variables in the equation.

The insistence of the early analysts on transference as the only mechanism
of therapeutic change may have been due to their realization that the transference feeling was the most affect-laden of all interactions and often represented the origin of the maladaptive pattern. In short-term treatment, we actively pull for affect in the context of *any* relationship being discussed. This
reduces our reliance on the transference interaction. Transference issues
sometimes play a minimal role in short-term cases with well-adjusted individuals who have limited focal problems and good alliance. The bulk of the

work can be done with current and past figures, and it can be sufficient for change to occur.

EXAMPLE: POINTING OUT TRANSFERENCE DISTORTIONS TO THE UNFORGIVEN TEENAGER

THERAPIST: You seem to be holding back the tears that are welling up inside of you. Would it be difficult for you to cry in front of me?

PATIENT: Sure!

THERAPIST: Sure? What would make it difficult?

PATIENT: I don't know how you'd react.

THERAPIST: How do you imagine I would react? [*Exposing the patient to the feared stimulus*]

PATIENT: Oh, you'd be cold and clinical. [*The transference distortion*]

THERAPIST: Cold and clinical? What would that mean? How would I feel inside if you were to cry?

PATIENT: You see this kind of thing all the time. You'd be doctorly on the surface, but you'd be thinking, "Oh here's *another one* blubbering all over the place."

THERAPIST: So you'd see me as bored and disinterested, just putting up with you?

PATIENT: Sure. Why would you want to listen to all this stuff, day after day, hour after hour? Aren't you sick of it? I sure would be. How do you stand it?

THERAPIST: How do I stand it!? You seem to feel as though your pain is an enormous burden on me. Listen to your words: "sick of it, here's another one." Can you see how you come to therapy with tremendous pain, and some part of you desperately must want to share that pain with someone, yet all that you can imagine is that I am going to be looking down on you if you do! I wouldn't want to cry either if I thought someone was going to treat me like that!

PATIENT [*Nodding*]

THERAPIST: I'd want to clam up tighter than a drum! [*Validating the defensive position*]

PATIENT: Yeah, that's how I feel.

THERAPIST: Does it really seem that I am that insensitive to you? Do I seem so cold as that? [*Contrasting the real relationship to the transferential perspective*]

PATIENT: Not so far. But you might be, if I cried.

THERAPIST: If you cried, somehow you imagine that seeing you cry would turn me off?

PATIENT: Definitely. My mother hated it when I cried.

THERAPIST: So you seem poised and ready for me to react the same way as your mother, rather than as your therapist, here to help you with your feelings.

PATIENT: Yes, I guess I'm doing that. [*Pausing*] I'm being awfully hard on you aren't I?

THERAPIST: Seems like you're making it awfully hard for yourself.

In the exploration of conflicts about feeling and the underlying transferential images, it can take part of a session or two to three sessions or longer for the issue to turn around (depending on the patient). But the process changes the inner representation of the therapist—and eventually of the self.

Countertransferential Issues

Because of the intensity of the experience in the therapist-patient relationship, therapists must be well prepared for their own countertransference reactions, both negative and positive. Patients invariably elicit reactions in us that we transfer from past relationships.

Throughout this type of treatment, the therapist must often pull for negative, unflattering, and disrespectful views of him- or herself. Therapists are like detectives, looking for clues, trying to discover who's guilty. However, it is decidedly unpleasant to discover that (in the patient's mind) *the guilty party is us:* long-suffering, hard-working, well-intentioned us. Sometimes, our patients hit the nail on the head, and their worst criticism of us is frighteningly correct. At other times, they are as grossly misguided in their appraisal of us as our parents were. We can find ourselves outraged and, worse yet, identifying with the patient's projections by behaving precisely in the way the patient transferentially imagined. This is a sticky position to be in but, alas, it is inevitable. There are excellent articles and books on countertransference, mentioned earlier, that help prepare us to handle our own unavoidable and imperfect human reactions (Bollas, 1986; Gabbard & Wilkinson, 1994; Winnicott, 1949). When countertransference hate is running high, the beleaguered therapist needs to find a compassionate colleague to talk to.

Even more challenging than negative countertransference is positive countertransference. Such reactions can include the therapist's need for omnipotence, for being idealized, for merger, for falling in love, or for sexual partners. Therapists are often drawn to this field because of unmet longings that need resolution. If such issues are resolved, we can better lead others through the same path. To the extent that such issues remain unresolved, our patients can fall prey to our own unmet needs and yearnings.

Because of the value of working intensely and closely with our patients, we need to be as tough-minded and clear about our own reactions as possible. This is the area in which the therapist's emotional intelligence needs to run high. When affect is strong, cognitive guidance needs to be equally strong. Standards and boundaries need to be especially clear. Danger needs to signal red flags in our minds. One of the main reasons for the rule of abstinence was that it put a control on the therapist's positive countertransference. Even more important than abstinence, however, is for the therapist to acknowledge countertransferential feelings and keep them in consciousness.

Abuses of the therapeutic relationship by psychoanalysts, like sexual abuse of parishioners by fundamentalist ministers, underscore that theoretical abstinence bought at the price of denial of feelings leads to acting out. *When such feelings are not addressed, there may be greater potential for abuse.* My experience is that if positive feelings between the therapist and patient are addressed and explored, there is a greater chance that inappropriate expression of such feelings will be controlled. In any case, because of the danger of countertransference abuse to the patient, the tormented therapist needs the support of not one but several colleagues. A guiding principle for dealing with any strong feeling is to institute cognitive guidance and control at early stages, when the feelings are just beginning to build. The problem is that the feelings often are just outside of awareness in the early stages. For this reason, I provide the following list of behavioral indicators that therapists should keep in mind that signal the buildup of potentially dangerous countertransference feeling. These indicators were identified by Robert Simon (1995).

1. Therapy sessions become extended in time
2. Excessive use of therapist self-disclosure
3. Therapist stops billing the client
4. Therapist's position of neutrality (i.e., *not* obtaining gratification at the expense of the patient) is eroded in little ways
5. Frequent use of the patient's name or nickname
6. Therapy sessions are scheduled at the end of the day
7. Extra-therapy contacts occur (Simon, 1995, p. 93)

This is only a partial list of indicators. For further information see Simon (1995), Pope (1990, 1994), Pope and Tabachnick (1993), or Gabbard (1989, 1995).

ANXIETY REGULATION IN SELF–OTHER RESTRUCTURING

The main goal of anxiety regulation during self–other restructuring is the desensitization of adaptive feeling toward others and toward the self. As noted earlier, *desensitization* means the reduction of the inhibitions or anxieties associated with adaptive affects. To do this, one must also replace inhibitory affects with pleasure-giving affects: One replaces shame with a mature pride, anxiety about closeness with trust of others, and the crushing effects of pain or anguish about attachment with joy, comfort, and security.

A secondary goal of anxiety regulation, therefore, is to keep the patient's moment-to-moment experience of the conflict within manageable limits so that the exposure to the feeling can continue. As long as the affective experiencing is proceeding (i.e., the patient is dealing with memories or reflections that are affect- or anxiety-laden), there is no problem. When patients cannot continue, however, and complain of difficulty, going "dead," or losing all feelings, anxiety regulation is necessary. The therapist must explore the conflicts (anxieties, shame, pain) until the patient has more control and is able to go back to the affect experience:

THERAPIST: You've just pulled away from the joy (or sadness, anger, or tenderness) that you were feeling here with me (or with a significant other). Can you sense that?

PATIENT: Yes, now that you mention it, I guess I did.
THERAPIST: What is the most uncomfortable part of that for you?

This gentle process of exploring anxieties constitutes a "graded exposure" to the feelings. The model presented in this book is analogous to Wolpe's (1958) graded hierarchy of successive approximations. For example, instead of the elevator phobic going directly on the elevator, the patient is encouraged to think first about being on an elevator, until the anxiety reduces. Next, the patient might stand 100 yards away from an elevator, until the anxiety reduces. Slowly, the conditioned phobia subsides. When there are phobias about attachment, which are ubiquitous, the patient needs to be exposed to successive degrees of closeness—to the therapist, to others, or to memories of past figures—until the anxiety subsides. After that, a little more affect experiencing is encouraged. Slowly, a more adaptive form of the affect reciprocally inhibits the maladaptive or inhibitory affects. I think of this process as the successive approximations to intimacy.

Techniques for Regulating Anxieties
In contrast to Weiss's (1990) dynamically oriented control–mastery theory and Beck's (1976) cognitive theory, both of which hold the modification of pathogenic beliefs to be the main change agent in psychotherapy, the model in this book sees the alteration of these pathogenic responses as *only one* of several ways to effect change. The disputation of logic is an important tool but not the only way to achieve the alteration of pathogenic beliefs and thus reduce anxiety, shame, or anguish. When shame (or any self-inhibiting affective response) is severe, working exclusively on a cognitive level often is insufficient for character change. In addition to effecting changes in maladaptive or pathogenic beliefs, it is necessary to assist the patient in building a new identity or sense of self, and this is done in three main ways:

1: By building inner representations of more affirming relationships, beginning with the relationship with the therapist. "Crucial to the process of growing up is the ability to internalize good people" (Vaillant, 1988, p. 157).
2: Through alteration in, or letting go of, deep attachments to earlier, more destructive relationships, from which the sense of self was created (emotional separation from maladaptive relationships).
3: By focusing on the inhibitory or self-attacking *affects* associated with maladaptive cognitions.

BUILDING AN ADAPTIVE SENSE OF OTHERS
The Receptive Capacity with Others: Building Assimilation
Just as the therapist works to build a receptive capacity in the patient for the therapist, it is equally important for the therapist to assist the patient in building a receptive capacity for experience with others—as many others as possible. How are significant others represented in patients' hearts and

minds? What do these people feel? What monsters or distortions are inno-
cent others turned into? Equally important, how are the hurtful behaviors of
abusive others denied or repressed?

For the short-term therapist to build a deep and bonded relationship with
the patient that will end in a relatively short time, there must be equally
solid and supportive relationships outside of treatment. Sometimes, it is
hard for patients to build such connections.

PATIENT: No one in my life has ever understood me so well as you, and I
don't believe anyone will.

THERAPIST: Then we need to help you find the people—who are all around—
who can be understanding. Some are better at it than others, but there is
care available that you may push away. I wonder if you do not know what
to look for or how to respond to that sort of connection? What do you
think?

Here the therapist is using several interventions: first, guidance; second,
teaching about capacities in others for understanding and presenting reality;
and third, a gentle, querying confrontation of the defenses against closeness.
To change the sense of others involves change in concepts and change in
aversive or inhibitory affects associated with others.

EMOTIONAL RECEPTIVITY

It is remarkable how common it is in our society to devalue praise or dismiss compliments, care, and concern rather than responding with a quiet
but deeply felt "thank you." The fears that block such taking in or resonating to what is given us have been highly ingrained through social injunctions against acting selfish, self-involved, big-headed, or egotistical. The fear
is that pride will make us arrogant. Yet with a moment's reflection it is clear
that arrogance is a result of insecurity, not of confidence. There are so many
cultural and religious injunctions against self-appreciation that it seems, at
times, as though many of our societal norms create psychopathology. The
origins of empathy are found in receiving enough so that one may, later, give
to oneself and to others with joy. Following is a list of tactics to help patients
receive the emotional gifts that are given:

1. Pointing out defensive avoidance of such experiences across a range
   of social interactions
2. Close and careful work toward accepting compliments or praise
   from the therapist, as demonstrated previously
3. Teaching about socialization to encourage the patient to rethink
   whether self-appreciation or feeling good about a compliment is bad

BASIC SKILLS: THE CAPACITY FOR EYE CONTACT AND THE SHARED SMILE

Tomkins wrote that one of the prime ways that adults recapture the type
of communion experienced in infancy is by "the mutual awareness of each
others' smile" (1962, p. 398). Stern addressed the aspect of "falling in love"

that is "to become imbued with the presence of an absent person, an almost constantly evoked companion" (1985, pp. 111–132). But such experiences extend beyond romantic love to the affirming moments of everyday living. Doesn't such communion potentially go on every minute of every day? Aren't children programmed to seek out the mother's or father's eyes, looking for attention, praise, joy, interest, or approval? Don't we all find ourselves scanning the faces of others seeking a response? Don't we all, from time to time, see a friend and find our faces lighting up? This response is the receptive capacity that is seriously blunted in many of our patients, especially those who have a difficult time being close to others. When patients have problems with closeness, the therapist needs to assess the capacity of the patient to make contact with others, especially eye contact and the shared smile.

The following example is of a woman who works in marketing and is well liked for her training seminars. It might seem that she would have no problem with eye contact, but that was not the case. Teaching requires a different set of skills from intimacy, and she had great difficulty with close relationships. The therapist was surprised by her answer to the initial question in the following example.

EXAMPLE: THE WOMAN WHO COULD NOT BEAR EYE CONTACT

THERAPIST: Can you look across a room and smile at someone who is looking at you?

PATIENT: No! Never!

THERAPIST: Never? What's so hard for you?

PATIENT: They might not smile back. I'd expect to see a frown. Anyway, I can't believe anyone would be looking at me approvingly. [*The inner representation of the other person is one that is rejecting or disapproving.*]

THERAPIST: Why not?

PATIENT: I just don't think there's anything special about me. [*The inner representation of self is accordingly negative.*]

THERAPIST: That's painful to feel. Wasn't there someone—anyone—whose eyes lit up when they saw you?

PATIENT [*Tearing up*]: I don't think anyone ever was glad to see me. [*The pain of rejection*]

This patient revealed that her mother had to marry because she was pregnant with her. Her parents loved her and did the best they were able to at the time, but her mother was depressed for years, and her father was emotionally detached. I explored her kinship network, attempting to find one relative who found her to be special, and there was one uncle who was kind. But the predominant response was to be shunned at family gatherings by the whole family in favor of her cousins. Her personal sense of shame was enormous, and eye contact was anathema.

THERAPIST: But now, how is it when you visit your mother? She isn't as depressed as she used to be.

PATIENT: She's really sweet now. She's glad to see me.

THERAPIST: How does she look at you when you arrive? Can you remember the last time?

PATIENT: Yes, last Sunday. I have to think, I didn't really notice. Yes . . . she was happy. She jumped up and hugged me. It makes me feel a little sad to remember it.

THERAPIST: It seems that you went for so many years without her responding fondly to you that you may not notice it now when it happens. [*Awakening receptivity in the current relationships*]

The therapist underscores the positive interaction and attempts to help the patient build a new inner representation of the mother to replace the image that she had carried for most of her life. The same process was repeated many times and extended to her father, as well, until she was strongly responsive to such interactions. The patient slowly built, with the therapist's support and encouragement, a sense of herself as someone who was valued and cherished.

For any patient who has problems with closeness, the ability to make eye contact is a major vehicle of change. The receptive capacity is made or broken here. If one cannot look at someone's face, one will not see whether or not a smile is there, nor will warmth in the other person be elicited. Patients such as in the preceding example need to alter inner models of others to include images of people whose eyes lit up when they saw them and who felt they were special.

The rebuilding of relationships is a complex process involving working on two fronts at the same time. First, the patient needs to build a new "sense of self" by identifying with and "internalizing" the caring and compassionate therapist. Second, the patient must simultaneously relinquish (analytically speaking) the inner representations of the noncompassionate early-life caretakers (the introject). In behavioral terms, this is the relinquishing of the way of responding that was learned through the relationship with the abusive caretaker. To give up deeply entrenched and maladaptive defenses, we must identify maladaptive relationships and relinquish them as well. The defenses that hold such maladaptive patterns in place are the functions against closeness, authenticity, and change. These aspects may be addressed early in treatment, but new relationships must be built before the old relationships are supplanted. Because of the tenacity of our early attachments (e.g., one has only one set of parents), it is typically no small matter to accomplish these decathexes and recathexes (or emotional disconnections and reconnections). *Only when a new identity has been fairly well developed and is familiar and feeling steady can the old identity be let go. Only when new, more adaptive coping responses are fairly well established can the old ways of coping be relinquished.*

Acquiring a new sense of self and a new sense of one's early-life relationships is one of the most difficult tasks to accomplish in a time-limited manner. The affects that are being warded off are primitive, overwhelming, and terrifying: generally the deepest rage, grief, and longing for care. Because this process is difficult, however, does not mean that it needs to ramble on and become protracted. *Indeed, precisely because of the depth and complexity of the problem, we need to be as focused and clear as possible about our objectives and how to achieve them.* As mentioned previously, building a new internalized relationship has been repeatedly observed to be achieved more rapidly through the *real relationship with the therapist.* Therapist involvement can result in tremendous strides; in contrast, *neutrality might draw treatment out much longer than necessary.*

The following is a therapeutic interaction that was related to me long ago, in which a real relationship between an older woman, Helen, and a younger woman, Mary, forever changed Mary's sense of others. Helen was not a therapist, but she became a model for me in therapy.

Case Example: Helen's Request

A young woman named Mary had had a paranoid and abusive mother who had succeeded in turning an initially benign but weak father against her. The first 18 years of her life were spent being blamed and scapegoated by both parents. If it had not been for loving grandparents, she might have been destroyed; as it happened, she was resilient and had a great many strengths. Nonetheless, it took little to make her think that she was being attacked or was unwanted.

In Mary's relationship with Helen, an inspiring older woman friend, bad feelings occurred frequently because Helen had a somewhat brusque manner. One day, Helen said something that felt particularly critical. Because Mary was struggling in therapy to learn to speak up when she was treated this way, she replied, "Helen, it feels like you are trying to hurt me when you speak to me like that." It was frightening for Mary to be so bold; her voice cracked, and there were tears in her eyes. Helen looked up, startled, because Mary had never spoken like that before. But Helen, unlike Mary's mother, was fundamentally a loving woman, with a tremendous capacity for care. She immediately stood up and walked over to Mary and hugged her.

HELEN: I had no intention of hurting you when I said that! You know how I am; I just say things, and sometimes I come off harsher than I mean to. But [*hugging her again*] I never, never would want to cause you pain! Can you believe that?

MARY: I believe you are telling me the truth. I don't think you are lying to me. But honestly, I don't feel it . . . it feels deep, deep down that you want to hurt me.

HELEN: Well, I can imagine you might feel this way given what you've told me of your mother [*Helen was remarkably astute in this interaction*], but I absolutely do not want to cause you pain. [*In what follows, she was even more astute, and she was not a therapist nor cognizant of therapeutics.*] I want you to think, and think hard in the days and weeks to come, about me, about what I've said, and that I don't want to hurt you. Now will you promise me you'll do that?

MARY: Yes, I will.
HELEN: Do you mean that?
MARY: Yes, I mean it. But right now it's so hard to believe.
HELEN: That's okay.

Mary was much older when she told me this story. This had been a pivotal incident in her young adulthood. In the weeks that followed Helen's request, each time Mary remembered this incident, she had to strain to feel it differently from the way she typically would have. During the third week, she finally "got it." She could feel inside that Helen cared about her instead of feeling that Helen wanted to hurt her. It was a totally new perception for her. True, her grandparents had been loving, but they had been so old and so gentle that they never, to Mary's recollection, ever had been harsh enough to test her this way. She had to learn that loving people can sometimes say things harshly but still care. This awakening opened an entirely new capacity in her, and she was forever changed, forever a little less paranoid. Today, we would say she built a new capacity, a new model, and shifted her inner representations from either all bad or all good to possibilities for mixtures of both.

This story so struck me that I have used it to illustrate this capacity to patients. I was also struck by Mary's trying so hard to believe and finally being able to feel the message 3 weeks later. Mary was not able to say what the factors of change were, except that she tried concentrating over and over again because Helen had asked her to. Nevertheless, the story made an impact on me. Now I pass on Helen's request when I say to patients: *I know you can't imagine it now, but try hard to see if you can come to believe that this person (it could be me, a parent, or a friend) feels real care for you.*

Like compassion for self, the capacity for receptivity does not grow immediately but over weeks with gentle encouragement. Not all people are so easily shifted as was Mary. Some require enormous repetition, and there may be some that cannot be reached.

CHANGING RELATIONAL PERSPECTIVES: OTHER POINTS OF VIEW

From a clinical perspective, to take in or internalize someone means building *a new capacity for remembering* the images and feelings that were experienced in relation to the other. Stern repeatedly noted that "these representations are not formed from external events or persons that have been internalized. They are not put inside from the outside. They are constructed from the inside, from the self-experience of being with the other. Nothing is taken in" (1995, p. 81). If the experience is positive, thoughts and feelings of warmth, care, joy, love, and protection *that came from others* are predominant. The need for recall cues to call someone else into one's presence varies greatly. Stern said that becoming maturely independent is the result of "continually building and rebuilding a more extensive set" of others within ourselves (1985, p. 244). Some patients have an inner representation of themselves that erects strong barriers to closeness with others, as demonstrated in the next example.

EXAMPLE: THE NURSE WHO COULD NOT BE CARED FOR

PATIENT: It's so hard to accept that people might want to give to me. I desperately need to be needed.

THERAPIST: What will happen if you give up being needed?

PATIENT: If I am not needed, there's no glue, no connection.

THERAPIST: What's the most uncomfortable part of that?

PATIENT: If I'm not a caretaker, if they don't need me, I have no place! No identity. Nothing! I would have no idea how to be with someone.

THERAPIST: How do you mean that?

PATIENT: When I'm not needed, I don't know what to do with myself. I just don't know how to Just Be. [*She has to hide behind the defense of caretaking, and cannot bear to let her real self show.*]

THERAPIST: You really have a struggle with just being present.

PATIENT: It's crazy. I can't imagine that I could actually be with people and not have to do all the work! [*This is a signal for the therapist to suggest the possibility that others might like her just as she is. This is done in a Socratic manner.*]

THERAPIST: Is it hard for you to imagine that just your *presence* might be a gift? [*The therapist is going to begin to shift the patient's self-image by changing perspectives.*]

PATIENT: Impossible!

THERAPIST: Have you ever just relaxed and been yourself with someone?

PATIENT: Never! I'm close to people, but only if I'm always taking care of them.

Because this patient's inner representations of others are so fear-laden, the therapist needs to work in the real therapeutic relationship to heighten her awareness of the feelings for her in others.

THERAPIST: What about with me? Can you sense how I experience you? [*The therapist's perspective*]

PATIENT: Oh, no! I can't even think about that!

THERAPIST: What's so scary about letting yourself enjoy my experience of you? Can we look at that?

From this point on, the therapist kept the focus predominantly on the patient's perception of the patient–therapist relationship. It was anxiety provoking, but with support, encouragement and some humor, the process was made comfortable for the patient. This patient spent 10 or more sessions going over her terror of relaxing and feeling good in the presence of the therapist and others; she also worked on experiencing that others might feel pleasure in her presence. Her barriers against closeness did not yield easily. She was 47 years old and had had severe trauma and loss throughout her childhood and adolescence. Over several months, major changes occurred, however, and follow-ups revealed a lovely flowering of connectedness with others.

In evaluating patients' receptive capacity, the therapist has to be aware of the sometimes subtle signals of these "games" or "dances" that are being en-acted interpersonally, which are basically defensive barriers to closeness. Sometimes patients do not report such responses as a problem because the responses are so ego-syntonic: so familiar and gratifying. The therapist has to notice these behaviors, such as always having to be the life of the party or always being in control or the teacher.

Addictive Attachment and Repetition Compulsion Based on Operant Conditioning

Because there is such frustration in trying to "unhook" patients from their maladaptive attachments, it is useful to present my understanding of some of the operant conditioning or learning pricinples that are at play and to offer another perspective on how to go about changing such repetitive behaviors.

People are born with a prepared "readiness" to respond to their parents. In abusive or neglectful situations, children have been reinforced by receiv-ing love on a variable interval schedule (i.e., sometimes they are given a warm or comforting response, but more often they are not, and it is unpre-dictable when the positive response will occur). Variable interval reinforce-ment is the hardest form of reinforcement to extinguish, because there is always the hope that the reward will come soon. For example, a child might conclude, "If I just try a few more times, or wait a little longer, I might get the response I want." (Mommy might smile; Daddy might play with me.) Neglected or abused children occasionally receive love, attention, and care, dispensed at unpredictable intervals amidst a steady stream of neglectful or abusive treatment. Such children are maintained at a heightened state of emotional deprivation, so that when a little warmth or contact is provided it is like an oasis on the desert—or a drug high. In behavioral terms, this con-stitutes "aversion relief." (In laboratory animals maintained in such states of deprivation, the frequency of the response being conditioned is the highest on variable and unpredictable interval schedules.) Because representations of others are "constructed from interactive experience with someone" (Stern, 1995, p. 81), all such children know of love is the variable and unpredictable moments of relief from pain.

In relationships, a little bit of "love" in a state of constant deprivation takes away the grinding pain or loneliness for a moment. People work fever-ishly for this moment of relief, a way of responding that has been called *rep-etition compulsion,* a label that describes the symptom but not the cause. Pat-terns are repeated because of an agonizing set of "relief of deprivation" contingencies. Consider putting a person who has been conditioned to re-spond to rare (but exhilarating) moments of human contact in the company of a new individual who is steady, loving, and caring. Such neglected people have learned to respond only to (a) little care and (b) a lot of neglect or abuse. Sometimes miracles happen, and they adapt to new, more nurturant relationships. More often, such a person finds maladaptive partners much more tantalizing than benign, comforting, but seemingly boring relation-ships. (After all, there is no "sting" in a comforting relationship: no rush or aversion relief.)

There are several reasons for addictive attachment. First, a steady, loving relationship can be strange to the deprived person; it can be experienced as dull or weird rather than rewarding. (Why are you smiling? What do you want from me?) The caring person is often devalued for having bad judgment (she must be pretty desperate to love me) because inner images are reminders that desirable people have *not* been caring, maybe with good reason (one thinks). Second, there is no state of deprivation to be released from, so there is no "drug high." Once one is addicted to intermittent care, there is a constant yearning for that "hit." Normal levels of care seem less exhilarating; the loyal, the true, the faithful seem dull or odd. Such contingencies are called *repetition compulsion* because it *appears* that the individual chooses the destructive conditions. What is really happening is reinforcement of a "generalized or prototypic happening" (Stern, 1995, p. 81). We learn what we live. The well-adjusted child is just as addicted to the constant loving relationship as the abused child is addicted to the abusive relationship. We want what we are used to, and it's hard to switch. The confusion about repetition compulsion results from difficulty in understanding why an abusive or neglectful partner is so compelling; it is the difficulty in understanding the nature of the reinforcement. It is not reinforcing to be loved if one never has felt loved or lovable. It is decidedly unpleasant, at least at first.

Providing constant loving care to a greatly deprived individual can be as difficult as giving a feast to someone who has undergone prolonged starvation. The stomach is shrunken and cannot tolerate the largess. If the steady care is allowed to penetrate (to be received), it elicits tremendous sorrow for what was missed. Many such individuals do not yet have the capacity to grieve, so the truly caring relationship feels aversive, uncomfortable, or unbearable, because unbearable feelings are generated. The person's emotional capacity needs to grow, through small caring interactions, just as the shrunken stomach needs gentle expansion by small amounts of food.

In summary, the response pattern described is not only the compulsion to repeat, but also a reinforced imprisonment. Such persons know *no other way of reacting* (even though they may desperately want to react differently on a conscious, intellectual level), because the reinforcement contingencies have them "locked in." On one hand, these people are rewarded by the exhilaration of intermittent release from pain; on the other hand, they would be *punished by unbearable emotional anguish* if they shifted too quickly to something better. This is not only a compulsion, it also is an entrapment or a*ddiction to a maladaptive attachment*. They cannot get out.

There are at least three structures that need to be built before such addictive attachment can be let go, each of which is a component of affect and self–other restructuring:

1. Inner representations of others as trustworthy and caring, especially the therapist
2. A new sense of self as worthy and able to receive care
3. The ability to grieve what has for so long been missing

SHIFTING MALADAPTIVE ATTACHMENTS:
ALTERING REINFORCEMENT CONTINGENCIES

The objective in building the three capacities listed is to alter the inner reinforcement contingencies. If the sense of self and others is compassionate, caring will be experienced as more rewarding than aversive. If grief can be borne, the tears that come with tenderness will be experienced as more relieving than punishing.

As soon as there is some ability to distinguish between love and need (or addiction), the therapist should begin to build the association of the negative affects with abusive partners and of the positive affects with the self. Where is the *anger* at the abuse? Where is the *contempt* or *disgust* at being treated so badly or abandoned so brutally? Where is the healthy pride (i.e., *joy* taken in oneself) to encourage an *interest* in finding someone better? Working with the full range of affects (especially in the relationship with the therapist) allows the restructuring of the inner representations of self and others and the undoing of the variable interval reinforcement of "human bondage." These are the "exit doors" out of the hell-like imprisonment of addictive attachment.

RECOVERY OF LOST LOVES: EXCAVATING OLD ATTACHMENTS

Are we not every minute of every day imbued with the presence of people from our past? They are our constant subliminal companions (Stern, 1985). In romantic love, such constant presence is vivid in our conscious awareness, but in everyday life, we cannot so easily separate figure from ground. Whose voice is playing in our head? Whose eyes watch us? Whose punishment do we fear, or whose praise do we crave? Are we even aware of the presence of these others, or do they guide us unseen?

The treatment process must identify the positive and negative voices that patients carry within. George Vaillant pointed out the following:

> We often emphasize grief and forget remembering. . . . Love must be told. Not so that it can be forgotten, but so that it may be rewoven into the tapestry of the present. . . . The source of psychopathology is that we forget the love and remember only the hate. . . . No one whom we have ever loved is totally lost. We deny gratitude and amplify envy! (1988, pp. 148–152)

The goal is to make peace with the negative and excavate the positive memories. Sometimes the loving people from the past are spontaneously remembered as the treatment process unfolds. When remembering does not occur spontaneously, the therapist can inquire about and investigate the special relationships from the past. This process also identifies patients' interpersonal strengths: whose love made them strong. If a patient is functioning fairly well despite past difficulties, I use as a rule of thumb that *someone, somewhere, must have loved them,* and I go hunting for that person. The therapist needs to ferret out *any past relationships* that were affirming but have been buried with the passage of time. So often, patients have to repress the memory of a loving relationship because it was too unbearable to face it in their childhood emotional climate. When one forgets the memory of a loving person, one forgets their love and the affirming sense of self that went with it. "So often the work of mourning is more to remember than to say good-bye" (Vaillant, 1988, p. 148).

Although we all need reminders of love from those in the present, the memories of loving people in the past make us receptive to the love and care that is currently given by others. The discussion of emotion-laden imagery sometimes elicits memories of loving people from the past who have been forgotten. At other times, the following questions can be helpful:

"What relationship made you feel the most special?"
"Whom have you had a crush on when you were young? Was the feeling returned?"
"Who felt joy in your presence?"
"Whose eyes would light up when they saw you?" (This question often brings tears of remembrance or tears of grief at the absence of such a person)
"Whose heart did you touch? Whose heart touched yours?"
"Whom did you love when you were a child, and what made that love so hard to bear?"

EXAMPLE 1: NED THE TAILOR

A busy female corporate executive had been raised by a demanding mother and a warmer, but self-absorbed father who worked 16 hours a day. When the patient was in first grade, she walked home after school each day and had to cross a busy street, which she was strictly forbidden to cross by herself. Her mother owned a coffee shop on the other side of the street, and the child was instructed to wait until her mother came to escort her across the street. When she arrived at the street corner, however, the mother often was not there. The little girl could see her mother through glass, behind the counter in the shop. She would jump and wave and call out, "Mommy, Mommy cross me, cross me! Get me, Mommy, come and cross me." This would go on day after day, with her jumping up and down and straining to get her mother's attention behind the plate glass window. Sometimes her mother eventually saw her, but more often, her mother did not look up. She remembered seeing her mother putting away glasses or chatting with customers, unmindful of her daughter's cries. Next door to her mother's shop was a tailor shop. Inside, Ned the Tailor would be watching the child jumping up and down trying to get her mother's attention. One day, as the patient was telling me about the longing to attract her mother's attention, she had a sudden memory that came with a flood of words and feelings:

PATIENT: I just remembered something. Ned, Ned the Tailor. He would be looking out through his window watching me, and he would come get me! I remember it now. Sometimes my mother would come, but more often, I think *he* would. He would come out the door, cross the street, pick me up in his big arms, and carry me back to my mother's shop. I remember his apron with thread all over it. He was the sweetest man. . . . I adored him. I loved being carried across the street. He was so tall and seemed so strong. I haven't thought of this in 25 years! Oh, how I adored him.

THERAPIST: Why do you think you had forgotten him?

PATIENT: I have no idea. Well, [*pausing*] maybe because my mother would make fun of him and me. She would tease me and say I had a crush on Ned. And I would feel so embarrassed. I would deny it. I guess I felt foolish. After a while, I got big enough to cross the street by myself, and Ned stopped coming to get me. I guess I just forgot him.

THERAPIST: Tell me more about how it felt to be with Ned.

PATIENT: Oh, I felt special. His face really lit up whenever he saw me. I never really thought about it, but I guess [*pausing reflectively and tearing up*] *he must have really loved me.*

We came back to these precious memories a number of times, so that they were full in her mind and heart and so she could savor them at length. Remembering her feelings with Ned awoke something that had been long buried in this woman. She had come to treatment because she could not commit to a man. She was charming and attractive, but she would let no one close to her. She had been married only briefly and was in her late thirties. Several months before she began therapy, she had broken up with Barney, a tall, handsome Coast Guard Captain who adored her. Barney had always said that the first time he saw her, he fell in love, but she did not respond to him in the same way. As she remembered Ned the Tailor, she realized that Barney reminded her of Ned. Over the next few months, she let herself become close to Barney once again. During the remainder of treatment, she explored her mother's jealousy of her loving anyone else, whether it be her father, her grandmother, her aunt, or even Ned the Tailor. She realized that she had cut off her attachments to try to win the love of her distant mother and that this led to a life of loneliness and isolation. A year later, she and Barney were married. Five years later, she and Barney have a wonderful marriage, and her issues about commitment are resolved.

EXAMPLE 2: REMEMBERING GRAMMY

Many patients exhibit the somewhat strange capacity for completely forgetting a person from the past or forgetting the love that came with the relationship. The woman in this example forgot the love of the grandmother she had lived with for the first 5 years of her life. Her mother, who had been extremely harsh, had always spoken derisively of her mother-in-law, and the patient had shut out the loving memories. As a result of treatment, she heavily grieved the loss of the grandmother and brought the precious memories back into her life:

I can remember it like it was yesterday. At the kitchen table, or in the backyard, Grammy was always doing chores. But no matter what she was doing, she would always be talking softly to me or smiling and winking. I felt special with her; noth-

ing I did was bad. She would let me eat whatever I wanted, even sugar out of the bowl. [Beginning to cry] *Grammy would sing little songs to me . . . and always, always, her sweet smile.* [Barely able to speak] *She never ignored me like my mother did. To Grammy, I was somebody—I was there.*

She contacted her mother and obtained some pictures of her grandmother, which she put on display in her living room so that she could see them each day and remember.

In both of the preceding cases, the memories emerged as a result of the therapist's exploring the relationship or issues related to the relationship. By sifting through both positive and negative aspects of these relationships, one brings the emotional content to the surface. I differ from Davanloo in that I find confrontation is *not* essential to get an accurate picture of past relationships; all that is needed is gentle focusing. The therapist should not assume that the first description of important past figures is necessarily accurate or complete. Repeated questioning is needed, with noting of contradictions and exploration when a relationship seems lopsided: too idealized or too devalued.

EXAMPLE 3: HOW GRAMMY WAS RECOVERED

Earlier in the treatment of the woman who remembered her grandmother's love, the therapist noted the bland response toward the grandmother: *You speak without much feeling about your grandmother, yet you lived with her for the first 5 years of your life. Can you tell me what you remember of her?* As the relationship was described, the therapist pointed out and questioned contradictions:

THERAPIST: Do you notice that you speak demeaningly of your grandmother, yet you have told me how devoted she was to you? Did she deserve devaluation for something you have not yet mentioned?
PATIENT: No, not at all. In fact, she was the kindest person I ever have known. My mother always put her down, I think because she was jealous of her.

This interaction led to the expression of much deeper affection for the grandmother but also an awareness that the grandmother was much less forceful than the mother. After the grandmother died, the patient came to depend on forcefulness, modeled after her mother, as a way to protect herself. As she revived the gentleness of her grandmother, she began to allow herself to become gentler as well.

The recovery of lost loves is of vital importance in the restructuring of the sense of self. The ways in which people lack receptive capacity needs further study and categorization so that we may better understand how to work through the serious blockages in human relationships. The importance of this ability cannot be understated. It may be one of the essential factors in healing.

Through encouraging the patient's adaptive feelings and building the capacity for closeness in the therapeutic relationship, the therapist connection becomes the new, good relationship (sometimes not as good as the patient has dreamed of, but good enough nonetheless). Remembering people differently, or restructuring the memory trace, is the result of building new felt experiences of others.

EXAMPLE 4: HOW THE DECEASED WOULD FEEL NOW

Another typical situation occurs when patients lament that their parents did not live long enough to know what their child accomplished. I encourage such individuals to spend time exploring what the parent might have felt.

THERAPIST: If your mother and father were sitting here today, hearing how much you long for their appreciation, what would they say? What would you most want to hear from them? How likely is it that they could say what you so want to hear, or at least feel it in their hearts. If they were sitting here today, how would each of them be feeling toward you?

PATIENT: Oh, I have no idea.

THERAPIST: You lived with these people for many years. In your heart, you know what they would feel for you right now. Let's take a few minutes to explore this.

Patients often want to skip away from such painful thoughts, but with some support and encouragement of the therapist, many are able to experience these "memories-to-be," and the grief is tremendously healing. Sometimes, unfortunately, there is the sad knowledge that the parent would not have responded in the longed-for way. That, too, needs to be acknowledged and borne, that is, grieved and eventually replaced by inner models of more nurturant figures.

By remembering and cherishing close experiences with others, one begins to care for and love oneself. If the interpersonal experience is negative, thoughts and feelings of coldness, neglect, anger, or abuse can be held in memory. We are social beings, and we learn what we live. By remembering such experiences, one learns that one is not lovable or worth caring for. We have to have the care and love of others in order to care for and love ourselves. Ample research supports this fact, from Harlow's monkey studies to Stern's mother–infant findings. The mother's attunement to the infant teaches the child the sense of self.

BUILDING AN ADAPTIVE SENSE OF SELF

Every aspect of this model of treatment is in service of building an adaptive sense of self. We know ourselves in part by knowing our defenses, our anxieties, and our feelings, as well as how they are implemented with ourselves and others. But we can come to be aware of these facets of ourselves only through the guidance and feedback of others. How others see us helps to build the concepts about ourselves. For better or for worse, how we are seen by others becomes the sense of self. The only mirrors we have for ourselves are the faces of others. How desperately we need those faces to be compassionate ones! We therapists also are mirrors for our patients, reflecting our patients to themselves. We hope that our patients are able to receive what we give to build a new and affirming part of themselves and that our mirroring will be healing.

In addition to the adaptive concepts of self that need to be built, patients must learn adaptive responsivity to a range of wants and needs. Gustafson suggested use of Gedo's (1979) schema for developmental deficits to guide the therapist in discerning and supplying "missing capabilities." The following list of areas of difficulty overlaps in many ways with the defensive functions discussed in chapter 4:

1. Inability to calm one's extreme tension states
2. Inability to defend oneself from assault
3. Inability to keep a buoyant sense of self or others, leading to disappointment and injury
4. Inability to work out conflict (e.g., competition)
5. Inability to tolerate the inevitable setbacks and frustrations of life as it imperfectly exists

Each of these levels can be reviewed, briefly, in light of the affects and relational issues that are involved. The ability to calm one's extreme tension states (Level 1) requires all of the affects: our biological endowment present at birth. The infant cries and reaches out to its mother when frightened or needing soothing and reaches out to the world when curious. We had to learn not to do so. Undoing that maladaptive learning means helping patients identify and feel deserving of their wants, interests, and needs. The inability to defend oneself from attack (Level 2) is an endowed capability. The 2-year-old automatically and emphatically says *no* and sets limits until taught that this is not acceptable. We need to free up our patients to feel their right to use appropriately their natural endowment of anger. The inability to retain the positive qualities of self or others (Level 3) results from the negative or inhibitory affects that thwart such buoyancy. Correcting this problem requires a strong association of positive feeling (interest and enjoyment) with the self and with others that balances or outweighs the negative feeling that inevitably emerges. I do not imply that we should try to feel positively about destructive or dishonest behaviors. But a holistic view of human nature, including our own and others' foibles, can balance the inevitable hate or disgust one feels with a deep appreciation of the pain and struggle we all face and sometimes do not overcome. It is helpful to remember that we are all mixed bags.

In resolving conflicts (Level 4), one has to respect one's own feelings and needs as well as those of others. This task necessitates the adaptive integration and balance of both positive and negative feelings associated with all human desires. In a similar vein, the inability to tolerate the inevitable setbacks and frustrations of life (Level 5) also requires the adaptive integration of appreciation and disappointment, but applied to life experience. As mentioned earlier, acceptance or spirituality is important here: the capacity for profound enjoyment and therefore appreciation of, hope for, and wonder at the world in all its complexity.

The ultimate goal of self–other restructuring is to allow patients to become their own good parent and to hold within and use everything good that they have been given. The goal in defense restructuring is to stop directing negative feelings toward oneself; the goal in affect restructuring is to free up positive and adaptive feelings; and the goal in the present objective is to associate positive feelings with the self.

EXAMPLE: THE WOMAN WHO DID NOT TRUST HER JUDGMENT

This married woman felt that she could not trust her own judgment, so I questioned her during the history taking about her decision making. I noted that she had made several mature choices in her life. I pointed out specific examples and questioned why she felt at such a loss to trust her judgment in the resolution of a conflict with her husband about marriage counseling. (They were in crisis and certainly did need counseling.)

PATIENT: I don't trust my judgment that my husband and I need marriage counseling because *he* doesn't want marriage counseling.
THERAPIST: Do you have any doubt that you yourself want marriage counseling, just from your view?
PATIENT: No! I know I want it, but I don't know if it's right 'cause he doesn't want it.

It took only minutes to point out that she was evaluating the worth of her judgments on the basis of other people's needs instead of her own. This tendency has been called living from the outside in rather than from the inside out. I pointed out that other people had to make up their own minds and she had to make up only *hers*. This insight was dramatic for her and sufficient to help her make significant changes in asking for things and also in helping her remember that other people might not want to do the same thing as she right away.

This woman's confused comments about her lack of judgment could have been misread easily as manifestations of borderline personality disorder or a serious identity disturbance. Indeed, I was not sure at first. The trick was to explore the less pathological possibility first: that she had a lot of strengths that were not being acknowledged because of her undue admiration of the opinions of others. Her father had been a prominent lawyer whom his daughter revered.

This policy of integrating the strengths in every problem area not only presents a new and more affirming view of the patient to the patient, but also can save an enormous amount of therapy time. If this woman had been pathologized by the therapist's agreeing that she had no capacity for making decisions, her therapy could have been endless. Because there was not an identity problem in the serious sense of the term, there would have been no beneficial response to treating it. Indeed, she would have lost additional self-esteem if she had been treated as though she had no sense of self. The clues to counter this diagnosis were everywhere. She had said she always chose men who were basically kind and decent to her. She had good friendships with women. She had happy, healthy children. It was highly unlikely that she had bad judgment to the extent that she feared. The problem was at the more superficial level of too much respect for the opinions of a successful husband (and previously, father). This submissive position had been encouraged by a critical mother. Yet her home life had been largely loving and stable. We do our patients disservice by not exploring the solutions at the healthier end of the continuum and not paying close attention to their strengths.

The Receptive Capacity of the Self Toward the Self

This chapter focuses largely on the interpersonal capacity for receptivity. It is important to remember, however, that one important area of receptivity is with oneself. Can we be as responsive to our own needs as to those of others so that both can be weighted and considered alongside each other? So often our patients' own wants and needs somehow "fall through the cracks" and disappear. The previous chapters deal with becoming more aware and in touch with one's affective experience, but in this section and chapter 8 I emphasize the use of one's feelings, needs, and desires for oneself by oneself. This means becoming one's own good parent. Throughout this manual, I stress the need for the patient to learn to identify, experience, and express wants and needs, all of which involve being responsive to oneself. Sometimes, however, the issue needs to be framed in explicit terms.

The following is a statement I make to most of my patients at some point in treatment: *In many ways you have inadvertently been reacting to yourself as your caretakers did, harshly and critically (or neglectfully). Maybe it's time now for you to begin to react to yourself in the ways that you need. What do you think? You cannot change how you were treated in the past, but you can change how you treat yourself now.*

The inner representation of the sense of self—one's view of oneself—can be ascertained by one's response to oneself. The main aspects of self focused on in this model overlap with those outlined by Stern (1985) and include self-awareness and self-agency in regard to defensive–coping behavior, conflict responses, and affectivity in relation to self and others. The more one "knows" one's feelings and responses and the major patterns they represent, the more sense one has of oneself as a "distinct, integrated body," and the more aware and in control one may be. The more we can transpose this inner and often unconscious self-experience into thoughts and language, the better we may be able to communicate our self-experience to ourselves and others.

SUMMARY

This chapter focuses on the interventions that can be useful in assisting patients in the alteration of the images of self and others. Within a real therapeutic relationship, anxieties associated with relationships with self and other are regulated. Interventions include the following:

- Enhancing the receptive capacity
- Changing perspectives on self and others
- Changing addictive attachments
- Repetition until anxieties about relationships are regulated

CHAPTER 10

The Flow of Treatment

The preceding chapters have described various aspects of the treatment process. This chapter presents the flow of treatment from start to finish to present a picture of how the different objectives and interventions are intermingled in clinical practice. I do not intend for my personal style to be taken as the only way to conduct treatment: Each therapist needs to develop his or her own style for comfortably conducting treatment. I present this description as a model for readers to bounce off: to follow, if comfortable, or alter, if not.

PREPARATION OF THE PATIENT

Preparation of the patient begins with the first contact. Sometimes this is face to face, but generally it is on the phone. "Can you give me a brief description of what you would like help with in treatment?" is the standard way that I begin. The aim is to determine whether the patient's problem areas are ones in which I have expertise. For example, substance abuse and eating disorders are problem areas for which I refer potential patients to colleagues who are specialists. A seriously suicidal or an extremely vulnerable patient might not be suitable if I am going to be out of town during the following month. If it is established that the patient's problems are ones I am trained to work with and feel able to treat adequately, I proceed. In that first telephone contact, I generally provide the patient with some information about the treatment. An example follows.

Introductory Remarks

The main objectives of treatment are presented in these remarks. I generally say something like the following:

Let me explain to you how I work so that you can see if it seems comfortable to you. In my work, I try to be as focused as possible on the problems you want help with in treatment. I am active throughout the session in questioning and giving feedback about these problem areas. During the initial evaluation session, with your help, we will try to make sense of why this problem is occurring and outline what we might do about it. At the beginning and end of treatment, I will ask you to list your main problem areas and rate them in terms of severity. I will also ask you to fill out some standard evaluation tests. Every 5 or 10 sessions, I will ask you to rerate the severity of your major problems. We will then see if you have made progress toward resolution of the problems. If not, we will focus on what more we need to do. I cannot say for sure how long treatment will last, but I am committed to working as efficiently and as rapidly as possible so you will spend no more time than is necessary. How does this sound to you?

If the patient is agreeable with this statement, I proceed to describe the process of videotaping:

I also offer the option of videotaping or audiotaping the therapy sessions. I tell you this before you arrive so that you have time to consider whether or not you want to have this done. I do not want you to make this decision without forethought. Many therapists are making this option available to their patients because it can be helpful to review the treatment process. People often choose to take the tapes home with them and review them between sessions, which can be a way to intensify the therapy process. I will enclose a consent form along with the evaluation instruments that you can review and consider. It will include several options, such as allowing me to view the tapes, use the tapes for consultation on your case, or use segments for training. Please understand that this is optional and that the tapes will only be used in ways with which you are comfortable and with your written permission. However, I strongly recommend that you consider taping at least for your own viewing, because so many patients have found watching the tapes to be enormously helpful.

In closing, I ask if the patient has any questions he or she wishes to ask.

A verbal contract for treatment is therefore established. I do not provide a written description of the treatment procedures to my private patients, although I may consider doing so in the future. A written contract is sometimes provided in more behavioral treatments, and all of our research patients receive a written description of general treatment procedures. Whether the description is written or verbal, it is important that the patient understand and agree to how treatment is to be conducted.

When a patient makes an appointment to begin treatment, I explain that I will mail a package of materials for him or her to fill out and bring to the first therapy session. This assessment battery (the Psychotherapy Assessment Checklist; PAC Forms) is described in detail in chapter 2. In the future, standard practice may include the option of a full diagnostic interview and relevant psychological testing, conducted in assessment laboratories by trained psychometricians.

Until such assessment support is available, I send the patient a letter with appointment date and time, directions to my office, and instructions to complete my assessment battery and bring it to the first session.

FORMAT OF TREATMENT

Initial Evaluation Session

When the patient arrives for the first session, I introduce myself and, leaving the patient in the waiting room, return to my office to review the Psychotherapy Assessment Checklist before beginning the session. I scan the forms, reviewing the severity of symptoms and the descriptions of the best and worst times in the patient's life. I am looking for degree of impairment in functioning across the lifetime, indicators of Axis I and II pathology, and an estimated GAF score. The main symptoms and problems are noted on the PAC Summary Sheet and further assessed during the session. These forms are designed to be quickly scanned and takes 3–5 minutes, after which the patient is invited into the office.

Because of the high motivation in most patients to begin talking about the presenting problems, any attempt at further assessment is often out of place in the beginning of the interview and can be done much more comfortably later in the evaluation. I have found it best to start with the same question that I asked during the first phone contact: *Could you tell me what problems you would like help with in treatment?* Variants include: *Could you tell me in more detail about the problems you want help with? Could we start by your describing in your own words the major problem or problems that brought you to treatment?*

If the patient does not describe a specific incident, the next question is: *Could you give me a specific example?* It is important that the patient's description of problems not remain on a vague or general level. When this is the case, the therapist needs to direct the patient to a specific occasion when the problematic behavior occurred. Examples should include real people and feelings in specific situations, not classes of people (my family, men), ideas (I feel confused), or general situations (when I'm at their house).

Evaluating the Patient at the Initiation of Treatment

PATIENT: I am usually shy and withdrawn.

THERAPIST: Can you describe a situation in which you were shy or withdrawn?

PATIENT: Well, I'm always like that in social situations.

THERAPIST: Can you recall a recent incident where you felt that way, so that you can describe exactly what happened, who was there, and how you felt?

Specific behaviors in interactions with real people are essential for an accurate analysis of the functions of the patient's maladaptive behaviors patterns on which therapy will be based. Affective connections are much more vividly drawn from specific behaviors than from vague generalities. Core psychodynamic issues (the scripts underlying the interpersonal scenes) are much more clearly revealed in specific behaviors (e.g., "What man has recently made you feel nervous?").

The main problems that brought the patient to treatment (generally those that are written down and rated as target or presenting problems) are each assessed for the patterns of defensive behavior, anxiety, and affects in interpersonal relationships, as described in chapter 3. These are the building blocks required to generate a core dynamic formulation, which often can begin to be discerned in the first few minutes of the session and comes into clearer focus with repeated examples. When a pattern is not clear after a few sessions, it could be due to the therapist's lack of experience in determining the core pattern, but more often it is symptomatic of the patient's degree of defensiveness. Inability to determine a treatment focus has been cited as a contraindication for treatment in earlier short-term models (e.g., Sifneos, 1979). In this model, lack of focus can be used as a signal that more preparatory work needs to be done (to build alliance or motivation), before the active work of short-term treatment can begin.

I have found that it is *optimal* (but not mandatory) to schedule 2 or 3 hours for this initial evaluation so that the therapist and patient have time to go into sufficient detail to generate an initial psychodynamic formulation for treatment. Many therapists do not have this flexibility in their schedules, so that such an evaluation may need to be spread out over three sessions. The extended time allows the therapist to probe issues in depth and rapidly identify the core patterns, and it often provides the patient with new and valuable ways of viewing of the problems early in treatment.

Determining a psychodynamic formulation can be confusing at first. However, the process is simplified by noting defensive behaviors and their adaptive affect-based alternatives. As noted in chapter 6, there are only a few "activating" affects on the I/F pole to choose from (the regulatory and pleasure-giving affect clusters) and still fewer inhibitory affects on the A pole (anxiety, guilt, shame, and pain). The interaction of the activating versus inhibitory affects and the resulting defenses are the basis of the core psychodynamic formulation. For example, if a patient is passive and needs to learn to become assertive, then anger or assertion might be the adaptive affect. Another possibility could be the need for self-care or self-esteem; undergirded by positive affects (interest–excitement or enjoyment–joy) attached to the self.

Thus, the goal of the initial evaluation is to make clear to patients the main defensive behavior patterns underlying their presenting problems, what adaptive responses are needed but are being warded-off, and the reasons why. It is also often possible (and common in patients functioning above 50 on the GAF) that affect restructuring and anxiety regulation can be begun, so that the patients have some degree of improvement in their main problems by the end of the 3 hours. This is generally a most gratifying process for both therapist and patient.

Schedule and Structure of Sessions

After the initial evaluation, my sessions are generally held on a weekly basis for approximately 50 minutes in the typical style of individual psychotherapy. The length of treatment is negotiated between the therapist and patient, and patients are encouraged to assume the role and responsibility of guiding and maintaining their own therapeutic progress as soon as possible.

Beginning Weekly Treatment

At the beginning of each session I recommend that patients begin discussing whatever is most salient to them. The core psychodynamic formulation provides a backdrop for each session and is a guide to return to when treatment becomes confused, but should not be rigidly adhered to. Patients must have the flexibility to discuss all topics of concern. *But whatever problem is brought up*, the therapist should assess its relation to the main focus by determining whether the topic is any of the following: (a) another example of the central psychodynamic pattern, (b) an example of a secondary or more peripheral dynamic conflict, or (c) a defensive avoidance of the main issues.

Weaving Together Treatment Objectives

Because there has been ample discussion of the implementation of the treatment objectives, this section briefly summarizes the main points. With patients who clearly meet criteria for active short-term interventions, my first objective is generally to bring them to an awareness of their defensive or maladaptive behavior patterns, including what feelings they are warding off and why. Second, I help patients develop a desire to give up their destructive defensive patterns.

With patients whose defensiveness is highly resistant to change or whose sense of self and others is severely impaired, work on self–other restructuring may have to precede or be interwoven with the defense restructuring. The building of compassion for self and of a sense that others can be trusted are essential for both defense relinquishing and affect experiencing. When these objectives are implemented in treatment *depends on the capacity of the patient.* For example, some patients come to treatment already seeing their defensive patterns, and they want to give them up:

PATIENT: I know I shut down and get passive in any conflict, and I want to stop doing that! [*In such cases, the therapist can quickly proceed to affect restructuring and explore the anxieties associated with the experience and expression of feeling.*]
THERAPIST: So let's see what goes on in a conflict. Can you describe a specific situation that comes to mind, and tell me what your were feeling at the time?

On the other hand, some patients begin experiencing certain emotions and then have a reemergence of defensiveness that blocks the experience. If this defensive response does not yield to gentle encouragement to continue, I return to defense-restructuring interventions to explore and attempt to regulate the anxieties that gave rise to the defenses:

PATIENT: I just don't want to look at this. I hate discussing these feelings.
THERAPIST: There must be strong feelings that cause you to shut down like that. What's the most difficult part of facing those feelings?

PATIENT: I feel sick inside, and I just can't stand it.

THERAPIST: So let's not proceed until the experience is more tolerable for you. Tell me about this sick feeling.

PATIENT: I just feel like a bad person and I can't shake it. [*This implies a strongly ego-syntonic defense that will not be removed without the therapist shifting the focus to the alteration of inner representation of the self.*]

THERAPIST: How does it make you a *bad person* to defend yourself in a conflict?

In this manner, the therapist moves back and forth among the treatment objectives, as one would tighten the lug nuts on a tire: a little attention to one and then to another, until the tire is secure. Defense, affect, and self–other restructuring are parallel objectives to which the therapist must attend; the timing depends on the patient's needs. A summary of the main treatment objectives and related interventions is provided in Appendix C.

Determining a Goal for Each Session

To work as efficiently as possible, I imagine at the beginning of each session what behavioral objective might be reasonable for the patient to try to accomplish. *The art of therapy involves knowing what might be an optimal step that could be realistically accomplished in each session and would constitute progress (however large or small) toward the resolution of long-standing and painful problems.* I ask myself the following questions at the beginning of each session:

- What is this patient's core conflict (as recorded on the 10 session summary form: see Appendix D)?
- What did we focus on in the last session, and how successful were we?
- What amount of change is likely today, given my patient's strengths and/or resistance?
- What can I realistically expect the patient to walk out of here being able to do that he or she is not able to do at present?
- How can I push for change in a way that neither badgers nor abuses but allies with the patient's present motivation and capacity for change?

The focus on realistic change makes therapy a challenge as well as fun. It is gratifying when patients make a step toward change, and it is food for thought when they do not. Of course, it is not realistic to expect to move patients toward their specified objectives in every session, but it is invigorating to try.

It is helpful to break down the change into small steps that are reasonable to accomplish in one session. Sometimes, that means doing something, and sometimes it means *not* doing something. With patients who are *too driven and performance-oriented*, I have suggested that they try *not* to achieve anything in treatment for a while and study how that feels (typically shameful), with the goal of their becoming proud of calming down. Counterdependent patients might be encouraged to stay in treatment somewhat longer to become more comfortable with dependency. Such interventions can be far more time-efficient that trying to badger change out of a performance-weary individual.

Most often, the treatment goals involve some aspect of the main objectives: offering portions of defense, affect, and self–other restructuring that the patient can digest in one session. Sometimes, the goal is just the vaguest awareness of a defensive pattern. Other times, the goal might be to feel a little more compassionate toward the self. Still other times, it might be to begin to feel.

Repetition is needed often. The therapist needs to be patient and confident that change will happen after a few weeks. When I have been focusing on a goal for a month or more and there is not even small movement, however, I collaborate with the patient to try to understand whether my focus is off, his or her motivation is lacking, or something else is interfering.

The 10 Session Summary Form

Following each session, I use the 10 session summary form shown in Appendix D to record the main themes of sessions and rate weekly treatment progress toward the achievement of therapeutic objectives. This record is tremendously helpful in two ways: (a) The summary of main themes keeps treatment on focus and (b) the rating of the degree of achievement of objectives indicates whether treatment is floundering or moving in a positive direction.

An example of the Unforgiven Teenager's summary form for her first 10 sessions is shown in Figure 10.1. Diagnostic summaries are recorded at the top right-hand corner of the form. The total Axis II items were 39.[1] She had no Axis III diagnosis; Axis IV stressors were mild; and her GAF score was 50. Her presenting problems are listed, and the ratings given. I rerated the severity of her problems after 10 sessions. (I did not start rating problems at five sessions until recently.) The core conflicts are listed and severity ratings given at Sessions 1 and 10.

For example, in Session 1, the Unforgiven Teenager did not recognize her masochistic defensive behavior (1A = 1.5) and she did not wish to give it up (1B = 1, because she felt she deserved to be punished). She showed only a low degree of affect experiencing (2A = 2) and no ability for adaptive expression (2B = 1). Her sense of self was poor (3A = 2, because she felt God hated her), and her sense of others was also quite low (3B = 3) because she

---

[1]The total number of Axis II items (that meet diagnostic criteria) is one of the best indicators of degree of defensiveness that I have found. I am assisted in assessing this by the PAC Forms (see chapter 2). The Unforgiven Teenager's total of 39 Axis II items was high; the typical patient in our research study has 15–30 items. There are 113 items on the Axis II (SCID-II) interview, and few outpatients have data that support more than 50 or 60 items. Research is needed on means and ranges of Axis II total items for different populations.

was distrustful and suspicious of others' motives. By Session 5 she repeatedly had been able to catch her masochistic reactions and hated to see herself doing that to herself (thus, ratings 1A and 1B are high: 8). Her affective responding and her sense of self and others shows a gradual improvement over the 10 sessions. This case is discussed further at the end of this chapter.

FIGURE 10.1
10 Session Summary Form.

					Session Number:	1	5	10
10 SESSION SUMMARY FORM					Axis I:___	Maj. Dep.		—
Short-term Psychotherapy Research Program at HMS					Axis I:___	Past Etoh		
Leigh McCullough Vaillant, Ph.D. (1/95)				*Total 39 items* Axis II.__A:	Paranoid (4 items)		—	
Patient Name/Initials:					Axis II__B:	Borderline (3 items)		—
The Unforgiven Teenager					Axis II__C:	Self-Def (9 items)		—
					Axis III:	—		
					Axis IV:	2		1
Presenting Problems: (One to three examples)					Axis V:	50		65

Presenting Problems	1	5	10
1) Come to terms with hurt and hostility to parents	11	6	6
2) Shame and guilt	11	8	3
3) Improve self-esteem	12	8	3

Core Conflict(s):		1	5	10
	1) Shame over sense of self	1	3	6-7
	2) (Note: Only one dynamic conflict			
	3) was focused on & rated in these 10 sessions)			

Pymt	Sess	Date	MAIN THEME(S) OF SESSION	1A	1B	2A	2B	3A	3B
	1	2/25	Anger toward father blocked. Grief over childhood, but shame & self hate since teens; Distancing me bothers.	1.5	1	2	1	2	3
	2	3/3	Can't stop the pain. Still blames herself as did her parents. Beginning to build compassion for self.	3	3	3	2	2	3
	3	3/10	Awareness of overwhelming loneliness; Huge sense of shame. God doesn't forgive her; Her relation to me.	4	3	3	2	2	4
	4	3/17	Overwhelmed by shame & loneliness. She's no-good-God will never forgive her. How I see her?	6	3	2	2	2	4
	5	3/25	No feelings this week; But clearly sees her masochistic pattern & hates treating herself that way!	8	8	2	2	3	4
	6	3/28	Drank a little this week (testing me?) Disgust for self but also increased sense of compassion for self & from me.	8	6	4	4	5	6
	7	4/7	Less paranoid but still feels unforgiven by God for teenage years. Yet growing sense of care for self	8	7	5	4	5	6
	8	4/14	Continuing shame-reduction; Slowly going over memories of teenage years, with compassionate view	8	7	5	5	5	6
	9	4/21	Shame decreased from "90% to 60%." Celebration! But feels frightened from being open & vulnerable	8	7	6	6	6	6
	10	6/25	Two-month maintenance session: More improved, Feels likeable and worthwhile. Not depressed.	8	9	8	9	7	7

After each session Rate 1) Degree to which Therapy Objectives were met for each conflict and, 2) degree conflict changed.
1 = Not at All   3 = Little   5 = Moderately   7 = Much   10 = Substantially

1A	Defense Recognition—	How much is defensive pattern (being focused on) recognized?
1B	Defense Relinquishing—	How much is defensive pattern aversive and desired to give up?
2A	Affect Experience—	How much is adaptive emotional response experienced and contained within?
2B	Affect Expression—	How much are wants and needs appropriately expressed in face to face relationships?
3A	Sense of Self—	To what degree is the sense of self adaptive?
3B	Sense of Others—	To what degree is the sense of others adaptive?

The process of rating each therapy session is one that most therapists are resistant to (myself included). Most find it hard to shift from the intuitive therapeutic process to the logical process of evaluation. Nevertheless, I think there is no better way to monitor one's treatment than session-by-session focus and ratings. Although reviewing videotapes is highly recommended, realistically it can only be done intermittently. In contrast, these weekly ratings take only a minute and can be done at the end of each session, thereby providing an essential feedback loop that we may keep consciously before us. If graduate programs made such session ratings mandatory during training it would help self-monitoring become a habitual part of our professional procedures. A blank copy of the 10 Session Summary Form can be found in Appendix D, which may be photocopied and enlarged for use in clinical practice.

Inclusion of Significant Others

If the patient consents, I often invite significant others to one of the first few sessions to obtain a broader perspective of the patient's family or social environment, to learn their perception of the patient's difficulties, and to prepare them for the rapid changes that may occur. I also invite significant others to join sessions midtreatment if therapeutic changes are causing difficulties for the partnership. If these problems cannot be clarified or resolved in such a session, I make a referral to couples counseling.[2] Often, a spouse or partner comes in during the final weeks of therapy to discuss the changes that have occurred and to plan for handling and maintaining those changes over time. This occurs only with the patient's consent and when it is in the patient's best interest.

Missed Sessions

In graduate school, I was taught that a therapist should never be so dependent on the revenue of one or two sessions in a week that a cancellation or missed session becomes a financial burden. Otherwise, one cannot maintain the necessary objectivity and compassion required to examine patients' issues concerning missed sessions. It was recommended that a therapy load be carried that allows for missed sessions so that patients are protected from our financial needs and so that we have the ability to be generous when the patient's history warrants it.[3]

Patients are not necessarily irresponsible or manipulative when they miss a session. (Often, both patients and therapists need to be reminded of this.) These symptoms are defensive reactions to underlying conflicts with *valid historical origins* that need to be understood. Patients miss sessions because

---

[2] I do not treat couples when one of them is or has been my patient because of the possibility of my bias toward the one I am closer too and the feeling of unbalanced loyalty the couple may experience.

[3] I generally allow one missed session and then negotiate for a cancellation policy involving notice within 24 hours to avoid being charged, unless there is sickness or emergency.

of *fear* of closeness or commitment, *shame* about issues being discussed, *pain* over the intensity of treatment, and so on. The therapist's task is to discover nonjudgmentally what those reasons are.

Dreams

Researchers such as Hobson (1987, 1994) have suggested that dreams may be nothing more than sleep-cycle epiphenomena that are more biological than psychological in origin. Regardless of etiology, in short-term psychotherapy dreams may function as projective tests and can be analyzed as in traditional dynamic therapy. Patients are asked to describe their associations to aspects of the dream or to view each aspect as representing a part of the self, and so on. The meanings that patients ascribe to their dreams can be helpful in formulating—or reformulating—a psychodynamic conflict or in signaling a process being worked through.

Gender Differences in Short-Term Treatment

In the development of this model I initially avoided gender or cultural stereotypes in psychodynamic formulations or offering of treatment. I frequently have seen men who are adept at closeness but have difficulty with assertion (e.g., the Ferryman), as well as women who are skilled in assertion but afraid to be close to others. The majority of patients, male and female, have responded positively to the empathic, anxiety-regulating approach, but a small percentage (in both sexes) routinely devalue any compassion that is offered. The point is that I have seen more similarities than differences across gender in patient response to short-term intervention. This is not, however, meant to diminish the importance of further study of gender issues in short-term treatment. Research is needed to ascertain the optimal interventions for gender differences.

Biology, Medication, and Psychotherapy

People often ask me if I think a problem is biological or environmental or if it is interpersonal or psychological. I do not view these sources as "either–or" factors but as points on a continuum. There generally can be found a component of each in every individual, to a greater or lesser degree. One individual can have a recurrent family history of depression, learned helplessness owing to societal discrimination, *and* intrapsychic conflict about assertiveness as a function of parental injunctions. In such cases, medication, coping skills, and psychodynamic exploration might all be useful.

Therapist Stance

The poem *Desiderata*[4] contains the following words, which offer therapists guidance: *Beyond a wholesome discipline, be gentle with yourself.*

The work of therapy is demanding. The standards for professional behavior must be high. Strupp and Binder (1984) and Benjamin (1993a) have of-

---

[4]Max Ehrman, 1927.

fered an excellent standard for professional conduct: Every therapeutic interaction should fall into one of the following categories of actions; any that does not is probably an error:

1. Interventions that facilitate collaboration between patient and therapist
2. Interventions that help the patient recognize present and past patterns
3. Interventions that block maladaptive patterns
4. Interventions that strengthen the giving up of destructive wishes and fears
5. Interventions that help the patient learn new, more adaptive patterns

The development of a "wholesome discipline" is no small achievement. Beyond the critical standard of professionalism and integrity, however, it is essential for therapists to hold a compassionate self-perspective.

How well are we prepared for all the challenges that therapy presents? In terms of our own affective life, how many of us have explored fully the depth of our rage and know how to handle our anger maturely all the time? How many of us have fully grieved and replaced all our losses? Who among us regularly enjoys a free and ever-passionate sexual life and feels the peace and joy that come from a fascinating job and a loving relationship? Don't we all feel like asking, at times, "What's wrong with me! I'm supposed to know how to handle these things!" Reality is where we start from.

Learning to handle our "selves" and our emotional life is the greatest challenge any one of us will ever face. Indeed, a lifelong process of growth may be the most profound challenge facing humanity. Each developmental milestone brings with it a whole new set of emotional responses to acquire and adjust to. We cannot expect to be perfect, and we cannot expect to function optimally all the time. Just as Winnicott taught us the value of the "good enough mother," we need to consider the value of the "good enough therapist." Malan characterized the good enough analyst as one "who is struggling with his own difficulty in understanding the patient's material, but gets there to a reasonable approximation in the end" (1979, p. 173). Furthermore, Jordan reminded us that "we cannot deliver perfect understanding, so we should not protect our narcissism. One should neither blame oneself nor blame one's patient, but handle empathic failures with humility and learning" (1994).

Although we should always strive to be the best we can be, the therapist does not have to be perfect nor have all of his or her own issues thoroughly worked out. The ability to join patients, to some extent, on their emotional journey (but always guarding against using patients for one's own gratification) is generally sufficient for change to occur. Of course, the more therapists are self-aware and emotionally in touch, the better able they are to guide their patients. Indeed, many colleagues report that they grow with their patients in the deep exploration of feeling. Years ago, a colleague of mine lamented that he cured a patient of impotency while he himself was plagued with it! (He was able to resolve his patient's problem even before he resolved his own.) Have we not all had the experience of seeing a distraught patient while moaning inwardly, "You think *you've* got problems! If you only knew what I've been through today!" The compassion we give our patients should also be directed toward ourselves. It is precisely that self-compassion that provides us with the vitality to keep working on the problems at hand. To repeat, *Beyond a wholesome discipline, be gentle with yourself.*

TERMINATION

When to Terminate?

Termination can be considered when either (a) the targeted behaviors have changed or (b) behaviors have begun to change and the patient feels confident that the change can be maintained. The initial consideration of termination should begin when the therapist sees the beginning of behavioral changes concerning the core conflict. Termination is appropriate when the patient feels that he or she can *maintain the gains without irrevocably slipping back* into old patterns. Often, the time between sessions is increased before termination to allow patients to carry on the therapeutic work and consolidate the changes on their own. The Unforgiven Teenager had 9 weekly sessions, 6 sessions a month or two apart to maintain those gains, and then 20 weekly sessions on a new problem.

Assessment of Treatment

The test of successful treatment can be put simply: To what degree have patients received what they sought in coming to treatment? Are the presenting problems resolved or on the way to being resolved? Are the behaviors of the core dynamic formulation (a) clearly seen, (b) no longer desirable, and (c) beginning to be replaced by more adaptive responses? Is the patient's sense of self and sense of others more adaptive than maladaptive? Is the patient able to *express* to others as well as *receive* from others the wants and needs that brought him or her to therapy? Have steps been taken toward this goal *in most if not every session?*

When change occurs, it must be made conscious rather than left as a vague idea. The therapist should help the patient to see precisely what factors led to the change. Patients should be asked to delineate the causes of the changes in their own words. Often, the answer is slow in coming and may be different from what the therapist expected. Nevertheless, it is crucial that patients know why they have changed. In periods of stress, people tend to slip back to where they were before. If they have a clear cognitive pathway out of the chaos, they are more likely to be able to reverse these inevitable returns to old patterns.

The patient does not always need to stay in treatment to reverse these lapses. One guideline to consider is whether the parents of the patient were available or whether they withheld guidance. Patients who have been left on their own often need to do such work within a relationship. Those who have had a more supportive environment might be better able to terminate and continue on their own.

It is helpful to do the following during termination or booster sessions:

- Assess the capacity of the patient to maintain therapy gains.
- Assess the impact of the patient's change on the interpersonal environment.
- Anticipate and plan for the future, especially handling of setbacks.
- Celebrate the progress made in therapy but also acknowledge what was not accomplished.
- Explore the full range of feelings of the patient for the therapist, not forgetting expressions of warmth and appreciation for gains made, as well as what the therapist could have done better.
- Consider the patient's need both to mourn and to replace the loss of therapy.

Follow-up or Maintenance Sessions Following Treatment

Maintenance sessions during the first year posttreatment are helpful and possibly essential in maintaining gains made in treatment. Certainly, there has been sufficient evidence of this from behavioral research. When there has been rapid and dramatic behavior change in lifelong patterns (especially when this has occurred within 5 or 10 sessions), maintenance sessions must be considered. Relapse is highly likely under such circumstances. Monthly or quarterly sessions help keep the individual on track. Maintenance of behavior changes can be assisted by having sessions every 4, 8, or 12 weeks until patients feel able to maintain gains on their own. Maintenance sessions can be spaced further and further apart until patients feel secure about "steering their own ship."

Character Changes Within a Loving Relationship

No matter how much work is done in therapy, significant character changes are made in sustained, loving relationships in the real world. The practice is the day-to-day relationship. The implicit goal of treatment is not to provide the ultimate relationship but to help the patient be able to find, maintain, and grow in a loving relationship outside of therapy (Hendrix, 1992).

DETAILED CASE EXAMPLES

Assessment of Changes: The Ferryman

Following are the initial assessment of the Ferryman, a summary of his treatment, and the assessment of change (see Figure 10.2).

This severely submissive man came to treatment because of low self-esteem and a divorce. Although his passivity was great, he was highly motivated and he had a strong ability to trust and connect with others, which permitted rapid changes. His core psychodynamic formulation involved defenses of passivity and dependency owing to fear of conflict over assertion

FIGURE 10.2
Assessment of the Ferryman.

Presenting problems:	Six-month follow-up[a]
1) Breakup of marriage, rating- 11 (severe problem)	4
2) Poor self-esteem, rating- 10 (severe problem)	3
Axis I: Dysthymia (20-year duration)	Absent
Axis II: Dependent, 6 items	Subthreshold, 3 items
Self-defeating, 7 items	Subthreshold, 4 items
Total Axis II items, 21	10
Axis III: None	None
Axis IV: 3—Moderate stress, divorce	2
Axis V: 60	75

Core formulation:
1) Passivity (D) due to fears (A) about feelings of anger (I/F)
2) Unresolved grief (D) over loss (I/F) of grandfather at age 13 due to pain (A)
3) Externalization of need for approval from others (D) due to shame (A) about self-worth (I/F)

[a]Gains were maintained and improved at 5-year follow-up.

of his wants and needs. Treatment predominantly focused on his capacity for assertion; however, the mention of his grandfather's death, the only time in his life he cried, signaled a relationship that was more significant than he wanted to admit consciously. He had almost entirely forgotten his grandfather's love, but the recovery of his grandfather's "lost love" gave him a new sense of self. "I'm growing a new person inside," he said. Here the symptomatic, interpersonal, and character changes occurred together: A 20-year dysthymic diagnosis was resolved during the first 17 sessions. Underlying this dysthymic diagnosis, as so often happens, was unresolved mourning. The following 18 sessions helped him with feelings of anger, adaptive assertion, and grief over his family life. At the 5-year follow-up, he was happily remarried and had improved further. No additional treatment was required, and the dysthymia did not recur.

After about 20 sessions, the patient and I reviewed the changes that were strongly apparent:

PATIENT: It's like I have so much more power now. I mean, I feel like I have a lot more power . . . or I'm just saying the way I feel. [*There is still a little hesitancy about being so forthright.*]

THERAPIST: Maybe we could take a few minutes to go over the changes that have happened that have made you feel more powerful. We've done some of this already, but I wonder if you can go over the treatment and see what stands out in your mind as having helped you.

PATIENT: I remember sitting in here and killing my mother and killing Cathy and Doug. [*Laughing*] I remember, I'm beating them up and, and really letting them suffer. [*Looking at the therapist and grinning*] I threw you through the wall once. I really got angry at you! [*I had been late for a session, and he was a punctual man, so he was angry.*]

THERAPIST: Yeah! [*We both laugh.*]

PATIENT: The, the memories of that anger, that . . . yeah, keeping that little bit of anger . . . has really helped me.

THERAPIST: In what way?

He goes on to explain that he can finally feel that his marriage is over, because he is freed up to feel the anger about his wife's affair and how she treated him.

PATIENT: So the way she played her part in the marriage makes it very easy for me to be mad.

THERAPIST: Is it the case that you never got angry at her before the way you do now?

PATIENT: No. I never got angry this way before. I'd never let my true feelings show.

THERAPIST: We've done a lot of work around your dealing with anger versus the old passive response that you used to do with her.

Although this patient was conscious of the usefulness of access to anger, he did not mention the remembrance of his grandfather. I decided to inquire about it as a factor in his changing:

THERAPIST: There are some things I remember particularly, and one was the real coldness of your family life, the emptiness with your mother and father, in sharp contrast to the discovery of the warmth from your grandfather. And you really felt the pain of that coldness in your family life during therapy. How do you see those two aspects affecting you now? That emotional work that we did?

PATIENT: The coldness, the feelings of this almost sanitary environment, didn't allow me to try out a lot of what I'm doing now. In other words, there was an inhibition to get angry. That was a very inhibiting environment. I had to be the good little boy.

THERAPIST: That's right.

PATIENT: Deep down, the good little boy. I wasn't allowed to lash out. I never did fight with other kids, never got to punch back.

THERAPIST: That's right. You told me your mother wouldn't allow you to fight.

PATIENT: I really never got, I really never got to punch back. I mean, I might have been pretty good at it! I at least might have decked a few of the people that punched me! Some of the bullies that used to bully me. [*The issue with anger is still predominant in his mind.*]

THERAPIST: So these feelings are building in you. Reliving that restrictive environment again, feeling the pain of that showed you why you were so withdrawn and inhibited.

PATIENT: Yeah. It was like a television family, my family. You don't see any activity, you know, ma and dad coming in, sitting around watching television, that type of thing. But you don't see them going out and playing ball or, you know, that kind of thing. So in a way, my life was partly like that. You sit on a couch and you watch TV, the whole family. You don't talk very much, so there wasn't that ability for interacting. No normal interaction.

THERAPIST: But in your case, there was the good little boy who had to be utterly quiet and let other people take control.

PATIENT: Yeah. [*Sadly shaking head*]

THERAPIST: And how has the love for your grandfather affected your life?

PATIENT: It's let me see that, though I've lost him physically, I haven't lost him. [*Choking up*]

THERAPIST: That makes you well up with tears, doesn't it?

PATIENT: Yeah. He's . . . he's inside of me still. Even more so now.

THERAPIST [Whispering]: Your eyes well up every time you really let yourself think of him [*Any mention of his grandfather would bring an emotional response.*]

PATIENT: Yeah. [*Also whispering*] Makes me proud to feel that. I have something there [*tapping his chest*] to give.

THERAPIST: It makes you proud to find the memory of him in you alive, and those feelings.

PATIENT: Keeping alive the memory of him helps me live better. And I feel good about myself.

THERAPIST: That's a big change.

PATIENT: Uh huh. And I'm a good person, but good for those who deserve it, not just anyone.

THERAPIST: And that's different, a different kind of feeling than you had about yourself before? This memory of this man you loved so. And that you'd pushed him out, memories of him.

PATIENT: And I'm marrying a person who lets me be me, and it feels good. I found somebody who, yes, is strong-minded and strong-willed, but *hey, I am too now!* And we sort of find our common grounds!

CASE EXAMPLES: OVERVIEWS OF TREATMENT

The following case examples demonstrate how treatment objectives play out in clinical practice. I trace the flow of treatment interventions in three cases that have been introduced earlier in the book: the Machine Builder, the Unforgiven Teenager, and the Girl Who Danced in Blood. In addition, I describe how the cases were initially assessed and how and when the various objectives were implemented.

The Machine Builder

ASSESSMENT SUMMARY

Figure 10.3 shows the initial and follow-up assessment of the patient called the Machine Builder.

This brief case was treated in four sessions (one 3-hour evaluation and three subsequent 1-hour sessions). This female graduate student came to treatment with severe anxiety that made her seriously consider leaving her professional career before it began, because she did not believe she could speak in front of people for job interviews or for the completion of her degree. A crisis was coming, because she needed to do both in the coming month. This young woman was of German descent, with a loving but reserved father and a mother who was cool to her and favored her brother. Any show of emotion was looked down on by all. Her father had been raised to believe that women did not have the logical capacity to do math; however, when his daughter showed him her high math scores, he was pleasantly surprised. During the initial evaluation, she mentioned that she went into the field of structural engineering (the German word for this term translates to "machine builder") because of her father's pride in her mathematical ability. When she was 16, he was dying of cancer; toward the end, he refused to eat, probably to hasten his death. His grief-stricken daughter would go to the hospital and try to feed him, but he would refuse.

FIGURE 10.3
Assessment of the Machine Builder.

Presenting problems:	Six-month follow-up[a]
1) Speaking in public, severity rating- 13 (couldn't be worse)	4
2) Eating in public, severity rating- 13 (couldn't be worse)	3
Axis I: Social phobia, 5 items	Subthreshold, 3 items
Axis II: Avoidant, 6 items	Subthreshold, 3 items
Total Axis II items, 17	11
Axis III: None	None
Axis IV: 2—Minor stress	1
Axis V: 50	70
Core formulation:	
1) Unresolved grief (D) over father's death due to fear and shame (A) over showing feeling (I/F)	
2) Defensive anxiety (D) that blocked expression of assertion (I/F)	

[a]Gains were maintained and improved at 3-year follow-up, but difficulty occurred in the fourth year in a high-pressure job.

At the beginning of the 3-hour evaluation, I asked what problem she wanted help with. She appeared to be nervous; her voice was shaking and her lips quivering. I immediately addressed her nervousness.

FOCUS: ANXIETY ABOUT FEELINGS

THERAPIST: You seem nervous, but like you're trying to cover it up.

PATIENT: Just one scratch is all it takes to get me going. [*Beginning to cry*]

THERAPIST: But isn't this the place for that?

PATIENT: Well, I feel like feeling nervous is not okay. I wonder whether it is normal to be this emotional?

THERAPIST: So you insult yourself for feeling emotional?

PATIENT [*Laughs*]: Seems absurd, but it seems nothing I can do to stop it. I just work so hard so that no one will see it.

THERAPIST: It's a terrible burden to bear alone. Then there is no one to comfort you.

The talking continues like this until her anxieties about being emotional with me are a little less severe. But after another hour, the conflicts about emotionality reappear.

PATIENT: It's an illness to be emotional. It's overwhelming.
THERAPIST: What is the worst fear?
PATIENT: I have a fear of it all spilling over. Then I won't just cry about a single thing. I'll cry over everything. People won't understand. No one seems as sensitive as me.
THERAPIST: So it sounds like you keep arm's length with everyone.
PATIENT: It's not conscious. I don't want to.
THERAPIST: You say emotion is an illness. Have you ever thought that feeling could be calming?
PATIENT: I never thought of it that way. Maybe I could just change. Start from scratch, and say, "Who cares what other people think!" But [*pausing*] I worry, I don't know . . . that a *beast* is gonna come out or something.

Her anxiety about showing emotion was great. Concerning the core conflict pattern, there was anxiety and shame about showing any feelings interpersonally, which underlay her fear of public speaking. Specifically, there was anxiety about defending herself in a conflict situation (assertion), as well as pain blocking her ability to grieve her father's death. There was a third, and probably most central, core issue, which I did not sufficiently address and will discuss later; I will let the reader see if it becomes evident in the case material. Because of the importance of mourning ungrieved losses, I focused next on grief.

FOCUS: WARDED-OFF GRIEF OVER FATHER'S DEATH
Early in the session, this patient mentioned her father's death, but she insisted that she would never want to cry about it. When I confronted this statement, she agreed it would be important to discuss the death, but she still skipped away from the topic repeatedly for almost 2 hours. When I pointed this out, she again agreed to pursue the topic, but she had a great deal of difficulty doing so. For almost 20 minutes, she talked about the fact that she never wanted to say good-bye to her father.

PATIENT: No last good-bye . . . I hate good-byes.
THERAPIST: What would be so bad about saying good-bye?
PATIENT: I couldn't do it. It feels too final. [*Pausing*] I couldn't say good-bye to my uncle when he was dying.

She then explains that she avoided her uncle's house when he lay dying but that she hoped he knew she loved him, because he treated her with special affection.

THERAPIST: So if you could put into words to him . . .

PATIENT: I wouldn't have said good-bye.

THERAPIST: What's impossible about it?

PATIENT: Knowing that it would have been the last time.

THERAPIST: What's the worst part if you had faced it?

PATIENT: Helplessness. I'd feel so powerless. I'd pretend it wasn't happening.

THERAPIST: Can we look at this fact of life together?

PATIENT: Does that mean to just accept death as a part of life? No! It's parting from everything dear to you. Everything seems so meaningless, you touch a few people, in the meantime you just worry that . . .

THERAPIST: There's so much pain around your father's death.

PATIENT: A last good-bye seems like an execution.

THERAPIST: Well, let's look at it. How would it be?

PATIENT: I'd be the weak one . . . . [Crying]

THERAPIST: You'd be sobbing [patient nodding, crying] head down on the bed, gripping his arm.

I continued to present imagery because the patient cried harder following each phrase. Some patients respond like this; others do not. If the patient responds to interventions by moving away from the affect, the therapist needs to remain silent or encourage the patient to describe sad images.

PATIENT: I hope somebody's gonna miss me this much. I'm not so sure they would. I wouldn't want to die. . .

THERAPIST: You'd be crying . . .

PATIENT: I'd try to hold onto life. I'd be like a little kid . . .

At this point, I remembered that she had told me she had been hospitalized at age 6, far from her parents' home. She had been terrified and had nightmares involving soldiers coming in the nighttime to kill the children on the ward. Yet when her parents came to visit her, she never told them how terrified she was. She was repeatedly flooded with terror about death, with no one to help soothe it. This memory seemed tied in with her fears of facing death.

THERAPIST: Like in the hospital . . . with no one to hold onto tight. How much it'd mean to have someone there. [Pausing as the patient cries] If your father had known, would he have held you tight?

PATIENT [Nodding affirmatively and sobbing]

THERAPIST: How hard would you hold him with your little arms?

I used the words little arms because images of the small child had led to a tremendous outpouring of sobbing in other patients. In this case, however, there is only a slight deepening of feeling.

PATIENT: I would fight for my life! [Here I heard some anger at her father, who died sooner than was expected because he refused to eat.]

THERAPIST: You wanted him so much to fight! There's so much sorrow, but there's anger there too. What would you have wanted to say to him?

PATIENT [*With great intensity*]: Why, why does he have to die? Why does he . . . have to leave me?

THERAPIST [*Pausing, then quietly*]: And what would he say?

PATIENT [*With calmness coming over her*]: I guess he'd say . . . he's not gonna leave me.

THERAPIST: With his arms around you. [*Attempting to keep the imagery going*]

PATIENT [*Choked up still*]: I guess he is still here . . . with me . . .

By this time, I was so moved by the intensity of her feeling for her father that the following words spontaneously came out:

THERAPIST: He fills the room, doesn't he?

PATIENT [*Her head falls in her hands and she sobs deeply.*]

A short time passes, and she raises her head, still deep in reverie. I was also moved to tears, so that when she looked up I had a few tears that I could not hold back running down my cheeks. She did not mention them.

PATIENT: He was afraid to die.

THERAPIST: He might have needed to cry, too. Both of you needed to let those feelings pour out.

PATIENT [*With anger*]: You'd think people would know this! Why do they think it's better not to communicate?

FOCUS: SHARED AFFECT WITH THE THERAPIST

Following this segment of intense affect experiencing, an issue emerged that required a shift to self–other restructuring. The patient had said repeatedly during this session that she would feel foolish if she cried. Yet, as described in the example of attunement in chapter 9, I had tears rolling down my cheeks, so I addressed how she felt about my showing my feeling. Her response was positive, and she was able to resonate or "receive" the feeling I shared with her.

Forever after, her sense of others and her sense of herself were softened in regard to sharing of feelings. Although we had focused more on her father's death than on the speaking phobia, both issues dealt with the core psychodynamic issue: that she was intensely ashamed to show feelings. During the following summer, she became close to a woman friend for the first time and felt comfortable confiding in her; therefore, the skills generalized from the therapeutic relationship. After this session, she also began eating in the university cafeteria with friends, although she did not mention it for a couple of weeks.

During the next two sessions, she was helped to see that her social anxiety (fear of public speaking) was in part due to her projection onto others that they would make fun of her or ridicule her. The therapist pointed out this pattern and demonstrated that she anticipated ridicule before anything had been said or done. We began with imagery of her speaking in front of groups. Even the imagery caused her to begin trembling.

When I pointed out that she was projecting onto others that they would criticize her before they actually did so, she saw that this was unreasonable. Her basic trust in people was strong enough to allow her to let go of some of these projections fairly rapidly, enabling her to speak in public with less anxiety. She was exhilarated by the freedom she felt, but her problems were not completely resolved. The issue came up again several times, as in the following example:

PATIENT: I feel like they'll judge me and think me stupid.
THERAPIST: Can you see how that thought makes you miserable? You really get hurt.
PATIENT: It's awful.
THERAPIST: Look at the pain you've gone through. [*Pointing out the negative consequences of the defenses*]
PATIENT: I need to stop doing that.

This realization, although motivating, was not sufficient to stop an entrenched defensive pattern. She also needed the ability to protect herself and to assert her wants and needs (affect restructuring), and she needed to feel that she was a person worthy of doing so (self–other restructuring).

Sessions 2 and 3 also focused on anger as a way to defend herself. The anger that emerged in the previous session had brought up a memory of being raped by a previous boyfriend who had come to her apartment, drunk. Because she knew him, she let him in, but then he forcefully raped her. She did not cry out and hated herself for not doing so. After a great deal of resistance, which I repeatedly pointed out and attempted to move her past, she finally began to experience some anger. But throughout this time, she was weepy and beaten down: much more scared than angry. At this point, there was a shift.

FOCUS: ANGER IN REACTION TO A RAPE
THERAPIST: How would you have wanted to be screaming for help?
PATIENT: I'd be fighting, trying to get away, kicking him, hitting. Fury! [*Gaining energy*]
THERAPIST: Where would you hit him?
PATIENT: Wherever I could. I'd kick him in the balls. [*Pausing*] This is the uncomfortable part. I want to push these feelings far away.
THERAPIST: Try not to do that. See if you can stay with it. When you think that he's in pain, what impulse do you feel when you think of that?
PATIENT [*Gaining strength*]: I *am* more aware of my body [*she straightens up in her seat*], in my heart and soul, it's stronger . . . he's bent over, he calls for help.
THERAPIST: What do you do then?
PATIENT: I'll kick again, scream loud. I'd just try . . . [*She is breathing heavily at this point.*] Punching, grab an object, baseball bat, beating him.

THERAPIST: All that energy flowing . . .

PATIENT: I feel a flush of adrenaline. He's being helpless, and I'm, *I'm* in charge now. [*With some degree of surprise*] I *can* take control.

THERAPIST: Now you have power, and he's quivering on the floor. What does that make you want to do?

PATIENT: I'd beat him until there was . . . nothing coming back.

THERAPIST: What damage is the bat doing?

PATIENT: It's hurting him badly. [*Hesitant; this is where a new level of resistance is emerging. Murderous impulses are close to the surface, and she is frightened and ashamed of them.*] I'm wondering, it's a sense of reality. I know this is just an emotional analogy. Could I go on . . . ?

THERAPIST: Well, in reality, you could be kicking and screaming, but in your feeling life, what is the honest response to a rapist?

I emphasize to her, as I do during all such imagery, the distinction between fantasy and reality. I am intentionally pulling for the murderous impulses, but with action well contained. Who, having been raped, would not have a natural desire to kill the rapist? This is an attempt to have her make peace with those feelings.

PATIENT: To kill him is not as far as I'd want to go. I have trouble with the reality. How can I emotionally kill someone?

THERAPIST: Well, let's see how your body feels.

PATIENT: Like I'm in control. [*Reflecting on that for a moment*] I could *do* that. I *could* help myself. I could *help* myself!

THERAPIST: You seem to be feeling so strongly that no one could hurt you.

PATIENT: It's so amazing. It seems to be there! Maybe I *can* be strong for myself. But I also feel nervous, anxious, like I discovered something I'm not supposed to discover. Like I got caught with my hand in the cookie jar.

THERAPIST: Sounds like it feels good but scary. What would be your father's reaction? [*I am intentionally pulling for supportive figures, as her anxiety builds.*]

PATIENT [*Startled*]: You mean if he walked in and saw me with the baseball bat?

THERAPIST: What would you want him to feel?

PATIENT [*Reflecting on this, a slow smile comes to her face*]: Proud! I know he would be proud that I could protect myself. Amazing. [*Pausing thoughtfully*] Everyone wants me to fight, and yet I don't do it.

THERAPIST: That's important to hold on to.

PATIENT: There's a *beast* in me. I'm gonna be able to do it. There's a beast inside like a dog. Now I know why people have those big dogs, to get it onto people. A sense of security.

After the fourth session, the Machine Builder was able to give a talk to her class and with exhilaration. At intake she had rated the anxiety about speaking at 13 (couldn't be worse) and after four sessions, it dropped to 1.5

(almost not a problem). The brief treatment got her over her crisis, and she no longer wanted to drop out of school. She also developed a friendship with a woman for the first time. A few months later, however, she was feeling that some of the anxiety was returning. She began to devalue her accomplishment and said that she probably was able to give the talk because her boyfriend helped her. In fact, her boyfriend was not with her the day of the talk.

CHARACTER CHANGES

At 6-month follow-up, the Machine Builder no longer exhibited two of the five behaviors that made up the criteria for avoidant personality. Over the summer, she went to all the parties she was invited to and surprised herself by comfortably looking people in the eyes and chatting. She even felt comfortable eating at parties and continued eating in the college cafeteria.

Unfortunately, this patient was moving away and not able to continue therapy for maintenance sessions for anxiety, or for the predominant issue that was not mentioned in the first session: her mother's neglect. (Her mother used to sit quietly with her hands folded while the patient's cousins teased and derided her, and she had openly favored her older brother.) The death of her father left the Machine Builder emotionally alone, feeling unprotected. Only long-term follow-up will be able to assess the impact of therapy on her Axis II personality disorder, but her behavior over the summer suggested that some of that work had begun. Unfortunately, a breakup with her boyfriend caused a setback in the fall, but she reported that she still maintained some of the changes. In this case, four sessions seemed insufficient to effect deep character change. My hypothesis is that more work (possibly 20 or 30 sessions) would have helped her to work through her issues of feeling abandoned and unprotected. I strongly recommended that she get further therapy for that purpose.

After graduation, she took a job in Europe. I lost contact with her for several years and was quite concerned because of the severity of her symptoms and the brevity of the treatment. I was concerned about relapse and was going to offer her free treatment if she returned to the area. When I finally located her 3 years later, she was doing remarkably well, although she did not express it quite that way. She was pleasant and excited to speak with me and quite happy to tell me she was engaged to be married, that she and her fiancé were returning to the States, and that they had accepted jobs.

FOLLOW-UP

THERAPIST: How are you doing with speaking in public?

PATIENT: Oh, not so great. I haven't really been challenged this year. I did interview for jobs in the States though.

THERAPIST: How did you do in the interviews?

PATIENT: Fine. I didn't have a problem.

THERAPIST: No anxiety?

PATIENT [*Pausing*]: No . . . I did okay, and I got the job!

THERAPIST: Well, it sounds like that was a challenge, the interviewing.

PATIENT: No, not so much. But this new company makes you give an oral presentation of your work every 2 months. So I will be challenged, and I'm worried about that. [*This is important, because I had emphasized to her that she would need to speak publicly quite a bit to get over her phobia about it.*]

THERAPIST: How about eating in public—how are you doing?

PATIENT: I don't know. Okay, I guess. The first month on my new job I didn't know anybody, and I didn't eat with them. But after a month or so I went to lunch with the group every day. It was no problem. We had a good time.

THERAPIST: You know we had such a few sessions—only four. Do you think that therapy had an impact on these problems?

PATIENT [*Reflecting for a moment*]: Yes, I do, definitely. I am more able to defend myself, and I'm not scared to show feelings . . . so that was a big help.

Considering the issue of transcendence, at this 3-year follow-up I asked her about the "beast" she had discovered in herself. She replied, "Oh, I no longer think of it as a beast. I feel it is personal strength and confidence." She was still burdened by anticipatory anxiety, however, although it no longer prevented her from functioning as it once had. I was pleased that the four sessions appeared to have given her enough emotional access to do well on interviews, eat with friends, and begin her professional life.

Earlier, I mentioned another core issue that had not been addressed sufficiently in the brief treatment of the Machine Builder. My hypothesis was that she needed to grieve the neglectful relationship with her mother, with the goal of building *a compassionate stance for herself and desire for self-care* to replace the *defensive and self-attacking anxiety*. She felt unable to protect herself in certain situations because she symbolically responded to herself as her mother had. She left herself unprotected because she had been left unprotected by her mother, who never came to her aid when she was attacked, and her father, who was more supportive but had died. Her inner representation of herself was that of a vulnerable and unprotected child, not the competent adult that she was. Indeed, she had described several dramatic examples in which she was able to stand up courageously for *others* who were being criticized. Clearly, she had assertive and protective skills in her behavioral repertoire but did not apply them to herself or on her own behalf.

At the 4-year follow-up, the anxiety returned. In contrast to the less pressured job in Europe, the American firm was high-pressured, competitive, and wanted their employees to show confidence at all times. She felt overwhelmed by their demands and returned to treatment for management of her anxiety. If I had understood the case as thoroughly as I do now (after dozens of times reviewing the tapes), I might have started from the beginning with the issue of being "left unprotected." Although I feel proud of the four sessions I provided and the effects that freed up her functioning, I realize that I might have been able to touch an even deeper level of her experience in those four sessions and provided her more freedom from anxiety. This is the constant challenge of short-term therapy: It is not merely a superficial way to "do it faster," but a challenge to strive to work as *intensively* and as *on the mark* as possible, as soon as possible. I had confronted her *anger* at her mother's neglect, and she had defended strongly against that. Had I focused on her *sorrow* about the mother's neglect and her longing for care and protection, however, it might have generated in her a deeper sense of her own losses and thus a greater capacity to care for herself.

The Unforgiven Teenager
ASSESSMENT SUMMARY

Figure 10.4 shows the initial and follow-up assessment of the patient called the Unforgiven Teenager.

FIGURE 10.4
Assessment of the Unforgiven Teenager.

Presenting problems:	*Six-month follow-up[a]*
1) Hurt and hostility toward parents- 11 (severe)	6
2) Shame and guilt- 11 (severe)	3
3) Poor self-esteem- 12 (almost couldn't be worse)	3
Axis I: Major depressive disorder, 7 items, 3 weeks' duration	2 items
Past alcohol abuse; sober for 3 years	
Axis II: Paranoid, 4 items (mild, but definitely met criteria)	Subthreshold, 3 items
Self-defeating, 9 items (severe)	Subthreshold, 4 items
Total Axis II items, 39	24 items
Axis III: None	
Axis IV: 2—Minor stress	1
Axis V: 50 (impairment moderate; few friends but fair	68
occupational functioning)	
Core formulation:	

1) Self-defeating/self-abusive or "masochistic behaviors" (D) due to shame (A) blocking self-acceptance or positive affect attached to self (I/F) or self-compassion
2) Isolation (D) to avoid closeness (I/F) due to shame and pain (A)
3) Passivity (D) in place of assertion (I/F) due to fear and shame (A)

[a]Gains were maintained at 3-year follow-up, with intermittent difficulty.

As described in chapter 1, this 34-year-old businesswoman came to treatment following a crisis in which she drank excessively and caused a scene. This woman felt such a degree of self-hate that she imagined God hating her and punishing her. Yet her presenting problem concerned the hurt and anger that she felt in relation to her parents. She met more than the minimum criteria for major depressive disorder, and the duration of symptoms had been 3 weeks. She strongly resisted the idea of taking antidepressant medication, but I told her that if her functioning became impaired, I would ask her to reconsider.

In the initial evaluation, I was unsuccessful in my attempt to confront defenses concerning anger. She only felt worse and blamed herself more, reflecting a pattern I have seen many times in patients with masochistic defenses. A rule of thumb is that I do not push for anger in such people until there is sufficient self-compassion to bear the intense force of their negative feelings. The first 9–10 sessions of treatment focused exclusively on her masochistic, paranoid defenses and her extremely poor sense of self, particularly in relation to the therapist and to God. She was a deeply religious woman, and her relation to her God was crucial to her cure.[5]

FOCUS: GRIEF AND CHANGING PERSPECTIVES

PATIENT: The pain won't go away. [*Points to chest*] Why can't I get rid of it? [*Choked up*]

THERAPIST: Let's look at it together.

PATIENT: It's not being loved by my parents. The thought of no one hugging me as a child really bothers me. I've never been hugged or loved in my life.

The real story was even more poignant. She broke her arm when she was 5 years old, and she did not tell her parents for 2 days because she was terrified that she would be punished. She just lay around holding her arm close to her body. It is hard to imagine how a 5-year-old child could be sufficiently trained to be afraid to show that degree of pain as well as how a parent could fail to notice.

PATIENT: I cried really hard this week when I was alone. I saw my parents in church, and they were so cold. I started crying right there in church, and they were sitting next to me, and they ignored me. But I feel guilty over never wanting to see them again. I blame myself. I must have done bad.

THERAPIST: You must have longed to be held.

PATIENT: They held onto themselves. I feel so guilty . . . I must have been really bad. [*She is weepy while speaking but holding back a great deal.*]

THERAPIST: What would some parents have done?

PATIENT: Put their arms around me? [*She asked this in a questioning voice.*]

THERAPIST: So who should feel guilty? [*This is too strongly stated, no doubt, because I was deeply disturbed by her stories. It would have been better to say, "Who is responsible for their not putting their arms around you—you or them?" [Therapists need not blame anyone but should assign responsibility for behavior.]*]

PATIENT: Why is it so difficult for them to care about me? I feel so undeserving.

THERAPIST: Well, from what you've told me, your parents have been critical of you all your life, and now you seem to automatically criticize yourself, too.

PATIENT: But I don't ask for help. I don't want to be rejected . . . it's too painful to be rejected. I hold it in.

THERAPIST: So you tend to push people away, and it's a cold and lonely exis-

---

[5]My colleagues and I have often speculated where to put the concept of God on the Triangle of Person. I think we might create a pyramid from this triangle and place God, spirituality, and the I–Thou relationship to the universal other at the apex.

tence that follows. So who else might feel bad in this situation? [*I am intentionally confronting her with a different perspective of others from the one she had held before.*]

PATIENT: My parents, I guess. [*The hesitance in her voice is a signal that she is not entirely with me.*]

THERAPIST: Can you see that?

PATIENT: Yes and no. It's hard to see it.

Her response elicits determination in me to shift her perspective. I feel stumped at first, because her self-blame is so severe, but then I try again to encourage her to view this scene from another perspective—to give her some intellectual distance on it.

THERAPIST: If you were sitting in the congregation and looking at this scene, a mother and father sitting in a church pew on either side of their daughter, who had her head bowed and was crying softly, what would you feel if you were watching?

PATIENT: I'd feel, "What's wrong with her?"

THERAPIST: Well, you might *first* wonder what was bothering the daughter. But what would you think about the parents' ignoring her?

PATIENT: What's wrong with the parents? [*Again, she asks this uncertainly.*]

THERAPIST: Yeah, why are they ignoring her? [*She is still unmoved by this imagery, so I persist further.*] What do you see if you imagine the three of them walking out of church?

PATIENT: Them walking off together and me left alone. In fact, that's exactly what happened. They walked away, my mother holding my father's arm. They didn't say anything. They just walked away. [*She is visibly jolted by the image she is seeing.*]

THERAPIST: It's a tragic picture, isn't it.

PATIENT: How can they do that! How can they just walk away! [*She drops her head and sobs, only briefly, but fully.*]

This is the first breakthrough into a compassionate view of herself. This will not be sufficient to change her inner representation of herself or others, but it is the first step on the pathway. She had to work through scenes like this one again and again to shift the deeply entrenched self-blame that she carried.

THERAPIST: How do you think God would see you in this situation? [*Her belief was that God was punishing her for being an acting-out teenager. I knew that in order for her own sense of self to improve, she would need to acquire a sense of a compassionate deity.*]

PATIENT: It seems like He sees me as disgusting.

I had never been given supervision on how to handle such a problem. I struggled for words that would be respectful of her deep beliefs but nevertheless would change her perspective.

THERAPIST: It seems like you might not be giving God much credit. I mean, maybe you're not giving God the credit he deserves for being understanding and forgiving.

PATIENT: I know, I probably should, but it's so hard for me to believe that I could be forgiven.

THERAPIST: It seems to me that God has forgiven you long ago, but that you do not let yourself feel that forgiveness.

Her sense of self did not change at that moment, but I came back to this issue dozens of times over eight to ten sessions. We spoke often of God's view of her. I encouraged her to talk to her priest and to consider (be more receptive to) the concept of forgiveness. I paired this intervention with much repetition of *her view* of *my feelings toward her*: Did I blame her, or did I see her in a compassionate way? Slowly over weeks, her sense of herself began to shift with the shift in how I felt toward her. My feelings were not directly stated, but she was Socratically questioned until she could sense compassion from me within her.

The Unforgiven Teenager learned to stop behaving destructively toward herself. She also learned to stop others from taking advantage of her. This happened through the experience of the caring relationship with the therapist. At first, she could not tolerate the therapist's warmth and concern, but with repeated focus on us, she began to metabolize the experience; that is, the positive feelings became strongly felt. When she was alone, she began to respond to herself with self-care, concern, and compassion (more like the therapist did), rather than the way she had been treated by her early-life caretakers.

Her major depressive disorder was no longer present by Session 10, and she reported that the first 9 sessions reduced her lifelong self-hate and masochism by 30%. Her problem with self-esteem was rated 6 (a moderate problem). Five months later (with five monthly maintenance sessions), she reported that her self-hate was almost entirely gone, and she rated her problem with self-esteem at 3 (only a little problem), down from 13 (couldn't be worse). Her paranoid behaviors had lessened so that she no longer met criteria for the Axis II paranoid diagnosis. She now felt likable, and she had friends for the first time in her life. She noted, however, that she did not feel that she had dealt with the intense feelings about her father, nor about her capacity for intimacy with a man. She felt that if she became involved with anyone, she would sabotage the relationship, as she had done so many times before. At 1-year follow-up, her depression had not returned. Two years later, she had not only maintained her growth but improved on these gains.

She returned to therapy the following year (for the batch of 20 sessions) to work on her enmeshed relationship with her abusive father and her problems with never having had a sustained, intimate relationship with a man. In these sessions, she made significant steps toward the difficult emotional separation from her father, but a job transfer to another city interrupted treatment. She continued therapy there with a highly experienced therapist.

The Girl Who Danced in Blood
ASSESSMENT SUMMARY

Figure 10.5 shows the initial and follow-up assessment of the patient called the Girl Who Danced in Blood.

FIGURE 10.5
Assessment of the Girl Who Danced in Blood.

Presenting problems:	*Six-month follow-up*[a]
1) Problems with boyfriend- 13 (couldn't be worse)	1 (absent)
Axis I: Major depressive disorder	Absent
Axis II: Histrionic, 5 items	Subthreshold, 2 items
Dependent, 5 items	Subthreshold, 2 items
Borderline, 3 items	Subthreshold, 1 item
Total Axis II items, 17	7 items
Axis III: None	None
Axis IV: 3—Moderate stress (breakup with boyfriend)	1
Axis V: 40 (suicidal gesture, some impulsivity but able to work and go to school)	80

Core formulation:

1) Suicidality or regressive fights (D) resulting from blocked assertion (I/F) due to shame from showing needs (A)
2) Competitiveness and guardedness (D) blocked closeness (I/F) due to shame and pain (A) of vulnerability

[a]Gains were maintained and improved at 6-year follow-up.

This college student had made a suicidal gesture (pouring out pills in her hand and then blacking out from anxiety) owing to the breakup with a boyfriend. During the first five sessions, she came to see that her suicidal feelings were linked to anger at her boyfriend that she turned on herself (i.e., I'm no good; I'm not worth anything), and she gained more control. She learned that she sought dependency on her boyfriend to bolster her self-esteem because she could not bear to be alone (i.e., to soothe, comfort, or care for herself). In the next 10 sessions, she saw that her poor self-esteem came from her loving, but sometimes downright sadistic and demanding alcoholic father, whom she loved and admired, nonetheless. Becoming aware that she treated herself like her father treated her (harshly and judgmentally) resulted in a strong wish to discontinue doing so. The suicidal feelings ceased after a few sessions and have not returned.

Initial change in character patterns began with her setting firmer limits on how her boyfriend could treat her, which was followed by an improvement in the relationship. She realized that she responded deferentially to him as she had done with her father, no matter how badly he treated her. After 15 sessions she said, "I'm learning a whole new personality. My friends tell me I'm completely different." But the work was only half done.

The more difficult part of the character change involved the full emotional separation from her parents. Sessions 20 through 30 focused on facing these difficult anger- and grief-laden feelings, which she had avoided all her life. She first sorted out the feelings toward her mother, and after some long talks, they became closer than they ever had been. Her father was much more difficult, but eventually she was able to face the depth of her rage toward him, as well as her love. Following this, she was able to respond to him in a much more forthright way. He responded well in return, so that they also were able to build a much better relationship.

At 5-year follow-up, she had just married. She was able to maintain her gains and continue growth without further treatment. Her mother wrote to me that she was "remarkably changed, so unlike how she was before—she is consistently happy, well-adjusted, and with a relationship to a wonderful young man." The following excerpts demonstrate the way the treatment was conducted.

At Session 19, she came in saying that she had been feeling increasingly angry at her father as she remembered some of the sadistic ways he had treated her. But she was uncomfortable about these feelings, and she had been having a lot of headaches. She had a headache when she arrived for this session, and I knew I needed to help her to be less afraid to feel angry to decrease the turmoil that was raging within her. As I encouraged her to talk about her feelings, however, she became silent, as was typical for her.

FOCUS: ANGRY FEELINGS

THERAPIST: Can you see that you are avoiding facing the feelings toward your father with your silence?

PATIENT: Mm hm.

THERAPIST: So you shut it all off and hold it in yourself. And haven't you done that all your life?

PATIENT: Yeah.

THERAPIST: And you as a child had to be very obedient to him.

PATIENT: Mm hm.

THERAPIST: So you see, it's a trained response. And anything you would have liked to do, you suppress, like you said you really would like to spring it at your father, actually. So can you follow through with it in fantasy?

PATIENT: Mm hm, yeah. [*But hesitant*]

THERAPIST: What is the worst part of facing your father?

PATIENT [*After some silence*]: The first thing that comes to me is that he'll say he's sorry. [*She becomes teary.*] And if he says he's sorry, then I won't be able to get mad. And that's so frustrating. There's all this . . . all this rage in me. I want him to know what it is!

THERAPIST: So let's go to it. Let's you and I look at the force of that rage. [*Until now, she has been cowering in her seat, but at this point she sits up.*]

PATIENT: Well, I know what it was, it was [*pausing*] . . . it was a lot of anger.

THERAPIST: What was the most angry part again? How does it feel inside you?

PATIENT [*Sniffs*]: Like something coming out. It's pathetic. Like I'm gonna explode.

THERAPIST: So let's see, let it explode here in therapy where it's safe [*anxiety regulation*] since you have had a lifetime of wanting to explode.

When confronting anger, the therapist needs to help the patient use words consciously to label the feelings and identify the physiological expression of anger: What does the body feel like? This tremendously controlled young woman keeps her turmoil inside and then gets so upset that she wants to kill herself. So after putting her in touch with the words and inner sensations, I offer her a harmless pathway: directing the angry and violent images into fantasy. I ask her what she would imagine herself doing to her father. But as I push her to look at the feelings, she regresses and becomes increasingly weepy.

PATIENT [*Weepily*]: All I do is I feel the tip of it. I would just start crying with him. [*The defensive weepiness is part of the aggression turned on herself, or the frustration that she cannot express. Yet she had just sat up and said she wanted to explode.*]
THERAPIST: Because you've always cried in these situations, now you don't have the habit to do it differently. [*Validating the defense*] Let's see if I can help you can push through that weepiness and experience your anger. [*Encouragement*]
PATIENT [*Crying*]: I don't want to. [*More regression*]
THERAPIST: You know, looking at these feelings in here does not mean you have to confront him. [*Anxiety regulation of the feelings before overt behavior is attempted*]
PATIENT: No [*sniffing*], but the feelings are hard.
THERAPIST: Maybe you're protecting your father? [Pause] Is that it?
PATIENT: I don't know, I, it's... [*Clears throat, pauses, crying*] I can't even imagine myself doing it. [*If imagining anger is impossible, then well-thought-out assertive behavior is greatly inhibited if not impossible.*]
THERAPIST: So let's try. [*I continue to encourage her to face the images.*]
PATIENT [*Sobbing*]: I can't do it!
THERAPIST: Yeah, uh huh. It's still blocked in you. Isn't this tragic? [*The costs of the defenses*] He taught you to shut your feelings up so effectively, didn't he? [*Patient is crying throughout*] And now you're defending against the anger at him, and I can't help you without your participation. [*The origin versus the maintenance of the defenses*]
PATIENT: Like I can't, I think it's, I can picture myself feeling it, but I don't feel it!
THERAPIST: Well, that's all right. Let's just go with the picture that comes to your mind, because that might make it easier to pull out the feelings later.

This is a graded, anxiety-regulating intervention, starting with thoughts and working toward feelings. In behavior therapy, this would be called "shaping," or reinforcing successive approximations to the desired behavior. I held the focus on anger, particularly because she got severe headaches when she felt mad but was unable to express her anger. I felt determined to continue if she was able to. I thought she was quite close to the angry feelings and just needed strong encouragement and holding of the focus to get to them. As it happened, it worked.

THERAPIST: Can you see yourself with your father? Can you just imagine what you would do?

PATIENT [*She shook her head as though an image came to mind*]: It seems like I was kind of like flying at him. It's like . . . [*Sighs, pauses, begins to cry; her face is contorted.*]

THERAPIST: What's the pain there? Let's not sink down into it! You . . . you see how you sink back into it? *Who is getting the beating now?* [*I say this with much feeling and emphasis, because she is clearly in so much pain. This is active therapeutic involvement.*]

PATIENT [*Pausing, sniffing*]: I am.

THERAPIST: Let's focus it off of you! [*Pause*] What happens when you fly at him? [*Again, I am not suggesting that she act out these feelings but that she portray them in fantasy.*]

PATIENT [*Sniffing, sighing*]: Well, it's silly, but I just, it's like I'm well, I don't know, airborne. It's just kind of like, I attack his face.

THERAPIST: Let's go with that. You want to attack his face. So let's think what you do with that attack. You'd really tear into him, wouldn't you? Because these feelings are very intense in you. So what do you see yourself doing?

PATIENT: I see myself ripping out his hair and hitting him in the face, and. . . [*She cringes and becomes silent.*]

THERAPIST: And now you're beating up on yourself again. What's the thought that's hurting you?

PATIENT [*Sighing*]: Well, I don't know. [*Sighs, cries a little, pauses*]

Often during her sessions, she would withdraw and become silent. Repeatedly, I had to point out, "When you shut me out, I can't help you. I don't know what's going on inside of you when you're closed like this." Clearly, she had learned to suffer alone, in silence.

The level of affect at this point is probably low-moderate. In contrast, the defenses are present to a greater degree: high-moderate. I am dragging the impulses through fairly strong defenses, therefore, something my colleagues and I generally try not to do. Optimally, we work with the defenses and anxieties until they are sufficiently reduced to permit affective flow. In this case, however, the young woman is suffering on a daily basis, from headaches. She has already said, in Session 15, "I'm learning a whole new personality." She was feeling better. Standing up to her boyfriend made her more ready to stand up to her father, but the idea of that was causing a lot of inner conflict, resulting in headaches. I felt it was time to push her through. I saw this as a phobic avoidance of anger and tried to expose her to it, to desensitize her reaction to it.

THERAPIST: What makes you hold back from speaking?

PATIENT: I don't know.

THERAPIST: It may be a way you control this interaction right here. I think by not sharing the images with me, then it's hard for me to know what you feel. And . . . you know, if you don't share it with me, I can't help you, you see? And then you slide back into the misery you've carried so long. Your head hurts. You feel tormented. So let's not do that. [*This is strong encouragement: offering support and pointing out consequences.*] Can we go back . . . to the image of lunging at him?

I present the image again, to bring her back to the scene as soon as possible. At this point, she works more collaboratively with me. When I watched the videotapes, all in a row, it was interesting to note that right before several breakthroughs to feeling, I had just said words to this effect: "You're blocking something here with me; can we look at that?" I described the withdrawal in two or three sentences and said, "Can we go to the feeling?" This intervention helped her, several times, to deepen the feelings.

PATIENT: He's screaming; I can see him screaming.
THERAPIST: How does it feel, to see your father screaming in pain? Like *you've* felt all these years.
PATIENT: There's more I want to do.
THERAPIST: So what do you want to do more?
PATIENT: I just keep doing it. I mean I'm, like I'm pulling him apart! [*Softly cries*]
THERAPIST: Oh, and . . . so there's a desire to pull him apart? [*She was clearly in upheaval and deeply thinking and sighing heavily.*] Let's keep on with that. [*I present images to help her continue.*] Is he laying down, are you over him?
PATIENT: Mm hm. [*Sniffing*]
THERAPIST: What else comes to mind? I notice you're still just sitting there with fists . . . [*Her hands were tightly clenched in fists.*]
PATIENT: I was just jumping up and down on him. How did I do that? How did I . . . ? [*She is shocked by the images that are now spontaneously coming to her mind.*]
THERAPIST: What comes to mind, let's see? You could be protecting him if you pull away.

She had said the week before, "I get these violent pictures in my head now, and I don't know how that happens. I want to throw a sofa at somebody." Although she wants to explode, she is also so resistant to it that she is weeping and becoming silent.

THERAPIST: You're pulling away from these images now. Could we go back? You're jumping up and down on his body. Where on his body are you jumping, where do you want to hurt him? [*I ask such questions because it is often the spot on the body where the patient was hurt that he or she wants to inflict the hurt.*]
PATIENT [*Silence*]
THERAPIST [*Pause*]: Are you pulling away from me now?

PATIENT: No, just thinking. In a way it wasn't me jumping on his body at that point. I mean, it was just like the ground became a pool of blood there, and him, but I was jumping up and down. And so I'm trying to figure how I can do that! How do I think these things!

THERAPIST: So you've taken him out of the scene. And you're alone again with the blood?

PATIENT: He's there, but. . . Oh, he's there. It's like warm, this pool of blood, and that's where his head is and, I'm, that's where I am!

THERAPIST: Okay. You're standing in this pool of blood that's his head. How does it feel, standing in that pool of blood?

PATIENT [*Pausing, but sitting up and looking less traumatized*]: I'm . . . like I'm dancing in it!

THERAPIST: Are you in as much pain as you were a few minutes ago?

PATIENT [*Looking surprised*]: No.

THERAPIST: Okay. So let's see, is there some pressure there? Is there some relief that you can find? [*I always try to find the relief in the experience of the feelings. If there is anguish or torment following such images, there is self-attack still occurring that must be lessened. There is often grief that follows angry images, because there is typically love along with the hate, but grief in its adaptive form is also relieving.*]

PATIENT: That's what it feels like. I, just, I feel like I just *jumped through something.*

THERAPIST: Okay. So is there anything else you want to jump through? Anything left? Any impulse toward your father? [*I often ask this, because patients so often want to get away from the aversive imagery.*]

PATIENT: To push him away. Or kick him away.

THERAPIST: Hm. Does that feel good to kick him? [*Again, this is fantasy, not reality; the suffering that the patient has gone through for years is about to be stopped.*]

PATIENT: Yeah.

THERAPIST: So how much do you want to keep kicking him? [*As I go on and on, she gets exhilarated.*]

PATIENT: I feel free, like I'm kicking the blood around. I'm . . . How do I do this! I'm dancing in it! [*Silence*] And then I just sit down in it!

THERAPIST: How does that feel?

PATIENT: It feels good, warm. I just put my hands out on either side. [*She makes swirling motions with her outstretched hands.*]

I wish now that I had explored this image more, for I did not fully understand it. Unfortunately, the session had run over, and we had to stop. My sense at the time was that sitting in the blood was being triumphant, but also being close to him. She loved her father too, and if positive affect was coming up, it would have been important to integrate it with the negative feelings. Fortunately, she was able to do that on her own: Her relationship with her father became much more assertive but loving as well. And her headaches stopped after that session!

Such violent images can be important in this process: On an emotional level, she was able to get this oppressive force off her. When patients become less tormented by their hostile impulses, they feel more able to support and defend themselves. Shortly after this session, she felt the courage to speak with her father about how hard he had been on her. She was calm and reasonable in her presentation; nevertheless, her father's initial response was to go on a 3-day binge.[6] After he settled down, however, the patient kept talking with him and was quite assertive in asking for his help with several things. This made the father feel needed and useful, and their relationship improved enormously. Five years after this session, she has never again felt suicidal, her relationship with both parents is excellent, and she is happily married. For readers who are hesitant to employ intensely angry imagery in therapy, I ask you to consider the results. In this woman with good impulse control, the fantasized anger hurt no one. The unfantasized anger could have caused enormous personal torment or even suicide.

This is a case demonstrating character change, and this session was a pivotal one, because strong changes followed it. Another point worth noting is that the anger was dragged out from under a lot of defensive weepiness. The impulse seemed quite strong, however, and the results were dramatic. Defenses can be present, therefore, and the affect does not have to be totally experienced to set the person free.

FOCUS: EXTENDING TREATMENT WHEN FEAR OF VULNERABILITY IS AN ISSUE (THE GIRL WHO DANCED IN BLOOD)

Shortly after the previously described session on anger, the following interaction took place:

PATIENT: I felt that . . . I'm getting better to the point where I don't need to come in, I don't know . . . if . . . I still have stuff that I need to be working on. Maybe I'm afraid to stop? But there have been some very noticeable changes that I, I've noticed and my parents have noticed and my friends have noticed.
THERAPIST: Okay. Tell me about them.

She described several changes in patterns. In one case, she began to get depressed about being criticized by her boyfriend, but as she caught herself, she told him she wanted to spend the weekend alone rather than with him.

PATIENT: And I was really thinking about breaking up with him. But the idea didn't upset me as much as it had [*when she had thought of suicide*]. It *did* upset me, but I wasn't going off the deep end about it. And [*pause*] I needed to do something that says to him that what he's been doing is out of line, that I don't want to be treated that way. So I ended up telling him that I just didn't want to see him this weekend. And I wasn't angry when I said it. I just said that we were getting on each other's nerves and I needed time to myself.

---

[6]It is not uncommon for parents to be defensive at first, even when confronted gently and respectfully. This father's initial reaction was on the extreme end.

THERAPIST: Mm hm.

PATIENT: And I haven't really been upset about it! And I felt like I've got like a measure of control back. And I've been a little upset. But I keep surprising myself. I'll go a couple of hours . . . doing something or I'm in a class or I'm doing something, you know, *I'd forget that I'm supposed to be upset about him,* and I'll like [*sigh*] remember, "Oh yeah," and then, like I'm not upset! [*She used to get hysterical if she didn't spend each night with him, and now she's saying she's asking for time apart.*]

THERAPIST: Hmm. What do you think caused that? [*Assessing change mechanisms*]

My understanding was that because she could emotionally face the fantasied death of her father (the emotional separation, as well as the force of her rage toward him), this strength generalized to her relationship with Steve; however, she could not articulate that.

THERAPIST: Have you been talking to yourself about it, and. . . looking at the pros and cons?

PATIENT: Yeah, it's true, but I guess what struck me was that—not that I don't love him as much anymore—but I guess I don't *idealize* him as much anymore. And I have to say that when I'm mad, I'm *really* angry about things. I mean I'm very angry about specific things that he does and to the point where I don't want to see him when he does them anymore, instead of like last fall when he'd still do things just to get me angry but I'd take it. Now I won't see him when he treats me badly.

THERAPIST: Last year, the worse he treated you, the more you were longing for him.

PATIENT: Hm. [*Nodding*]

THERAPIST: But, you know, you've gone back and forth in your moods about whether were feeling better or whether you were in danger. [*She had felt that she was still in danger of becoming suicidal if they broke up.*] Last week I got the impression you still felt frightened.

PATIENT: Mm hm.

THERAPIST: And what shifted after last week?

PATIENT: This weekend, basically, I just decided that I don't want to be treated like that. I mean, I'm not certain that I'm not going to shift back. And I am still kind of worried about school ending, just not as frantic about it. [*When school ends, they have work commitments in distant cities.*]

THERAPIST: He's leaving a few weeks before you do. My strong suggestion would be, although you may be feeling very good between then and now, but just to stay in therapy each week and indulge yourself in sorting out all the things that you'll need to work on or that might come up after he leaves, after your supports are gone. Let the work we've done sink in deep. You haven't had to lean on anybody. And you're smart, and you're capable, and you could probably take the ball and run with it, from now on. Except that I would just say, well, why don't you learn to do a little more leaning?

This piece is not as eloquent as I might have liked, but it does represent the point I try to convey to patients who have been counterdependent, that is, afraid of being dependent on others. I encouraged her to stay in therapy 2 or 3 months longer, to accustom herself to being in a relationship in which she is the focus of the attention. I think this is the shortest term solution to the problem of counterdependency. We had had only 30 sessions at that point. (In total we had 44 sessions.)

THERAPIST: Does that make sense—to stay in therapy a little longer?
PATIENT: It does. It probably does, because my first thought was that I feel silly coming in for therapy when I, when I guess it looks to me that I might not need it.
THERAPIST: Hm, yeah. You still have that critical voice in you that, you know, you were intensely critical of yourself for feeling so needy just a few months ago.
PATIENT: Yeah, I know.

She is so ashamed of being vulnerable that the minute she has a decrease of symptoms and is feeling stable again, she wants to terminate. I am trying to make that reaction conscious.

FOCUS: ASSESSING CHANGES
THERAPIST: What do you think of the work we did that helps you get this distance from Steve? And do you think it was work we did, or has it been parallel things happening outside, or some combination? If you were to look back and review, what would you say?
PATIENT: I think it's stuff in therapy and I think it's stuff outside. The . . . what we worked on in here, I think, was the stuff about recognizing when I'm actually angry at somebody else instead of taking it out on *me*. Now I don't react [*the way she used to*]. Well, I mean I do, I guess, but I know what it is right away. Now when I, when something happens, or somebody says something mean, or I'll get into an argument and I'll get a sick feeling, I usually know then that I'm angry at somebody else and I'm just feeling it in myself, and I can try to direct it outside. I'm not always that great at it right away, but at least I know it a little bit, whereas before I would just sit there and feel sick.
THERAPIST: You used to go into the sick feeling and get lost in it.
PATIENT: Mm hm. Right.
THERAPIST: That's what led to the suicidal gesture.
PATIENT: Yeah. So that was a pretty big thing.
THERAPIST: Yes. Yes, and so now you see it. You're catching it. And, you know, these things are like emotional push-ups. The more you catch it and work on it, the stronger you become.
PATIENT: Yeah, I can see that happening.
THERAPIST: So, of the things that helped you change, one was recognizing the anger.

PATIENT: Oh, also just being able to come in and tell you situations and have you be able to point out to me that I am overreacting to some situations or that I am . . . overthinking things.

THERAPIST: Okay. So that one change is that you're able to catch your anger and when you're turning it on yourself. The other is catching yourself when you're overreacting, when there's not really that much to be mad at. Or what we so often had said came from some old memory. [*I repeat the reasons she gave for the change in behavior, making a verbal list of changes to make them conscious and remembered.*]

PATIENT: Yeah. Cuz that was the other thing that was helpful too, was being able to separate when I was angry at my *dad* and when I was angry at *Steve* and not getting all mixed up between the two. And even now I can see what I do. I overreact to something that can generally make me angry because it reminds me of something in the past.

THERAPIST: It's understandable, isn't it, that you would react like that? [*I now bring up something that she has not addressed.*] One thing that I felt was notable that we did in here . . . was that you began to learn to lean on somebody and let yourself ask for help.

PATIENT: Um. Yeah, that was a hard, that was a hard thing to get.

THERAPIST: Was that helpful to you?

PATIENT: It was helpful. And it's still going to be hard. [*Slight laugh*] I mean, I still do get a silly kind of feeling. I don't think that has ever gone away. You know, right now staying in therapy feels like I'm asking for something that I should be able to handle on my own and . . .

When I hear those words, I know the basic character structure of shame at being vulnerable is not completely resolved. This alerts me to two main foci—the feelings with the father and the shame over vulnerability—which are closely linked.

THERAPIST: So we can see the very important movement you've made and the pieces that are left.

PATIENT: Yeah.

THERAPIST: There is still that feeling that you should do it on your own, that you shouldn't have to need somebody, as though people really get through life without the care and support of others, or that it would be "silly."

I start work on anxiety reduction around vulnerability, which follows about 10 minutes of assessment of her changes. Before jumping back to the work on shame, however, I could have taken some time to talk about how much better she feels and what a pleasure it is to have these burdens off her. I sometimes do not slow down enough to relax and appreciate the changes.

FOCUS: SHAME CONCERNING DEPENDENCY

PATIENT: I guess because I feel like somebody's going to look at me and criticize me for not being able to handle whatever is going on. I mean . . . I'm very careful about who I talk to about anything that's bothering me or any problems because I don't want to be looked at as unstable or not being able to handle my own situation. That's very scary.

THERAPIST: It's scary to have people look at you and criticize you. How do you think *I* look at you?

PATIENT: I don't know. [*Slight smile*]

This response was amazing to me. I had been working in a highly empathic manner with her each week for months. Yet she did not recognize the feelings of compassion that I strongly felt.

THERAPIST: You haven't quite gotten away from the feeling that there might be criticism coming from me? [*Here is the need to shift into self–other restructuring.*]

PATIENT: I mean, just even now, I think that's silly, that there might be criticism, like what I'm going through is a kind of a silly thing.

THERAPIST: Oh. That I'd be looking down my nose at you? Or trivializing what you say?

PATIENT: Yeah.

THERAPIST: Is there anything I've done that would indicate that?

PATIENT: No. Which, I mean, makes me feel silly even bringing it up.

THERAPIST: But it's no shock to us, is it, that you might transfer that on to me and imagine me being critical of you? Because you had very strong learning growing up, didn't you, not to show a need? And that you were really condemned for it in a very humiliating way when you did. So right now it's understandably hard for you to believe that I don't think you're silly. [*Strong validation of the projection to reduce her shame*]

PATIENT: Yeah, I mean, it's such a strange thing because I can tell myself that you obviously don't think I'm silly because you're a professional and . . . you just wouldn't think that.

THERAPIST: Uh huh.

PATIENT: But on the other hand, I just can't wipe away that feeling of being stupid.

THERAPIST: Of course. We learn on different levels. Intellectually, you can understand this, but emotionally it's hard to feel.

Her position is a little ego-dystonic. Intellectually, she can appreciate that I might not be criticizing her, but emotionally the old pattern is still there. Affects are sluggish things to change.

PATIENT: I'm feeling like ridiculous right now, talking about it.

THERAPIST: Right. You were cringing just then. And blushing. Is it embarrassing to tell me this?

PATIENT: Yeah!

THERAPIST: Well, what's the most difficult part right now? [*At this point, I proceed with anxiety regulation around sharing feelings with me.*]

PATIENT [*Pause, little laugh*]: Hm. It's painful, it seems—I'm not really sure why. I guess . . .

THERAPIST: Let's see what comes up. [*She's opening, and she's embarrassed.*]

PATIENT: I don't know. This is . . . I feel like sometimes I should come in with the right questions or the right situations, and sometimes I have questions that I don't know if I should bring in.

And so it goes. The rest of the session focuses on her and me: how she feels and how she thinks I feel versus what I really seem to be feeling, and so on. During the next three sessions, we stayed on this focus of defensive patterns that avoid closeness because of shame. It was so painful to open up because her father had been so harsh.

FOCUS: GRIEF AND THE EMERGENCE OF PAST MEMORIES

A few sessions later, a memory emerges in which her father is screaming at her: *I had fallen down and cut my lip badly and was bleeding all over. I was so scared of all the blood. I was screaming. But he screamed louder, "Don't you scream like that until you're ready to die! Put a laugh on your face! Now." He was screaming louder and louder, "Laugh, do you hear me, laugh!" And I was sobbing, trying to put a laugh on my face.* [She is crying and choking it back as she tells this story, probably as she did back then.] *How could he be so mean! How could someone treat a child like that!* [Sobbing]

Here is a further emotional separation from her father's abuse. She is able to feel strong grief as well as compassion for the memory of herself as a child, a restructuring of the inner representation of herself. She is also able to voice a different form and level of anger at her father for his cruelty at that moment. In fact, he was quite tender with her at other times, which made his temper outbursts more painful.

Suddenly, I better understood her angry imagery earlier in treatment. The fact that it was her father's head that she wanted to attack makes more sense (his face was in her face, and he was screaming at her). The reversal of an assault reflects a pattern I have often seen when angry imagery emerges. What was done to the patient is fantasized being done in return. It was her face that was cut and bleeding as a child, and her father was screaming at her to laugh when she was bleeding. In her fantasized reaction, many years later, she attacked his face and drew his blood, probably expressing the feelings she was having at that traumatic moment, long ago, in reaction to him. Considering transcendence, although she danced in her father's blood in her fantasy, she used assertion to create a new and loving relationship with him.

SUMMARY

This chapter provides an overview of treatment: how it begins, how it ends, and the flow of sessions in the restructuring of defenses, affects, and attachments. The initial evaluation, the interweaving of the main objectives of treatment, and the termination procedures are described. Several case examples are provided to demonstrate the treatment process.

CHAPTER 11

Disorder-Specific Modifications of the Short-Term Anxiety-Regulating Model

RELATIONSHIP OF PATIENT-SPECIFIC FORMULATIONS
TO DISORDER-SPECIFIC FORMULATIONS

It has become increasingly popular in the field of psychotherapy to tailor treatment to diagnosis (e.g., differential therapeutics; Frances, Clarkin, & Perry, 1984). As I discussed in chapter 3, however, one needs to address both the symptom (DSM diagnosis) and the environmental source (the psychodynamic conflict) of the problem. My treatment model focuses on the *learned source of the symptoms*, which is a patient-specific psychodynamic conflict involving affective responses and people. An analogy to treating the symptoms would be treating acne symptomatically with astringent lotions, without an accompanying change in diet, or treating an infection with cold baths to reduce the fever, without medication for the infection.

If such a psychodynamic source-oriented approach had been easy to implement, the Freudian–Meyerian reaction-pattern DSM-II would not have been replaced by the disorder-oriented (often symptom-oriented) DSM-III, -III-R, and -IV. The problem is a thorny one. First, not all psychotherapy patients want a "change in diet," which would mean paying attention to intrapsychic conflicts. Second, as discussed in chapter 3, identifying the metaphorical and dynamically meaningful source of a symptom is a skill that has been difficult for therapists to master consistently. Finally, the DSM-III/DSM-IV models rightly emphasize the biological component of mental disorder, which was minimized by the more conflict-oriented DSM-II. Sometimes, reducing symptoms with medication (e.g., for hallucinations and mania) is more realistic, or treating panic with cognitive therapy is more efficient than attempting to go to the psychodynamic root of the problem, which may not be easy to identify or change. The biological specificity of the symptoms is as important as the formulation of conflict. We often can only alleviate the symptoms of a biological defect, but now, increasingly, there is the potential to "cure" conflict.

David Barlow (1993), writing from the vantage point of cognitive therapy, and Glen Gabbard (1994), writing from a psychodynamic viewpoint, have suggested complementary solutions to treatment of the disorders in DSM-IV. Barlow and his colleagues provide a comprehensive, data-based array of cognitive treatment interventions for many DSM-IV disorders (Barlow, 1993). The overlap between the work of Barlow and his colleagues and that of Gabbard offers an impressive state-of-the art compilation of cognitive approaches for Axis I psychological disorders. The overlap between Barlow's work and my integrative psychodynamic approach is in the area of amelioration of symptomatic distress: the active techniques to reduce maladaptive responses, as represented on the defense and anxiety poles of the Triangle of Conflict. My model incorporates many cognitive techniques, therefore, although it differs from the cognitive model in positing underlying conflict-laden affects, or "affect phobias," and extends cognitive and behavioral techniques (exposure, desensitization) not only to the regulation of the inhibitory affects (e.g., anxiety) but also to the treatment of the maladaptive avoidance of the *regulatory or pleasure-giving affects.*[1] The term r*egulatory affect* refers to the functioning of the impulse–feeling pole of the Triangle of Conflict, not just fear but the full *range of affective reactions:* anger, grief, tenderness, excitement, joy, and so on. *This holistic group of affects has been not been adequately addressed as a source of pathology by either traditional psychodynamic theory or cognitive theory.*

Gabbard (1994), in concert with such authors as Lorna Benjamin (1993a) and Nancy McWilliams (1994), has argued for the understanding of psychodynamic issues underlying each of the DSM-IV diagnoses and provided clear descriptions and research evidence of effective dynamic and interpersonal approaches. To read the work of Gabbard alongside that of Barlow, *disorder by disorder,*[2] helps to integrate a psychodynamic understanding of the major Axis I diagnostic groups with the power of cognitive therapy to effect symptomatic change in each of these diagnostic groups. Furthermore, the theories of these two authors overlap in a number of ways. This chapter endeavors to further that potential integration by offering a perspective that can encompass aspects of both.

It is beyond the scope of this chapter to go into great detail for each diag-

---

[1]Progressive cognitive therapists are also beginning to use exposure for desensitization of uncomfortable affects other than anxiety. Debra Hope, Ph.D., personal communication, 1996.

[2]Unfortunately, Barlow's text does not include treatment of Axis II disorders, except for Linehan's chapter on borderline personality disorder, presumably owing to lack of empirical support. For a cognitive perspective on treatment of personality disorders, the reader is referred to the work of Beck and Freeman (1990).

nosis; there are entire books devoted to this topic. Instead, my goal is to integrate *diagnostic-specific knowledge* into this short-term treatment approach and to view these diagnostic groups from an integrative psychodynamic perspective. Specific research in support of this short-term model is discussed in detail in chapter 12.

Table 11.1 presents the Axis I and Axis II categories for the patients who provided some of the chief clinical examples used throughout this book. The Unforgiven Teenager and the Ferryman met criteria for depressive disorders. The Machine Builder met criteria for social phobia. Each of these patients also met criteria for one or more Axis II diagnoses. These cases demonstrate quite different symptom pictures, but they reveal highly overlapping affective psychodynamic "sources" of the symptoms.

TABLE 11.1
**The Relationship of Diagnoses to Conflicted
Affective Reactions in Three Cases**

Case	*DSM diagnoses*	*Affects focused on in the major core dynamic formulations*
Machine Builder	Axis I: Social phobia Axis II: Avoidant	Grief, anger, closeness to therapist and others
Ferryman	Axis I: Dysthymia Axis II: Dependent	Anger, grief, sense of self-respect
Unforgiven Teenager	Axis I: Major depression Axis II: Paranoid, self-defeating, borderline features	Self-acceptance, closeness, anger

Whatever the symptom picture, I submit that resolution of conflicts about affect was more effective than symptom relief alone would have been. Problems with regulation of anger, grief, and the affects associated with attachment were predominant. Also prominent among patients are problems with interest, joy, and sexual desire. Of course, these patients were selected for short-term dynamic psychotherapy. For patients who do not desire conflict resolution, one may consider medication, cognitive therapy, or other approaches. As the patient-specific approach suggests, each patient is different.

The Ferryman was a 36-year-old man who had been depressed for 20 years until he was able to grieve his grandfather's death and thereby recover the memory of his grandfather's love. The Machine Builder's inability to grieve led not to depression but to anxiety in the form of social phobia. When she mourned her father's death in the therapist's presence, her anxiety dropped dramatically. Her anxiety dropped further when she was encouraged to become *angry* at the rapist and at people who criticized her.

In addition, both of these patients had Axis II pathology combined with their Axis I diagnoses. The Machine Builder's avoidant personality disorder was improved by helping her to become conscious of how she projected negative feelings onto others. The Ferryman's dependent personality disorder was improved by helping him see how much he asked others to validate his worth, when in fact his self-worth seemed far more helped by his remembering his grandfather's love. In these cases, the DSM diagnoses were not treated specifically. Rather, the focus was on the *presenting problems* that the patient wanted help with and the core psychodynamic pattern that emerged from the analysis of these problems. *Knowledge of the Axis I and II pathology (i.e., the symptomatic or defensive responding) helped guide the short-term treatment toward the specific defenses to be restructured, the affects needing to be experienced, and the necessity for alteration in representations of self and others.* For time-efficient therapy, the Meyerian and DSM-IV models must be integrated.

The Unforgiven Teenager had a more severe personality disorder. She met criteria for 39 (out of a total of 113) items on the SCID-II diagnostic interview, whereas the Machine Builder had only 17, and the Ferryman, 14. In addition to Axis I major depressive disorder, the Unforgiven Teenager met criteria for paranoid personality disorder, self-defeating personality disorder, and many other traits across a number of other categories. She also manifested three items diagnostic of borderline personality disorder.[3] After 10 sessions that focused on reduction of shame around her relationship to herself (self-care, self-compassion, relationships to others), her depression was no longer present, and she no longer met criteria for paranoid or self-defeating personality disorder. There was no mystery to this process. She learned, in the relationship with the therapist, to like herself and to feel compassion for herself; subsequently, she no longer believed that people were talking about her behind her back. She learned to be somewhat more assertive with her parents and people who mistreated her, and she therefore felt less vulnerable to and suspicious of others. The main "source" of her depression was her self-hatred, and when that was altered (by helping her feel accepted by God and by the therapist), her Axis I disorder resolved. It is also possible that the same results might have been achieved with the new antidepressant medications. There are many paths to the top of the mountain. The choice of the path was clear in this case, however; she refused medication.

The main point is that underlying these distinctly different DSM-IV disorders are similar, thwarted responses of the patients' basic motivational system. If one reviews the many cases in this book, which reflect a variety of diagnostic categories, one repeatedly sees problems with expression of grief, anger, feelings about attachment to self and others, and sexuality, excitement, and joy as well. The issue in short-term treatment is how, given the disorder at hand, to improve adaptive expression of affects.

---

[3]The borderline items identified for the Unforgiven Teenager were (a) not knowing who she was, (b) not knowing whom she wanted for friends or lovers, and (c) feeling bored or empty inside. She knew what her values were, and they were strong. Her impulse control, over the course of 1 year, was basically strong.

GENERAL MODIFICATIONS TO DEFENSE RESTRUCTURING WITH RESPECT TO DIAGNOSIS AND FUNCTIONING

The way defenses are pointed out and restructured must vary across Axis I and Axis II diagnoses and (as emphasized in chapter 2) with the patient's general level of functioning on the Global Assessment of Functioning Scale. The problem is that, as Table 11.1 illustrates, it is rare for patients to have a *single* Axis I or Axis II diagnosis or to have Axis II symptoms that fall entirely within a single disorder or even diagnostic cluster. Just as patients have relatives with many forms of polygenic psychiatric disorders, patients are a complicated blend of many symptoms. (Current research suggests that there is no single gene for schizophrenia, unipolar depression, alcoholism, or panic disorder.) It is as helpful to know the *total number of Axis II criteria*, therefore, as it is to know that a patient meets criteria for a distinct personality disorder. Each of the items on the Axis II questionnaire can be seen as representing a form of defensive behavior. The more Axis II criteria the patient meets, the greater the patient's defensive repertoire and the greater the need for self–other restructuring, defense restructuring, or both, before beginning affect restructuring. For this reason, it is useful for the therapist to have some assessment of Axis II disorders (well grounded in descriptions of behaviors) before the first session.

The degree of anxiety that is elicited by defense restructuring may be the best guide for how the therapist should proceed. If attempts at anxiety regulation are successful (i.e., the patient is calmer or more comfortable after discussing the fears with the therapist), the therapist can safely return to pointing out defenses and feelings. If attempts at anxiety regulation are not successful and the patient stays angry, flooded with anxiety, or feeling victimized, the therapist should consider moving to self–other restructuring, cognitive therapy, or supportive forms of treatment.

GENERAL MODIFICATIONS TO AFFECT RESTRUCTURING WITH RESPECT TO DIAGNOSIS AND FUNCTIONING

The modifications in this stage are highly dependent on patient level of functioning and the degree to which Axis II-based pathology interferes with interpersonal relatedness. For affect experiencing, the main difference across disorders is the degree of anxiety, guilt, shame, or pain associated with the underlying feeling. In general, the lower the level of functioning, the greater the degree of self-attacking (or other-attacking) responses. This relationship was demonstrated in the case of the Unforgiven Teenager, who had a high level of Axis II pathology. Her main presenting problem was anger at her father; unlike the Ferryman or the Machine Builder, however, when I tried to explore angry feelings, she immediately became self-attacking. (Anguish about herself as being "bad" was so strong that it threatened to disrupt her functioning.) This response led me to pull back and work on defense restructuring and self–other restructuring to build a more affirming sense of self. The more impaired the patient's general functioning, the less safe it is to uncover highly conflicted affects, unless there is a hospital or residential "holding environment" with highly trained individuals who can be with the person around the clock.

Modifications to affective experiencing can be highly patient-specific. For example, the alexythymic patient (see Sifneos, 1973), who lacks the capacity to image affect, is generally totally blocked in treatment at this point. Such patients need laborious work in building new inner representations of affective behavior. Sometimes, role-playing affective behaviors or watching others show emotions (in group therapy, for example) is helpful in awakening affect awareness. Obsessional patients (see example at the end of this chapter) need relentless focus on affect, whereas histrionic patients need a stronger focus on cognition and understanding.

GENERAL MODIFICATIONS TO SELF–OTHER RESTRUCTURING WITH RESPECT TO DIAGNOSIS AND FUNCTIONING

Of the three main objectives, self–other restructuring requires the least modification across different patients and diagnoses. Building receptive capacity and changing perspectives on self and others can be applied in a fairly similar fashion across patients, without concern for eliciting maladaptive responses. Such work, by its very nature, typically is experienced by the patient as supportive and validating. Patients with more severe disorders tend to need a more extended focus on self–other restructuring than those with milder disorders.

AXIS I DISORDER-SPECIFIC MODIFICATIONS

In the following discussion, I briefly address how this short-term anxiety-regulating model may be used to impact most effectively on specific Axis I diagnoses. Often, Axis I disorders (as well as Axis II disorders) reflect defensive behaviors; however, people often ask how depression or anxiety can be seen simultaneously as having a biological predisposition and as a defense. The answer is that these mood states result when defenses break down and depression and anxiety function defensively to block adaptive feeling. (Such breakdown is discussed in chapter 4.) For example, when patients can no longer look on the bright side (*suppression*) or *rationalize* their problems, and they do not have the ability to grieve, they may become depressed. When someone can no longer use the defense *repression* for soothing, anxiety emerges. When more adaptive defenses are not working or more adaptive emotional responses are blocked, it is a result of the excessive inhibitory mood states of anxiety, shame, guilt, and pain functioning defensively.

The goal of my treatment model is to identify which of the affect-based responses is blocked and to desensitize that response so that the need for the symptomatic reaction (Axis I or II) is lessened or eliminated. To offer a metaphor, we can not cure dyslexia, but we can teach dyslexic patients to read, and to do that, shame reduction may be a crucial factor; also critical, however, is the information about the patient's innate biology that is conveyed in the diagnosis of dyslexia.

Schizophrenia

I have not attempted to treat schizophrenia with this model of therapy, although historically there have been many who attempted to do so using dynamic psychotherapy (e.g., Fromm-Reichmann, 1950; Karon, 1992; Karon & VandenBos, 1981). Today, there is ample research demonstrating that schizophrenia is a disorder largely rooted in biology, although research with twins documents that nongenetic factors account for over half the variance. To a greater or lesser degree, depending on the patient's family history, psychotic defensive reactions can be accentuated or even elicited by anxiety, guilt, shame, or pain inhibiting basic wants and needs. Bertram Karon (1992) noted that the primary affect of schizophrenia is terror, and the therapist is challenged to handle the terror in the psychotic projections. To the extent that such anxieties or "terrors" can be regulated through psychotherapy (preferably, with the support of an inpatient setting and medication), the severity of the schizophrenic decompensation *may be* attenuated by anxiety and shame regulation and by gaining mastery of regulatory affects as described in this model. Gabbard's findings suggest that "patients who can integrate a psychotic experience into their life may benefit from exploratory work in the context of psychotherapy, while those who seal over a psychotic episode will probably not benefit and may perhaps even be harmed by persistent exploratory attempts" (1994, p. 196).

Mood Disorders

Gabbard (1994) and Strupp and Binder (1984) have stated that no definitive conclusion can be drawn regarding the effectiveness of highly expressive psychotherapy or short-term dynamic therapy for mood disorders, because the methods have not been rigorously tested for these disorders. Gabbard suggested that the lack of rigor is in part due to lack of development of specific interventions for specific symptoms in dynamic models, a problem that this model of integrative and anxiety-regulating psychodynamics (with explicit objectives and interventions) is intended to resolve. Gabbard pointed out that a modified version of dynamic psychotherapy called *interpersonal psychotherapy* (IPT) has been rigorously tested and found successful, particularly for the more severe forms of depression (1994, p. 231). Because IPT employs *common factors* used in dynamic treatment (e.g., interpersonal deficits, pathological grief), Gabbard concluded that his results lend support for the dynamic treatment of depression. On the other hand, there is abundant evidence for successful treatment of depression by cognitive therapy (Young, Beck, & Weinberger, 1993), which focuses on cognitive restructuring in depression but also is beginning to incorporate "early maladaptive or core schemas." The increasing integration of the common factors in established psychotherapeutic treatment techniques for depression is called for. The model advocated in this book employs many of these common factors.

Treatment of depressive reactions in this short-term model needs no major modification to the basic treatment approach. Accumulating single-case research is lending support to its effectiveness, as exemplified by three of the cases in this book. The Unforgiven Teenager resolved her major depressive disorder in 10 sessions, the Ferryman resolved a 20-year dysthymic condition in the first 17 sessions, and the Girl who Danced in Blood resolved long-standing suicidal and depressive tendencies in the first 10 sessions of her treatment. Each of these patients had Axis II disorders that were resolved as well, and long-term follow-up has shown these gains to be maintained. Improvement was accomplished through restructuring of defenses and affects and *through altering of the sense of self and others.* Much more research is needed in this area, not only to establish the degree of effectiveness, but also to establish empirically the processes that contribute to success.

Like other severe impulse disorders, frank mania is a contraindication to this short-term anxiety-regulating model.

Anxiety Disorders

Gabbard stated that "whenever anxiety forms part of the clinical picture, the psychodynamic psychiatrist must enlist the patient's collaboration in identifying the developmental origins of the anxiety" (1994, p. 251). From his review of the literature, Gabbard concluded that "all these data taken together suggest that the etiology of panic disorder may well involve the unconscious meaning of events, while pathogenesis may involve neurophysiological factors triggered by the psychological reaction to the events" (1994, p. 251).

Many patients with anxiety disorders (with GAF scores above 50) have been treated successfully by this short-term anxiety-regulating model (e.g., panic disorder, phobias, generalized anxiety disorder).

The resolution of an anxiety disorder sometimes is dramatic and rapid, as it was for an immigrant woman who spoke limited English, had little formal education, but was a basically well-functioning wife and mother. When the therapist (a psychology intern I supervised) pointed out that she seemed to be having panic attacks whenever she was angry at her husband (the first step in defense restructuring), this was a revelation to her. Because her relationship with her husband was fairly good, she was then asked if she felt able to tell her husband what she was upset about. She found that with a little instruction she was able to assert herself comfortably, and her husband responded well. After five sessions, the panic attacks stopped altogether. In this case, mere recognition of the defensive pattern was sufficient to correct the problem.

It is important for therapists to know that such rapid changes are possible, although rare. Anxiety disorders can be difficult to treat and to resolve, and therapists should draw from the rich contributions of cognitive therapy. There are several reasons for the difficulty in treating anxiety disorders. First, there is the biological contribution. I have conceptualized dynamic psychopathology in general as fundamentally an "internal phobia," or phobic response to affective responses. However, results from behavior therapy and neurobiological research (e.g., LeDoux, 1993) have shown that it is often exceedingly difficult to extinguish phobic responses. Increasing evidence suggests that structural changes may be environmentally induced in limbic synapses that permanently maintain an anxiety-laden response (Kandel, 1983); therefore, anxiety regulation may sometimes cure by inducing additional learned reactions or new cognitive schemas (i.e., by further synaptic modification; Baxter, 1992). Acquisition of such skills takes *time and repetition*, a process probably analogous to physiotherapy in rebuilding muscle tissue. Presumably, the previously described woman's panic response was less deeply ingrained biologically than in other cases and not too long-standing.

In contrast, the Machine Builder's lifelong social phobia was reduced to permit continued professional functioning, but it was not entirely eliminated. Her severe level of anxiety was helped by a few sessions of intensive interpretation of dynamic conflict, restructuring of defenses, and exposure to shared affective experience. She was able to speak and eat in public, and she was able to move on into a professional position. Because of her avoidant personality disorder, however, I had to modify the approach to address issues of closeness and distance to others. At follow-up, although she was functioning quite well, she was still having anticipatory anxiety about giving presentations, and when a great deal of pressure was put on her in a later job, the anxiety returned. In chapter 10, I speculate about additional work that might have been done on conflicts concerning her mother's neglect or with maintenance sessions. The objective of short-term treatment sometimes is not to cure the problem altogether but to help get the change under way so that the patient can continue the long-term desensitization process.

Much support for this integrative psychodynamic approach comes from the identification of effective common factors in cognitive research. For example, cognitive behavioral group therapy for social phobia (Heimberg, Becker, Goldfinger, & Vermilyea, 1985; Hope & Heimberg, 1993) demonstrates the effectiveness of *imaginal or simulated exposure, in vivo exposure,* and *cognitive restructuring.* The treatment model in this book builds on this excellent work by addressing, in addition to the cognitive issues, the dynamic components of human functioning, that is, restructuring of the full range of affects and relationships.

Concerning obsessive–compulsive disorder, Barlow (1993) wrote that "successful therapy. . . is markedly different both in structure and in content from the usual therapeutic approaches. . . . Few therapists feel self-efficacious enough to undertake this therapy" (p. 189). Although my model's dynamic approach would conceptualize obsessive–compulsive disorder in part as a defensive response to conflict, the research literature suggests the existence of a strong biological component requiring medication (see Gabbard, 1994, for a review) and the effectiveness of a well-established behavioral treatment (e.g., Riggs & Foa, 1993).

Posttraumatic Stress Disorder

After reviewing the literature on posttraumatic stress disorder (PTSD), Gabbard concluded that "no treatment is wholly satisfactory for PTSD"

(1994, p. 277). My integrative psychodynamic model offers a treatment alternative that can be empirically examined.

The PTSD reaction is regarded in this model as a defensive affective response, analogous to the response of anxiety flooding the defenses in deeply entrenched panic disorder. Because the symptoms of PTSD are qualitatively different from the usual defensive symptoms, it requires specific attention. PTSD happens when unbearable trauma becomes irreversibly etched into memory and the mechanisms of vigilance. When stimuli in the environment (or inner stimuli) provoke memories of past trauma, the *standard defenses do not work;* the trauma is elicited again and again. PTSD is less reversible than most operant-conditioned defensive reactions that are maintained by their positive consequences. PTSD more closely resembles classical conditioning, in which a response is *elicited rather than reinforced.* Bessel Van der Kolk and his colleagues (Van der Kolk, Boyd, Krystal, & Greenberg, 1984) developed a model of PTSD that was similar to animal models of *inescapable shock* and compatible with my view.

The psychotherapeutic *solution* that is offered by this model is to alter the patient's reaction to the sense of not being able to escape: The patient must acquire the affective capacity to *imagine escaping or fighting back with full affective arousal.* In that way, a different, mutually exclusive, and *more adaptive emotional reaction to the memory of a trauma* is elicited: *anger* rather than *anxiety,* and *grief* (that relieves and resolves) rather than *anguish.* For the person who feels out of control, this affective response provides a sense of mastery of the situation, not only in memory but also in anticipation of the future. I propose the following hypothesis: *To the extent that a more adaptive and reciprocally inhibiting emotional response is elicited and can be tolerated, the painful PTSD response will be reduced.*

However, the problem of eliciting competing affective reactions in PTSD patients is due to: (a) the inability of these patients to access affect, (b) *a flooding of anxiety following any affective arousal,* and (c) the lack of motivation due to the aversiveness of such instances. If the patient is not able to bear the intense affective experiencing required to compete with the trauma reaction, the treatment experience will be aversive and harmful. This precarious reactivity in PTSD patients *necessitates preparatory and graded interventions.*

The approach described here is intended for moderately well-functioning people. The Machine Builder was taught to feel anger rather than anguish in response to a rape (see chapter 10). (She imagined a baseball bat in her hand *and felt powerful* whenever she thought of the incident; she felt self-compassion when she decided that her father would have wanted her to fight.) She also knew with certainty that, if it were reasonable to do so, she would fight back or at least yell if it happened again. These feelings and images appeared to provide reciprocal inhibition of her previous reaction of anguish, shame, or anxiety each time she thought of the rape. The approach in this case, as in a number of others, was somewhat successful in reducing the sense of trauma and providing a sense of control. Even so, the Machine Builder found the images of fighting the rapist very aversive, and the intensity of the images had to be reduced in the two following sessions for her to imagine them at all. Much research is needed to assess the efficacy of these interventions on a broader scale.

Somatoform Disorders

Neither Gabbard nor Barlow addresses somatoform disorders. Because somatic reactions are a common occurrence in short-term treatment, I deal with them here on a conceptual level. Somatoform disorders can be thought of as a defensive displacement of some inner pain or turmoil. What does our body tell us about our pain? Do we try to avoid it, or do we try to look at how we avoid it—and then turn back and face it? Such patients need special attention paid to the recognition of their affects. They need to learn that anger makes their stomach hurt or that anxiety makes their head ache, makes them feel they are choking, or produces chest pain. Evoking such responses in the therapy session (by confronting painful topics) can be most helpful in demonstrating the association between the physical symptom and the underlying affect. The somatic reaction can be conceptualized as a defensive reaction that signals underlying conflict about unexpressed wants and needs. It goes without saying that this dynamic formulation should be made only if a medical disorder is ruled out.

Sexual and Gender-Identity Disorders

Although the therapist needs to be vigilant for biological contributions to such disorders, Gabbard has stated that the psychodynamic approach is often the treatment of choice. In this model, my general guideline for interpreting many sexual and gender-identity disorders is to see them as *defensive responses to anger, grief, or (most often) unmet longing for love.* Because I have discussed treatment of conflicted sexual feelings and sexual perversions in chapter 7, I only briefly review my approach to treatment here.

I treated a transvestite using defense restructuring. We came to see how his cross-dressing had begun at age 7 when he would put on his mother's clothing and feel close to her in so doing. It was terribly painful for him to realize that his mother virtually had never hugged him or shown affection toward him. Being literally inside of her clothing was his way of feeling held. We were able to arrive at this realization within 10 sessions. He became much more resistant, however, when we moved toward changing his cross-dressing. He had come to therapy because his girlfriend wanted him to stop cross-dressing, and he was initially highly motivated to try. When we began the process of shifting his attachment from clothing (representing his mother) to his girlfriend, however, he abruptly terminated therapy. In retrospect, I believe it was too painful for him to make this sacrifice, and he did not have sufficient "readiness" to respond to the active interventions of short-term treatment. He needed preparatory work first, such as building much stronger bonds to me and to the people in his current life, before he could give up his attachment to and tremendous longing for his mother.

Impulse-Control Disorders

Like obsessive–compulsive disorder, impulse-control disorders (e.g., eating disorders, substance abuse, or pedophilia) are a contraindication for affect restructuring. Behavioral and cognitive treatments are needed to help build the capacities to control behavior. However, self–other restructuring and some aspects of defense restructuring can be useful in helping such patients to understand and manage their impulses. On the most conscious level, patients can be helped to recognize the costs of their defensive behaviors as well as the benefits. The *primary gain* of such disorders is typically to avoid some aversive affect state. The *secondary gain* is the soothing quality of the action. Whatever short-term comfort that is obtained needs to be evaluated in relation to the long-term costs, which are typically great.

Learning to anticipate the negative consequences to the *self* can increase the patient's motivation to gain control over the disorder. What is known in alcohol treatment as "spoiling the patient's drinking" is almost identical to defense relinquishing. Painstakingly, the patient learns that the defensive "soothing" behavior—alcohol—is foe, not friend. I ask patients to stop in the moments before taking a drink, binge eating, or engaging in a sexual fetish or obsessional ritual to note what is felt at that moment: What is the affect— the sorrow, anger, or loneliness—that is too painful to bear? What painful affect is the patient avoiding by the (defensive) eating (or not eating), drinking, or acting out? This analysis of affective conflict can lend a valuable dimension to the treatment. It is important, however, for the therapist to be aware of the necessity for behavioral treatment of impulse-control disorders. Because such behaviors may be reinforced by external factors even more strongly than intrapsychic factors, *environmental contingencies must be a major focus of the treatment* in severe addictions. Insight *alone* (i.e., defensive pattern recognition) is of next to no value, although we do not yet know the value of affect restructuring.

AXIS II DISORDER-SPECIFIC MODIFICATIONS

The DSM-IV Axis II personality disorders are defined by qualitative criteria that characterize a "prototype" for each of the diagnostic categories. These diagnostic categories are grouped into three clusters, or families: cluster A, odd or eccentric behavior; cluster B, emotional or dramatic affect; and cluster C, anxious or fearful behavior. This clustering is intended to suggest a central affective style uniting the members of the group and to acknowledge that clusters, rather than specific disorders, run in families. A common criticism of the DSM classification of personality disorders is its lack of specificity. Patients frequently fulfill criteria for more than one diagnosis or exhibit characteristics of several diagnostic categories without meeting criteria for any one (Frances & Widiger, 1986; Widiger & Frances, 1985). In addition to overlap of personality syndromes, there is frequent contamination by overlap with symptoms of Axis I disorders. In other words, personality disorders reflect the patient's genetic makeup *as well as* defensive character armor resulting from past experience.

Benjamin wrote that "a simple focus on behavioral symptoms or traits . . . will not often lead to successful treatment of personality disorders. . . . Traits are unlikely to change without transformation of underlying wishes and fears" (1993a, p. 377). Gabbard (1994) and others have directed therapists to a source-oriented approach to personality disorders. Vaillant (1993) hypothesized that personality disorders reflect an effort to provide an illusion of object constancy and to master problems with feelings associated with attachment. "For every symptom there are reasons" (Benjamin, 1993a, p. 385). "Maladaptive patterns are driven by wishes that internalized other persons will offer love, approval, forgiveness, apologies, admiration, reparation, and so on (1993a, p. 101).

Benjamin has described each of the personality disorders from the interpersonal "wish for attachment" perspective. She made the bold generalization that every psychopathology is a gift of love, which forces us, for a moment, to step into the patient's shoes. I have thought of Axis II disorders as representing a *longing for love,* but Benjamin's point is that therapists need to be intensely aware of the *invitation for a loving relationship* that is being conveyed (albeit not in the clearest nor most adaptive fashion) through the psychopathology. When we intervene from that perspective, we have a far better chance of making a healing connection with the patient. Benjamin added that "the patterns of their disorders reflect their attempts to adjust to ... pain" (1993a, p. 390). Although Benjamin's work grew out of an interpersonal focus and mine from a short-term dynamic focus, we have arrived at similar conclusions. We also agree that a major role of therapy is, in Benjamin's words, "to help the patient endure the intense anxiety that often comes with giving up old ways" (1993a, p. 390).

My short-term model has been derived from research on long-standing personality disorders, discussed in detail in chapter 12. The methods presented in this section have been shown to be effective with Axis II disorders. In reading the discussion that follows, however, the reader should remain mindful that personality is a mixture of conflict-shaped character and genetically shaped temperament (e.g., Plomin, 1994; Tellegen, Lykken, Bouchard, Wilcox et al., 1988). I focus on the psychodynamic components to emphasize the portions of Axis II disorders that are more amenable to therapeutic change.

Cluster A: The Odd, Eccentric, or Withdrawn Personality Disorders:
Paranoid, Schizoid, and Schizotypal

Severe examples of these disorders (especially schizoid and schizotypal) are not frequently seen in outpatient settings, but many outpatients have *traits* in each of these categories. To the extent that patients' pathology reflects these Cluster A disorders, the therapist needs to work primarily in two areas: defense restructuring around the defensive warding off of closeness and self–other restructuring to help modify the negative impressions of others. Cluster A defenses—projection, idealization, devaluation, and autistic fantasy—primarily avoid the *anxiety* about social contact. The *primary gain* of the defensive pattern is the avoidance of relationships that are too close for comfort. The *secondary gain* is the omnipotent safety of being alone. Such patients can be thought of as being "allergic to people." No doubt shame plays an important role and needs to be regulated; however, the initial anxiety about closeness seems paramount in treatment of individuals with Cluster A traits. The *replacement*, or missing, capability that is required is for other people (beginning with the therapist) to become soothing or comforting to the individual (starting at a safe distance, then moving closer).

People with Cluster A pathology often experience deficits in basic trust and cannot begin work on defense restructuring without concomitant work on self–other restructuring, with emphasis on learning to trust others. This means that developing an alliance is paramount, although to do this requires more than support. The therapist has to help patients see how they hold others in fantasy and how they project onto others. Just as most patients need to learn to bring their emotions into consciousness, Cluster A patients need to bring their internalized, sometimes autistic relationships into consciousness. Beginning with the relationship with the therapist, patients with such maladaptive patterns must learn to rebuild the basic trust that we were all born with. Such people had to learn that others were untrustworthy or to be exquisitely sensitive to others' reactions, so that ordinary hurts by others were exaggerated. In either case, healing involves acquiring a less anxiety-ridden experience of others: first with the therapist and then with others.

Cluster B: The Acting-Out, Impulsive Personality Disorders: Histrionic, Narcissistic, Borderline, Antisocial

In contrast to Cluster A pathology, in which the patient views *others* badly, in Cluster B it is the *self* that is experienced (either consciously or not) as bad, inadequate, or shameful. Although the extroverted Cluster B patient usually has too *little* stranger anxiety rather than too much (as in Cluster A), patients can present with aspects of both clusters. In Cluster B pathology, the impulse-ridden reactions (the narcissistic patient's rage at insults, the borderline person's anguish over rejection, the histrionic patient's defensive emotionality, and the antisocial individual's need-driven tantrums) all can be seen as *defensive affects* that result from *the pain of unmet longings*. Patients with *severe* levels of these disorders typically are not responsive to short-term dynamic approaches and are better treated with more supportive and skills-building models (e.g., Linehan, 1993a).

Many patients in short-term treatment have moderate Cluster B traits (if not the full diagnosis), which can be responsive to this treatment (e.g., the Unforgiven Teenager; the Woman with Butterfly Feelings). Impairment in how such patients perceive themselves requires compassionate mirroring and validating by the therapist. Such interventions are crucial for rebuilding the impairment in sense of self and breaching the Cluster B defensive structures of acting out, projection, devaluation, hypochondriasis, and splitting. To the extent that there is a lack of connection to others, there may need to be a period of mirroring of the patient or idealization of the therapist to facilitate the restructuring of the inner representations of others. The goal is to help such individuals develop trust and closeness in the shortest amount of time possible. (This discussion is highly condensed and presupposes knowledge of theoretical issues such as presented by Kohut, 1977; Benjamin, 1993a; Gabbard, 1994; Linehan, 1993a; and others.)

It is helpful to look at the factors that hold Cluster B defensive patterns in place. The overarching *primary gain* of Cluster B defensive behaviors is the avoidance of "abandonment depression" (Masterson & Klein, 1990) and of the painful longing for closeness. The *secondary gain* of the defensive pattern is the embellishment of an inadequate sense of self and the manipulation of others. Because all four of the disorders have features in common, I focus on two in the following discussion.

The borderline and narcissistic disorders represent clearly contrasting challenges to the therapist. The defenses of the narcissist work too well, and the defenses of the borderline do not work well enough. As a result, the therapist feels too distant from the narcissist (or the antisocial) and all too close to, and even assaulted by, the borderline (or histrionic) patient's last line of defense, which typically is explosive defensive affect.

Borderline Personality Disorder

In working with patients with these more impulse-ridden personality disorders, one has to proceed with defense restructuring as though one were walking in a minefield. If defense restructuring is not handled carefully, patients with such traits are in danger of fragmentation due to pain. Here again, self–other restructuring, together with affirming and reparative interventions, is needed to create a therapeutic alliance that permits self-cohesion and defenses to be altered. In *borderline defensive behaviors,* the *primary gain* of the defenses is the partial (though never complete) avoidance of the pain of abandonment. Masterson and Klein (1990) emphasized, however, that this response pattern is so pain-ridden because the borderline defenses fail and flood the patient with traumatic and overwhelming pain and anxiety. The *secondary gain* is the intermittent relief obtained through various forms of dissociation, hypochondriasis (help-rejecting complaining), or acting out (defensive feeling and impulse-ridden behavior). Because patients with borderline pathology are unable to avoid emotional pain, they must do things of sufficient intensity (e.g., wrist cutting, promiscuity, bingeing) to distract themselves and change their internal state.

These patients differ greatly from narcissists, who gain a great deal from their defensive structure and have much to lose by giving it up. It is not that the borderline's self-abuse is so desirable; it is its power of *aversion relief* that leads to the compulsive and impulsive borderline responses. Consider the learning principles that hold the defensive behaviors of these disorders in place, especially their highly reinforcing quality. It feels *good* to the Cluster B to behave in a charming or manipulative manner. But it is also negative reinforcement (a frequently misunderstood concept) that holds such defenses in place. Negative reinforcement is not punishment but a reward for the withdrawal of an aversive stimulus. (For example, one is rewarded, or reinforced, for putting on one's seat belt because doing so stops an aversive buzzer.) For the borderline patient, creating a staff uproar through wrist cutting puts rejection by one's lover (a far more painful experience) literally out of mind. Engaging in a barroom brawl or a con game takes the antisocial person away from emptiness. Such defenses are maintained by *negative reinforcement* because they *put a stop to unbearable emotional pain.*

The challenge in Cluster B pathology is that so much must be *built*; so much restructuring of the self and others must be done before these defensive behaviors can be replaced. As explained in chapter 2, borderline patients, like schizoid patients, are often not suitable for a full short-term uncovering treatment. But a few sessions of active interventions that make clear the destructive defenses can save months of therapy time. In addition, many moderately well-functioning individuals have aspects of impairment of self that I call "borderline pockets," or limited disturbances in sense of identity and relatedness in individuals who usually have good impulse control. It is for such people that the short-term techniques are particularly helpful. Statements such as the following might introduce a discussion: *It seems like you get confused about what kind of people are good for you and what kind aren't. Can we take some time to examine some of the people in your life and see what relationships have been comforting and which have not?* (This should include the comforting versus uncomfortable aspects of the therapist–patient relationship.)

The focus here is on building a capacity that is absent in the patient: the ability to feel the difference between constructive and destructive, if distracting, relationships. Some identification of the patient's emotional responses in these relationships is important. What is consciously liked or disliked must be identified, just as hurtful and adaptive behaviors are identified in the defense-restructuring phase. It would be incorrect, however, to elicit the depth of the emotion (either positive or negative) in relationships unless there is good impulse control.

Patients who have borderline identity disturbance and lack of impulse control should not be confronted regarding defenses and uncovering warded-off feelings until they have acquired effective cognitive control over labeling and expression of affects. Patients with borderline personality disorder often have no idea what they feel but are usually just as blocked in regard to adaptive anger, grief, or closeness as those with other personality disorders. Because of the amount of defensive affect displayed by the borderline patient, this may not be initially apparent. Their explosive or impulsively vented affects are indicators of defensiveness, not a sign of adaptive affective responding but an indicator of deficit pathology that calls for building of structures rather than uncovering of conflicts. Indeed, Monsen and his colleagues (1995) have demonstrated the effectiveness of building "affect consciousness" (i.e., building conceptual awareness of inner experience) in borderline patients.

NARCISSISTIC PERSONALITY DISORDER

It is beyond the scope of this book to describe fully how to treat narcissistic disorders and disorders of self. For further understanding of the theory and treatment of narcissism, the reader is referred to Baker (1991), Baker and Baker (1987), Masterson and Klein (1990), Gabbard (1994), Stolorow and

Atwood (1992), Stolorow and Lachmann (1980), and Kohut (1971, 1977). This section provides the reader with some basic guidelines for treatment of disorders of self in a short-term anxiety-regulating framework.

In the narcissistic pattern, the *primary gain* of the defenses is the avoidance of the pain associated with longing for a sense of worth or value from others. The *secondary gain* is the safety that is provided from the pain of vulnerability. If one never becomes close or becomes vulnerable to another, one is never devastated by the pain of abandonment (Masterson & Klein, 1990). Another component of *secondary gain* of the defensive pattern is the sense of power, stature, and control one achieves if one can successfully use someone else as an "object" to one's advantage or to embellish the sense of self (narcissistic supplies). Narcissistic defenses are highly reinforcing and equally resistant to change. The patient will need to replace the safety of cool detachment with (a) the *joy* of authentic connection to others, (b) the *joy*, pride, or respect of sense of self in relation to others, and (c) the ability to *grieve* losses rather than be so potentially devastated that one dares not care (which emerges from the growth of the first two components). These affective experiences, however, are difficult to reach owing to the barrier of the defenses and require intensive restructuring of the sense of self in relation to others. The therapist needs to be well-versed in the developmental deficits that need reworking: the degree of mirroring, idealization, and twinship (e.g., Kohut, 1971, 1977) that needs to be worked through in the patient–therapist relationship. Indeed, the affirmation or shared idealization from the therapist is crucial for the restoration of self-esteem. Such patients need the therapist as a self-object on whom they can rely to fill gaps in their sense of self. In such cases, "something outside the patient (the empathically responsive therapist) and something inside—a function such as initiative or interaction or organization—are both recognized to be missing" (Lichtenberg, Lachmann, & Fosshage, 1992, p. 127).

The rapid uncovering work of the direct application of short-term therapy is not appropriate for treatment of narcissistic personality disorders.[4] I have seen such patients respond just as the therapist is encouraging them to and, thus, twist themselves into apparent openness and false feeling without real change. This process carries the danger of creating yet another layer of "falseness" on top of the already false self.

In less severely disordered patients, aspects or traits of a false self and other milder narcissistic "pockets" of defenses might be addressed more readily in a short-term treatment. These defensive behavior patterns are closely tied with the individual's identity, however, and even when mild, do not yield easily. Only with understanding, appreciation, and validation can the individual tolerate being seen accurately (probably for the first time) without being overwhelmed with shame. Even after a strong alliance is built, there is still danger of rupture if the defenses are pointed out too

[4]I do not believe one can give up a narcissistic character style (that comprises the whole identity) in an outpatient setting without a year or two of careful and deeply empathic work.

abruptly or before the patient is prepared. Even gentle clarification can rupture the alliance. Defenses so close to the core of the individual should not be taken away unless something more viable has been built to replace it (e.g., new and more adaptive skills, better relationships, a healthier sense of self). Teaching the patient with narcissistic traits the costs of the defenses is not sufficient. New emotional foundations must be built. To help someone become authentic with another human being when that has never before been done necessitates a longer (although time-conscious) treatment process.

Examples of anxiety-regulating responses for narcissistic patients include the following:

> *You must have needed so much to be brave or strong that the scared side of you has to stay hidden.*
>
> *You were so rewarded for doing what your mother wanted, how could you have done otherwise!*
>
> *It is extremely difficult to share such deeply held secrets. You need to know that you can take your time opening up to me. I will not push you faster than you can bear. It is important that you feel safe with me.*

CASE EXAMPLE: NARCISSISTIC PERSONALITY DISORDER

If the major defensive function is to hide one's identity by creating a false self, the therapist needs to mirror it, accept it, and appreciate it before trying to alter it. Otherwise, the fragile sense of self of the individual will not be able to tolerate the exposure, as the following example demonstrates.

PATIENT: I saw a dent in your car, and I became worried that you had been in an accident.

THERAPIST [*Exploration of the preceding comment yielded nothing until the therapist made the following suggestion*]: Could we look further at your feelings about my possibly having an accident, because there was some disagreement between us in the last session. Could you be feeling some anger at me and a wish to cause me harm?

Here I mistakenly interpreted the defenses against a possible negative feeling! Pointing out defenses against anger is a typical thing to do in short-term treatment, and this patient appeared to be quite high functioning, at least occupationally. However, I failed to take into account the severe impairment in her interpersonal relationships. She had never had the experience of being authentic with anyone, and to do so with me at this point was impossible.[5]

---

[5]Earlier in my career, I continued such confrontation of anger with two patients. Although they had narcissistic disorder, I believed the alliance was strong enough to manage it. In both cases, I was wrong. Both patients (one male, one female) became outraged and terminated irreconcilably, which I greatly regretted. Since then, I have learned to modify my approach when the level of the patient's outrage suggests narcissistic injury. In this case, fortunately, I made a more corrective response.

PATIENT [*Looking devastated and deeply injured, barely able to speak*]: How could you think I would wish harm on you? Don't you know how much these sessions have helped me? Don't you know how much you mean to me, and how scared I am that I might lose you? I was terrified to think that you might have been in an accident and been hurt! How could you think that of me! [*The affect expressed was, in large part, fury.*]

THERAPIST: Oh, I must have really misunderstood your very strong protective feelings of me! That must feel terrible! [*With feeling*] I am so sorry.

At deeper levels, the patient probably did have anger at me, and certainly she was furious at my misunderstanding her, but at this stage in treatment she could not bear the sense of rupture it would cause to face the angry feelings. Besides, she did have positive feelings and dependent longings for me, and fortunately I realized how much she needed me to acknowledge and accept this side of her first.

THERAPIST: That must feel really terrible.

PATIENT: Yes, it does! My mother never saw anything positive in me.

THERAPIST: So I must feel just like your mother. Misunderstanding how much I mean to you. That must make you feel so alone.

PATIENT: It sure does. Nobody has ever understood me. And I can't trust anyone. I thought you understood me. Now I feel like you have no idea who I am.

Following is a dramatic departure from traditional approaches of any theoretical persuasion. I am working with real feelings in the real relationship.

THERAPIST: I'm really sorry that I misunderstood your comment. You've told me of the unbearable loneliness when you were a child, and it makes me a little choked up to see in your face that my comment brought back those painful memories. [*I said this only because it was absolutely true. Seeing the enormous degree of pain she was in at the moment, I did feel "a little choked up." No doubt my reaction was unconsciously intensified by my prior experience of the two patients who had been so hurt. My affect was sufficiently evident for her to notice it, and I struggled to put words on it.*] I feel touched that you were worried about me, and it makes me sad that I completely missed that.

PATIENT [*Silent, but looking at me intermittently*]: Your face looks sad. [*More silence*] That makes me feel better, 'cause it seems like I do matter to you after all.

The rupture was healed in that moment, and treatment proceeded with increasing closeness and exposure of herself. Later in treatment, she was to refer to this session as a watershed. If I had not responded in this manner, the rupture might have taken months to heal, or she might have dropped out.

This type of self-disclosing behavior entails a different sequence of interactions from any I had been trained to do. It is also a departure from the standard short-term approach. However, flexibility is the hallmark of patient-specific treatment. This example demonstrates the rapid shifting from defense restructuring to self–other restructuring to mend a rupture in the alliance. The more false the personality, the more crucial that the therapist be real. Of course, such real self-disclosures lose their power unless they are done only occasionally, carefully considered, and expressed with restraint (Hill, 1989). In this case, the involved, concerned therapist approach healed a potentially damaging rupture in a time-effective manner.

Authentic acceptance of the narcissistic defensive stance by the therapist creates a safe environment for individuals to begin to face themselves compassionately; therefore, such a stance is *the most rapid path to the defenses that eventually will be relinquished.* Later, this patient came in week after week telling me of things she had done of which she was ashamed. I did not point them out to *her;* she pointed them out to *me!* Because I was worried that she would have a backlash of shame, I was reassuring about her confessions and strongly validated her for whatever she revealed to me.

THERAPIST: I'm sure you had a good reason for (doing the specified behavior). Of course! I can imagine you (responding this way), because it would have been unbearably painful for you to do otherwise. [*On several occasions, following such responses by me, she would tear up and say the following quietly.*]

PATIENT: Thank you. You make it safe for me to look at these things. I'm so ashamed of the dishonest ways I have behaved.

This is not a singular experience with one patient. This type of interaction is common with patients who have never allowed themselves to be close or interpersonally genuine. The danger in this approach is that the therapist will collude with the patient's illusions that she has no negative feelings and thus undergird the patient's pathology. It should go without saying that this would not be a suitable solution. When patients cannot bear to face negative aspects of themselves without threatening rupture in the treatment, however, it is crucial to build a positive sense of self and a strong alliance. Patients have felt able to acknowledge many negative or socially unacceptable behaviors because they have previously experienced me as accepting or at least understanding of *whatever* they have done. Always, however, the therapist must blend the total *acceptance or understanding of past behavior* with the encouragement of *responsibility for future behavior.*

HISTRIONIC PERSONALITY DISORDER

The histrionic patient predominantly uses defensive patterns of dissociation and repression as well as defensive affects. The primary gain of histrionic defensive emotionality is to avoid other, more painful or conflicted affects. The secondary gain results from the distraction that the defensive emotion provides, as well as the sense of worth or closeness that is achieved from flirtation and manipulation—if only temporarily. The replacement that is needed is cognitive recognition and control of the defensive affects as well as anxiety regulation of adaptive affects. If the patient's GAF score is above 50, this type of patient is often responsive to short-term dynamic treatment. If functioning and impulse control are poor, more cognitive or ego-building approaches are indicated.

ANTISOCIAL PERSONALITY DISORDER

Gabbard stated that "outpatient individual psychotherapy of the severely antisocial patient is doomed to failure" (1994, p. 548). Michael Stone (1993) subtitles his book on the psychopathic personality *Within and Beyond Treatment*. Benjamin headed her chapter on the antisocial personality with the words "this disease is beyond my practice" (1993a, p. 191). Such is the level of difficulty faced in changing the character structure of persons with antisocial personalities. Yet Gabbard (1994), Benjamin (1993a), and Vaillant (1975) all have described how to handle less severe forms of this disorder.

The patient with antisocial personality presents an opposite picture from every other patient in this book except for some aspects of those with narcissistic personality disorder. (Narcissistic patients with GAF ratings below 50 often also meet criteria for antisocial personality.) In such cases, the anxiety regulation that is required is to *increase, rather than decrease,* anxiety, guilt, shame, and pain to normal levels, as well as to build a sense of compassion that might bring these people into the bonds of humanity.

In contrast to the heightened empathic mirroring and acceptance required for treating narcissistic personality disorder, "correct empathy" for patients with antisocial personality is often not showing too much empathy lest they think they are dealing with a "sucker." Just as one must titrate closeness for the schizoid patient, one must titrate empathy for the antisocial person. In both cases, these feelings are aversive. Such people have conscience or superego responses that are too harsh and at the same time contain lacunae. They also have severe deficits in attachment. Underlying these defects, however, their fundamental wishes and desires often are like those of the rest of us (Vaillant, 1975). Benjamin (1993a) emphasized the need for experiences that increase attachment and interdependence in antisocial patients.

Cluster C: The Anxiety Personality Disorders: Avoidant, Dependent, Depressive, Negativistic, Obsessive

Working to restructure Cluster C defenses is what defense restructuring and short-term dynamic psychotherapy were originally intended for. For patients whose level of functioning is moderate or better and who do not have pronounced features of Cluster A or B personality pathology, the therapist can begin pointing out defenses from the start and work toward the giving up of those defenses as soon as possible. The primary gain of the Cluster C defenses is the avoidance of feelings that would be experienced in various situations (sometimes with others, sometimes with oneself). The secondary gain varies according to disorder: The dependent personality obtains the safety of some form of attachment; the avoidant person obtains the safety of distance; and the obsessive patient obtains the safety of control.

AVOIDANT PERSONALITY DISORDER

Patients with avoidant defenses shun closeness to a large degree because of shame or fear of rejection. The *primary gain* is the avoidance of the terrors of social interaction, and the *secondary gain* is the comfort of isolation. The *replacement* that is needed is enjoyment and interest in social interaction obtained through the reduction of the inhibitory affects associated with feelings experienced and expressed toward others.

DEPENDENT PERSONALITY DISORDER

The defenses of passivity and compliance are typically used to avoid loss of the dependent, or child, role. For some, giving up a dependent role means bearing the anxiety (or terror) in taking on adult responsibility. To others, giving up the dependent role means ripping away the only structure for living that they have ever known. Certainly, one would not readily relinquish defenses that held such a structure in place. In such patients, the *primary gain* of the dependent responses is the comfort of the attachment to and dependence on others. The *secondary gain* is the avoidance of *the aversive feelings involved in* dependence on oneself and the overwhelming fears *involved* in being alone or on one's own. The *replacement* that is needed is more positive feeling about the self and about being alone that are free from severe inhibitory affects. In such instances, the therapist must identify *what specifically reinforces the defensive pattern* so that the patient may find alternative and more adaptive rewards.

THERAPIST: You may not want to give up the passive behavior because that would thrust you into taking on adult responsibility . . . and we can see why that would be uncomfortable for you. You were punished severely whenever you tried. But what happens if you continue on in this pattern?

PATIENT: I know. [*With tears in her eyes and visibly shaking*] But my mother has made decisions for me for my whole life! To give it up is terrifying!

THERAPIST: Why don't we explore what would be the most frightening parts of you making the decisions.

PATIENT: It seems impossible to even imagine.

THERAPIST: I don't doubt it! But let's explore it together, and maybe it will be easier to begin to think through that way. [*Encouragement to expose oneself to the feared situation*]

DEPRESSIVE PERSONALITY DISORDER

Depressive (formerly called self-defeating) personality disorder may be the most straightforward of the behavior patterns to treat and one of the most responsive to short-term intervention. The *primary gain* is the avoidance of conflict that might threaten attachment (e.g., If I am assertive of my wants and needs, I will not be loved or accepted). The *secondary gain* includes the approval or care that is received from others because of the passive behavior. The *missing capability* that needs to be acquired is the care for self that includes setting of limits and asking for things, both aspects of constructive self-assertion of basic needs.

NEGATIVISTIC PERSONALITY DISORDER

Passive–aggressive personality disorder has been dropped from Axis II, but unfortunately this defensive pattern has not been dropped by our patients. Because these patients are generally largely unconscious of what they are doing, the disorder is difficult to identify through patient self-report or even by interview. An attempt at improving this category is now referred to as the negativistic personality disorder. Whatever the name, one must know how to work with this quite serious interpersonal problem. The therapist needs to be vigilant for the patient's report of inexplicable or unjustified anger from others. The *primary gain* of passive aggression is the avoidance of direct interpersonal conflict (that the individual feels powerless to handle). The *secondary gain* is even more compelling and enormously reinforcing, that is, the pleasure of fighting back from a protected position. It is compelling and enormously reinforcing to do something infuriating and get away with it by denying it. This is a common pattern in the adolescent. Sins of omission, or *not* doing something that is wished (working slowly, making indirect but subtly cutting comments, being chronically late, forgetting things), can drive others crazy. When such individuals do not take responsibility for the covert hostility it can drive others even crazier. The spouse, the boss, or the parents may be screaming in frustration, but the passive–aggressive individual is saying, "Who me? What's *your* problem?"

The spouses of passive–aggressive people are taught not to respond to reduce the reward value of the behavior. Before passive aggression is given up, the individual must develop new and equally safe ways to fight or to become separate, as well as to value and enjoy closeness. At a deeper level, passive–aggressive people must be helped to "feel" the damage they are doing to the potential for interpersonal closeness. The individual who revels in opposition or passive aggression has had serious deficits, or ruptures, in the experience of attachment to others. Not until interpersonal closeness is seen as worthwhile and desirable will the passive–aggressive person relinquish the delights of covert attack.

OBSESSIVE–COMPULSIVE PERSONALITY DISORDER

Obsessive defenses present some difficulty to penetrate, but unlike the Axis I variant, the Axis II disorder often has been responsive to short-term dynamic interventions. Davanloo (1980) said that the therapist needed a "bazooka" to break through massive defensive barriers of such patients, which he said were like 3 feet of concrete. His anxiety-provoking techniques required that the therapist persist in confrontation of defenses for full sessions until a breakthrough was achieved. When I began speculating on what alternative approach might also work with this difficult disorder, I recalled that in the Tao Te Ching it is said that the softest thing in the universe can overcome the hardest thing in the universe, like water eroding away stone. I speculated that drawing attention to tenderness inherent in the patient–therapist relationship would be equally successful in eroding the obsessional defenses. I began, like Davanloo, relentlessly pointing out the defensive barrier but, unlike Davanloo, doing so as gently as possible. First, I focused on tenderness, closeness, and especially, sorrow. I validated the obsessional defenses as *once* necessary, and I addressed the feelings of closeness that were probably frightening and being pushed away. Holding this focus produces a slow, steady "awakening" of affective life in such people. The session-by-session effects are not explosive or dramatic, but over time the change is clear. The total time in treatment appears to be about the same as for Davanloo's anxiety-provoking methods with similar patients: 40 sessions on average.

The maladaptive or defensive behaviors are primarily isolation of affect, reaction formation, displacement, and intellectualization. The *primary gain* is the avoidance of unpleasant feelings within oneself or in connection to others. The *secondary gain* is the peaceful quietness of relative nonfeeling. Things are in control. If Cluster A responses indicate an allergy to people, obsessional personality disorder reflects an allergy to feeling. What is needed is to help the patient experience feeling as comfortable instead of chaotic. These people are the most deserving of the term *affect phobia*, and much anxiety regulation is needed. It is helpful to remember that feeling is always present and can never be totally blocked; the therapist does not have to break through to anything. It can be sufficient to acknowledge whatever small amount of felt experience is present and to encourage and build on that.

Because of the frustration experienced by therapists who try to reach the feeling life of patients with obsessional personality disorders, I present a segment from such a case to demonstrate how one might proceed within this model. The standard approach of restructuring defenses and affects is employed but with an intensified and constant focusing on the affect, which is ever-present but denied. In contrast to Davanloo, who focuses intensively on the defensive barrier, I focus intensively on the affect. Defenses are continually pointed out, but affect is continually titrated. As affective experience becomes more and more conscious and the conflicts around affective experiencing are reduced, the defenses seem to melt away—again, as water eroding a stone.

EXAMPLE: THE MAN WITH "MOSQUITO FEELINGS"

This 33-year-old man came to therapy because of a 15-year history of poor relationships, less than optimal job performance, and a wish to be able to have feelings. Several women had complained that he was emotionally detached and distancing.

PATIENT: These three sessions have been really hard for me. When I'm alone, feelings flicker. They sting me like mosquitoes, but then they're gone, just like that.

THERAPIST: I had no idea. I couldn't see it on your face. I'm glad you told me. Let's stay with those feelings here with me. If you let it out here . . . [*After some silence I proceed with the imagery.*] If we look at these feelings in fantasy, would you be crying here with me?

PATIENT: No, I don't sob.

THERAPIST: Okay, but let your thoughts wander. How would I be viewing you if you were sad here with me?

PATIENT: Oh, I'm okay with that. You'd be happy for me if I could cry, I know that. [*This is intellectualization and isolation of affect. He believes what he says, but his affective response is the opposite.*]

THERAPIST: Intellectually, I think you do know that, but I wonder if, on an emotional level, you might feel some shame or discomfort of some kind?

PATIENT: I don't know, I don't think so. I haven't cried so often in my life, so I can't tell.

THERAPIST: It's such a lonely image you paint. You've told me of huge demands put on you as a boy. You gave a lot, but there were so few arms to cry in. So where could you learn to let down?

PATIENT: Yeah. [*Sadly*]

THERAPIST: That's such a long, lonely road.

PATIENT: Yeah, I suppose . . . [*He tries to minimize the feeling that is welling up.*]

THERAPIST: Suppose? You don't feel it strongly then? [*I should have stated this in the affirmative. Possibly on the order of, "Suppose? Maybe the feelings are stronger than you realize."*]

PATIENT: Maybe I need to get comfortable and relax.

THERAPIST: So this place must be made safer for you.

PATIENT: But it *is!*

THERAPIST: But maybe it could be more so. [*Pausing*] I want to hear the worst part of it—what's been upsetting you in these last sessions.

PATIENT: My life seems so dead, so wasted. I've been going through the motions. Why didn't I know?

THERAPIST: Those sound like hard feelings to bear alone.

PATIENT: But they're hard to express until I find them myself. [*He had told me several times before that he wasn't putting up a barrier to me. He did not know what he felt, himself.*] Thoughts are always in my mind, tiredness, distraction. I feel incapable of overcoming it. I'm afraid I can't change.

THERAPIST: It's an awful feeling to carry around, to feel stuck. How do you bear that? [*I intentionally focus on the affective part of his communication, but he, once again, responds in a defensive manner.*]

PATIENT: Oh, it's not so bad. I just think of something different.

THERAPIST: But there's still a fear there . . .

PATIENT: What do you have to do to not be afraid? What do you have to do to cry easily? That's the big one!

THERAPIST: Yeah, that's what you've wanted so much. [*Pausing*] So we'll start by touching the flickers. [*This is really the heart of the work with an obsessional character style: touching the flickers of the feelings, then fanning the flames. Then a question came to my mind.*] Are you more restrained with others than in here?

PATIENT: No, I'm restrained all the time.

THERAPIST: What are you feeling right now?

PATIENT: Just confused. [*This is a typical obsessional response on an intellectual level. I speak with him briefly about what the confusion is, but then I pull the focus back to feeling.*]

THERAPIST: I wonder what you might be feeling in your body right now? [*This alerts him to an inner sensation.*]

PATIENT: Heavy. . . . Something keeps me holding back, almost tangible, as though there's something there, a lid right across my chest. [*He makes a straight, horizontal motion across his chest.*] A lid to slide off. Wooh! Wouldn't that be a relief!

THERAPIST: All those feelings would come bubbling up, and pour out and be shared here, from inside to outside—here.

PATIENT: Coming here makes it come the closest to the surface. I feel pressure against that lid.

THERAPIST [*I wait a moment. He seems unable to label what is inside of him, so I model the feeling, and speak in a whisper*]: My experience of being with you is—sad.

PATIENT [*With great emphasis*]: Well, that's the same way I feel!

THERAPIST [*We sit silently for a moment*]: We're both sitting here full of sadness . . . [*Pausing; His face seemed filled with sadness and he is silent. So I put words on it, but quietly and slowly.*] . . . brimming with the pain of what you've been through. [*Pausing*] It's palpable between us. [*The sadness on his face was truly making me ache inside. This is the shared experience of the affect, which may be so crucial to the walled-off obsessional patient.*]

PATIENT [*Silence; then he looks at me with tears in his eyes, as though unable to speak.*]

THERAPIST: The feeling is welling up more in you now.

PATIENT [*Nodding, slowly*]: The lid is sliding just a little bit now, just a little bit. . .

THERAPIST: This is always with you. You don't have to push it. [*Silence*] Mmmm. [*I sigh with the buildup of feeling.*]

PATIENT [*Silent for a while*]: When closest to crying, I started to feel good again. It's hard for me to grieve over a memory that I've thought so often, but . . . [*He intellectualizes a bit but still conveys a very sad tone.*]

THERAPIST: You're an intensely feeling man deep down, and you've shared a fullness of feeling with me today. What's going on inside of you—now?

PATIENT: Relief, calmer . . . moving in that direction I wanted to go . . . thank God.

THERAPIST: So we don't have to push it. We went from flickers of your body to the sad feelings I felt in my body and back to deep sad feelings in your body, and that's a long way.

The session was almost over, and I was intent on reinforcing successive approximations to feeling. This session was one of many steps in his emotional growth. By Session 30, he was far more able to identify his feelings and share them with me as well as with others. He found himself much more able to take an assertive and dominant position at work. In the subsequent 6 months, he met a warm loving woman, and for the first time in his life, he developed a deeply bonded and caring relationship. He told me of crying fully in her arms with the sense of the blessing that had befallen him. She came to one of his follow-up sessions, and their mutual warmth shone. At 3-year follow-up, they had married and this continues to be an extremely happy and stable relationship. The growth process in this man was not dramatic, as it might have been if I had taken a more anxiety-provoking approach. There was a gentle erosion of the defensive structure, with small and not always continuous steps taken to develop a greater awareness of affectivity.

SUMMARY

This chapter integrates the patient-specific approach with the disorder-specific approach by identifying how to work with defenses, anxieties, and adaptive feelings across various Axis I and Axis II disorders. Some of the major modifications across disorders involve: (a) the degree of supportive versus exploratory interventions that are used, (b) the degree to which self–other restructuring is needed to permit defense and affect restructuring, and (c) the noting of pitfalls that could cause treatment ruptures.

The disorder-specific approach alone does not adequately represent the specific patient, who may have several different disorders or traits of many syndromes. Examining specific disorders can alert the therapist to the range of defensive styles that are employed.

CHAPTER 12

Theory and Research

Part 1: Overview of Theory and Rationale: Assumptions and Change Mechanisms

When I was in graduate school and seeking guidance in how to conduct therapy, I avidly read the works of such gifted therapists as Frieda Fromm-Reichmann and Franz Alexander. I repeatedly encountered passages in their writings indicating that a specific interpretation broke through to the patient's deepest issues and led to the resolution of the case.

As a result, I would feel lost, frustrated, and demoralized; as a fledgling therapist, I could not begin to construct the intermediate steps leading to the enormous intuitive leaps taken by these gifted clinicians. I did not doubt their accomplishments but I knew that I could not do likewise on my own. It made sense when, about that time, Calvin Hall and Gardner Lindzey (1978) made their strong point that no theory should be subscribed to that cannot be scientifically tested.

For these reasons this book attempts to make explicit what often has been left to intuition, and to generate some flexible guidelines to help therapists when intuition fails or when inexperience leaves them confused. Crucial to this clarification process has been continual review of videotapes with colleagues and the adjustment of techniques on the basis of repeated observations and research evidence to strive for theory that is grounded in data (e.g., Glaser, 1978; Glaser & Strauss, 1967; Rennie, Phillips, & Quartaro, 1988). My goal has been to convey as simply as possible the art of dynamic psychotherapy; it has been a humbling process. As Henry and colleagues pointed out, "by their very nature, psychodynamic constructs have been the most intractable to scientific scrutiny" (Henry et al., 1994, p. 499). I am aware that my operational definitions are rough approximations of clinical reality. There is a beauty and mystery to the psychotherapy process that constructs will never completely capture. Science follows clumsily behind art and spirit! Nevertheless, striving to make explicit some of the ways that psychodynamic psychotherapy effects change is the only way to examine the model empirically. It is the only way therapists can continue to grow in the ability to heal patients.

This book contains a number of points that are departures from traditional approaches, as well as a number of assumptions, rules, and definitions that I wish to make explicit. The central facet of my integrative model is the manner in which *affects are categorized, impacted on, and altered.* The following lists summarize the major components of the model. The rest of Part 1 of the chapter amplifies these assumptions and change mechanisms.

The assumptions are as follows:

1. An integrative position is essential for a comprehensive model of psychotherapy.
2. On the basis of extensive infant research, human nature may be considered benign unless provoked.
3. An updated psychodynamic theory must revise the Freudian structural model to include the full range of affects.
4. Affects constitute our biologically endowed basic motivational system and, in contrast to drives, are amenable to psychotherapeutic change.
5. Distinguishing specific functions of affects is essential to understanding, predicting, and altering psychopathology: the defensive, inhibitory, and activating (or adaptive) affective functions.
6. The psychodynamic conflict formulations represent the major maladaptive affect patterns and guide treatment objectives and interventions.
7. Principles of operant and respondent conditioning are major agents of psychodynamic change.
8. Integration of interventions are needed to achieve psychodynamic treatment objectives.
9. Relational theory must be integrated with intrapsychic theory to guide the adaptive solution focus.
10. Effective treatment must be patient-specific.

In summary, the intrapsychic structure represents what needs changing (how one reacts to self and others). The principles of learning-based conditioning represent the major mechanisms of change. Relational theory suggests what form that change might take (the optimal solution focus).

The change mechanisms are as follows:

1: The systematic *desensitization of anxiety associated with affects and attachments.* This process entails the restructuring of affects and images in the procedural memory trace and the regulation of conflicts or anxieties associated with affective experience in relationship with others.
2: The *acquisition of missing concepts or capabilities.* This task involves the building of new models in the memory trace, including declarative

knowledge (e.g., affective, cognitive, and relational concepts) and procedural knowledge (e.g., learning new ways of responding).

3: *The acquisition of an integrated perspective of intrapsychic and interpersonal relatedness.* Affect experienced and shared by the patient and therapist in the real therapeutic relationship is a major change agent.

These change mechanisms and their underlying assumptions are believed to account for most of the variance in psychotherapeutic change. I elaborate on each one in more detail in the following discussion.

ASSUMPTIONS

The Need for an Integrative Position

For many years, therapists have understood the need to integrate the disparate worlds of psychoanalytic and cognitive–behavioral psychotherapy. The pioneers who began the exploration of psychotherapy integration, Marvin Goldfried (1992), Paul Wachtel (1977), and others in the Society for the Exploration of Psychotherapy Integration, have taught that the therapists of the future must be adequately trained to provide a holistic approach to the biopsychosocial individual. We need to assess and treat environmental contingencies, family and interpersonal systems, maladaptive cognitions, and blunted affect, as well as recognize genetic predispositions (temperament and family history; Kagan, 1994; Whybrow, Akiskal, & McKinney, 1984). We must be able to evaluate the relative contributions of nature versus nurture in any given case. The greatest challenge is to integrate the skills, methods, and insights of affect-based intrapsychic psychotherapy with the power of cognitive and behavioral therapy within a sensitive relational perspective.

Dynamic therapists have been turned off when behaviorists have applied punishment or reinforcement, ignoring the needs of the whole individual. Such criticism is generally leveled at an unenlightened behaviorism that has not assumed a holistic perspective. Consider the bedtime fears of a child who is biologically overly anxious. The child needs the mother's care and soothing. If the mother mistakenly tries to soothe the cries by letting the child stay up, she inadvertently reinforces the terror around going to bed. If the mother is only placating or *soothing,* she and the child will become ruled by the child's anxieties. If the mother is only punishing of the crying behavior, the bedtime crying behavior will in fact stop, but the price paid will be the silencing of the child's voice. None of these ways of responding is optimal. The child's emotional needs must be attended to; the metaphorical meaning of the child's crying must be understood. The child's bedtime behavior also needs to be altered, however. The basic theory underlying this model is that the patient's anxieties need to be soothed with help from the therapist, with active successive steps taken to teach the patient to self-soothe until autonomy is well established. Progressive behavioral approaches are evolving that take into consideration not only symptoms but also affects, relationships, and self-care.

Behaviorists and cognitive therapists who do not acknowledge the existence of "unconscious emotion" (i.e., inner affective experience that is not yet verbally labeled) are missing a crucial aspect of the human being. Sometimes the change agent is the cognitive alteration of erroneous beliefs, but other times the agent of change must be the recognition of the metaphorical meaning of behaviors and the desensitization of conflicted affects. Although initially psychodynamically trained, many of the leading behaviorists became disenchanted by the lack of clarity and frequent ineffectiveness of dynamic intervention. Today, dynamic constructs increasingly are being operationalized; David Malan has been the pioneer. To ignore the impact of intrapsychic factors on the individual and the capacity of the mind for representation through metaphor is to remain unnecessarily blind.

Likewise, dynamic therapists who ignore the influence of reinforcement contingencies, conditioning principles, or cognitive distortions on the individual's behavior are also remaining unnecessarily blind. In addition to the aforementioned considerations, equally important is the relatedness of the individual in the social milieu. Finally, the ardent environmentalists from both the behavioral and psychodynamic camps who ignore biological predisposition and genetic loading are remaining equally blind. Any comprehensive therapy of the future must take all these vital components of psychotherapeutic healing into consideration.

The Benign Quality of Human Nature

As discussed in chapter 1, abundant infant research has demonstrated that the affective nature of the human infant is benign unless frustrated (Emde, 1992; Lichtenberg, 1983; Stern, 1985). Evidence is also found in Jerome Kagan's observations of infants' "joys of play and sensory delight" (1992, p. 127) and Phyllis Greenacre's (1960) comments on the infant's love affair with the world. This perspective on human nature necessitates a shift from the Freudian structural position, which held that our basic motivators were bestial impulses (sex and aggression) that needed to be controlled, to an awareness of the natural biological endowment of affective responsivity in the infant that needs guidance and modulation.

Freudian Structural Theory Must Be Revised to Include the Full Range of Affects

My short-term anxiety-regulating model is based on Malan's (1979) conceptual schema of the Triangle of Conflict and the Triangle of Person; it is a revised structural model that follows Freud's fundamental principle of psychoanalysis. Called by Malan the universal principle of psychodynamics, this schema describes the barrier of defense and anxiety, which wards off a range of conflicted impulses and feelings. It is employed worldwide and endorsed by many modern dynamic theorists. *The principle that defenses inhibit adaptive affective responding owing to anxieties or conflicts is operative in every human being.*

Treatment is based on an extension of the Freudian structural model to replace the dual-drive theory of sex and aggression with a theory of the full range of affects and drives. Defensive behavior arises from conflict associated with this range of affective responding. Psychopathology is seen as the thwarting of basic motivation (i.e., human affective expression) resulting from excessive inhibitory reactions (affect–belief combinations), lack of capacity for adaptive responses, or both.

SYSTEMATIC PSYCHODYNAMIC OBJECTIVES

My theory contains an intentional, systematic organization of psychodynamically based treatment objectives. These objectives, which have evolved from Freudian structural theory as described by Malan's (1979) Two Triangles, are intended to be flexible guidelines that assist therapists in the scientific evaluation of dynamic psychotherapy. They are as follows:

1. The alteration of maladaptive response patterns through defense recognition and relinquishing
2. The exposure to warded-of feelings (considered objects of phobia) through affect experiencing
3. The relearning of suppressed skill or the learning of new skills: affect reintegration and expression
4. The alteration of the inner representations of self and others: self–other restructuring

OPERATIONALIZATION OF PSYCHODYNAMIC CONSTRUCTS

To further clarify the treatment mechanisms, dynamic constructs are described whenever possible in terms of observable behaviors. This process, made possible in large part by the use of videotapes and audiotapes, enhances clarity in clinical training and permits scientific investigation.

Tomkins's affect theory has been incorporated to describe the functioning of the I/F and A poles. In this model, the *unconscious* is operationalized as *inner experience that has not acquired a verbal label*. By labeling and focusing on previously unnamed impulses and feelings (drives and affects), we no longer have to grapple with an amorphous unconscious. The concept of *affects* (especially the physiological experiences) that have not acquired a verbal label reduces the confusion and brings us closer to tangible reality than we were before. For example, research by Tomkins, Ekman (1992a, 1992b), and Izard (1990) on facial expression has brought the study of affects into the realm of science.

Furthermore, operationalizing the term *neurosis* as "conflicts about feelings" refers one to the functions of the anxiety pole, where one finds an amalgam of *beliefs and self-inhibiting or self-attacking responses that thwart or block adaptive responding*. This construct is much more tangible than that of *neurotic conflict*.

Defensive behavior exists on a continuum from the most to the least adaptive. Defensiveness is not seen as destructive or maladaptive unless it blocks the expression of an affect that is needed for adaptive purposes. This defense continuum is based on Vaillant's hierarchy (1977, 1993), in which defensive behavior is shown to range from mature and adaptive to immature and maladaptive forms. It is on the less mature forms of defensiveness that this therapy focuses for change. Defensive behaviors function to take the place of warded-off adaptive expression of wants and needs (by avoiding affects, closeness, authenticity, and so on). Defenses are called on in interpersonal situations when we do not dare to express ourselves directly. The more severe the defensive function (as defined in chapter 4), the greater the psychopathology, that is, the earlier the developmental impairment and the greater the strength of the inhibitory functions of anxiety, shame, and pain.

The term *defense* is retained to convey the psychodynamic meaning of something done to keep something else outside of the awareness due to some form of conflict. Of course, not all defensive behavior is a problem. Indeed, life throws so much at us that we need to filter experience. But when that defensive behavior becomes problematic for the individual, it comes into the realm of pathology and must be made explicit. (See chapter 1, Part 2, for operationalization of constructs in this model.)

Defenses are the responses resulting when anxieties or conflicts block the expression of primary feeling. Defenses can be thoughts, feelings, or behaviors that serve to avoid or protect us from the experience or expression of uncomfortable feeling. Defenses can also take the form of affective expression (i.e., defensive feelings) used to avoid a primary feeling (weepiness to cover anger or irritability when one is afraid to show tenderness).

Affect Is a Basic Motivational System Amenable to Psychotherapeutic Change

Silvan Tomkins's model emphasizes that *affects, rather than drives, are the basis of human motivation.* Affects activate our behaviors, influence our decisions, spur our choices, and impel us to act. Appropriate experience and expression of our affects is fundamental to adaptive functioning. Because affect-laden associations are learned through experience, they are amenable to change through psychotherapeutic intervention.

Certainly, cognitions and beliefs serve to guide and direct basic affective motivations. The interwoven nature of cognition and affect suggests that approaches involving either one offer valid methods of change that will impact on the other. Nevertheless, ultimate alteration in affective responding (affect restructuring) is a fundamental mechanism of character change.

Affective blunting, which is the severe inhibition of the inner experience or the outer expression of our basic motivations, is postulated to be the fundamental basis of human maladaptive responding and, therefore, of psychopathology. *Effective treatment depends on regulating the inhibition to permit adaptive activation of affects resulting in a more constructive response.*

Distinguishing Defensive, Inhibitory, and Adaptive Affects
Is Essential in Understanding Psychopathology

There is a blind spot in our culture that fails to distinguish among (a) defensive affects, (b) inhibitory affects, and (c) adaptive affects. Furthermore, we fail to recognize that much expressed affect is defensive. Defensive affects are affects used to replace or avoid conflicted feelings. Defensive affects result from activating affects being too strongly inhibited by aversive A pole affects. Examples include smiling when one is sad, or acting interested when one is bored but afraid to say so. (Defensive affects are discussed at length in chapter 7.)

Anxiety, guilt, shame, and emotional pain are the biologically endowed affects for inhibition. If these inhibitory affects (i.e., the A pole) were not in operation, there would be no need for defenses; affects, in the form of wants or needs, would simply be expressed. But because emotional expression often needs to be interpersonally modulated, the inhibitory affects have evolved to control or guide their expression (Tomkins, 1962). In therapy, we try to reduce the aversive levels of the inhibitory affects, affects that no longer serve *self-control but result in self-attack or self-abuse.* (I'm stupid, worthless, bad, and so on.)

In contrast to Freudian "hydraulic" libido theory, the model described in this book does not hold that activating affects are stored up or dammed up energies needing to be released. Rather, these affects represent adaptive motivations, action tendencies, and a readiness to respond to life experiences, to other people, or to inner needs (signaled by the drives, thoughts, or other feelings). *Adaptive affective expression is not catharsis but cognitively guided, fully controlled adaptive interpersonal expression of wants and needs.* These distinctions among activating, inhibiting, and defensive affects are discussed in detail in chapters 4, 6, and 7. The relationship of affect to attachment is central to psychopathology and is discussed in detail in chapter 9.

The Core Psychodynamic Formulation Guides the Treatment

The core psychodynamic formulation is the identification of the most salient and repetitive pattern or patterns of defenses and anxieties that block adaptive affective responding. The core pattern is hypothesized to carry most of the weight of the patient's disorder. Resolving the major psychodynamic conflicts in a patient's life should significantly reduce the character disorder, or pathology: the long-standing and inappropriate or maladaptive behavior patterns. The formulation of the psychodynamic conflict is presented in detail in chapter 3.

Restructuring the character pathology involves three treatment objectives: defense restructuring, affect restructuring, and self–other restructuring. The specific content of these objectives (i.e., the specific function of the defenses, the specific affects that are conflicted, and the specific reasons why they are conflicted or inhibited) are determined by the psychodynamic formulation. These specific formulation-based objectives represent the *solution focus,* that is, the regulation of the anxieties or inhibitory affects that block affective experiences needed to resolve problems in the patient's life.

Principles of Operant and Respondent Conditioning
Are Major Agents of Psychodynamic Change

The principles of operant conditioning (the frequency of the occurrence of a behavior is altered by its consequences, e.g., reinforcement, extinction, punishment; Cautela, 1966, 1973; Cautela & McCullough, 1978; McCullough, 1982; Skinner 1938, 1953) and respondent conditioning (Pavlov, 1927; reciprocal inhibition, Wolpe, 1958) offer guidelines for how to change behavior, whether it is covert–intrapsychic, overt–intrapersonal, or interpersonal. Intrapsychic phenomena are not seen in this model as a "black box" but operationalized as self-reported images (of self in relation to others through identified defensive, anxiety-based, and affect-based behaviors). The conditioning principles used to alter the inner affective experience as well as instrumental behaviors or interpersonal functioning include reinforcement (primary and secondary gain), extinction, desensitization, punishment and identification of negative consequences, and reciprocal inhibition.

In addition (again, from learning-based conditioning principles), this model holds that to the degree that pathology is learned or conditioned,[1] it is, in part, a phobic response to affective expression, a lack of essential intrapsychic or interpersonal concepts or capabilities, or both. (Many learning-based hypotheses concerning alteration of psychodynamic functioning also are discussed in McCullough, 1991b.)

From a cognitive therapy perspective, acquired maladaptive beliefs underlie maladaptive responding. My approach is in agreement with cognitive therapy, but adds that the *beliefs are maladaptive because they thwart, punish, or inhibit adaptive self-experience or expression of conflicted or unlabeled adaptive affects.*

Integration of Interventions Needed to Achieve Psychodynamic Treatment Objectives

Both long- and short-term dynamic psychotherapies seek to analyze defenses that ward off conflicted affects. The methods for achieving the psychodynamic objectives in this model, however, which are designed to shorten the process or make it more efficient, are drawn from a diversity of theoretical orientations, including cognitive, gestalt, supportive, self psychology, object relations, and interpersonal therapies. Examples of the methods, such as guided imagery to assist in exposure, therapist empathy and affirmation to reinforce more adaptive models of attachment, and cognitive restructuring to assist in desensitization, are described throughout this book.

In summary, the treatment is a highly integrative approach with psychodynamic goals and the incorporation of interventions from a range of theoretical orientations to achieve those goals in a time-efficient manner. Under-

---

[1]Operant conditioning is defined as "a process in which the frequency of occurrence of a bit of behavior is modified by the consequences of the behavior" (Reynolds, 1975, p. 1). In this model, the behavior is adaptive affective responding. By the term *conditioned avoidance*, I refer to *learned* associations or linkages. For example, an infant naturally cries when hurt, but many of us, in growing up, have learned that crying is shameful; there is a linkage, or association, between crying and shame. Shame is the negative consequence of the crying, and thus crying is decreased in frequency. This conditioned association is one of the main linkages that this therapy seeks to "decondition" or help the patient to "unlearn."

lying this treatment is the hypothesis that learning-based conditioning principles are major factors in maintaining maladaptive behaviors and in promoting behavior change.

Integration of Relational and Intrapsychic Theories Defines the Form of Adaptive Change

The intrapsychic self grows, develops, and changes only in an interpersonal milieu. Recovery of the positive affect associated with past persons in memory is a mechanism hypothesized to effect change through the desensitization of the conflicts related to positive feelings associated with that relationship and the sense of self. Recovery of positive affect has the power to alter the sense of self by promoting the memory of earlier models of positive attachment. Of course, positive affect associated with current persons in the patient's life can also assist in the desensitization process and in building new relational models. For the same reasons, the real relationship with the active, involved therapist is a major agent of change.

Relational theory is integrated with intrapsychic theory to guide both the patient and the therapist in their construction of the optimal solution focus. The needs of the self must be considered in an optimal balance with the needs of others in the social milieu or society. One must not be sacrificed to the other. As reviewed by Stanley Guisinger and Sidney Blatt (1994), individuality and relatedness are not treated as opposing values but as integrated constructs. A stable and compassionate sense of self can occur only within a matrix of caring relationships. Mitchell pointed out that "human fulfillment is sought in the establishment and maintenance of relationships with others" (1988, p. 403). Jordan and her colleagues (1991) emphasized the essential nature of the "self-in-relation."

Defenses, inhibitions, sense of self, and self-expression are acquired only in relationships with others. The regulation of conflicts around attachment—the need for responsivity from others and by the self—is crucial to the healing of psychopathology. The optimal, or adaptive, response for the patient is one that transcends the dichotomy of self versus other to integrate and balance the needs of both.

Effective Treatment Must Be Patient-Specific

As noted in chapter 2, patient receptivity to treatment interventions varies according to the patient's level of functioning, preparedness for psychodynamic treatment, his or her specific biological predispositions, and the compatibility of the desired change with the patient's relational milieu, whether personal, social, or cultural. If a patient is motivated, is psychologically minded, and responds well to therapist interventions, the prognosis is better and the treatment is briefer. Proper supports (residential or inpatient settings) may compensate for a GAF rating below 50 in such patients. The reverse typically is not true, however: If the GAF level is high, but motivation, psychological-mindedness, and patient response to treatment are low (e.g., alexythymia), prognosis is poor and short-term treatment is contraindicated without substantial preparatory work.

Response to treatment is also impacted by a patient's biological predisposition or affective temperament. Therefore, biological boundaries of learning (e.g., Seligman & Hager, 1972) must be considered as they might apply to each patient. For example, patients with bipolar I disorders are much less responsive to psychotherapy than are patients with depressive disorders. Kagan's (1994) research on inhibited versus uninhibited children highlights the necessity of considering biological predisposition. Kagan notes, however, that a nonanxious mother can often decrease the inhibition of an inherently anxious child. Therapists should endeavor to do the same for their patients.

CHANGE MECHANISMS

Central to this treatment model's objectives is the adaptive management of affect. The first objective is to remove or reduce the blocks to affective expression (i.e., defenses and anxieties) by defense restructuring, and the second objective is to assist the patient in acquiring new, adaptive modes of affective experience and expression (affect restructuring). The third objective, self–other restructuring, is called on when needed to identify, affirm, and make more adaptive the concepts of feelings associated with self and others.

Desensitization of Conflicts

If one seeks to impact effectively on such conditioned avoidance reactions, the principles of learning-based conditioning (both operant and respondent) need to be incorporated into the psychodynamic framework. One of the major interventions follows the principle of desensitization to help patients overcome their phobia of internal reactions or affects and dare to feel once again. Through the use of imagery, the patient is exposed to the conflict-laden affects until the anxieties are regulated to adaptive levels and the adaptive affective expression is modulated rather than thwarted or inhibited.

Similar to a dog flexing its leg on hearing a tone that had been paired with an aversive shock, defensive avoidant behavior occurs when affects become sensitized through association with aversive experience to elicit fear or anxiety. From a respondent conditioning perspective (e.g., Wolpe, 1958), reciprocal inhibition occurs when an adaptive affective response competes with an anxiety response. From an operant conditioning perspective, repeated exposure to the phobic inner stimuli (i.e., conflicted or sensitized affects) without aversive consequences results in reduction of the anxiety. Desensitization can be seen, therefore, as the process of extinction of a conditioned response (defensive behavior) by the presentation of the conditioned stimulus (an affect) without the presence of the unconditioned aversive or fear-eliciting stimulus (social punishment, shame, neglect, or abuse). Through the process of repeated exposure to affect without aversive consequences, the experience and expression of the affect becomes less closely linked with anxiety and freer. In fact, both operant and respondent mechanisms appear to be operative, and research is needed to assess their relative contributions. The main premise is that principles of learning-based conditioning are brought to bear on inner affective and cognitive reactions rather than on external stimuli only.

The primary goal of this treatment approach is the desensitization of conflicted affects: the freeing up of self-expression in relation to others including the ability to laugh when happy, cry when sad, set limits or defend when attacked, and work and love with tenderness, enthusiasm, and joy.

Acquisition of Missing Intrapsychic Concepts and Capabilities

We should not attempt to alter what has been sustaining to our patients unless we can help them to replace the altered responses with a more adaptive variant. Not only do we need to break associations and reduce inhibitions, we also need to replace lost functions and build new concepts and capabilities.

Building new concepts and capabilities is important both for the resolution of conflict as well as deficit pathology. These new capabilities include the labeling of specific maladaptive behaviors or defenses, labeling of affects (identifying response patterns in defense restructuring), mastery of affect skills (affect experience and expression), and affirming or building of relational experience (self–other restructuring).

Acquisition of Missing Relational Concepts and Capabilities

The needs of the self and of others must be taken into consideration in a balanced way in the treatment of psychopathology and in the guiding of the patient toward adaptive functioning. Much goes on within us that is, unfortunately, separate and distinct from what goes on between us and others.

Psychotherapy cannot be focused solely on the individual's inner experience and outward expression of feeling—in a vacuum. We are encased in a social milieu, and all our actions and reactions need to take that milieu into consideration. The art of living is in large part the ability to (a) express what is experienced within in a way that can be best received by others and (b) adaptively experience within what is expressed by and received from others. Furthermore, we need to learn to give to and to receive from *ourselves* as well as others. Human connection, attachment, and mutuality are the optimal result of personal development and growth.

THE RELATIONAL ROLE OF THE THERAPIST IN CHANGE

This model puts greater emphasis on the real relationship than on the transferential relationship. Although transference distortions are important to resolve, the real, affectively shared human relationship between the patient and the therapist may be more fundamental to character change than transference phenomena.

The role of the therapist is to (a) assist in the desensitization of conflicted affects and attachments, (b) offer a new or "good enough" model for attachment, and (c) help validate, clarify, and label inner experience, when necessary.

In this model, the therapist collaborates with and is an ally of the patient. This collaborative (rather than confrontive) and emotionally present therapist stance is essential to creation of the "holding environment," in which rapid growth and change can take place. This stance provides a "continuous, graded, corrective emotional experience" at every point in the session. One does not "manipulate" the transference. Instead, genuine human contact is experienced in the real relationship. The relationship with the therapist is the vehicle of transmission of affect and carries in it the power to harm or to heal.

Much psychotherapy research points to the power of the alliance in therapeutic change, but thus far the full range of the different types of alliances has not been well described or sufficiently researched.

THE OVERARCHING PRINCIPLES IN THIS THERAPY MODEL

The overarching principles that encompass the psychodynamic, learning, and relational theories are (a) the universal dialectic of activation versus inhibition, or separation versus attachment (thesis versus antithesis, yin versus yang), and (b) the equally universal struggle for synthesis and resolution of conflict. Affects associated with attachments are the activators of relational experience, the theses. Defenses, anxieties, and separation are inhibitors of relational experience, the antitheses. To regulate these experiences when they are out of synchrony, this model employs the activating forces of reinforcement through positive experience and the inhibitory forces of extinction (neutral consequences) and punishment (identification of negative consequences) all embedded in a range of interventions. It is in the regulation and balance of these opposing forces that healing takes place and we find peace.

Part 2: Research in Support of Short-Term Anxiety-Regulating Psychotherapy

It has been said repeatedly that research does not influence clinical practice. I am proud to say that this model, short-term anxiety-regulating psychotherapy, is one of the exceptions. This treatment model has been developed and repeatedly revised in light of clinical observations and research findings. It is based on the impressive work of Malan and his colleagues, reflecting a 50-year history of careful study of "the science of psychodynamics" as applied to brief psychotherapy. This model retains the fundamental components of Malan's model of the two triangles and many of its basic principles. It has grown further on the basis of clinical trials conducted at Beth Israel Medical Center in New York City (1982–1990) and the University of Trondheim, Norway (1988–1999; a clinical-trial comparison of this model with a cognitive–experiential model, is approaching completion), as well as ongoing research at Harvard Medical School (intensive study of the single case).

Research support for this model is cited here beginning with the most general level of analysis, psychotherapy as a whole, and including research on common factors, brief psychotherapy in general, clinical trials in this model, and the process levels of research analysis of this model.

GENERAL RESULTS OF PSYCHOTHERAPY RESEARCH

Years ago, Morris Parloff (1984) said that the effectiveness of psychotherapy had been demonstrated with "monotonous regularity." Today, after hundreds of research studies and many meta-analyses, this finding of the effectiveness of psychotherapy remains consistent. Psychotherapies in general have positive effects that are both statistically significant and clinically meaningful. Michael Lambert and Allen Bergin pointed out that "psychotherapy facilitates the remission of symptoms . . . and often provides additional coping strategies and methods for dealing with future problems" (1994, p. 180). The average treated person was better off than 80% of the untreated sample (Lambert & Bergin, 1994, p. 144). The authors were careful to note, however, that not everyone benefits to a satisfactory degree. The average effect of psychotherapy is equivalent to 1 standard deviation (SD) unit, which is statistically large by standards developed by Jacob Cohen (1988). This amount of change exceeds the average effects of 9 months of reading instruction in elementary school ($SD = 0.67$) or a trial of antidepressants ($SD = 0.41$–0.80). "Thus the effect sizes produced by the application of psychotherapies are typically as large as or larger than those produced by a variety of methods . . . employed in medical and educational interventions" (Lambert & Bergin, 1994, p. 147).

The comparison across a wide variety of treatments reveals that differences in outcome between various forms of therapy are not as pronounced as one might expect. Lambert and Bergin (1994) conclude that no one form of therapy is *consistently* better than another. The typical psychotherapy patients, however, show gains that surpass those resulting from pseudotreatment conditions and placebos. When the effects of psychotherapy are compared to those of medication for many diagnoses, psychotherapy is found to be as good or better. Compared to the meta-analyses of 10 or 20 years ago, the amount of change caused by psychotherapy is increasing from about 0.67 SD to 1.0 SD, on average.

This strong level of effectiveness has also been demonstrated in the first major clinical trial completed on the short-term dynamic treatment of personality disorders (Winston, McCullough, & Laikin, 1993; Winston et al., 1991), which is the precursor to the present model. There was an average of 1 SD change in outcome measures ($M = 0.97$) after 40 sessions of brief, active, and focused psychotherapy. This positive outcome was even more impressive because it was obtained in a population of patients with personality disorders, who are typically unresponsive to treatment. At follow-up after 1.5 years, not only were these gains maintained, but there was slight improvement as well (Winston et al., 1993). In an extensive review of the overall effectiveness of brief psychotherapy, Mary Koss and Julia Shiang reported that "there is now considerable empirical evidence showing that brief therapy, practiced in various forms, is efficacious with specific patient populations" (1994, p. 676).

COMMON FACTORS INCLUDED IN THIS MODEL

Lambert and Bergin (1994) examined the effectiveness of psychotherapy from the perspective of techniques, common factors, and alliance. In this section, I focus on the results for common factors. It has been hypothesized that different therapies embody common factors that are curative, even though these factors may not be explicitly stated by the theory of change central to the treatment model.

There is substantial research support for the idea that common factors across different treatments account for much of the improvement in patient outcomes. Lambert and Bergin (1994) strongly recommended that therapists intentionally incorporate them. These common factors fall into three categories: (a) *support factors* (e.g., reassurance, structure, therapist skill, mitigation of isolation), (b) *learning factors* (e.g., advice, affective experiencing, corrective emotional experiencing, feedback, insight, changing expectations), and (c) *action or behavioral factors* (e.g., mastery, facing fears, taking risks, modeling, practice).

Each of these common factors has been intentionally incorporated in the model presented in this book. For example, *support factors* include validation of the defensive behaviors, anxiety regulation throughout the treatment, and an empathic, open, and accepting stance of the therapist in the real relationship. *Learning factors* include teaching patients to identify defensive patterns and label affects, to note the negative consequences of the defenses, to distinguish defensive from adaptive functions of feelings, to express affect adaptively, and to view themselves and others in a different light. *Action factors* in this model include the repeated exposure to fearful and conflictual situations and experiences. Extensive research by Barlow (1988, 1993) and his colleagues has supported the value of exposure. Barlow was far ahead of his time when he hypothesized the following:

> It is possible that the crucial function of exposure, instead of facilitating extinction, is to prevent the action tendencies associated with fear and anxiety. (1988, p. 311)
>
> It is possible that attention to action tendencies forms an important part of the treatment of other emotional disorders [depression as well as anxiety]. (1988, p. 312)
>
> In any case, the majority of therapeutic approaches to anxiety disorder in general and phobia in particular have stumbled on the necessity of directly countering the action tendency of escape associated with panic. Escape behavior may be blatant, as is the case with phobic avoidance, or more subtle, as with the variety of cognitive avoidance strategies seen in panic disorder. One must prevent escape or other avoidance responses, both cognitive and behavioral, and must strongly encourage approach behavior. [*Overwhelming evidence supporting the usefulness of this approach is presented throughout this book.*] (1988, p. 312)

A procedure such as relaxation may be useful not because of any arousal-reducing properties, but because it directly substitutes a different action tendency for chronic vigilance.

In summary, the overwhelming evidence from emotion theory is that an essential step in the modification of emotional disorders is the direct alteration of associated action tendencies. Laughter, humor, and associated facial expressions induced during successful paradoxical intention . . . —a technique successfully used to counteract fear and anxiety . . . —may be effective not because of changes in self-statements, as is often assumed. Rather, prevention of behavioral responses (including facial expressions) associated with fear and anxiety, and the substitution of action tendencies associated with alternative emotions, may account for the effectiveness of this technique. (Barlow, 1988, p. 312)

Additional research support for exposure and empathy is cited in a review of predominantly experiential and dynamic studies by Greenberg and Safran (1987, pp. 85–95). This strong support for exposure from several theoretical vantage points demonstrates how theoreticians are moving toward a unified model of psychotherapy incorporating many of these common factors, which have been repeatedly demonstrated to be effective.

RESEARCH AT THE BETH ISRAEL
BRIEF PSYCHOTHERAPY RESEARCH PROGRAM

The Beth Israel Medical Center (BIMC) program was established in 1982 to study short-term dynamic psychotherapy for patients with Cluster C personality disorders with GAF functioning above 50 (McCullough & Winston, 1991; Trujillo & McCullough, 1985; Winston et al., 1989). Patients received a standard assessment battery and were randomly assigned to one of two treatment conditions, which varied the amount of confrontation and focus on affect. All sessions were videotaped and coded for psychotherapy process variables. Between 1983 and 1991, 64 patients received 40 sessions of psychotherapy (designed for long-standing character problems as measured on the SCID-II). Coding of the videotaped sessions was completed in 1992. A number of studies, reviewed here, have been published, and others are now in preparation for publication. Manuals have been developed for three short-term dynamic treatment models that have emerged from this program: dynamic supportive psychotherapy (Pinsker, Rosenthal, & McCullough, 1991), brief adaptational psychotherapy (Pollack & Winston, 1991), and short-term dynamic psychotherapy (Laikin, Winston, & McCullough, 1991). The latter manual was a precursor to this book.

The Beth Israel program demonstrated empirically that improvement in symptoms and social adjustment resulted from decreased defensiveness and increased affective expression for patients with Axis II disorders (Cluster C, plus histrionic patients, all with multiple additional Axis II criteria; Winston et al., 1991). These were patients whose level of functioning was moderate (GAF > 50) and who thus could respond to the rapid exploratory form of treatment (McCullough, 1993b). At the 18-month follow-up, not only were these gains maintained, but the patients had improved (Winston et al., 1994). This study offered a maximum of 40 sessions, but subsequent pilot studies have shown comparable results in 20 sessions or less when patients are assisted rather than confronted to change. In conclusion, this short-term treatment model for Axis II pathology (which increases patients' awareness and control of defenses and affects) has support, both theoretically and empirically. Further research is needed, however, on the impact of treatment objectives on Axis II criteria and to assess the number of sessions required to achieve these objectives.

RESEARCH IN PROGRESS AT THE
UNIVERSITY OF TRONDHEIM, NORWAY

At the Short-Term Psychotherapy Research Program in the Department of Psychiatry, University of Trondheim in Norway, this short-term anxiety-regulating therapy model is currently being examined in a repeated-measures comparative process outcome design. The main purposes of the study, directed by Martin Svartberg and Tore Stiles, are (a) to compare the outcomes of short-term anxiety-regulating psychotherapy (START) and cognitive–experiential psychotherapy (C–ET), (b) to examine the course of improvement both during and after treatment, and (c) to study a series of process variables and their impact on outcome. Fifty patients meeting DSM-III-R criteria for Cluster C personality disorders (i.e., avoidant, dependent, obsessive, passive–aggressive, and self-defeating) were randomized to 40 sessions of either START or C–ET. All sessions have been videotaped. START therapists are eight experienced psychiatrists and psychologists who participated in an 8-year program of training and supervision by Leigh McCullough Vaillant. Cognitive therapists are six equally experienced psychologists who also participated in a long and intensive training program. Patients have been assessed repeatedly during and after treatment on dimensions such as general symptomatology, depression, anxiety, personality functioning, internalized objects, and social adjustment. The final follow-up assessment will take place in 1999.

REVIEWS OF PSYCHOTHERAPY PROCESS STUDIES

An extensive review of more than 2,300 empirical findings by David Orlinsky and his colleagues (1994) highlighted specific processes that have been consistently related to outcome. "These include, among others, the overall quality of the therapeutic relationship, therapist skill, patient cooperation versus resistance, patient openness versus defensiveness, and treatment duration" (Orlinsky, Grawe, & Parks, 1994, p. 364). Several of my group's studies (described later in this chapter) were included in this review, and our findings were in line with those of many others on the effects of defenses, affects, and the therapist–patient relationship on psychotherapy outcome. Orlinsky's review lends supports to the effectiveness of the processes incorporated in my model.

Specific Process Studies of Short-Term Dynamic Psychotherapy

As research director of the BIMC program in New York City, I designed and supervised a number of process studies that lend support to this model.[2] One of the initial steps in the BIMC program was designing a coding procedure for the assessment of psychotherapy process, which underwent continual development and revision during the first 4 years of the program and culminated in the Psychotherapy Interaction Coding System (PIC System; McCullough, 1991a). The PIC System demonstrated adequate-to-good reliability ($Rs = .55–.90$), exhibited excellent predictive validity ($R^2 = .64$), and yielded strong process–outcome relationships (e.g., McCullough et al., 1991; Taurke, Flegenheimer, McCullough, Winston, Pollack, & Trujillo, 1990). The PIC System assesses therapist interventions (e.g., interpretation, clarification, support) and patient responses (e.g., affect, defense, cognitive elaboration) minute by minute throughout the session. Although the PIC System produced an enormous amount of highly specific data, it also pointed toward the next step in coding of therapy process: the need *to place patient–therapist interactions in a relevant context of treatment objectives*. This was one impetus to the identification of specific treatment objectives, which led to the clinical and research studies described in the following sections.

OBSERVATION OF VIDEOTAPED SESSIONS

The intensive coding of hundreds of hours of videotaped sessions revealed repetitive patterns that represented obstacles to treatment progress. (The obstacles, outlined in chapter 1, contributed to the establishment of the main treatment objectives.) These repeated clinical observations, along with the studies discussed subsequently in this chapter, led to modifications in the confrontational approach (e.g., Davanloo, 1980), replacing confrontation with clarification and supportive interventions to assist the patient in the difficult assimilation of the analysis of defenses and experiencing of affect (Laikin, Winston, & McCullough, 1991; McCullough, 1991a; McCullough, Bacheldor, & Bullitt, 1988). Both defensive and affective behaviors were rendered more manageable through regulation of the associated anxiety, guilt, shame, or pain that plagues patients with personality disorders and typically impedes therapeutic progress (McCullough, Bacheldor, & Bullitt, 1988). Techniques from many orientations have been included in the various steps of the treatment model to enhance the patient's *exposure to and mastery of the specific treatment objectives*.

This model was intentionally standardized through the focus on *objectives rather than interventions*, for the following reasons:

1: Objectives make explicit the subgoals of treatment and provide guideposts for the therapist that help in organizing the enormous amount of complex clinical material.

[2]The research was funded by Beth Israel Medical Center (see McCullough & Winston, 1991, for a detailed description of the methodology).

2: The focus on objectives allows therapists some flexibility in the method used to achieve those objectives; they can make use of their clinical skill and intuition in addition to the methods suggested. Too rigid an adherence to interventions described in a treatment manual has been demonstrated to have a small negative relationship to outcome ($r = -.10$; Hoglend & Heyerdahl, 1994).

3: Standardized objectives allow a comparison with other treatments that strive to achieve similar goals (both long- and short-term psychodynamic psychotherapies) but do so through the use of different interventions (e.g., free association versus high therapist activity, or the development of a transference neurosis in contrast to exposure to affective experiencing).

4: Clinical experience and research have supported this method of standardization.

RESEARCH IN SUPPORT OF DEFENSE RESTRUCTURING

Although our series of hypotheses predicted that confrontation would lead to decreased defensiveness, increased affective responding, and better outcomes, a series of studies demonstrated the efficacy of *supportive, empathic, and clarifying* methods above that of *confrontive* methods in the alteration of defenses. Salerno and colleagues (Salerno, Farber, McCullough, Winston, & Trujillo, 1992) demonstrated that higher total frequencies of therapist confrontation of defenses in the transference *did not, as we had hypothesized, predict improvement at outcome*. In a subsequent study (Makynen, 1992), researchers further examined confrontations that were sustained over several minutes, hypothesizing that it was the *continued confrontation* that would "break through" the defenses. Again, counter to expectations, this method did *not* predict improvement. Anu Makynen's study was a strong contributor to the growing awareness of the need for a graded and empathic procedure for recognition and relinquishing of defenses. In exploratory analyses of the coding data, it was noted that when confrontations were given *along with a supportive or empathic statement by the therapist* (Foote, 1989; Rubin, 1990), the result was a greater likelihood of expression of affect, a higher rating of therapist alliance, and (especially in lower functioning or more "difficult" patients) a higher probability of improvement at outcome. Patients seemed to be much more able to take in the painful information contained in a therapist's confrontation or interpretation when it was paired with a statement that reflected understanding or care.

After analyzing these studies, which examined which patient responses followed particular therapist interventions, our research team decided to look at patient–therapist interaction from the opposite perspective. Christine Joseph (1988) compared the likelihood that a given therapist intervention (e.g., questions, clarifications, confrontations, interpretations, self-disclosure, support) would precede affective responding versus defensive responding. We hypothesized that confrontation would elicit significantly more affective responses. But Joseph, like Makynen (1992) and Salerno et al. (1992), demonstrated that, of the eight interventions, confrontation elicited the most defensive behavior. Clarification was the only variable that significantly elicited affect. Apparently, listening carefully and reflecting back what the patient said prepared the patient to respond in a less defensive and more open and affective manner.

Studies such as these have led many clinicians to question seriously whether the anxiety-provoking techniques are the best, or only, method for altering defenses. My inclination to back off and be more gentle was supported by these studies. When anxieties emerge, therapists do not have to intensify the confrontation of defenses to achieve "breakthroughs" to feeling (as in Davanloo's, 1980, anxiety-provoking methods). Our studies, and studies of others at that time (e.g., Wallerstein, 1986, on the Menninger Clinic study) were demonstrating that emotional depth could also be elicited by support, validation, and the provision of a safe and encouraging relationship in which the patient can face difficult issues. As therapists moved toward empathy and clarification over confrontation, however, the therapist stance remained active, focused, and involved and thus continued to differ markedly from the less active psychoanalytic and Rogerian approaches.

RESEARCH IN SUPPORT OF AFFECT RESTRUCTURING

Three studies have supported the need for sustained attention to affective experiencing. Franklin Porter (1988) demonstrated that the overall frequency of patient expression of affect did *not* correlate with outcome. Nor did the total frequency occurrence of defenses predict poor outcome. This finding was initially discouraging because the findings ran so counter to clinical experience; however, these data led us to consider that our initial hypothesis might have been too general. A revised hypothesis predicted that patient affect experiencing and defensive reactions to the therapist are predictive of outcome only *when in response to therapist intervention*. This hypothesis was strongly supported by the following study, and it underscored the importance of understanding the context of a patient's response.

Additionel research (McCullough et al., 1991) demonstrated through rated videotapes that the patient's affective response to transference interpretations significantly predicted improvement at outcome ($P = .01$; Multiple $R^2 = .66$; Unique Variance $= .22$) (1991, p. 531). This relationship was previously theorized by both Glover (1931) and Merton Gill (1982) and empirically demonstrated by Malan (1976) and Marziali (1984). The strength of this relationship was increased by the fact that transference interpretation followed by affect experiencing was a rather uncommon occurrence. (There were 61 occurrences in 64 coded sessions, i.e., less than 1 *per session*. No such responses occurred in the four cases with the poorest outcomes.) This finding emphasized the efficacy of *eliciting patient affect under specific therapeutic conditions* and the need to understand how to remove the obstacles to and increase the occurrence of such responses.

In a sample of 16 patients with personality disorders, Taurke et al. (1990) demonstrated that the ratio of affect expressed to defenses expressed was predictive of improvement. (The greater the ratio of expressed affect to defenses, the greater the improvement at outcome.) Patients started with an average of 1 episode of expressed affect per every 5 defensive responses at admission. At termination, the five most improved patients showed an average of 1 affective response for every 2 defensive responses. The five least improved patients showed no change in the 1:5 affect:defense ratio shown at admission. This study provided direct support for Malan's conceptual schema holding that lowering defensiveness in relation to affective expression contributes to improvement in outcome.

Viewed as a whole, these studies underscore the need for techniques to elicit affective expression as well as to *overcome the defensive obstacles* to affective expression. Several objectives in the short-term anxiety-regulating treatment model described in this book were derived from the research described.

THE SHORT-TERM PSYCHOTHERAPY RESEARCH PROGRAM AT HARVARD MEDICAL SCHOOL

The Short-Term Psychotherapy Research Program for Personality Disorders is being conducted at Beth Israel Hospital and Brigham and Women's Hospital at Harvard Medical School. This study is continuing to build on the 15-year programmatic body of research on short-term psychodynamic treatment of personality disorders described in this chapter. The current study employs a single-case multiple baseline experimental design with intensive analysis of videotaped psychotherapy sessions. An initial goal of the program has been the development of a method for rating how adequately a therapist has assisted a patient in meeting the specific treatment objectives descirbed in this book. This has resulted in a rating manual entitled *The Achievement of Therapist Objectives Rating Scale (ATOS Scale)* (McCullough, Vaillant, Meyer, & Cui, 1996) that will be further described. The long-range goal of this research program is the further specification of therapeutic change mechanisms that substantially reduce suffering and improve the functioning of patients with personality disorders.

The Achievement of Therapeutic Objectives Scale

Research is under way to test the objectives in this treatment model using a scale developed for that purpose, the Achievement of Therapeutic Objectives Scale (ATOS; McCullough, Vaillant, Meyer, & Cui, 1996).[3] One rates on a scale of 1 to 100 the degree to which each of the treatment objectives has been met. Ratings are made of the patient's recognition of defenses, the motivation to give up defenses, the intensity of experiencing affect, the ability to express wants and needs interpersonally, and the maladaptive inner representation of self or others. The identification of objectives, together with the rating of the degree the therapist assists the patient in achieving those objectives, offers a new and potentially useful method for assessing thera-

---

[3]This manual may be obtained from the author by sending a self-addressed ($1), stamped 9- x 11-inch envelope to the Short-Term Psychotherapy Foundation, Box 466, Dedham, MA 02026.

pist adherence to the model as well as therapist competence in applying the model.

The ATOS ratings are given for each session and are correlated with various residual measures of pre-post change at termination and follow-up of treatment, for example, severity of target complaints, ratings on the affect consciousness interviews, diagnostic criteria for Axis I and Axis II (total number of criteria), and ratings on the Global Assessment of Functioning (GAF) Scale. Preliminary data on reliability and validity are excellent, and a series of studies of the ATOS-based process–outcome relationships is under way.

SUMMARY

There is substantial research that lends support to the mechanisms incorporated in this model. In addition to general research findings on psychotherapy and research supporting the efficacy of common factors incorporated in this model, there have been numerous studies supporting the particular model, developed at Beth Israel Medical Center in New York City. A clinical trial comparing this model to a cognitive-experiential treatment is near completion at the University of Trondheim in Norway and the model is being tested in a single-case experimental design format at Harvard Medical School.

Epilogue: Future Directions

The short-term anxiety-regulating model of therapy described in this book represents my understanding of the subject and that of many colleagues at the close of 1996. Much work has been done before, and much will follow. I offer a *testable model* that has a demonstrated capacity to change long-standing and maladaptive character patterns. Now is the time to go on to the next phase of the research: experimentally examining the efficacy and breadth of application of the various objectives and interventions of this treatment model. I suspect that parts of this model will withstand the passage of time, and parts will change.

The parts that I hypothesize to have the greatest staying power are the therapeutic objectives: the restructuring of defenses, affects, and relationships by the regulation of the associated anxieties or conflicted affects. These objectives follow from Freud's original principles and were simplified and operationalized by Malan; I integrated them with other orientations. The universal principle of psychodynamic psychotherapy that Malan described (namely, that defenses and anxieties block true feeling concerning self and others) has withstood the test of time, and I suspect it will continue to do so.

The parts of the model that are likely to change, and that I hope will evolve and improve, are the interventions that assist in the achievement of those goals. Although some of these interventions may also have staying power, I hope that my colleagues and I and future generations of psychotherapy researchers will continue to discover more time-conscious and effective ways to achieve each of the major treatment objectives.

Looking to the future, what are the foci for the growth and development of psychotherapy? Foci that I would select include patient-specific treatment, assessment laboratories, videotaped assessment of treatment, what I call "airline pilot standards," and single-case experimental design. Finally, I believe the information gained about the brain–behavior interface through brain-imaging technology ultimately will allow us to link psychotherapeutic interventions with brain function.

Future research likely will benefit from the continuing leadership and inspiration provided by David Orlinsky and Ken Howard, not only through their creation of the Society for Psychotherapy Research, which has provided a crucible for the development of this young science, but also through their comprehensive studies of issues such as process–outcome relationships, generic change mechanisms, and dose–response ratios (e.g., Howard, Kopta, Drause, & Orlinsky, 1986; Orlinsky et al., 1994).

PATIENT-SPECIFIC TREATMENT

At this writing there is great controversy concerning which is better: long-term or short-term treatment. Rather than debating the merits of these two options, psychotherapists should be seeking the optimal treatment mechanisms (interventions, goals, and time required) for each patient. It is not that one psychotherapy is more effective than another but that there are increasingly standardized and effective interventions (e.g., exposure methods) that need to be specified for individual patients. I hope that in the next decade we will see the continuing development of effective mechanisms of change (cognitive, dynamic, and other methods) that can be provided for particular patients.

Research is also needed to identify the *approximate minimum number of sessions* necessary to achieve specific psychotherapeutic goals. We need to weigh the benefits of rapid movement in outpatient treatment versus intensive restructuring during a brief hospitalization with subsequent supportive, reconstructive treatment. It is my dream that we rigorously examine experimentally the potential for inpatient care to provide a supportive structure for character change (e.g., Volkan, 1971, 1972; Volkan & Showalter, 1968).

ASSESSMENT LABORATORIES

The mental health field desperately needs improved assessment of psychotherapy patients both before and after treatment. It is not realistic to expect a therapist to perform the rigorous function of a psychometrician and also provide treatment, much less to do so in 6–12 sessions, as mandated by managed care. Just as physicians routinely send patients for laboratory tests before and after treatment, so should psychotherapists send patients for assessments (DSM-IV diagnoses, symptom levels, and life-functioning information); the report would be in hand when the therapist first meets with a patient and would be used to guide treatment decisions and determine potential interventions. To assess change, these data should routinely be collected at the end of treatment as well. With the addition of videotaped sessions, such testing would tremendously enhance examination of data in experiments with single-case designs. Such a large-scale assessment effort has already begun (Howard, Leuger, Maling, & Martinovich, 1993; Orlinsky et al., 1994).

Such scrutiny of therapy outcomes might seem frightening to some, but let me reassure the reader that such examination of therapy has been ongoing for decades, with much success. In Europe and the United States, there are scores of research therapists who have submitted their work for close and careful scrutiny. They have considered it an honor and a privilege to do so. Some cases are successful, and some are not, but the study of these cases has given researchers the opportunity to examine what worked and what did not. As a result, therapists have grown individually, and the field has grown. Individual therapists need constant feedback on treatments; we need not be afraid of assessment, nor should we be punished when we are less than perfect.

VIDEOTAPED ASSESSMENT OF TREATMENT

Perhaps it will become increasingly routine for patients to permit video recording of treatment, as is frequently done in surgery and in athletic coaching. There are many reasons to consider doing so (see Alpert, 1996, for a detailed discussion):

1. The camcorder technology is making office recording easy and inexpensive.
2. Experience shows that therapists often have more inhibitions concerning videotaping than do patients.
3. Videotaping allows the therapist, like the football coach, to understand how important events were sequenced.
4. Videotaping allows the therapist to assimilate therapy content that, without repeated viewing, might be too emotion-laden to tolerate.
5. It allows high-quality supervision by showing, not telling.
6. It offers protection for the therapist (from distorted patient allegations) as well as for the patient (in the assurance that the therapist permits his or her work to be reviewed).
7. It allows the patient also to review what has happened.
8. It is a cost-efficient way of intensifying therapy.

AIRLINE PILOT STANDARDS

There are impressive standards for training of airline pilots that far exceed those used in the training of psychotherapists. Before a pilot is entrusted with taking a commercial plane into the air, hundreds of hours of practice in the test cockpit are required. In contrast, beginning psychotherapists often are assigned patients without ever having observed a psychotherapy session being conducted and without the opportunity to practice. As well-documented single-case designs (with videotaped sessions) begin to accumulate, I hope that practice programs can be developed for therapists-in-training. I would like to see standards evolve for "hours logged" at the videotape machine, not in passive watching but in interactive coding, responding, and anticipating of the next move.

Furthermore, the airlines have established regulations for maximum number of in-flight hours per week permitted for a pilot. In this vein, Benjamin noted that the intense work of well-executed psychotherapy "requires intense concentration from the therapist. . . . I believe that psychotherapists, like airline pilots, become unsafe, if they are overworked, upset, distracted, in altered states or too tired" (1993b, p. 88). We need research to evaluate the maximum number of treatment hours that permit optimal therapist functioning. I propose that such standards for training and conduct of treatment be considered for psychotherapists or for the medical profession as a whole.

SINGLE-CASE EXPERIMENTAL DESIGN

Abundant clinical trials have demonstrated that psychotherapy works, but we are only beginning to understand how, for whom, and under what conditions. The only way that we will be able to answer the pressing questions of patient-specific treatment is by constructing carefully controlled, intensively studied, single-case experimental designs. In the coming decades, we need a worldwide aggregation of not hundreds but *thousands* of well-executed single-case experimental designs (following a standardized format) to detail specific mechanisms of change.

These studies need to be designed with sufficient specificity, behavioral grounding, and standardization that comparisons among treatments can be made even decades from now. Inevitably, methods will change and treatments will change, but if carefully documented, the frequency, intensity, and duration of both treatment interventions and maladaptive behavior can be compared across time.

BRAIN–BEHAVIOR INTERFACE
ILLUMINATED THROUGH BRAIN IMAGING

Recent advances in neurobiology and neurological technology have great potential for contributing to psychotherapy research. There have been increasingly vivid and dramatic demonstrations of alteration in brain activity related to alteration in behaviors. This relationship has been shown for schizophrenic symptoms (Andreasen et al., 1995), for happy and sad states (George et al., 1995), for emotions such as hope (Gottshalk & Fronczek, 1995), and for changes induced through the cognitive therapy of obsessive–compulsive patients (Baxter, 1992; Baxter et al., 1992). *Brain imaging technology has forever illuminated the "black box."*

In addition, there is increasing understanding of *where* in the brain psychotherapeutic change may be found. Functional changes have been demonstrated, as measured by positron emission tomography (PET) or single photon emission computed tomography (SPECT). Furthermore, structural changes in the brain have been demonstrated by magnetic resonance imaging (MRI). A dramatic example is Baxter's demonstration of caudate glucose metabolic rate changes with both drug and behavior therapy in patients with obsessive–compulsive disorder (Baxter et al., 1992).

LeDoux's (1993) research on the declarative memory functions of the hippocampus suggest this as a potential area for studying the declarative knowledge acquisition underlying defensive pattern recognition or for imaging the restructuring of the representations of self and other. The procedural memory mechanisms underlying character change will be more difficult to pinpoint, but there is research suggesting the possibility of deconstructing this complex process. Studies of the limbic cortex (e.g., Aggleton, 1992; MacLean, 1972, 1985) have demonstrated brain–behavior relationships potentially related to affect and attachment. Social approach and avoidance behaviors have been associated with activity in the amygdala and related structures (Aggleton, 1992; Brothers, 1990; Insel, 1992; Kling & Brothers, 1992; Winslow & Insel, 1991). Attachment-related behaviors have been associated with the anterior cingulate gyrus (MacLean, 1985).[1] Responses in the amygdala to reward-related processes (e.g., Everitt & Robbins, 1992) and to the memory of reward (e.g., Gaffan, 1992) suggest potential links of amygdaloid function to the process of conditioning; this work is fundamental to understanding change in the present model.

Theorists such as Edelman (1987, 1988, 1992) and Kandel (1983) have offered explanations for *how* psychotherapeutic change might come about on the neuronal level. Edelman proposed that plasticity of neuronal networks can occur through "neuronal group selection" on the basis of environmental contingencies throughout the life span. Edelman (1987) called the process "neural Darwinism" and offered a neuron-based explanation for Freud's concept of *Nachtraglichkeit* (the retranscription of the memory trace): the continual "reentrant" signaling (or reverberating neural circuitry) that occurs between perceptual activity in real time and value-laden memory (1992, p. 119). When we help patients build new memories, new connections are built among and within these "reentrant maps" for both declarative and procedural memory throughout the brain.

In addition, Kandel (1983) offered a model of synaptic functioning in which classical conditioning is seen as an amplified form of presynaptic facilitation. Kandel suggested that "normal learning, the learning of anxiety and unlearning it through psychotherapeutic intervention, might involve long-term functional and structural changes in the brain that result from alteration in gene expression" (1983, p. 1291). The reader is referred to this classic article, which charts relationships between molecular biology and the metapsychology of anxiety reactions in psychotherapy.

We are developing sophistication in the (a) specification of therapy objectives and interventions, (b) methodology and technology used to measure behavioral change robustly on many levels, (c) understanding of areas of brain function, and (d) understanding of how neuronal networks might be continually altered throughout the life span. Although there is much more work to be done, these exciting developments are leading us into a new era in which psychotherapy research will be brought into the realm of "normal science" (Kuhn, 1970).

---

[1]The involvement of the anterior cingulate gyrus was brought to my attention by Greg Friscione of the Harvard Medical School (personal communication, 1995).

CONCLUSION

As this book came to completion and the title, *Changing Character*, was decided on, I found myself wondering whether my patients would concur that their character had changed. Shortly thereafter, I had a session with a woman who I felt had made remarkable progress. Since adolescence she had kept tight control over her emotions, maintained much emotional distance from others, and demonstrated a lifelong obsessional character style. The woman who now sat before me chuckled as she told me how much more relaxed she had become, how much better her relationship with her spouse was, and how she no longer had a need to keep such tight control over things. Her maladaptive patterns of rigidity and emotional isolation were substantially altered. Here was a great example of character change, I thought, so I asked her if it was *her* experience that she had changed her character. Her response was illuminating:

No, I don't think I've changed my character. [Pausing to think further] *I think I'm more myself than I ever have been. I feel like the core of me has been disinhibited.* [She stopped at that before reflecting further.] *Of course, I had to give up a certain defensiveness that felt safe and sustaining. I lost a certain amount of rigidity and* [pausing and chuckling] *... I learned the merits of risk-taking!* [Laughing heartily] *But from all that, a certain confidence has emerged. Now I'm less isolated, and I feel much more connected to people.*

Her moral character—her basic values, or the core of her—felt the same. Many patients since then have given me the same answer: "No, my character hasn't changed. I'm more myself than ever!" The real change in this treatment deals with destructive and sometimes inhuman defensiveness, what William James called the "plaster" of character, Wilhelm Reich called "character armor," and David Malan called "long-standing, repetitive and inappropriate patterns of behavior." My patient reminded me, yet again, that adaptive character change means freeing our patients (and ourselves) from the barriers to feeling. Adaptive character change means that our core of benign and relationship-oriented humanity—the best within us—may be set free.

Appendix A

GAF Ratings for the Practice Case Examples

THE MAN WHO LOVED ICE SKATING   GAF RATING: 70

Explanation of GAF Ratings

Symptoms (70) Symptoms of occasional irritability, loss of temper, and with-holding response to wife were in the category of "some mild symptoms." Because they were occasional rather than constant, he is put in the top of this category. But the above category of "transient and expectable reactions" is too mild a rating.

Social Adjustment (75) Slight impairment in social functioning. The diffi-culties with his wife are serious, but his overall functioning with friends and children is good to excellent.

Occupational Functioning (92) He loved his job and was highly respected, but not a leader.

THE UNFORGIVEN TEENAGER   GAF RATING: 50

Explanation of GAF Ratings

Symptoms (50) Although she met criteria for major depression, she was able to function without medication, thus the rating of "moderate" rather than "severe."

Social Functioning (52) She had one close confidante (her sister, with whom she spoke weekly), so the rating is above 50. She does not have other friends, and never had a close love relationship, so the rating is low in this category.

Occupational Functioning (65) She managed a large department and was respected for her work, although she had some difficulty with her boss and coworkers.

THE PERSONAL ADS MAN

GAF RATING: 42

Explanation of GAF Ratings

Symptoms (42) His symptoms are rated in the serious category partly because of their chronicity as well as severity. He never truly felt happy, and was mildly depressed most of his life; he feels like a fake, and his self-esteem is poor.

Social Functioning (45) The fact that he has no close friends puts him in the 41–50 category. His rating falls in the middle of this range because he is socially involved with dating (although compulsively) and colleagues (although superficially). He does not isolate himself like many people in this category. He does have the capacity to be congenial and somewhat witty.

Occupational Functioning (55) He is doing his job as a college teacher satisfactorily, which would give him a rating at least in the 60s, but he is given a rating of 55 because he derives no satisfaction from his work.

WIFE WITH A SOUL MATE

GAF RATING: 40

Explanation of GAF Ratings

Symptoms (40) Her depression was sufficiently severe that it is impairing her ability to function—not totally, but significantly. Also, her judgment, mood, and decision making are unstable. Impairment in several areas places her in the 31–40 category, but she is rated at the top of this category because she had sufficient judgment to get to a therapist before she did something impulsive.

Social Functioning (47) Although she is married and has friends (which would place her in the 51–60 category), her marriage has serious problems and she has not been able to confide in anyone. Thus, she is rated in the top third of the 41–50 category.

Occupational Functioning (45) She is functioning as a housewife, but with much difficulty.

THE MACHINE BUILDER

GAF RATING: 50

Explanation of GAF Ratings

Symptoms (50) Her anxiety symptoms were sufficiently severe that they were threatening her professional functioning, so she was rated in the 41–50 category. However, she was continuing to function (although with difficulty) and had gotten herself to therapy, so she was rated at the top of this category.

Social Functioning (52) She had a boyfriend with whom she could confide a little, although she confided in no one else. And although she could be friendly with other students, she had much difficulty speaking and eating in public and going to parties. Thus, she is rated in the lower quadrant of the 51–60 category.

Occupational Functioning (60) She was involved and interested in her career and a good student (which would place her in the higher 60s or 70s), but she was experiencing severe difficulty with one crucial aspect of her career, which lowers this rating to 60. (It could be argued that it should be lower, but she enjoyed what she did and for the most part did it well.)

THE NAILBITER   GAF RATING: 42

Explanation of GAF Ratings

Symptoms (42) Her anxiety symptoms and fingernail biting were severe, causing her constant difficulty and impairment in functioning, mood, and judgment. This places her in the lower quartile of the 41–50 category. The reason that she was not rated lower on symptoms is that she had good reality testing, and these symptoms were highly ego dystonic. She was motivated for help, though pessimistic.

Social Adjustment (51) She did not have many friends because she felt so inadequate, but she was close to her sister and had been able to confide in her husband and mother, although in a dependent way. Her ability to confide puts her in the 51–60 category, but her excessive dependency is what causes this rating to be at the lowest point on this range.

Occupational Adjustment (45) Serious impairment in several areas. She had difficulty with domestic chores and with child care, although she was coping independently for the first time in her adult life.

THE FERRYMAN   GAF RATING: 60

Explanation for GAF Ratings

Symptoms (60) His diagnosis of dysthymia put this rating in the 51–60 category, but because it was mild and his functioning was good the highest rating in this category was given.

Social Adjustment (60) He had a number of meaningful interpersonal relationships and was a good father (rating of 61–70 or better), but he had serious difficulties in his marriage and occasional conflicts with workers, which put his rating in the "moderate difficulty" range, although at the higher end.

Occupational Functioning (60) This man had very good skills with patients but trouble taking criticism, which implies some problems at work that need addressing. However, it was unclear whether these problems were mild or moderate, thus the rating in between.

THE ARTIST WITH JAW PAIN   GAF RATING: 30

Explanation of GAF Ratings

Symptoms (30) Her behavior was influenced by the delusion that she was being spied on; however, her reality testing was otherwise intact. She has severe jaw pain without any known medical basis. Her behavior in the interview was somewhat inappropriate in that she could not wait to divulge conflictual material. There was disturbance in identity.

Social Functioning (51) She had friends, and ones she could confide in, but her relationships were often fraught with conflict and distrust.

Occupational Functioning (48) Dropping out of school due to the aforementioned symptoms constitutes serious impairment (41–50). However, she was working as a waitress at a busy restaurant and functioning well in that capacity, so she was given a score in the top part of this range.

THE STALKER   GAF RATING: 25

Explanation of GAF Ratings

Symptoms (25) His behavior is considerably influenced by delusions (e.g., the neighbor will marry him) and serious impairment in communication and judgment.

Social Functioning (25) He has no friends, and his behavior is grossly inappropriate.

Occupational Functioning (25) "No job" is an example given for this range, and no home.

THE BICKERING DAUGHTER   GAF RATING: 82

Explanation of GAF Ratings

Symptoms (82) "Some mild symptoms" (rating 71–80) is more than what is constituted by her symptoms. Because bickering with her father was an isolated and "minimal" symptom but recurrent and long-standing, she is rated in the lower end of the 81–90 range.

Social Functioning (95) Excellent family relations, many good friends, and socially active.

Occupational Functioning (95) Excellent, much satisfaction, competent, and a leader.

Appendix B

Core Psychodynamic Conflict Formulations
for the Practice Case Examples in Chapter 3

THE MAN WHO LOVED ICE SKATING

Psychodynamic Conflict 1: Inhibition and Displacement of Anger

WHAT adaptive feeling is avoided? Anger–assertion.

HOW? Defenses: Reaction formation (excessively protective, pleasing, and compliant), passive aggression (refusal to respond), somatization (diarrhea), displacement and acting out (yelling at the children).

WHY? Because of conflicts/anxieties: Guilt.

In narrative form: With his wife he is compliant (D), passive–aggressive (D), and has diarrhea when angry (D) due to guilt (A) taught to him by his mother that he should never express anger (I/F) toward women because they were fragile and needed to be protected. With his children he sometimes lost his temper (D) (displacement, acting out) when actually angry at his wife.

Defensive function: Avoidance of conflicted angry feelings toward wife.

Optimal solution: Help him to appropriately assert his needs with his wife and not to displace his anger onto his children.

Comment: This man had conflicts predominantly around anger toward women, but not with grief or feelings associated with attachment. His attachments to his children, friends, and coworkers were close and strong. After one session of focusing on his displacement of anger toward his children, he felt enormously upset with himself, completely stopped these outbursts, and directed his issues appropriately toward his wife. (Note that in this case guilt—or adaptive remorse—was increased rather than decreased.) As he realized that his wife could not respond to him in a fully adult fashion, he spontaneously grieved the limitations in the relationship. He resolved that he would not leave his wife at that time because of the children.

In contrast to the Machine Builder and the Ferryman (chapter 3), for whom a predominant problem was conflict about grieving, once he saw the limitations in his marriage this man was able to grieve fully.

THE GIRL WHO DANCED IN BLOOD

Psychodynamic Conflict 1: Blocks to Assertion

WHAT adaptive feeling is avoided? Anger–assertion.

HOW? *Defenses:* Suicidal thoughts, gestures, regressive fights; turning against the self.

WHY? Because of conflicts/anxieties: Shame over showing neediness or wanting.

In narrative form: She uses masochism (anger turned inward) (D) and suicidal thoughts, feelings, and a suicidal gesture (D) when angry (I/F) with her boyfriend. She is conflicted about her feelings of anger (I/F) because she is ashamed to show need or ask for what she wants (A) and fears rejection for being needy (A).

Defensive function: Avoidance of angry feelings.

Optimal solution: She needs to be able to feel comfortable with anger, so that she may more easily assert herself (I/F).

Comment: Her regressive fighting represented a form of defensive anger blocking adaptive assertion as well as the wish for closeness.

Psychodynamic Conflict 2: Avoidance of Closeness

WHAT adaptive feeling is avoided? Vulnerability, openness with others (the sharing of the range of feelings, positive and negative, with others).

HOW? Defenses: Reaction formation (competitive rather than collaborative), dissociation (guarded, distant stance), defensive anger (regressive fighting without resolution).

WHY? Because of conflicts/anxieties: Shame and pain over being seen as weak or vulnerable.

In narrative form: This patient uses competitive and guarded behaviors as well as temperamental outbursts to avoid revealing feelings of vulnerability or intimacy (I/F) in close relations with others due to the shame of showing weakness.

Defensive function: Avoidance of closeness or intimacy.

Optimal solution: She needs to learn how to drop her guarded and competitive stance (D) or her regressive arguments (D) and allow herself to be more open, receptive, and trusting to sharing the range of feelings (I/F) (tenderness, sadness, joy) in close relationships. She believed she was worthwhile and that people liked her (at least under certain conditions), but she was afraid others would humiliate her or look down on her (A) as her father had done, so she kept up her guard (D). However, to safely open up she also needs to be able to protect herself (conflict 1).

Comment: In contrast to the Man Who Loved Ice Skating, this patient's inhibition over assertion was due to shame rather than guilt. Shame was the main inhibiting factor in both her dynamic formulations. Also, she had many more barriers to closeness than did the Man Who Loved Ice Skating, but not as much as the Unforgiven Teenager, who follows. Grief is an inevitable part of psychopathology, but as demonstrated in these cases it emerges in different ways. In this case, grief arose as she became aware of both her anger at her father and her love for him. Her conflicts about grief were moderate and similar to aforementioned issues; shame over showing vulnerability.

THE UNFORGIVEN TEENAGER

Psychodynamic Conflict 1: Masochistic Warding-off of Self-acceptance

WHAT adaptive feeling is avoided? Self-acceptance or positive feelings attached to the self, such as interest–excitement (adaptive self-interest) or enjoyment–joy (adaptive pride).

HOW? Defenses: Reaction formation, acting out (drinking and sexual behaviors in past), masochism–passive aggression (self-hate), projection (God hates her, others dislike her).

WHY? Because of conflicts/anxieties: Shame, guilt, emotional pain (distress–anguish), from lack of affirmation from early-life caregivers.

In narrative form: She uses reaction formation (D) and self-hate (D) in place of positive feelings toward herself (I/F) due to enormous shame (A) and pain (A) of there being few affirming people in her early life (deficit in positive affects received from others).

Defensive function: Lack of motivation for change due to pain and anxiety (terror) associated with emotional separation from her parents. Although painful, these relationships are familiar and the only ones she has known, thus her "addictive attachment."

Optimal solution: Restructuring of inner representation of self (e.g., by building a capacity to accept positive feelings [compassion] from the real relationship with the therapist as well as through recovery of loving relationships in the past) in order to enhance adaptive self-interest and healthy pride.

Psychodynamic Conflict 2: Isolation to Avoid Closeness

WHAT adaptive feeling is avoided? Vulnerability, openness with others (the sharing of the range of feelings, positive and negative, with others).

HOW? Defenses: Withdrawal (staying alone), projection (feeling hated, disliked), inhibition in receptive capacity (turning down invitations).

WHY? Because of conflicts/anxieties: Shame (feeling undeserving), pain over lack of love.

In narrative form: She uses withdrawal (D) and staying alone (D) to avoid closeness (I/F), because of feelings of inadequacy due to shame and pain of loneliness and neglect (A).

Defensive function: Avoidance of closeness.

Optimal solution: The ability to better trust others, or feel more positive feelings associated with others (this focus on her *feelings associated with others* reflects a subtle shift from conflict 1, which addressed her *feelings about herself.* Both these capacities are in part dependent on her ability to be receptive to others' positive feelings toward her.

Psychodynamic Conflict 3: Passivity Blocking Anger–Assertion

WHAT adaptive feeling is avoided? Anger–assertion.

HOW? Defenses: Masochism, hurt, passivity (compliance to parents).

WHY? Because of conflicts/anxieties: Guilt, shame, fear.

In narrative form: She uses passivity (D) and self-criticism (D) to avoid asserting herself or experiencing angry feelings (I/F) because she feels guilty (A) about feeling negatively, ashamed and undeserving to ask for things for herself (A), and terrified that she would be rejected (A), especially by her parents.

Defensive function: Ambivalence over change about separation from parents.

Optimal solution: Ability to stand up to parents and bear their possible rejection.

Comment: Although grief is a crucial issue in this case, it emerged in different ways throughout the treatment. During the first 10 sessions, she could feel a little grief for the loneliness of her childhood. However, the enormity of the pain she carried over the neglect and abuse by her parents was initially unbearable and highly defended against. I reasoned that she could not begin to feel this level of sorrow for herself until she could stop hating herself, begin facing her parents' serious limitations in care giving, and build some new and more caring relationships. Therefore, the first 10 sessions of this treatment focused on improving her feelings toward herself and others, and her ability to assert or protect herself from abuse. Only later was she able to begin work on her inhibition over grief about early-life neglect, which constituted a fourth dynamic conflict.

Her conflicts about grief were much greater than the Girl Who Danced in Blood. The Unforgiven Teenager felt enormous shame over crying in front of me, felt undeserving of that degree of care for herself, and was terrified of the tremendous pain involved. It is also important to note that she was severely blocked in most of the basic affects, for example, affects associated with attachment to self and others, anger, grief, interest–excitement, and joy.

These three cases demonstrate three levels of severity of defensiveness. The Man Who Loved Ice Skating was defensive only around one affect, anger–assertion. The Girl Who Danced in Blood defended against anger as well, but also against sharing of feeling in close relationships. The Unforgiven Teenager was the most impaired with problems with specific feelings, with sharing of the range of affects in close relations, and with affects associated with her inner representations of self and others.

It is also important to note that the Unforgiven Teenager has greater deficit pathology than the other cases. Therefore, we see that she carries much greater shame, guilt, anxiety–terror, and pain, as well as the inevitable severe relational (i.e., self–other) conflicts that result from deficit pathology.

Finally, it is important to note how idiosyncratic these conflicts are. There are different levels of severity of defensive functions that include conflict and deficit pathology. All three cases have blocks toward anger, but the Man Who Loved Ice Skating is conflicted due to guilt, the Girl Who Danced in Blood is inhibited due to shame and anxiety, and the Unforgiven Teenager has much more severe degrees of all of the inhibitory affects.

In addition, each of these patients defends against angry feelings in somewhat different ways, although each uses some form of inhibition as well as acting out. The Man Who Loved Ice Skating displaced his anger by lashing out inappropriately at his children. The Girl Who Danced in Blood acted out by using defensive anger in regressive fights rather than appropriate assertion. The Unforgiven Teenager acted out by drinking and sexual encounters. In regard to inhibition, the Man Who Loved Ice Skating was passive–aggressive and compliant with his wife. The Girl Who Danced in Blood turned her anger on herself and made a suicidal gesture. Though much more traumatized, the Unforgiven Teenager said she would never consider suicide because her religious beliefs forbade it; thus, she turned anger on herself through a chronic self-hate and a projected belief that God hated her. These variations in styles underscore the idiosyncratic "fingerprint" of personality and the need for treatment to be targeted to specific dynamic constellations.

Appendix C

Overview of the Main Treatment Objectives and Interventions

DEFENSE RESTRUCTURING

Objective 1A: Defense Recognition (Chapter 4)
- Identify defenses, anxieties, and feelings
- Determine the function of the defensive behavior
- Validate defensive patterns as once adaptive
- Note strengths interacting with defenses
- Generate a tentative hypotheses about the core dynamic pattern
- Repetition of patterns until defenses, anxieties, and affects are clearly recognized

Objective 1B: Defense Relinquishing (Chapter 5)
- Identify consequences: the costs and benefits of the defenses
- Distinguish the origin from the maintenance of the defensive pattern
- Elicit grief over losses due to defenses
- Repetition and active therapist involvement to reduce conflicts associated with giving up of defenses
- If no grief, assess and build compassion for self
- If no compassion for self, build sense of relationship and identity (i.e., go to self–other restructuring)

AFFECT RESTRUCTURING

Objective 2A: Affect Experiencing (Chapters 6 and 7)
- Identify and explore verbal, physiological, and action tendencies in fantasy
- Exposure to and containment of affect in fantasy
- Induce benign (i.e., well-controlled) regression with guided imagery
- Therapist encouragement and shared affect to assist facing conflicts
- Repetition of imagined scenes until conflict is regulated (i.e., desensitized)

Objective 2B: Affect Expression (Chapter 8)
- Assess current relationships for adaptive integration of all feelings
- Assess receptive as well as expressive capacity of feelings in relationships

- Role-play difficult interactions
- Provide teaching and skills training when necessary
- Repetition until conflicts about interactions are regulated (i.e., desensitized)
- Return to previous stages where necessary

SELF–OTHER RESTRUCTURING

Objective 3A: Alteration of Inner Representation of Self (Chapter 9)
- Identify adaptive and maladaptive inner representations of self
- Build receptive capacity by the self toward the self (i.e., capacities of self-compassion, self-care, etc.)
- Change perspectives on the self: how the self is viewed by the self and others
- Assist responsivity (expressive and receptive capacities) through exposure to feelings in guided imagery
- Alteration of sense of self through exposure to the care of others (through receptivity); in current and past relationships and in the real therapeutic relationship
- Repetition of imagined scenes until conflict about pride, respect, and enjoyment in self is regulated (i.e., desensitized)

Objective 3B: Alteration of Inner Representation of Others (Chapter 9)
- Identify adaptive and maladaptive inner representations of others
- Build receptive capacity to others to balance expressive capacity (capacities of trust, vulnerability, etc.)
- Change perspectives of others: how others are viewed by the self and others
- Assist responsivity (expressive and receptive capacities) through exposure to feelings in guided imagery
- Replace addictive attachments with adaptive attachments
  Recovery of lost loves through exposure to positive feelings in guided imagery
  Building receptivity in current relationships and in real therapeutic relationship
- Repetition of imagined scenes until conflict about attachment is regulated (i.e., desensitized)

TERMINATION *(Chapter 10, along with flow of treatment)*

Termination can be considered when: (a) the main problem behaviors have shown significant change, and (b) the patient feels able to maintain the gains.
- Time between sessions can be extended to two or more weeks
- Thoroughly assess contributions of treatment to change
- Anticipate and plan for handling setbacks
- Identify areas that need more work
- Encourage full expression of affects (positive and negative) between patient and therapist (e.g., what was most valued, what was least helpful, what more could have been done)

Appendix D

			Session Number:	1	5	_0

10 SESSION SUMMARY FORM
Short-term Psychotherapy Research Program at HMS
Leigh McCullough Vaillant, Ph.D. (1/95)

	Session Number:	1	5	_0
	Axis I:___			
	Axis I:___			
Patient Name/Initials:	Axis II___A:			
_____	Axis II___B:			
_____	Axis II___C:			
	Axis III:			
	Axis IV:			
Presenting Problems: (One to three examples)	Axis V:			

1) _____

2) _____

3) _____

Core Conflict(s):
1) _____
2) _____
3) _____

O b j e c t i v e s

Pymt	Sess	Date	MAIN THEME(S) OF SESSION	1 A	1 B	2 A	2 B	3 A	3 B
	1								
	2								
	3								
	4								
	5								
	6								
	7								
	8								
	9								
	_0								

After each session Rate 1) Degree to which Therapy Objectives were met for each conflict and, 2) degree conflict changed.
  1 = Not at All   3 = Little   5 = Moderately   7 = Much   10 = Substantially

1A	Defense Recognition—	How much is defensive pattern (being focused on) recognized?
1B	Defense Relinquishing—	How much is defensive pattern aversive and desired to give up?
2A	Affect Experience—	How much is adaptive emotional response experienced and contained within?
2B	Affect Expression—	How much are wants and needs appropriately expressed in face to face relationships?
3A	Sense of Self—	To what degree is the sense of self adaptive?
3B	Sense of Others—	To what degree is the sense of others adaptive?

References

Aggleton, J. P. (1992). The functional effects of amygdala lesions in humans: A comparison with findings from monkeys. In J. P. Aggleton (Ed.), *The amygdala: Neurobiological aspects of emotion, memory, and mental dysfunction* (pp. 485–504). New York: Wiley-Liss.

Alexander, F., & French, T. M. (1946). *Psychoanalytic therapy.* New York. Ronald Press.

Alpert, M. C. (1991). Is intense affect necessary? *STDP Newsletter, 1*(4), 1–2. Riverside Medical Center, Denville, NJ: STDP Institute Publications.

Alpert, M. (1992). Accelerated empathic therapy: A new short-term dynamic psychotherapy. *International Journal of Short-Term Psychotherapy, 7,* 133–156.

Alpert, M. (1996). Videotaping psychotherapy. *Journal of Psychotherapy Practice and Research, 5*(2), 93–105.

American Psychiatric Association. (1994). *Diagnostic and statistical manual of mental disorders* (4th ed.). Washington, DC: Author.

Andreasen, N., O'Leary, D. S., Cizadlo, T., Arndt, S., Rezai, K., Leonard Watkins, G., Boles Ponto, L. L., & Hichwa, R. D. (1995). Remembering the past: Two facets of episodic memory explored with positron emission tomography. *American Journal of Psychiatry, 152,* 1576–1585.

Arkowitz, H. (1989). The role of theory in psychotherapy integration. *Journal of Integrative and Eclectic Psychotherapy, 8,* 8–16.

Arlow, J. (1985). The concept of psychic reality and related problems. *Journal of the American Psychoanalytic Association, 33,* 521–535.

Ascher, L. (1980). Paradoxical intention. In A. Goldstein & E. B. Foa (Eds.), *Handbook of behavioral interventions: A clinical guide.* New York: Wiley.

Bacal, H. (1985). Optimal responsiveness and the therapeutic process. In A. Goldberg (Ed.), *Progress in self-psychology* (Vol. 1, pp. 207–227). New York: Guilford.

Baker, H. (1991). Shorter-term psychotherapy: A self-psychological approach. In P. Crits-Christoph & J. P. Barber (Eds.), *Handbook of short-term dynamic psychotherapy* (pp. 287–322). New York: Basic Books.

Baker, H., & Baker, M. (1987). Heinz Kohut's self psychology: An overview. *American Journal of Psychiatry, 114,* 1–9.

Balint, M. (1968). *The basic fault: Therapeutic aspects of regression.* London: Tavistock.

Balint, M., Ornstein, P. H., & Balint, E. (1972). *Focal psychotherapy: An example of applied psychoanalysis*. London: Tavistock.

Barlow, D. H. (1988). *Anxiety and its disorders: The nature and treatment of anxiety and panic*. New York: Guilford.

Barlow, D. H. (Ed.). (1993). *Clinical handbook of psychological disorders: A step-by-step treatment manual*. New York: Guilford.

Barlow, D. H., Hayes, S., & Nelson, R. O. (1984). *The scientist practitioner: Research and accountability in clinical and educational settings*. New York: Pergamon Press.

Basch, M. F. (1976). The concept of affect: A re-examination. *Journal of the American Psychoanalytic Association, 24*, 759–777.

Basch, M. F. (1985). Empathic understanding: A review of the concept and some theoretical considerations. *Journal of the American Psychoanalytic Association, 31*, 101–126.

Bass, E., & Davis, L. (1988). *The courage to heal: A guide for women survivors of child sexual abuse*. New York: Harper & Row.

Battle, C., Imber, S., Hoehn-Saric, R., Stone, A., Nash, E., & Frank, J. (1966). Target complaints: A criterion of improvement. *American Journal of Psychotherapy, 20*, 184–192.

Baxter, L. R. (1992). Neuroimaging studies of obsessive–compulsive disorder. *Psychiatric Clinics of North America, 15*, 871–884.

Baxter, L. R. (1995). Neuroimaging studies of human anxiety disorders: Cutting paths of knowledge through the field of neurotic phenomena. In F. E. Bloom & D. J. Kupfer (Eds.), *Psychopharmacology: The fourth generation of progress* (pp. 1287–1299). New York: Raven Press.

Baxter, L. R., Schwartz, J. M., Bergman, K. S., Szuba, M. P., Guze, B. H., Mazziotta, J. C., Alazraki, A., Selin, C. E., Ferng, H., Munford, P., & Phelps, M. E. (1992). Caudate glucose metabolic rate changes with both drug and behavior therapy for obsessive–compulsive disorder. *Archives of General Psychiatry, 49*, 681–689.

Beck, A. T. (1976). *Cognitive therapy and the emotional disorders*. New York: International Universities Press.

Beck, A. T., & Freeman, A. (1990). *Cognitive therapy of personality disorders*. New York: Guilford.

Beck, A. T., Rush, A. H., Shaw, B. F., & Emery, G. (1979). *Cognitive therapy of depression*. New York: Guilford.

Beebe, B., & Lachmann, F. M. (1992). The contribution of mother-infant mutual influence to the origin of self and object representations. In N. Skolnick & S. Arshaw (Eds.), *Relational perspectives in psychoanalysis* (pp. 83–117). Hillsdale, NJ: Analytic Press.

Beebe, B., & Lachmann, F. M. (1994). Representation and internalization in infancy: Three principles of salience. *Psychoanalytic psychology* (pp. 127–135). Hillsdale, NJ: Erlbaum.

Benjamin, L. (1974). Structural analysis of social behavior. *Psychological Review, 81*, 392–425.

Benjamin, L. (1993a). Every psychopathology is a gift of love. *Psychotherapy Research, 3*(1), 1–24.

Benjamin, L. (1993b). *Interpersonal diagnosis and treatment of personality disorders*. New York: Guilford.

Bennett, M. J. (1989). The catalytic function in psychotherapy. *Psychiatry, 52,* 351–362.

Beutler, L. E. (1986). Systematic eclectic psychotherapy. In J. C. Norcross (Ed.), *Handbook of eclectic psychotherapy* (pp. 94–131). New York: Brunner/Mazel.

Binder, J. L., Henry, W. P., & Strupp, H. (1987). An appraisal of selection criteria for dynamic psychotherapies and implications for setting time limits. *Psychiatry, 50,* 154–166.

Blanck, G., & Blanck, R. (1974). *Ego psychology: Theory and practice*. New York: Columbia University Press.

Bollas, C. (1983). Expressive uses of the countertransference: Notes to the patient from oneself. *Contemporary Psychoanalysis, 19*(1), 1–34.

Bollas, C. (1986). *Being a character: Psychoanalysis and self experience*. New York: Brunner/Mazel.

Bollas, C. (1989). *The shadow of the object: Psychoanalysis of the unthought known*. New York: Columbia University Press.

Bollas, C. (1995). *Cracking up: The work of unconscious experience*. New York: Hill & Wang.

Bowlby, J. (1969). *Attachment*. New York: Basic Books.

Bowlby, J. (1982). *Attachment and loss: Vol. I. Attachment* (2nd ed.). New York: Basic Books.

Brenner, C. (1957). *An elementary textbook of psychoanalysis*. New York: Doubleday.

Brenner, C. (1976). *Psychoanalytic technique and psychic conflict*. New York: International Universities Press.

Brenner, C. (1982). *The mind in conflict*. New York: International Universities Press.

Broner, N. (1992). Two types of brief psychodynamic psychotherapy: The interaction of patients' internal-external locus-of-control orientation with highly structured and moderately structured treatments (doctoral dissertation, Union Institute). *Dissertation Abstracts International, 53*–05B.

Brothers, L. A. (1990). The social brain: A project for integrating primate behavior and neurophysiology in a new domain. *Concepts in Neuroscience, 1,* 27–51.

Budman, S. (1980). *Forms of brief psychotherapy*. New York: Guilford.

Burke, W. F., & Tansey, M. J. (1991). Countertransference disclosure and models of therapeutic action. *Contemporary Psychoanalysis, 27*(2), 351–384.

Burns, D. D. (1980). *Feeling good: The new mood therapy*. New York: William Morrow.

Burns, D. D. (1989). *The feeling good handbook: Using the new mood therapy in everyday life*. New York: William Morrow.

Cautela, J. R. (1966). Treatment of compulsive behavior by covert sensitization. *Psychological Record, 16,* 33–41.

Cautela, J. R. (1973). Covert processes and behavior modification. *Journal of Nervous and Mental Disease, 1,* 157.

Cautela, J. R., & McCullough, L. (1978). Covert conditioning: A learning theory perspective on imagery. In J. L. Singer & K. S. Pope (Eds.), *The power of the human imagination* (pp. 227–254). New York: Plenum Press.

Clark, D. (1989). Anxiety states: Panic and generalized anxiety. In K. Hawton, P. Salkovskis, J. Kirk, & D. M. Clark (Eds.), *Cognitive behavior therapy for psychiatric problems: A practical guide.* New York: Oxford University Press.

Clyman, R. B. (1992). The procedural organization of emotions: A contribution from cognitive science to the psychoanalytic theory of therapeutic action. In T. Shapiro & R. N. Emde (Eds.), *Affect: Psychoanalytic perspectives* (pp. 349–382). Madison, CT: International Universities Press.

Cohen, J. (1988). *Statistical power analysis for the behavioral sciences.* Hillsdale, NJ: Lawrence Erlbaum.

Costa, P. T., & McCrea, R. R. (1990). Personality disorders and the five-factor model of personality. *Journal of Personality Disorders, 4,* 362–371.

Costa, P. T., & Widiger, T. A. (1993). *Personality disorders and the five-factor model of personality.* Washington, DC: American Psychological Association Press.

Crits-Christoph, P., & Barber, J. (Eds.). (1991). *Handbook of short-term dynamic psychotherapy.* New York: Basic Books.

Crits-Christoph, P., Cooper, A., & Luborsky, L. (1988). The accuracy of therapists' interpretations and the outcome of dynamic psychotherapy. *Journal of Consulting and Clinical Psychology, 56,* 490–495.

Csikszentmihalyi, M. (1990). *Flow: The psychology of optimal experience.* New York: Harper & Row.

Cummings, N., & Sayama, M. (1995). *Focused psychotherapy: A casebook of brief intermittent psychotherapy throughout the life cycle.* New York: Brunner/Mazel.

Curtis, J. T., Silberschatz, G., Sampson, H., & Weiss, J. (1994). The plan formulation method. *Psychotherapy Research, 4,* 197–207.

Dahl, H. (1978). A new psychoanalytic model of motivation: Emotions as appetites and messages. *Psychoanalysis and Contemporary Thought, 1,* 375–408.

Dahl, H. (1991). The key to understanding change: Emotions as appetitive wishes and beliefs about their fulfillment. In J. D. Safran & L. S. Greenberg (Eds.), *Emotion, psychotherapy and change* (pp. 130–165). New York: Guilford.

Dahl, H., & Teller, V. (1994). The characteristics, identification, and application of FRAMES. *Psychotherapy Research, 4,* 253–276.

Damasio, A. (1994). *Descartes' error: Emotion, reason and the human brain.* New York: Avon Books.

Darwin, C. (1920). *The expression of emotion in man and animals.* New York: Appleton-Century-Crofts.

Davanloo, H. (Ed.). (1978). *Basic principles and techniques in short-term dynamic psychotherapy.* New York: Spectrum.

Davanloo, H. (Ed.). (1980). *Short-term dynamic psychotherapy.* New York: Jason Aronson.

Davanloo, H. (1987). Intensive short-term dynamic psychotherapy with highly-resistant depressed patients: Part I. Restructuring ego's regressive defenses. *International Journal of Short-Term Psychotherapy, 2,* 99–132.

Davis, M. (1992). The role of the amygdala in conditioned fear. In J. P. Aggleton (Ed.), *The amygdala: Neurobiological aspects of emotion, memory, and mental dysfunction* (pp. 255–306). New York: Wiley-Liss.

DeLaCour, A. T. (1986). Use of the focus in brief dynamic psychotherapy. *Psychotherapy, 23,* 133–139.

Demos, V. (Ed.). (1995). *Exploring affect: Selections from the writing of Silvan S. Tomkins.* New York: Cambridge University Press.

Dewald, P. A. (1971). *Psychotherapy: A dynamic approach* (2nd ed.). New York: Basic Books.

Drake, R. E., & Minkoff, I. S. (1991). *Dual diagnosis of major mental illness and substance disorder.* San Francisco: Jossey-Bass.

Edelman, G. (1987). *Neural Darwinism: The theory of neuronal group selection.* New York: Basic Books.

Edelman, G. (1988). *Topobiology: An introduction to molecular embryology.* New York: Basic Books.

Edelman, G. (1992). *Bright air, brilliant fire: On the matter of the mind.* New York: Basic Books.

Ekman, P. (1984). Expression and the nature of emotion. In K. Scherer & P. Ekman (Eds.), *Approaches to emotion* (pp. 319–340). Hillsdale, NJ: Erlbaum.

Ekman, P. (1992a). An argument for basic emotions. *Cognition and Emotion, 6,* 169–200.

Ekman, P. (1992b). Facial expressions of emotion: New findings, new questions. *Psychological Science, 3,* 34–38.

Ekman, P., & Davidson, R. J. (1993). Voluntary smiling changes regional brain activity. *Psychological Science, 4,* 342–345.

Ekman, P., & Davidson, R. J. (Eds.). (1994). *The nature of emotion: Fundamental questions.* New York: Oxford University Press.

Ekman, P., Levenson, R. W., & Friesen, W. V. (1983). Autonomic nervous system activity distinguishes among emotions. *Science, 22,* 1208–1210.

Eliot, T. S. (1917). *Prufrock and other observations.* London: The Egoist Ltd.

Elliott, R. (1983). "That in your hands": A comprehensive process analysis of significant events in psychotherapy. *Psychiatry, 46,* 113–129.

Emde, R. N. (1983). The pre-representational self and its affective core. *Psychoanalytic Study of the Child, 38,* 165–192.

Emde, R. N. (1992). Positive emotions for psychoanalytic theory: Surprises from infancy research and new directions. In T. Shapiro & R. N. Emde (Eds.), *Affect: Psychoanalytic perspectives* (pp. 5–44). Madison, CT: International Universities Press.

Endicott, J., Spitzer, R. L., Fleiss, J. L., & Cohen, J. (1976). The Global Assessment Scale: A procedure for measuring overall severity of psychiatric disturbance. *Archives of General Psychiatry, 33,* 766–771.

Engel, G. L. (1977). The need for a new medical model: A challenge to biomedicine. *Science, 196,* 129–136.

Epstein, L., & Feiner, A. H. (1979). *Countertransference.* New York: Jason Aronson.

Erikson, E. (1978). *Childhood and society* (2nd ed.). New York: Norton.

Everitt, G. J., & Robbins, T. W. (1992). Amygdala-ventral striatal interactions and reward-related processes. In J. P. Aggleton (Ed.), *The amygdala: Neurobiological aspects of emotion, memory, and mental dysfunction* (pp. 401–430). New York: Wiley-Liss.

Ezriel, H. (1952). Notes on psychoanalytic group therapy: II. Interpretation. *Research Psychiatry, 15,* 119.

Fairbairn, W. R. D. (1952). *An object-relations theory of the personality.* New York: Basic Books.

Fairbairn, W. R. D. (1963). Synopsis of an object-relations theory of the personality. *International Journal of Psycho-Analysis, 44,* 224–225.

Farrell, A. D., Stiles, P. A., & McCullough, L. (1987). Identification of target complaints by computer interview: Evaluation of the computerized assessment system for psychotherapy evaluation and research. *Journal of Consulting and Clinical Psychology, 55,* 691–700.

Feiner, A. H. (1979). Countertransference and the anxiety of influence. In L. Epstein & A. H. Feiner (Eds.), *Countertransference* (pp. 105–128). New York: Jason Aronson.

Fensterheim, H. (1994). Hyperventilation and psychopathology: A clinical perspective. In B. H. Timmons & R. Ley (Eds.), *Behavioral and psychological approaches to breathing disorders.* New York: Plenum Press.

Foote, J. (1989). Interpersonal context and patient change episodes (doctoral dissertation, New York University). *Dissertation Abstracts International,* 51–12B.

Forward, S. (1989). *Toxic parents: Overcoming their hurtful legacy and reclaiming your life.* New York: Bantam Books.

Fosha, D. (1992). The inter-relatedness of theory, technique and therapeutic stance: A comparative look at intensive short term dynamic psychotherapy and accelerated empathic therapy. *International Journal of Short Term Psychotherapy, 7,* 157–176.

Fosha, D. (1995). Technique and taboo in three short-term dynamic psychotherapies. *Journal of Psychotherapy Practice and Research, 4,* 297–318.

Frances, A., Clarkin, J., & Perry, S. (Eds.). (1984). *Therapeutics in psychiatry: The art and science of treatment selection.* New York: Brunner/Mazel.

Frances, A., & Widiger, T. (1986). The classification of personality disorders: An overview of problems and solutions. In A. Frances & R. Hales (Eds.), *Psychiatry update: American Psychiatric Association annual review* (pp. 240–257). Washington, DC: American Psychiatric Press.

Frankl, V. E. (1960). Paradoxical intention: A logotherapeutic technique. *American Journal of Psychotherapy, 14,* 520–535.

Freud, A. (1936). *The ego and the mechanisms of defense* (C. Baines, Trans.). New York: International Universities Press.

Freud, A. (1954). The widening scope of indications for psychoanalysis [Discussion]. *Journal of the American Psychoanalytic Association, 2.*

Freud, S. (1930). *Civilization and its discontents. Vol. 8.* In J. Strachey (Ed. and

Trans.), *The Standard Edition of the Complete Psychological Works of Sigmund Freud.* London: Hogarth Press.

Freud, S. (1955). Lines of advance in psychoanalytic therapy. In J. Strachey (Ed. and Trans.), *The Standard Edition of the Complete Psychological Works of Sigmund Freud.* London: Hogarth Press. (Original work published 1919)

Freud, S. (1955). Mourning and melancholia. In J. Strachey (Ed. and Trans.), *The Standard Edition of the Complete Psychological Works of Sigmund Freud* (Vol. 14, pp. 237–258). London: Hogarth Press. (Original work published 1917)

Freud, S. (1956). *Collected papers* (Vol. 4, J. Riviere, Trans.). London: Hogarth Press. (Originally published 1917)

Freud, S. (1957). Instincts and their vicissitudes. In J. Strachey (Ed. and Trans.), *The Standard Edition of the Complete Psychological Works of Sigmund Freud* (Vol. 14, pp. 117–140). London: Hogarth Press. (Original work published 1915)

Freud, S. (1959a). Inhibitions, symptoms and anxiety. In J. Strachey (Ed. and Trans.), *The Standard Edition of the Complete Psychological Works of Sigmund Freud* (Vol. 20, pp. 75–175). London: Hogarth Press. (Original work published 1926)

Freud, S. (1959b). Turnings in the ways of psycho-analytic therapy (J. Riviere, Trans.). In *Collected papers* (Vol. 2). New York: Basic Books. (Original work published 1919)

Fromm-Reichmann, F. (1950). *Principles of intensive psychotherapy.* Chicago: University of Chicago Press.

Gabbard, G. O. (Ed.). (1989). *Sexual exploitation of professional relationships.* Washington, DC: American Psychiatric Press.

Gabbard, G. (1990). *Psychodynamic psychiatry in clinical practice.* Washington, DC: American Psychiatric Press.

Gabbard, G. (1994). *Psychodynamic psychiatry in clinical practice: The DSM-IV edition.* Washington, DC: American Psychiatric Press.

Gabbard, G. O. (1995). Transference and countertransference in the psychotherapy of therapists charged with sexual misconduct. *Psychiatric Annals, 25*(2), 100–105.

Gabbard, G., & Wilkinson, S. M. (1994). *Management of countertransference with borderline patients.* Washington, DC: American Psychiatric Press.

Gaffan, D. (1992). Amygdala and the memory of reward. In J. P. Aggleton (Ed.), *The amygdala: Neurobiological aspects of emotion, memory, and mental dysfunction* (pp. 471–484). New York: Wiley-Liss.

Gedo, J. (1979). *Beyond interpretation.* New York: International Universities Press.

Geller, J. D., & Farber, B. A. (1993). Factors influencing the process of internalization in psychotherapy. *Psychotherapy Research 3*(3), 166–177.

George, M. S., Ketter, T. A., Parekh, P. I., Horwitz, B., Herscovitch, P., & Post, R. M. (1995). Brain activity during transient sadness and happiness in healthy women. *American Journal of Psychiatry, 152*, 341–351.

Gill, M. (1982). *Analysis of transference* (Vol. 1). New York: International Universities Press.

Gill, M. (1983). The interpersonal paradigm and the degree of the therapist's involvement. *Contemporary Psychoanalysis, 19,* 200–237.

Gilligan, C. (1982). *In a different voice: Psychological theory and women's development.* Cambridge, MA: Harvard University Press.

Glaser, B. G. (1978). Theoretical sensitivity: Advances in the methodology of grounded theory. Mill Valley, CA: Sociology Press.

Glaser, B. G., & Strauss, A. (1967). *The discovery of grounded theory: Strategies for qualitative research.* Chicago: Aldine.

Glover, E. (1931). The therapeutic effect of inexact interpretation: A contribution to the theory of suggestion. *International Journal of Psychoanalysis, 12,* 397–411.

Goldfried, M. (1992). *Converging themes in psychotherapy.* New York: Springer.

Goleman, D. (1994). *Emotional intelligence.* New York: Bantam Books.

Gottshalk, L. A., & Fronczek, J. (1995). Defense mechanisms and hope as protective factors in physical and mental disorders. In U. Hentschel, G. J. W. Smith, W. Ehlers, & J. G. Draguns (Eds.), *The concept of defense mechanisms in contemporary psychology: Theoretical and clinical perspectives* (pp. 339–359). New York: Springer-Verlag.

Greenacre, P. (1960). Considerations regarding the parent-infant relationship. *International Journal of Psychoanalysis, 41,* 571–584.

Greenberg, J., & Mitchell, S. A. (1983). *Object relations in psychoanalytic theory.* Cambridge, MA: Harvard University Press.

Greenberg, L. S. (1980). The intensive analysis of recurring events from the practice of gestalt therapy. *Psychotherapy: Theory, Research, and Practice, 17,* 143–152.

Greenberg, L. S. (1984). A task analysis of intrapersonal conflict resolution. In L. N. Rice & L. S. Greenberg (Eds.), *Patterns of change: Intensive analysis of psychotherapy process.* New York: Guilford.

Greenberg, L. S. (1986). Change process research. *Journal of Consulting and Clinical Psychology, 54,* 4–11.

Greenberg, L. S. (1991). Research on the process of change. *Psychotherapy Research, 1,* 3–16.

Greenberg, L. S. (1992). Process diagnosis of levels of emotional processing. *Journal of Psychotherapy Integration, 2*(1), 19–24.

Greenberg, L. S., & Safran, J. D. (1987). *Emotion in psychotherapy.* New York: Guilford.

Greenberg, L., Elliott, R., & Lietaer, G. (1994). Research on experiential psychotherapies. In A. E. Bergin & S. L. Garfield (Eds.), *Handbook of psychotherapy and behavior change* (4th ed., pp. 508–542). New York: Wiley.

Greenberg, L., Rice., L., & Elliott, R. (1994). *Process experiential psychotherapy.* New York: Guilford.

Greenson, R. R. (1967). *The technique and practice of psychoanalysis.* New York: International Universities Press.

Greenson, R. R., & Wexler, M. (1969). The non-transference relationship in the psychoanalytic situation. *International Journal of Psycho-Analysis, 50,* 27–39.

Guisinger, S., & Blatt, S. (1994). Individuality and relatedness: Evolution of a fundamental dialectic. *American Psychologist, 49,* 104–111.

Gustafson, J. P. (1981). *The complex secret of brief psychotherapy.* In S. Budman (Ed.), *Forms of brief psychotherapy* (pp. 83–130). New York: Guilford.

Gustafson, J. P. (1984). An integration of brief dynamic psychotherapies. *American Journal of Psychiatry, 141,* 935–944.

Gustafson, J. P. (1986). *The complex secret of brief psychotherapy.* New York: Norton.

Halgren, E. (1992). Emotional neurophysiology of the amygdala within the context of human cognition. In J. P. Aggleton (Ed.), *The amygdala: Neurobiological aspects of emotion, memory, and mental dysfunction* (pp. 191–228). New York: Wiley-Liss.

Hall, C. S., & Lindzey, G. (1978). *Theories of personality* (3rd ed.). New York: Wiley.

Harlow, H. F. (1958). The nature of love. *American Psychologist, 13,* 673–685.

Harlow, H., & Harlow, M. K. (1962). Social deprivation in monkeys. *Scientific American, 207*(5), 136.

Harlow, H. F., & Zimmermann, R. R. (1959). Affectional responses in the infant monkey. *Science, 130,* 421.

Hartmann, H. (1958). *Ego psychology and the problem of adaptation* (D. Rapaport, Trans.). New York: International Universities Press. (Original work published 1939)

Heimberg, R. G., Becker, R. E., Goldfinger, K., & Vermilyea, J. A. (1985). Treatment of social phobia by exposure, cognitive restructuring and homework assignment. *Journal of Nervous and Mental Disease, 173,* 236–245.

Hendricks, G., & Hendricks, K. (1993). *At the speed of life: A new approach to personal change through body-centered therapy.* New York: Bantam.

Hendrix, H. (1990). *Getting the love you want: A guide for couples.* New York: HarperCollins.

Hendrix, H. (1992). *Keeping the love you find: A guide for singles.* New York: Pocket Books.

Henry, W. P., Strupp, H. H., Schacht, T. E., & Gaston, L. (1994). Psychodynamic approaches. In A. E. Bergin & S. L. Garfield (Eds.), *Handbook of psychotherapy and behavior change* (4th ed., pp. 467–508). New York: Wiley.

Herman, J. (1992). *Trauma and recovery: The aftermath of violence—from domestic abuse to political terror.* New York: Basic Books.

Hill, C. (1989). *Therapist techniques and client outcomes: Eight cases of brief psychotherapy.* Newbury Park, CA: Sage Publications.

Hinsie, L. E., & Campbell, R. J. (1960). *Psychiatric dictionary* (3rd ed.). New York: Oxford University Press.

Hobson, J. A. (1987). Dream bizarreness and the activation-synthesis hypothesis. *Human Neurobiology, 6,* 157–164.

Hobson, J. A. (1994). *The chemistry of conscious states: How the brain changes its mind.* Boston: Little, Brown.

Hoglend, P., & Heyerdahl, E. (1994). The circumscribed focus in intensive brief dynamic psychotherapy. *Psychotherapy and Psychosomatics, 61,* 163–170.

Hope, D. A., & Heimberg, R. G. (1993). Social phobia and social anxiety. In D. Barlow (Ed.), *Clinical handbook of psychological disorders: A step-by-step treatment manual* (pp. 99–136). New York: Guilford.

Horowitz, L. M., & Rosenberg, S. E. (1994). The consensual response psychodynamic formulation: Part I. Method and research results. *Psychotherapy Research, 4,* 222–238.

Horowitz, M. J. (1976). *Stress response syndromes.* New York: Jason Aronson.

Horowitz, M. J. (1994). Configurational analysis and the use of role-relationship models to understand transference. *Psychotherapy Research, 4,* 184–196.

Horowitz, M. J., Fridhandler, B., & Stinson, C. (1992). Person schemas and emotions. In T. Shapiro & R. N. Emde (Eds.), *Affect: Psychoanalytic perspectives* (pp. 173–208). Madison, CT: International Universities Press.

Howard, K., Kopta, S. M., Drause, M. S., & Orlinsky, D. E. (1986). The dose-effect relationship in psychotherapy. *American Psychologist, 41,* 159–164.

Howard, K. I., Leuger, R. J., Maling, M. S., & Martinovich, Z. (1993). A phase model of psychotherapy outcome: Causal mediation of change. *Journal of Consulting and Clinical Psychology, 61,* 678–685.

Insel, T. R. (1992). Oxytocin, a neuropeptide for affiliation: Evidence from behavioral, receptor autoradiographic, and comparative studies. *Psychoneuroendocrinology, 17*(1), 3–35.

Izard, C. (1990). Facial expressions and the regulation of emotion. *Journal of Personality and Social Psychology, 58,* 487–498.

Jary, M. L., & Stewart, M. A. (1985). Psychiatric disorder in the parents of adopted children with aggressive conduct disorder. *Neuropsychobiology, 13(1–2),* 7–11.

Jordan, J. V. (1991). The relational self: A new perspective for understanding women's development. In J. Strauss & G. R. Goethals (Eds.), *The self: Interdisciplinary approaches* (pp. 136–149). New York: Springer-Verlag.

Jordan, J. V. (1994, February 15). *Relational issues in psychotherapy.* Grand Rounds, Brigham and Women's Hospital, Harvard Medical School, Cambridge, MA.

Jordan, J. V., Kaplan, A. G., Miller, B., Stiver, L. P., & Stiver, J. L. (Eds.). (1991). *Women's growth in connection.* New York: Guilford.

Joseph, C. (1988). Antecedents to transference interpretation in short-term psychodynamic psychotherapy (doctoral dissertation, Rutgers University). *Dissertation Abstracts International, 50–04B.*

Kagan, J. (1992). A conceptual analysis of the affects. In T. Shapiro & R. N. Emde (Eds.), *Affect: Psychoanalytic perspectives* (pp. 109–130). Madison, CT: International Universities Press.

Kagan, J. (1994). *Galen's prophecy.* New York: Basic Books.

Kandel, E. (1983). From metapsychology to molecular biology. *American Journal of Psychiatry, 140,* 1277–1293.

Kaplan, H. S. (1974). *The new sex therapy.* New York: Brunner/Mazel.

Kaplan, H. S. (1983). *The evaluation of sexual disorders.* New York: Brunner/Mazel.

Karon, B. P. (1992). The fear of understanding schizophrenia. *Psychoanalytic Psychology, 9*, 191–211.

Karon, B. P., & VandenBos, G. (1981). *Psychotherapy of schizophrenia.* New York: Jason Aronson.

Kernberg, O. F. (1983). Object relations theory and character analysis. *Journal of the American Psychoanalytic Association, 31*(Suppl.), 247–272.

Killingmo, B. (1989). Conflict and deficit: Implications for technique. *International Journal of Psycho-Analysis, 70*, 65–79.

Kitayama, S., & Markus, H. R. (Eds.). (1994). *Emotion and culture: Empirical studies of mutual influences.* Washington, DC: American Psychological Association.

Klein, M. (1975). *Envy and gratitude and other works (1946–1963).* New York: Free Press.

Kling, A. S., & Brothers, L. A. (1992). The amygdala and social behavior. In J. P. Aggleton (Ed.), *The amygdala: Neurobiological aspects of emotion, memory, and mental dysfunction* (pp. 353–379). New York: Wiley-Liss.

Kohut, H. (1971). *The analysis of the self: A systematic approach to the psychoanalytic treatment of narcissistic personality disorders.* New York: International Universities Press.

Kohut, H. (1977). *The restoration of the self.* New York: International Universities Press.

Koss, M. P., & Shiang, J. (1994). Research on brief psychotherapy. In A. E. Bergin & S. L. Garfield (Eds.), *Handbook of psychotherapy and behavior change* (4th ed., pp. 664–700). New York: Wiley.

Kuhn, T. (1970). *The structure of scientific revolutions* (Rev. ed.). Chicago: University of Chicago Press.

Lachmann, F. M. (1988). Psychoanalytic therapy of developmental arrests. In N. Slavinska-Holy (Ed.), *Borderline and narcissistic patients in therapy* (pp. 47–58). Madison, CT: International Universities Press.

Laikin, M., Winston, A., & McCullough, L. (1991). Short-term dynamic psychotherapy. In P. Crits-Christoph & J. Barber (Eds.), *Handbook of brief dynamic therapies* (pp. 80–109). New York: Basic Books.

Lambert, M. (1994, June). *Discussion group on outcome measures.* Society for Psychotherapy Research, York, England.

Lambert, M., & Bergin, A. E. (1994). The effectiveness of psychotherapy. In A. E. Bergin & S. L. Garfield (Eds.), *Handbook of psychotherapy and behavior change* (4th ed., pp. 143–189). New York: John Wiley.

Lazarus, A. A., & Messer, S. B. (1991). Does chaos prevail? An exchange on technical eclecticism and assimilative integration. *Journal of Psychotherapy Integration, 1*(2), 143–158.

Lazarus, R. (1991). *Emotion and adaptation.* New York: Oxford University Press.

LeDoux, J. E. (1992). Emotion and the amygdala. In J. P. Aggleton (Ed.), *The amygdala: Neurobiological aspects of emotion, memory, and mental dysfunction* (pp. 339–351). New York: Wiley-Liss.

LeDoux, J. E. (1993). Emotional memory systems in the brain. *Behavioral and Brain Research, 58*(1–2), 69–79.

Lerner, H. G. (1989). *The dance of anger: A guide to changing the patterns of intimate relationships.* New York: Harper & Row.

Leuner, H. (1969). Guided affective imagery (GAI): A method of intensive psychotherapy. *American Journal of Psychotherapy, 23,* 4–23.

Leuner, H. (1977). The role of imagery in psychotherapy. In S. Arieti & G. Chrzanowski (Eds.), *New dimensions in psychiatry: A world view.* New York: Wiley.

Leuner, H. (1978). Basic principles and therapeutic efficacy of guided affective imagery (GAI). In J. L. Singer & K. S. Pope (Eds.), *The power of the human imagination* (pp. 125–166). New York: Plenum Press.

Levenson, H. (1995). *Time-limited dynamic psychotherapy: A guide to clinical practice.* New York: Basic Books.

Lichtenberg, J. D. (1983). *Psychoanalysis and infant research.* Hillsdale, NJ: Analytic Press.

Lichtenberg, J. D. (1989). *Psychoanalysis and motivation.* Hillsdale, NJ: Analytic Press.

Lichtenberg, J. D., Lachmann, F. M., & Fosshage, J. L. (1992). *Self and motivational systems.* Hillsdale, NJ: Analytic Press.

Linehan, M. M. (1993a). *Cognitive-behavioral treatment of borderline personality disorder.* New York: Guilford.

Linehan, M. M. (1993b). *Skills training manual for treating borderline personality disorder.* New York: Guilford.

Linehan, M. M., & Kehrer, C. A. (1993). Borderline personality disorder. In D. Barlow (Ed.), *Clinical handbook of psychological disorders: A step-by-step treatment manual* (pp. 396–441). New York: Guilford.

Longabaugh, R., Stout, R., Kriebal, G., McCullough, L., & Bishop, D. (1986). DSM-III and clinically-identified problems as an approach to treatment. *Archives of General Psychiatry, 43,* 1097–1103.

LoPiccolo, J., & LoPiccolo, L. (Eds.). (1978). *Handbook of sex therapy.* New York: Plenum Press.

Luborsky, L. (1962). Clinicians' judgments of mental health. *Archives of General Psychiatry, 7,* 407–417.

Luborsky, L. (1977). Measuring a pervasive psychic structure in psychotherapy: The core conflictual relationship theme. In N. Freedman & S. Grand (Eds.), *Communicative structures and psychic structures* (pp. 367–395). New York: Plenum Press.

Luborsky, L. (1984). *Principles of psychoanalytic psychotherapy: A manual for supportive-expressive treatment.* New York: Basic Books.

Luborsky, L., & Bachrach, H. (1974). Factors influencing clinicians' judgments of mental health: Eighteen experiences with the Health-Sickness Rating Scale. *Archives of General Psychiatry, 31,* 292–299.

Luborsky, L., & Crits-Christoph, P. (1990). *Understanding transference: The CCRT method.* New York: Basic Books.

Luborsky, L., Crits-Christoph, P., Mintz, J., & Auerbach, A. (1988). *Who will benefit from psychotherapy? Predicting therapeutic outcomes.* New York: Basic Books.

Luborsky, L., Popp, C., & Barber, J. P. (1994). Common and special factors in different transference-related measures. *Psychotherapy Research, 4*(3, 4), 277–286.

Luborsky, L., Popp, C., Luborsky, E., & Marks, D. (1994). The core conflictual relationship theme. *Psychotherapy Research, 4*(3, 4), 172–183.

MacKain, K., Stern, D. N., Goldfield, A., & Moeller, B. (1985). The identification of correspondence between an infant's internal affective state and the facial display of that affect by an other. Unpublished manuscript.

MacLean, P. D. (1972). Cerebral evolution and emotional processes: New findings on the striatal complex. *Annals of the New York Academy of Science, 193,* 137–149.

MacLean, P. D. (1985). Evolutionary psychiatry and the triune brain. *Psychological Medicine, 15,* 219–221.

Magnavita, J. (1993). The evolution of short-term dynamic psychotherapy: Treatment of the future? *Professional Psychology: Research and Practice, 24,* 360–365.

Makynen, A. (1992). The cumulative effects of confrontation on patients' immediate responses in time-limited dynamic psychotherapy (doctoral dissertation, Columbia University Teachers College). *Dissertation Abstracts International, 54*–01B.

Malan, D. M. (1976). *The frontier of brief psychotherapy.* New York: Plenum Press.

Malan, D. M. (1979). *Individual psychotherapy and the science of psychodynamics.* London: Butterworth.

Malan, D. M., & Osimo, F. (1992). *Psychodynamics, training, and outcome in brief psychotherapy.* London: Butterworth-Heinemann.

Mann, J. (1973). *Time-limited psychotherapy.* Cambridge, MA: Harvard University Press.

Marziali, E. (1984). Prediction of brief psychotherapy from therapist interpretive interventions. *Archives of General Psychiatry, 41,* 301–304.

Masterson, J., & Klein, R. (1990). *Search for the real self: Unmasking the personality disorders of our age.* New York: Free Press.

McCullough, L. (1982). I image, therefore I learn? Invited comment on B. R. Bugelski's article "Learning and imagery." *Journal of Mental Imagery, 6,* 44–47.

McCullough, L. (1991a). Davanloo's short-term dynamic psychotherapy: A cross-theoretical analysis of change mechanisms. In R. Curtis & G. Stricker (Eds.), *How people change: Inside and outside of therapy* (pp. 59–79). New York: Plenum Press.

McCullough, L. (1991b). Psychotherapy Interaction Coding System Manual: The PIC system. *Social & Behavioral Science Documents, 18*(2), 50.

McCullough, L. (1992). Toward reliability in identifying ego defenses: Clinical techniques. In G. Vaillant (Ed.), *Ego mechanisms of defense: A guide for clinicians and researchers* (pp. 171–180). Washington, DC: American Psychiatric Press.

McCullough, L. (1993a). Psychotherapy outcome measures: A core battery. In N. Miller, L. Luborsky, J. Barber, & J. P. Docherty. *Psychodynamic treatment research: A handbook for clinical practice* (pp. 469–496). New York: Basic Books.

McCullough, L. (1993b). Short-term dynamic psychotherapy: A "melting pot" of cross-theoretical methods and techniques. In G. Stricker & J. Gold (Eds.), *Handbook of integrative psychotherapies* (pp. 139–150). New York: Plenum Press.

McCullough, L., & Winston, A. (1991). The Beth Israel Psychotherapy Research Program. In L. Beutler & M. Crago (Eds.), *Psychotherapy research: An international review of programmatic studies* (pp. 15–23). Washington, DC: American Psychological Association.

McCullough, L., Bacheldor, S., & Bullitt, C. (1988). *Intensive content and process analysis of transference interpretations and the effects on outcome.* Paper presented at the twenty-first annual meeting of the Society for Psychotherapy Research, Wintergreen, VA.

McCullough, L., Farrell, A., & Longabaugh, R. (1986). A microcomputer-based mental health information system: A potential tool for bridging the scientist-practitioner gap [Special issue on psychotherapy research]. *American Psychologist 14*, 207–214.

McCullough, L., Winston, A., Farber, B., Porter, F., Pollack, J., Laikin, M., Vingiano, W., & Trujillo, M. (1991). The relationship of patient-therapist interaction to outcome in brief psychotherapy. *Psychotherapy, 28*, 525–533.

McCullough Vaillant, L. (1994). The next step in short-term dynamic psychotherapy: A clarification of objectives and techniques in an anxiety-regulating model. *Psychotherapy, 31*, 642–654.

McCullough Vaillant, L., Meyer, S., & Cui, X. J. (1996). The achievement of therapeutic objectives scale manual (ATOS). Unpublished manuscript. The Study for Adult Development, Department of Psychiatry, Brigham & Women's Hospital, 75 Francis Street, Boston, MA 02115.

McWilliams, N. (1994). *Psychiatric diagnosis: Understanding personality structure in the clinical process.* New York: Guilford.

Menninger, K. (1963). *The vital balance: The life process in mental health and illness.* New York: Viking Press.

Menninger, K. (1958). *Theory of psychoanalytic technique.* London: Imago.

Miller, A. (1983). *Drama of the gifted child.* New York: Basic Books.

Miller, A. (1990). *Banished knowledge.* New York: Doubleday.

Miller, A. (1993). *Breaking down the wall of silence.* New York: Meridian.

Millon, T. (1969). *Modern psychopathology.* Philadelphia: Saunders.

Millon, T. (1987). *Millon Clinical Multiaxial Inventory Manual* (3rd ed.). Minneapolis, MN: National Computer Systems.

Mitchell, S. A. (1988). *Relational concepts in psychoanalysis: An integration.* Cambridge, MA: Harvard University Press.

Modell, A. H. (1971). The origin of certain forms of pre-oedipal guilt and the implications for a psychoanalytic theory of affects. *International Journal of Psychoanalysis, 52*, 337–345.

Modell, A. H. (1976). "The holding environment" and the therapeutic action of psychoanalysis. *Journal of the American Psychoanalytic Association, 24,* 285–307.

Modell, A. H. (1990). *Other times, other realities: Toward a theory of psychoanalytic treatment.* Cambridge, MA: Harvard University Press.

Monsen, J. T. (1994). Personality disorders and intensive psychotherapy focusing on affect-consciousness: a prospective follow-up study. Oslo: Psykologisk institutt, University of Oslo.

Monsen, J. T., Eilersten, D. E., Melgaard, T., & Aadegaad, P. (1996). Affects and affect consciousness: Initial experiences with the assessment of affect integration. *Journal of Psychotherapy Practice and Research.*

Monsen, J. T., Odland, T., Faugli, A., Daae, E., & Eilersten, D. E. (1995). Personality disorders: Changes and stability after intensive psychotherapy focusing on affect consciousness. *Psychotherapy Research, 5*(1), 33–48.

Nathanson, D. L. (1992). *Shame and pride: Affect, sex and the birth of the self.* New York: Norton.

Nathanson, D. L. (Ed.). (1996). Knowing feeling: Affect, script and psychotherapy. New York: Norton.

Norcross, J. C. (Ed.). (1992). *Handbook of psychotherapy integration.* New York: Brunner/Mazel.

Norcross, J. C., & Grencavage, L. M. (1989). Eclecticism and integration in counseling and psychotherapy: Major themes and obstacles. *British Journal of Guidance and Counseling, 17,* 227–247.

Norcross, J. C., & Neapolitan, G. (1986). Defining our journal and ourselves. *International Journal of Eclectic Psychotherapy, 5,* 249–255.

Orlinsky, D. E., & Geller, J. D. (1993). Patients' representations of their therapists and therapy: New measures. In N. E. Miller, L. Luborsky, J. Barber, & J. Docherty (Eds.), *Psychodynamic treatment research: A handbook for clinical practice* (pp. 423–466). New York: Basic Books.

Orlinsky, D. E., Geller, J. D., Tarragona, M., & Farber, B. (1993). Patients' representations of psychotherapy: A new focus for psychodynamic research. *Journal of Consulting and Clinical Psychology, 61,* 596–610.

Orlinsky, D. E., Grawe, K., & Parks, B. (1994). Process and outcome of psychotherapy—Noch Einmal. In A. E. Bergin & S. L. Garfield (Eds.), *Handbook of psychotherapy and behavior change* (4th ed., pp. 270–378). New York: Wiley.

Panskepp, J. (1982). Toward a general psychobiological theory of emotion. *Behavior & Brain Science, 5,* 407–422.

Parens, H. (1992). A view of the development of hostility in early life. In T. Shapiro & R. N. Emde (Eds.), *Affect: Psychoanalytic perspectives* (pp. 75–108). Madison, CT: International Universities Press.

Parloff, M. B. (1984). Psychotherapy research and its incredible credibility crisis. *Clinical Psychology Review, 4,* 95–109.

Pavlov, I. P. (1927). *Conditioned reflexes* (G. Anrep, Trans.). New York: Oxford University Press.

Peck, M. S. (1983). *People of the lie.* New York: Simon & Schuster.

Perry, J. C. (1994). Assessing psychodynamic patterns using the idiographic conflict formulation method. *Psychotherapy Research, 4*(3, 4), 239–252.

Perry, J. C., & Vaillant, G. E. (1989). Personality disorders. In H. I. Kaplan & B. J. Sadock (Eds.), *Comprehensive textbook of psychiatry* (Vol. 2, 5th ed., pp. 1352–1387). Baltimore: Williams & Wilkins.

Perry, J. C., Augusto, F., & Cooper, S. H. (1989). Assessing psychodynamic conflicts: I. Reliability of the Idiographic Conflict Formulation Method. *Psychiatry, 52,* 289–301.

Pine, F. (1984). The interpretive moment. *Bulletin of the Menninger Clinic, 48,* 54–71.

Pine, F. (1990). *Drive, ego, object and self: A synthesis for clinical work.* New York: Basic Books.

Pinsker, H., Rosenthal, R., & McCullough, L. (1991). Dynamic supportive psychotherapy. In P. Crits-Christoph & J. Barber (Eds.), *Handbook of brief dynamic therapies* (pp. 220–247). New York: Basic Books.

Plomin, R. (1994). *Genetics and experience: The interplay between nature and nurture.* Thousand Oaks, CA: Sage.

Plomin, R., & DeFries, J. C. (1990). *Behavioral genetics: A primer.* San Francisco: Freeman.

Plutchik, R. (1962). *The emotions: Facts, theories and a new model.* New York: Random House.

Plutchik, R. (1984). Emotions: A general psychoevolutionary theory. In K. R. Scherer & P. Ekman, (Eds.), *Approaches to emotion.* Hillsdale, NJ: Erlbaum.

Pollack, J., & Winston, A. (1991). Brief adaptational psychotherapy. In P. Crits-Christoph & J. Barber (Eds.), *Handbook of brief dynamic therapies* (pp. 220–247). New York: Basic Books.

Polster, I., & Polster, M. (1973). *Gestalt therapy integrated: Contours of theory and practice.* New York: Brunner/Mazel.

Pope, K. (1990). Therapist-patient sex as sex abuse: Six scientific, professional, and practical dilemmas in addressing victimization and rehabilitation. *Professional Psychology: Research and Practice, 21,* 227–239.

Pope, K. (1994). *Sexual involvement with therapists: Patient assessment, subsequent therapy, forensics.* Washington, DC: American Psychological Association.

Pope, K., & Tabachnick, B. (1993). Therapists' anger, hate, fear, and sexual feelings: National survey of therapist responses, client characteristics, critical events, formal complaints, and training. *Professional Psychology: Research and Practice, 24*(2), 142–152.

Porter, F. (1988). The immediate effects of interpretation on patient in-session response in brief dynamic psychotherapy (doctoral dissertation, Columbia University Teachers College, 1987). *Dissertation Abstracts International, 48,* 87–24076.

Prochaska, J. O., DiClemente, C. C., & Norcross, J. C. (1992). In search of how people change: Applications to addictive behaviors. *American Psychologist, 47,* 1102–1114.

Prochaska, J. O., Norcross, J. C., & DiClemente, C. C. (1994). *Changing for good: The revolutionary program that explains the six stages of change and teaches you how to free yourself from bad habits.* New York: William Morrow.

Prochaska, J. O., Rossi, J. S., & Wilcox, N. S. (1991). Change processes and psychotherapy outcome in integrative case research. *Journal of Psychotherapy Integration, 1*(2), 143–158.

Prochaska, J. O., Velicer, W. F., DiClemente, C. C., & Fava, J. S. (1988). Measuring processes of change: Applications to the cessation of smoking. *Journal of Consulting and Clinical Psychology, 56*, 520–528.

Quackenbush, R. L. (1991). The prescription of self-help books by psychologists: A bibliography of selected bibliotherapy resources. *Psychotherapy, 28*, 671–677.

Ratey, J. (Ed.). (1995). *The neuropsychiatry of personality disorders.* Cambridge, MA: Blackwell Science.

Redpath, W. E. (1995). *Trauma energetics: A study of held-energy systems.* Lincoln, MA: Barberry Press.

Reich, A. (1951). On countertransference. *International Journal of Psycho-Analysis, 32*, 25–31.

Reich, A. (1960). Further remarks on countertransference. *International Journal of Psycho-Analysis, 41*, 389–397.

Reich, W. (1949). *Character analysis* (3rd ed., enlarged). New York: Orgone Institute Press.

Rennie, D. L., Phillips, J. R., and Quartaro, G. K. (1988). Grounded theory: A promising approach to conceptualization in psychotherapy. *Canadian Psychology, 29*, 139–150.

Reynolds, G. S. (1975). *A primer of operant conditioning* (rev. ed.). Glenview, IL: Scott Foresman.

Rich, A. (1973). *Diving into the wreck: Poems 1971–1972.* New York: W. W. Norton.

Riggs, D. S., & Foa, E. B. (1993). Obsessive compulsive disorder. In D. Barlow (Ed.), *Clinical handbook of psychological disorders: A step-by-step treatment manual* (pp. 189–239). New York: Guilford.

Robinson, R. G. (1995). Mapping brain activity associated with emotion. *American Journal of Psychiatry, 152*, 327–329.

Rounsaville, B. J., Chevron, E. S., & Weissman, M. M. (1984). Specification of techniques in interpersonal psychotherapy. In J. B. W. Williams & R. L. Spitzer (Eds.), *Psychotherapy research: Where are we and where should we go?* (pp. 160–172). New York: Guilford.

Ruben, C. B. (1992). *Toward an integration of cognitive and object relations therapies: An illustration focusing on dysphoria, hostility, and rejection.* Ann Arbor, MI: UMI Dissertation Services.

Rubin, M. (1990). The relationship between the therapeutic alliance, transference interventions, and treatment outcome in short-term dynamic psychotherapy (doctoral dissertation, Columbia University Teachers College). *Dissertation Abstracts International, 54*–05B.

Sabin, J. E. (1994). The impact of managed care on psychiatric practice. *Directions in Psychiatry, 14*(9), 1–36.

Safran, J., & Greenberg, L. (Eds.). (1991). *Emotion, psychotherapy and change.* New York: Guilford.

Salerno, M., Farber, B., McCullough, L., Winston, A., & Trujillo, M. (1992). The effects of confrontation and clarification on patient affective and defensive responding. *Psychotherapy Research, 2*(3), 181–192.

Salovey, P., & Mayer, J. D. (1990). Emotional intelligence. *Imagination, cognition and personality, 9*(3), 185–211.

Santrock, J., Minnett, A. M., & Campbell, B. D. (1994). *The authoritative guide to self-help books.* New York: Guilford.

Schacht, T. E., & Henry, W. P. (1994). Modeling recurrent patterns of interpersonal relationship with structural analysis of social behavior: The SAS-CMP. *Psychotherapy Research, 4*(3, 4), 208–221.

Schafer, R. (1959). Generative empathy in the treatment situation. *Psychoanalytic Quarterly, 43,* 4–25.

Schafer, R. (1983). *The analytic attitude.* New York: Basic Books.

Scherer, K. R., & Ekman, P. (Eds.). (1984). *Approaches to emotion.* Hillsdale, NJ: Erlbaum.

Seligman, M. E. P. (1975). *Helplessness: On depression, development and death.* San Francisco: Freeman.

Seligman, M. E. P., & Hager, J. L. (Eds.). (1972). *Biological boundaries of learning.* New York: Appleton-Century-Crofts.

Shapiro, T., & Emde, R. N. (Eds.). (1992). *Affect: Psychoanalytic perspectives.* Madison, CT: International Universities Press.

Shengold, L. (1989). *Soul murder: The effects of childhood abuse and deprivation.* New Haven: Yale University Press.

Sifneos, P. E. (1972). *Short-term psychotherapy and emotional crisis.* Cambridge, MA: Harvard University Press.

Sifneos, P. E. (1973). The prevalence of "alexithymic" characteristics in psychosomatic patients. *Psychotherapy and Psychosomatics, 22,* 257–262.

Sifneos, P. E. (1979). *Short-term dynamic psychotherapy: Evaluation and technique.* New York: Plenum Press.

Sifneos, P. E. (1991). Affect, emotional conflict, and deficit: An overview. *Psychotherapy and Psychosomatics, 56*(3), 122–166.

Simon, R. I. (1995). The natural history of therapist sexual misconduct: Identification and prevention. *Psychiatric Annals, 25*(2), 90–93.

Skinner, B. F. (1938). *The behavior of organisms.* New York: Appleton-Century-Crofts.

Skinner, B. F. (1953). *Science and human behavior.* New York: Macmillan.

Skinner, B. F. (1961). *Cumulative record.* New York: Appleton-Century-Crofts.

Skinner, B. F. (1969). *Contingencies of reinforcement: A theoretical analysis.* New York: Appleton-Century-Crofts.

Smith, M. (1975). *When I say no I feel guilty.* New York. Bantam Books/Dial Press.

Smothermon, R. (1980). *Winning through enlightenment.* San Francisco: Context Publications.

Soldz, S. (1993). Review of the book *Understanding transference: The core con-*

flictual relationship theme method, by Luborsky & Crits-Christoph. *Psychotherapy Research, 3,* 69–73.

Spiegel, D. (1993). *Living beyond limits.* New York: Fawcett Columbine.

Spitz, R. A., & Wolf, K. M. (1946). The smiling response: A contribution to the ontogenesis of social relations. *Genetic Psychological Monographs, 34,* 57–125.

Spitzer, R., Williams, J., Gibbon, M., & First, M. (1988). *Instruction manual for the Structured Clinical Interview for DSM-III-R-Client version (SCID-P 6/1/88).* New York: Biometrics Research Department, New York State Psychiatric Institute.

Stamfl, T. G., & Levis, D. J. (1967). Essentials of implosive therapy: A learning-theory based psychodynamic behavioral therapy. *Journal of Abnormal Psychology, 72,* 496–503.

Stern, D. N. (1977). *The first relationship: Mother and infant.* Cambridge, MA: Harvard University Press.

Stern, D. N. (1985). *The interpersonal world of the infant: A view from psychoanalysis and developmental psychology.* New York: Basic Books.

Stern, D. N. (1995). *The motherhood constellation.* New York: Basic Books.

Stettbacher, J. K. (1991). *Making sense of suffering: The healing confrontation with your own past.* New York: Dutton.

Stolorow, R. D., & Atwood, G. E. (1992). *Contexts of being: The intersubjective foundations of psychological life.* Hillsdale, NJ: Analytic Press.

Stolorow, R. D., & Lachmann, F. M. (1980). *Psychoanalysis of developmental arrests: Theory and treatment.* New York: International Universities Press.

Stone, M. H. (1993). *Abnormalities of personality: Within and beyond treatment.* New York: W. W. Norton.

Storr, A. (1992). *The integrity of the personality.* New York: Ballantine Books.

Strupp, H. H. (1989) Psychotherapy: Can the practitioner learn from the researcher? *American Psychologist, 44,* 717–724.

Strupp, H. H., & Binder, J. L. (1984). *Psychotherapy in a new key: A guide to time-limited psychotherapy.* New York: Basic Books.

Szasz, T. S. (1963). The concept of transference. *International Journal of Psycho-Analysis, 32,* 432–443.

Taurke, E., Flegenheimer, W., McCullough, L., Winston, A., Pollack, J., & Trujillo, M. (1990). Change in affect-defense ratio from early to late sessions in relation to outcome. *Journal of Clinical Psychology, 46,* 657–668.

Tavris, C. (1982). *Anger, the misunderstood emotion.* New York: Simon & Schuster.

Tellegen, A., Lykken, D. T., Bouchard, T. J., Wilcox, K. J., et al. (1988). Personality similarity in twins reared apart and together. *Journal of Personality and Social Psychology, 54,* 1031–1039.

Thoma, H., & Kachele, H. (1985). *Psychoanalytic practice: I. Principles.* Berlin: Springer-Verlag.

Tomkins, S. S. (1962). *Affect, imagery, and consciousness: Vol. I. Positive affects.* New York: Springer.

Tomkins, S. S. (1963). *Affect, imagery, and consciousness: Vol. II. Negative affects.* New York: Springer.

Tomkins, S. S. (1970). Affect as amplification: Some modifications in a theory. In R. Plutchik & H. Kellerman (Eds.), *Emotions: Theory, research and experience* (pp. 141–164). New York: Academic Press.

Tomkins, S. S. (1981). The quest for primary motives: The biography and autobiography of an idea. *Journal of Personality and Social Psychology, 41,* 306–329.

Tomkins, S. S. (1984). Affect theory. In K. R. Scherer & P. Ekman (Eds.), *Approaches to emotion*. Hillsdale, NJ: Erlbaum.

Tomkins, S. S. (1991). *Affect, imagery, and consciousness: Vol. III. Negative affects: Anger and fear*. New York: Springer.

Tomkins, S. S. (1992). *Affect, imagery, and consciousness: Vol. IV. Cognition*. New York: Springer.

Tomkins, S. S. (1995). Script theory: Differential magnification of affects. In V. Demos (Ed.), *Exploring affect: Selections from the writing of Silvan S. Tomkins* (pp. 312–410). New York: Cambridge University Press.

Trujillo, M., & McCullough, L. (1985). Research issues in short-term dynamic psychotherapy: An overview. In A. Winston (Ed.), *Short-term dynamic psychotherapy: Clinical and research issues* (pp. 81–102). Washington, DC: American Psychiatric Press.

Vaillant, G. (1975). Sociopathy as a human process: A viewpoint. *Archives of General Psychiatry, 32,* 178–183.

Vaillant, G. (1977). *Adaptation to life*. Boston: Little, Brown.

Vaillant, G. E. (1988). Attachment, loss and rediscovery. *Hillsdale Journal of Clinical Psychiatry, 10*(2), 148–164.

Vaillant, G. (1993). *Wisdom of the ego*. Cambridge, MA: Harvard University Press.

Vaillant, G., & McCullough, L. (1987). A comparison of the Washington University Sentence Completion Test (SCT) with other measures of adult ego development. *American Journal of Psychiatry, 144,* 1189–1194.

Vaillant, G. E., & Perry, J. C. (1984). Personality disorders. In J. Kaplan, A. Freedman, & B. Sadock (Eds.), *Comprehensive textbook of psychiatry Vol. 4* (chap. 22). Baltimore: Williams & Wilkins.

Van der Kolk, B., Boyd, H., Krystal, J., & Greenberg, M. (1984). Post-traumatic stress disorder as a biologically based disorder: Implications of the animal model of inescapable shock. In B. Van der Kolk (Ed.), *Post-traumatic stress disorder: Psychological and biological sequelae* (pp. 124–134). Washington, DC: American Psychiatric Press.

Volkan, V. (1971). A study of a patient's "re-grief work" through dreams, psychological tests, and psychoanalysis. *Psychiatric Quarterly, 45,* 255–273.

Volkan, V. (1972). The linking objects of pathological mourners. *Archives of General Psychiatry, 27,* 215–221.

Volkan, V., & Showalter, C. R. (1968). Known object loss, disturbance in reality testing, and "re-grief" work as a method of brief psychotherapy. *Psychiatric Quarterly, 42,* 358–374.

Wachtel, P. L. (1977). *Psychoanalysis and behavior therapy: Toward an integration*. New York: Basic Books.

Wachtel, P. L. (1984). On theory, practice, and the nature of integration. In H. Arkowitz & S. B. Messer (Eds.), *Psychoanalytic therapy and behavior therapy: Is integration possible?* (pp. 31–52). New York: Plenum Press.

Wallerstein, R. S. (1986). *Forty-two lives in treatment: A study of psychoanalysis and psychotherapy*. New York: Guilford.

Walter, J. L., & Peller, J. E. (1992). *Becoming solution-focused in brief therapy*. New York: Brunner/Mazel.

Watson, D., & Clark, A. (1992). Affects separable and inseparable: On the hierarchical arrangement of the negative affects. *Journal of Personality and Social Psychology, 62,* 489–505.

Watson, D., Clark, A., & Tellegen, A. (1988). Development and validation of brief measures of positive and negative affect: The PANAS scales. *Journal of Personality and Social Psychology, 54,* 1063–1070.

Weiss, J. (1990, March). Unconscious mental functioning. *Scientific American,* 103–109.

Weiss, J., Sampson, H., & the Mount Zion Psychotherapy Research Group. (1986). *The psychoanalytic process: Theory, clinical observations, and empirical research*. New York: Guilford.

Whybrow, P. C., Akiskal, H. S., & McKinney, W. T. (1984). *Mood disorders: Toward a new psychobiology*. New York: Plenum Press.

Widiger, T. A., & Frances A. (1985). The DSM-III personality disorders: Perspectives from psychology. *Archives of General Psychiatry, 42,* 615–623.

Williams, N. (1994). *Psychoanalytic diagnosis: Understanding personality structure in the clinical process*. New York: Guilford.

Wilson, J. M. (1993). DSM-III and the transformation of American psychiatry: A history. *American Journal of Psychiatry, 150,* 399–407.

Winnicott, D. W. (1949). Hate in the countertransference. *International Journal of Psychoanalysis, 30,* 69–74.

Winnicott, D. W. (1965). *The maturational process and the facilitating environment: Studies in the theory of emotional development*. London: Hogarth Press.

Winslow, J. T., & Insel, T. R. (1991). Endogenous opioids: Do they modulate the rat pup's response to social isolation? *Behavioral Neuroscience, 105*(2), 253–263.

Winston, A., Laikin, M., Pollack, J., Samstag, L., McCullough, L., & Muran, C. (1994). Short-term psychotherapy of personality disorders. *American Journal of Psychiatry, 151,* 190–194.

Winston, A., McCullough, L., & Laikin, M. (1993). Clinical vignettes of brief psychotherapy [Special issue on psychotherapy process research]. *American Journal of Psychotherapy, 47,* 527–539.

Winston, A., McCullough, L., Pollack, J., Laikin, M., Pinsker, H., Nezu, A. M., Flegenheimer, W., & Sadow, J. (1989). The Beth Israel Psychotherapy Research Program: Toward an integration of theory and discovery. *Journal of Integrative and Eclectic Psychotherapy, 3,* 345–357.

Winston, A., McCullough, L., Trujillo, M., Pollack, J., Laikin, M., Flegenheimer, W., & Kestenbaum, R. (1991). Brief psychotherapy of personality disorders. *Journal of Nervous and Mental Disease, 179*(4), 188–193.

Winston, A., Pinsker, H., & McCullough, L. (1986). A review of supportive therapy. *Hospital and Community Psychiatry, 37*, 1105–1114.

Winston, A., Pollack, J., Trujillo, M., McCullough, L., Laikin, M., & Flegen-heimer, W. (1990). Efficacy of brief adaptational psychotherapy. *Journal of Personality Disorders, 4*, 244–250.

Wolpe, J. (1958). *Psychotherapy by reciprocal inhibition.* Stanford, CA: Stanford University Press.

Young, J. E., Beck, A. T., & Weinberger, A. (1993). Depression. In D. Barlow (Ed.), *Clinical handbook of psychological disorders: A step-by-step treatment manual* (pp. 240–277). New York: Guilford.

Zetzel, E. (1956). Current concepts of transference. *International Journal of Psycho-Analysis, 37*, 369–375.

Zinker, J. (1977) *The creative process in gestalt therapy.* New York: Brunner/Mazel.

Index